They Slept Upon Their Rifles

The Kuykendall family roots go deeper in Texas than most oak trees. This book is a family history, but it's also the history of Texas.

—MIKE COX
Austin, Texas

In *They Slept Upon Their Rifles*, sixth-generation Texan Marshall Kuykendall introduces the newcomer to what University of Texas historian Walter Prescott Webb called the "high adventure" of researching the past. To one who knows and loves Texas history, he introduces us to the Kuykendall clan, rooted deeply in Texas (the Old 300) and American history. It is a great and compelling story.

—RON TYLER
Former Director,
Texas State Historical Association

Few American families can tell a story that covers ten generations as they moved from the Atlantic to the Pacific. The Hardemans and the Polks come readily to mind, but none have had a chronicler who tells their story with the verve, candor, and humor that characterizes this account.

—AL LOWMAN
Past president of the
Texas State Historical Association

They Slept Upon Their Rifles

The story of the Captain Robert H. Kuykendall family in America and the entry of the family with the Anglo Settlement into Mexican/Texas in Stephen F. Austin's Colony in 1821.

(Includes allied families-Early, Hardin, Moore, Shannon, Swift)
(Includes the Kuykendalls from Texas in the Civil War)
(Includes the Texas Kuykendall Death Records from 1903-2000)

Marshall E. Kuykendall

"We sleep with our rifles besides us in the best of times."
John Sevier, Elizabethton, Tennessee
1785

Cover Picture: Marshall E. Kuykendall, Jr.

Illustrated by the late Charlie Shaw.

Designed and typeset by Pat Molenaar.
All pictures cleaned and enhanced by Jennifer and Pat Molenaar.

Copyright © 2005
By Marshall F. Kuykendall
Published By NorTex Press
An Imprint of Wild Horse Media Group
P.O. Box 331779
Fort Worth, Texas 76163
1-817-344-7036
www.EakinPress.com
ALL RIGHTS RESERVED
1 2 3 4 5 6 7 8 9
ISBN-10: 1-57168-993-1
ISBN-13: 978-1-57168-993-1
Library of Congress Control Number 2005928354

Dedication

This work is for my family. I know they tell folks not to bring up Texas history in front of Dad because it will ruin a good evening. They are probably right. Once this family research gets in your blood, it can make you a real bore during family OR non-family functions.

I think what I really want to accomplish is, I want my own family and those interested, to be able to access interesting information about our family. I want them to be able to obtain this history in the public domain. Not under some old ladies bed, who hid it in a cardboard box and wouldn't let a soul see it for fear the family ghosts would soar to light. Such was the case of my dear Aunt Dorothy, my father's sister, who has long since gone to some other place not accessible by modern communicational means. Dear Aunt Dorothy managed to tear out most of the prime pages from a one-hundred-year-old Kuykendall ranch diary that she thought should not be seen by present nor future generations. It was probably not done by malice, just prejudice. She also felt that viewing the Kuykendall Family Bible would set us back emotionally. It was not until a few years ago that I was finally able to see it and it had at least fifteen immediate family members who were either very vague to me or completely unknown. We will never know why.

Several years ago, I obtained an extensive diary out of California, written by one of my mother's ancestors from Bell County, Texas. It talked in detail about the comings and goings of that particular family in that early day county before 1900. There was only one small thing missing. The author felt it was not in our best interest to know the proper names of all the players. So she purposely changed every single family member's name to someone else. I won't say it is worthless, just a great disappointment. And I never tried to decipher it—wasn't worth the effort.

Since I got started in this family history adventure, I have written some fifteen or twenty biographies, some good and some not so good, some thirty pages long, and a bunch one or two pages in length. The early ones were the ones that did not have the research in them I presently wish I had done. Nothing will take the place of long, hard, footnoted research. The good news is that the Barker Texas History Center at UT-Austin was kind enough to accept all of those papers and now those interested parties, whether my immediate family or others, will have access to that information, and won't have to crawl under some wonderful old lady's bed like I did to find it.

It was through Doug Barnett at the Barker Texas History Center at UT-Austin that I got my first real shot at doing some fairly decent writing when he asked me to rewrite the Kuykendall section of the 1986-96 *Hand Book of Texas* published by the Texas State Historical Association. I am grateful to him, Ron Tyler, and George Ward of the Texas State Historical Association for putting up with me and allowing me to do that work. It propelled me into a better place as an amateur writer. I thank them for it.

To my wonderful family, past and present, who were, and are, chock full of wonderful stories—it's now my time to get even.

Contents

Acknowledgments vii
Foreword ix

——THE BEGINNINGS——

1. The Dutch Colony of New Amsterdam 1
2. The Indian War Paths and the Great Wagon Road 3
3. Maps 7
4. The People 9

——THE BIOGRAPHIES——

PRIMARY

5. Adam Kuykendall 15
6. Captain Robert H. Kuykendall of Austin's Colony 39
7. R. H. (Gill) Kuykendall 59
8. Wiley Martin Kuykendall 71
9. Robert Gill Kuykendall 93
10. Wylie Moore (Bill) Kuykendall 111
11. Marshall Early Kuykendall 175

ALLIED

12. William Erastus Moore 183
13. Arthur Swift 201
14. Captain Abner Kuykendall of Austin's Colony 203
15. Captain Gibson Kuykendall of Austin's Colony 212
16. Barzillai Kuykendall of Austin's Colony 220

17. William Kuykendall of Austin's Colony.............................. 232
18. J. Hampton Kuykendall.. 239
19. Joseph Kuykendall of Austin's Colony 258
20. Rev. Marshall Daniel Early, Baptist Minister 267
21. Col. Joseph Hardin, Father-in-Law of Adam Kuykendall 277

——RECORDS AND NOTICES——

22. Kuykendall Death Notices, State of Texas, 1903-2000 293
23. Kuykendalls, Texans, in the Civil War 330

Notes 365
Index 385

Acknowledgments

The information that I put on these pages was not done by me at all but a host of fine researchers who preceded me. I will admit that the information on my own personal family was from my sources, but the bulk of the data was from researchers I have known and many that were before my time.

The family Bible of research goes to Dr. George Benson Kuykendall of Oregon, who privately published his Kuykendall Family of America in 1918. Dr. Kuykendall's account in the book of his travel as a young boy with his family along the Oregon Trail is witness to the very history of this country. While there are mistakes in any good work, this book gave the family the foundation to work and search for their ancestors. Interestingly, my brother, Gil, had a copy of this fine, rare book, but I had to work from a Xerox copy for many years to do my research. It is only in the past few years that I was able to obtain an original edition of this exemplary book which is impossible to find in any rare book store. And that book was a gift to me by Arlene Saffell of California, one of the premier researchers in this country today.

But in order not to run for pages and pages, let me list, in my opinion, who the premier researchers are in this country on the Kuykendall Family in America:

Mrs. Velma Kuykendall Winn of Auburn, California,
Mrs. Herman P. (Arlene) Saffell, of El Segundo, California,
Mr. Eugene L. Kuykendall of Sloatsburg, New York, now deceased,
Mr. Gifford White of Austin, Texas, now deceased,
Ms. Betty Kuykendall Price of Mt. Gilead, North Carolina,
Mrs. Betty Kuykendall McCrosky of Glen Flora, Texas, now deceased.

Do not think you are being left out. As noted, my name is not mentioned, because I don't feel I am in the class with these folks. While we are all semi-experts in some of the details of our own family, I would have never been able to start my historical and genealogical writings without the information these particular people provided.

Much of this information was located in the public information domain of this country, primarily in the county courthouses of our states. The balance, of course, is in private hands. Remember, that one hundred percent of this information was done long before the so-called computer age. It was hours and hours in every courthouse in this country, where Kuykendall family information could be found or gleaned. It was person or persons who spent countless days in search for a particular lost document. It was thousands of personal letters written to and from interested participants. It is from a thousand owned, lost and found, family Bibles, where the center portions showed the old writings of our aunts and grandmothers of all the children they birthed and the thousands they buried—some in marked graves, but most in lost places. It is to these folks that we owe our gratitude. I am so sorry I let both my grandmothers and all my aunts die before I awoke to the history that was in my own family.

Now that the computer age is upon us, many fine folks are joining the fray to share their personal family information with us. It has opened a wonderful new chapter in family research and what is even better, it is instantaneous. Just press a button on our keypads and there it is.

The only problem with this new information is that it is being placed or dumped into cyber space without benefit of *clergy*. (*It ain't been blessed.*) The translation being the *dumpee* did not do the research, but found it dumped by someone else and entered it in his or her computer "as fact" and dumped it to you and me. For those who started looking into their family histories yesterday, this is a travesty. Most of us are spending too much of our present time undoing this new activity and rebutting the incorrect information instead of spending more time in the courthouse. *Such is the way.*

Foreword

Marshall Kuykendall, one of the greatest and kindest men I have ever known, asked me, as an historian and friend, to write a foreword to his history of the Kuykendall family. For me this was a great honor. Here was the scion of one of the first families of Texas (the Old Three Hundred) asking me to introduce him and his amazing ancestors to posterity. Of course I said yes. I have known this bear of a man with the enthusiasm of a child for at least forty years. He has always delighted me and I never get tired of his Texas stories because he *is* Texas with a great big smile. He is perhaps the best man Texas has yet produced—"bettern Sam Houston hisself." I can say this because it wasn't anybody else who walked beside my gurney to the operating room of Seton Hospital when I was heading toward my quadruple heart bypass with me not knowing whether I would make it or not.

I think few if any historians or genealogists have ever had as much fun compiling a family history as Marshall has had. The sheer glee with which he described his progress—a progress that didn't come easy for him—was always a delight to share with him. Now, except for a few required touches here and there, Marshall has completed his historical journey. I am sure people will be fascinated by it. Before I read it, I was not all that interested in either genealogy or Texas social history, though I am considered a western historian. But the tale of the Kuykendalls as they migrated with other Dutch and Scots-Irish families down from upper New York around the late seventeenth century has fascinated me. They, being early Dutch settlers headed south from near Albany, New York, towards Pennsylvania so as to avoid the fierce League of the Iroquois, the six most powerful Indian tribes in the eastern back country. The family was, however, always on a wilderness frontier. Their story, as they moved along the Appalachians via mountain passes and Indian war trails, bears a striking resemblance to the famous western writer, Louis L'Amour's sage of the Sackett family. Their journey was almost always out ahead and their adventures with Indians and the wilderness, killing bears and all sorts of wild game to survive certainly matches the Sackett sage in "True Grit."

As the excellent maps in this account indicate, they made their way down the great Valley of Virginia, beyond the Blue Ridge Mountains to the Wilderness Road which some family members took through the Cumberland Gap, the north to the Ohio River where they climbed on knocked together wooden keelboats and floated, as a great many would-be settlers did, down the Ohio and the Mississippi to the mouth of the Arkansas River and Arkansas Post. Marshall's branch of the family made their way overland, passing over mountains, swollen rivers, through great woods and Indian hunting grounds down the Natchez Trace until they finally stopped in Cadron Settlements on the Arkansas River in 1810. Before that, however, Adam Kuykendall, son of Peter Kuykendall, born in Anson County, North Carolina, ca 1756, became the founder of Marshall's branch of the family. He fought in the Revolutionary War in North Carolina. The family lived near the battle site of King's Mountain twenty-seven years before the Revolution.

Adam's son, Robert H. Kuykendall, was an Indian trader with a firm that employed numerous traders. Some of the Kuykendalls intermarried with the Hardins, making the latter-day dangerous Texas outlaw, John Wesley Hardin, a distant relative.

Adam's sons, Robert, Abner, and Joseph, moved into Texas (Mexican Territory) from Arkansas because in 1820 Governor William Clark persuaded the Osages to surrender some of their lands in Arkansas, Missouri, and Oklahoma to the Cherokees. Eastern Indian removal to the west had been considered since James Madison's presidency and the Creek War where General Andrew Jackson, patrol of the Scots Irish settlers moving into Georgia, soundly defeated the Creeks and their British sponsors at the battle of Horseshoe Bend. By 1819 half of the Cherokee Nation had ceded their eastern land and were moving into Arkansas, six thousand of them rounded up by Andrew Jackson. Though in 1821 John Marshall and the Supreme Court declared this illegal, Jackson and white settlers paid no attention, and the Cherokees willingly moved west. While presidents Monroe and John Quincy Adams largely ignored the ongoing "removal," when Andrew Jackson became president, he pushed through a strong Indian Removal Bill in 1830. He never cared what John Marshall, his enemy, ruled.

It is ironic that families like the Kuykendalls were also pushed westward as a result of Indian removal into foreign territory, but perhaps it was a good thing as it got them out of Arkansas and into Texas where they thrived. They were granted lands as part of Stephen F. Austin's Colony, later called "The Old Three Hundred," referring to the first families that settled there. The Choctaw and Chickasaw got their Arkansas land with no federal remuneration to the Kuykendalls. Meanwhile in Georgia's former Indian lands, eastern Scots-Irish were busily digging for gold in America's first Gold Rush.

Robert and Joseph Kuykendall actually met Moses Austin at Nacogdoches, Texas, shortly after they crossed the Red and the Brazos rivers. However, Robert H. Kuykendall had scouted out Galveston Island as early as November 1819, and Robert, a hard man, hanged one of Jean La Fitte's pirates for trying to rob him. When Robert Kuykendall settled in a log cabin on the land grant east of the Colorado River between Peach and Caney Creeks, he was continually attacked by the Karankawa Indians who were rumored to be cannibals. Robert soon became captain of a militia protecting the settlers, and he was granted two extra leagues of land for his services. Captain Kuykendall, in a fight with Indians in spring 1826, was wounded in the head, probably by a tomahawk. He went blind and he became paralyzed but lived until some time in 1830 when he died as a result of a doctor's trepanning (drilling holes in the skull) operation.

Robert H. "Gill" Kuykendall, his son, served in Martin's unit of scouts during the Texas Revolution. In a sense this group of scouts were the first Texas Rangers. Gill's son, Robert H. Kuykendall III, joined the 6th Texas Infantry in the Civil War. He was captured in a fight near Arkansas Post and imprisoned in Camp Butler, Illinois, where he died on 20 April 1863.

Another son of Gill was Wiley Martin Kuykendall, a true cowboy who not only ranched but made several long cattle drives north to markets and railheads. In the Civil War, Wiley joined the 1st Texas Cavalry and fought in the Red River Campaign and other bloody fights before he also was captured and paroled at Victoria, Texas, 8 August 1865. Wiley went to work for the south Texas cattle baron, A. H. (Shanghai) Pierce, a true scalawag if there ever was one. Wiley married Shanghai's sister, Susan E. Pierce, on 22 April 1869 in Matagorda County. Readers who see her likeness on page 73 will note that the Kuykendall men, especially the author of this memoir, strongly resemble her, down to the present. Interestingly, Wylie and Robert Kuykendall adopted a heart for their brand. While Wylie went up the cattle trail to Kansas in 1871, Susan Kuykendall took charge of the farm. As she wrote, "I practiced diversification ... I milked the cows, helped break horses [bucking broncos!] marked and branded calves, took on sewing, washing, ironing and ran a boarding house, having as borders, eight children whose fathers and mothers were dead." She also survived a hurricane that destroyed the town of Indianola. She added, "In the marketing, branding and selling season, I used to get up at 3 o'clock in the morning, and at 4 o'clock I would have breakfast ready ... We would then go in alone to the prairies, and when the sunrise came, we would have a herd rounded up and on the way to the pen ... In the year of the big snow ... in February, 1864, I picked up and raised forty-four motherless calves, besides saving many cows that were on the left, and skinning others that I found dead." This was the life of a cattleman's wife in the late nineteenth century! One wonders, where was Wiley?

The Will Moore family comes into the picture about this time. Moore, a friend of Wylie's, was also a cowboy and worked for Shanghai Pierce. He fought in the Civil War and later against Grant at Shiloh in the Mississippi River Campaign. He had four horses shot out from under him while riding with Terry's Texas Rangers. He was then severely wounded at Murfreesboro, Tennessee, in 1862, but survived to fight again. Moore returned hime in 1865. His daughter, Maggie, married R. G. "Gill" Kuykendall and became the present author's grandmother.

Later the family moved north to Onion Creek, between Kyle and Buda, Texas. The present author lives nearby today. Gill Kuykendall acquired 11,000 acres.

I cannot wind up this foreword without saying something about the author's wild and crazy father, Wylie Moore (Bill) Kuykendall. Much of his life was recounted in a diary by Wylie's Aunt Dora Inez Moore who never married and lived with Bill

Kuykendall's family for most of the rest of her life. To Marshall Kuykendall her diary has been a godsend.

Wylie or Bill, besides being a major rancher and cowboy, was a ladies' man. He drove fast cars when they came on the market and squired many girls—Thelma, Mary, Helena, etc. He built a house on the 11,000-acre ranch. Once he went to California and came back with a beautiful movie star to whom he gave the family diamond. Her name was Marjory Honey who stayed at the ranch and went to wild parties with Bill (Wylie). He didn't marry her either. Indeed he was beginning to match the Hollywood lothario, Howard Hughes.

Wild Wiley dabbled in oil wells in Luling while his brother Ike caught the mumps, and his testicles shrunk to the "size of an English pea and the other was just a little bitty son of a bitch." Poor Ike, he couldn't capitalize on all the big parties that began to take place on the Kuykendall's 101 Ranch, named after the movie ranch from Oklahoma. Suddenly Wylie married Mildred Williams of Lockhart on Sunday, April 17, 1921. They had a daughter named Lamond. Lamond was often left with Ike and Aunt Dora. As we shall see, Bill wasn't much for children. In 1925 Mildred dumped Bill, probably because he wasn't home very often.

In 1926, when he was twenty-seven years old, Wild Bill married Alice Hamlett of Austin who was fifteen years old. And as Alice put it "all hell broke loose the next day." Alice was made to eat in the children's dining room! Alice's mother said "she would just die" when she found out they were married. Alice's sister and brother kidnapped her from Bill's ranch and took her to Panama. Bill wasted no time going after her and bringing her back! Then Bill enrolled at South West Normal School [LBJ's alma mater] to play football! In 1929 he had a grand national rodeo on his ranch. Bill got along splendidly with Alice. Their first child, Gil, was born in 1929. Then two years later on 13 October 1932, Marshall, author of this book, was born. Alice was 21.

During the Depression, Bill took up polo! He was so good that he traveled all over the U.S. and Mexico, usually winning, and earning money on side bets, too. Bill had discovered that central Texas bred the most surefooted polo ponies.

Gil went on to the University of Texas. Marshall, a homely, little boy had first been sent to San Marcos Military Academy where he suffered mightily from teachers and schoolmates alike. Later, Austin High was a relief. Then off to Kyle High School, where he played six man football. Afterwards Marshall went to Sul Ross Cowboy College and then Southwest Texas University. After graduation from SWT, he joined the Air Force ROTC, and learned to fly B-25s. Bill, never the good father, got jealous of Marshall's flying ability, went out to Ragsdale Aviation in Austin, bought a plane, climbed into it, and took off with no lesson whatever. Earlier he shot a ranch trespasser in the belly and was no-billed because of trespassing. You couldn't do that today.

Wild Bill died of stomach cancer on 11 October 1976. Always the cowboy, he declared that when he died he would end up in a "pile of cow manure." Instead he ended up in the Kyle Cemetery, followed by Alice much later on 24 August 1993.

Marshall is perhaps best known for his splendid Take Back Texas movement that battled so-called "environmentalists" to a standstill when, using the federal government as a shield and for funding, they tried to run families, sons and daughters of the great long lost pioneers who built Texas and America, off their land in favor of cave beetles and yellow throated warblers. He got no help from Texas Governor Ann Richards whom he thought was his friend of long standing. But she was running for governor and needed, she thought, the "environmental" vote—all twenty-four of them!

I do hope that Marshall and his wife, as well as his fine children, Marshall, Mary Alice, and Sarita, and their children live forever.

—WILLIAM H. GOETZMANN
Austin, Texas

The Beginnings

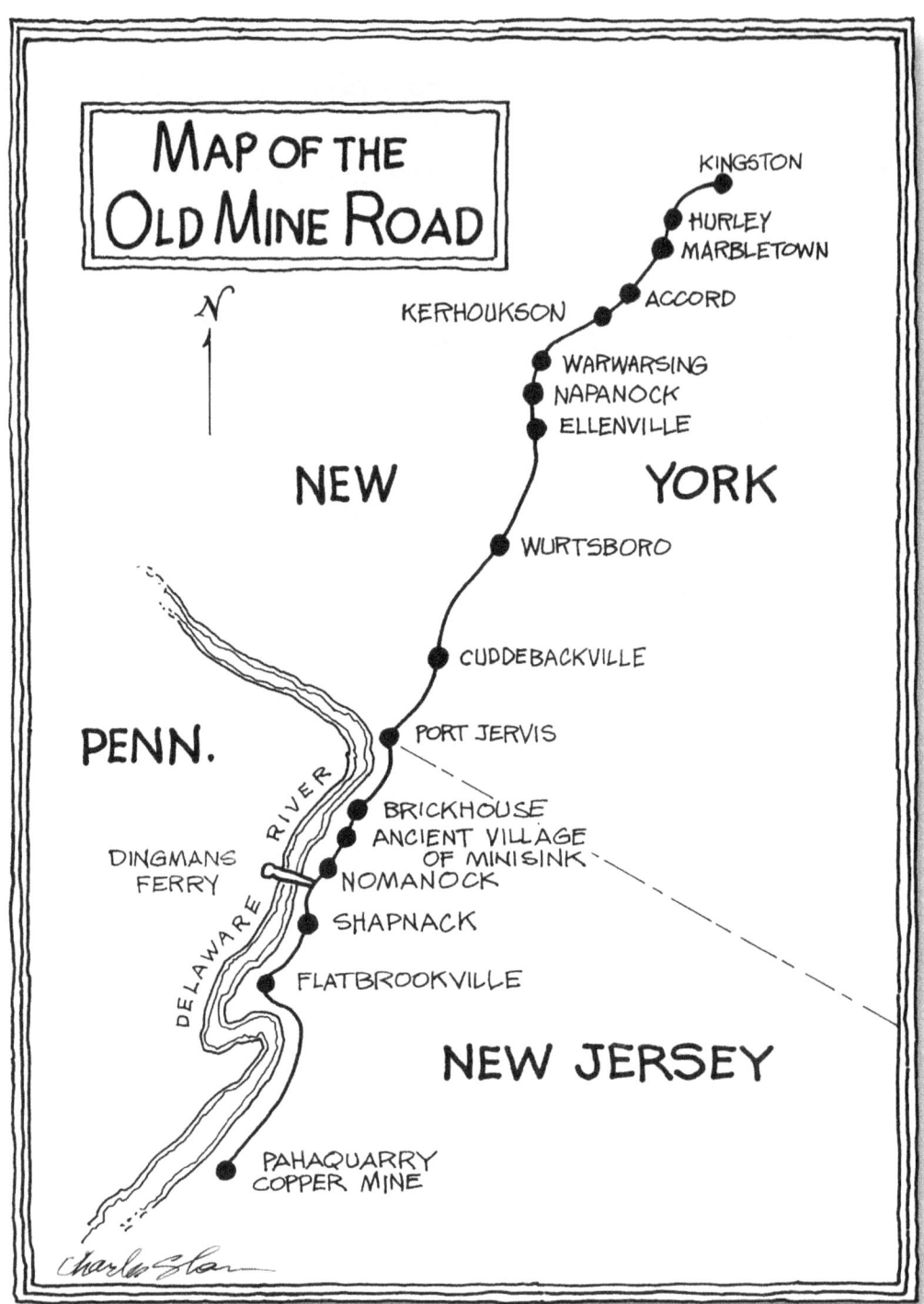

Chapter One

The Dutch Colony of New Amsterdam

What's so fun about being able to write this story is the fascinating history of the Kuykendall family of America. This family has been in this place we call America since, if not day one, then certainly day two. Our family, Dutch in origin, came to this country via the Dutch West Indies Company in ca. 1645 to settle in New Amsterdam along the newly named Hudson River, which to you and me, is present upstate New York. (Colonized by the Dutch in 1613-1624.) To make it even more fun, the family's name was not Kuykendall when they entered, but Jacob Luurszen, known as the *emigrant*. It was his son, Luur Jacobsen, who introduced the name in the family baptismal records about 1700 or 1704 into the American records. As stated in Eugene Kuykendall's fine personal family history published in 1984:

"There is no evidence the toponym "van Kuykendall" ever existed in the Netherlands or was ever used by Jacob Luurszen. Luur Jacobsen apparently introduced the name when we first see it recorded in 1700. This was at the time when the old Dutch Patronymic system was phased out in America and new surnames were adopted by mandate of the British."(Letter from Gene Kuykendall via Genforum to Angela Anderson, dated 29 Nov. 1999, author's possession.) NOTE: The New Amsterdam Dutch Colony was taken over by the British in 1664.

Much old and new research has been done and is being done at present to try and explain the name Kuykendall, what it means and where in Holland or the Netherlands it could come from. To my knowledge, none of that information has ever been proven.

Such translations as "Chicken Valley," "Church in the Valley," and "Curve in the River" have been spoken about. The name was probably invented by then young Luur Jacobsen to discern the names of his children and make them different. Perhaps it was from a place known as KUYK-EN-DALE. And perhaps young Luur wanted to give some foundation to his family name. But it's never been found if there is such a place in Holland. Good folks are presently scouring the early Dutch West Indies records and the New Amsterdam Church records of New York State to try and find a clue. We shall see.

Many of our family and their friends were by the very nature of this vast wilderness, made into frontiersmen the day they arrived. Most of our ancestors were "mechanics" or carpenters or stone masons. That is why they were allowed to emigrate and join the Dutch Colony. But the moment they arrived in this new land, their civilized past had to be rebuilt. I'm sure the first generation tried their best to build their churches and little villages along the Hudson (*1609, Henry Hudson*) and get some semblance of order back in their lives. But as soon as the second generation hit the ground, many of our families immediately headed off into the wilderness, leaving their families and the villagers behind.

Chapter Two

The Indian War Paths and the Great Wagon Road

By 1700, the tax records show our family moving down the Hudson River into the areas of Fort Orange (Albany, New York), Raychester (Accord, New York), down the Old Mine Road (basically Route 209 in New York State), into the Minisink Valley (Delaware River area below Port Jervis, New York in Sussex County, New Jersey, near Montaque), and into Machackemeck, and Deerpark DRC (Port Jervis, New York) and into Mamakating Hollow (Mamakating Township, New York—villages of Wurtsboro, Summitville, and Phillipsport).[1]

By and large, the Kuykendalls were always "Frontiers people," "Long Riflemen" or "Over Mountainmen" as they were later called. If one is interested in geography, follow the Appalachian Mountain chain down southwesterly from the upper Hudson River and follow them as they course through that area into eastern Pennsylvania, into what is now eastern West Virginia, then on into western North Carolina or present eastern Tennessee.

What the settlers found as they traveled down inside that range of mountains was a vast network of ancient Indian Warpaths and trails. These marked paths showed the way to find the river crossings, the springs, the *licks*, and the difficult mountain passes such as the Cumberland Gap over and through the steep mountain ridges. So while other groups of newcomers where plying their trades along the coast of then North America, our families were exploring the vast forests that lay within the Appalachian range.

Along these ancient marked trails were built the great wagon roads of northeast America at the time. The most famous of which ran from outside of Philadelphia,

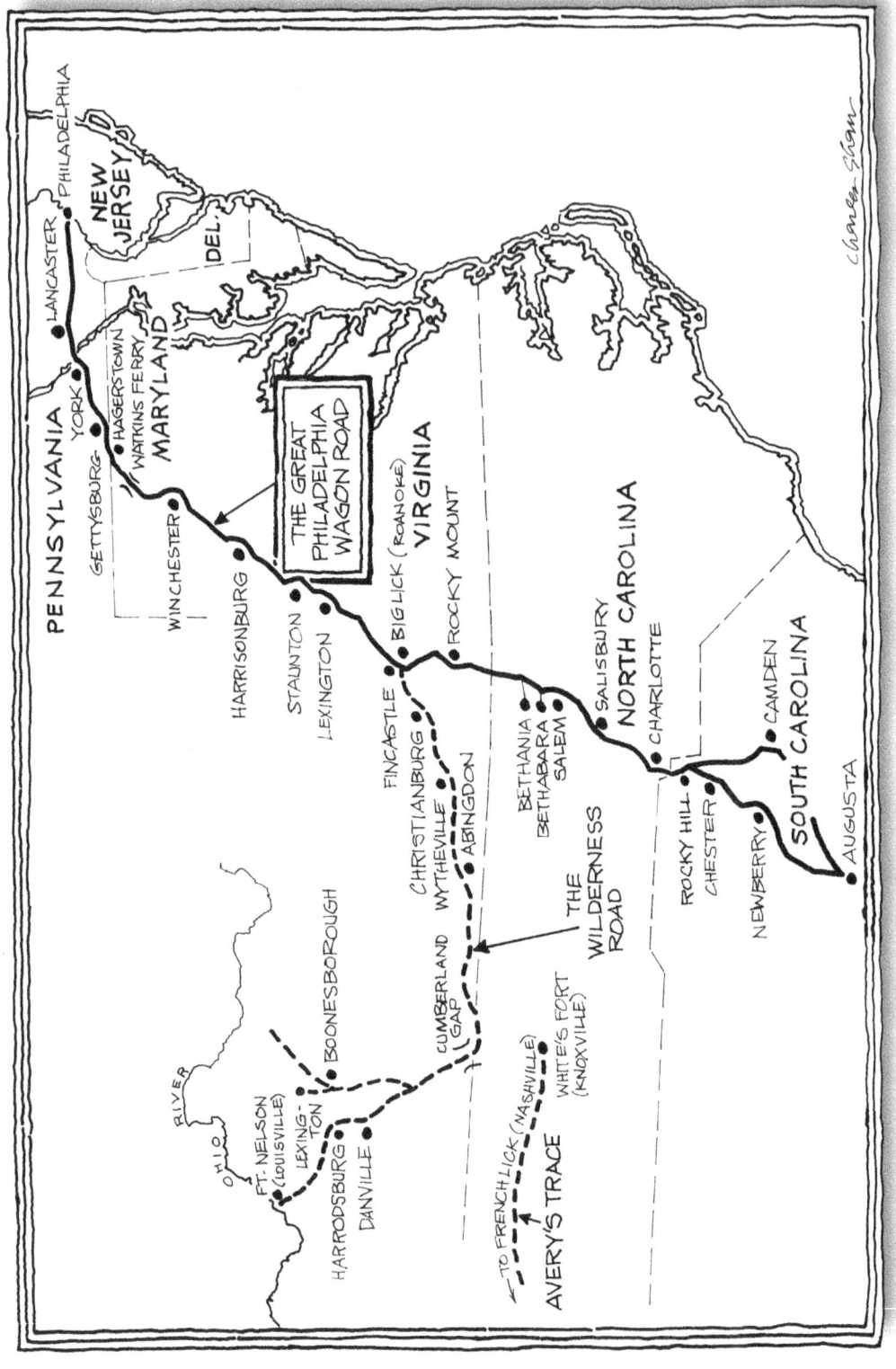

southwesterly across Virginia and into western North Carolina and eastern Tennessee. Our families would take this great migration route on their trek into the western North Carolina country in the mid 1700s. This important Indian trail or warpath was very well traveled. This was part of the great warpath that joined the Iroquois Confederacy in the north with the Catawba and Cherokee nations in the south.

Interestingly, the reason our families did not go due west out of the Hudson River Valley was because of the "Iroquois Confederacy." It was originally composed of the Cayuga, Mohawk, Oneida, Onondaga, and Seneca Indians, which was then called the Five Nations. In 1722, the Tuscarora were admitted and henceforth the English referred to the group as the Confederacy of Six Nations. It was the area north of what was to be called the River Ohio, west of the Hudson River Valley and basically south of the Great Lakes, probably over to near what is now the Mississippi River. This Federation discouraged or denied settlement by the newcomers (Europeans) into their region, hence the movement of our particular families down the interior of the Appalachian chain.[2]

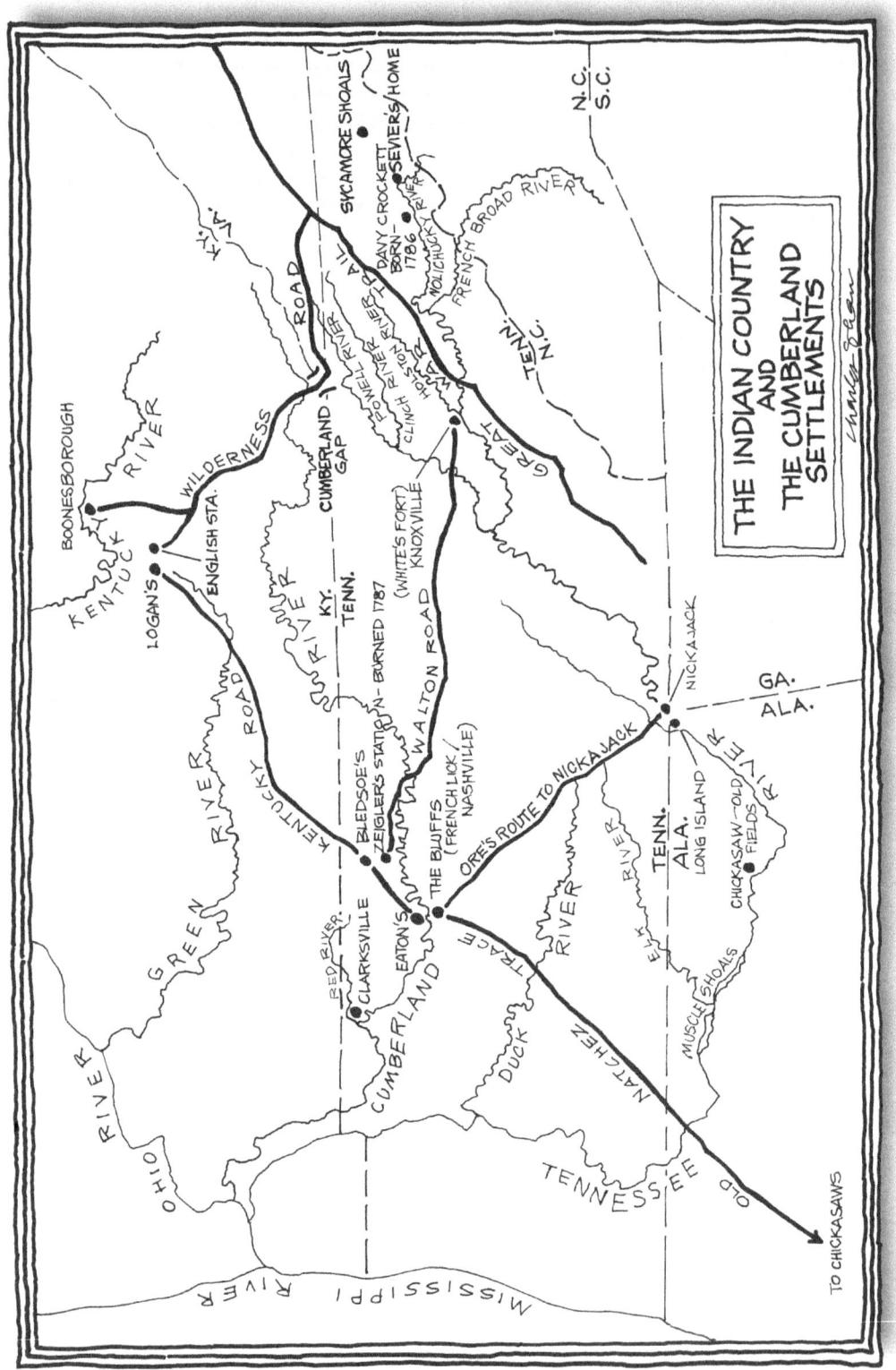

Chapter Three

Maps

Shown on many pages are several maps of those early regions showing the possible routes and trails used by our early ancestors in their search for new lands and the *"Western Waters."* The term used by many early explorers for the elusive route and rivers that would allow them access to the Pacific Ocean and points west.

Even though several hardy souls penetrated the dense forests west of the known coastal settlements of early English/ European occupation in the late 1600s (1673) and stumbled onto parts of the Great Lakes, and the Ohio River, real exploration would not take place for over 100 years. (Remember, I said English; the French had been in Canadian North America much longer) It is reported that Dr. Thomas Walker[1] of Virginia working for a land company named the Loyal Land Company, while exploring lands in that region for settlement, stumbled upon the Cumberland Gap (south western Virginia) and wrote about it in his journal dated 13 April 1750. Elisha Walden* would be the next well known "Long Rifleman" to make his way through the Cumberland Gap in 1761 and again in 1763 on extensive hunting forays. The most famous of the Long Riflemen, the man who made Kentucky and his own name a household word, Daniel Boone, would not make his way through the Gap until May of 1769. It is he that most people think about when they think of the so called "discovery" of what is now the state of Kentucky. This discovery of a passage through the great Appalachian wall into what is now known as Tennessee and Kentucky areas would allow hundreds of thousands of future settlers to pour into a region that heretofore had been blocked for settlement by the mountains. It is inconceivable today for one to understand that the civilized world in 1700 ended for the European settler at this particular mountain range until the discovery of these passages. And, it was found because the explorers were following an ancient Indian War Path.

I am not suggesting that there weren't other routes including the many streams and rivers that were used as highways in those days, I am simply stating this was the probable route of our particular family.

While we are looking at the maps and possible routes our ancestors took after leaving North Carolina and venturing into the Tennessee and Kentucky wilds, one must focus on the rivers. And really one river in particular—the Cumberland. It is so interesting that both the Cumberland and the Tennessee Rivers head up in eastern Tennessee and eastern Kentucky, flow southwesterly, then west, then northwesterly, until they empty into the River Ohio. Amazingly, the mouth of both the rivers is very close, with the Cumberland being slightly upstream from the other and just downstream from Henderson, Kentucky or Red Banks, as it was called by some in those days. Having said that, that's the end of the similarity. While both offered great advantages of travel to the frontiersman and his family as a frontier expressway so to speak, the Tennessee River was fraught with danger. Both were no piece of cake, as the marauding Indians would and could harass the unexpecting traveler with a hail of arrows and lead when the boats attempted to land or ventured too close to the shore. However, the Tennessee River was different in 1779 to 1790, as our ancestors made their way west to view their lands given to them for their services during the Revolution, the Tennessee dipped down much further south into what is now northwestern Alabama before turning back northwest into western Tennessee. This giant turn south for this major river and thoroughfare sent it directly into the heart of the Cherokee Confederation. Those few hardy souls who attempted this particular route ran into grave consequences.[2]

It is the belief of some researchers of our particular branch of Kuykendalls that some went overland into central Tennessee and some used the Cumberland River from the Elizabethton, Tennessee, area or the then Washington County, Tennessee, area. The overland group probably followed the Robertson route. Both routes would end up at the "French Licks" or Nashboro. However, the overland route to middle Tennessee was probably the most used until one got past the French Licks area and on into the Red River area at present day Clarksville, Tennessee. The river was too shallow up near Elizabethton.

Chapter Four

The People

In order to start naming members of Captain Robert H. Kuykendall's family, we must first name the generations. We are known as the southwest branch of the family.

1. Jacob Luurszen, the emigrant, was born in Holland ca. 1616, possibly in or near Wageningen, Holland. Jacob and his wife Stijntje Douwes (1617-after 1682) had possibly five children. Jacob died at Beverwyck (now Albany, New York) ca. 29 April 1655.

2. Luur Jacobsen, the second child of Jacob, was the first son born in the New World and he was baptized on 29 May 1650 in New Amsterdam, New York. His wife was Grietje Aertze Tack (b.1663–d.after 1720) and they had eleven known children. It is my belief that we descend from their sixth child and son named Matheus or old Matthew. (Some researchers believe it should be his brother, Cornelius. It has never been proven that Cornelius went south.) Luur died after 1720, possibly near Minisink, Delaware River Valley below present day Port Jervis, New York. (Note his movement southwest.)

3. Matheus, or Matthew, Luur's sixth son, was born ca. 1690 in or near Rochester, now Accord, New York. He was probably married twice. His first wife was Jannetje Westvael (b. before 1700, d. unknown). His second wife was Mary, last name unknown. There were eight known children according to the records of researcher Gifford White. Old Matthew lived near his brother, Jacob, in Sandyston Precent, Sussez County, New Jersey, on the Delaware River, and was there as late as 1731.[1] Old Matthew died supposedly in the summer of 1754 in Anson County in western North Carolina, now Mecklenburg County[2] (Note his movement southwest.)

4. Petrus, or Peter, the second child of old Matthew, was baptized on 28 January 1719 in the New York Dutch Reform Church at Minisink (below Port Jervis, New York) Died/Will 1783, Washington County, North Carolina, now Tennessee. His will is in Vol. 3, page 126 of the Winn Records.[3] Peter was married to a Mary, last name unknown, but most researchers tend to believe she was a Hampton. (The Hampton name will be used in the family after this time.) Peter had ten known children. Peter moved with his father from the Port Jervis area to what is now West Virginia and settled for a time along the banks of the South Branch of the Potomac River on lands granted to his father in 1749 by Thomas Lord Fairfax of Virginia. Peter and other family members owned 11 of the South Branch River lots. Old Matthew sold this land in 1751. Peter would then show up on many land transaction in the western North Carolina and South Carolina areas. Peter did not name a wife in his Will of 1783. She was probably deceased. (Note his movement southwest.) (Note map of Kuykendall's Fort on Lot #7, which was originally sold or granted to John Kuykendall on the 15th of June 1749. Lot #5 belonged to Abraham Kuykendall; Henry Kuykendal later owned a portion or all of Lot #7. In all, the family owned Lots #1,5, 6, 7, 8, 9, 10, 12, 17, 35, and 58.)[4]

5. Adam, the third child of Peter, was born ca. 1756-58 in Anson County, North Carolina. He is the father of our particular branch of the Kuykendall family, which migrated to Missouri Territory in 1810 (Arkansas) and then on into Mexican Texas. He married Margaret Hardin (1758-1835) before October of 1779. She was the daughter of Col. Joseph Hardin of Virginia and Tennessee and they had seven known children. Adam died in Arkansas before the census of 1830 and Margaret died there before the census of 1840. Adam's biography will follow. Adam Kuykendall was a Revolutionary Soldier as noted in his biography.

6. Robert H. Kuykendall was the third child of Adam and Margaret Hardin. Robert was born near Princeton, Kentucky, in 1790 (census report) as the family moved through that area on their migration southwest. This is the first time we see a middle initial used in the family and it will never be revealed to us. It is possibly Hampton but most assuredly it is Hardin, after his mother. Robert H. Kuykendall was one of the three brothers who went to Mexican/Texas with Stephen F. Austin in the fall of 1821 as members of what is now known as *Austin's Old 300*. Robert H. Kuykendall married Sarah Ann Gilleland (1797-1857), the daughter of William Gilleland. Gilleland Creek just east of Austin, Texas, is named after her brother James, who was killed by the Indians near there. Robert and Sarah had six known children. Robert died probably in 1830 as the result of an Indian fight in late 1827 or 1828. Robert's extensive biography will follow.

7. R. H. "Gill" Kuykendall, sheriff and rancher, was the first child of RHK, Sr. He was born ca. 1816 in Arkansas Territory near the Cadron Settlement as the family passed through that region. He was married twice. First to Electra Shannon and second to Matilda Earp. He had two sons by Electra and one daughter by Matilda. He was a veteran of the War of Texas Independence. He was killed by the indians or outlaws in 1846. His biography will follow.

8. Wiley Martin Kuykendall, rancher, the second son of RH, was born in 1839, probably in Ft. Bend County, Texas. He became a Chisum Trail cattle driver after the

great war. Wiley married Susan Pierce, sister to Abel Head (Shanghai) Pierce. He was a Civil War veteran. He died in 1920. His biography will follow.

9. Robert Gilden (Gill) Kuykendall, rancher, was the first son of Wiley M. and Susan P. Kuykendall. He was born in 1870 in Matagorda County, Texas. He married Margaret Martha (Maggie) Moore. He died in 1905. His biography will follow.

10. Wylie Moore "Bill" Kuykendall, rancher, was born at Ashby, Matagorda County, Texas, on 3 March 1899. He was married twice, first to Mildred Williams of Lockhart, Texas, and second to Alice Hamlett (27 October 1910–August 1993) of Austin, Texas. He had a daughter, Lamond Kuykendall by his first marriage and two sons, Robert Gilden (Gil) (1929) and Marshall Early (1932) by his second. He died on 12 October 1976 and is buried in the Kyle Cemetery in Kyle, Hays County, Texas. His wife, Alice, is buried next to him. His biography will follow.

The Biographies

—PRIMARY—

Adam Kuykendall, Frontiersman, Revolutionary Soldier
—Illustration drawn by Charlie Shaw

Chapter Five

Adam Kuykendall

Adam Kuykendall (1756-1828) was born ca. 1756, probably in Anson County, North Carolina. (Mecklenburg County was not formed until 1762, effective 1 Feb. 1763.) He was the son of Peter (1719) and Mary (Hampton?) If she was in fact a Hampton, as some researchers have suggested, then she probably was the sister of Col. Andrew Hampton and possibly Adam Hampton, if Adam Hampton was, indeed, a brother and not a son. The other interesting connection to this family is that the name Adam first appears in the Kuykendall line at this juncture and not before. It seems logical that Peter named his son after one of his Hampton brothers-in-law. To further confuse the issue, there has been some speculation by researchers that it was old Matthew, Peter's father, who married a Hampton and not Peter. Matthew's second wife, Mary, may have been the Hampton. Remember, the two families had been together since their settlement together on the South Potomac in the 1740s when they received land from Lord Fairfax.

The county seat of Mecklenburg County (1763) was Charlotte, which began as a tiny settlement in 1748. However, the area in which the first Kuykendalls lived, who came to North Carolina, stretched from what is now Lincoln County (Kirkendall's Creek and Dutchman's Creek) and Gaston County, south to as far as York and Chester counties (Fishing Creek); West and north to Cherokee, Cleveland, and

---

There is much confusion between researchers whether Peter was the son of old Matthew or the son of Cornelius. There will be no attempt in this writing to clear up that matter. However, this writing is based on the premise that Peter, the father of Adam was the son of old Matthew. The only known facts are that Adam was the son of (a) Peter Kuykendall, who filed his Will in Washington Co Tenn. in 1783 and stated the names of all his children in that Will.

Rutherford counties (Kings Creek near Kings Mountain). This area is about a one hundred mile radius of Charlotte. The fact that the area is so large shows to what extent the family went to acquire land over so a large area during the time. As different land offices opened, members of the family and their friends would immediately travel into those areas and buy more land. This family was always very aggressive in the acquisition of lands and the fact that so many deeds actually moved, it simply means that they had gone to that area or county to purchase more land. The deeds of Peter and Abraham Kuykendall, which are scattered throughout many counties in western North Carolina and South Carolina, not to mention eastern Tennessee, are a prime example of persons very actively acquiring more land. There is some difficulty in identifying all of the family members as they moved from one area to another and there was then the problem of overlapping generations of sons and grandsons bearing the same first names by the time they spread into Tryon County (Rutherford/Lincoln) on the First Broad River, Second Broad River, and Sandy Run (probably Cleveland County) (There is a Sandy River in Chester County, South Carolina, also.) However, most researchers are in agreement that all of this activity, which started originally in old Anson County, North Carolina, ca. 1754 and then spread out to the other counties was probably the work of a single family of Kuykendalls, all the sons and daughters of old Matthew (1690) and his first wife, Janetjen Westfall, namely Simon (1716) (no further info), Abraham (1720s), Peter (1719), James (Jacobus) (1721), John (ca 1720s), Elisabeth I (1726-died), Elisabeth II (1728), and Jacob (after 1730), who was probably Matthew's son by his second wife, Mary. After old Matthew's death ca 1754 in Anson County, North Carolina, Mary would marry Martin Armstrong.[1]

In North and South Carolina, land acquisition at the time the family was there, was in a sense a free-for-all. Some one would give a vague description of a tract, then a warrant was issued for the piece to be surveyed, after which a grant might be issued. There was no pre-definition of what a tract might look like, that is, tracts were not laid off in regular shapes or in sections and townships like they were later done in the western U.S.A. It was up to the surveyor to make sure the boundaries of one tract didn't overlap with the lines of another, and since only one or two surveyors worked a given area, this did not tend to be an immense problem, even though overlapping did occasionally occur. To date, neither North Carolina nor South Carolina have ever created a mapping system that shows those original land grants and only a few individuals have pieced together land grant maps that cover their area of interest.[2]

The major rivers of North Carolina in the Piedmont (central) and eastern regions are the Roanoake River, the Tar, Neuse, Cape Fear, Yadkin-Pee Dee, and the Catawba Rivers, which flow southeasterly toward the Atlantic Ocean. The Roanoake, the Tar and the Neuse rivers empty into the Sounds and the Cape Fear River flows directly into the Atlantic. The Yadkin-Pee Dee and the Catawba Rivers both flow into South Carolina before reaching the sea. In the western part of the state are the Little Tennessee and French Broad rivers, which both flow toward the Mississippi River and the Gulf of Mexico.[3]

In Colonial times, inland waterways provided the best means of transportation. Land roads often followed the Indian trails or warpaths. Using the waterways as a guide, one will note how close to the major streams all the land records occur. In the North Carolina and South Carolina land grants, the records show that Peter

Kuykendall had 200 acres on Fishing Creek adjacent other Kuykendalls, the Woods and the McDowels, on the north side of Dickens Fork of said creek. The deed was dated 15 November 1762 and the survey was done by Arthur Dobbs. Records dated 25 April 1767 also reflect that Peter had 400 acres on the north side of Fishing Creek. This land adjoined or was in the area of his two brothers, Abraham and James. This survey was done by William Tryon. Other neighbors is this area were a possible aunt, Rebecca Hardin Kuykendall, wife of John Kuykendall (son of old Matthew); Andrew Woods, Martin Armstrong, the Humphreys, Beatys (Bettys) and the Millicans.

The different branches of Fishing Creek were called Humphreys Branch, Beaver Dam Branch, and the South Fork. Abraham Kuykendall had land on the north side of the Broad River and on the Sandy River as early as 1752. The land described above has gone through many county changes and is probably located today in present York County, South Carolina, just southeast of Kings Mountain. *(See Holcomb below.)*

One will notice from old maps of the period the difference in the boundary of today between North Carolina and South Carolina and the original one of early records. It is easy to see why so much of the land was in South Carolina after the line was resurveyed. In the introduction of the Tryon Abstract book of Brent H. Holcomb, he states "Tryon County was formed from Mecklinburg in 1769, Mecklinburg having been formed from Anson County. in 1763. At its formation, Tryon County extended north to Earl of Granville's line and west to the Indian Line of 1767 *(a portion of which is now the line between Greenville and Spartanburg Counties, South Carolina)*. The eastern boundary was the Catawba River. Tryon County included all or part of the North Carolina counties of Lincoln, Gaston, Cleveland, Rutherford, Henderson, Polk, Burke, and McDowell and the South Carolina counties of York, Chester, Union, Cherokee, Spartanburg, Greenville, Laurens, and Newberry. The first courts of Tryon County were held in what is now York County, South Carolina. The courthouse site was moved to present day Gaston County, North Carolina, when the border survey of 1772 determined the other site to be in South Carolina.

When the border survey was made, the South Carolina county system as is known today was not yet set up. The Tryon County lands south of the border were then in Craven or Barkley counties and/or Camden or the "Ninety Six District." This is one of the reasons so many records of those days will be found in county courthouses located in South Carolina. One will also realize the immense area that the settlers operated in during the period.[4]

As stated earlier, evidence suggests that old Matthew, father of Peter (1719), James, Abraham, John, and Jacob, migrated from New York State on down into North Carolina, going by the way of the South Fork of the Potomac River, near Roanoke, Virginia, now West Virginia, where old Matthew and his son Peter received parcels of land from Lord Fairfax. If any sons of Cornelius traveled with their uncle Matthew, they probably stayed in West Virginia.[5]

Earliest mention of the North Carolina Kuykendalls is a list from the Anson County North Carolina records of married and single men in the Spanish Alarm of 1747-1748. The Spanish American War of 1739-1748, known in Europe as the War of Jenkin's Ear (1739-1744) and King George's War (1744-1748), or combined as the "War of the Austrian Succession" was known in North Carolina as the "Spanish

Alarm." Upon the outbreak of England's war with Spain, North Carolina raised four companies of 100 men each to join other Colonial troops in the siege of Cartagena (in present-day Columbia, South America). One company commanded by James Innes set sail from the colony in 1740 and returned after two fever-ridden years with only 25 survivors.[6]

In addition to the 400 men raised for the Cartagena expedition, it was necessary for the colony to raise forces for the defense of its coast. Spanish attacks on North Carolina shipping and port towns were continuous from 1741-1748. The town of Beauford was taken and plundered by them in 1747, and Brunswick met the same fate in 1748. The Treaty of Aix-la-Chapelle (1748) ended the war in Europe and in America as well, and the Spanish depredations along the North Carolina coast came to an end.[7]

The Militia returns of 1748 (North Carolina) for Captain Samuel Coborn show a list of the married men with the names of John, Abraham, James, and Peter Kuykendall among its members. This was recorded in Blandon County, North Carolina, as Anson County was not formed until 17 March 1750. At that time, Peter (1719), son of Matthew, would have been 29 years old and consistent with the ages of the other men in the company. Had this been Peter (1733), son of Cornelius, he would have been only 15 years of age at the time. Therefore from this record, one knows that this Peter (1719), whose wife was Mary, possibly a Hampton (from deeds before 1754), was the son of old Matthew. However, it must be noted again that to date no concrete proof has been found as to actually which Peter was really Adam's father other than the Peter whose Will was recorded in Washington County, Tennessee, in 1783.[8]

Adam's father, Peter, had come south as a young boy originally from his birthplace in Minisink, New York, probably over the Great Wagon Road which ran from New York State southwesterly through Philadelphia or southwest from Port Jervis, New York, to near Allenton, on to Harrisburg, crossing the Potomac River in the Hagerstown-Harpers Ferry area, then southwest by Harrisburg, Virginia, then the Lexington, Fincastle, Roanoak area, entering into North Carolina and crossing the Yadkin River at Shallow Ford Ferry close to Bethania and Farmington, on through Mocksville to Salisbury, North Carolina, then from Charlotte, North Carolina, to Rock Hill, Chester, Newberry, South Carolina, etc. From Salisbury, another road turned west-southwest toward Georgia. Another road was from Charlotte Town into the lower western part of North Carolina. (*See the Map of the Great Phildelphia Wagon Road.*)[9]

Another description of the great Wagon Road was written by Dr. Harry Y. Gamblo, pastor of the Calvary Baptist Church of Roanoak, Virginia, and reads as follows:

> When Gen. Braddock was defeated by the Indians on July 9th, 1755, near Pittsburg, all the frontier was thrown into a state of disorder. The western parts of Pennsylvania, Maryland, and Virginia were left exposed to the incursions of the Savages; the frontier settlements were generally broken up and the inhabitants were driven into the interior, some fled in one direction, and some in another, as attachments to distant friends, or as prospects of safety or interest directed. At this time many moved south-ward along the Great Wagon Road. This famous road began at the Schuylkill River Ferry on the east side of Philadelphia. The Schuylkill rises to the

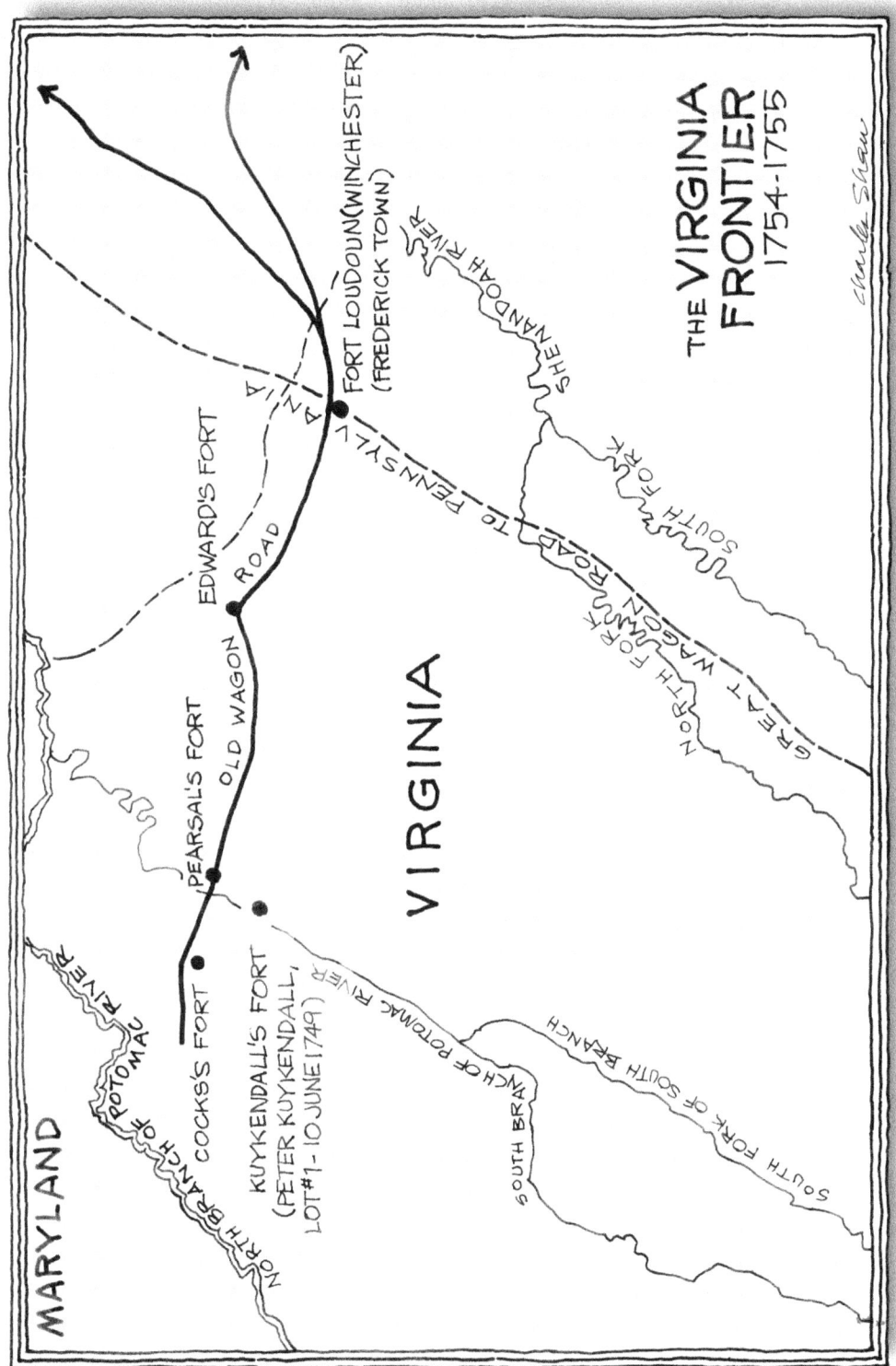

Map of the Virginia Frontier, 1754-1755

south of Hazelton, near the center of eastern Pennsylvania, and flows southward through Schuylkill Haven thence to Port Clinton where it is joined by the Little Schuylkill. The larger river then flows south through Reading, then in a southwesterly direction through Pottstown and Norristown to the southern Philadelphia area where it joins the Delaware.

Beginning at the Schuylkill River Ferry, the road ran west through what is known as the Pennsylvania Dutch Country to Lancaster, Pennsylvania, thence to Harris Ferry on the Susquehanna River (midway between Lancaster and York) and on to York, Pennsylvania. The road then moved in a gradual southwestern direction crossing part

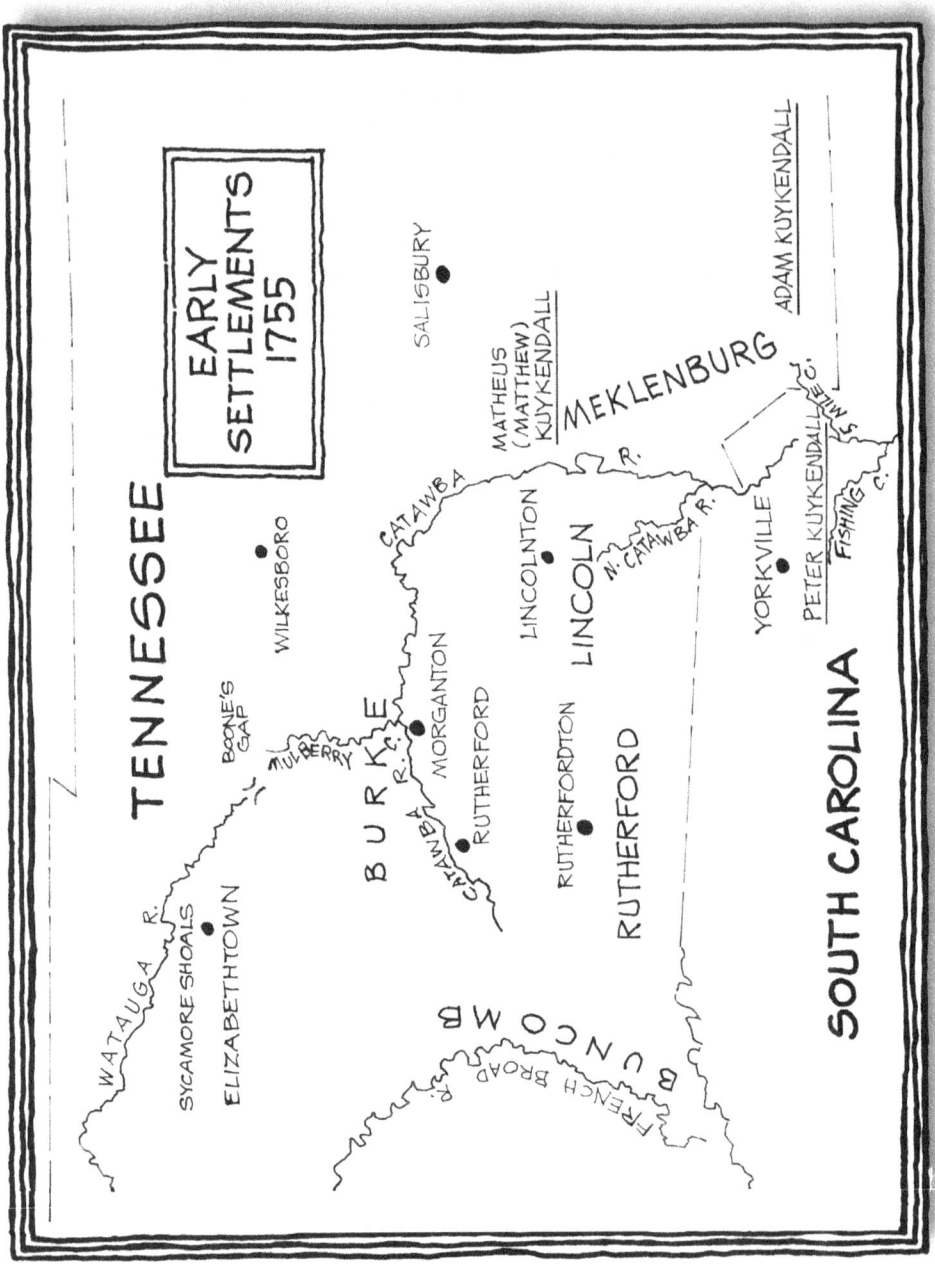

Early Map of South Carolina.
—Drawn by Charlie Shaw

of what is now Maryland to William's Ferry on the Potomac River, then stretched southwest across the tip of now West Virginia to the beautiful plateau of the Winchester, Virginia, area just south of the most eastward thrust of present day West Virginia. From Winchester, the road ran to present day Strasburg, where the northern reaches of the Blue Ridge suddenly sprawl eastward as if by natural accommodation to open the mouth of the great valley of Virginia lying between the Appalachians on the west and the Blue Ridge on the east.

Much of HWY Rt. 11, running through the valley follows the bed of the Old Wagon Road. At some points it parallels or bisects the old road. The new Interstate HWY 81 through the valley runs some distance west of the old road. Entering the beautiful valley and hugging close to the Blue Ridge, the road ran from Strasburg or near the present day towns of Tom's Brook, Woodstock, Mt. Jackson, New Market, Mauzy and through the Lexington area to Buchanan where the James River was crossed at Looney's Ferry and where the Appalachian Range makes a southeasterly thrust to meet the Blue Ridge. Moving toward the present site of Roanoke and with diminishing ruggedness of the Blue Ridge permitting more frequent passages of safety to the east, the road turned eastward through the Staunton Gap, then southward crossing the Blackwater, Irvine, and Dan Rivers and then on to Wachovia, North Carolina, on a tributary of the Yadkin River. After about 1756, the road ran on to the Trading Ford on the Yadkin River near present day Salisbury, where it intersected other old trails originating in Virginia and leading into the south and southwest from the Trading Ford.[10]

Peter Kuykendall (1719), son of old Matthew, must have tarried along the way, for records state that in December of 1743, he (along with Jonathon Coburn, Isaac Thomas, and James Delheryea) was ordered to mark off a road from Noah Hampton's Mill (present day West Virginia) to a road on the Great Cacapon River, near James Coddy's Fort. The Noah Hampton Mill was known as the old Stackhouse Mill on the Capon River, which would be located today about halfway between Romney, West Virginia and Winchester, Virginia.

On the 10th of June 1749, this Peter received some land from Lord Fairfax of Virginia on the south branch of the Potomac River. (Lot #1, 420 acres) Peter's father, Matthew (1690), also received a grant from Lord Fairfax, to-wit, Lot #5, 337 acres in 1749. Old Matthew sold this tract in 1751 and supposedly moved to Anson County, North Carolina. The records reflect that Peter sold his land in 1753. At any rate, it has been established that old Matthew (1690) left New York with half his sons and possibly some of his brother Cornelius's sons and rambled all the way down to Anson County, North Carolina to Dutchman's Creek, where the old man died ca. 1754. Before his death, old Matthew deeded his son Peter land on the Catawba River (1 March 1754) in what was then Anson County, North Carolina. After Anson County was split, this land would be located in Mecklinburg County, North Carolina. It is assumed by researchers that Peter moved to North Carolina in order to claim this sale or gift from his father. Later in 1771, when the border changes between North Carolina and South Carolina, this land probably falls into what was then known as Craven Count, South Carolina, then the Camden District, then York County, South Carolina, as it is known today. After all is said and done, if indeed this Peter is the son of old Matthew (1690-1754) and is the same Peter (1719-1783) whose Will is filed in Washington County, Tennessee, in 1783, then this Peter is the father of our Adam.

Note: There was a "Fort Kuykendall" established in this same area that was located on Lot #7 conveyed to James Kuykendall by Thomas Lord Fairfax on the 15th of June 1749. It had been built by some of the Kuykendall families living on the South Potomac River and was completed by some time in 1754 or 1755. Several of the Kuykendall families purchased four of the South Branch lots directly from Lord Fairfax and by 1768 they had acquired eleven of these lots, having more of these parcels than any other frontier family there at that time. The Lot owners of numbers 1, 5, 6, 7, 8, 9, 10, 12, 17, 35, and 58 were Peter, Matthias (old Matthew), John, Benjamin, Nathaniel, Abraham, Jacob, and Henry Kuykendall. (Not in order of ownership.) George Washington in his writings referred to this Fort on many occasions.[11] (See map of Kuykendall fort on page 19.)

Note: Young George Washington had been in the surveying party on the Fairfax tract.[12]

Peter's Will was recorded in Washington County, Tennessee, in 1783. Researchers know that Abraham (1720s), Peter's brother, was administrator of the Will, and that a John Kuykendall was a witness. This John probably was a nephew.[13]

The Kuykendall brothers had land scattered all over the area, some on Kings Creek near Kings Mountain and some on Fishing Creek and Dutchman's Creek off of the Catawba River. (Some reseachers believe Adam was kin to the family who lived near Kings Mountain.) (See Matthew Kuykendall's Revolutionary Pension Report.) Researchers state that John, son of old Matthew, died in 1762 in what was then Anson County, North Carolina. (Old Matthew died in Anson County. ca. 1754). Yet a John Kuykendall witnessed Peter's "Will" over in Tennessee in 1783. One would think he would be a nephew, the brother being deceased. This John was probably the son of Abraham, b. ca. 1752, who would have accompanied his father over to Washington County, Tennessee. There was another nephew, John, b. ca. 1760, son of the John who died in Anson County in 1762, but it seems unlikely that he would have gone over the mountains at that time.[14]

Researchers know that there are at least two deeds signed "Abraham Kuykendall of Washington County" recorded in Buncombe County, and his son Matthew was one of the two Matthews at the Battle of Kings Mountain. (This same Matthew named his son Abraham H. Kuykendall after his father.) Descendants claim this to be the same Abraham (1720s) of Henderson County, North Carolina, who died ca 1812 and is buried at Mud Creek Cemetery in what is now Henderson County (Flat Rock), North Carolina. Researchers know from Peter's son Matthew's pension application that he was visiting his relatives near Kings Mountain (Kings Creek) during the time of the battle. This Matthew, son of Peter, will be known as Matthew, the Pensioner.[15]

Again, there are two Matthews in question at the Battle of Kings Mountain, one of them in Campbell's Regiment and the other one who was in the "vicinity" but not in the battle who was in Col. Charles McDowell's Regiment, Capt. Joseph McDowell's company. The one in the "vicinity" who filed the pension application in 1832, was Adam's brother, and is the one who died in Butler County, Kentucky. The other Matthew listed in Campbell's Regiment and also listed in the "Kings Mountain Heroes" (?) was the son of Abraham. There has been much confusion between the two Matthews, first cousins to one another, because they were both born about the same year, 1758.

At this point I want to insert a part of Matthew's pension application statement because it states where Matthew lived over a good many years and shows an interesting parallel to Adam Kuykendall's movements over the same period of time. Matthew states:

> that he was born in Mecklinburg County, North Carolina (originally Anson) on October 24th, 1758, that he lived in Burke County, North Carolina a few years after he was wounded (at the Cow Pens, January of 1781), when he moved to Washington County, North Carolina (later Tennessee) and lived there 3-4 years, when he removed to Davidson County, Tennessee (formed in 1783) and lived there 8-10 years, when he removed to Logan County (formed in 1792)(that part of which is now Butler County), Kentucky, where he now resides.

Burke County, North Carolina (created from Rowan in 1777) joins the Tennessee border next to the Washington District, later known as Washington County, Tennessee. Washington County was created in 1777 from Wilkes and Burke counties. Adam lived in Washington County about this time. Matthew then moved over the mountains into the same county as Adam. Later the records reflect that they both show up on a jury panel in Sumner County, Tennessee. Sumner was created from Davidson in 1786, where Matthew said he lived. Matthew then moved to Logan County, Kentucky. So did Adam. *They just lived in different parts of Logan County, and when the new counties were formed from Logan County, Adam ended up in the Henderson County part and Matthew was in the Butler County part.* Around 1809-10, when Adam and his bunch started their migration into Missouri Territory (Arkansas), his brother Matthew, who would have been around 52 years of age at the time, and who lived some distance away, decided not to be up-rooted again and elected to spend the rest of his life in Butler County, Kentucky. Not so with the others—new lands meant new adventures, and the bulk of them were off again, many of them in their 50s and 60s.[16]

Adam Kuykendall deeded a tract of land in 1779 as follows: DEED, 18 Oct. 1779 between Adam Kirkendall of the County of Rutherford and State of North Carolina and Joseph Carpenter, 232 acres on both sides of Knob Creek. (signed) Adam Kuykendall, Marg't Kuykendall. (witnesses) Saml. Carpenter, J. Stevenson, and Saml. Young.[17]

As stated above, when Adam was about 23 years old, he sold a piece of land in Lincoln County, North Carolina (present day Lincoln County is 75 miles north of present day York County, South Carolina) and probably took his family and maybe his father, Peter, and moved to Washington District (now Tennessee), which was still a part of North Carolina, where he shows up on the tax rolls in 1781, with 150 acres and some livestock. Adam probably moved over the mountains into present day eastern Tennessee in the company of his father-in-law, Col. Joseph Hardin, either soon after the sale or just after the battle of Ramsour's Mill, which had occurred near their lands on Knob Creek in Lincoln County, North Carolina, on June 20, 1780. (Joseph Hardin was one of the officers in that battle and Adam's brother, Matthew, was also in the battle.) Many of these participants had to flee with all their possessions after that battle to escape the Tories. Ramsey said, "Many where forced, in their turn, to forsake their plantations, and transport their families beyond the mountains to the securer retreats of Watuaga and Nollichucky." This also coincides with movement of the British General Ferguson and his troops into that same area near the mountains that separated North Carolina from Tennessee, Gilbert Town, near present day Rutherfordton, and from which point he sent the threatening message to the Over Mountain people that if they did not lay down their arms and cease opposition to the Crown, "he would march his army over, burn and lay waste their country and hang their leaders." The reaction by Sevier, Shelby, and the other leaders was instantaneous and they immediately decided to attack Ferguson before he could attack them, which sparked the great battle at Kings Mountain later in October. Interestingly, many of the families including the Kuykendalls and the Hardins, who escaped over the mountains probably in the summer of 1780, would join the Over Mountain Men from Tennessee in October in their historic forced march out of eastern Tennessee on their way to their victory at Kings Mountain.

Ramsey states, "The refugee Whigs mustered under Col. McDowell. (See Matthew Kuykendall's Pension application.) All were well mounted, and nearly all were armed with a Deckhard Rifle. This rifle was remarkable for the precision and the distance of its shot. It was generally three feet six inches long, weighed about seven pounds and ran about seventy bullets to a pound of lead. It was so called from Deckhard, the maker, in Lancaster, Pa.—Each man, each officer, set out with his trusty Deckhard on his shoulder, a shot-pouch, a tomahawk, a knife, a knapsack and a blanket completed the outfit."

A letter from Shelby and others to General Gates:

"A statement of the proceedings of the Western Army, from the 25th of September, 1780, to the reduction of Major Ferguson and the army under his command.

On receiving intelligence that Major Ferguson had advanced as high up as Gilbert Town, in Rutherford County, and threatened to cross the mountains into the "Western Waters," Col. William Campbell, with four hundred men from Washington County, Virginia (now Tennessee); Col. Isaac Shelby, with two hundred and forty men from Sullivan County, North Carolina (now Tennessee), and Lt. Col. John Sevier, with two hundred and forty men from Washington County, North Carolina (now Tennessee), assembled at Watauga on the 25th of September, where they were joined by Col. Charles McDowell, with one hundred and sixty men from the counties of Burke and Rutherford, who had fled before the enemy to the "Western Waters."

Matthew Kuykendall states in his Pension Application that McDowell allowed him to visit his family who lived near Kings Mountain and he missed the battle, but joined up with them just afterwards to march with them and help guard the prisoners. Ramsey: "The flints were taken from their locks, and the most vigilant espionage kept over the prisoners by the troops—at sundown, they met the men they had left on foot on their hurried march to the battle. The march was continued pretty close to the mountain till the fourteenth, when a court-martial was held at Bickerstaff's Old Field, in Rutherford County."—and several Tories were executed by hanging.

Ramsey: "the hunting shirt, with its fringes, wampum belts, leggins and moccasins, the tomahawk and knife; these with the well known death-dealing aim of these matchless marksmen, created in the European military, a degree of awe and respect for the hunting shirt which lasted with the war of the Revolution."

Two years later, Adam appears as a taxpayer in Greene County (separated from Washington County) and shows to be a co-signer on a $10,000 bond with Col. Joseph Hardin (his father-in-law) in the August Court in the same county. Adam's father, Peter died between February and May of 1783 and in the "Will," Adam received five shillings. The "Will" was recorded in Washington County, Tennessee. When Tennessee as the Southwest Territory was separated from North Carolina in early 1790, a small part of Tennessee's Washington County remained in North Carolina and was statutorily outside any North Carolina county during the 1790 Census. Whether this area was counted or not has not been determined. See map guides to the federal censuses in any State genealogical library.[18]

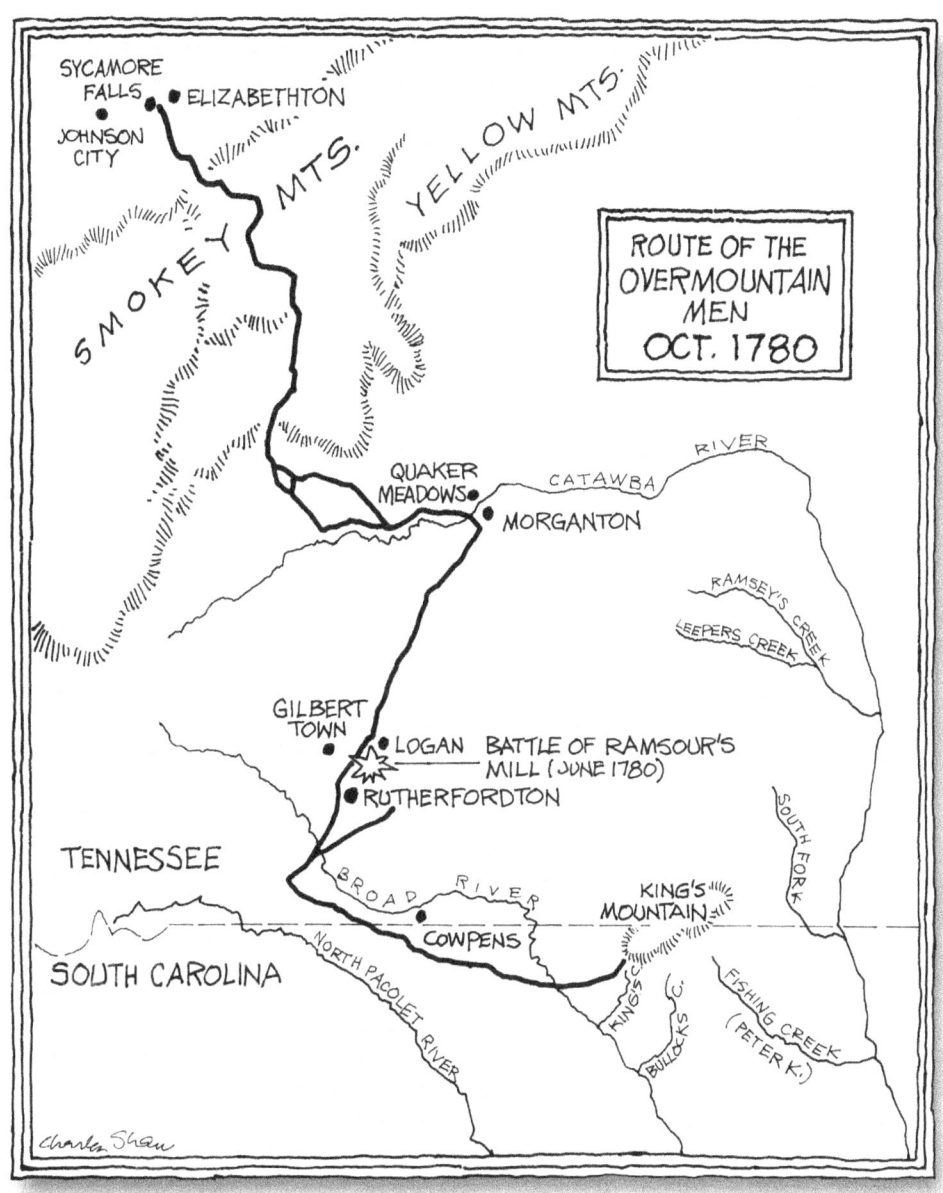

Peter Kuykendall's children as mentioned in the Washington County, Tennessee, Will of 1783 were: Adam (to Arkansas), Matthew (to Butler County, Kentucky), Peter Jr. (to Missouri), Elisabeth, Jane, Mary, Ruth, Rebecca, Affray (Affay) and Jesse Young K.[19]

Adam received Land Warrant #1604 in payment from North Carolina for his services during the Revolutionary War that was located in Davidson County, Tennessee, (later Sumner County). He sold or gave this land to Benjamin Hardin III in 1788 probably on the same day he received it. The deed states: "Know Ye: that we have granted unto Benjamin Hardin Sr. (III), assignee of Adam Kuykendall, a private in the Continental Line of said state," etc. (Researchers argue over whether the statement pertains to Adam or to Benjamin, but the consensus is that it refers to Adam as the "soldier" in the Continental Line.) In May of 1780, the General Assembly of North Carolina had passed a resolution to give officers and soldiers, in its *"Line of Continental Establishment,"* a bounty in lands in proportion to their respective grades. These lands were to be laid off in what was known as *"Middle Tennessee."* Adam later shows up on the Tax List for Sumner County in 1788, 1789, and in 1790 he appears on a Jury List for the county, and was excused from jury duty along with his brother Matthew in 1791. As stated earlier, the records show that Adam was married to Margaret Hardin, daughter of Joseph Hardin and Jean Gibson Hardin (of (K) Nob Creek, North Carolina), later of Greene and Knox County, Tennessee. Obviously, Adam and Margaret had gotten married prior to October 1779 (above mentioned deed) and prior to leaving for Tennessee.

(*Note*: In order to fulfill a recruiting promise made by the state to soldiers enlisting in the regular army (Continental Line) during the Revolutionary War, North Carolina set aside a large tract of land in what subsequently became Davidson and Sumner counties, Tennessee. After the war, and until as late as 1841, North Carolina issued more than 6,500 warrants for grants of bounty lands. Until 1797 the grants were made by North Carolina, but after 1800, the grants were made by Tennessee.)[20]

When the family left eastern Tennessee on their way out west to the middle district, it has been assumed by researchers that they probably went northwest out of Washington and Greene counties, crossing through the Cumberland Gap into present day Kentucky, then either loaded onto "keel" boats on the Cumberland River and floated down to the "French Licks" (Nashville) or went overland on what was to be known as "Robertson's route of 1779" via the Kentucky Trace. This overland route was via the Cumberland Gap and the Kentucky Trace to Whitley's Station on Dick's River; then on to Carpenter's Station on the waters of the Green River; then to Robertson's Fork on the north side of that stream; then down the river to Pitman's Station, crossing the river at that point and descending that river to the Little Barron River, crossing it at Elk Lick; then passing the Blue Spring and the Dripping Spring on the Barren River to Big Barren; then up to Drake's Spring to a bituminous spring; then to the Maple Swamp; then on to the Red River, at Kilgore's Station; then on to Mansco's Creek; and from there on into French Lick (Nashboro or Nashville). It wasn't until several years later that the Tennessee Militia would build a newer and more direct road from the area around present day Knoxville over to the "Bluffs" or Nashville.

However, recent letters from the Tennessee Historical Society reveal that most of the settlers of this period probably went from the Watuaga, Washington, Greene

Keel boat on the Cumberland River

County areas through the Cumberland Gap then overland via the Wilderness road into Kentucky to Boonsboro-Harrodsburg-Bardstown area, then down the Kentucky road via the present Glasgow region into Sumner and Davidson counties of Tennessee or the French Licks, Nashville. That is the route now followed by the modern Hwy. US 31E. The feelings were that the Cumberland River ran too shallow in the upper regions for our ancestors to successfully use that river at that point. Also, the Cherokee Indians under Chief Dragging Canoe controlled the Tennessee River and played havoc with all the poor settlers who were either brave enough or dumb enough to attempt travel on the particular stream. Hence the more probable use of the more northern land route into Kentucky then looping down into Tennessee.[21]

Note: In 1790-1800, Sumner County, Tennessee encompassed a great part of north-central Tennessee, joining Kentucky on the north and the Cumberland River on the south and/or crossing over it for a goodly distance. Those people using the Cumberland River could have easily stopped off anywhere. Several of the Kuykendalls and the Hardins did just that and settled or had land along the Red River in north-central Tennessee; the Red which empties into the Cumberland at Clarksville, Tennessee. This area would have been at that time both in Davidson and Sumner counties. Davidson on the western side and Sumner on the more easterly side.[22]

Note: Col. Joseph Hardin and his wife, Jean Gibson Hardin, had fourteen children—nine sons and five daughters, to wit: Joseph Jr., John, Jane, James, Benjamin, Robert, Elender, Mary E., Margaret, Benjamin II, Amos, Rebecca, Gibson, and Robert II. These Hardins are known as the "Knob Creek Hardins" to differentiate them from the "Hickory Creek Hardins."[23]

Col. Joseph's brothers and sisters were Benjamin III (married to Catherine), John (married to Elizabeth Kuykendall, probably the daughter of old Matthew (1690)), Sarah (married to Col. Frederick Hambright), and Rebecca, who was probably married to John Kuykendall (son of old Matthew), and brother to Peter (1719)[24]

Benjamin I and Sarah Hardin were the grandparents of Col. Joseph Hardin. (See Will of Benjamin Hardin, Surrey County, Virginia, and recorded in Will Book 8, page 382 of said county, book dated 6 Feb. 1732-39, Jan. 1734. Also see Will of Sarah Hardin recorded in Isle of Wight County, Virginia, in Will Book 8, page 261, dated 6 January 1747.)[25]

In Tommie Cochran Patterson's *Biography of Col. Joseph Hardin*, dated 1931, it is stated that an "old day book" in possession of the family in Hardin County, Tennessee, gives the name of Joseph's father as Benjamin II and states that Joseph was born near Richmond, Virginia. Col. Joseph Hardin was supposedly born there on 18 April 1734, and he died on 4 July 1801, and is buried in Hardin's Valley, Tennessee. His grave is located in the Hickory Creek Cemetery near Concord in Knox County, Tennessee. (It is now known as the Mt. Pleasant Baptist Church Cemetery near Concord and just north of present day Lenoir City in western Knox County, Tennessee.)[26]

Major Joseph Hardin, his brother Benjamin III, his father-in-law, James McAfee, his brother-in-law, Frederick Hambright, and Joseph (Pulaski) Kuykendall, among others, are mentioned as signers of the celebrated Tryon Declaration of Independence dated 14 August 1775.[27]

Joseph Hardin and his brothers and sisters came to North Carolina from Virginia and they first appear on Deed Records in Anson County, North Carolina, in 1753.

The three brothers were later all veterans of the Revolutionary War. A history of Col. Joseph Hardin states he received a total of 8,100 acres of land in Military Grants between 1788 and 1803 for his services during the war.[28]

The colonel's son, Joseph Hardin, Jr., went to Arkansas ca 1816 and settled in old Lawrence County, Arkansas, then later moved to Clark County, Arkansas, and died there ca. 1850. Three other sons of the colonel were killed by the Indians—Benjamin at "Licklogin" in Greene County, Tennessee, John at "Lookout Mountain," and Robert at "Flinn's Lick," Kentucky. Another Joseph Hardin, son of Benjamin IV, went to Davidson County, Arkansas, ca 1811 and was sheriff there and shows up on many records of the period. He died in that county in 1826.

Note: The great Texas gunfighter, John Wesley Hardin was the great-grandson of Col. Joseph Hardin. His father was James Gibson Hardin, son of Col. Joseph's son, Benjamin II. Benjamin I was killed at Licklogin in Greene County, Tennessee. The colonel then named his next son Benjamin II.[29]

Joseph (Pulaski) Kuykendall (son of John who died in 1762) was in Greene County, Tennessee, with the family and served on the August 1783-84 Court under Col. Hardin. A Matthew, probably Adam's brother, was also with the family and served on the May 1784 Court with the colonel. Matthew, Adam's brother, was pensioned for his services during the Revolutionary War, as mentioned earlier. He went to Butler County, Kentucky. A John Kuykendall, probably a brother to Joseph (Pulaski) and a son of old John was with them also and is listed in the August Court for 1784. Matthew Kuykendall, Adam's brother, married Jane Hardin, daughter of John and Elisabeth Hardin. This John was the colonel's brother.[30]

It was noted earlier that while in Greene County, Tennessee, in 1788, Adam sold or gave his Davidson County Revolutionary Land Grant Warrant #1604 to Benjamin Hardin III. Four years later in 1792, Adam's signature appears on a "List of the Male Inhabitants" of Logan County, Kentucky, along with Abner, his son. It states he is located in the village of "Red Banks," the present name of Henderson, Kentucky, on the red banks of the Ohio River. The records reflect that his land was located on "Highland Creek" near "Whitelick" in Henderson County, Kentucky. (Note: it was first Logan County, out of Russellville, Kentucky, then Christian County, and lastly, Henderson County, Kentucky.) Present day Henderson, Kentucky, is located on the high red bluffs overlooking the mile wide Ohio River, created by the "Transylvania Co." in the year 1797 out of 200,000 acres granted to the company by the state. The first settlements were located in and around the old Stockade village of "Red Banks," Kentucky. (Henderson, Kentucky, was later named after Col. Richard Henderson, the leader of the company.) An original plat of the town is in the courthouse and on the list of partners of the "Transylvania-Louisa-Co." are the names of many North Carolinians.[31]

Before Henderson was formed, the residents of the area had to travel to Russellville, Kentucky, to court. On 23 December 1794, the court in then Logan County, Kentucky, appointed commissioners "to view" a road from the Red Banks on the Ohio River to Russellville, keeping on the south side of the Green River. Morton Maulding, William Gates, Reason Bowie, and West Maulding were the commissioners. Those appointed by the commissioners to plan the road were Benjamin Hardin, Morton Maulding, Ab Hardin, James Stewart, John McCombs, and Joseph Worthington.

Note: William Gates was the father-in-law of Abner Kuykendall, Adam's oldest son.[32]

The records state that Adam was on the Tax Roll for Logan County, Kentucky (at Red Banks), in 1793 and again in 1795. In 1797, Logan County was changed to Christian County and he shows up on that record. In 1799, the county name was changed again, this time to Henderson County and Adam was on that Roll also. (Keep in mind that Adam had probably not moved, just the county names had changed.) In October 1799, the Court returned two indictments against Amos, the son of Adam, one for swearing and the other for riding through the roads of town (Henderson), naked. Note: *"Drunk, rode up the streets like Indians."* Adam's name appears on the Tax Roll for the county again on 1 October 1800. Adam's name appears again on the Henderson County Tax List in 1801, 1802, 1803, 1804, and 1809.[33]

Records state "on Tuesday, the 2nd of July 1799, the First Court Criminal Common Law and Chancery Jurisdiction held its sitting in the village of Henderson, Kentucky. A grand jury was then impaneled, consisting of citizens of the area. William Gates served as a member of this first grand jury." Records further reflect that as late as the July term of 1810, the Court appointed Abner Kuykendall (son of Adam), Wm. Gates (Abner's father in law), and Humphrey Barnett to view a road from the town of Henderson to the main fork of Highland Creek. The road crossed Canoe Creek about 100 yards above the old ford on the Trace to Diamond Island. Again, note that William Gate's wife, Catherine Hardin, the daughter of John, was Margaret Hardin Kuykendall's aunt.[34]

One needs to bear in mind that the Kuykendall family had been in North Carolina/South Carolina since probably as early as the 1748 Spanish Alarm War and 1752 (earliest deeds to Abraham and Peter are dated 1752). This put the Kuykendalls in the Kings Mountain area 27 years before the American Revolution. It also had them living around the area which became a hot bed of unrest a few years later as the revolution heated up between all the factions of the Tories and the non-Tories, known as the Whigs. It is very likely that a lot of these families living so close to the warring factions and being involved in the different Colonial Militias, left a good many of them refugees and is a very good reason why the family probably moved into Washington County, Tennessee. (See the bio of Col. Joseph Hardin by Patterson which states that when the family farms were overrun by the British and/or the Tories, the families had to move across the mountains for safety.) So even though records show the family in Washington County, Tennessee in 1781, the family had obviously been there a year or so earlier.[35]

The records have stated that Adam's brother Matthew received a land grant for his services during the revolutionary war. This is rather plausible when one reads the Roster List of the names in the great battle at Kings Mountain, South Carolina, on 7 October 1780. The list contains the names of two Matthew Kuykendalls, Adam's brother and his cousin; Joseph (Pulaski) Kuykendall, son of old John and also a cousin to Adam, and Joseph's brothers, Benjamin (killed by the Indians in Sumner County, Tennessee, on June 2, 1791) and Simon Kuykendall. The list also contains Abraham, John, and Joseph Hardin, Jr., and Major Joseph Hardin's brother-in-law, Lt. Col. Frederick Hambright, who was one of the officers in command.[36]

It should be noted that by 1792, Adam and Margaret had probably had four boys, Abner, born ca. 1777, 15 years old by now, Amos, born ca. 1781 would be 11, Robert H. born 1790, was 2, and Joseph born ca. 1791, was 1 year old. While at Red Banks,

Peter will be born ca. 1797; there are no birth dates recorded showing when Sally and Adam Jr. were born.[37]

Looking at the birth dates leads one to surmise that Abner was probably born in the Carolinas, that Amos could have been born either in Lincoln County, North Carolina, or Washington County, Tennessee. Since Robert was born ca. 1790, he was probably born somewhere en route on the move from eastern Tennessee to northwest Kentucky on the Ohio. Other research has suggested that Robert was born in or near Princeton, Kentucky. That thought leads us to the Cumberland River.[38]

There were many Indian traces, warpaths, trails, and frontier wagon roads throughout western Tennessee and Kentucky by this period. But the greatest high-way system of the time was the rivers, and one of the most important was the Cumberland River. Also, the Tennessee River drops down from eastern Tennessee into the Alabama area, running southwesterly and then in eastern Alabama it turns abruptly northward and runs into Tennessee and Kentucky to enter the Ohio River strangely enough only a short distance downstream from where the Cumberland empties into the Ohio also. Another main stream of the period was the Green River, which runs from central Kentucky easterly, turning north to enter the Ohio River just upstream from Red Banks or Henderson, Kentucky. The third stream is the Kentucky River which runs north through the state near present day Danville, Kentucky, and Frankfort, Kentucky, to enter the Ohio River just upstream from the Falls of the Ohio (Louisville).

Therefore, the settlers could leave eastern Tennessee going northwest through the Cumberland Gap and with some difficulty in eastern Kentucky get on one of the rivers, all of which would eventually lead to the Ohio River.

It seems, however, that one of their favorite choices was the Cumberland. The Tennessee River covers much more territory and did leave the very area that all the family lived in, but if one took the Tennessee River during that period, it would take the settlers directly through the middle of the Cherokee Indian Nations and from 1760 to 1793, there was terrible unrest, warfare, and bloodshed with the Indians all throughout this region. (See the diary by Col. John Donalson, December 22, 1779, to April 24, 1780, of his harrowing trip down the Tennessee River.) It is believed that most of the female Kuykendall family members went west using the Cumberland while probably some of the men and older boys went overland on earlier, probably by "*Robertson's route of 1779.*" In doing so, the Cumberland River would take the settlers right near the present day location of Nashville, Tennessee, through both Sumner and Davidson counties, then on near Princeton, Kentucky, and by turning upstream on the Ohio for a short distance, they would arrive at Red Banks, Henderson, Kentucky. However, it seems more likely that the family did not start using the Cumberland until after it passed the French Licks or Red River area.

It should be stated here that several of the family members, along with some of the Hardins, did settle along the Red River nearby which empties into the Cumberland near Clarksville, Tennessee.[39]

After Adam Kuykendall shows up on the 1804 Tax List in Henderson County, Kentucky, he then appears on a Memorial, along with his sons Amos, Abner, and Robert (and with Jonathon Hampton and others) north of the "River Ohio" in Indiana Territory, dated 16 March 1808. The Memorial is addressed to William Henry Harrison, Governor of the Indiana Territory and is signed by many settlers of the area.[40]

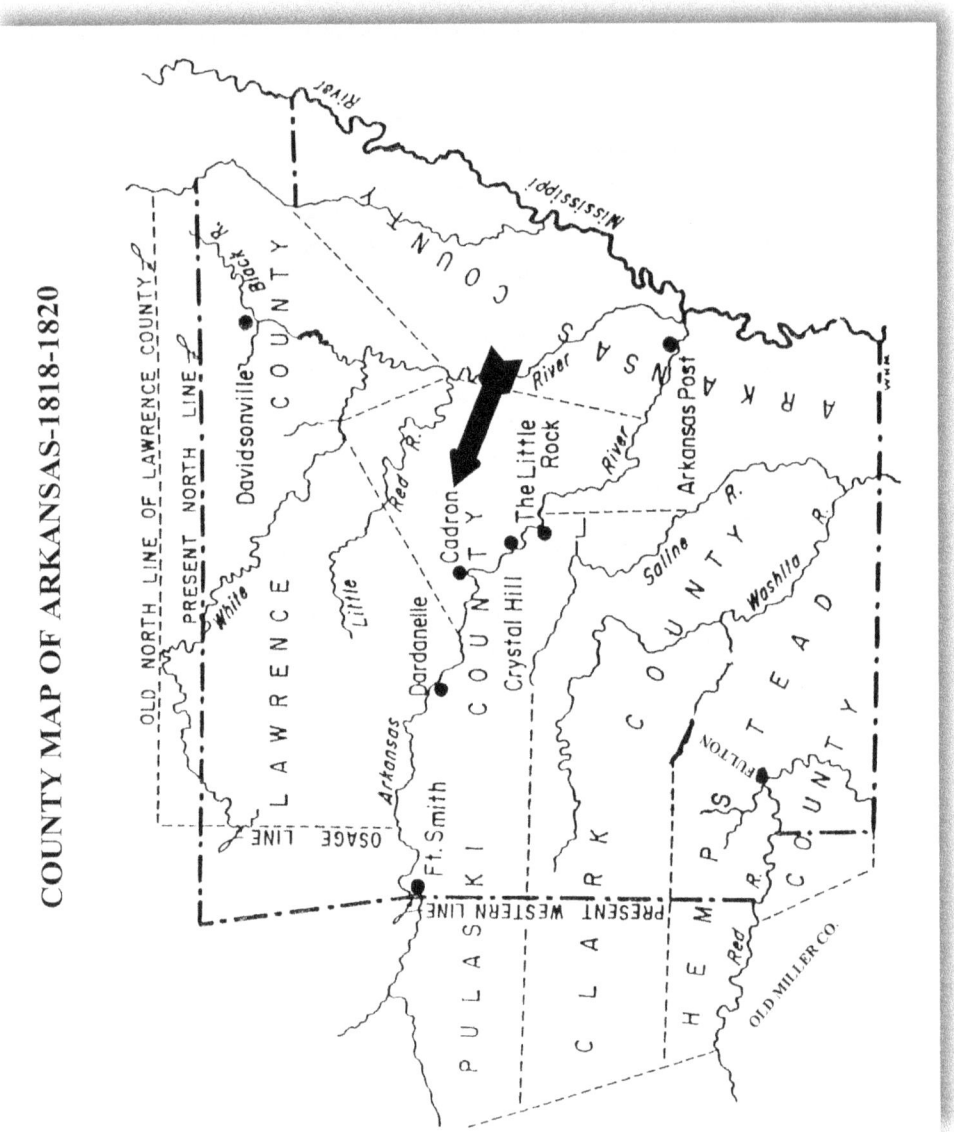
COUNTY MAP OF ARKANSAS-1818-1820

There have been no deed records to date found for the family in the Indiana Territory. As noted earlier, Adam again appears south of the Ohio River on the Henderson County Tax List of 1809.[41]

Shortly after March of 1808, it is obvious that the Kuykendalls and the related families of the Gates and the Hardins began their move into Missouri Territory (Arkansas). The records show that Abner Kuykendall, Adam's son, was in Arkansas (Missouri Territory) at the Cadron Settlement at least as early as February 15, 1810, when Abner and his brother Amos, were witness to a "Power of Attorney" from John Bain to Patrick Darby. The records also reflect that Adam Sr. and William Gates lived nearby at or near the same time. Records show that Abner's land was "joining the northwardly shore of the Arkansas River at the first rock bluff below where Murphy has been for some years past, the said Abner and Sally (Gates) his wife, having actually inhabited and cultivated upon the lands aforesaid for three or four successive years prior to the said 12th of April, 1814."[42]

Many of the migrating families of the period crossed the Mississippi River at the Chickasaw Bluffs (Memphis, Tennessee). They walked or rode horses and mules all the way to the Cadron Settlement. Probably the most popular mode of travel, however, was by water in flat-bottomed "keel" or flat boats that they floated down the Ohio and the Mississippi Rivers. When they came to the mouth of the Arkansas River they poled and pulled themselves upstream until they reached the Cadron Settlement at the mouth of Cadron Creek where the creek empties into the Arkansas River.[43]

Adam and Margaret Kuykendall settled near their sons at a point known as Red Hill on the Arkansas River a short distance below the mouth of Cadron Creek. No deed for his pre-emption claim has been found.[44]

It should be noted here that Peter Kuykendall, Adam's son, was appointed Captain of an Arkansas Militia Company, Second Regiment, on 10 October 1820. He was also appointed a commissioner of the Cadron Township to locate the county seat.[45]

Peter was also one of the 144 men who signed a Memorial to the President from the county of Arkansas, asking him not to move the Indians on to their lands. Dated 30 January 1820.[46]

In the census reports of 1829-1830, Adam is not listed as the head of his household, but Margaret his wife is so listed in 1830 in Conway County, Arkansas. The report states the household consists of all females: 1 under 5; 1 aged 20-30; 1 aged 40-50, 1 aged 50-60, and 1 aged 70-80. Margaret, Adam's wife, was listed as the head of the household in that census of 1830 but she does not show up on one after that date. She presumably died between 1830 and 1840. Some researchers have stated that Margaret was living with her son Peter in the census of 1850, but that is erroneous. The Margaret shown on that roll is shown as 73 years of age and would be much too young to be the mother of the older brothers, Abner and Amos.[47]

Further proof of the family being at the Cadron was recorded when Amos sold his improvement on the Arkansas River, five miles below the mouth of the Cadron, to Martin S. Tuttle. This conveyance is not dated, but on September, 26, 1817, Tuttle assigned it to James Lemons. Both the census by the sheriff in 1829 and the U.S. census of 1830 showed Amos and his wife, Betsy, living in the Hardin Township of Conway County. In the 1850 census, they were still in the same township, and a James Kuykendall, aged 22, lived with them. Additional proof of the family being there are

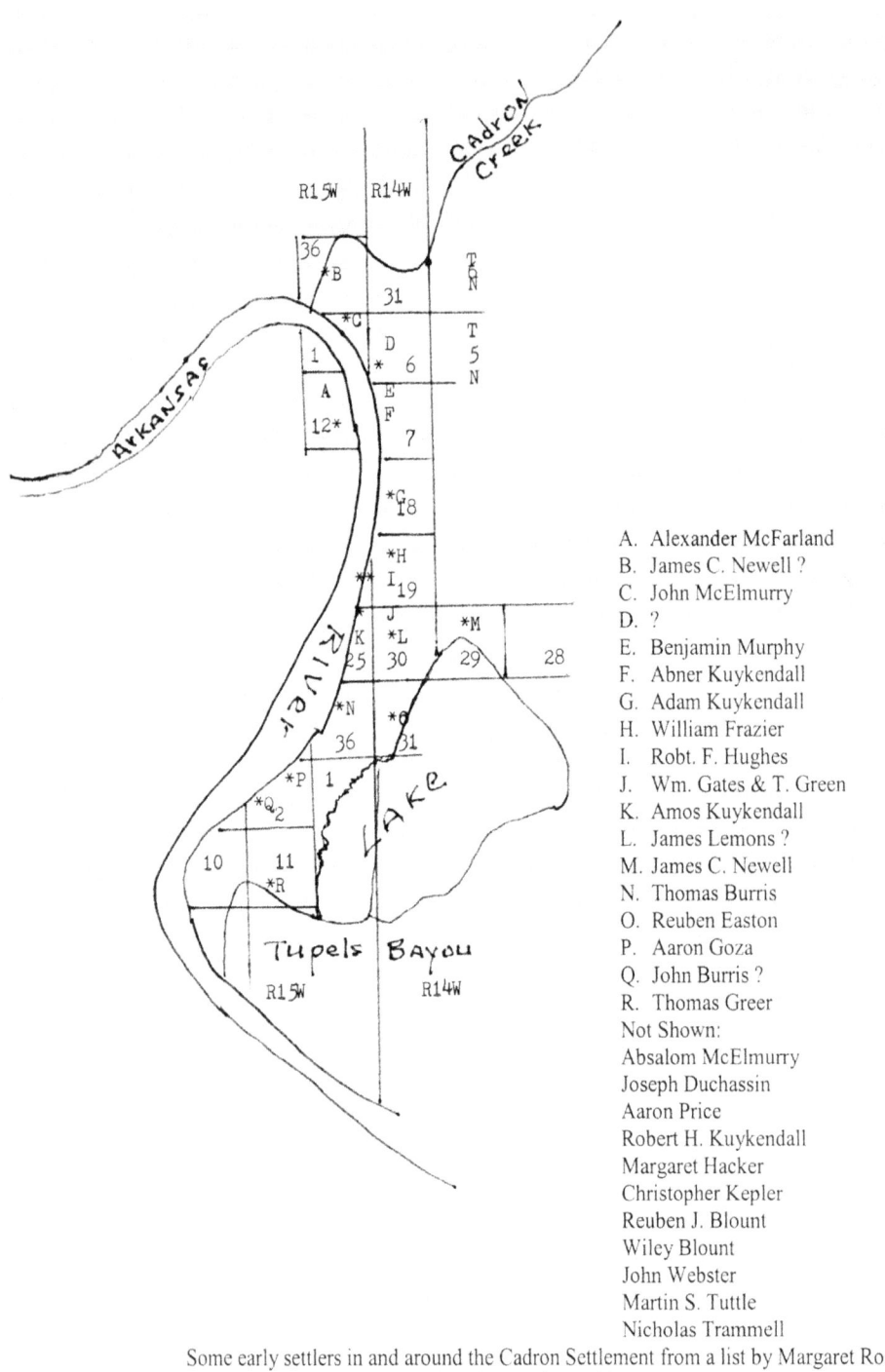

A. Alexander McFarland
B. James C. Newell ?
C. John McElmurry
D. ?
E. Benjamin Murphy
F. Abner Kuykendall
G. Adam Kuykendall
H. William Frazier
I. Robt. F. Hughes
J. Wm. Gates & T. Green
K. Amos Kuykendall
L. James Lemons ?
M. James C. Newell
N. Thomas Burris
O. Reuben Easton
P. Aaron Goza
Q. John Burris ?
R. Thomas Greer
Not Shown:
Absalom McElmurry
Joseph Duchassin
Aaron Price
Robert H. Kuykendall
Margaret Hacker
Christopher Kepler
Reuben J. Blount
Wiley Blount
John Webster
Martin S. Tuttle
Nicholas Trammell

Some early settlers in and around the Cadron Settlement from a list by Margaret Ross Smith, from the Pulaski Co. Historical Review, 1956.

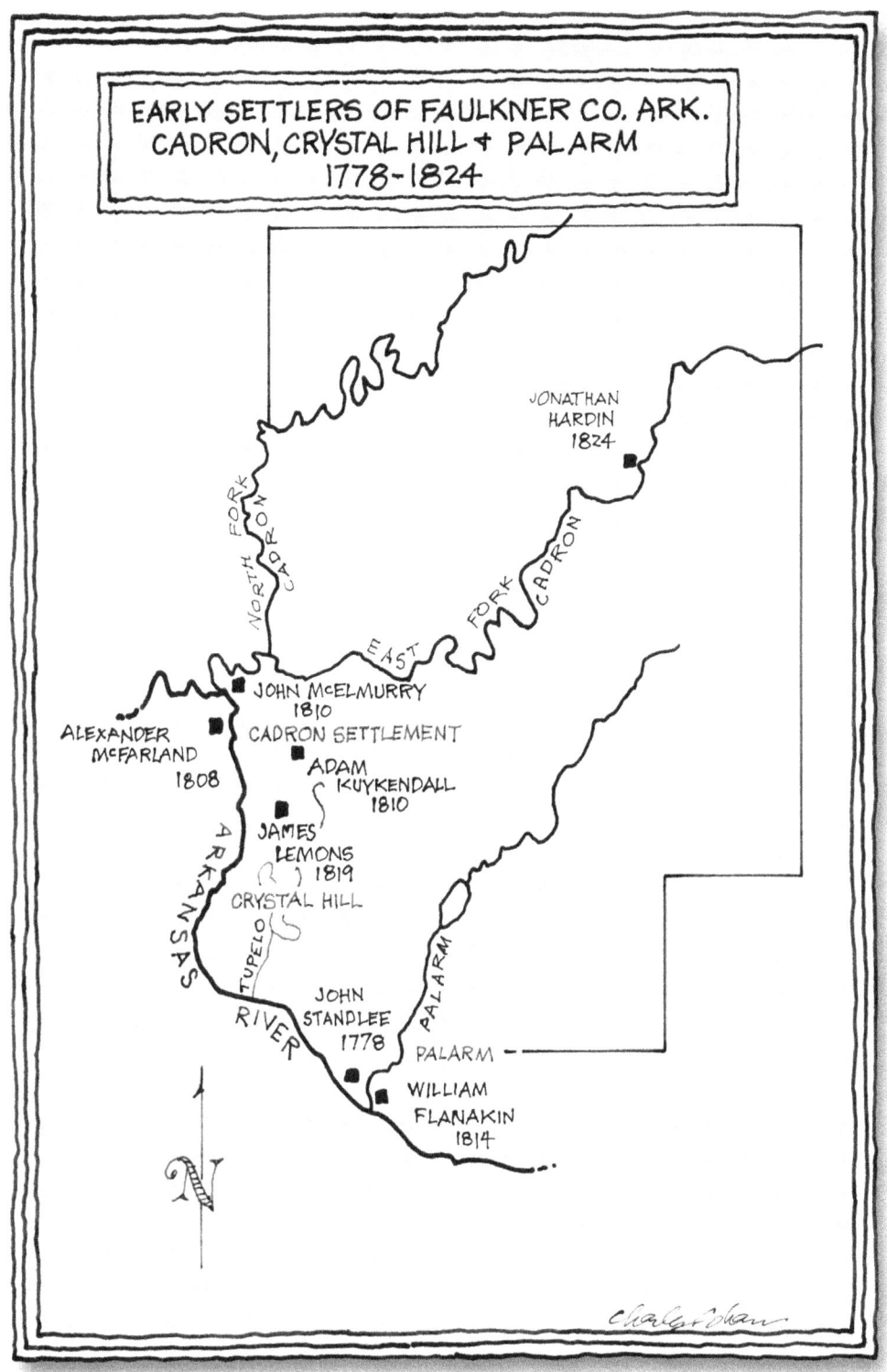

the Deeds of Transfer by Robert Kuykendall to some slave children dated 1816 and recorded at the Village of Cadron.[48]

Adam Jr. and his wife, Falbey Goza Kuykendall, are also shown in the 1829-30 census as living in the Cadron Township with their two sons and one daughter.[49]

All three of these sons, Peter, Amos, and Adam, Jr. had moved further up river by the census of 1840 and are shown in Conway County as owners of land in Township 7 North (T-7-N), Range 14 West (R-14-W) of Conway County, Arkansas. Amos was elected to the Arkansas Territorial Council in 1829.[50]

Joseph, the other brother, may have lived at the Cadron before he went to Texas, but no record has been found of him in that area. (He is not to be confused with Joseph Kuykendall, who was from Christian County, Kentucky, and who died in Pulaski County, Arkansas in 1828, and who was a first cousin to old Adam.) Joseph, Adam's son, a member of Stephen F. Austin's Old 300, settled in Ft. Bend County, Texas, and didn't die until after the Civil War.[51]

Robert H. Kuykendall, son of Adam and brother to those noted above, was an Indian trader. He was associated with Alexander McFarland and McElmurry as an Indian trader. There is no doubt that he lived at or near the Cadron settlement, for on June 3, 1816, he sold a mulatto boy and girl to Frances Vaugine and identified himself as "of the township of Cadron." No record has been found of his pre-emption claim and he probably lived with or near other members of the family. If he had had a claim, he would have sold it before he went to Texas.[52]

Other settlers in the area were Jacob Pyeatt, a Revolutionary soldier, and his family who settled at Crystal Hill ca 1812. Soon after their arrival at that place, the increase in immigration created a need for a ferry, and Jacob established one which ran between his home and that of Samuel Gates on the south side of the River (Arkansas). Samuel was the son of William Gates, was the brother-in-law to Abner Kuykendall, and was the son-in-law of Jacob Pyeatt.[53]

Another settler, Thomas Williams was in Arkansas very early, for on March 26, 1816, he sold to Sylvanus Phillips his "only settlement and improvement claim," situated near a cypress bayou which is believed to be the waters of White River or the river Mississippi. The settlement and improvement claims were based on his residence prior to 1803. His home at Crystal Hill was identified only as "on the bank of the Arkansas River about 25 miles below the Cadron by land." On July 29, 1811, two instruments were drawn by these people. One was a power of attorney from John Williams, possibly a brother to Thomas, to John Johnson of Stewart County, Tennessee, drawn at the Cadron, and the 2nd instrument was a deed of gift from Nancy Williams, wife of Thomas, to her son Robert Gilleland, conveying to him "every part of property to me belonging or in my possession." It was witnessed by David Yarbrough of Crystal Hill and Betsy Green of Cadron, and by John Bain, who acknowledged and filed the deed at "Arkansas Post" on August 11, 1811.[54]

Nancy Johnson Gilleland was the widow of William Gilleland of Davidson County, Tennessee, and she had remarried Thomas Williams on September 15, 1802 in Tennessee. The above is noted because Sarah Ann Gilleland, daughter of Nancy, married Robert H. Kuykendall, son of Adam and Margaret, probably in or near the Cadron or Crystal Hill Settlements, ca 1814.[55]

In the fall of 1821, Thomas Williams and his wife Nancy, along with all their family which included 13-year-old John Ingram, went to Texas to join the Stephen F. Austin Colony. *(Actually they accompanied the Kuykendalls.)* Thomas and Nancy went on down to the Colorado River and settled near her son-in-law, Capt. Robert H. Kuykendall, who was made captain of the colonial militia for the Colorado District by Stephen F. Austin.[56]

Adam and Margaret Hardin Kuykendall had seven known children that survived infancy:

Abner, b. ca 1777-1834, m. Sarah (Sallie) Gates. (Died in Texas.)
Amos, b. ca 1781-ca. 1845, m. to Elizabeth (?). (Died in Arkansas.)
Robert H. b. ca 1790-1830, m. Sarah Ann Gilleland. (Died in Texas.)
Joseph, b. ca 1794-ca 1873, m. 1st, Rosana (Annie), 2nd, Eliza J. Jones. (Died in Texas.)
Adam, Jr., b. ca 1796-ca 1845, m. Falbey (Falray) Goza. (Died in Arkansas.)
Peter, b. ca 1997-ca. 1845, m. Sarah Hacker, daughter of Frederick Hacker. (Died in Arkansas.)
Sally, (unknown b.) m. 1st, Wiley Blount; 2nd John Murray. (Died probably in Arkansas.)

Of the seven, three would go to Texas with Stephen F. Austin in 1821, Abner, Robert, Joseph as the earliest members of Austin's Old 300. The records do not reflect that any of the other children ever left central Arkansas. (Earlier researchers had thought that perhaps Peter had ventured into Texas but no record exists to date to prove that.)[57]

Old Adam probably died before 1828 at or near the "Cadron" and Margaret, his wife, died sometime between 1830 and 1840 since the 1840 census of Conway County does not show her on its records. No Will nor Probate for either has yet to be found. It should be noted that all the records for Conway County, Arkansas, were destroyed by a tornado and flood in 1859 and probably all these records were lost at that time.[58]

Robert H. Kuykendall

—Illustration drawn by Charlie Shaw

Chapter Six

Captain Robert H. Kuykendall of Austin's Colony

Robert H. Kuykendall (1790-1830)—frontiersman, Indian trader, colonist. (One of Stephen F. Austin's earliest members of the Old 300.) He was the son of Adam and Margaret Hardin Kuykendall. He may have been born in Kentucky near present-day Princeton or Henderson, Kentucky, because he was born about the time his family was moving from Sumner County, Tennessee, into Kentucky. In 1792 Adam Kuykendall's signature appears on a tax list of inhabitants from Charleston (Red Banks), Kentucky, along with his eldest son Abner.[1]

Adam moved into Logan County, Kentucky, at or near Red Banks near the present town of Henderson, Kentucky. Adam and his family had left Tennessee between 1788 and 1789, because Adam sold or gave his Revolutionary War Grant to Benjamin Hardin III in 1788 according to North Carolina records. Russellville, Kentucky, was the location of the county court for Logan County at the time. The records state that Adam was on the Tax Rolls for Logan County at Red Banks, Kentucky, in 1793, 1795, 1797, 1799, and 1 October 1800.[2]

"On Tuesday, the 2nd of July, 1799, the First Court of Criminal Common Law and Chancery Jurisdiction held its sitting in the village of Henderson, Kentucky. A Grand Jury was then empanelled, consisting of citizens of the area." William Gates served as a member of this first grand jury. In the July term of 1810, the court appointed Abner Kuykendall, Robert's older brother, Wm. Gates and Humphrey Barnett "to view" (to plan) a road from the town of Henderson to the main fork of Highland Creek near Adam's home. The road crossed Canoe Creek about 100 yards above the old ford on the trace to Diamond Island. (*Note*: William Gates was married to Catherine Hardin, possibly a daughter of Benjamin Hardin III. Adam was married to Margaret Hardin, daughter of Col. Joseph Hardin. Joseph, John, and Benjamin Hardin III were brothers. Adam's son, Abner, was married to Sally Gates, Wm. and Catherine's daughter, therefore the children would be cousins to one another.)[3]

Since the Tax Rolls show that Adam was in Sumner County, Tennessee, in 1790 and the records show that he was excused from jury duty there the following year, along with his brother, Matthew, it is very probable that Robert was born in that area and not in Kentucky as has previously been stated. The year 1790 has been determined as correct for his year of birth because in the 1823 Census of the Colorado District of Texas, Robert states that his age at the time was 33.[4]

After earlier moves from Sumner County, Tennessee, into Logan County, Kentucky, and a brief stay north of the Ohio River in Knox County, Indiana Territory, Adam, with his entire family, along with the allied families of the Hardins and the Gates, all began their move down the Ohio-Mississippi rivers into that part of the Missouri Territory known as the Arkansas Territory.[5]

As stated earlier, Abner Kuykendall, Robert's older brother, and other members of the family were in Arkansas (Missouri Territory) at the Cadron Settlement as early as February 15, 1810. Records state that Abner's land was "joining the northwardly shore of the Arkansas River at the first rock bluff below where Murphy had been for some years past, the said Abner and Sally (his wife) having actually inhabited and cultivated upon the lands aforesaid for three or four successive years prior to the said 12th day of April 1814."[6]

Many of the migrating families of the period crossed the Mississippi River at the "Chickasaw Bluffs (Memphis, Tennessee) and walked or rode their horses and mules all the way to the Cadron Settlement but probably the most popular mode of travel was by water in a flat bottomed keel boat down the Ohio and Mississippi rivers to the mouth of the Arkansas River, then pole and pull the keel boats upstream until they reached the Cadron Settlement near the mouth of Cadron Creek where it empties into the Arkansas River not far from present day Conway, Arkansas.[7]

Robert H. Kuykendall was an Indian trader at this time in Arkansas. There is no doubt that he lived at or near the Cadron Settlement because records show that he sold three slaves there in a period from 1815-1816. The first sale was on August 10, 1815; the second sale was on June 3, 1816; and the third sale was on June 6, 1816. The third deed reads as follows:

> "DEED: 6th August A.D., 1816, County of Arkansas, Territory of Missouri, Vol. B., page 536: TO WIT: This indenture made and entered into by and between Robert Kuykendall of the Township of Cadron in the County of Arkansas and Territory of Missouri of one part, and Francis Vaugine of the Township of Arkansas in the same County and Territory of the other part. Witnessed that the 1st, Robert Kuykendall, for and in consideration of the sum of four hundred dollars lawful money of the United States to him in hand will & timely paid before the signing, sealing, and delivering of these presents, the receipt of which payment is hereby acknowledged, has granted, bargained & sold & does by these presents, grant, bargain & sell to the said Francis Vaugine & to his heirs and assigns forever, all the right Title & Claim & interest of him, the said Robert Kuykendall, of, in & to a certain "mulatto girl" named

ANN, about nine years old, and the said Robert Kuykendall does by these presents bind himself, his heirs & assigns forever, to warrant and defend the right & title to the said mulatto to the said Francis Vaugine his heirs & assignes, forever against the claim or claims of all & every person or persons what-so-ever claiming or to claim the said mulatto by, through or unto him, the said Robert Kuykendall. In Witness whereof the said Robert Kuykendall has hereunto set his hand & seal at the Township of the Cadron, this 6th day of June AD, 1816 and of our Independence, the fortieth.

ROBERT KUYKENDALL (SEAL)

signed, sealed & delivered in the presence of Jesse Joy—Benjn. Murphy."[8]

No record has been found of a pre-emption claim in Robert's name, however he did participate in a lawsuit against the government at a later date in order to get monies for lands or improvements that had been taken away from him in the Choctaw and Cherokee removal on or into their lands that he and the family claimed. But to date no record of the sale of any land by Robert in Arkansas has been found.[9]

Robert H. Kuykendall was probably a hunter and Indian trader associated with John McElmurry and Col. Alexander McFarland. By 1810, McElmurry had 100 whites and Indians traders in the field, conducting a vast fur trade through the northern Arkansas tribes. McElmurry disposed of his pelts through the "Notrebe County" at Arkansas Post located at or near the mouth of the Arkansas River. It is very likely that Robert worked for him from time to time.

McFarland and his family had settled at the Cadron in 1808. In the summer of 1812, he headed a group of traders, among them was Robert Kuykendall, John Lemons, Wm. Ingles, and Benjamin Murphy, who went out from the Cadron Settlement to the upper Red River to trade for horses and mules. Before they left the Cadron, the Cherokee Chief, Tallantusky, gave McFarland some trading materials, presumably planning to share in the profits. The trading party made every effort to avoid the hostile Osage Indians, but while McFarland was alone in camp, a band of Osage came in and murdered him and plundered the camp. The date is given as either 13 or 17 August 1812.

When news of the tragedy reached the Cadron, Chief Tallantusky set out to find the murderers and retrieve his stolen goods. In October, at the mouth of the Verdigris River, his search ended. The Osages had gathered there to trade, among them were the band of murderers triumphantly bearing their loot. Wm. Ingles, Robert Kuykendall, and Benjamin Murphy were there as traders and witnessed the meeting between the Cherokee Chief and the Osages. Among the items in possession of the Osage were two short swords and other items that the Chief had given McFarland to trade. Ingles, who apparently spoke both Cherokee and Osage acted as interpreter and through him Tallantusky demanded and got his property back as well as a full confession of the crime.

In 1813, Lydia McFarland, widow of the Colonel, filed a claim with the United States Government for the loss of her husband and his property. The claim was supported by depositions made in 1814 by Lemons, Murphy and Robert Kuykendall. In June 1814, Governor William Clark wrote to the Cherokee Agent, Maj. William L. Lovely, that he had sent Pierre Choteu, the Osage Agent, to demand that the murderers of McFarland and others, be turned over to the government, but they were not given up.[10]

The Cadron Settlement was the most important settlement in Arkansas except

Arkansas Post in the pre-territorial period. On 20 April 1814, William Russell wrote to William Rector: "On the north side of the River Arkansas, there are scattered settlements, from about 10 miles below Arkansas Village up to 10-15 miles above Cadron Creek, mostly on private claims, except a settlement of perhaps 40-50 families at, near to, and above Cadron Creek, which are mostly on public lands. (*Note*: It is the families' removal from this particular area that will spark the future lawsuit against the government.) The lands immediately on or near the river (both sides) are very rich, but become poor as they approach the dividing ridges on both sides, except on the creeks and small water courses, which would afford some small settlements. The Cadron Settlement of this period is not to be confused with the town of the same name, which was laid out in 1818 and covered the pre-emption claim of only one settler, John McElmurry. The Cadron Settlement became a part of Conway County, Arkansas, when that county was formed in 1824.[11]

Robert's father and mother, Adam and Margaret Kuykendall, settled near their son Abner at a point known as Red Hill on the Arkansas River, a short distance below the mouth of Cadron Creek. Old Adam and his wife did not accompany their sons into Texas in 1821.[12]

Margaret's father, Col. Joseph Hardin, along with her uncles, John and Benjamin Hardin III, were all very active in the Revolution and all held commissions. (See the biography of Col. Hardin in a later chapter.)[13]

Abner, **Robert**, and Joseph, would initially enter Texas in the fall of 1821 with Stephen F. Austin.[14]

There was another Joseph Kuykendall, the son of John (1717-1752), living near by in Pulaski County, Arkansas, who was a first cousin to Adam. He was born ca 1752 in North Carolina, and was also a Revolutionary soldier. He had moved to Arkansas from Christian County, Kentucky, a short time after Adam. His Will names six sons and three daughters, none of whom went to Texas with the sons of Adam, not at least in the early days of the colony. His son, James M. Kuykendall, was the long-time sheriff of Lawrence County, Arkansas. Two of his other sons, Benjamin and Dempsey, are well documented in the county.[15]

Robert's brothers, Amos, Adam Jr., and Peter, remained in Conway County, Arkansas, the rest of their lives. (Sisters are there also.) Amos and his wife Elisabeth appear on the Conway County census rolls, Hardin Township, in 1850. They had a son named James, aged 22, living with them. Peter and his wife Sarah moved to Union Township of Conway County and were there in the 1850 census. Neither Amos nor Peter are shown on any further census records. Adam Jr. and his wife, Falray Goza, had been living at the Cadron but he moved upriver as the census of 1840 in Conway County reflects.[16]

These families and many others among Austin's original 300 colonists had moved into Missouri Territory (Arkansas) after the Louisiana Purchase of 1803. After the Panic of 1819 struck the U.S.A. proper, the U.S. Government ordered the Choctaw Indians moved from the east side of the Mississippi River to the west side and settled them on lands west and north of the Arkansas River on lands on which many of the early settlers lived, including some of the Kuykendalls. In parts of the area, there was so much friction that the U.S. Government soldiers were deployed to move the settlers from their lands or burn them out.[17]

Map of Arkansas in 1817 showing Indian boundaries

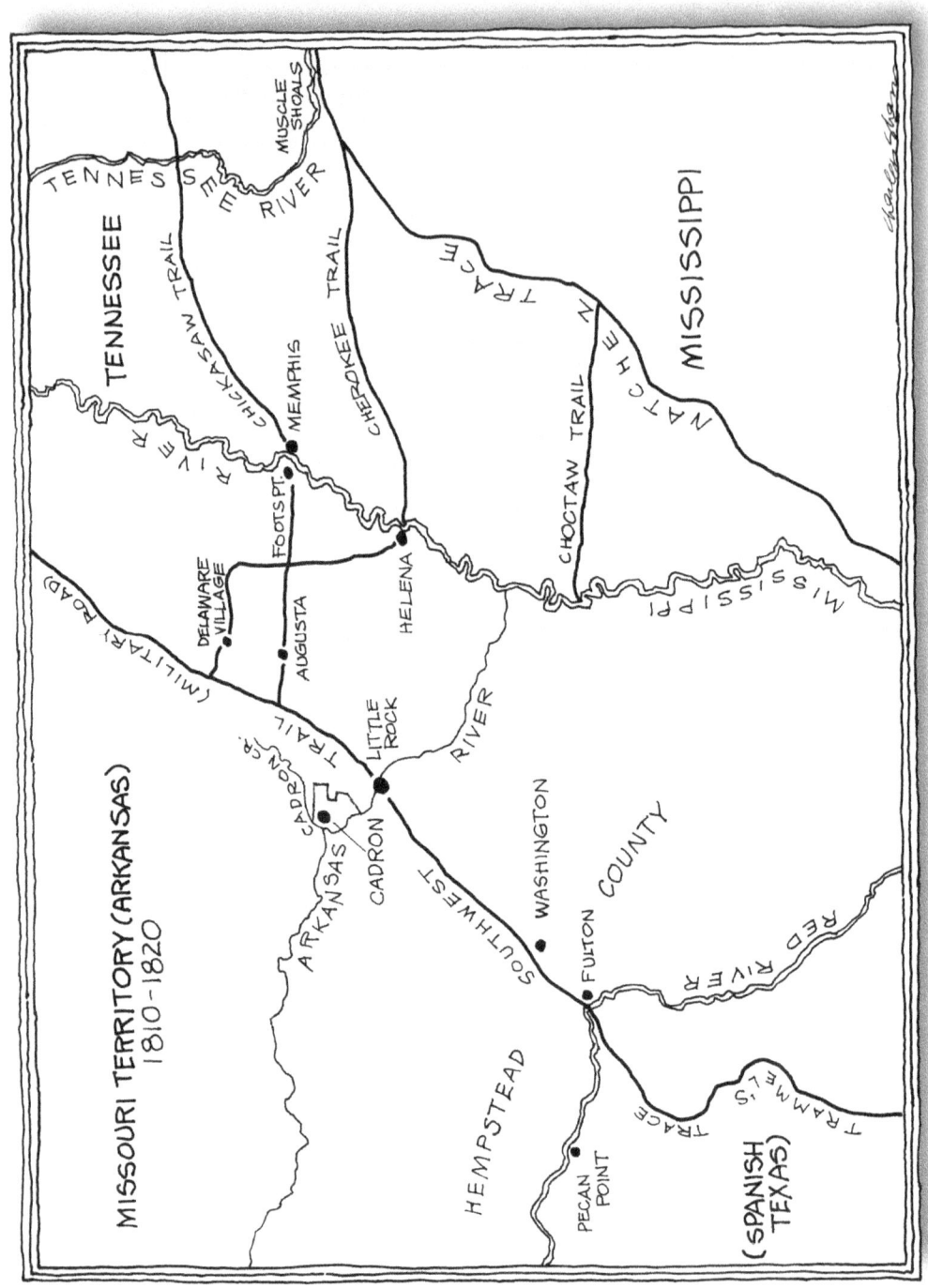

Abner Kuykendall and his family left the Cadron area prior to May 16, 1820, and moved down into the southwest area of present day Arkansas. (See biography of Abner Kuykendall in another chapter.)[18] This was near Pecan Point on the Red River in what was soon to become Miller County Arkansas.[19]

Robert H. Kuykendall married Sarah Ann Gilleland of Tennessee, daughter of William and Nancy Johnson Gilleland of Davidson County, Tennessee, probably in the Cadron Settlement area ca. 1814-15, but no marriage license has ever been found. After William's death in Davidson County in 1800, Sarah's mother, Nancy, married Thomas Williams in 1802 in Tennessee and then they all moved with the family into Arkansas and eventually settled on the Buzzard Creek Branch of the Red River above Pecan Point before 1821. They later moved with the family into Texas.[20]

The Pecan Point area was near the critical area that was to become Indian Land in 1820-21. The Choctaw and Cherokee land boundary line ran northeast from Fulton, Arkansas, on the Red River to Lewisburg on the Arkansas River, then more northeast to Batesville on the White River, taking up half of the present-day state of Arkansas.[21]

A protest in the form of a "Memorial" to the President of the U.S. by the citizens of the Territory of Arkansas was sent in early 1821, pointing out that the settlers had moved to the western part of Arkansas with the promise that the land(s) would be theirs: "We reflect that our frontier settlements were made under the circumstances which entitled them to anticipate the usual indulgence and benevolent protection of our government hitherto extended to other sections of the United States." The signers encouraged the President to prevent ratification of the Indian Treaty as it was written. The "Memorial" was signed by 367 of the citizens of Arkansas, including Claiborne Wright, Bailey English, William and Samuel Gates, Owen and John Shannon, Joseph and Abner Kuykendall, Wyatt Hanks, Jonathon Hampton, Henry Wyatt and Martin Varner, to mention a few.[22]

It should be noted that Abner Kuykendall would name all of his sons after his friends that are listed on this Memorial: William, after his father-in-law; Samuel Gates Kuykendall after his brother-in-law; Wyatt Hanks Kuykendall and Jonathon Hampton Kuykendall after his two friends who had been traveling along with the family for so many years. Wyatt Hanks Kuykendall died on the ill-fated Mier Expedition in 1842 and J. Hampton Kuykendall became one of the early scholars and historians of Texas.[23]

Many tried to get compensation for improvements placed on their lands before the Indian Treaty. Robert Kuykendall gave a Power of Attorney to Richard C. Patton of Arkansas to collect from the federal government what was owed him, but nothing ever came of his claim and just before his death in late 1830, Robert named his brothers, Abner and Joseph, administrators of this claim should any monies ever be paid to his estate. (This pertains to the areas where the settlers were forcibly removed from their lands in the Indian removal period of 1819, 1820, and early 1821.)[24]

It is ironic to note that at the very time the settlers were being forced from their homes in Arkansas, Moses Austin was to receive his land grant from the Mexican government to move or settle 300 families into the area known as Texas. In June 1821 Moses Austin died and his son, Stephen F. Austin, who was a circuit judge of the First Judicial District of Arkansas (July 1820) moved from Little Rock to New Orleans in December of that same year. Deciding to cooperate with his father on the Texas venture, he was back in Natchitoches, Louisiana, when he heard of his father's death. He proceeded at once to San Antonio to meet Governor Antonio Maria Martinez and come to a general understanding of the proposed colony. This was in August 1821.

Returning immediately to New Orleans, Austin published the terms and conditions of the proposed colonization in all of the newspapers and invited colonists to come to Texas, stating that the settlements would be along the Brazos and Colorado rivers (down) to the coast of Texas. The long depression, followed by the Panic of 1819 (in the U.S. proper), coupled with the critical movement of the Indians onto the settlers' lands in Arkansas, made the setters eager to take advantage of the offer. It also should be noted that many hundreds of the settlers were already on the northeast boundary of Texas at the time (Pecan Point on the Red River), and many had already encroached across the border on many horse gathering expeditions and Indian trading forays. It is fairly certain that Robert Kuykendall had been among these people. (See the statement to follow.)[25]

The settlers in Arkansas got the word shortly thereafter and Abner Kuykendall left Arkansas Territory (Miller County) in September or October of 1821, probably in the company of Abner's father-in-law, William Gates and his family. When they arrived in Nacogdoches, Texas, they were joined by their other brother, Robert H., who *"had been residing in Texas for some time."*

> Robert and Joseph Kuykendall saw Moses Austin near Nacogdoches (on his return from San Antonio de Bexar). They had been routed from Arkansas by the US (Gov) granting the land to the Choctaw and Chickasaw Indians; they (the Kuykendalls) were ripe for removing, and were looking for a new home when they met Austin, who explained to them the object of his visit to San Antonio. As soon as Moses returned, he made a proclamation for the settlers, and the Kirkendalls & the company above named came over immediately and settled as we have stated.—Andrew Robinson, Abner Kuykendall, Robt. H. Kuykendall and Joseph Kuykendall, and families, all making 22 old and young. They left Arkansaw September 1821—reached the Brazos & crossed at that place, Abner K. went 4 miles below; Robt. and Joe K.—left first day of Janry 1822 for Colorado & stopped 12 miles below La Grange; remained there 2 or 3 years, sold his place to Ross and removed 5 miles below Richmond where he has lived ever since, this was Joe; Abner went to head of Peach Creek where Dr. Williams now resides.—Buckner and Peter Powell came to Colorado soon after Joe Kuykendall—Martin Varner followed the Kirkendall(s) in and settled near Washington.—Bill Gibbons & Chas. Garret, came with their families with the Kuykendalls—they parted near the Trinity. Gibbons and Garret took the upper road and settld at the Atuscasito crossing on the Brazos. Garret died 1849 at Joe Kuydndal on the Brazos."[26]

The Indian traders of the period traveled all over in search of trade and pelts, but they were required to obtain a passport to enter the Mexican Territory. It is very probable that all of the active traders knew of the early forays into Texas by Phillip Nolen in 1801 and Anthony Glass in 1808. There were thousands of wild horses and mules in Texas during this period and if they could be caught and smuggled down the contraband trail that existed in deep east Texas to the coast at the time, lots of money could be made. Current researchers are not sure why Robert was in Texas earlier in the summer of 1821, it could be for the reasons given above, or he might have been sent to actually view the area between the Brazos and Colorado rivers so he could report to the settlers and his own family where the best lands were for forming their settlements. History has yet to give the answer.

Note: New information has been uncovered that places Robert Kuykendall on Galveston Island in the fall of 1819. That place was at one of the ends of the Trammel Trace or main smugglers' road that the pelt traders or horse smugglers would have used. Exerp: A man named Brown had been executed by the pirate Jean LaFitte because he had raided the coast of Louisiana against Lafitte's orders. This was around the 7 November 1819.

> "A few weeks after the execution of Brown, another man was hung. He was a Frenchman named Francois, also one of LaFitte's men, against whom a Mr. Robert Kuykendall made complaint to LaFitte of his having engaged in a plot to rob him. He (LaFitte) ordered Francois to be arrested without investigating the truth or falsity of the charges against him, and turned him over to Kuykendall, with permission to punish him as he pleased, and, accordingly, he had him hung."[27]

Robert H. Kuykendall had been scouting in east Texas for several months prior to October 1821, when he met his three brothers, Abner, and Joseph in Nacogdoches, Texas.[28]

The families then went southwesterly and crossed the Brazos River on the La Bahia Road crossing on 26 November 1821. There they all camped about a month.[29]

There were some fifteen families in the area. Some of them were Elizah Allcorn, his wife Nancy, their 24-year-old son James, William, about 12, Thomas, 11, Elliot, 8, and 4-year-old MaryAnn; there was John McNeese and his wife and at least two sons, Parrott and Ivy McNeese; Thomas Boatright and his wife and their oldest son Richard, two younger boys and little Betsy Boatright; Andrew Robinson and his family; Daniel Gilleland (Robert's brother-in-law) and his family and the three Kuykendall brothers and all of their families which tallied close to 17 persons in all in their family alone. It is very likely that Thomas Williams and his wife, Nancy (Robert's father-in-law and his wife's (Sarah Ann's) mother) along with their children were probably in the group.[30]

After 1 January 1822, Robert, his brother Joseph, along with Daniel Gilleland, and their families, proceeded to the east bank of the Colorado River near the La Bahia Road crossing and started the river's first settlement at that point, which is very close to present day Columbus, Texas.[31]

After many Indian depredations in the summer of 1822, Robert H. Kuykendall headed a party of settlers in an attack on the Karankawa Indians at the mouth of Skull Creek, where the Indians were defeated with considerable loss.[32]

In December 1822, the Baron de Bastrop arrived at the upper settlement on the Colorado River to organize the colony. The settlers met near the present town of Columbus, Texas, where they took an oath of allegiance to the Emperor Iturbide and held an election for civil and militia officers which resulted in the selection of Robert H. Kuykendall as captain of the militia for the Mina District (Colorado) and alcalde of the (Colorado) district (temporary) when militia officers were elected. Robert's house was the election site when James Cummins was later elected alcalde of the (Colorado) district. Later, a group of horse thieves were captured by Robert and his

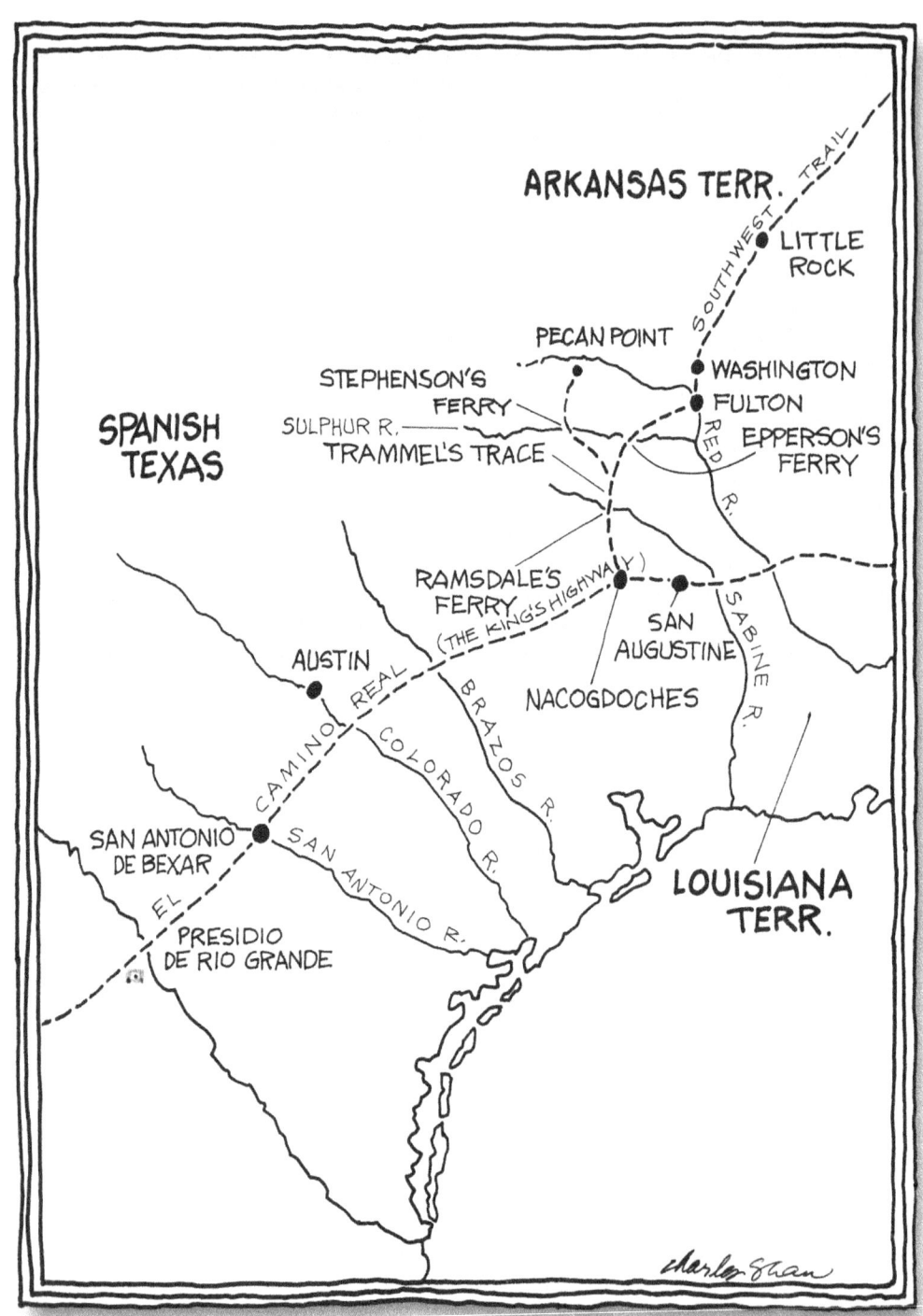

men. They were found guilty, were executed and their heads were cut off and placed on tall poles alongside the La Bahia road as a warning to others: "after these examples, the border ruffians ceased their depredations within the bounds of Austin's Colony." (It should be noted here, that the election of Robert as the captain of the militia may place him as one of the very first captains of a (Ranger) Rang(e)-ing Company to be formed in Texas.)³³

In March 1823, Robert joined with John Tumlinson to write a letter to Governor J. F. Trespalacios at San Antonio from the District of Colorado Province of Texas, explaining their need for protection from the Indians and sighting several instances of acts by the Indians against the settlers. In the same letter, they sent the "first census" report of Texas from the Colorado District and listed the inhabitants of the Colorado River area. It is in this report that Robert states the ages for himself and his family members by name. Robert states that he is 33 years of age, that his wife Sarah is 27, young Robert (Gill) is 8, Molly is 5, Jane is 3, and baby Jose Felix Trespalacios, known as Joseph F., is 4 months old. The letter is signed by both John Tumlinson and Robert Kuykendall.³⁴

Plaque on courthouse grounds, Columbus, Texas

In June 1823, Robert led a party of men to the mouth of the Colorado River to meet the supply boat, the *Only Son*, bringing Col. William Kinchelow and 20 families to Texas, who had chosen land on Peach Creek (present day Wharton County) on which to settle. While on this trip, Robert and his men encountered a group of Indians in the Skull Creek area again. A battle ensued and the Indians were dispersed with several of them having been killed or wounded.³⁵

On 13 July 1823, Robert wrote another letter to the Governor at San Antonio:

Colorado 13 July 1823

Sir, our affairs at present seem to be some what critical in consequence of the frequent depredations of the Indians. On or about the 6th of the present month, Mr. Tumlinson, our Alcalde, started to St. Antonio for the purpose of transacting some business with the Gov. of that place. After crossing the Guad., he and his companion were met by some of the Waco Indians in company with one Spaniard. After some insolent observations and conduct by the Indians, they shot and killed Mr. Tumlinson. ____ Newman, who was with Mr. Tumlinson, you will see in your city who will give you every information you may wish on the subject. From the latest information we have been able to collect, there will be no arrivals from Orleans by water shortly likewise, there are no Indians at or near the mouth of the River, neither has there been since Lt. Morrison took his position at that place. We therefore solicit that he and his company may be drawn from that position and placed in that part of the country where they are most needed, at least for three or four months, every man in our position is essential as the upper Indians are numerous and show strong symtoms of hostilities, you will therefore be good enough to take into consideration our request and act agreeably to your own discretion.

We feel it a duty we owe our countryman to revenge his blood, and the time is not far distant when we will teach those savage people better sence that to sport with the lives of our countrymen.

God grant you many years, your most obedient and very humble servant,—

                Robert Kuykendall
                (Rubric)[36]

In 1824, Robert was again chasing the Karacawas. In recalling the experience Thomas M. Duke later described Robert Kuykendall as a "man of extraordinary fleetness."[37]

In June or July 1824, the Karankawas killed a calf of Robert's a few hundred yards from his house. He sent his 10-year-old son Robert (Gill) for help and concealed his wife and family in a thicket nearby. After reaching their hideout, it was discovered that a baby of the family was missing that had been carried by a Negro slave. She said she had dropped the baby while crawling through the rail fence. As soon as possible, the family went back and found the baby fast asleep in the corner of the fence where it had been dropped, hidden by the tall grass. Ingram was the first man to Robert's assistance. A dozen or more neighbors quickly assembled and they tracked the Indians to the Colorado River and found the Indians on the far side. Spurring their horses to a gallop, they plunged into the river under a hail of arrows and gave flight to the savages. One of the settlers was wounded in the elbow and one Indian was killed.[38]

In Stephen F. Austin's request to the Baron de Bastrop dated 9 July 1824 for two leagues of land for Robert, Austin states that Robert deserves the land because "he had a large family, was one of the first settlers, and has always protected the other settlers from the savage Indians." Austin and Bastrop granted Capt. Robert Kuykendall two leagues of land in recognition of his service during the early days of the colony as captain of the militia for the Mina District. The land was described as follows:

July 16, 1824—One league, 4,428 acres of land east side of the Colorado River.
July 16, 1824—One league, 4,428 acres of land west side of the Colorado River.[39]

Robert established his home on the league of land east of the River near the old

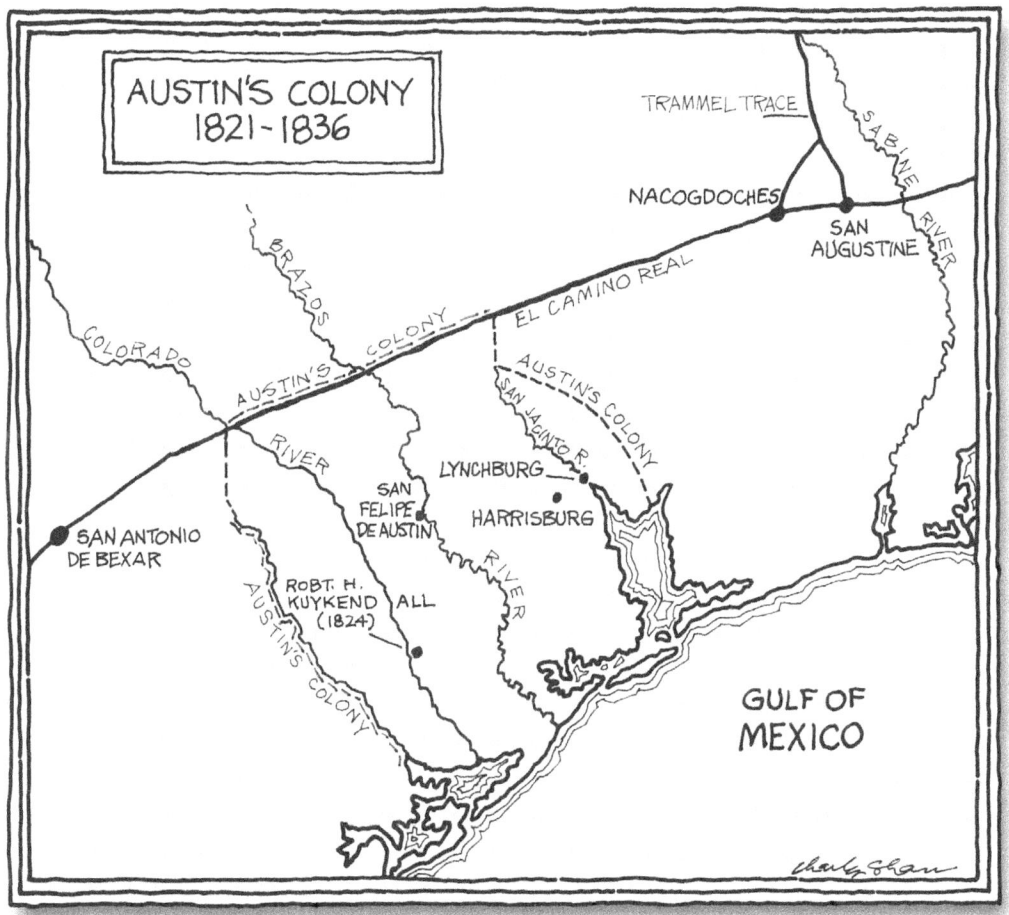

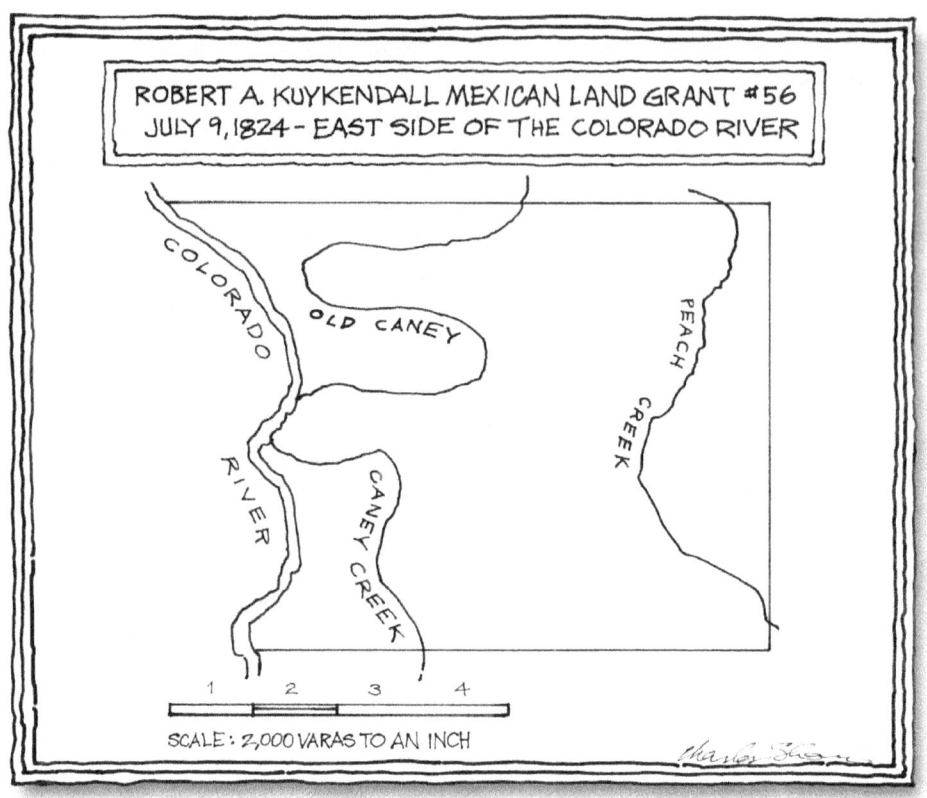

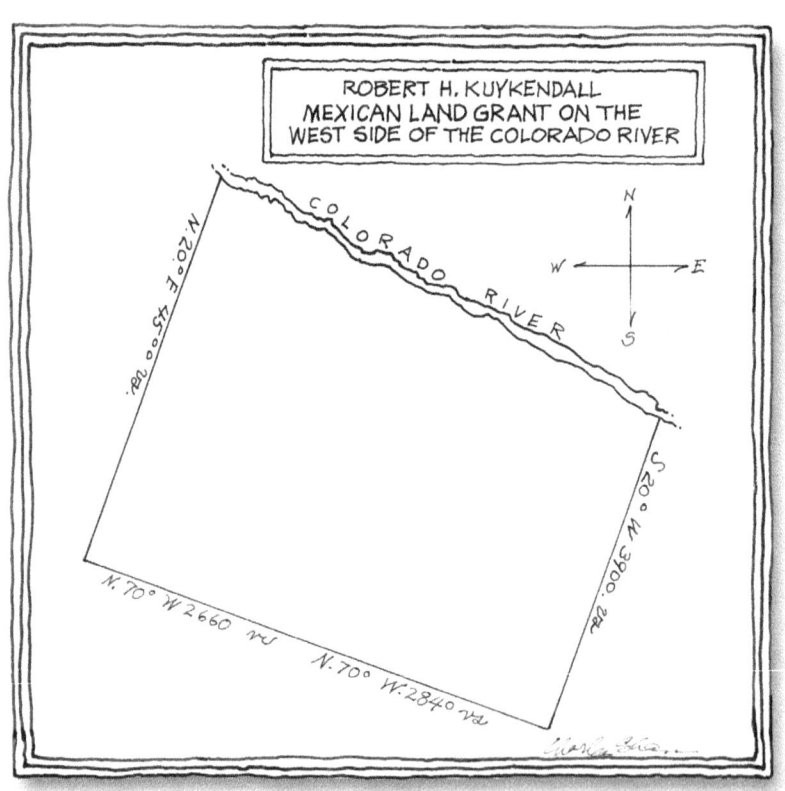

Robert Kuykendall's land grant at Glen Flora, Wharton County, Texas

Indian crossing on Peach Creek, close to the present-day village of Glen Flora in Wharton County, Texas. His home was known as the Pleasant Farm Plantation, Bay Prairie, as the area was called that laid between the Colorado River and the Bernard River.[40]

Spanish Camp is located two miles east of Glen Flora at the springs on Peach Creek. Mexican soldiers under Gen. Santa Anna camped there in the spring of 1836. Looting was prevalent and the Kuykendall home was probably ransacked and burned since it was only a short distance away.[41]

In 1829, Robert wrote Austin a letter in which he talks about his hopes and his health:

> Col. Stephen F. Austin
> D. Sir, I have drawn an order on you for twenty-five dollars in favor of Mr. Barker, which sum I took the liberty of drawing for from your letter to me. Mr. Wightman has undertaken to teach school for twelve months and the above amt. is a balance due for payment of a house and lot in Matagorda to enable me to move there for the purpose of schooling my children. I shall furthermore wish to pay through you at the expiration of the school, fifty dollars to Mr. Wightman, which accounts I will refund you as soon as it is in my power. My health still continues indifferent. I have very little hope of getting much better and shall always continue grateful for your kindness. Since I last saw you, I have had two sons (twins) born, one named Benjamin and the other Thomas. I remain with every sentiment of esteem,
>
> Robert Kuykendall[42]
> (punctuation added) (rubric)

Later, RHK would write probably his last letter to Stephen F. Austin:

> Sir,
> You will please to receive this order for the amount of forty eight Dollars in payment for land according to your offer to me and I will adjust the same with you according to agreement on account of Elias Wightman it being for tuition.
>
> Matagorda 3 Jany 1830
> In presents of   R. G. Kuykendall
> *(Very shaky, uncertain hand)*   Robert (X) Kuykendall
>   (his mark)
> R. Kuykendall—order for $48.—Accepted March 13, 1830, S.F. Austin.[43]

Note: Here is young "Gill" Kuykendall, probably 14 or 15 years of age, trying to witness his dying father's hand. In later years, he would sign all his papers, R.H.K.

In a letter dated January 1, 1830, from Austin to Commissioner General Juan Antonio Padilla, Austin requests that two important individuals with particular merit receive additional land for their services during the early days of the colony. Josiah H. Bell as alcalde and Robert H. Kuykendall as commander of the militia.

> Both rendered very important serviced and by their dexterity and just management contributed to the advancement of the enterprise in its enfancy during my absence in Mexico and for them I request that an increase of land be granted to complete the amount of 3 Sitios inclusive of what they have received. Villa de Austin,
>
> Stephen F. Austin   (Rubric)

There is no record that Robert ever received this increase.[44]

Capt. Robert H. Kuykendall received a bad injury in an Indian fight sometime after the spring of 1826 which gradually impaired his health to the extent that he became blind and paralyzed. Joseph, Robert's brother, tells in a deposition given in an old court case held in Matagorda County that "my brother was hit over the head by a gun barrel while he was fighting the Indians and the injury caused his death."[45]

Between the 20th and the 27th of March 1830, Dr. Robert Peebles performed a "trepan" on Robert's skull. Judge Robert M. Williams, while editor of the *Texas Gazette* at San Felipe, stated in the paper that Dr. Peebles has just trepanned the skull of Capt. Bob Kuykendall with success, and "this proves that we have in our colony, fine doctors." After the operation Robert went to his summer home in Matagorda to recuperate and probably died there late in 1830. He was presumed to be buried in the old Matagorda Cemetery. Subsequent hurricanes have washed away most of the early gravestones and his headstone has been lost. However, a Historical Marker has recently been placed at the cemetery in his honor purchased by Mr. and Mrs. Hubert Johnson (Donna McCrosky) and the Matagorda, Texas, Cemetery Association. It has a "Veteran of the Republic of Texas" bronze medallion from the Daughters of the Republic of Texas on the monument.[46]

Just before Robert's death, he gave a Power of Attorney to his brother Joseph, covering all matters and canceling the one he had given to Richard Patton in Arkansas given earlier pertaining to the lawsuit against the U.S. Government. It was dated August 6, 1830. Robert made his Will on the same date and signed his mark, because he was totally blind and very ill at the time. It was witnessed by E. M. Wightman, Pumley Barnet, John Haddon, and Thomas J. Tone, and was filed the next day. His untimely death no doubt cut short a bright future and robbed Texas of an outstanding leader. He was kind, charitable, and most generous to the less fortunate. There was a civil case concerning land against his estate that was tried in Matagorda County, Texas. Among these papers were depositions from friends and neighbors stating that Robert and his good wife, Sarah, never turned away anyone from their door. If they were hungry, they fed them, if sick, they nursed them, if homeless, they gave them shelter until such time as they could provide for themselves.

Capt. Robert H. Kuykendall was well educated for his time and place. He was always in a place of responsibility in the colony, and was closely associated with other leaders in the counsel of both war and peace. He wrote a smooth, flowing, and legible hand as shown by his letters and signatures.

After his death, the Colorado County Court appointed his brothers, Abner and Joseph, as administrators of his estate and made his son, R.H.K., guardian of the minor children. The two leagues of land, the lots in the village of Matagorda, and all the livestock were divided between Sarah and all the children.

After Robert's death, William B. Travis, Administrator, turned some money over to E. Roddy for Dr. Peebles from Robert's estate for the medical expenses incurred.[47]

Robert and Sarah Kuykendall had six known children that survived infancy:

1. R.H. (called Gill) b. ca. 1816, probably in Arkansas. Supposedly died or was killed between Victoria, Texas, and San Antonio in late 1846 by either Indians

or outlaws. He married Electra Shannon of Montgomery County, Texas, daughter of John Shannon, ca 1835, reaffirmed in 1837 by license in Austin, County, Texas. Two sons were born to them: Robert, ca 1837, and Wylie Martin, born 22 October 1839 in Ft. Bend County, Texas. Electra died after 1841 and R.H. remarried Matilda Earp in 1844 with one issue, a daughter named Jane. There is no further information on Jane. (See biography on RHK in another chapter.)

2. Molly (Mary) b. ca 1818, probably in Arkansas, married Howard Decrow 18 October 1837.[48] They had four children: Elijah b. ca 1837 died at birth; Thomas E. b. ca 1838; Sarah Emma, b. ca 1842; and L.E.K. (daughter) b. ca 1844, died at birth. Howard Decrow does not show up on the 1850 Matagorda County census. The Matagorda County Historical Book does state however, that both Mary and Howard died in 1856. The probate court granted John Moore guardianship over the two remaining children after the deaths of the parents. John Moore was married to Sarah Ann Kensey, half sister to Mary.

3. Jane, b. ca 1820, also probably in Arkansas, married James Fitzgerald, no further information has been found.

4. Joseph Felix T., b. in November or December 1822 in Texas. His signature appears on the estate papers in 1842; no further information, possibly never married and probably died soon afterwards.

5. Albert Benjamin (twin) b. 21 January 1829, Pleasant Farm Plantation, Bay Prairie, Texas, married Elisabeth Elliot on 9 February 1855. He lived in west Matagorda County near the Tres Palacios River. He served on several Matagorda Court committees (road, jury, etc.). He was a stock raiser. He died 9 November 1865 in Matagorda County. His wife, Elisabeth, died in 1866. Both are buried in the Williams Cemetery on Wilson's Creek in Matagorda County near the village of Blessing, Texas. They had two known children: William T. and Kate. Kate married Samuel Grant on 25 December 1876.[49] Benjamin is supposedly buried under an old oak tree in the cemetery.

6. Thomas (twin) b. 21 January 1829, married Sarah Ann Gainor of Edna, Texas, on 7 December 1850. He died in Matagorda County, Texas, on 11 January 1904, and was buried near Wilson's Creek near Ashby. They had five known children: (1) Benjamin W., born ca 1854. Never married, lived in Markham, ran the livery stable, died in 1918, buried at Hawley. (2) Annie, born in 1858, Matagorda County, married Henry S. Abel on 24 June 1877. They lived at Wharton. Annie died in Houston. Henry died ca 1885. Both are buried in a family plot in Wharton County. (3) Willie (Wilburne)(daughter), b. 1862, married her cousin, Wilburn Harry Gainer, b. 1863, d. 1918. Willie died on 13 December 1920. Both are buried at Hawley. They had three children: Henry A. b. 1888, d. 1944; William Thomas (Bill) b. 1892, d. 1976, never married; and Jimmie (daughter) b. 1897, d. 1965, married Carl Haggard and they had three sons: Archie, Ward, and Wilburn. (4) Mattie Amanda, b. 12 April 1865 at the Kuykendall Ranch on Tres Palacios Creek in Matagorda County. She died 15 July 1934 at her home in Markham, Texas, Matagorda County, and is buried in the Hawley. Mattie married John Harrison McCrosky on 24 April 1890. They

had two children: John Harrison McCrosky, Jr., b. 1891, d. 1938, married Betty Randolph McLendon 20 January 1920 and they had one child, Betty Jane; and Thomas Kuykendall McCrosky; b. 1892, d. 1959. He was married twice. First to Asa Griggs, second unknown, with four total children: John Voss, Thomas Griggs, Peter, and Peggy. (5) Emma Kuykendall, b. 13 November 1866 at the Kuykendall ranch on Tres Palacios Creek. She never married and lived with her sister, Mattie Amanda. She died 22 December 1935 and is buried in the McCrosky plot in the Hawley.

There is no record of any other children born to Robert and Sarah.[50]

In the probate records of 1842 of Capt. Robert H. Kuykendall's estate, which are quite long, are the signatures of all the living heirs. Sarah G. Kuykendall and her children signed the documents in many different locations which show their names very clearly. Young Robert, who is 26 years old at the time, always signs his name as RHK, but on one page, Sarah lists all of her children by name and writes out the name of her first born son as "Robert Gilleland Kuykendall." This clears up the mystery of the *Gill Kuykendall* who was with Wiley Martin in 1836 and the *Mrs. Gill Kuykendall* who Fenn talks about in the *History of Ft. Bend County, Texas*. Even though his mother wrote that as his name, and the fact that he went by the nickname of Gill, he always signed all his papers, R. H. Kuykendall.[51]

Sarah Ann Gilleland Kuykendall, daughter of William and Nancy Johnson Gilleland, was born on 4 December 1797, probably in Davidson County, Tennessee. After Robert's death in late 1830, Sarah married Peter Kensie, ca 1833. He came to Texas from Kentucky ca 1830. They had one child, a daughter named Sarah Ann. Kensie died shortly thereafter and Sarah gave power of attorney to William Casneau to try and get the land that had been granted to Kensie. Sarah then married Thomas J. Tone on 31 December 1837. Tone was deputy surveyor under E. R. Wightman and also administrator of Kensie's estate. Tone died without children and Sarah asked for administration papers of the Tone estate in 1853.

Sarah's daughter, Sarah Ann Kensie, married John Moore on 26 May 1845. After the death of Tone, old Sarah went to live with her daughter just south of the present village of Blessing, Texas. She died there after a short illness in 1857 and was buried in the Moore family cemetery. Later her grave and several others were moved to the famous "Old Hawley" cemetery (Deming's Bridge) located one mile east of Blessing on the east side of Tres Palacios Creek just off Hwy. 35 and FM 459 in Matagorda County. It is the oldest grave in the beautiful cemetery and is located in the Moore plot with a headstone that reads:

SARAH TONE
In memory of our mother
Born December 4, 1797
Died October 13, 1857[56]

R. H. Gill Kuykendall, 1815-1846
Texian

—Illustration drawn by Charlie Shaw

Chapter Seven

R. H. (Gill) Kuykendall
1815-1846

R. H. Kuykendall, called by the nickname of Gill (after his mother's maiden name) was born ca 1815 in Arkansas Territory to Robert H. Kuykendall, Sr., and Sarah Gilleland Kuykendall. His father was one of the earliest members of Stephen F. Austin's Old 300 Colonists into Mexican/Texas in the fall of 1821. He probably was born in the area known as the Cadron Settlement since Robert Sr. and all of his immediate family lived in that general vicinity at that time.

Abner Kuykendall, Robert Sr.'s older brother, and other members of the family were in Arkansas (Missouri Territory) at the Cadron Settlement as early as 15 February 1810, when Abner and his brother, Amos, were witness to a Power of Attorney from John Bain to Patrick Darby.[1]

The settlers had been told not to make any improvements west of the Kiamichi River. The orders actually came from the Secretary of War John C. Calhoun through Gen. Andrew Jackson, then commanding officer of the Southern Division of the United States Army. He (Jackson) told Maj. William Bradford at Ft. Smith, Arkansas, in May 1819, that the "illegal" settlers must be removed. Most simply went south into the Miller County, Arkansas, area.[2]

It is known that Robert Kuykendall was an Indian trader and had been trapping and trading for several years in what is now known as western Arkansas and eastern Oklahoma and had been with his father-in-law, Thomas Williams. Both were hunters with William English and others at the mouth of the Verdigris River in October 1812. He certainly would have been moved by the Army had he built improvements on Indian lands. It is fairly certain that Robert moved south into the Pecan Point or

Fulton, Arkansas, areas earlier than his brothers Abner and Joseph. He possibly bypassed these areas and went on into Spanish Texas several years before Austin's grant for the 300 families came into effect. It is stated that he had "been scouting east Texas" for several months prior to October 1821 when he met his brothers at Nacogdoches and went west with them to the Colorado River. (Brazos River)[3]

It also should be noted that many hundreds of the settlers were already on the northeast boundary of Mexico/Texas at that time (Pecan Point) and many had already encroached across the border on many horse gathering expeditions and Indian trading forays. It is fairly certain that Robert H. Kuykendall, Sr., had been among these people.[4]

Originally researchers thought that Abner, accompanied by Joseph, entered Mexico/Texas in the fall of 1821 where they then met up with their brother, Robert H. But statements noted in the Mirabeau B. Lamar Papers have found that Joseph was with his older brother, Robert, in Nacodoches earlier.

Lamar wrote: "Robert and Joseph Kirkendall saw Moses Austin near Nacadoches (on his return from San Antonio de Bexar). (See bio. on Capt. RHK, Sr.)[5]

In December 1822, when young RHK was 7 years old, the Baron de Bastrop arrived at the upper settlement on the Colorado River to organize the colony. The settlers met near the present town of Columbus, Texas, where they took the oath of allegiance to the Emperor Iturbide and held an election for civil and militia officers which resulted in the election of Robert H. Kuykendall (Sr.) as captain of the militia for the Mina District (Colorado) and alcalde of the (Colorado) District (temporary) when militia officers were elected. Robert's house was the site when James Cummins was later elected alcalde of the (Colorado) District.[6]

In March 1823, Robert Sr. joined with John Tumlinson to write a letter to Governor J. F. Trespalacios at San Antonio from the District of Colorado province of Texas explaining their need for protection from the Indians and citing several instances of acts by the Indians against the settlers. In this same letter, they sent the first census report of the colony from the Colorado District and they listed the inhabitants of the Colorado River area. It is in this report that Robert Sr. states the age of himself and his family members by name: Robert states that he is 33 years of age; Sarah, his wife, is 27; young Robert (Gill) is 8; Molly is 5; Jane is 3; and baby Jose Felix Trespalacios is 4 months old. The letter is signed by both John Tumlinson and Robert Kuykendall (in their own hand).[7]

In June or July 1824, the Karankawas killed a calf of Robert's (Sr.) a few hundred yards from his home. He sent his 10-year-old son Robert (Gill) for help. A dozen or more neighbors quickly assembled and they tracked the Indians to the Colorado River and found the Indians on the far side. One of the settlers was wounded in the elbow and one Indian was killed.[8]

Robert Sr. established his home on the league of land east of the Colorado River near the old Indian Crossing on Peach Creek, close to the present village of Glen Flora, Wharton County, Texas. His home was known as the "Pleasant Farm Plantation, Bay Prairie," as the area was known that lay between the Colorado and Bernard rivers.[9]

After Robert Sr.'s death (ca 1830), the Colorado County Court appointed his brothers, Abner and Joseph, as administrators of his estate and made his son, R. H.

(Gill), guardian of the minor children. (Gill would have been 15 years old at the time.) The two leagues of land and the lots in the village of Matagorda and all of the livestock were divided among the children.

During the Texas Revolution, young Gill Kuykendall served under Wiley Martin in his unit of scouts that patrolled the Colorado River crossings in the Ft. Bend, Texas, area. After April 1836, he shows up in Capt. Washington H. Secrest's company of Washington cavalry, June 1836, and was discharged on 23 October 1836.[10]

MEMORANDUM OF APPLICATION FOR LAND
IN AUSTINS & WILLIAM'S COLONY

Name: Kuykendall, R. H.
Where from: Resident
Date of Arrival: Citizen
Date of Application: 1st of June 1835
Profession: farmer
Remarks: wants land in Buffalo Bayou next to Riniman.[11]

June 7th 1836

Robert H. Kuykendall joined my company of Texian Volunteers on the 7th of March for three months, whose term of service expired on the 7th of June and having served honorably and faithfully during that period is entitled to an honorable discharge from the Army of Texas.

Wyly Martin
Capt. Of Texian Volunteers[12]

I hereby certify that Robt. H. Kuykendall served in my company of cavalry with credit to himself & honor to his country from the twenty fifth of June to the twenty fifth of September & is this day honorably discharged for the term of three months.

September 25th 1836
John P. Gill
1st Lieut. of
Columbia Cavalry

Approved: William B. Travis
Sec. of War
File # 648: $24.00
Robert H. Kuykendall: filed 27th of Feb. 1837
Examined same day, admitted to audit
For $24.00
Military
24 June 1836
27 Feb. 1837
no draft 888[13]

REPUBLIC OF TEXAS
KNOW ALL MEN TO WHOM THESE PRESENTS SHALL COME:

THAT Robert H. Kuykendall, having served faithfully and honorably for the term of three months from the Seventh day of March 1838 and being honorably discharged from the ARMY OF TEXAS is entitled to three hundred twenty acres of Bounty Land, for which this is his certificate.

And the said Robert Kuykendall is entitled to hold said Land, or to sell, alienate, convey, and donate the same, and exercise all rights of ownership over it.

THIS CERTIFICATE WILL BE TRANSFERABLE BY ENDORSEMENT,

With a Deed, before any competent authority, with witnesses to the same.
IN TESTIMONY WHEREOF, I have hereunto set my hand,
At Houston this day of November 29th, 1837.

          Approved 23rd of July 1840.
          B. T. Archer, Sec. Of War.[14]

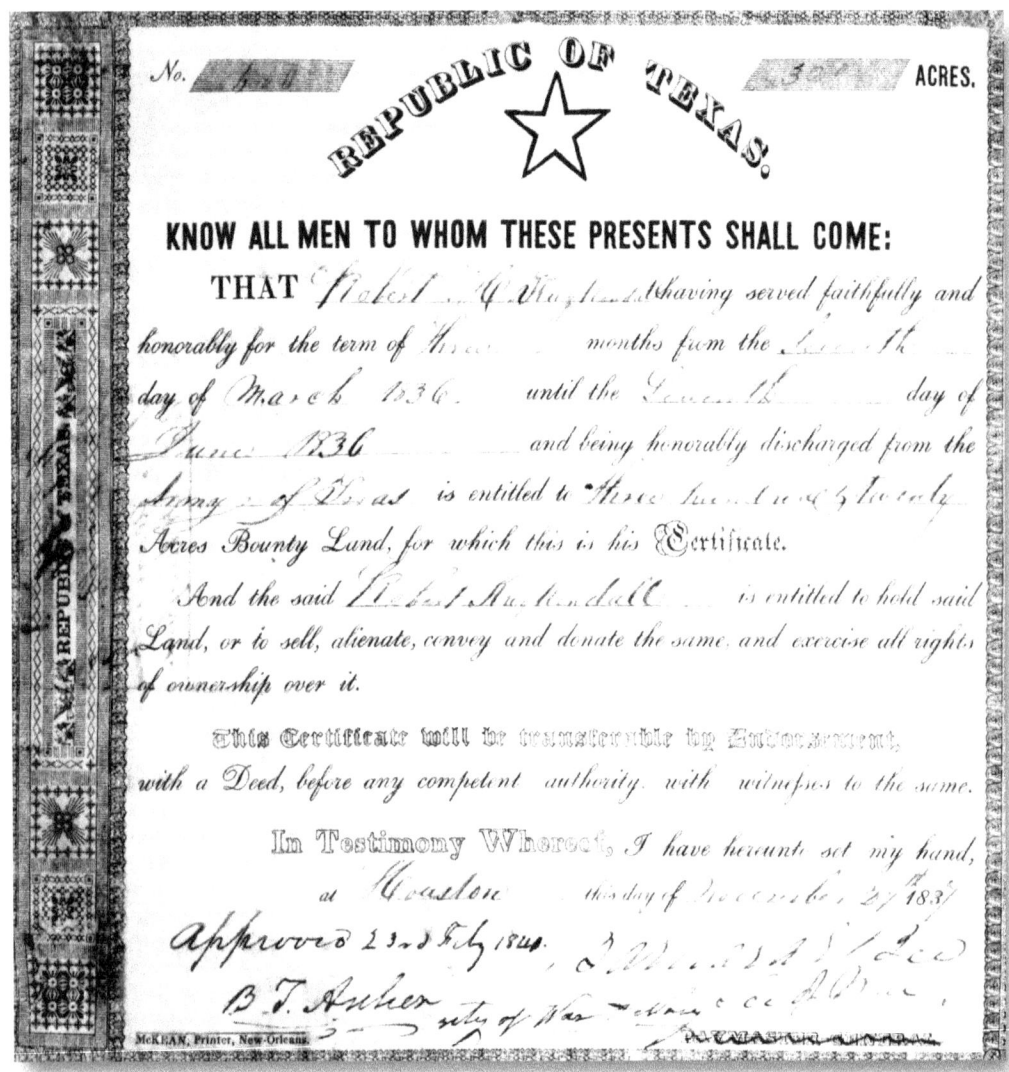

Republic of Texas
County of Ft. Bend:} Know all men by these presents that I, Robert H. Kuykendall, for and in consideration of the sum of one thousand dollars to me in hand paid by George M. Dobson, the _____ and payment of which is hereby acknowledged, have sold, transferred and assigned over to the said Dobson all my rights, title & interest in and to the land for which I am entitled by the written certificate and I hereby authorize the said Dobson to locate and obtain a title for the same in his own name & _____ _____ ratifying & confirming the same and binding myself, my heirs, & assigns by these presents to make good such transfer and assignment by giving a more & formal title should the same be required by the said Dobson, his heirs, Executors Administrators or assigns given under my hand this 1st day of February 1838.

    Witnessed: Joseph H. Barnard   *Robert H. Kuykendall*
    Sworn to by: *Wyly Martin*
    Chief Justice
    Exeficio Notary Public Ft. Bend County[15]

Republic of Texas:

Ft. Bend Co: In consideration of two hundred dollars to me in hand paid by Randolph Foster, I sign over to him the said Foster all my rights, title, and interest to the written land certificate for three hundred and twenty acres of land, January 12th, 1840.

                                        Robert H. Kuykendall

Wyly Martin[16]

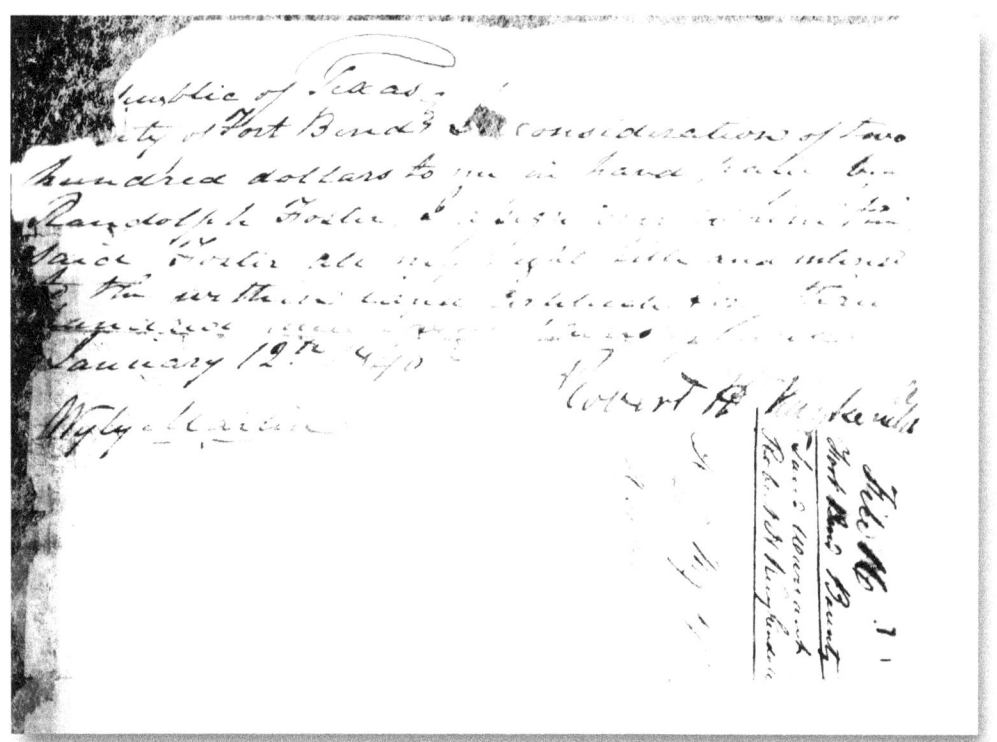

Bounty and Land Grant to Robert H. Kuykendall, (Jr):
"No. 82:
This is to certify that Robert H. Kuykendall has appeared before us the Board of Land Commissioners for the County of Ft. Bend and provides according to law that he arrived in this Republic in July of 1825 (incorrect) and that he is a married man and entitled to one League & one Labor of land upon the condition of paying at the rate of one dollar & twenty cents for each Labor of pasture lands & two dollars & fifty cents for each Labor of irrigable lands which may be contained in the survey secured to him by this Certificate.

Given under our hands this 1st February 1838
R. Jones President[17]

On January 19, 1841, the Texas Legislature passed an act which created a new county, Ward County, out of lands that had until then been part of Colorado and Matagorda counties and which included the community of Egypt. After, on February 4th, 1841, they scheduled district court sessions for it, the new county differed from the two counties from which it was created in only one regard: the residents of Ward County remained in the same congressional districts they had been in before Ward County was created. The legislature appointed Virgil A. Stewart as the county's first chief justice, and Stewart set about organizing elections. On February 24th, 1841, a district clerk, county clerk, county surveyor, six justices of the peace, and two constables were elected, and a county seat, at the proposed town of Fulton, was approved. Two candidates for sheriff tied, forcing a runoff. The winner of the runoff refused to accept the job, so a third election was held, on May 15th, 1841, and Robert H. Kuykendall, the son of the former militia captain, was elected.

A lawsuit was initiated by Benjamin Franklin Stocklin challenging the constitutionality of the law which created Ward County and on February 4th, 1842, the supreme court declared Ward County unconstitutional.[18]

In the probate records of 1842 of Captain Robert H. Kuykendall's estate are the signatures of all the living heirs. Sarah Gilleland Kuykendall (her's by an "X") and her children signed the documents in many different locations which show their signatures quite clearly. Young R. H., who is 26 years old at the time always signs his name, "R. H. Kuykendall." But on one page his mother, Sarah, lists all of her children by name and lists the name of her first born son, not as RHK but as "Robert Gilleland Kuykendall. This clears up the mystery of the *Gill Kuykendall* who was with Wylie Martin as a scout in 1836 at Ft. Bend and the *Mrs. Gill Kuykendall* Fenn talks about in the *History of Ft. Bend County, Texas*. Even though his mother told the court that her son's name or nickname was Gill, he always signed all his signatures, RH Kuykendall. His mother, by her signature, could not read nor write, and therefore could not tell what his signatures were.[19]

R. H. Kuykendall married Electra Shannon of Montgomery County Texas in 1835 which was re-affirmed on 7 November 1837 by license in Austin County, Texas. Two sons were born to them, Robert H. K. (Jr. or III), born ca 1837 and Wiley Martin

Kuykendall, born 22 October 1839 in Ft. Bend County, Texas. Gill's wife, Electra, died sometime after 1841 and Gill remarried a Miss Matilda Earp on 30 May 1844. They had one daughter named Jane. After Gill's death in 1846, there is little or no further information about Matilda or her daughter, Jane.

Son, Robert H. K. III, died on 20 April 1863 during the Civil War. He never married. (See notes on RHK III below.)

Son, Wiley M., married Shanghai Pierce's sister Susan in 1869 and died at Cuero, Texas, in 1920. He is buried at the famous old Hawley Cemetery at Blessing, Matagorda County, Texas. (See bio. to follow.)

The record of a Will found in Montgomery County, Texas, states:

"To all to whom these presents shall come, Know Ye that I, John Shannon of the County of Montgomery in the Republic of Texas do make and order this day this my last Will and Testament in manner and form as follows to wit:

"It is my will and desire that at the death of my wife Charlotte, all my estate then remaining undivided be equally divided among my above named children. My daughter Electra Kuykendall I consider has received a full and equal portion of my estate with the rest of my children, etc."

8th day of February AD 1838 and Second year of Independence of the Republic of Texas.

signed: his mark
(Known as the "Black Box"   *John (X) Shannon*
files of Montgomery Co.)   mark[20]

R. H. Kuykendall to John Fitzgerald:

"This indenture made the twelfth day of November in the year one thousand eight hundred and forty four between Robert H. Kuykendall of the County of Colorado Republic of Texas of the first part and John Fitzgerald of the County of Ft. Bend and Republic aforesaid of the second part witnessed. That the said party of the first part by this act acknowledges himself to be indebted to the said John Fitzgerald in the sum of four thousand five hundred dollars on a note with even date herewith and payable on the first day of January one thousand eight hundred and fifty five with interest at the rate of ten per cent per annum, payable annually from and from after the first day of January next (1845) and for the payment of said sum of money well and truly to be made he by this instrument especially binds and hypothecates in favor of the said John Fitzgerald a certain tract or parcel of land consisting of seven hundred acres being and situate in the County of Ft. Bend on the east side of the Brazos River and being the same that was conveyed to the said Kuykendall by the said Fitzgerald by deed of even date hereof, and which is thus described in said instrument (vis): the league of land of which said tract is a part was originally granted to my father David Fitzgerald by the Mexican Government in the year eighteen hundred and twenty four as will more fully appear by reference to the original deed of concession.

The said seven hundred acres of land is bounded as follows, to wit: South by a tract of land sold by me to Mrs. Fann (which was also originally a part of the league granted to my father aforesaid.) West by a tract of land also off said league sold by me to Johnathon D. Waters. North, partly by the said tract of Waters, partly by another tract originally a part of said league sold by me to Mrs. Perry. And bounded on the East end by another tract off said league sold by me to John D. Colder and since owned by Willis M. Battle. And the said Robert H. Kuykendall for the same purpose hereby further especially binds and hypothecates seven Negro slaves being the same that were sold unto the said Robert by the said John as will more fully appear by a certain bill of sale executed by the said John of even date with this instrument and which Negro slaves are of the following names and age, to wit: John, aged about fifty years; Winny, aged about thirty seven years; Ike, aged about twenty two years; Patience, aged about twenty two years and her child, aged about eighteen months; Lark, aged about eleven years and Martha, aged about eight years. And the said R. H. Kuykendall hereby further declares that he by this instrument authorizes the said Fitzgerald to take possession Judicially or extra Judicially of the said land and Negro slaves as aforesaid and to hold the same as a pledge until the final payment and satisfaction of said demand. And to the observance of this obligation he binds himself, his heirs, executors and administrators and with himself and property submits to the tribunals of the County which of right ought to have cognizance of the matter, that they may compel him to comply with this obligation by all the rigors of the law. And he renounces all law that might favor him and signs this instrument before the undersigned witnesses (using his scroll for seal) the day and date above written."

(Signed) *R. H. Kuykendall*

Witnesses:
J. Hampton Kuykendall (1st cousin)
Joseph Kuykendall (Uncle)

(Interestingly, future children and grandchildren of Wiley would be named Ike and Winnie—MEK)

REPUBLIC OF TEXAS
COUNTY OF FORT BEND

Personally came and appeared before me, Mills M. Battle County Clerk of said County, J. Hampton Kuykendall one of the witnesses to the foregoing instrument of writing, and after being sworn in due course of law, declares and says that he saw R. H. Kuykendall sign, seal, and deliver the same for the uses and purposes therein expressed, and himself with the other witness signed the same as witnesses.

Given under my hand and seal of office at Richmond the 19th day of January 1845.

Mills M. Battle,
County Clk.

Filed for Record the 19th & recorded the 28th January 1845.
Mills M. Battle, County Clk., & Recorder
By his deputy N. S. Rector[21]

The State of Texas
Colorado County

To the Honl. Chief Justice of said County, your petitioner, Patrick Fleming states that one Robert H. Kerkendol departed this life on the day of _____ 1846, intestate, and that no administration has been taken out of his estate—that he is indebted to your petitioner and others & that unless he or some person is appointed he has no remedy to collect his debt with others and they will be lost wherefore _____ _____ your honor to grant him letters of administration on the estate at the next term of our court of said Kerkendol, this Sept. 15th, 1848.

(Signed) P. Fleming[22]

In October 1846, J. Hampton Kuykendall (RHK's first cousin), decided to seek employment as an interpreter with the American Army in Mexico under the command of Gen. Zachery Taylor. Enroute he stayed overnight at his brother William's house on Garcitas Creek near present day Victoria, Texas. It was at this juncture that JHK recorded the last known information about his cousin, R. H. Gill Kuykendall, one of his fondest boyhood friends. JHK stated that RHK was camped nearby on Garcitas Creek and that he went there to visit with him. He mentioned that RHK was there with all his family, belongings, and cattle, camped out on the prairie like a "vagabond" and that he was such a "misanthrope."(?)[23]

Betty McCrosky, one of the first, original researchers of the Kuykendall family in Texas made a statement in her papers that she thought RHK was killed by Indians or outlaws on his way to San Antonio from the Garcitas Creek area. If there is a deposition to that effect in court records, it is unknown to this writer. His body was never found.

Robert H. Jr.'s second marriage was to Matilda Earp on 30 May 1844. To that union was born one daughter, Jane. The records do not reflect her birth date, nor what happened to her after her father's death. Nor do we have a record of who she might have married had she lived long enough. On 12 January 1847, Matilda filed a petition stating that Robert was dead. On 2 November 1847, Icabod E. Earp, brother to Matilda, petitioned for the guardianship over the persons and properties of Robert H. K. III, and Wiley M. Kuykendall, minors of RHK, Jr., deceased. (There is no mention in his petition about Jane.) It can be assumed that he did not win this petition, because the 1850 Census of Ft. Bend County, Texas, shows the two orphan boys, Robert H. and Wiley M. Kuykendall are living with their great uncle, Joseph. (Joe Kuykendall, younger brother to Captain Abner and Captain Robert H., lived on his league on the Brazos River just south of present day, Richmond, Texas, until his death ca 1870.[24]

Shortly after living with their great uncle, Joseph, south of present day Richmond, Robert disappears from the records until the Civil War. Wiley, however, is taken by his family Negro slave, Lark, down into Matagorda County to live with his uncle Thomas near Wilson's Creek and the Tres Palacios. There is considerable history recorded about him in later years as will be noted in his biography.

All that is known of Robert H. Kuykendall (III) is that he joined the 6th Texas Infantry during the Civil War and fought with that unit until its surrender to federal forces at Arkansas Post (Ft. Hindman), Arkansas, on 16 February 1863. Many of the personnel were exchanged to join other units but the records reflect that young RHK III, Private, died as a prisoner of war at Camp Butler, Illinois, on 20 April 1863 and is buried in the National Cemetery there near Springfield, Illinois, in the Confederate Section "D," grave number 378.[25]

A personal tribute to Robert H. Kuykendall from his cousin, Jonathon Hampton Kuykendall:

To ROBERT H. KUYKENDALL

My friend in boyhoods balmy days,
We sported o'er these plains,
But memories of those happy days,
Is all that now remains.

How often did our simple hearts,
Then yearn for manhood's years,
Ah! Little deem'd we that our wish,
Would bring us woes and tears!

And now we stand at life's mid Arch,
Our friendship unestranged,
Our hearts are true to boyhood's pledge,
Though all things else have changed!

We've chased the phantom happiness,
A long and weary round,
As erst we chased the butterfly,
But her we have not found!

And every step we've ta'en in life,
Seems further from the goal,
And every sunny-winged hope,
Has flitted from the soul!

Our span will soon be measured out,
Our brief career soon close,
And in our mother's earth's embrace,
We'll find at last repose!

And in the grave of dreams may come,
Be they of boyhood's days,
Ere time unseal'd the fount of grief,
Ere fancy dimmed the Rays![26]

Wiley M. Kuykendall

Chapter Eight

Wiley Martin Kuykendall

Wiley Martin Kuykendall (1839-1920), pioneer cattle trail driver, was born in Ft. Bend County, Texas, on October 27, 1839, to R. H. (Gill) Kuykendall and Electra (Sectra) Shannon (Montgomery County). He was the grandson of Captain Robert H. Kuykendall, one of Stephen F. Austin's earliest members of the original "Old 300." He was named after a family friend and prominent colonist, Wyly Martin.[1]

His mother died when he was very young (ca 1844) and his father failed to return home from a trip to San Antonio in late 1846. He was presumed killed by Indians or outlaws. Wiley's father had served in the Texas revolution under Captain Wyly Martin as a scout.[2]

Very little is known about Wiley's father and little or nothing about his mother. There are several muster rolls that reflect RHK's service during the Texas revolution. There are also scattered deed record transactions in Austin County signed by R. H. Kuykendall on lands received by him for his services during the revolution. The records reflect that Robert H. Kuykendall was elected sheriff of Ward County-Judicial on 15 May 1841, and served until the county was abolished in 1841 by the Texas Supreme Court. Ward County-Judicial was a part of present day Wharton and Colorado counties.[3]

It has been stated that after Wiley's father's death, Wiley left Ft. Bend County riding a mule behind his Negro man-servant named Lark. Lark dropped him off in the village of Matagorda where he lived for a while with his grandmother, Susan Kuykendall Tone and his uncle Thomas Kuykendall. He got along well and was soon dubed "Mr. Wiley" before the fuzz on his face turned to whiskers.[4]

Wiley got a job punching cattle at the age of 10, and at 15 was trailing cattle to

Missouri. Bill Hurnden was the owner of the herd on this trip and he paid Wylie $25 per month. The herd consisted 600 "beeves" and he signed on as a "hand" to trail the herd from Matagorda County to Weberville, Missouri. "We went by Columbus, Texas, crossing the Colorado River near Bastrop, then on into north Texas and entered the Indian Territory (Oklahoma) at Preston. After passing through the Creek, Cherokee, and Choctaw Nations, the Indians became so troublesome that the owner of the herd secured an escort of United States soldiers to guard them as they went on into Missouri. We were gone nine months. We encountered all kinds of weather conditions during this long drive. In some sections we encountered droughts and heat and in others rains and cold. At the time there were no roads and bridges, and we had to ford and swim the streams as we came to them. Altogether, this was the hardest trip I ever made. I am the only survivor of the five white boys and the five Mexicans hands who carried this herd through to Missouri. Half the wages which the owner of the beeves agreed to pay me is still due me."

"I was 12 years old before I ever had a pair of shoes. I worked for 25 cents a day to get money enough to buy me a pair. I worked a number of years for 50 cents a day and had to clothe myself. After coming back from Missouri, I worked for W. B. G. Grimes. The first year he paid me $25 per month, and after that he paid me a dollar a day. This raise made me feel like I had at last struck luck that was placing me upon the road to fortune. I worked upon the ranges at this price until the war began, when I enlisted in Buchel's regiment of Texas cavalry. When the war was over I came home without a dollar, and again I went to work on the ranges."[5]

By 1857, he was trailing 600 head to Quincy, Illinois, nearly 10-15 years before the big cattle drives out of Texas were to start.[6]

The August Conference—1857

Minutes of the Trespalacios Baptist Church, Matagorda County, Texas.

The Trespalacios Church, after divine service met in conference on Saturday before the first Sabbath in August, Brother Haynie, Mod.—H. Yeamans, Ch. Clk.

1st. The minutes of the last Conference were read.

2nd. The door was opened for reception of members and while we sang a hymn, Elijah Deckrow, Wiley Kuykendall*, and Matilda Deckrow came forward and gave satisfactory experience, and were received. After which Conference adjourned.

Sabbath morning after divine service the door of the Church was opened for reception of members, and while singing a hymn, Emma Deckrow and Joseph Williams came forward and what the Lord had done for their souls, and were received. And in the afternoon were Baptised.

*Note: He was received at the May Conference.

September Conference—1859

The Trespalacios Baptist Church after divine service met in Conference on the first Sabbath in September and chose Brother Moore, Moderator. After the first and second rules were dispensed with, there was a charge brought against Brother Wiley Kuykendall for disorderly conduct. On motion and seconded there was a Committee appointed to wait on Bro. K. and reclaim him to the fellowship of the Church. Brethern John Smith, John B. Smith and Robert Partain appointed committee.

John Moore, Mod   Horace Yeamans, Ch. Clerk

October Conference—1859

The Trespalacios Church after divine service met in conference and chose Brother Moore, Mod. The case of Bro. Wiley Kuykendall was brought up. The Committee was not ready to report, etc.

          Bro. Moore, Mod.
          Horace Yeamans, Clerk

March 4, 1860

The Trespalacios Baptist Church after divine service met in Conference on the 4th of March. Bro. Loudermilk having excepted the call of the Church presided as Moderator.

1st. The door of the church was opened for the reception of Members.

2nd. The Committee that was appointed to wait on Bro. Wiley Kuykendall made a report that said Bro. Kuykendall refused to make reconciliation whereupon a motion was made and seconded to exclude Bro. Kuykendall from the fellowship of the Church. He accordingly was excluded. Having no other business the Conference adjourned.

          Bro. J. J. Loudermilk, Mod.
          Horace Yeamans, Ch. Clk.[7]

Wiley joined the Confederate Army on 10 April 1862 at Camp H. E. McCulloch, near Victoria, Texas. He served in Capt. James C. Boren's Company "D," Yager's Battalion (Buchels), Texas Mounted Volunteers. Also, known as "Company D, Yager's Battalion Texas Mounted Volunteers" or 1st Texas Mounted Rifles, and 1st (Yager's) Cavalry and 1st Regiment Texas Cavalry.[8]

His "Regimental Descriptive Book" shows that he joined on April 10, 1862, at Camp McCulloch, for the term of the war. He was 21 years old, 5 feet 8 inches tall, with grey eyes, light hair, born in Texas, and was a stock raiser. It was signed by Col. Garland.[9]

He appears to have been promoted to 3rd sergeant in November or December 1862 and his name appears on the company muster rolls in March 1863. There is an entry that a "W. Kuykendall, Pvt. 1st. Tex. Cavalry" appears on a list of prisoners of war surrendered and paroled at Victoria, Texas, prior to August 8, 1865. His residence is shown as Matagorda County, Texas.[10]

The 1st (Yager's) Regiment Texas Cavalry was formed about May, 1863, by the consolidation of the 3rd (Yager's) Battalion Texas Cavalry, the 8th (Taylor's) Battalion Texas Cavalry and Captain Ware's Company Texas Cavalry. It was also known in the field as the 1st Regiment Texas Mounted Rifles.[11]

This Confederate unit served along the Texas coast until March 1864. It would later see extensive action in the Red River Campaign. It was then known as Yager's Texas Cavalry Regiment (1st Texas Cavalry) which was formed in May 1863 as a consolidation of the 3rd (Yager's) Battalion Texas Cavalry, and Captain Ware's company of Texas Cavalry. (See above) At one time Terrell served in this regiment as a major.

From the time the 1st Texas joined General Taylor at Mansfield on April 5, 1864, until the return to Texas with Terrell's brigade, the regiment served gallantly, suffering many casualties. In the battles of Mansfield and Pleasant Hill alone, the regiment had nine killed, fifty-one wounded and four missing.[12]

By consolidation of organizations about May 1863, Wylie became a private of County "D" 1st (Yager's) Regiment of Texas Cavalry. The muster roll for January and February 1864 show him present. On or about 1 April 1865, all the men of the brigade who were without horses were given furloughs to return home to Texas and remount themselves.[13]

His name appears on a list of prisoners of war paroled at Victoria, Texas, prior to 8 August 1865. His home was shown in the records as Matagorda County, Texas.[14]

To date there have been no records found that state when and where Wiley fought, nor when he actually left his unit to return home to Matagorda County. J. Hampton Kuykendall, Wiley's uncle from Victoria, Texas, and William and Talbot Kuykendall, cousins, of Tilden, Texas, also served in the same company. William in a later diary account of the war states he saw extensive action in the Red River campaign but he does not mention Wiley's name. (MEK personal files) Other cousins from Bell County, Robert and George Kuykendall were in Company "K." In the diaries of J. Hampton Kuykendall, he states they "served on the Rio Grande around Brownsville guarding the river from blockade runners."[15]

Wylie Kuykendall

Susan E. Pierce Kuykendall

"I was married April 22, 1869. I went to work on the ranges for wages, and my wife took charge and managed the farm. For ten years I worked day and night, making as many as ten trips up the old cattle trail to Kansas in charge of herds for W. B. G. Grimes and others. After I quit going up the trail I began to buy and raise cattle for myself."[16]

(signed) Wiley Kuykendall

"Mr. Robert Kuykendall,

Dear Sir; I was indeed happy to pass and see your mother and father. I had not seen your father in about forty years. It was a real pleasure to meet your mother, she is a very attractive person.

I was very sorry indeed that I can not give you the information that I would have about your great grandfather. I know that he use to talk about his uncle Tom (Thomas Kuykendall) that raised him, his brother, and his sister. He and his brother went to war. (Civil War) When he returned his sister was missing, they never knew what became of her. Then he got a job working for Mr. Pierce as trail boss. There he met Miss Susan Elizabeth, Mr. Pierce's sister. That was your (great) grandmother. His Uncle Tom disinherited him because he married a Northern and he was from the South. He (Uncle Tom) never had anything to do with him as long as he lived."[17]

In late 1865 or early '66, Wiley went to work for A. H. (Shanghai) Pierce and Jonathon E. Pierce as range boss on their El Rancho Grande ranch at Demings Bridge (present-day Blessing, Texas) Matagorda County, Texas.

"Mr. Wiley was one of Pierce's first recruits. He came cow-driving but wound up courting the Pierce brothers' sister, Susan. When Shanghai saw what was going on, he stormed at his sister, "I'm not hunting a brother-in-law, just a cow hand. If you marry that man, you'll starve to death. You can't do anything with him. He has Kuykendall fits."[18]

Wylie married Susan E. Pierce, sister to Shanghai and John Pierce, on 22 April 1869 in Matagorda County, Texas.[19]

Now that "Mr. Wiley" had become a brother-in-law, he took over as roundup boss. His love for Susan, liquor and longhorns was only exceeded by his energy. As a boss he was harder than Shanghai, long before dawn each morning, he crawled out from under his blanket, lighted his big, smelly black pipe with a coal out of the camp fire, and called the cook. Together they boiled a big black pot of coffee, cup after cup of which he drank piping hot. Then, very softly, he called to the sleeping cowboys:

A.H. "Shanghai" Pierce as a young man.   *Jonathan E. Pierce*

"Come, boys. Come. Get up and hear the little birds singing their sweet praises to God." (Then continuing loud and harsh) "Almighty Damn Your Souls! GET UP!"[20]

With Jonathon Pierce in control at "El Rancho Grande" headquarters, and Wylie Kuykendall calling out the boys on the range, the A. H. & J. E. Pierce cattle company was a substantial reality.[21]

Wiley and Susan had five children: Robert Gill (1870-1905), Isaac Bradford (1874-1875), Isaac Green (1876-1896), Eugeone Burshell (1878-1879), and Electra Miranda (1883-1965).[22]

John Wesley Hardin, the well known Texas gun fighter, showed up in the area, which alarmed Shanghai terribly. The state police were out looking for the boy bandit and he took cover in the cow camps in and around Matagorda County. Charlie Siringo had gone back over to the Pierce camp to work again and was well aware of Pierce's

R. G. Kuykendall   *Isaac G. Kuykendall*   *Electra Kuykendall*

alarm over the marauding Wes Hardin. One night, said Charlie, "while I was employed by the great and only Shanghai Pierce, a young man who was jovial and full of fun came riding into camp." Mr. Wylie recognized John Wesley immediately, but kept his identity secret until he had ridden away the next morning. When Shanghai learned of his brother-in-law's finesse in steering Wes out of his path, he confessed, "that Wiley is a hunney."[23]

What has not been stated in the history books about Wiley, is that he and John Wesley Hardin were cousins. The Hardins and the Kuykendalls had been traveling together ever since old Adam Kuykendall, Wiley's great-great-grandfather married Margaret Hardin in the late 1760s. Wes Hardin was from that same lineage. (MEK personal files)

Later around 1871, Wiley trail bossed for another outfit. "About the middle of August 1871, we pulled out again with a fresh supply of horses, six to a man, and a brand new boss, Mr. Wiley."[24]

Young Matagorda County cowboys, ca 1870

"Fred P. O. Indian T Y"
Mr. A H Pierce,
Dear Sir,
 not having herd from you since we left I thought I would write you so that you would know whare to find us I am now camped on Bitter Creek between the Washata & Canadian Rivers You had better write to us here as we will remain in this visinity some time unless we receive orders from you to move on we have not had eny rain yet and this is the first place that I have been where we could improve the Cattle and horses. Wylie's men have been having the measles Bob Logan has them now but is getting all right my cattle have been running badly but are getting all right now the grass and water is fine and cattle ought to improve very fast I have 2000 head in my herd,

Brand	Owner	Year
AS	ABNER SMALLEY	1837
←	THOMAS & ELIJAH DECROW	1837
28	LAWRENCE KINCHELOE	1838
88	GEORGE M. COLLINSWORTH	1838
SI	SETH INGRAM	1838
O	NANCY PARTAIN	1838
D AND SD	SILAS DINSMORE	1839
H (NOW H)	M. SEXTON & M. SAVAGE	1843
⇁	GALEN HODGES	1844
⋙	MARY VAN DORN	1845
⇂	MOSES VAN DORN	1845
∀	GEORGE W. WARD	1845
⊖	JOHN MOORE	1845
♡	ROBERT & WILEY M. KUYKENDALL	1845
AH	ALBERT C. HORTON	1848
☰	JAMES H SELKIRK	1848
℘	D.D.E BRAMAN	1849
℘	HORACE YEAMANS	1850
Y	WILLIAM SARTWELLE	1851
N	NORMAN SAVAGE	1851
K	THOMAS KUYKENDALL	1851
SR	FREDRICK W. ROBBINS	1852
V	ISAAC VAN DORN	1853
AP	A.H. "SHANGHAI" PIERCE	1854
D	D. HARDEMAN	1854
8	ROBERT H. WILLIAMS	1855
12	JOHN FRANCIS HOLT	1855
6	NORMAN SAVAGE	1857
SB	WILLIAM B. WADSWORTH	1858
⊿	JOHN F. MCNABB	1858
⌒	CHRISTIAN ZIPPRIAN	1859
X-S	JOHN S. SANBORN	1860
WBG	W.B GRIMES	1860
H	JAMES B. HAWKINS	1860
2	JOHN DUNCAN	1872
S2	C.A. SIRINGO	1873
H	GOTTLIEB BAER	1874
D	ABEL H. PIERCE	1880
TC	THOMAS E. CORNELIUS	1891

Matagorda County brands

july 24 '56

Dear Marshall you asked me for some information just received answer from Aunt Ella P. Dunn I wrote at once and forgot

I spent so much time with my grandmother and father, all day each day just listening that I believe I may be right.

I think Mr. Tom Miller pastured cattle on Grandfather Kuykendall's Matagorda County ranch when my father was a boy of 12 saying "Son why don't you take the brand 'JO'." In those far off days a brand could be registered and no one else could use it. A.H. Pierce was my grand mother's brother. Abel Head "Shanghai".

I remember my mother saying that my father "went up the trail" a little boy, came home a man. "Going up the Trail" was a six months horse back ride. A boy of sixteen or 18 might come back a man after that ride??

From the age of 2 or 4 I spent much time with grandmother and Grandfather P. From 2 to 20.

Continued on next page

had to let Wylie have one of my hands to help him out have had no chance to sell any cattle yet, etc.[25]

Susan Pierce Kuykendall: "In 1867, I came down from Little Compton, R. I., to Texas, landing at Indianola. This town had just passed through a scourge of yellow fever. I remained there a week at the home of Dan Sullivan. From there I went on a sail boat up the Trespalacios to the home of Mr. Downs. From there I took shipment on the back of a rough cow pony to Rancho Grande, where my brothers, A. H. and John Pierce, were then living. The distance from Mr. Downs' to the Rancho Grande was twelve miles, and I went in a lope across the prairies, it being the first time I had ever been on the back of a horse. I reached my destination feeling tired, sore, cripple, like I had been shipwrecked on land."

"I lived there until I was married to Wiley Kuykendall, April 22nd, 1869. We lived there until November. He was on the prairies cow driving working for wages. From Rancho Grande we went into camp near Demings Bridge (present-day Blessing, Texas) on the Trespalacios, where we had bought 400 acres from Nancy Parton, one of the early settlers in that community. January following, (1870) we moved into the house which we had built. Mr. Kuykendall then went to Mexico to buy horses and mules and was gone nine months. The next year (1871) he went up the trail to Kansas. I took charge of the farm and ran it. According to the work I had to perform I am sure you will say that I practiced diversification thoroughly on this farm. I milked the cows, helped break horses, marked and branded the calves, took in sewing, washing, ironing, and ran a boarding house, having as boarders, eight children whose fathers and mothers were dead. Of these, only two paid me for their board. My house was a kind of rendezvous for cattle men and travelers."

"During the night of the storm that destroyed Indianola (16 September 1875), I thought my house would surely be blown away, and we went to a pile of hay and sat there all night in the cold wind and rain up to our armpits in water, but the house did not go. The waters of the Colorado (River) and the Trespalacios ran together, flooding the country. We had a fearful time during the storm. I hired a Mexican and a Negro as farm hands, but they could not agree and fought, so that I could not get them to work my crop. The only way that I could make them earn their salt and wages was to work with them. In hoeing corn, I would work the middle row, making the Mexican take the row on my right and the Negro on my left. In this way I got my crop worked. I have done every kind of work on the farm except plowing."

—Letter courtesy Marian K. Taylor

"From this place we moved to the Colorado, where we bought one-fourth of the Cox league. Here we had to live in a log cabin until we could get our house moved from Trespalacios. This was in 1887. Here we ran both a farm and a ranch, extending my field of labor. I had to do the work of both man and woman. Wiley was in Kansas

> Little Compton Nov 5th 1899.
> Dear sister Susan
> It has become my painful duty to convey the sad tidings of our brother Horatio's death to you. He died yesterday morning about 9-30 Oclock. He was a very great sufferer and death must have been a relief to his poor body but it was dreadful hard to have him go; and it was hard to see him so distressed for breath. He died of paralasys and dropsy. We did all we could to save him but nothing could keep him. I cannot write more now. Yours in love
> Miranda

in charge of a large herd of cattle. It was on this farm where my Negro and Mexican help gave me so much trouble to keep them from wasting so much time fighting. I made a good corn crop, and in gathering it I drove the wagon and made my Negro and Mexican pull the corn and load and unload the wagon."

"I have often hoed corn in the hot sun with my baby strapped on my back. When he would go to sleep, I would lay him on a pallet at the end of the row, and his little brother would stay there and watch and take care of him. I have run the hay mower, hay rake, and pitched hay all day, besides cooking breakfast, dinner and supper for the hands and the boarders, and washing the dishes after these meals had been dispatched. While the

Wylie Kuykendall, ca 1900

Susan Kuykendall, ca 1900

hands were resting I was at work. One year I made beds for my potato crop with my hoe and worked them myself. I made over 400 bushels. I had a fine horse that got his leg broken, and there being no one on the place to attend to him, I went to work and set and splintered the broken limb. He had cost us $1,200. My surgery practice on this horse was successful and he afterward proved to be a valuable animal to us. I have also set the broken limbs of cows."

"After moving to the Colorado (River) and going into the cattle raising industry, I used to go out on the prairie and help make the roundups in the marketing and branding seasons. On my cow pony, I could head a cow or tail a beef as good as a cowboy. When the time for selling came the cattle were driven into the 'call pen' and I was always there and kept the tally. I knew the mark and brand of every animal of the cow species that passed through the chute into the pen where the cattle that were being sold were kept. As soon as one bunch of cattle was worked over they were turned loose, and the hands would go for a fresh bunch. While they were gone, I would cook and have dinner ready when the hands would return with a fresh herd."

Exhibiting a photograph, Mrs. Kuykendall said: "I am the woman you see sitting under those shade trees keeping the books. I planted those trees with my own hands."

"In the marketing, branding and selling season, I used to get up at 3 o'clock in the morning, and at 4 o'clock I would have breakfast ready. We would eat it and while the men were saddling the ponies I would wash the dishes. We would then go in alone to

The Pierce family in Little Compton, Rhode Island.

Pierce homestead, Little Compton, Rhode Island.

Cox League Map, Matagorda County, Texas

the prairies, and when the sunrise came, we would have a herd rounded up and on the way to the pen. Working the range in those days meant hard work and plenty of it."

"In the winter time I used to get up, cook breakfast, eat it and have the dishes washed by daylight. I would then hitch my old horse, Whiskey Pete, to my little wagon and make a round in the pasture carrying cotton seed and hay to the cows that were down, or needing feed to carry them through the winter. I have made these rounds in sunshine, rain, sleet and snow. I would pick up the little calves and take them home and raise them. The year of the big snow, which I think was in February, 1894, I picked up and raised forty-four motherless calves, besides saving many cows that were on the lift and skinning others that I found dead."

"Sometimes the cold would be fierce while I was making these rounds. On a cold, rainy day, Wiley and I were raising an(d) old Brama cow that was on the lift, and as soon as we got her on her feet, she hooked and threw me on my back in the mud. Well, I rose to my feet and while I may not have used any ugly words, I could not but help thinking 'damn it.'"

"Often I have worked until 12 o'Clock at night running the treadle of the sewing machine with one foot and the cradle with the other."

"During these years of strenuous toil and privations, I often went to camp meetings and dances. I could not enjoy the camp meetings much because I had to work too hard cooking and feeding others and washing dishes. I saw but little pleasure in the dances, I being a Pierce left that enjoyment to others. I could take an old cow's tail across my shoulder and raise her from the life with greater ease and grace than I could trip the light fantastic."

"In 1902, Wiley's health gave way and we sold out on the Colorado, ranch, cattle, sheep, and horses, and moved to Hays County, where we bought a farm of _____ acres.

Wiley Kuykendall on horse, Susan and Laura in the buggy, Buckeye Ranch, Matagorda County, Texas, ca 1900.

This place was magnificently improved, and on which was a fine residence with twenty-two rooms. This was too much room just for holding myself, my husband and little granddaughter, so we sold it and came to Beeville, where we boarded eight months. We then went back to Hays County, buying a home in San Marcos. We still have this house, but on account of Wiley's ill health and he not being able to hear good, we board in Victoria during the fall, winter and spring months and travel north in the summer. Next summer we may go to the mountains of Colorado in our car, which I am learning to run myself so that I will not be dependent upon chauffeurs."

"We raised three children of our own, but only one of whom is now living. We have also raised thirteen orphans, Winnie Arnett, our little granddaughter, being the last. She is now 13 years old and we have her in school in Victoria."

"In our younger days we worked hard, economized and laid up enough to support us in our old age. Now we have retired from our business, and we are taking life by sections."

"I have sheared as many as forty sheep a day. One year I had Horace Yeamans shearing for me. I did the cooking, and sheared sheep for sheep with him. He said I liked to made him work himself to death trying to keep up with me."

"I want it distinctly understood," said Mrs. Kuykendall, "that we made everything that we own by our own hard labor, and without any assistance from anyone, and it is nobody's business how we use, enjoy, and dispose of it."[26]

Isaac G., Wiley's son was sent to Indian Territory with a bunch of cattle in the summer of 1896. He contracted pneumonia and died there. His last letter read:

> Tulsa I. T.
> Oct. 14, 1896.
> Dear Mother,
> I got your letter last night. about those pants I guess you had better send them as it will be very cold this winter an send them by express with the rest to Tulsa I. T. in cair of Jay Foresythe Jay Foresythe.
> I think that cattle will be

worth more next year I don't know what they are worth now. we have bin branding cattle that Foresythe bout they was natives of this country. I don't know what he gave for them. I guess that I will get this letter off this week. I will close with love to all

Ike

Ike died the first week of December 1896.

Wiley and Susan ranched the "Buckeye Ranch" on the Colorado River near Blessing and Ashby, Texas. They sold their property in Matagorda County in 1901-02, and moved to Hays County. Their son, Gill (Robert G.), and his wife Maggie also sold their property, and the whole family moved at the same time, Wiley buying on the Blanco River and Gill buying on Onion Creek.[27]

Wiley was in Cuero, Texas, trying to buy some cattle on 25 January 1920 when he

Wiley Kuykendall, ca 1900

contracted pneumonia. He died there in the Muti-Hotel six days later on 31 January. Dr. S. P. Boothe of Cuero was the doctor in attendance. After his death, he was taken by train to Blessing, Texas, and buried in the Kuykendall plot in the famous old Hawley cemetery (originally Deming's Bridge) next to his children and under the shadow of the great statue of his brother-in-law Shanghai Pierce.

Susan Elizabeth Pierce Kuykendall died the following September 26th in Blessing, Texas, and was laid to rest next to her husband.[28]

THE MUTI HOTEL
ZINGELMANN & SEEKAMP, PROPS.
AMERICAN PLAN

CUERO, TEXAS   Sept. 30th 192(0)

Dear Laura,

I am glad to hear from you & Laura we all will miss mother terribly. You see Winnie & I were in Chicago & they sent for us and when we arrived mother was terribly ill & all the Dr. we called could not do any good. When Mother died to tell the truth I was so broken up I couldn't think & as mother was unconscious most of the time she might not have known you—

Well we are broken up now—no mother, no home & not much of anything but we'll try to help you some no matter how little we may have so you must write to me often enough so I can keep run of you (etc)

    Sincerely,
    (signed)   Ella K. Dunn
    Cuero, Texas
    c/o Muti Hotel[29]

Obituary, *Matagorda County Tribune*, February 6, 1920:

"Wylie Kuykendall died Cuero, Texas yesterday. Buried at Hawley Cemetery Blessing, Tex."

Letter written by Ella Kuykendall

Susan P. Kuykendall with Ella and little Laura, ca 1900

Obituary, *The Victoria Advocate*, February 3, 1920:

The funeral of William Kuykendall aged 80 years, whose death occurred Saturday afternoon in Cuero was held Sunday afternoon at the old family home in Blessing. The funeral was largely attended as Mr. Kuykendall was a well known settler of the coast country.

Deceased was a widely known cattleman of South Texas and a brother in law of the late Shanghai Pierce, land owner and railroad builder, whose lands formed the sites for many of the towns along the Southern Pacific Railway. Mrs. Kuykendall survives her husband.

Wiley M. and Susan P. Kuykendall had the following children:

Robert Gill, b. 15 May 1870, Matagorda County, Texas—d. 19 December 1905, Hays County, Texas.

Isaac Bradford, b. 15 October 1871, Matagorda County, Texas—d. 23 June 1875, same.

Isaac Green, b. 13 June 1876, Matagorda County, Texas—d. 1 December 1896, Indian Territory.

Eugeone Burchell, b. 13 September 1878, Matagorda County, Texas—d. 23 June 1879, same.

Electra Miranda, b. 15 April 1883, Matagorda County, Texas—d. 26 January 1965, Bexar County

TEXAS STATE BOARD OF HEALTH
BUREAU OF VITAL STATISTICS
STANDARD CERTIFICATE OF DEATH

Reg. Dis. No. 333
Registered No.
29946

1 PLACE OF DEATH
County: Matagorda
City: Blessing

2 FULL NAME: Mrs. Susan E. Kingdom(?)

PERSONAL AND STATISTICAL PARTICULARS

3 SEX: Female
4 COLOR OR RACE: White
5 SINGLE, MARRIED, WIDOWED OR DIVORCED: Widowed
6 DATE OF BIRTH: Nov. 20, 1840
7 AGE: 79 yrs. 10 mos. 6 ds.
8 OCCUPATION: housewife
9 BIRTHPLACE: Rhode Island
10 NAME OF FATHER: J. E. Pierce
11 BIRTHPLACE OF FATHER: Rhode Island
12 MAIDEN NAME OF MOTHER: Hannah A. Head
13 BIRTHPLACE OF MOTHER: Rhode Island
14 THE ABOVE IS TRUE (Informant): Mrs. Dunn

Filed 10/13 1920

MEDICAL PARTICULARS

16 DATE OF DEATH: Sept. 26, 1920

17 I HEREBY CERTIFY, That I attended deceased from Sept. 13th 1920, to Sept. 25th 1920, that I last saw her alive on Sept. 25th 1920, and that death occurred, on the date stated above, at 8 A.m.

The CAUSE OF DEATH was as follows:
Empyema of Gall Bladder
(duration) yrs. mos. 14 ds.

Contributory (Secondary):

Did an operation precede death? no
Was there an autopsy? no
What test confirmed diagnosis? no

(Signed) A. B. Morton, M.D.
Sept. 30, 1920 (Address) Bay City, Tex.

19 PLACE OF BURIAL: Hawley Cemetery
DATE OF BURIAL: Sept. 27, 1920
20 UNDERTAKER: J. B. Taylor
ADDRESS: Bay City, Tex.

STATE OF TEXAS
COUNTY OF TRAVIS

I HEREBY CERTIFY THAT THE ABOVE IS AN EXACT PHOTOGRAPHIC COPY OF THE ORIGINAL CERTIFICATE FILED IN THE BUREAU OF VITAL STATISTICS, TEXAS DEPARTMENT OF HEALTH, AUSTIN, TEXAS.

ISSUED MAY 3 1965

STATE REGISTRAR

Wiley Kuykendall, ca 1920

Wiley Kuykendall's grave stone, Hawley Cemetery, Matagorda County, Texas

Robert Gill Kuykendall

Chapter Nine

Robert Gill Kuykendall
1870-1905

Robert Gill Kuykendall was born in Matagorda County, Texas, on 15 May 1870, to Wiley Martin Kuykendall and Susan E. Pierce. There is some confusion as to his real middle name. It is shown by McCrosky as Gill. One letter states that it is Gilbert, and his wife, Maggie, told Alice Kuykendall that it was Gilden. Alice, therefore, named her first born son, Robert Gilden K., after his grandfather. Gill is correct, shortened from Gilleland. Wiley's grandmother was Sarah A. Gilleland and she called her first son by that nickname of Gill.[1]

Gill, as he was called, married Margaret Martha "Maggie" Moore in Matagorda County on 21 August 1890. Maggie was the daughter of William Eurastus "Will" Moore and Mary C. Swift. Will Moore was from an old family of the area that had settled in Indianola in 1845. Will's father, Robert Baxter Moore, was killed in the great hurricane of 16 September 1875, at

Maggie Moore Kuykendall

MARRIAGE LICENSE ROBERT GILL KUYKENDALL TO MAGGIE M. MOORE 21st AUGUST, 1890, MARRIAGE RECORDS, VOLUMNE B, PAGE 79, MATAGORDO COUNTY, BAY CITY, TEXAS; PAGE 19

Indianola. He had lived there for many years and had built many buildings in the town. The Moores are a well-known pioneer family of Matagorda County, Texas.

Mary Swift was the daughter of Arthur Swift and Martha Baker. Both of the Swifts owned much property in Seguin, Texas, and Arthur was one of the original signers of the town charter of Seguin. He had moved there in the late 1830s, probably from Tennessee, along with Ben and Henry McCulloch. (The Swifts were English and had settled in Virginia via Burmuda prior to the Revolutionary War.) There must be some connec-

Grandmother Swift

James McCulloch Baker

Nazareth Convent,
Victoria Texas,
Jan 16th 1888

My Dear Aunt Dora,

Your welcome and appreciated letter was received yesterday evening. It is so cold this morning that I can hardly leave the fire long enough to write. did you ever see such cold weather, I don't think I ever did. it has been snowing real hard all the morning. I guess these last spells will be bad on the cattle have we lost many yet.

Oh! I'm very well I haven't

Letter from Maggie Moore to Aunt Dora, 16 January 1888 (page one) missed a day from school since I've been here. I am real fleshy expect I would weigh about one hundred and twenty five lbs.

~~Aunt Dora I wish you would~~ tell me something nice to make for the folks. I've been thinking of making a cape for Ice and Inez. it would not cost more than $2. to make one for each of them and they would be real pretty. I want to make something for aunt Kate. I wish you would tell me what you think would be nice. I want you to tell me what you ~~think about it when next you write~~

Tell Uncle Ed that I have will write to him as soon as the weather gets a little warmer. I have the letter composed, but it is too cold to write it.
Write soon to
    Your loving niece
      Maggie Moore

Letter from Maggie Moore to Aunt Dora, 16 January 1888 (page two)

Victoria,

HOS Ranch Jan. 11th
1890
Miss Maggie
Dear little sweet
heart I am very sorry
that I can not come after
you tomorrow. ~~Father~~
Father wants me to go
to Mattagorda sunday
for him. I did not
want to go a bit but
of course I hafter
please him once and
a while. I would

have come down to see
you tonight but
cow ~~drove~~ all day and
I rode all my horses
down so I could not
come hope you will
not be mad be cause
I did not let you
know before. but I did
not have a chance my Dear
I will come from Matagorda
to see you tomorrow
night if I get back in
time. I am a going to
ride dirty and I
will only hit the ground
in hy places.
you must look for me

I hope you'd had
a nice time while
you was gone.
it seames like it
has been a month
since I saw you.
you bet I had a lonsom
old time after you left
us ~~at town~~ last sunday
well I must stop for
it is bed time
I hope this letter
will find you well
and happy
good night Sweeting
I ~~remaine~~ remain your
loving G.

I got my Trevor brother
to bring this letter
to you because I
knew you would wait
for me

I suppose
You got your
son horse yet that
is victoria did it
you

Letter from Gill Kuykendall to Maggie Moore

tion with that family since Martha's father's middle name was McCulloch. Both died of the fever before the Civil War and Martha's father, Judge James McCulloch Baker, of De Witt County raised the four daughters of Arthur and Martha.

It is interesting to note that Arthur died "intestate" and owned much property. When all the estate was settled and sold off, nothing remained. The lawyers must have gotten everything or it was sold off at 10 cents on the dollar to other leading citizens. Whoever buried Arthur and Martha conveniently failed to put up any kind of marker. They must have figured it was going to dip into the profits they were making off the estate. To this day no grave marker has ever been found for these two leading citizens of Seguin, Texas.

Zack Miller of the famous "101 Ranch" in Oklahoma came to Gill and Maggie's wedding and gave them the "101 cattle brand" as a wedding present for them to use in Texas. The brand is still used today by the Kuykendall family. Wiley had pastured cattle on the 101 Ranch in Oklahoma for many years and he and Zack Miller were old friends from the trail driving days after the Civil War. (Ranch photos of the period show the 101 brand on the Kuykendall horses.)

Both Gill and his father moved to Hays County in 1901 and purchased two ranches, Wiley the HO on the Blanco River, which contained 3,700 acres, and Gill the Hutchison Ranch on Onion Creek, which contained 11,000 acres.

R. G. Kuykendall home, Matagorda County, Texas, ca 1900. Note the 101 brand on Gill's horse. Dorothy is on the ground, Marion is on the second horse, Wiley W. (Bill) is on the second floor of house.

Gathering cattle for the move from Matagorda County to Hays County. Gill Kuykendall is third from the right.

May 1, 1902.

11,500 acres in Hays County.

The above ranch is located above the center of Hays County and contains about 11,500 acres of deeded land with perfect title. It is divided into eight pastures with five wire fence and cedar posts, everlasting water in each, taking in 5 miles of Onion Creek, four wells and wind mills and pump jacks, three large lakes with lasting water and a number of tanks, making it one of the best watered ranches in Texas. The land is about half prairie and half timber, is all covered with fine mesquite grass. The ranch house is a good rock building of five rooms and a hall, and three out buildings. The foreman's house near by is a frame building of three rooms. There is a large barn with a number of stalls and a storage capacity for 150 tons of hay, corn, cotton seed and etc.. Five good stock pens with chutes and three large corrals that will hold 1000 cattle each. There are five farms on the property with house and barn on each. The International & Great Northern Railroad is only six miles away. It is 12 miles to San Marcos, county seat of Hays county, and 18 or 20 miles to Austin, the state Capitol.

This is a splendid proposition for maturing steers or for a fine stock farm, or both. While all the land is good for grazing purposes, there is an abundance of rich agricultural land for all purposes.

Price $4.50 per acre. If desired, reasonable terms will be given. This is a large list of other improved ranches and stock farms for sale by,   Geo., B. Loving Company, Ft Worth, Texas.

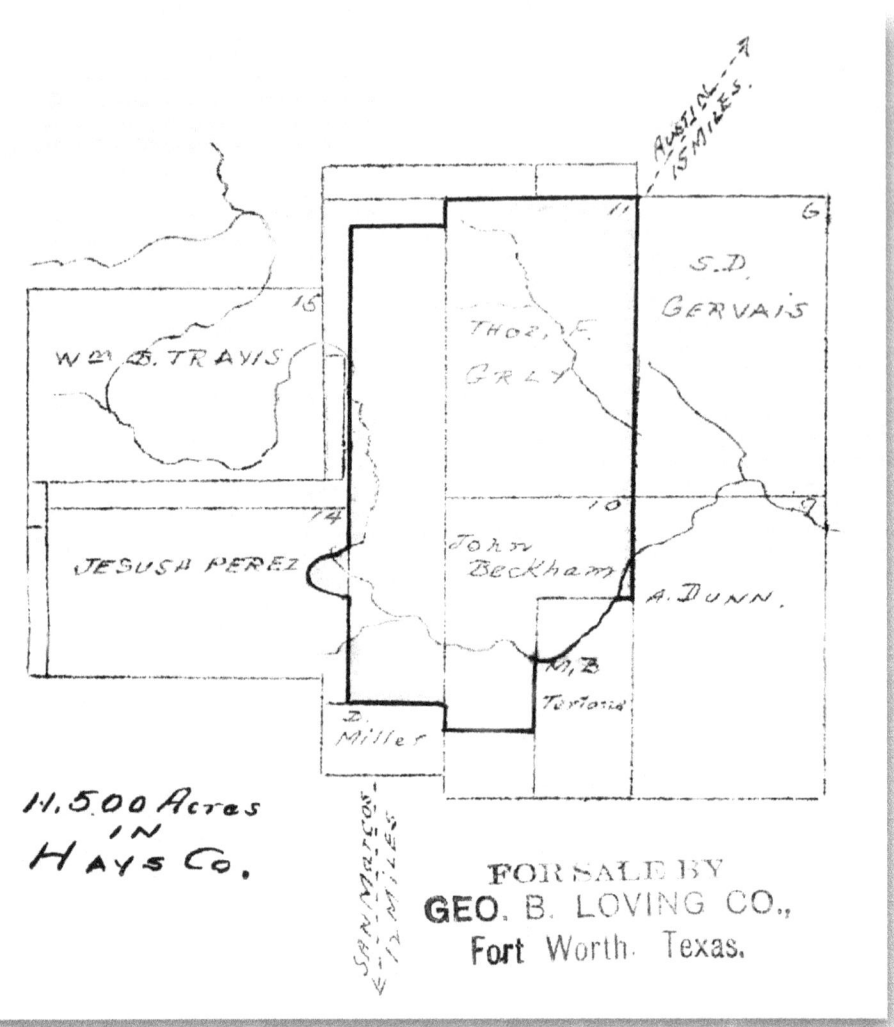

Geo. B. Loving Company
LAND, CATTLE AND RANCHES
Ft. Worth, Texas
May 1, 1902

Mr. R. G. Kuykendall
Ashby, Texas
Dear Sir:—

  Replying to yours of the 28th enclosed we hand you (a) sketch of 11,500 acres in Hays County, considering location improvements and etc. this is certainly a very desirable property at the price named in the description, $4.50 per acre. If this property interests you we will be glad to put you in direct communication with the owner who lives in Austin, and will be glad to show it to you at any time it may suit you to look at it.

Yours truly,
signed   Geo. B. Loving Co.[2]

D. G. JONES,

DEALER IN
GROCERIES, HARDWARE, GENTS FURNISHING GOODS, AND UNDERTAKING SUPPLIES

Dripping Springs, Texas, Mar. 29th, 1904.

This instrument witnesseth that an agreement has this day been entered into between R. E. Spaw of Dripping Springs and R. G. Kuykendall of Kyle, whereby said R. E. Spaw agrees to deliver to said R. G. Kuykendall at Driftwood, one hundred (100) good, average cows of this section, from three to eight years old, both inclusive, on or before the 29th of April, 1904, for the sum of eleven dollars per head, and the said R. G. Kuykendall on his part pays to said R. E. Spaw, two hundred dollars ($200) receipt of which is hereby acknowledged, as a payment on said cows, balance to be paid on delivery of said cows.

R. E. Spaw
R. G. Kuykendall

Gill obviously was quite a rounder and perhaps a heavy drinker. It has been noted that he killed a man in a drunken brawl in Matagorda County over a fence dispute in October 1900 before they left there. That might have been one reason the family left Matagorda County.

Eudora I. Moore, Maggie's aunt, is the real source of all the sad details that are known of Gill's life at that point because she lived at the ranch at Buda and kept a daily diary. Eudora, or Aunt Dotty, as she was known, was an old maid, virgin school teacher whose motto surely was, "Lips that touch wine will never touch mine." She was constantly commenting that little Miss So and So had to get with THAT MAN and go through that terrible ordeal (of marriage). Eudora managed to leave out the ordeal!

Gill must have tried poor Eudora's soul. In the fall of 1905, while on a return trip from Kyle, Hays County, Texas, Gill fell from his horse into Onion Creek in the dead of winter and developed pneumonia. He took to his bed in October of that year and as his condition worsened, he drank more and more and would not eat, and finally died on December 19 at the Kuykendall Ranch at Buda. Eudora dutifully noted in her diary, "Thank God, Gill was finally gone and maybe Maggie would now have some peace!"

His body was taken by train to Blessing, Matagorda County, Texas, and he was buried in the Kuykendall plot in the Hawley Cemetery next to his brother Ike, who died in 1895. Gill was 35 when he died and Ike was 20. Both died of pneumonia in the prime of their lives. Wylie and Susan never were able to talk about either of them for the rest of their lives.

Gill was a big man, well over six feet. Shanghai Pierce, his uncle, was 6 foot 5. The pictures of Gill show him as a very well dressed man riding fine looking horses, all bearing the 101 brand. Gill's sense of humor was obvious, one of the early pictures shows all the cowhands around a pen full of cattle on the coastal plains of Texas and in the picture Gill is standing on his head *with his ten gallon Stetson hat on*. With Gill's death, the ranching helm of the family was lost and his widow, Maggie, now had the responsibility of running the ranch.

Gill and Maggie had the following children:

Ishmal, b. 25 May 1891, Matagorda County, Texas—d. same day, buried unknown.

Cornelia, b. 14 August 1892, Matagorda County, Texas—d. same day, buried unknown.

Marion (Taylor), b. 4 August 1893, Matagorda County, Texas—d. 31 August 1973, Hays County, Texas, buried on the 101 Ranch, Hays County, Texas. No issue.

Dorothy (Hoskins), b. 7 September 1895, Matagorda County, Texas—d. 7 May 1986, Burnet County, Texas, buried on the 101 Ranch, Hays County, Texas. Two children.

Ester, b. 12 October 1896, Matagorda County, Texas—d. same day, buried unknown.

Wylie Moore, b. 3 March 1899, Ashby, Matagorda County, Texas—d. 11 October 1976, buried Kyle Cemetery, Kyle, Hays County, Texas. Three children.

William Isaac, b. 14 August 1904, 101 Ranch, Hays County, Texas—d. 12 September 1980, buried in the Phillips Cemetery, Dripping Springs, Hays County, Texas. No issue.

Eudora Inez Moore, ca 1870

Gill, Maggie, Wylie in her arms, Dorothy and Marion on the ground. Matagorda County ca 1900.

New York Life Insurance Company.

346 & 348 BROADWAY, NEW YORK.

John A. McCall, President.

THE GREAT INTERNATIONAL LIFE INSURANCE COMPANY.

AUSTIN BRANCH OFFICE.

CHAS. R. STARLY
E. G. BEWLEY, Agency Director.
JNO. O. HEATH, Cashier.

AUSTIN, TEX., 12/28/05.

Mrs. R.G. Kuykendall,
   R.F.D. #2, Buda, Texas.

Dear Madam:-   RE POLICY NO. 976439 - R.G. Kuykendall -deceased.

    I am in receipt of your favor of the 25th advising us of the death of your husband, and I have furnished our agent, Mr. J.N. Houston, with proper blanks for making proofs of death, and he will call on you in a very short while.

    In signing your name to any of the papers be sure it is signed Maggie and not Mrs. R.G. Kuykendall.

                                       Yours truly,

                                         Jno O Heath
                                            Cashier.

PRESSLER & ROBINSON,
SUCCESSORS TO
(HERMAN PRESSLER & CO.)
REAL ESTATE,
Rental, Fire Insurance and Loan Agents.
FARMS AND TEXAS LANDS.
819 CONGRESS AVE.

HERMAN PRESSLER
EUGENE B. ROBINSON

AUSTIN, TEXAS, 12/22nd 1905

Mrs. W. L. Kuykendall
Buda Texas —

Dear Mrs. Kuykendall,—

When my eyes fell upon the cruel page announcing the sad intelligence of the death of your husband, I was grieved and shocked beyond expression. My relations with him had always been so pleasant — He was always so cheerful strong and full of life, that it is hard realize he is gone —

In this hour of darkest grief and sorrow, may a kind Providence bless you and yours — He only can bring comfort and sooth the pain of grief like yours —

In deepest sympathy, I am earnestly,
Your Friend
E. B. Robinson —

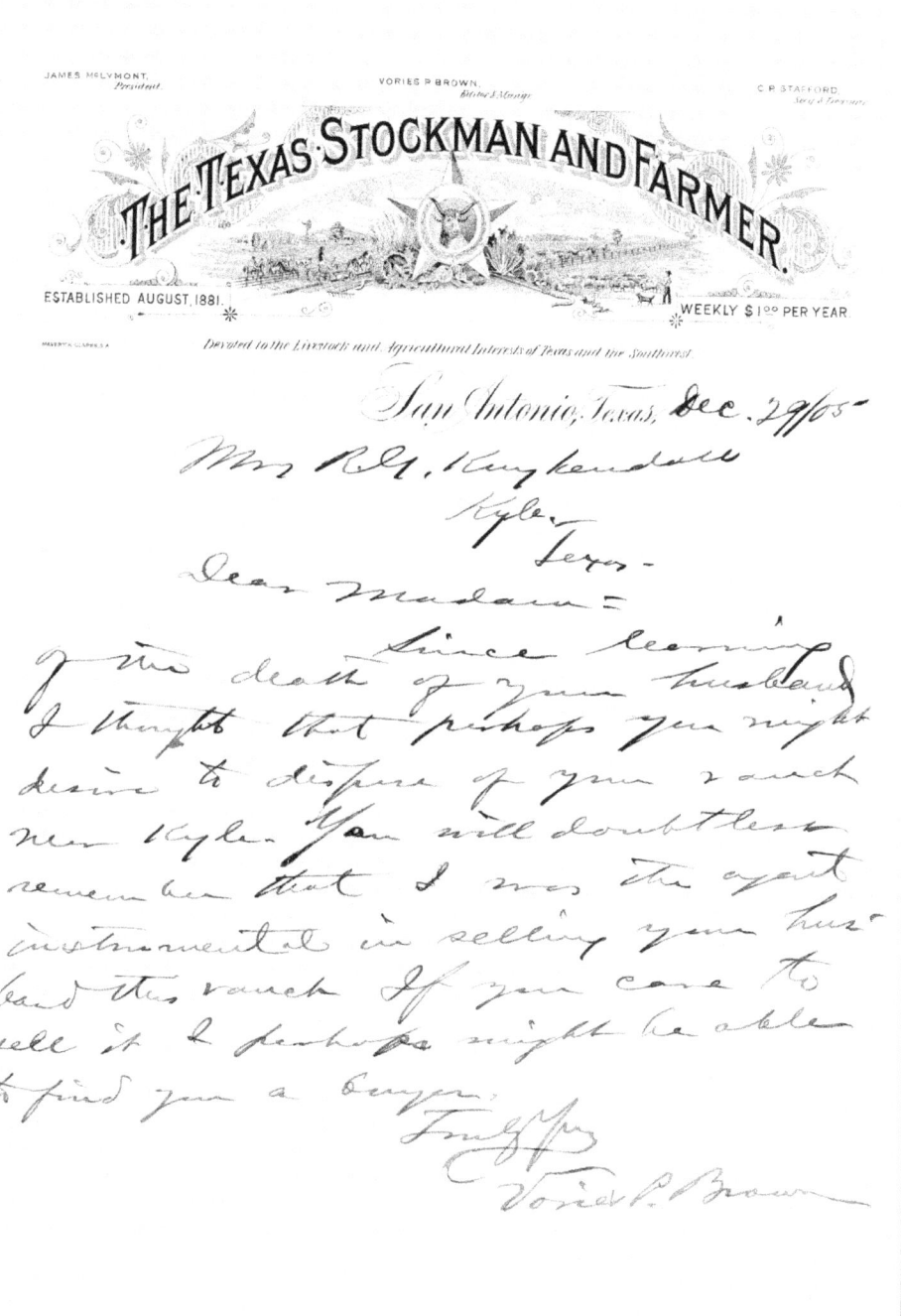

San Antonio, Texas, Dec. 29/05

Mrs R.G. Kuykendall
Kyle,
Texas -

Dear Madam =
    Since learning of the death of your husband I thought that perhaps you might desire to dispose of your ranch near Kyle. You will doubtless remember that I was the agent instrumental in selling your husband this ranch. If you care to sell it I perhaps might be able to find you a buyer.

Truly yrs
Vories P. Brown

T. B. DUNN
ATTORNEY
AT LAW......

HOUSTON, TEXAS, Dec. 26, 1905.

Dear Tom,

    Your letter of yesturday received today, and in answer to same, will say, that if Mr. Gill died without leaving a will, then under the law his wife will have to qualify as administratrix of the estate, as well as guardian of the person and estate of the children.

    Article 1689 Sayles Statutes, provides for the above, also provides, that where deceased left no will, then the surviving spouse shall have one third of the personal estate and the balance shall go to the children, the surviving spouse shall also have a life interest in one third of the land, after having a homestead set aside to her.

    Unless these probate proceedings are had, she can not sell any of the land, cattle, or anything belonging to the estate, until the children arrive at the age of twenty one years. Hence probate proceedings are necessary, as you can perceive.

    In the probate proceedings however, Mrs. Kuykendall need not appear in Court but once, and then only for a few moments.

    You will observe that I am presuming that Mr. Gill died intestate, (that is without a will). Of course if he left a will it will have to be probated, but I would have to see the will before I could intelligently advise.

    All are quite well, but miss you and Ella very much.

                Affectionately yours,

                    T. B. Dunn

T. B. DUNN
ATTORNEY
AT LAW

HOUSTON, TEXAS. December 27, 1905.

Dear Tom,

In writing to you yesterday in reference to the estate of Mr Gill Kuykendall, I was interrupted by a client before I had concluded same, hence hastily closed.

What I want to say, in addition to what I advised in that letter is; that Mrs Kuykendall is entitled under the law to half of the community estate and the children are entitled to the other half. The division as mentioned in yesterdays letter applies to his separate estate.

It will be necessary for the estate to be administered upon, for the purpose of apportioning the estate between the heirs, i. e. between Mrs. Kuykendall (as surviving wife) and the children; to have the home-stead set aside, to them, and separated from the balance of the estate, to have allowances made to the wife, aslo for the support and education of the children, for the purpose of collecting any money which may be due the estate, either cash in bank or due from individuals, to pay any claims, pending against the estate, to loan money, or sell anything which may belong to the estate.

Should Mrs Kuykendall fail to qualify as guardian of the children, and as administratrix of the estate, then any creditor of the estate, or other person interested, could do so, to the exclusion of her.

I am still going on the hypothisis that there was no will, as you mentioned none in your letter.

There are a number of things in connection with estates of decedents guardian-ships etc., which it is almost impossible to set out and discuss in detail, by letter. However I have given you the main principles and reasons, which for the present, are sufficient for a clear understanding of what is necessary in the premises.

I trust that this, in connection with my letter of yesterday, will be sufficient, and give both you and Mrs Kuykendall full information.

Affectionately yours,

To
Mr. Thos. B. Dunn, Jr.
Kyle, Texas.

Bill Kuykendall on "Smooth Sailing," 101 Ranch, Buda, Texas, ca 1942.

Chapter Ten

Wylie Moore Kuykendall

Wylie Moore Kuykendall (1899-1976) was always known as Bill in his adult life. He was called Wylie in his early years but when his polo playing days emerged in the 1930s someone incorrectly thought his initials W.M. meant William, and called him Bill and the name stuck for the rest of his life. He was the son of R.G. and Maggie Moore Kuykendall and was born on their ranch near Ashby, Matagorda County, Texas, on 3 March 1899. Ashby no longer exists but the cemetery there is just south of present day Blessing, Texas. The Kuykendall ranch was called the Buckeye Ranch at the time.

When Bill was two years old, the family sold out in Matagorda County and moved to Hays County on a ranch on Onion Creek just west of present day Buda and Kyle, Texas. The 11,000-plus acre ranch was the largest ranch in Hays County until its breakup at the end of the twentieth century.

Not many details are known of his early childhood other than glimpses and short sketches. His father, Gill Kuykendall, died when he was six years old and Joe Cruze of Wimberley, Texas, was the foreman at the time. I remember him telling me that he had only one memory of his father, where he was horseback with him over west of the homeplace and it started getting dark and the wolves in the area began to howl and he became fearful and his father told him everything would be all right.

The other short stories were of him learning to ride with Joe Cruze and the trouble he got into when they jumped an old wormy cow down near the Hays City corner of the ranch. Joe tried to rope the old cow and missed and Dad, who was riding a little Shetland pony, didn't, and all hell broke loose when the old rangey cow hit the end of Dad's little cotton rope which was tied fast and tight to his saddle horn. The old cow could, of course, outrun the little Shetland pony. Dad said they were only hitting the ground about every 75 yards and the big cedar break was looming when Joe finally got his second loop going and was able to rope the cow and save a double disaster.

Aunt Dora Inez Moore, Maggie's aunt, lived at the Kuykendall ranch during all of these years and taught the children at home to some extent. The diary by Aunt Dora notes that Wylie stayed in different homes in Kyle from time to time after 1909. His first seems to have been with a Mrs. Hall in September 1909. She noted his teacher was Miss Maggie Gross. His education was very limited at best and always scattered. An example was a note in the diary dated 17 March 1910, "M. (Maggie) brought Wiley home to stay—suppose I will teach him." Whereas his brother Ike went to Texas A&M in the 1920s, Dad's education was never that formal. I do not know if he graduated from any high-school. I do know he attended SMA (Staunton Military Academy) before WWI but how he got there and for how long, was never told to me. He also attended SWT (Southwest Texas) in San Marcos in 1926 for one semester after he and Alice were married because he wanted to play football. He was 27 years old at the time. I know that he tried to join the army during WWI but caught the flu during the great epidemic of 1918, and did not have to serve. Dad was able to make his way through life by his wits and his good looks, but he was nearly illiterate.

The diary in 1908 notes that Laura (Kuykendall), the Negro daughter of Ike Kuykendall, Wylie's uncle, was staying at the ranch where she was brought there on several occasions by the older Kuykendalls (Wiley and Susan). One of the comments by Aunt Dora on 12 August 1909 was, "Wylie and Laura got into a row and it came near to being a general fuss as I didn't like to see him whipped by a Negro, bad as he is."

Maggie Kuykendall, Wylie's mother, was having a very hard time trying to manage and run the 11,000 acres. She was being ably helped by Joe and Will Cruze ever since the death of her husband, Gill, in 1905. The diary states on many occasions, however, that Joe Cruze was very enamored with Maggie and seemed to be in different stages of trying to court her over many years. All during this time they were all trying to keep the ranch going, but finally on 9 April 1910, Maggie informed all that she had sold all her cattle and had leased the 11,000 acres to a Mr. Blocker for three years. (Possibly Joe Blocker?) There was also a Mr. Nolan and a Mr. Searight of Austin involved in the lease. Will Cruze went to work for Mr. Blocker during this period.

In September 1910, Wylie was boarded in Kyle with Mrs. Cleveland. However, in October, it states that he boarded in a new place and then went to stay with Mrs. Will Gross. "January 15, 1911: M. & J. went to town with Wylie. I think Mrs. Gross is getting tired of him. He certainly can be aggravating at times and yet I feel sorry for the poor kid, having to stay away from home with most anybody who will keep him."

All of 1912 and half of 1913 are missing from the diary.

"March 3rd, 1914. This is Wylie's birthday, fifteen years old. It rained some today. The eve a norther blew up. It is right cold already. They finished the yard fence today—all but hanging the gate on the front."

The diary also notes the Laura Elisabeth Kuykendall (1895-1981), the Negro daughter of Ike Kuykendall, deceased, came and stayed from time to time at the 101 Ranch from 1909 through about the middle of July 1914, when she moved with her grandparents, Wiley and Susan Kuykendall, to Beeville, Texas. They had cared for and

Wylie and Dorothy, ca 1915

educated her since birth and she constantly traveled with the older folks or stayed with her Aunt Ella Kuykendall Dunn, the daughter of Wiley and Susan. As she got older, it became must more difficult for the elderly grandparents to care for a Negro child as they traveled about the country. An excerpt from a letter from her daughter states: "The grandparents began having trouble with my mom (getting) into hotels. The owners wanted her to go out back with the help. The old people refused. They would sit up all night in the train stations so that they could keep her with them."

However, on July 11th, there is an interesting entry: "Laura's baby has been sick since Tuesday, gave it some castor oil this afternoon." I did not know Laura was married, or even pregnant. She would have been 19 at the time. However, a letter from Laura Veasey Williams states Laura's baby was born in January 1914. There is no mention of it in the diary.

"July 25th, 1914. Laura wanted D. (Dorothy K.) to take her to Kyle as she could do nothing here, could not carry her baby? or wait on her. So they got off this morn. L. (Laura) will go to San Marcos and stay until her foot gets well. I doubt if she comes back at all."

"January 3rd, 1915. Kyle. We moved here yesterday, Wylie, Ike and I. The boys came on the wagon and I came in the buggie with Maggie. There were four wagons besides what we brought in the buggie. We got things pretty well fixed up yesterday eve and I cooked breakfast on the new stove. The boys went to the moving picture show last night and to church and Sunday school this morning. Miss Cornelia Wallace asked us over to dinner so I didn't have to cook any. Hope the boys do well at school."

"January 5. The boys began school yesterday. Ike came home feeling bad and did not go back in the afternoon. Stuck a pen knife in his knee last night but is not very lame today."

"January 16. I am all alone in the little house. Ike went home with his mother yesterday and tonight Wylie is at a moving picture show with his girl."

"January 26. No one here today. Had the mischief with Wylie tonight about going down-town—a girl wanted him to go with her. He didn't go, but gave me some pretty rough talk."

*Ike Kuykendall
101 Ranch House, ca 1918*

Maggie, Ike, and Aunt Dora
101 Ranch, Buda, Texas, ca 1918

Left to right: H. C. Storey of Cotulla, Texas, Jack Storey, Dorothy Kuykendall, Julia Storey, Grace Nance, Nell Storey, ca 1915.

Wylie was at the age when girls suddenly appeared in his life and the diary records his many outings. He moved back to the ranch after school was out the middle of May.

It is interesting to note that the family at this period did all their schooling, shopping, and traveling into Kyle. If they went to Austin or San Marcos, it was always by train. In fact, all of their travel for years and years was always by train. The diary states over and over the difficulty in crossing Onion Creek. They were constantly having to wait on the creek to go down, were stuck in it, or had to wade across, either to walk home or be picked up by family members.

"May 30. Sunday. Wylie went to Kyle to take the train to San Marcos."

"June 7. Ella Jordan and her son, Ben and granddaughter Gladys came in their car. Dorothy and Wylie met them at the creek."

In the middle of June 1915, Wylie makes his first trip to Kansas City with cattle from the ranch belonging to Mr. Toalson and Mr. Nolen. Also, Mr. Blocker must still be pasturing cattle on the ranch with Nolen, because he is still showing up from week to week, eating meals at the Kuykendall house.

One thing of interest was for some reason or another, the Kuykendall house had been a zoo of guests for years and it was to continue as long as Aunt Dora kept her diary. All the women (Maggie and Dora) did was cook and clean house for a zillion people who seemed to descend on the good graces of Maggie Kuykendall. Dora constantly complains about her long hours over the stove or having to clean house after fourteen people who showed up at 6 P.M. for supper and to spend the night. It got even worse after the siblings started being old enough to have all of their friends show up. The ranch seemed to be the most popular place in central Texas for a whole bunch of people a whole lot of the time.

Years 1915 and 1916 seem to be big ones of transition for Wylie. He bought a bunch of steers in Fort Worth on his way home from Kansas City. Had them delivered to Kyle by train. Found out about girls. Ranch caught on fire. Horse ran away with Winnie. All the ranchmen and steer buyers in the country descend on the 101 ranch. All of the friends of Marion, Dorothy, Wylie, and Ike are constantly either at the ranch or trying to get to Kyle so they can get on the train to go somewhere to a party or a dance. Life picked up for a sixteen year old. It was not to change one iota for the next ten years. Wylie got bigger, the travel got further and the girls got hotter. The depot in Kyle burned down. And the car had four flats on every trip. Life can be hell when one operates in the fast lane.

Schooling got more scattered and Wylie started staying out later and longer. And the girls' names began to change, one after another. The diary stated that electric lights were put in the 101 ranchhouse in 1916 and every person's name ever recorded in Kyle or Buda will be stopping by the ranch for a visit and a meal. Maggie bought a new car, and of course, Wylie went to San Marcos, or Seguin, or Austin. Martha? got her finger bitten by a rattlesnake and Maggie wrapped in up in a kerosene rag.

In July 1916, the family decides to all travel to Colorado. Mr. Joe Blocker dies just after the family leaves. I assume he is the Blocker who has part of the ranch leased. They stay there until the fall.

Aunt Dora moved back to Kyle in September and on September 21st stated: "The soldiers, 15,000 of them came through town (Kyle) today. Infantry, Cavalry, and artillery. Wagons, trucks, etc. I have not seen so many troops since the Civil War."

Is is sad that the diary is missing most of the pages for 1917 and half of 1918. These were critical years for Wylie and the family. Wylie supposedly joined the army in San Antonio in 1918 but was sent home after contracting the flu in the great epidemic of that year. I do know for a fact that Wylie went to SMA (Staunton Military Academy) at Staunton, Virginia, for a year or maybe two semesters. There are many pictures of him there as shown in an old album that we gave to the Austin History Center in Austin, Texas. I remember him telling me he had gone. Since the pages of the diary that we have do not mention this, one would assume he was there in the fall of 1917 and possibly the spring of 1918 because he is back home to get bitten by the cat in the next paragraph. I also think he played football while in Virginia.

On 12 October 1918, Maggie got badly bitten by a rabid cat and Wylie was bitten trying to get the cat off his mother. Both had to go through Pasteur Institute in Austin for treatments.

In December (1918) Wylie goes with the Kyle football team to play with them against Lockhart. They won the game. The diary never mentioned he ever practiced. I think he simply wanted to play and went with them. He is also 19 years old. "Kinda" old for a poor little high-school boy. Any sort of help, however, is always appreciated. Ike was on the same team so I guess it was just brotherly love. Aunt Dora says Wylie got pretty "banged up."

It is probably important to state that in this point of Wylie's life he had reached physical maturity. He was nearly six feet tall and quite a good looking young man. He started having many girlfriends, mostly from the San Marcos and Lockhart area.

Wylie obviously now has his own car, because the diary states that on 2 April 1919, he was in San Marcos in "his car" and could not get home because Onion Creek was on a snort. Also, in this same month, there is talk about building Wylie his own home. Why he needs one is not stated. The ranch was not to be divided between the four siblings until 1933, yet here is Wylie getting a new home built for him. The diary states:

"April 26, 1919. The folks were down during the week (to Kyle where Dora was temporarily living) to meet a carpenter from Austin and to talk to Mr. Charlie Wallace (of Kyle) about lumber and plans for the house they are to build for Wylie."

The girls' names begin to change at a faster rate. Thelma, Mary, Helena, etc. However, on June 11, Wylie buys a little roadster. Aunt Dora

Wylie's house

call it a "Flivver." She is contantly stating that Wylie goes here and Wylie goes there in "his Flivver." Wylie's house must be finished by August, because guests are now beginning to stay there also. Interestingly, this was no simple cottage. It was a large two story four bedroom ranch house without verandas. (I should know because I was raised in that house.) Quite a spread for a 20-year-old.

Having not traveled far enough, Maggie and the family decided to make a run to California by car in August 1919. Wylie is left temporarily at his home. The family goes through Hillsboro, Henrietta, Estelline, Texico, Willard, Quenado, New Mexico, St. John's, Arizona, Canyon City, Kingman, Needles, and then into Los Angeles. Making the trip in the summer is unheard of for the time period. Interestingly, the road in Arizona was made of wood—because of the sand. It seems that Maggie, Marion, Dorothy, and Aunt Dora all traveled in the same car. There must have been a man somewhere but the diary only mentions a "Jack" somebody. (Maybe Jack Sledge of Kyle.) However, it was Dorothy's car that they drove in. Those making the trip seem to be Maggie Kuykendall and three of the siblings, Marion, the oldest (1893), Dorothy (1895), Ike (1905), Aunt Dora, and Jack. It is my recollection that Maggie leased the big house and that part of the ranch for two years, hence the reason for the trip to California.

The diary makes scant mention of Lester during these years. That is Lester Taylor. I do not remember how he shows up in the equation, but I think he was in the army during WWI and was stationed at Fort Sam Houston in San Antonio. He was from Cleveland, Ohio. He would have known the family then. I think Marion went to school for a time in San Antonio and since she was a very attractive heiress to one of the largest ranches in central Texas, I'm sure the handsome army officers would have known all the young things at the main schools there.

The family gets letters from home stating Wylie is at his new house and Marion gets a letter from Lester. The letter states he is back in the U.S. He has probably been in Europe with the army. He is back in Cleveland, Ohio. Dora says she doesn't know whether he is coming for Marion or whether Marion is going to him (2 September 1919).

"September 30th. Marion left for Philadelphia today at 8:50. I wonder what the outcome of her trip will be?" They get a wire from Marion on October 18 that states she thinks she will stay there. (?) A letter from Wylie suggests he wants to lease his ranch (?) also. Maggie decides to go home for a month to check on him.

"November 4th. Maggie leaves for Texas for a month."

"February 2, 1920. A telegram came for Dorothy from her mother at Blessing (Texas) that Mr. Kuykendall (Wiley M.) died Saturday and was buried yesterday."

"February 20. A letter from Maggie states they will leave home a week from Monday 23, to come out here. Mr. Kuykendall willed each of Gill's children $5,000, $20,000 in all.

"March 2. Maggie wrote that if nothing happened to prevent they would start Sat. the 28th."

"March 10. (1920) Maggie, Nora (Cope), and Wylie got in this morning about 8:30—traveled all night.

"March 14. Sunday. Had a letter from Marion yesterday, she is counting on Ike and myself being with her next year. I never dreamed of ever living with Marion—but feel sure will get along nicely together." Obviously, Marion and now Dr. Lester Taylor have gotten married. However, typical of Aunt Dora, many important details (like marriage) are always left unstated.

In March 1920, Aunt Dora makes several interesting entries in her diary stating that Wylie is out and about (in California) with his friend Jimmy Mac. attempting to take his place selling bread. She says J. is probably going back to Texas on about the 1st of April and that Wylie will take his place selling bread. What bread? Why is the part owner of 11,000 acres in central Texas doing out in California selling bread for a living? Well, later the diary states Jimmy has decided not to go to Texas after all, so poor Wylie has lost his opportunity for a new job.

However, not having a job has not kept Wylie from getting a new girlfriend. "March 28. Sunday. Wylie took a new girl Marge Honey in his "flivver.""

Dad told me that he drove to California in an open racing type car and that he had tied a large set of cow horns to the radiator for effect. I cannot imagine that he drove all the way across the desert with his mother in an open racing car. The record does not mention anything one way or another.

"April 9th. (1920) Wylie and Margery Honey here a little while yesterday, also Sammy Wilson. W. got his "flivver" smashed up last night. He came home sometime in the night—slept till nearly noon, then went off—we don't see much of him. The folks are talking of going home on the 5th or 6th of May and leaving Ike and me here until school is out. Wylie will stay here too."

"April 14. Wylie brought company here yesterday afternoon—Margery Honey and Sammy Wilson. They spent the night here and are still here at this writing. Ike went to bed like a sensible boy. I do hope he will not fritter his life away on things that count so little in life. The folks expect to leave here on the 5th of May, that is, Maggie, Dorothy, and Nora. I don't know what Wylie will do."

"April 17. Wylie brought his girl, Marjory Honey, here yesterday eve—she took supper and stayed all night. Seems to be a very nice girl and much in love—she and Wylie are on the eve of matrimony it seems."

"April 19. Wylie brought company home with him last night and they are still in bed while the women of the family have done nearly a half a day's work."

"April 24. Wylie and the two girls have gone to a party tonight given by Mr. and Mrs. Honey. The car is in the shop so they hired one—the car and chauffer costing ten dollars. Wylie and Marjory are to be married quite soon. Think it will be announced tonight."

"April 25. Wylie did not come home last night, but stopped this morning to change clothes. Mr. Honey was taking him to the Country Club to play golf."

"April 27. Mrs. Honey here today, came to talk matters over regarding her daughter and Maggie's son. The wedding is not to be as soon as first contemplated. W. is to go home and fix a place for the "bird.""

"May 4. Mrs. Heep and Herman came yesterday—stayed all night and are here for lunch. Dorothy sold the Buick this morning."

"May 11. Left Los Angeles this morn. We went through Riverside today. Are spending the night in the desert between Mecca and Light."

"May 16. Sunday. Got to El Paso last night—stopped at the St. Regus Hotel."

"May 17. Traveled all night Sunday and got to Ozona late this afternoon. Got supper in Ozona and went out to Glady's."

"May 18. Stayed with the Pierces until nearly sunset then started on our way. Got about 27 miles on our journey and found so much mud had to turn back—lost our way but a man directed us and we went back to Ozona. Traveled all night."

"May 19. Traveled all day yesterday over the worst roads possible—crossed rivers in over 20 places. Some men help us up a high hill where high water had left some debis. Got to San Marco about 2 A.M. All the Cope family came to welcome us home."

"May 21. The boys (Wylie and Ike) got home Tues. morning."

From the time Wylie got home from California until the middle of August, the diary is full of his comings and going, from this party to that one, staying out several nights a week, working cattle in the day time, partying at night. This in the middle of August there is this entry:

"August 15. Sunday. A gloomy day. Only Marjorie and the family here. We like Marjorie very much. She seems to be a sweet child and is bright intellectually. All the family are in love with her, don't really know how it is with Wylie, who really is the central figure in the matter."

On 19 August 1920, Aunt Dora and Ike left on their expected trip to Cleveland to stay with Marion. It is obvious that she has married Dr. Lester Taylor by now, but of course, Dora never mentions it. She's not real hot on women getting married and having to do unnatural things with men, so she seldom talks about folks getting married. When she does, she talks about the miseries they are about to face. However she does mention that Dorothy and Marjorie accompanied her into Austin. Wylie and Herman Heep were already in town and met Dora there. Wylie had been partying with Herman in Austin a lot in the past month so figure he was helping others with their religion while Marjorie, who had come all the way from California to see and probably marry Wylie, cooled her heels.

It is here that I need to insert a story that Alice (my mother) told me. It seems that while Dad (Wylie) was in California in 1920, he fell in love with a soon-to-be silent movie actress, who followed him home to the 101 ranch at Buda. In the course of her being there, Wylie gave her "the family diamond" which she, of course, had on her finger. One day while they were all working cattle out in the big pens at the ranch, Marjorie, who had been sitting up high on one of the rails watching all the hoopla and fiddling with her new big diamond, just happened to fiddle it off of her finger by accident and it fell into the pen full of rustling cattle.

Several days went by, I'm told, and with her constantly covering up her left hand so no confession would be necessary. When finally Wylie noticed it missing, he, of course, demanded to know "where in the hell it was," and in a fit of squalling she confessed her mortal sin. Wylie in the true spirit of a forgiving lover and husband-to-be, threw all her belonging into her trunk, hauled her into Buda, pitched her on the first train going west and sent her back to California for her sins. He then rushed back out to the ranch, jerked the screen door off of the main house, got out the wheelbarrow and shovel, went out to the pens, shoveled up every scrap of dirt out of about 4 acres upon the screen and after sifting for about one whole day, found the diamond ring. "Those dadgum uppity California women. One has to 'learn-um' a thing or two." His honor restored, Wylie cleaned up, changed clothes, cranked up his "flivver, and went into Austin with Herman Heep to spend the night with their new girlfriends. Life however rough, must go on. (This happened between the 20th and the 25th of October 1920)

"September 23. A telegram from Maggie last night stating that she and Dottie were on the way to Blessing and advising Marion to go down. Think she is going."

"September 25. Marion left last night for Texas."

"September 28. Lester got a telegram from Marion today. Mrs. Kuykendall is dead and the funeral was to be today. (the 27th)"

Susan Pierce Kuykendall, the wife of Wiley M. Kuykendall, died in September of 1920. Old Wiley died earlier that same year. The diary is filled with information about both of them and there seemed to always be some friction between the older group and Maggie and her children, which seemed to come from Ella Kuykendall Dunn, the only surviving child of the older folks. My father, Wylie, never liked her until the day she died. We were never able to find out the cause of this animosity. It kept us from being able to know Aunt Ella better. She died in the early 1950s.

"March 1, 1921. (Cleveland) Had a letter from Maggie yesterday, from what I hear, Dottie and a young widower, Lawrence Hoskins, are getting pretty thick."

"March 13. Sunday. We had letters from home yesterday. Dottie is going to marry Lawrence Hoskins in the fall if nothing happens(?). She will have three stepchildren, little girls."

"April 3. A letter from Dottie informs us she will be married in June as soon as Ike and I return; and *Wylie* also expects to marry in June"???

Wylie has obviously been practicing some religious activities unknown to Aunt Dora and her diary, because on April 22, she received a telegram from Dottie that Wylie had married Mildred Williams of Lockhart on Sunday, April 17, 1921.

Dora and Ike start for home on June 15, 1921.

"June 20, 1921. Got to Austin at 8 P.M. Friday eve. Maggie, Wylie and Mildred were there to receive us."

"June 26. Sunday. Well, old diary, lots of things have happened the past week. Dottie was married Wednesday at 1:30 P.M." (June 22, 1921) She and Lawrence are off to Colorado on their honeymoon.

Even though Wylie has his own home and is now married, it seems that everyone always takes most of their meals down at the main house where his mother lives. They will also spend the night there and breakfast the following morning. This practice goes on for as long as Wylie and Mildred are married even when they have as many as four servants working for them. They then bring their servants with them and they ALL eat down there.

At this period the family has bought back all the cattle from the different folks who have the ranch leased just in time to enter the tick eradication period in the state of Texas. I remember Dad stating that they had just bought the cattle back at a fairly high price when the cattle market and the price of grown cattle fell from near $100 to $14. Whether the price broke because of market or the tick fever eradication program is unknown. I do know, however, that all the ranchers had to dip their cattle in an arsenic dip solution every two weeks for a year or more. One can imagine the stress it placed on the livestock, the horses and the help during that period. Being the largest outfit in the county, the family was obviously quite overburdened during this time period. One of Dora's entrys states: July 1921. "They collected cattle yesterday and dipped a bunch of steers which they shipped this morning. (three carloads) Have been collecting and dipping all day. We had eleven men to dinner and nearly as many for supper yesterday. Had two inspectors, a Mr. Waller and Hestor. The men worked til night, dipping cattle and horses—dipped in all over 900 head of cattle—nearly a thousand with the steers they shipped." Dora followed up with this statement: "Mildred (Wylie's wife) has taken dinner here every day and is doing some sewing. She is beginning to look "quite" important."

Then later in July, she states that Maggie and Ike doctored wormy cattle nearly all day while Wylie and Mildred went to Lockhart in Wylie's new car, an Essex. She felt provoked that Wylie would go off and let his mother do all the cow work. Such is life when you have a new wife who looks important and a new Essex all at the same time.

Throughout all of August 1921, the men had to constantly dip the cattle, and as many as twenty odd folks would dine at the main house each day. Herman Heep came by to eat and Dora thought he was a fine looking young man. Winnie and her beau were to come, but she had to tend to her mother, Ella Kuykendall Dunn. Dora says, "one thing for sure, no one was longing for her. We had all we could do without them." Still that animosity between the two families. Later Dora states: "It is dreadfully hot today. A Negro and a Mexican drove up to get wood a while ago—wanted a drink. I handed the Negro a gallon bucket and the devil drank first though the Mexican was nearly white." Dora comes from a different time.

The balance of the summer continued very hot and dry and Wylie added to the equation by buying a bunch of high priced Brahman cattle that were to be delivered on September 3. Then on September 9, a storm hit and it rained for days, nearly washing out the bridge over Onion Creek at Buda. Wylie and Mildred continued their trips thither and yon and continue to eat and lodge at the main house instead of their own home. They always brought their help with them.

October brings much more of the same. Dora states that Mr. Blocker was by and he was looking very bad. Then on October 26, she states that he died. This is William B. (Bill) Blocker. (1850-1921) *The Hand Book of Texas*, Vol. 1, page 596, states: "that he ran cattle near Kyle, Hays County."

Mildred, who is pregnant, delivers her baby girl at 9:15 on Armistice Day (November 11, 1921) and she is named Lamond.

What is interesting about this period in the diary is the entry of dozens of well known families from Kyle and Buda who either worked at the ranch this summer helping with the dipping or just coming by to dine and spend the night. Maggie and Dora were at it 24 hours a day.

The year ends the same way it started and 1922 is no different. The family is constantly having to dip the cattle and Wylie and Mildred are still traveling about. Folks are still pouring into the ranch as if it is the Hilton of Hays County.

During May 1922, Ike, who had gone back to Texas A&M, contracted the mumps. I only bring this up because Ike never had any children and one time *"a hundred years later,"* while hunting on the Rawls ranch in the Big Bend, I asked Uncle Ike why. His comment was classic. *"I had the mumps when I was a young man and they went down on me. Now, I have one nut about the size of an English pea and the other is just a little bitty son of a bitch."* History at its best.

Later in the late summer, Wylie dabbled in some oil wells in Luling. I'm sure this has to do with Herman Heep because Herman made his first big money in the Luling oil field and he and Dad were big friends. Also, there seems to be a strain between Wylie, Mildred, and the Hoskins—Wylie's sister Dorothy and Lawrence Hoskins. *There also seems to be a growing strain between Wylie and Mildred.* Later, that fall, for reasons unknown, Maggie decides to buy the meat market in Buda. Working 28 hours a day at the ranch was not enough. The balance of 1922 is filled with killing cattle and hauling them into the market at Buda. Everyone is involved. One thing I never understood, even though Dorothy and Lawrence live in Gonzales, they are always at the ranch working there. Now both are working at the market too. In October, Dora states that Wylie and Mildred are now taking most of their meals at the main house. I assume they have abandoned the use of their own home.

In the meantime, Dorothy rushed home to Gonzales to give birth to Lawrence Worth Hoskins on November 1922—her first child. Lawrence is spending most of his time at the market in Buda and Dorothy joins him before the year is out. 1922 ends in a cloud of dust of constant cattle work and cooking and cleaning.

In January, Wylie fractures his skull by running into something at his house. Dora gets her copy of the January 1922 *Confederate Veteran* magazine which has published her article "Reminisces of Indianola."

February brings a big snow to the 101 and all the pipes froze solid. The balance of the late winter and spring passes with the normal frenzy of activity and travel. Mildred is spending more and more time at her folk's home in Lockhart.

"June 15. Next week will be cattle dipping and after that company—guess the house will be full all summer."

"July 6. Wylie stopped here this morning on his way to Buda. He wants to work in the market. I certainly wish he was dependable."

Lem Scarbrough of Austin and Nelson Puett of Fentress were at the ranch for a short while. Now the ranch visitors are coming from other towns and villages.

Wylie and Mildred have left little Lamond at the main house while they are off partying. Wylie turns his hound dogs loose? President Harding died. Wylie decided to sell his Luling oil interests. No need to make any long term investments. Ike quits A&M to work at the ranch since there is no one there to to do the work that is needed. Maggie stays in Buda with Mrs. Heep all the time. The Mexicans are there shearing a thousand head for Mr. Toalson (sheep and goats). Wylie and Mildred have gone to the fair in Austin. Wylie and Ike went hunting. A wolf got into the turkeys and killed a pile of them. Mr. Williams, Mildred's father, is showing up more often? Cattle prices are at an all time low. Roy Stubbs of Johnson City comes by to sell Wylie some horses. Herman Schlemmer of Kyle spends Christmas day at the ranch. And the turbulent year ended in another cloud of dipping cattle and a cold norther. So much for 1922.

January 1923 passed with Aunt Dora staying in Kyle. She writes on Tuesday, January 9 that Wylie hurt his head some time ago and had it X-rayed and found out it was fractured. January 12. Wylie is doing better. January 18. Dottie states she now has two copies of the *Confederate* magazine with her contribution about "Reminisces of Indianola."

Later that month, Wylie and Mildred take little Lamond to Lockhart with 105 fever. It soon went down and she got better. Much travel for all the family back and forth from the ranch to Lockhart during this period.

February 4, Sunday. "The earth is white with snow this morning. Ike went to Lockhart (in Wylie's car) to bring Mildred and the baby here. She waited late so Beatrice Williams could come, it rained all day and the ground was slippery, just out of Luling the car slipped and turned over. They had to break out the windows in the car to get out. Some Negros righted the car for them and aside from the broken door it was not injured to any extent. It was almost a miracle that no one was injured."

"February 23. A gloomy day, foggy and raw. Frances Puett here to supper last night, Nelson came later"

"February 27. Tues. No rain today but it has turned cooler. A letter from Dolph tells of the death of Mrs. Dr. Rugeley. She will be sadly missed in Bay City. One more old southern woman has gone to join the throng on the other side."

"April 19. Do not feel well today. Went to town to see Mrs. Jones in the afternoon. She is a dear old lady, a typical woman of the Old South. She had three brothers in Terry's Texas Rangers, one was killed at Bolling Green, Kentucky." More tales of the Civi War, which is always on Dora's mind.

Aunt Dora goes to Bay City for a visit and mentions her brothers, Ed and Dolph Moore, the Partains, Mrs. Law, Mrs. Traylor, Mrs. Rachael Clement, and many of the old timers of the area. She got home by train on the May 27. Wylie picked her up and took her to the ranch.

"June 3, continued, Joe Cruze was here yesterday, told me about his father's last days and his burial by the old Confederate Veterans."

"June 13. Wylie's horse got away with the saddle on and when they finally caught him, W. mounted him and spurred and jerked him unmercifully, no wonder the poor thing is afraid to be caught."

"June 15. Friday. Next week will be cattle dipping and after that company—guess the house will be full all summer."

"June 19. I am thankful to say that the dipping is over for this time. We have had a crowd, sixteen, to feed yesterday and more today.

"June 20. Queen Elizabeth Nance and Herbert Whisnant here this afternoon."

It seems the family had opened a meat market in Buda during this year and the family had been very busy killing beeves at the ranch and hauling them into the market. On July 6, Dora makes an entry in her diary that Dorothy, Wylie's sister, has told him that he is no longer employed at the market. The following day she enters: "Wylie stopped by here this morning on his way to Buda. I certainly wish he was dependable."

"July 9. Wylie and Mildred went to Austin, left Lamond here. They were to be back early and was 2 A.M. when they arrived and I had not slept a wink."

During this whole summer, little Lamond has been quite ill, having bouts of high fever every few days. "August 19, 1923, 101 Ranch, Hays County, Texas. Lamond is better than she was far from a healthy baby. I fear for her future health if she lives over this period. Her liver is not normal and I know not what other derangements she may have. She needs a regular, quiet life and she has not had it and I fear she never will."

"August 24, Friday Night. We have no rain yet, things are literally drying up, cattle are suffering and they fear the cattle will have to be shipped."

"August 26, Sunday night. A fine rain began falling this afternoon and is still raining at 10 P.M."

"September 14, Friday, Morn. A great disappointment has come to me. I fear that

Ike's school days are over. (at Texas A&M) There is no one to take care of the ranch unless he stays to do it. There is no money to do anything with unless it is borrowed. He says his expenses at A&M will be greater this year than ever before as he is now an officer and will have to dress better."

"September 27, Thursday. The Mexicans came Tues. eve with their shearing outfit—worked all day yesterday and today. They sheared over a thousand head for Mr. Toalson and worked on Mr. Foster's and Maggie's today."

"October 2, Tuesday night. Wylie and Mildred went to the fair in Austin this afternoon. Wylie killed a calf last night. He and Mildred took supper here."

"October 6, Saturday Night 10 oclock. M&W did not get home till dark tonight. Wylie promised Ike his car to have tonight and was to come home and do the chores for him. W&M stayed the night."

"October 17. Mildred spent the day here and she and Wylie spent the night. A wolf got after the Turkeys this morning. Ike shot at it several times but it got away."

The year 1923 ended with a steady flow of people at the ranch who had to be fed. Cattle were being dipped on a weekly basis so they could be shipped. The cars were constantly being stuck or flooded in Onion Creek. Every soul who ever lived in the towns around the ranch were either on the ranch shipping cattle, dipping cattle, shearing goats, hunting, fishing, or having a gay time while Dora cooked and washed dishes. At the same time Wylie and Mildred kept up their party pace.

January 1924 was ushered in with a blast of freezing weather that froze all the pipes at the ranch and most of the pipes burst. The month passed as did the previous one with folks coming and going as usual.

"February 21. Yesterday was a cold, cloudless day and today is colder. Wylie's Brahma Bull "Red Wasp" died and was dragged off yesterday. This is the second fine bull he has lost and several Brama cows and others are about to die. It is hard on the boy for he paid a big price for them and thought they would do wonders. Hard times are sure striking this family. Never were in such a plight before."

"March 16, Sunday noon. I went to sleep last night thinking about where my burial place is to be. I always used to think that I would rest at Ashby between Mother and brother Will. In fact he suggested that space be left between the two graves for me. Sister Mary, Little Ella and baby Winnie are buried there. Father, Spencer and dear brother Baxter are buried at Indianola and brother Joe at Alexandria, Louisiana, where he fills a soldier's grave. Will's first wife, Gussie Butterfield, rests near Elliott's Ferry on the Colorado, so our dead are widely scattered. I think perhaps it would be just as well for me to be buried here near the house. It would save trouble, time and expense, though, if I happened to be in Matagorda County, Ashby would be my choice. That is a lovely spot where Wilson's Creek flows into the broad Trespalacios and where large liveoaks with their Spanish moss forever stand sentinel."

The balance of March saw Wylie going into Austin to try and convince Govenor Pat Neff to open some sort of game reserve on the 101 Ranch. Obviously, Wylie was unsuccessful.

During the next month or so, Wylie and Mildred began to have different schedules on whom and when would be at the ranch. Wylie spent several nights there when he was keeping little Lamond himself.

"June 8. Sunday afternoon. Mrs. Williams and Mildred were here Friday night. They talked of family problems."

"June 10, Tuesday night. Wylie and Mildred went to Austin yesterday, did not get home until after midnight. This A.M. Mildred came and said W. was sick or something was the matter. Maggie and Ike went up there and found him up. Mildred said she was going home. (Lockhart) M. helped Mildred get ready. Washed dishes etc.??? They came here to dinner and left soon after. I hated to see little Lamond leave, she is such a sweet child. It is a bad business, I'm afraid."

July saw Wylie and Herman Heep staying in Austin quite a bit, going to parties and such.

"July 13, Sunday. Wylie and Herman did not appear this morning. Mrs. Williams has been up (at Wylie's place) getting Mildred's things in order. Lawrence (Dottie's husband) will go to Gonzales this eve and will take Mrs. W. and Lamond home. (Lockhart)"

"July 15, Tues. P.M. Wylie and Herman got back from Waco Mon. Morn just as we were rising, went to bed and slept awhile."

Wylie's sister, Dorothy, moves into his home. On August 5, Wylie and Aunt Dora go to Corpus and then to Kingsville. Wylie is trying to get a job there working for one of the ranches. That is when he ordered the pistol holster and rig that I now have. Dad told me that he had it made at the King Ranch store either in 1924 or 1925. This shows the exact date.

The following is so typical of Dora's writing: "August 12. Mildred and Lamond came home with Dottie. Spent the night up there. Mildred had a spell of cholera morbus. About 9 A.M. Wylie drove up with his new outfit of cowboy furnishings, stayed till about four oclock, Mildred went away with him. W. went to the Reunion at Camp Ben McCulloch. Lamond is with us. Tommy (the deer) frightened by dogs ran into fence and broke his neck."

"August 23 (1924) Dottie went to Mrs. Williams and talked to Mildred. She had left the house clean and did not want Mildred to bring a party up there (to the ranch) as she had planned to do. A lot was said on both sides and Mildred came up to talk to Maggie about it. She was very indignant and said a lot of things here. I did not know she hated Ike as she does. Think she hates the whole family."

"August 29. Friday. Mildred has written to both Maggie and Dorthy, very scathing letters as well as untrue. Have not heard from Wylie in some days—think he will be wise to stay away awhile if he doesn't want to get into trouble."

"Sept. 7. Sunday. Wylie came about sunset yesterday. He left his wagon of goods here until he returns Tues. or Wed.—is going to Kingsville."

In October, Wylie went out west to Mountain Home and the Junction area to work for several cow outfits. Their names are not available. This was the result of his going back and forth to Kingsville to try and get some work. Again, the question is asked, if the K's had been ranching their own ranch, why would Wylie be off looking for ranch work elsewhere? Whatever he was doing out there did not keep him there long as he was home off and on several times before the end of the year.

"November 17. Monday. My birthday, 77 years old . Wylie has two men here tonight, guess he thought we did not have enough to do, etc." Whatever Wylie was doing in Kerr County did not need his constant attention, because he was home most of December 1925. In one of her comments Dora says Wylie has some new venture in mind.

The year of 1924 ends with Wylie going to as many parties, fairs, and rodeos as he can. Tons of folks are still passing through the Kuykendall homestead as if it were still the Grand Hilton of Central Texas. Every known family name from Kyle, Buda, and Austin are mentioned. And Dora at 77 years of age is still doing most of the cooking and cleaning. What's also interesting is the fact that Wylie is still squiring Mildred around to some of the parties.

Now we enter the phase where there is no diary in which to refer. The years 1925 through 1928 are missing. The next books found are 1929, 1930, and 1932. Dear old Aunt Dora Inez Moore went to her great reward in the sky in 1933. She got her last wish and was buried between her mother and brother in the old Ashby Cemetery on Trepalacios Creek in Matagorda County, Texas.

The loss of these years is very disappointing because these were critical years for Wylie. He would finally divorce Mildred or she probably dumped him in 1925. I'm sure her string just ran out trying to put up with him. Also, Wylie went to Mexico for several months during 1925 to work for the same cow outfit he had contracted with out in Kerr County in 1924. His job was to gather wild cattle off a ranch those folks had down there. The ranch in Mexico was located somewhere up the San Rodrigo River which is just upstream from Eagle Pass and Piedra Negras. When he bought the ranch in Mexico in 1956, he would always tell everyone he had ranched there before. He was referring to the 1925 time. The story he told was that he had been down there for a year but knowing Wylie, he probably only lasted a few months.

The reason that is mentioned is because he remarried in July 1926. Alice Hamlett was down in Seguin visting friends when she met this dashing 26-year-old cowboy named Wylie Kuykendall. He was down there at the time attending the same parties. Wylie always mentioned that there were more good looking young girls in and around Seguin and Lockhart than the rest of Texas and he wanted to be sure they received the right kind of religious upbringing that he could give them.

> "At Christmas (1925) time I wrote Cousin Patty in Seguin and asked to come for a visit. Cousin Patty was Patty Cassidy from Waco. Her mother, Aunt Corrine, was my father's aunt. Patty was married to a Dr. Neighbors and they had a small son named Allan. I went to Seguin for the holidays. I attended several dances where I met a dashing, divorced young rancher named Bill Kuykendall. (A name he acquired later.) It was a fun week out of the Austin atmosphere I so hated. Then back to the Austin routine. One day in January 1926, Mother (Faye Early Hamlett) and I had gone shopping. I was waiting for her outside of Scarbroughs on 6th and Congress, when a car stopped and Bill got out. Bill and I dated all that spring. He was 26 years old and I was 15. He was a delight to be with, extremely handsome, not mixed up in any Austin memories and (he) lifted me out of my brooding. So, on July 16, 1926, Bill and I were married in San Marcos, Texas. The ceremony was at a minister's house and a friend of Bill's and his date were witnesses. We went to the ranch afterwards and all hell broke loose the next day."
>
> —Alice Hamlett Kuykendall, 1990.

To say all hell broke loose was an understatement of the decade. When Wylie hauled his child bride out to the ranch, all of the Kuykendall clan had an absolute fit. So much so that she was banished to the other dining room and not allowed to take meals with the family when Wylie ate at the "other house" as Grandmother Kuykendall's house was called. Mother would tell me later in life that she never got over that humiliation. When the news of Alice's secret marriage leaked out, the balance of the manure hit the fan in Austin. Faye, Alice's mother, who was called Mona, went to bed weeping and allowed as how she would just die there. Brother William was called up from Houston where he lived to help clear up the mess.

In the meantime, sister Corinne and her Army husband,

Alice at 15 and wild Bill at 27

John, had just been transferred to duty in Panama. Brother William went out to the Kuykendall ranch and told Wylie and all that Mona was gravely ill over the incident and Alice needed to go with him to get matters settled. What no one knew was William had conspired with Corinne to wisk dear underage Alice away from Wylie and get her on a train for New Orleans with the intent of putting her on the next boat for the Canal Zone. There they could hide her until the marriage could be annulled. Alice and the bunch got to New Orleans and while they are waiting for the Banana boat to hual them to Panama, a knock was heard on the hotel door—it was the New Orleans police. Turns out ole Wylie had contacted the Texas Rangers and they in turn had put the dots together and found out where Alice had been taken. The officer at the door wanted to know who had been kidnapped and Alice held up her hand and allowed as how it probably was her. With that, the policeman hauled the whole bunch, Alice, William, Corinne, and little Jack down to the station house, where Wylie was reached by phone and he agreed to drop the charges if Alice would come home. They all agreed and Wylie dropped the charges of kidnapping. As soon as they were out of the building, though, ole conniving Corinne hauled Alice down the the wharf and put her on the next boat for Panama.

Needless to say, Wylie jumped on the next train for New Orleans. He then flagged down the next boat, which interestingly turns out to be the same boat that Alice had taken the week or so before. This particular boat made a weekly banana run to the Canal Zone from New Orleans.

While in Panama, Alice was in need of a job, so she applied in town at a kindergarden school to teach piano. She boarded the army bus and while on the return trip back to the Post, she noticed a taxi following them. Turns out, Wylie had stepped off the boat just in time to see Alice get back on board the bus for the Post. So he whistled up a taxi and followed them until it stopped. What ensued was basically this. Wylie had proof that dear ole Corinne had tampered with Alice's letters and telegrams to Wylie telling him where she was and he never received any of them. That just happens to be a "federal offence." When he got through telling Corinne and Captain John what would happen to their army career if he pressed charges, John in turn, told his wife Corinne to back off and the matter was settled once and for all. With Alice in tow, Wylie boarded the same boat and took his child bride back to the 101 ranch in Buda, Texas.

What I find most intriguing about this whole episode was that Wylie had married an underage girl without her mother's permission. All of which was very much against the law, but Wylie was able to turn it all around and make the family believe they had broken the law by taking Alice away from him. Things are different when you live in the wild west.

Wylie moved back into his own home on the west side of the 101 ranch, but the date is unknown, and Dorthy moved back to the "other house" to live with her mother, Maggie. In the fall of 1927, Wylie enrolled at SW Normal in San Marcos (South West Texas) as a freshman in order to play football with Barney Knisple, an old buddy. He is shown in the school annual *The Pedigog* for that year. What a 27-year-old newly married rancher and part owner of the largest ranch in Hays County is doing going back to school to be on the football team was never explained.

Then in the late summer of 1929, Wylie hits upon the idea to have the 101 Ranch at Buda, Texas, put on the Kuykendall Rodeo. He sold advertisements to the local businesses in Buda and Austin telling everyone to attend the event of the season and the ads came out in the Austin paper on September 29, 1929. The first rodeo was held on October 5, 1929. Later that same month, the world was plunged into a world-wide depression. One thing Wylie always had was perfect timing. His motto was to wait until cattle were at some historic high and buy all you could. It seemed his business decisions over his entire life were made as if some small voice spoke to him in the middle of the night and told him to go forth. And sure enough, about every five to ten years, he would come home, make an announcement, and go forth once again. It was exciting if one could keep up, and the thing about Alice was she could keep up.

A note in Aunt Dora's diary on June, 7th, 1930 written while she was staying in Wharton: "A letter from Maggie to Dottie with circulars of the rodeo which Wylie is giving Sunday, June 15, etc."

"Sunday, June 15, 1930. Left (Wharton) this A.M. 4:30 got breakfast at Schulenberg. Reached the rodeo grounds at eleven A.M., had a good drive. Ed, Connie, George

Scenes of the rodeo at the Kuykendall 101 Ranch in Buda, Texas, with Bill Kuykendall riding pickup.

and the puppy (Tyge) constituted our crew. There were hundreds of autos already on the grounds. Saw Maggie, Ike, Worth, and little Marion. Soon after arrival, met Sherman Birdwell and another man at the gate. Told them who we were and they passed us free. Saw Alice and the baby (Gil), he is a good looking baby and very large, also saw Mrs. Hamlett (Alice's mother) and William (Alice's brother) and wife. Most everyone was strange to me."

However, I am getting ahead of myself. As nature will have it, marital bliss carries

More 101 Ranch Rodeo scenes.

its own rewards and on June 26, 1929, Alice gave birth to a bundle of joy in the form of one Robert Gilden (Gil) Kuykendall, my brother. I'm sure Wylie was off fishing on Onion Creek when this happened because events of this nature were not something he found very important.

"Monday, June 16, 1930. Rained real hard about 3:30 A.M. Leaked in the room. Maggie looks well, but I guess is pretty tired. Connie helped get dinner ready. They (Ed and Connie) left at 1:15 P.M. Wish they could have stayed longer. Got the gift Mildred sent me mother's day, some lovely handkerchiefs. A year today since I left the ranch." Aunt Dora spent the last year in Cleveland with Marion (Wylie's sister) and her husband, Dr. Lester Taylor, with a brief stay on the coast, before going back to the 101 Ranch at Buda.

Alice and Gill

Sometime in 1930, the little voice spoke to Wylie once again and he was off and running again on his new vocation, *polo*.

"Tuesday, June 17, 1930. The carpenters worked here today. Ike is going to be home for a while at least. Wylie and his man, Mr. Austin, left for Junction yesterday to play polo, took three horses."

It seems that during this period, Wylie and Alice seem to be staying down at the "other house." This must be the period that Alice talked about when the Kuykendall family took their meals in the dining room, but made her eat in the kitchen by herself or with the hired help.

"Tuesday, June 24, 1930. Wylie and Alice and little Gilden came at dinner time. A. left immediately after."

Why in the world would someone want to get into the most expensive, exclusive sport in the universe—polo—

Bill and Alice, ca 1930

at any time much less when the whole world is broke? There were food lines in every city of this country. Everyone was out of work, and the Okies were heading out to the promise land.

The Kuykendall ranch ran lots of livestock, including lots of horses, and they were short of cash like everybody else in this country. When you stop and think about it, the place to be during a worldwide depression is on a farm or on a ranch. If there is no debt, you can always raise a garden, raise chickens, eat eggs, eat beef, etc., and, if you can raise good horses you can still sell them to (1) the army (cavalry), and (2) rich folks who play polo. For once it was brilliant—or kind of brilliant. Wylie got ahold of old Roy Stubbs of Johnson City and told him to start looking for some real good ponies.

Wylie knew everyone in Austin, so he approached Niles Graham, one of the owners and partners in Enfield Realty Company, to be his sponsor. Niles and his brother, Murray, owned big homes and Niles had stables out behind his home on Niles Road where Wylie said they could keep their horses. Murrah loved the idea and together they formed the Woodlawn Polo Club and started the Westenfield Polo Field—a polo field that was in the area of MoPac in west Austin today, near the street that is named Polo. Their first polo team would include Ralph Robinson, from the Robinson Ranch on the Pedernales River, Slim Austin, one of the Crofts from Johnson City, and Bill Kuykendall of the 101 Ranch at Buda, Texas. The polo club was located on Graham's property at the end of Niles Road, west of the old Pease place.

At some point here Wylie started using the name Bill. He always hated the name Wylie and Bill sprang up by accident. His initials were WMK and folks thought the WM stood for William. He loved it, started using it for the rest of his life, signed all his legal papers that way and never used the name Wylie again.

"Saturday, June 28, 1930. A hot day, Ike went to Kyle. Bill Wylie came in the truck and brought a horse." This is the first time in Dora's writing that she mentions his name change.

Murray Graham put the word out that games were going to be played on their polo field in west Austin and teams from Georgetown, Stonewall, Dripping Springs, as well as San Antonio were formed. There was a Fleming Brother's polo team formed at Cedar Valley made up of O. D. and L. S. Fleming, J. C. Pope, and L. Hardin. While Murrah agreed to play, the breakdown went like this:

Niles Graham, team owner; officers—Niles Graham, Pres., Murrah Graham, V.P., Ralph Robinson, Sec., Sutton Croft, Asst. Sec., and Bill Kuykendall, coach and club manager.

Murrah Graham, T. C. Steiner, Dean Smith, and Bill Kuykendall started for the Austin Club. M. Cabniss served as goal keeper. Bill's embryo polo quartet would make their initial bow at the old Fleming Ranch, 6 miles west of Cedar Valley, between Dripping Springs and Austin.

Bill gathered up some 16 polo ponies purchased for the club, including some bought from the 101 ranch at Buda, Texas. Improvements were made to the already existing stables on the Graham Estate in Enfield. Veteran polo player, Sidney Donaldson of Kyle, Texas, agreed to join the team and the team started with Donaldson in the number 4 slot, Bill in number 2, Ralph Robinson in number 1, and Sutton Croft in the number 3 slot. There was also the possibility of Stonewall, Texas, stars Hilman Ellebrocte, George Dutton, and Alton Fleming coming in to join the fray.

Teams from Junction, Stonewall, Fredericksburg, and O.W. Carwell's Georgetown four were among the first to come to Austin for the games.

Some of the early membership of the Woodlawn polo club were: Murray Graham, Niles Graham, Ralph Robinson, Sutton Croft, Wallace Roberts, Bill Kuykendall, George Dutton, Alton Fleming, Charlie Cabaniss, Slim Austin, and Bill Olive.

"Sunday, August 24, 1930. Wylie and a Mr. Robinson were out this morning. Brought Pete (Bunton) and he was going to take some horses, three I think, to Austin."

"Wednesday, August 27, 1930. Alice came just after Dottie here. We had dinner and after that, Wylie came. Dottie and Worth went to Austin to see Wylie's horses. She and Alice rode (together). Later Worth showed Dottie the way to Wylie's house." Obviously, Bill and Alice had moved into their own house in Austin.

"Sunday, August 31. 1930. Bob Barton came to see Maggie about pasturing some goats. He is going to teach in the Buda school this term."

"Sunday, September 21, 1930. We were all invited to take dinner with the Hammanns in Austin today. Went to Wylie's first. He was training polo horses, hard work it seemed to me for both horse and man. Alice was making a custard pie for dinner. The baby was in his crib, we talked to the little fellow a few minutes. The Hammanns treated us royally, had a nice dinner."

"Monday, September 22, 1930. Maggie found a note from Helen Hall (later Michaelis) here last eve—she wants Maggie to keep house for her—rather late in the day to ask her, after she has got the house fixed up to stay here."

"Friday, October 10, 1930. Ike spent the night at Wylie's. Said little Gill is walking."

"Wednesday, October 22, 1930. Mr. Heimer died last night. Ike went to Joe Cruze's to inform him."

"Tuesday, November 4, 1930. The election was held in the Picture Show bldg, an old white headed man was judge, Mr. Wayland. Mrs. Staten Lindeman was assistant. I voted the straight Democratic ticket. The Governors was the one I was most interested in. We went to Clay's store (Or Clem's) Then went to Mrs. Heep's for dinner. Saw Zoe Heep and two of her children. Mr. (Roy) Stubbs came to see Maggie about some mules. Dr. Lauderdale said my face was better. He is a pleasant man."

"Wednesday, November 5, 1930. Ike looked at some plows yesterday at Buda and Kyle. We saw Mr. Schlemmer, Turner Harwell, who spoke to us and said he was going to send me the News. On the way home talked to Mr. E. Toalson, also some Mexicans. Took Hubby Heimer home to the Roger's place, etc."

"Friday, November 7, 1930. Two years ago today, my brother Dolph (Moore) passed away. I can scarcely realize it has been that long a time."

"Sunday, November 16, 1930. Went to Will G. Barber's residence according to Mildred's invitation to take a birthday dinner. We had a lovely dinner which was given for Lamond and me. Two cakes, one with 9 candles and one with 83."

"Sunday, December 7, 1930. Sun shown part of the day. We worked fast trying to get ready for the company. Mildred, Will G. (Barber) and Lamond, also Mrs. Heep came. Later Mr. and Mrs. Barton—Helen Heep, Dorothy Heep and little Jim Barton arrived." Things at the Kuykendall Ranch Hilton never changed for poor old Aunt Dora.

"Wednesday, December 10, 1930. Wylie came this afternoon and brought Mr. and Mrs. Cruseman. He is a native of Holland and speaks with a foreign accent, is a fine looking man. They all went hunting."

Aunt Dora's diary ends the year of 1930 with some addresses in the back and one is for W. M. Kuykendall, 308 West 12th St., Austin, Texas.

The year 1931 is missing from Aunt Dora's diary, but she writes one last book for 1932. January 1, 1932, opens, "This is has been a bright sunny day, cool enough to be pleasant. I have kept a diary so long that it has become a habit with me and I should feel lost without it. Wylie Bill came this A.M. to help cut up the three hogs they killed yesterday, brought Peter Bunton to assist. Ike and Georgia (Ike must have married in 1931, because Georgia was his first wife.) took the sausage meat to Buda to be ground."

One of the trophies that exists from those days states: "Elimination Houston Invitation Polo Tournament March 1931 Won By—" So, obviously Bill played polo throughout 1931 all over Texas.

Dora is invited by Dorothy (Bill's sister) to go with her to Harlingen, Texas, where Dorothy is now living. The notation is so typical of Aunt Dora. "Saturday, January 9, 1932. Getting ready to go home with Dorothy tomorrow. She is very good to want me, hate to leave the ranch for some reason, as think I can make work a little lighter for Maggie, as there are a few things I can do, such as trimming lamps, cleaning up the kitchen in the morning, seeing that the wood box is filled, etc, that will likely fall to her lot, though Georgia seems willing to help and Ike also." Bless old Dora's heart, at 80 something, she's still hanging in there.

"Tuesday, January 12, 1932. Dorothy had a few lines from Marion stating that she had lost her baby and that it was born dead, she is still in the hospital, too bad, but better the child than herself." This is the first knowledge I ever had that Aunt Marion ever had a child.

Thursday, January 21, 1932. A letter from Maggie this A.M., Abel Pierce had his operation in Bay City and it was a success. Joe Cruze's youngest son, Curry died, and Maggie and the boys were going to the funeral the day she wrote."

Harlingen, Texas. "Sunday, January 24, 1932. Cold today, and cloudy and wet. Hokey and Winnie (Phillips) got here after supper tonight."

"Thursday, February 4, 1932. Also a letter from Maggie (today) inclosing one from Marion, who is still unsettled in her domestic affairs." Aunt Marion would divorce Dr. Lester Taylor in the early '30s. Looks like it's getting ready to happen.

"Thursday, March 24, 1932. Letter this A.M. from Maggie inclosing two from Marion. She is very unhappy and thinks of going to Europe with Miss Billings. There is another woman in the case."??? There is a possibility that dear old Lester was having an affair.

"Saturday, April 9, 1932. Left Harlingen at 6 A.M. with Mr. Biggin, my companion was Miss Montgomery. Had some trouble finding Mrs. Heeps (in Buda) as he drove past her house."

"Sunday, April 10, 1932. A cool norther this A.M. (at the 101 Ranch) Ike and Georgia were at Mrs. Heep's waiting for me. It was 9:30 P.M. and I surely was put out. Ate a good lunch at Alice's. Wylie came in for a few minutes. He starts with his horses for Boston tomorrow. Herman Greenhaw is going with him." I knew Bill had played polo at one time in Boston. He had been invited to play there.

"Monday, April 11, 1932. Wylie and Herman Greenhaw left for Boston, Massachusetts, today with 9 horses."

It is surprising that Bill would have been invited to a major eastern tournament so early in his career. However, here is a related story he told about it. He was invited up there to play as number 4 in a big tournament. When the game was over, all the players were invited to some big estate on the outskirts of Boston to attend an after game party and supper. Obviously, Bill had something to drink which would be proper, and then he went up to the room provided for him to rest a minute and freshen up before going back downstairs. He decided to lie down on the bed for just a moment and he still had his boots and spurs on. He lay down and hooked his spurs over the footboard so as not to get his boots on the bedcovers and went sound asleep. He awoke the next morning just before dawn. He had slept through the whole affair and no one felt comfortable in waking him up. He slipped out of the house quietly, never knowing to the day he died who the family was where he had stayed. That was the only time he ever played in Boston.

"Thursday, April 14, 1931. Mexican girls washed. Alice and Mr. Stewart here to dinner. Little Gill is the very picture of health."

"Friday, April 15, 1932. Heard from Wylie, he had reached Cleveland, but the horses went to Boston." Bill would have gone that way to stay with his sister, Marion.

"Thursday, April 21, 1932. Alice's brother, Marshall (Hamlett) and wife came today. Mildred (Bill's first wife) came a little before dinner, she has a precious boy." (Will Barber??)

"Monday, April 25, 1932. A letter from Dorothy and one from Wylie in Boston."

"Wednesday, May 18, 1932 (from Bay City) Letter from Dottie, inclosing one from Marion. She is planning to go to France with Miss. Billings."

"Sunday, May 21, 1932. A letter from Maggie today, nothing satisfactory about it, she is with Mrs. Heep." For some reason Maggie got in a twit and left the ranch to go into Buda to live with Mrs. Heep.

"Thursday, May 26, 1932. Did not sleep any scarcely last night for thinking of the affairs at the ranch—never dreamed that I should be cast out in my old age from what has been my home all these years. Did not think that Ike would not ever answer my letter, and I have been generous to them. Have given of my scanty hoard till there isn't much left. Dottie is at the ranch this week. They may be having a hot time for all I know."

"Wednesday, June 1, 1932. Had a letter from Maggie, M. was at the ranch and thought she was going to have her house, not settled yet."

"Friday, June 10, 1932. A letter from Maggie. She is going to let Georgia have her house for 3 weeks to entertain her family. Wants me to stay that length of time here. (Bay City) I never dreamed that Ike would go back on his own mother as he has and he would not even answer my letter."

"Friday, June 17, 1932. I lay awake a good deal last night thinking of affairs at the ranch, and of Marion. Our family seems to be so broken up, and Ike, who has always been so near to me seems so far away since he has married."

"Monday, July 11, 1932. Left Wharton at 4:30 A.M., got home (ranch) about ten oclock. 178 miles, made good time. Stopped at Buda to telephone and met Ike there. Maggie was running the place alone.?"

"Friday, July 15, 1932. Maggie is having a time trying to get the stock and everything watered, not enough wind to turn the mill, has to run the engine and it stops every now and then, hot and terrible day."

"Thursday, July 21, 1932. Maggie had a nice chicken dinner, butter beans, potatoes, hot biscuits and ice cream dessert. Ike, Georgia, Alice and little Gill ate with us."

"Saturday, July 23, 1932. Maggie and I went to Buda with Alice to vote. Don't know that my voting did any good but at least I voted against Mrs. Ferguson and for Judge Wilhelm."

"Monday, July 25, 1932. Alice came down and will spend the night here, probably stay for some time as she is quite alone up there."

"Tuesday, August 2, 1932. Had a telegram from Wylie, he had sold some horses in Cleveland." Getting back to the polo events, one of the successes for Bill during these years during the depression was that he trained all his own polo ponies. When he traveled, he would sell these horses before he came home. That is how he made his living through the depression years and how he paid his bills at the ranch.

"Thursday, August 11, 1932. Also a letter from Dottie (she had gone back to Harlingen). She is nearly killing herself taking quinine to prevent pregnancy. I could say a lot about the other sex—something ought to be done to them it looks to me like."

"Friday, August 12, 1932. A warm day. Alice came this A.M., brought vegetables etc. She said Gill had been in a bad humor ever since she left. At dinner time he cried as loud as he could before coming to the table. Alice went for him, he asked "are you going to whip me hard?" She did give him a resounding spanking. At dinner time he wanted grape juice. It was prepared for him, before tasting it, he threw his spoon with force on the table. Alice made him leave the table without tasting it. Poor kid, he has a hard school, but at least he will not be spoiled by being humored, as many a child has been."

"Friday, August 19, 1932. Alice and Gillie got here late in afternoon. She says Wylie's to start for home on Monday."

"Friday, August 26, 1932. Alice had a message from Wylie today stating that a horse belonging to an Austin man, Mr. (blank) broke his leg and had to be shot. Wanted Alice to telephone the news to the man. M. had a long letter from Marion yesterday. She was still in Paris, but going to Lucerne and later to Florence. Poor girl and I think she hates the idea of giving up Lester (husband), seems really to pity him."

"Monday, August 29, 1932. Alice had a letter from Wylie written at Cleveland and he was with Lester. Should not think he would have gone there after what has transpired."

"Tuesday, August 30, 1932. Wylie got here early this A.M."

"Wednesday, September 7, 1932. After we had retired last night, here came Dottie, Worth, Marion, Florence and Elizabeth. They were hungry and ate supper. Today is Dottie's birthday and that is the way she is celebrating it. Alice and Gill, Ike and Georgia, and Marcelle Stubbs ate dinner (lunch) here, twelve of us in all." The Kuykendall 101 Ranch Hilton is still open for business.

"Sunday, October 2, 1932. Wylie was here a good while this A.M. talking to his mother about breaking the Kuykendall Will."??? (The Will that was written by Wiley and Susan Kuykendall.)

"Wednesday, Octber 12, 1932. Wylie and Alice went to Austin. She was not feeling well. Hope Alice gets along all right and her baby will be a boy." First time Aunt Dora ever mentioned that Alice was pregnant.

"Thursday, October 13, 1932. Alice's baby boy born this A.M., name Marshal." Marshall Early Kuykendall. I was named for Alice's grandfather on her mother's side, Marshall Daniel Early. (His biography will be included later.)

"Friday, October 14, 1932. Wylie took Gillie to Austin to see his little brother this A.M., should like to hear what he has to say about him."

"Tuesday, October 18, 1932. Maggie and Gillie got home about 5:30 (from Austin), think Wylie is going tomorrow to play polo at Ft. Worth."

"Wednesday, October 19, 1932. Wylie and Doc Greenhaw got off with some horses for Ft. Worth this A.M. He to play polo. I took a dose of salts this A.M. and feel fine." Aunt Dora was big into purgatives. She figured a big cleanout every now and then was good for what ails you.

"Thursday, October 20, 1932. Cooler today. Mrs. Earl Crews here to dinner, also the negro Rueben. Mrs. Crews is Herman Greenhaw's sister. Mr. and Mrs. Roy Stubbs took Mrs. C. to Buda. Gillie was pretty bad this A.M., I hate to lose my temper with the child, he's so pretty and smart. Took a long nap this P.M., just feel trifling."

"Friday, October 21, 1932. While cleaning up the dishes had a time with Gill, first had to go upstairs to the toilet with him, then he came down and got my jacket and kept hitting me with it, then he pulled my dress up, then he came on one side and spat at my face, then went the other side and took better aim. I slapped, just couldn't help it, then he went up the the bathroom and I followed to see what mischief he was into, just got my toothbrush and put it in a different place." Sounds like brother Gill got into a twit.

"Sunday, October 23, 1932. Wylie came, he brought Alice home, came to get Gillie, some coffee, etc. had his fingernail torn off and leg bruised, playing polo I suppose. It seems quiet here without Gill. The Stubbs went to Johnson City."

"Tuesday, October 25, 1932. Mr. Voght here at dinner. A very well educated man and interesting talker, paid M. (Maggie) some money on pasturage which I'm sure was quite acceptable."

"Thursday, October 27, 1932. (Alice's 22nd birthday, she was born in 1910) Annie Heimer here looking for turkeys which roosted here last night. Wylie and Gill came and stayed a while. W. got home from Ft. Worth about 3 A.M., his party beat the others in polo game."

"Friday, October 28, 1932. Mr. Robinson (Ralph) took supper with us last night, a very pleasant man and intelligent." One of Bill's teammates on the polo team.

"Saturday, October 29, 1932. Went to see young Marshal Kuykendall this A.M., did not take my microscope (?) so couldn't see him very well. Alice was in bed, had a bad cold, Gillie met us in the yard and invited us in. That is a nice looking house, and very comfortable in winter." She is referring to Bill's house on the west side of the 101 Ranch that was built for him in ca 1918.

"Sunday, October 30, 1932. Wylie got home early this A.M. His party won the polo game, guess he was the champion player. We came home early to see Mrs. Heimer, have been talking to her about cows, calves, horses, pigs, chickens, turkeys and worms, ending up with quilts."

"Monday, October 31, 1932. A norther today but not cold. Pete (Bunton) worked here to today and is spending the night, stayed to look after Stubb's cows, as they went to Seguin." Pete Bunton and his wife Mary, who were from the old Black Colony just west of Buda, worked for the Kuykendall family all of their lives as did their son, L.D. Bill and L.D. were the same age, both born in 1899.

"Saturday, November 5, 1932. Two letters from Marion. (Bill's sister) She is not planning to come back this winter, says she can live cheaper over there, she and Lester are separated for ever, strange things happen."

"Saturday, November 12, 1932. First ice last night. Wylie got home last night, his party beat in the polo game. He is quite a star in the polo firmament."

"Thursday, November 17, 1932. A nice letter from Lois with a birthday card, eighty five today. Cold and wet, the rain is badly needed." Eudora Inez Moore was born in Victoria, Texas, on Nov. 17, 1847.

"Monday, November 21, 1932. M. (Maggie) had a long letter from Marion. She is still in Florence (Italy) will not be back until April, will be in Cleveland a short time, then to Texas."

"Tuesday, November 22, 1932. Mr. Robinson drove up a large herd of cattle late this afternoon, Wylie was with him, penned them here for the night, all red with white faces, Herefords, I presume."

"Wednesday, November 23, 1932. They worked all day with the cattle, branded and marked the calves, Wylie came in bloody and dirty, ate dinner and at it again."

"Sunday, December 4, 1932. A quite uneventful day, Wylie went to San Antonio to play polo. Alice also went in their car. W. took two horses in his truck."

"Wednesday, December 7, 1932. Ike killed two hogs, Pete & Rueben here, Pete stayed all night. Wylie played polo in San Antonio."

"Saturday, December 24, 1932. This has been a rather turbulent day. Wylie came this A.M. to wash, Ike and Georgia came later, Wylie said something that made Ike angry, he came in the house and his mother said something. He used some profane language, left his cream in the slop bucket, took some packages and left. Dottie got angry and said a good deal to us. I went with her up to Wylie's, got a good look at the baby (Marshall) this time, I'm afraid he has a hard time before him. I washed dishes all morning."

Thus ends Aunt Dora's lifetime of keeping journals. She probably kept a journal for as long as she could in 1933, but it has been lost. Bless her heart, she moved up to Hays County when the family moved there in 1901 from Matagorda County, to be with her, niece, Maggie Moore Kuykendall. She helped run the Kuykendall Ranch Hilton until the day she died, which would be on November 8, 1933, one year later. She died at the ranch and her body was taken to Matagorda County by train to be buried in the old Ashby Cemetery there. She got her wish and was buried between her mother and her brother, Will, in the space that had been provided for her.

She was a prolific writer and her journals were published over the years in different newspapers around the state. She was in old Indianola, Texas, when the Army unloaded the camels. In the back of the 1932 book she has a note: "Jefferson Davis was Secretary of War under President Pierce. He established our short lived Camel Corps of the Army, 1853-1857." She was standing on the wharf there when they were unloaded. A contributor on several occasions to the *Confederate* magazine, her articles appeared several times. She went to as many Confederate reunions as she could attend. Most of her brothers had been in the war.

The reason I have gone to such great lengths to copy her diary into this writing was to show the every day life of such an interesting, turbulent family as the Kuykendalls of Hays County. However, each journal and especially the 1932 journal, is chock full of a zillion names of folks who came, ate, lived, and died through the 101 Ranch at Buda, Texas. The entries placed have sidetracked this book enough and it was thought the addition of every single detail would be too cumbersome for anyone to read. Now, let's press on.

Eudora Inez Moore

Bill Kuykendall became a very well known polo player in a very short time. He only played from 1930 to 1939. In one of the first tournaments he was in at Arlington, Texas, his fledgling, inexperienced team won the tournament. He and his team of four, had only one groomsman, and only took two or three horses apiece to play in this major tournament. The horses were unroached (longmaned) and their tails were not tied up. The reason for both was so your mallet didn't get tangled up in the horse's mane and tail. A polo game is very grueling and has several periods called "chukkers"(periods). (An Indian name from India, where polo was started.) The maximum duration of play in a match is eight chukkers of 7½ minutes each with intervals of three minutes after each chukker.

The horses are required to run full out through one of these chukkers and all polo players had to bring enough horses to change at least one time per chukker, which meant they brought eight to ten horses per player. Bill and his group took only about eight to ten horses total, for all of them. And they didn't have a groomsman for each player, unheard of in the social circles of polo playing, where everyone could afford a groomsman. How uncivilized. The groomsman was the fellow who saddled the horses, got them ready to play, and held them at the ready so when a player needed to rush over and mount another horse, the horse was saddled and ready to go at moment's notice. I think Greenhaw went with them on this first trip to hold the horses. All of them.

When Bill and his group arrived in Arlington, Texas, for the big shindig, the social group of polo folks there would have very little to do with these upstarts from the Hill Country of Texas. Remember that in 1932, the Army calvalry had big, well-known polo teams. Teams from Fort Sill, Oklahoma, and Fort Sam Houston in San Antonio were present. I think fourteen teams were represented in this particular tournament, some of the very best in the southwest.

Polo players have handicaps just like in golf. They are handicapped from one goal to ten goals, meaning that's how many goals each player could possibly make in any given game. Needless to say, Bill's team was almost in the minus numbers, since they had so little experience. I think they were rated at about four or five goals total for their team. The other teams were so highly rated that they thought that would not be a problem.

The tournaments are structured in brackets where the winners advance and the losers drop out. For instance, if Bill's team was scheduled to play, let's say the good team from Wichita Falls, Texas, when the game started, Bill's team already had a five-goal advantage. Then Bill's team beat the other team on the "flats," meaning they beat them seven to six actual goals. In other words, Bills team scored seven actual goals, and the other good, well-known team could score only six actual goals. The teams were stunned.

Bill's team played the next team in line and beat them also. The players were so impressed with the ruffians from the Hill Country that they sent down their groomsmen from the other teams, roached Bill's horse's manes and tied up their tails. It was a gallant thing to do. Bill's team ended winning the tournament and their names made the rounds as the newcomers to watch out for.

I asked Bill, my dad, how he did it. His answer was simple and interesting. There were plenty of top-notch horseman among the cavalry and among the private teams. Men who knew how to ride well and could hit a polo ball. Dad and his teammates were top cowboys, who rode superb horses and could hit the polo ball fairly well. The difference was in the horses and the horsemanship. Dad's horses could outrun just about everybody on the field and the cowboys were better horsemen than the others on that particular day, by and large. So

Bill Kuykendall and polo trophy, ca 1932.

they simply outhorsed them and were able to steal the ball away enough to score enough goals to win the games.

Here are the actual stats of that tournament from the 1933 Year Book of the United States Polo Association, page 62, 347 Madison Ave., New York, New York:

THIRD ANNUAL FALL TOURNAMENT
El Ranchito Polo Club, Arlington, Texas

FIRST GAME: October 22, 1932, Umpire, Capt. F. H. Barnhart
Georgetown (team name) 11 goals (Earned 8, Handicap 3). No. 1, O. M. Cardwell, No. 2, L. Starke; No. 3, Alton Wier, Back, Bill Kuykendall
Wichita Falls (team name) 4 goals. (Earned 4). No. 1, Ernest Fain; No. 2, Horrace Robbins, No. 3, Aubrey Floyd, Back, J. Smith
FIRST SEMI-FINAL: October 26, 1932, Umpire, George Prendergast
Georgetown: 12 Goals (Earned 7, Handicap 5). No. 1, O. M. Cardwell; No. 2, L. Starke; No. 3. Alton Weir; Back, Bill Kuykendall
Ft. Sill, Okla. 7 Goals (Earned 7). No. 1, Capt. C. E. Sargent; No. 2, Maj. H. D. Jay; No. 3, Maj. C. A. Baehr; Back, Lt. J. B. Horton.
FINAL GAME: October 29, 1932, Umpires, Capt. F. H. Barnhart and Geo. Prendergast.
Georgetown: 13 Goals (Earned 8, Handicap 5) No. 1, O. M. Cardwell and W. W. Cardwell; No. 2, L. Starke; No. 3, Alton Wier; Back William Kuykendall.
El Ranchito: 7 Goals (Earned 7). No. 1, A. B. Wharton, Jr; No. 2, L. E. Weeks; No. 3, Cecil Childers; Back, B. H. Stephens.

Dad bought most of his horses from Roy Stubbs of Johnson City, Texas, or further west in the Junction country. There was a reason for that. Horses raised in real rough, rocky, country will *never* fall with you. Horses raised in blackland or sand, where most folks think they should be raised, will fall all the time when put to the test. Dad, bless his heart, was rough on horses and if one fell with him under any condition, he was gone from the ranch by sundown, no questions asked. You take Sutton Croft, or Ralph Robinson, or dad, men who rode horses every day for their livelihood. These men would run a horse across the slippery rocks in the bottom of the Pedernales River or the honeycomb rocks around Onion Creek and rope a big brahma bull on a short 30 foot rope tied to their saddle and dare their horses to fall with them. These men were Texas Hill Country cowboys, and damn good ones.

Dad's could take his big, black stallion, Smooth Sailing, play polo on him for a month, come back to the 101 Ranch at Buda, change from English saddle to stock (western), and rope the biggest brahma bull in the county and jerk him flat as a pancake every day of the week and twice on Sunday—and never break stride and never fall down. These horses were tough and the men tougher. Dad's entry into the polo arena was off to a good start and he was finally coming into his own.

The 11,000 acre Kuykendall 101 Ranch was divided among the four siblings in 1933. Bill, my dad, got the western portion, some 1,826 acres, with his 1918 house, and about three miles of cypress, bottom Onion Creek. Our house was about one and a half miles due west of the "other house," which we called Grandmother's house (Maggie Kuykendall). I do not remember a time when Grandmother was not there along with Aunt Dorothy or Aunt Dottie as we called her. Obviously Dottie had

Marshall, Alice, and Gil, ca 1937

In both pictures, Bill Kuykendall is on far right and Mike Butler is third from right.

Gates Mills, Ohio, ca 1936. In both pictures, Bill Kuykendall is on far right.

moved back home from Harlingen by the time my memory kicked in (1936 etc.). Her husband, Lawrence Hoskins, was in a horrible car wreck and became very disfigured. I barely remember him. Something happened to cause them to get a divorce in the middle '30s.

At any rate, Dad must have leased his portion of the ranch about 1935, because we moved to Shreveport, Louisiana, where Dad became the manager and horse trainer for the City Service Gasoline Company at their Hunt Club and stables on the west edge of town. They also sponsored a polo team that Dad joined. I think we lived there about two or three years. The team was called the Shreveport Riding and Polo Club and they played all over the country. One of the trophies in my possession is inscribed:

> Wm. Kuykendall
> June 9, 1935
> Dayton, Ohio.

The other one is inscribed:

> El Ranchito
> Consolation Tournament
> November 1935.

I do not know where that was played.

Some of the clubs that were in the Southwestern Circuit are: Austin Polo Club, Border Polo Asso., El Ranchito Polo Club, El Valle Club, Houston Riding & Polo Club, Polo Asso. of Dallas, San Antonio Polo Club, and the Shreveport Riding & Polo Club.

The Texas army stations that also were in the same circuit were: Fort Bliss, Fort Brown, Fort Clark, Fort Sam Houston, Fort McIntosh, Fort Ringold, Fort D.A. Russell, Kelly Field, Maxwell Field, and Randolph Field.

Some of the names on the Shreveport team were: Herschell R. Scivally #1; O. Knutsen, Jr. # 2; Kenneth Hickman # 3, and William Kuykendall, back or #4.

On one of the tournaments Bill Kuykendall was assisted by Mike Butler of Austin, Texas. Other well-known players were: Roy and Harold Barry; Billy Skidmore; John and Charles M. Armstrong; J. T. Mather; S. P. Farish; and Leon O'Quin, to name just a few.

Other men who played on teams with Bill were: York Ratliff, Cecil Childers, Capt. H. K. Coulter, Wilson Southwell, Lt. C. G. Benharm, Dudley Milliken, Jay Floyd, Horrace Robbins, C. H. Featherston, Doc Wier, Capt. W. H. Craig, Maj. J. A. Watson, William Berry, Aubrey Floyd, Earnest Fain, Luther E. Weeks, Maj. D. M. Scott, F. B. Asche, Wynn Humberson, H. R. Scivally, Jim Peppar, Dr. A. V. Young, Harold Berry, O. Knutsen, Jr, Kenneth Hickman, Leon O'Quin, Ross Malone, Lt. Col. T. W. Hastey, Mike Butler, Billy Skidmore, and Dr. Rayworth Williams.

My next polo memory was being in Gates Mills, Ohio, just outside Cleveland in 1939. My mother Alice and I had driven up there probably that summer from the ranch at Buda. I remember it well because Dad played with Courtney Burton and the Knutsens against one of the national polo teams from Mexico. Their leader and captain was Gen. Jesus Jamie Quiniones, from the town of Villa Acuna, Mexico, just across the river from Del Rio, Texas. It was such an event that Dad and Courtney had arranged for the general and his team to receive the Key to the City of Cleveland from the mayor and a big parade was held in their honor. Alice and I got to ride in a big Pontiac touring car with the top down. Later there was a big shindig held in their honor at the polo club at Gates Mills where the Burtons lived. I was allowed to attend and have the pictures to prove it.

Gen. Jesus J. Quiniones and Bill Kuykendall in Villa Acuna, Mexico, ca 1939.

There were two tournaments held against the Mexican polo team and I think the first was held in 1938 in Mexico City were Dad and Courtney were invited to play. However, it could have all happened in the summer and fall of 1939. I don't remember. What I do remember is Dad telling me they played twice, once in Mexico City using Mexican horses and Dad's team lost, and once in Gates Mills, Ohio, using their own horses, where they won.

What is interesting about the tournament held in early September 1939 was the fact that until this month of the twentieth century, all

Bill Kuykendall and his teammates played against the National Mexican Polo Team, summer of 1939, in Mexico City. The team is dressed in white, standing from center to right: Tom Mather (holding trophy), Bill Berry, Bill Kuykendall, and Harold Berry.

Poloists Battle for Gold Cup

Gen. Jesus Jaime Quinones of the Mexican Army polo team (left) is shown casting a wistful eye on the gold cup for the international polo matches which are being played at Hunting Valley Field. Windsor T. White, one of the original riders in Cleveland polo 27 years ago when the game was started here, will present the cup. He is shown above on the right. The Mexican Army team and the Hunting Valley team meet at Hunting Valley tomorrow afternoon at 5 o'clock and Sunday afternoon at 3:30.

Bill Kuykendall, between chukkers.

the armies of the world had active calvary units. Most of the cavalry units in the U.S. had polo teams. On 29 September 1939 that changed forever for America and for Europe because Hitler and Nazi Germany invaded Poland and began WWII. The horse cavalry that was known the world over vanished with the death of the Polish Officer Corp Cavary against German Panzer tanks.

That fall of 1939 was the end of Bill Kuykendall's career as a polo player. He had risen to four goals (his handicap), mother said six, but there is no proof. Having a four goal handicap was quite good. Mother said the reason Dad always played "back" or #4 was because he had one of the "finest backhands" in the Southwest. It seems Dad always had some of the best horses on the field and he could outrun the opposition as they headed for their own goals, get ahead of them, and backhand the polo ball back down the field, thus keeping them from scoring.

The war for America started after 7 December 1941. Late in the year of 1942 or early 1943, I remember mother staying up in her room and crying a lot. It seems that Hays County Judge Charles Decker had called Bill during that period and informed him that all of the Kuykendall family ranch and many other ranches west of Buda and Kyle were to be condemned and turned into a massive Army base. The Judge told Dad he had been ordered to close all the roads west of these towns by a ceratin date. The news was devastating to all concerned. This started a lifetime of dislike and distrust between my family and Lyndon B. Johnson.

Throughout 1942 Dad had been

Bill Kuykendall, Onion Creek, 101 Ranch, Buda, Texas, ca 1940

contacted by his army friends, who told him they wanted to survey the Kuykendall family ranch and help with ranching efforts, such as reseeding and many other conservation practices. Unknown to my father was the fact that this was a lie and the real reason they were on the ranch was to conduct a survey of how the ranch might best be used as a future military base. This farce was a product of Lyndon Johnson's relationship with the city of San Marcos, Texas. Johnson felt that Texas needed a massive army base, and Johnson wanted it there so it would benefit the town where Johnson had gone to school.

My memory of those days was that Dad was gone a lot and mother was still upstairs. Mother told me that the army base near San Marcos was cancelled due to the fact that Dad had considerable influence among his old army polo buddies. She told me that the land had in fact been condemned and that when the paper work came down to an army general in Fort Worth to sign (possibly the Army Corps of Engineers), who had played polo with my father, he contacted my father, got the information on what really was happening, and refused to sign the final papers.

I have never run these records, nor have I attempted to get these records through the "Open Records Act." What I do know is that some time in early 1942, all the poor folks in the Killeen, Texas, area lost their lands to a massive army base to be known as Fort. Hood. "On January 14th, 1942, it was announced that a tank destroyer tactical and firing center would be established near Killeen, Texas. Some 300 farming and ranching families were required, on short notice, to give up their lands." (*The Hand Book of Texas*, Volume 2, page 1104.) I wonder if those folks ever voted for Lyndon B. Johnson after that.

When the war ended in the summer of 1945, my father had another vision. He figured that since there had been a massive depression after WWI, surely there would be one after WWII. The only problem with this scenario was the depression after WWI came after some twelve or thirteen years, not one year. After much thought of a day or so, Dad sold all the cattle on the ranch and leased his pastures to Vernon Cook of Austin.

Dad got involved with a man named Harry Lowther from Chicago who had in-

Mona in later years with Alice and her sister Corrine

Bill in center with Marshall and William Hamlett, Alice's brothers, on either side)

Ice House, Cotulla, Texas, ca 1946
Left to right: LaVerne Allen, Helen Story, Bill Kuykendall, and Sheriff Hogue Pool

Deer hunting camp on the Doby Ranch, ca 1946. Alice Kuykendall is second from left, Sheriff Hogue Pool is fifth from left; Helen Story, sixth from left, Cassie is on Helen's left, Marshall E. Kuykendall at age 13 is second from right, and Bill Kuykendall is on far right.

Bill Kuykendall and the Lowther saw

vented a "saw" that would cut down trees. This saw was something like you have never seen before. It was just like having a wheelbarrow with a large Briggs and Straton engine on it and out in front was a huge whirling saw blade about 36 inches in diameter whirling at 900 million mph run by belts from the engine. One had to manhandle this beast up to a cedar tree in the Hill Country of Texas and attempt to cut or saw it down. Dad thought he was going to get richer than ten feet up something and he became the distributor for the "Lowther C-Saw Company" all over Texas.

So from 1946 until 1948, Dad traveled all over Texas demonstrating this beast. He figured he needed a better location for his shop or store, so he bought a brick building from the Watson Milling family on one of the corner streets in Buda for his main office and Lowther C-Saw Shop. This building later became the Montague Grocery.

I recall that Dad was always flying back and forth to Chicago on Trans-Texas Airlines to confer with Mr. Lowther. Sometime during this brief tenure, Mr. Lowther and Dad were offered a smaller saw that would also cut trees down that ran off a little engine and incorporasted a chain device. It was later called a chain-saw. My Dad and Mr. Lowther passed on this invention stating it would never work.

Dad wasn't into small boys being under foot much and I guess neither was Alice, because my brother, Gil, had been living in Austin with Alice's mother, Mona, for some time. About 1942 or '43 the mud or the trip to the school bus over on the Buda road, or whatever, caused Bill and Alice to place me in foster care during each week in Buda. They would haul me into Buda on Sunday evenings or perhaps early Monday mornings and leave me with the family of the week and I wouldn't get to go home until Friday afternoon.

The first family I remember was the Armbrusters. I don't remember their first names, but they had a house full of boys. We lived first out on the Buda to Driftwood road across from the Giberson Dairy. Then they moved into downtown Buda, and we lived just on the east side of the railroad tracks from where the library is today. I remember the first night I spent in that particular house and the freight train came thundering through Buda, I thought the old house was going to fall off its foundation. What's also funny is I never remember it again. I guess little boys learn to sleep through anything.

It was war time and everything was scarce and I suspect the few dollars Dad gave to the Armbrusters was welcome as could be.

Mrs. Armbruster always cooked white bread in an iron skillet in margarine—there wasn't any butter. She flopped them over until they were toasted, then poured karo syrup over the top of them. I called them Armbruster pancakes and I thought they were great. I don't have any teeth left from those days but never you mind. They were great!! The other thing Mrs. Armbruster would do was take your chewing gum from you before you went to school each day and paste it above the woodstove so when you got home "of an evening," she'd peel it off the old wallpaper and give it to you. It helped to be frugal in those days. Of course, having a house full of boys, it was sometimes hard to keep up with who got which, but "we didn't care none."

Later, probably in 1944-45, Dad and Alice moved me back across the main street to live in the Montague Café with Miss Molly and her husband. I'm here to tell you those were fine folks and I will always remember them with love and affection. I was also there the evening that son Bill came home from the great war. (Probably late spring of '45.) I came bounding in the café and Miss Molly grabbed me and told me not to go in the back bedroom and wake up her son Bill, "cause if you wake him up, he'll hit you." My eyes got as big as mama's sauce pans and you can bet I didn't go in there for some time. Many years later, this fine man's son would be our "High" Sheriff in Hays County.

Some time in late 1947 or '48, Dad's ole time buddy, Herman Heep, approached him and told him that a Houston oil man by the name of Pat Rutherford wanted to buy a ranch in the Hill Country. Our home place had at that time, 3,600 acres in it and about three or four miles of cypress-lined Onion Creek through the middle of it, including the old Butler House and Butler Spring. Dad had gotten about 1,800 acres in the family ranch division of 1933. He later added about 1,800 more acres from a purchase he made from John Greenhawe (Ike Kuykendall's portion) some time around 1944 or 45. John Greenhawe had bought Uncle Ike's 3,000 acres in 1941 for $21 per acre.

At any rate, this oil man was willing to pay $50 per acre for this stunning ranch and Dad knew that was double what his brother had received so he sold our ranch. I remember because I was upstairs in our house when Alice called me into her bedroom and told me they had sold the ranch. I was 15 years old at the time and I was heartbroken.

Before this time, about 1945-46, Dad and Alice thought I had it too easy living with those fine folks in Buda, so they enrolled me in the San Marcos Baptist Academy. What was good about that, Dad thought, was I couldn't come home every weekend so he didn't have to fool with me then either, it being a military school and all. Well, I'm here to tell you, if you ever want to send your little squalling thirteen-year-old son to prison, send him to the San Marcos Baptist Academy. The 1903 Enfield rifle was bigger than I was and I had to carry that sucker every time I marched. I hated it and still do. I have tried my whole life never to think about that sorry place nor ever visit it again under pain of death. You have never seen so many disfuctional kids in your life. It was a dumping place for unwanted, unruly, and undone kids. Probably still is.

I cried on every letter I sent to the ranch so Alice would see the tear stains on the paper until they finally relented and sent me to live in Austin with Mona, Alice's

Tear-stained letter and MEK in SMA uniform, 1945.

mother. Turns out the real reason was brother Gil had just moved out to go to the University of Texas and there was a vacancy, so to speak, at Grandmother's house at 1215 Parkway. The little yellow house is still standing there today. So I was staying there during the week and going home again on weekends when the ranch was sold in 1947.

In the old days, there were just three higher grade schools in Austin—Austin High School on West 12th Street, University Jr. High on 19th Street, and Allen Jr. High over near East 9th or East 10th Street. All of our friends in West Austin sent their kids to UJH, of course, so when we sold the ranch, Dad and Alice enrolled me in UJH, so I could be with "my own kind." But coming from out of town and probably from a school district south of Austin, I could only get into Allen Jr. High, much to the chagrin of my folks and my friends. So I socialized with the underprivileged until I was able to transfer to Austin High in the spring of my sophomore year. I think that was in the spring of 1948.

In the meantime, Dad and Alice closed the deal on our new home place. Dad then somehow wrangled his sister, Auntie Marion K. Taylor, into a lease/purchase of her 1,500 acres of land that abutted the old Kyle to Driftwood road known today as FM 150. So while I am weaving my way through the educational process of the Austin schools, Bill and Alice are building their dream home on the south side of the 1,500 acres next to the Kyle road. It, along with barns, corral, etc., would be finished by the summer of 1948. So we moved from our apartment on West 18th Street back to the ranch that summer in time to enroll me in Kyle High School for the fall term and my junior year.

In 1948, dad was still involved with Mr. Lowther in his "C-Saw" business. At sales end Dad still had no cattle on his portion of the ranch. With his new found wealth, Dad was able to completely clear the cedar from Auntie Marion's portion, build his new home and restock the 1,500 acres with cattle. He also bought Alice a 1948 Lincoln Continental convertable two-door, 16 cylinders, pea-green car. It was fancy and even had electric push button windows. You just press the buttons and the windows went up and down by themselves. What would the Ford engineers think of next?

While Dad was getting the ranch cleared of 50 years of neglect and plenty of cedar growth, he hired old man Joe Cruze of Wimberley to help him build one of the first deer-proof fences in Central Texas. Old Joe was a character. He always wore a Stetson hat and a red bandana around his neck. And the first thing he said upon meeting you each day was, "Have you heard any news?" And you'd better answer or mumble something, because nothing else was going to take place until you did.

The Kuykendall ranch was still the largest ranch in Hays County in 1948 (all family members included), even though Uncle Ike had sold his portion in 1941. Somewhere back in the '30s, Dad became very interested in protecting his fishing on Onion Creek and his deer and turkey population. He also got crossways with the hound-dog owners, who ran their hounds through the Kuykendall ranch. I find this interesting, because in the old days, dad had sure run his hound dogs through some-

Group of Buda, Texas, ladies, ca 1948. Maggie Kuykendall is on front row, second from left.

one else's place, but earlier on, that's what country folks did. Times were changing. More people were moving in and somewhere in the scheme of things, Dad got real crossways with the hound-dog boys and let it be known that there would be no more free hunting on the Kuykendall ranch nor could one run their hounds there anymore. Well, folks got real snorty about that, especially the dog boys. After a while some let it drop, but the fringe outlaw boys sent word they were going to hunt whereever they damn well pleased and the honeymoon was over between Bill Kuykendall and most of the small owners nearby in the county.

It was about this time that Dad no longer participated in anything outside of the ranch, such as ropings, rodeos, or the Reunion at Driftwood. He simply no longer visited to any great extent with his old lifelong ranching friends. He never was a social coffee drinker, anyway, so you never saw him down at the corner café a 6 A.M. drinking coffee with his buddies and gossiping about who did what to whom. He figured it was none of their damn business what he did and he sure didn't give a damn what they did. He gravitated more back to the old West Austin society group that he had known forever. He even joined the Austin Country Club, even though he did not play golf. I think it was also to help out brother Gil, who was becoming a very well known golfer on the University of Texas golf team in 1948.

Remember, Dad was a cowboy and one fine roper. He could have easily become a professional had he wanted to do so. I bring this up, because during the late '30s and early '40s when Dad caught someone's dog, he would get on the old crank phone, call up "Central" and tell her to connect him with old so and so. When the dog owner got on the phone, Dad would tell him he had his hound in the pens and for him to come and get him. During

Bill Kuykendall on the 101 Ranch, ca 1940

this time, Dad told some fellows to keep their dogs off the ranch and one of the owners mouthed off, that "Bill Kuykendall would never catch one of his hounds" in a million years.

During these turbulent years, if Dad thought there was going to be trouble, or if he thought someone was going to sneak on the ranch, he kept ole Smooth Sailing, his black stud horse, saddled in the pen with nothing but a hackamore on him. On short notice, he could run out to the corrals, slap a bridle on ole Smooth, and he was in business. And of course, his 30-30 Winchester was always in the scabbard.

It was not long after the mouthing-off episode, that Dad heard the hounds running through the ranch again. He hopped on Smooth and before the night was over had roped, in the dark mind you, all four of this loudmouth's hounds. The fellow could not believe it when Dad called him and told him what he had done and for the fellow to come get his "gawddam" dogs before Dad killed all of them. Needless to say, that stopped that particular fellow from trying that again. Anyone who could consistantly rope a jumping goat off the back of a big stud horse could certainly rope a dog. However, this had no effect on the hardcore tresspassers of the area who had always hunted and fished where ever they wanted, when they wanted. So the tensions between Dad and these outlaw types worsened.

I remember getting up one morning and going out to the pens, probably about 1940. Dad had hired an old boy from Wimberley who had one ear missing. I don't remember his name or how he happened to lose his ear, but that particular morning, he had a brand new bullet hole in his leather jacket which he was proud to show me. In fact, the bullet had grazed his upper arm near his shoulder and had left a burn scab where it had burned him as it went through the jacket. Seems he and Dad had slipped out the night before because they had gotten word some fellows were going to sneak in the ranch on the south side of the Kyle road which would have been then in Auntie Marion's part of the ranch. Dad and Ol' Earless eased over in the Lock Pasture, as we called it, and "lay" up to wait on their friends. Dad was in one cedar thicket and Ol' Earless was in another. Not much time passed, until two and possibly three fellows, one or two with headlights and one with a flashlight, started working their way toward Earless. When they got about 30 yards from him, he said he rolled over just a bit to get a better look at the folks and when he did, he broke a limb underneath him and it snapped. Instantly, the fellow with the flashlight fired his gun at the noise. And just as instantly Ol' Earless, bless his heart, let fly at them with Dad's ol' trusty 32-20 Colt single action six shooter, and damn if he didn't shoot the flashlight out of the outlaw's hand. After that I'm sure there was a big double runoff by all foks concerned and much popping through the cedar breaks.

Right after I spoke to him, he and dad rode back over in the pasture and found the flashlight with the bullet hole smack dab through the bulb and the exit hole just about where a man's finger would be. Dad got in his pickup and went down to San Marcos to report the near shooting to the sheriff. While there, they were able to locate and question the fellow they suspected, who had his left forefinger in a bandage. Said he'd cut it on a broken coke bottle.

Dad caught another fellow one night over on the bluff overlooking Onion Creek in the old Nook Pasture. Dad was lying up in a pile of brush when this fellow walked right by him. Dad stuck his Winchester Model 64 30-30 in the small of the fellow's back, and said in a real low voice, "I've got you now, you son of a bitch." Dad said the old boy crapped in his pants right there on the spot. He started kicking him in the ass and every time he kicked him, the old boy would crap some more. He said he broke that particular fellow from "sucking eggs" any more. If he told me his name, I don't remember it.

This whole episode of thieves, outlaws, and professional tresspassers continually coming on the Kuykendall Ranch came to an abrupt halt sometime in 1948 or '49 just after we'd moved into the new house on the south side. I awoke one morning to the yard full of Sheriff's vehicles. Alice told me to stay inside the house, that something bad had happened over in the Nook Pasture. Turns out Dad had found out somehow that some fellows were going to sneak in the Nook Pasture on our northwest side of the ranch. So he called my crazy cousin Worth Hoskins and his own brother, Ike, to come down here and help repel the invaders. All the family had armed themselves and was lying up once again in the brush in the pasture. Luck would have it that the tresspassers with headlights attached walked right up on Dad. Dad eased up and pointed his rifle at the head fellow, turned on his own flashlight and hollered for the fellow to stop. The man had killed a young doe earlier in the evening and was walking with her over one of his shoulders and carrying a rifle in the other. In an instant he rolled her off his shoulder and was in the process of bringing up his rifle when Dad shot him in the brisket. I'm here to tell you that nothing in this world will stop trespassing and the "will" thereof more than to be perforated from front to back with a 180 grain soft-nosed 30-30 bullet traveling at 1,800 feet per second from an old trusty Winchester Model 64. Dad killed him dead as a hammer. And with that killing, most of the other outlaws or would-be outlaws figured the price of trespassing on the Kuykendall Ranch got a bit too high to pay. There was a second fellow with the guy that night. I heard that when the shot was fired, he broke to run down through the cedar breaks and didn't get home until sometime the following day with most of his clothers ripped off him from the brush. Needless to say he decided to retire from his past transgressions. What I never understood was how Dad always knew when the folks were coming. I asked him one time and he said the outlaws would leave him a sign, like deer guts in the mail box or a cedar branch hung in the high fence somewhere, that they were coming. It was like a deadly game of you-can't-catch-me. But how he actually knew the exact night, I never found out and he never told me.

Dad was "No Billed" by the Hays County Grand Jury for the shooting. It seems that not only had Dad called the Sheriff's Department in Hays County, but he had also called some of his friends over at the Texas Rangers in Austin, requesting help on that particular night. None was available so Dad had to go it alone.

An interesting side story to that episode happened many years later when I heard that a book about Driftwood, Texas, was going to be sold at the old Driftwood store. I went by the store to buy the book since it contained information on all the folks in the vicinity and talked about all the ranches in the area. Being the history buff that I am, I wanted one of the copies for my library. I picked up a copy and glanced in the index to find out which pages would mention my family and there was not a single mention of the Kuykendall Ranch nor the Kuykendall family. Now that was kind of odd, since the Kuykendall Ranch nearly joined the store and was the biggest ranch in the county. I was fussing about the lack of ingredients in the book when one of the

Bill Kuykendall with the same rifle he used to shoot a trespasser.

neighbors kind of saddled up next to me and suggested that I keep my objections to myself, since either the author or one of the main contributors was the daughter of the man Dad had perforated. He is buried in the cemetery at Driftwood. I put on my hat and left.

In 1950, or thereabouts, Dad leased the 4,000 acre Circle C ranch from Polly Blanton Covert, later to be Wilson, and then to be Brooks, ranch. He ran Hereford cattle there as I remember, and had the Polk boys helping him run it.

I transferred from Austin High to Kyle High School when we moved to the south side of the ranch. The school bus came in front of the ranch and Mr. Montague was the driver. Moving back into a small town was quite fun for me. I was beginning to know what a cute girl looked like and Kyle High had a pile of them. When one is in a small school, one is involved in every single aspect of that school and I was suddenly pulled into all the sports that the school had, mainly six-man football.

Both brother Gil and I were late bloomers and growers. I was only about five foot five when I moved to Kyle my junior year. I probably didn't weigh 140 lbs. Gil was about the same at that period of his life. There were about eight or nine kids out for football that fall and I was prime meat to be on the second squad of the Kyle High School Panthers. Kyle needed every man to maintain its football program and I was the new, necessary man. The term "man" in this text is used very loosely.

A man named Black was our coach in the fall of '48 and he nearly killed all of his

Kyle High School Panthers. Left to right, back row: Superintendent James L. Childs, Edgar Arnold, David Allen, Edward Schmeltekopf, Marshall Kuykendall, Alton Hagedorn, Truman Guttery, Eugene Schnautz, and Coach Weldon Moody; front row: Jack Gold, #10 unknown (possibly Schulle), Edward Simon, Bill Bassett, Jack Dalton, Doyle Tyler, and Owen Dorman.

Six-man formation, fall 1949: halfback Alton Hagedorn, right end Truman Guttery, quarterback David Allen, center Edgar Arnold, left end Marshall Kuykendall, and fullback Edward Schmeltekopf.

players getting us in shape. The football field was a piece of fairly level old cotton patch near the school that someone had marked off in the required chalk lines and goal posts. Before each game, the elders of the school and necessary volunteers, would walk the entire field and throw out all of the bigger rocks they could lift and find.

My male classmates were David LaVern Allen and Edward Schmettekopf. I forget which class Jack Peoples was in. I mention his name because I was on the second team that first year and in about the second or third game, Jack broke his leg clean off and that was the only way I got to play.

Things rocked along fairly normally for the next year or so. Dad was running his Polled Hereford Cows on the ranch and I graduated from dear old Kyle High in the spring of '50.

I didn't want to go to a big college the fall of '50 and had hoped to go to one that had a fine ranch and range management school, so I chose Sul Ross State College in Alpine, Texas. Dad and I went out there that summer and turns out he had gone to school in San Marcos with a bunch of the Mitchells of Marfa. So while I was checking out the school, he was visiting with his old friends. During those visits, the Mitchells invited us to hunt mule deer with them that coming fall. Mr. Mitchell had a deal made with the Rawls family to hunt on the Rawls' Mesa ranch down below Casa Piedra. The old Rawls' ranch had about 55-60,000 acres and at that time all the Rawls were still alive, Grandpa Rawls, Jack Rawls, and Junie Rawls. Grandpa lived or stayed down at the "Alazan" place; Jack stayed up at the old headquarters where the good landing strip was, and Junie stayed over on the northwest side. I think Junie and his wife were the only ones then to live on the ranch, the rest lived in Marfa and came out (65 miles) every day or so. However, Jack did have a little Air Coupe airplane about as big as a gnat which he flew all the time. Interestingly, all the Rawls and Mitchells were little tiny men. Most wore Lucchese cowboy boots about a size 5 or 6. They were a tough bunch, all dried up from a zillion years of living in the Chihuahuan desert. Grandpa drove an old black Ford pickup and carried a black doctor's bag on the seat next to him and a gallon jug of SoTol juice on the floor. In that doctor's bag he had his trusty 44-40 Colt sixshooter and a spare box of shells or two.

Hunting scene on the Rawls Ranch, ca 1952. Bill K. is on right and MEK is in dark jacket.

One day while we were visiting, I finally got up enough nerve to ask him if I could shoot that thumb-buster at a tin can. He said, "Sure!" and drug out his 44-40 and handed it to me. In the meantime he pitched a beer can out about 20 feet and told me to shoot at it. I eared back that ol' six-shooter and aimed and aimed and finally touched one off. I vaguely remember that I hit the canyon wall some 100 yards away and never came close to that tin can. Grandpa, who was blind in one eye, borrowed it back, swung the gun in both hands above his head, pulled it down to eye level in one smooth motion and let fly and blew the hell out of Mr. Tin Can. My admiration for that fine ol' man greatly increased that day.

I entered Sul Ross that fall close to my eighteenth birthday and Dad kept the lease on that fine ranch for the next eighteen years. Those were some of the finest times of my life.

As fate will have it, the Korean War started that fall and since the draft was still in effect, all us young men were notified that we'd better be in a ROTC outfit during college or we would be in Korea before too many suns went down. I checked out several schools and it turned out the South West Texas State Teachers College in big San Marcos had an Air ROTC outfit. So, after only one semester at Sul Ross, I transferred there to finish out my college career.

I do want to tell one story about Sul Ross that I remember. They had a fine Rodeo Club. I was too scared to join, I think. One bunch of boys that were in it was the Mays brothers. Now remember, when I was 18, I was still not very big and I certainly was not mature in any way. So to be confronted with the great, big ol' Mays boys, who I'm sure rode in horseback 100 miles every day to school, was enough to scare a little fellow like me. I think their names were Harley, Clyde, and I don't remember the third one's name. I'm here to tell you those boys were tough. During one of the rodeos the school had, one of the boys came out of the bucking chutes on the meanest horse God ever made and rode him into the ground. After the 8-second whistle, he just swung off that ol' horse and was walking right in front of where I was sitting in the bleachers. He had a big grin on his face from the good ride he had just made, and blood was coming out of his ears and his nose and he thought nothing of it. As I said, those boys were tough.

While I was winding my way through college and the Air ROTC, Dad still worked our ranch and the Circle C ranch over near Brodie Lane that he had leased. My folks and the Coverts, that's Polly and Clarence Covert, were big buddies and saw each other all the time. Clarence was from the Covert Buick family in Austin and of course, Polly was from the Yates family group of West Texas and she owned the Circle C ranch that Dad was leasing.

In the early '50s, when the major Texas drought was just starting and the grass was beginning to fail and be burned up, Dad hit upon the idea to buy a little farm down toward Kyle where we could grow hay for our livestock. Now only 7 miles separated our two places, and how Dad figured it was going to rain more there than it did on our home place has never been that clear to me. Since he had already used up the fortune that was going to last forever that we'd gotten from the Pat Rutherford ranch sale, Dad had, of course, borrowed the money from the Schlemmers at the Kyle Bank to buy the farm.

In the spring of '54, I graduated from SWT and entered the Air Force that summer to begin my three years duty and my flight training. I was stationed first at Bartow, Florida, at the airbase there. It just so happen that the Maxeys lived in nearby Frostproof, Florida, and that's where Dad had bought some steers in 1953 to ship to Kyle. I don't remember how they all met. Gil had been in the Air Force earlier and had been stationed, I think in Georgia. Since we knew the Maxeys from earlier times, Gil had gotten to know them too, and started dating one of their daughters, Laura Jean Maxey. So in the winter of '55, February, I think, Gil and Jeanie got married at Frostproof. I believe it was the day or so after I had graduated from my class at Bartow, so it was very convenient to be able to attend. Many folks from Austin, including Bob and Verna Mae Morrison, were there.

I was then stationed in San Angelo, Texas, at Goodfellow Airforce Base where I completed my flight training in one of the last classes of B-25s, a WWII medium bomber. I was in the Class of 55-T. From there I was stationed at Lockbourne AFB, near Columbus, Ohio, through all of 1955 until the summer of 1956.

It was at this time that our old neighbor, Max Michaelis, was up from his Mexican Ranch visiting his wife and family at their Kyle ranch. He ran into Dad and told him about an adjoining ranch in Mexico that could be bought and why didn't Dad call Lat Maxey in Florida and they all go down and look at it. Well, Dad did and Lat Maxey flew up immediately and they all flew down to the Mexican ranch in Michaelis's airplane. They spent a few days at the Michaelis "El Fortin" ranch and were able not only to inspect the "Sierra Hermosa" as the ranch was called, but bought it while they were

Marshall E. Kuykendall
Bartow AFB, Bartow, Florida, Fall 1954

MEK graduation class of 55-T, Goodfellow AFB, San Angelo, Texas, August 1955. MEK is standing eleventh from the left

there. The ranch was and is fabulous. It had approximately 90,000 acres of valley, with the east and west fence lines being the top hogback of the big mountain range. There were four house groups on the ranch, one being the main headquarters and the other three being line shacks or houses for cowboys and their families. It also had a 5,000 foot airstrip and a rock hangar large enough to house two DC-3s, which the Mexican owner had. In the hangar at the time were two stage coaches, one a town coach with crystal glass windows and one an open coach, just like a Wells Fargo coach in the movies. The ranch had about 1,100 grown highland Hereford cattle and 200 Thoroughbred horses. It also had $10,000 cash in the Bank at Muzquiz, Coahuila. Dad and Lat bought the ranch for about $3.50 per acre, lock, stock and barrel and got the $10,000 in the bank. Those were the old days when one could still buy a fine ranch in Mexico for about one and a half times the value of the cattle on the ranch. In other words, one could inventory the cattle, add a fraction to their market value, and that was what the ranch was worth in 1956. And the hired hands went with it. Dad and Alice immediately moved to the Mexican ranch.

I was stationed at Lockbourne AFB when I got word they had bought the ranch. I came home on Christmas leave that winter and was able to fly down and see it for myself. I always thought it looked like a John Wayne movie set, it was so fine. It's hard to imagine going from a 1,500 acre ranch in central Texas to a 90,000 acre ranch in Heaven.

It was during this time period that Dad and Alice were up at the Kyle ranch for something and while there, attended a party in Austin at the Country Club. It turns out the commander of the base at Bergstrom, General Clarence Edmonson, was at the same party. Everybody was having a gay time and as the whiskey flowed, someone mentioned to the fine general, that Bill Kuykendall's son was an officer in the Air Force, and why in the world didn't the general have this splendid young officer working for him at Bergstrom AFB. About six weeks later I was stationed at Bergstrom. Miracles and politics happen. I spent the next year until I mustered out in July 1957, working for this fine man. He is another story. Full Bird Colonel at age 29, flying P-38s over Germany in 1944 and 1945. He was a Tiger. God, I loved him.

When I got out of the AF, my dear Aunt Marion sent me to Europe for six weeks. She wanted to be sure if I was to become a heathen in Mexico, that at least I would be a well educated and traveled one. As soon as I got home I immediately went to the ranch in Mexico. With my record as a pilot, I became the pilot and handyman cowboy for the Rancho Sierra Hermosa. The only thing I needed to learn was how to land an airship on those little, bitty short landing strips in Mexico. Our strip was good—great approach, 5,000 feet and all that, but the Michaelis strip was about 2,100 feet and you

Marshall E. Kuykendall
Sierra Hermosa Ranch, Coahuila, Mexico, 1956

had to set it down about eight feet inside the fence and get it to stop before you ran out of runway and brains at the same time. It took me solid year to learn how to do it. And in the meantime, I scared everybody who rode with me.

When I went to Europe in 1957, I spent several nights with John Henry Faulk and his wife, Lynn. So later, on one of my trips from the Mexican ranch to Austin, we found out John Henry was in town. We invited him to accompany me back to the Mexican ranch. It was during this time that I met the beautiful aspiring actress, Karen Koock, just home from summer stock in Vermont. I thought she was a really fine looking woman but at the time she thought I was just some cowboy hick from the sticks and she had her mind made up to go back to New York. I think her mother locked her in a closet at Green Pastures (in south Austin) until she would agree to at least be pleasant to this cowboy and remember her manners. Well, she was kind to yours truly and one thing led to another and we were later married. Then I did the worst thing you can do to a beautiful bride who wishes to live in New York. I hauled her to the Mexican Ranch so she could live real close and slightly downhill from my two crazy parents.

By the summer of 1960, my relationship with my crazy father hit a low point of all low times when I was attempting to start a Fairbanks Morse engine one day so we could get our 45 mile water pipeline flowing. Dad was showing the system to someone who had flown into the ranch and I was getting ready to start it all to show them. The old single cylinder engine needed to be hand cranked and after about two cranks, the engine backfired and jerked the crank out of my hand. That crank is loose on the wheel and if it backfired and then flew off at 900 miles per hour, it could kill every body from there to Muzquiz. I don't know what made me do it, but the instant it backfired and blew out of my hand, I slapped at it and some how managed to grab the crank and jerk it off the fly wheel. I was damn lucky. There was nothing wrong with anything I did, but in a very typical Bill Kuykendall fashion, Dad started cussing and doing a little dance out in front of our guest and saying just how dumb I was. The one thing Dad was good at was humiliating you in

Marshall E. Kuykendall in Mexico

the front as many people as he could. He had done that all of my life. I guess after all those years I had had enough. I was nearly 30 years old, I was married, I was responsible, but I was living on *his* ranch and *downhill* from the big house. And I was about to pay the price for insubordination. When he stopped cussing me, I walked toward him and I still had the crank in my hand. I wasn't going to hit him with it, but as I got close to him, I said in a very clear voice that he could and should stick that crank up his butt where the sun would not shine on it. Of course, I said this in front of our guest. Now it's all right for a father to humiliate his children in front of others but it is not all right for them to do it to him. That was one of the lowest points in our relationship and there were many, but that one ended in John Wayne fashion.

Marshall E. Kuykendall in Mexico

I went back to my house and told Karen that we were finished on the ranch. The next morning after having slept on it and I'm sure, conferring with Alice, Dad drove his Jeep down to our house and asked me to come outside. There he very solemly told me that I would have to leave the ranch, that the 90,000 acres was not big enough for the two of us. Karen and I packed up all our belongings and made about five trips by plane to our Kyle ranch and that was the end of my tenure in Mexico. I was and still am heartbroken over not being able to live there any more. Under normal circumstances or abnormal circumstances, I would have never left the ranch nor Mexico. But Bill Kuykendall was too much.

In late 1961, one of the neighbors, Alden McKeller, who ranched over near Muzquiz, flew into the Mexican ranch and told Dad that he knew some folks in Laredo who would buy the ranch if Dad wanted to sell it. Alden told Dad he would like to be paid a $10,000 commission if Dad decided to do it Dad told him he'd think about it.

Shortly thereafter, Dad got real sick with his first bout of stomach cancer. Dr. Raleigh Ross operated on him and he was in Brackenridge Hospital for a while. I went up to visit him and as usual did everything I could to convince him to let me go back down and run the ranch. Dad was 61 years old and I was 30. My proposition to him was simple. I'll live on the Mexican ranch and run it and he would live on the Kyle ranch and run it. He could come down once a month and bring his list of things for me to do. While there, he could scream his head off at me, call me all the bad names he could think of and then leave and come back the next month with a new list of things to do, and we'd start all over. That way at least I wouldn't have to listen to him every day like I'd done all my life. We both got a little chuckle out of my proposition, but I was deadly serious. He said he might just agree to it. The door knob to his room hadn't closed behind me before he was calling Alden McKeller at his home in Rositas to tell him he'd agree to sell to the Laredo folks. Dad and Lat met later in Laredo, Texas, with the buyers, Radcliff Killam and John Hurd. They closed the deal shortly thereafter.

I did not mention that while the folks owned the ranch, it was the social thing to do to have everyone from Austin come down for visits. It was great! Anyone who could wrangle up an airplane was welcome. They came in droves. One of Dad's best buddies was Cactus Pryor from Austin. Cactus came down on numerous occasions and he and Dad remained good friends until Dad died.

I need to tell you the story about Dad's airplane adventure. Now remember, Dad was extremely competitive. The reason he never would teach me how to rope, bulldog or anything like that was because he couldn't stand it if I could do something he couldn't do. Or maybe yet, do something better than he could. It was one thing for Gil to be sent away and then get his degree in something that kept him off of the ranch and, therefore not in competition with his Dad. But, not me, I always wanted to be rancher, and therein lay the rub. I went to college and got a degree in range management. Dad never would admit it but it really chapped his butt when I would suggest some new ideas on how to run *his* ranch. Well, guess what, I had gone through flying school and I could fly and *he* couldn't. That really got to him, so somewhere in the scheme of things, Dad went to Austin and bought a Cessna 172 from Bobby Ragsdale. I was still at Bergstrom during this time.

Anyway, Dad drives out to the airport with his boots and spurs on and buys himself a Cessna 172 from Bobby. Writes him a check like "white folks" are supposed to do. Gets Bobby to get him an instructor, tells the instructor to get in *his* airplane, and off they go. And the story goes, after several days and about 7.5 hours of flying, Dad gets where he can at least find the airport. The instructor mistakenly gets out of the airplane and tells Dad to shoot a landing by himself. Somehow Dad takes off, makes it around the airport and lands it again without killing everyone all the way to Kyle. He opens the window to the side of the airplane, thanks the instructor for a job well done, jams the throttle forward and goes crow-hopping down the runway, spurring the damn thing at every jump just like an old bronco and flew the airplane all the way to the ranch in Mexico. Bobby Ragsdale told me later that he didn't see Dad again until he had nearly 200 hours on the airplane, all on a "student ticket." You've got to admit, the old man had "huevos"!

Dad and mother retired back to the Kyle ranch in 1962. Dad had built a lake on Potter Creek and he spent his last years down there fishing and shooting everything that crawled, loped, and swam. I always laughed about the lake and told all my friends who wished to swim there to be sure and wear their best steel bottomed shoes 'cause Dad would throw his beer bottles out in the lake and shoot them. So I'm positive that the bottom of that lake has about four feet of broken beer bottles in it.

Dad got into trapping coons and any other creature that would stick its nose in one of his live traps. He would then shoot them and hang them on the fence along the Hwy 150 for all his neighbors to see. Since it was the '60s that particular highway got its share of the wonderful flower children from the University of Texas nearby.

Sunday or weekend drivers would ventured out into the beautiful Texas Hill Country to get a glimpse of the great scenery and a whiff of the fragrances of nature. Then just as they were really getting into the wonders of nature, they would venture upon Dad's 300 yards of dead coons, possums, skunks, etc., that if downwind, the stench would have made the hair slip on a Grizzly Bear.

So, as luck will have it, Dad was out cruising one day in his trusty Ford Bronco and as he turned the corner on Hwy 150 to head down toward his stash, he noticed a flowered Volkswagon parked near his trophies. When he got up near them, there was a scraggly haired old hippie boy with two girls in their typical long skirts made out of flour sacks and their hair, of course, in braids, out near the fence. To hear Dad tell the story, they were howling and wailing about the fate of these poor defenseless animals when he drove up. Now Dad always carried an arsenal of weapons in his truck. He figured he'd better be ready in case an army of coons attacked him because of his evil ways. He had his .22 Magnum rifle, his 12-gauge shotgun and his .38 pistol and .22 Magnum pistol. One couldn't be overarmed. Dad drove right up to those crazies just as they were *really* getting into their wailing and carrying on, stepped out of his truck, and let fly in the air with his trusty .38 pistol. As he touched off the round, he let out a yell something like; "Whatthehelldoyouthinkyouaredoinghere?" Or something to that effect.

Well, to hear Dad tell it, the hippies simply exploded with fright, and broke to run for the flowered van, thinking that the very devil himself had suddenly appeared, knocking off big chunks of hair, skin, bone, flour-sack dresses, and Volkswagon paint as they dove into their van. They went screeching off into the sunset and made my father's life a lot happier because of it. He loved it.

Dad developed stomach cancer about 1975. Dr. Raleigh Ross operated on him a couple of times. The last time, he simply closed him back up and told Alice there was nothing else he could do, that the cancer had consumed Dad's stomach. Dad died two days before my birthday on October 11, 1976. He had been at home until the end and was only in the hospital a few days. Just before he died, Raleigh came down the hall and told us he was going quickly but he was lucid for a bit if we wanted to see him. I went in and he woke enough to know who I was. I looked at him for moment and then asked him; "Ol' man, when you die, where do think you'll end up?" He answered,; "In a pile of cow manure!" I walked out of his room and he died a few minutes later. We buried him on my birthday in the Kuykendall plot in the Kyle Cemetery at Kyle, Texas.

Interestingly, his lifelong friend, Max Michaelis, died the same day on his ranch in Mexico. A crazy, wild era had ended.

The day after we buried Dad, some of the good ol' boys from the neighborhood stopped on the highway in front of his ranch house in broad daylight and killed all eight or ten of his big, trophy Mufflon sheep with a .22 rifle. They did it out of meanness. I guess it was payback time for Dad not letting someone on the Kuykendall ranch. They sure as hell didn't have the guts to do it when he was alive.

Alice stayed out at the ranch for a while, then she moved into Westminster Manor in Austin, where she lived until she died of pancreatic cancer in 1993. Mother told me after Dad died that he had been a difficult husband and a poor father. By the time she died, he had improved.

Alice Hamlett Kuykendall was born in Temple, Texas, on 27 October 1910 to

Alice Forbes (Faye) Early and William A. Hamlett. Her parents graduated from Baylor University in 1896 and were married the day after their graduation. Dr. Hamlett was a well-known Baptist minister, who later became pastor of the First Baptist Church of Austin when it was situated directly in front of the Governor's mansion. While in Austin, they lived on Washington Square. In 1913 Dr. Hamlett sold out in Austin and moved his entire family to the Holy Land, wanting to preach there and practice his ministry. His efforts were tharted, however, because the Holy Land was a British Protectorate and the Brits denied them entry. They moved back to Austin. As mentioned earlier, Alice's grandfather, her mother's father, was Marshall Daniel Early, a prominent and renowned Baptist minister from Arkansas.

Alice contracted cancer in the summer of 1993 and died at Seton Hospital in Austin, Texas, on 27 August 1993. She is buried in the Kuykendall grave plot in the Kyle Cemetery at Kyle, Hays County, Texas.

Interestingly, I did not get an obituary of my father.

As mentioned, two sons were born to this union, Robert G. (Gil) Kuykendall, 26 June 1929 and Marshall Early Kuykendall, 13 October, 1932. Gil married Laura Jean Maxey of Florida in 1955 and four children were born to this union: Kirk, Laura, Maxey, and Wylie. My marriage to Karen Koock Kuykendall resulted in three children: Marshall Jr., Mary Alice, and Sarita.

So ends the story of Bill Kuykendall. If you have a better one, you can tell your own!

Alice and Bill, ca 1948

Maggie M. Kuykendall
1871-1950

Marion Kuykendall Taylor
1895-1973

Little Marion K. Hoskins
1920-1936
Dorothy K. Hoskins
1895-1986

KUYKENDALL 101 RANCH MAUSOLEUM

IN 1902 MAGGIE MOORE KUYKENDALL AND HER HUSBAND ROBERT GILL KUYKENDALL OF THE 101 RANCH IN MATAGORDA COUNTY BOUGHT 11,073 ACRES IN HAYS COUNTY, ESTABLISHING A RANCH BY THE SAME NAME. WHEN GILL DIED IN 1905, SHE AND FOREMAN JOE CRUZE RAN THE RANCH UNTIL IT WAS DIVIDED AMONG HER CHILDREN IN 1933. THE MAUSOLEUM WAS BUILT IN 1925. MAGGIE'S NINE-YEAR-OLD GRANDDAUGHTER, MARION HOSKINS, WAS INTERRED HERE IN 1936, AND MAGGIE WAS LAID TO REST NEXT TO HER IN 1950. A SECTION WAS ADDED IN 1973 FOR MAGGIE'S DAUGHTER, MARION KUYKENDALL TAYLOR. THE ASHES OF DOROTHY KUYKENDALL HOSKINS, LITTLE MARION'S MOTHER, WERE SPREAD ON THIS SITE IN 1986.

HISTORIC TEXAS CEMETERY 2006

HISTORIC DEDICATION
SATURDAY
15 JUNE 2002

Welcome to the dedication of the Kuykendall 101 Ranch Mausoleum and the unveiling of the Historic Texas Cemetery plaque placed on that location. This Historic marker was placed here in memory of the Pioneer Rancher **Margaret Martha (Maggie) Moore Kuykendall** and her children and grandchildren who are buried with her. Miss Maggie, as she was called by all who knew her, kept this ranch intact after the untimely death of her husband, Gill, in 1905. It was the largest operating ranch in Hays County until the end of the century, owned in the later years by the Rutherford family. Maggie's father, Captain Will Moore, was a prominent cattle buyer, Confederate Veteran, store keeper, and postmaster of the village of Ashby, Matagorda County, Texas. Will Moore served in Company K of the famous "Terry's Texas Rangers". Her father-in-law, Wiley Martin Kuykendall, was the grandson of Captain Robert H. Kuykendall, one of Stephen F. Austin's original members of the "Old 300". Wiley M. Kuykendall was married to Susan Pierce, A.H. (Shanghai) Pierce's sister, and was trail boss for many years of the Pierce's "Rancho Grande" ranch in Matagorda County, Texas. Wiley M. Kuykendall was a Confederate Veteran having served in "Yager's 3rd Mounted Texas Cavalry". He went "up the trail" 11 times trailing longhorns to Dodge City and points north after the Civil War. Maggie's grandfather, Robert Baxter Moore, was one of the founders of Old Indianola, Texas, one of the greatest seaport towns in Texas. He was killed in the great storm of the 16th of September 1875, when the town of Indianola was destroyed. It is in this memory that this Historic Plaque is dedicated.

MEK as a young man on the 101 Ranch.

Chapter Eleven

Marshall Early Kuykendall
13 October 1932

Most of my early stories of my life are contained in the biography on my father. My first marriage was to Mary Karen Koock of Green Pastures and South Austin, Texas. To that union were born three children: Marshall Jr, born on 28 December 1960; Mary Alice, born on 20 April 1962, and Sarita, born on 8 May 1963. I have to admit a certain irony to most of these dates. My family has been lifelong friends of the Robinson family of Austin and Austin White Lime. Mama Al Robinson was born on 20 April and George (Bo) Robinson's first daughter was born on 8 May. Life will play tricks on you if you are not alert.

In the early naming patterns of America, one did not name a son after himself until several children were born. I hope having the affliction of my particular name will not hinder my son from his life's purpose. Naming Mary Alice after her two grandmothers was an easy choice. Both Alice Kuykendall and Mary Faulk Koock were amazing women. Now Sarita is a different matter. She is not named for Sarita Kennedy and/or Sarita, Texas, but she is named after Sarita Burton, the daughter of Courtney Burton, the fine gentleman polo player from Gates Mills, Ohio, who in 1937 sent his daughter Sarita and her German governess to be our guest at the Kuykendall 101 ranch at Buda, Texas. I never forgot her name. With such a fine name as Sarita, one does not need a middle name.

Marshall Jr. is married to Margaret Williams of Dallas, Texas. She is the daughter of Jim and Lois Williams of Highland Park. To that union were born two children: Wylie Williams, 2 September 1993, and Jennie Alice, 6 May 1996.

Mary Alice is married to Jerry Naiser of Baytown, Texas, and they reside in

Austin. To that union were born Haley Nichole, 11 September 1995, and Catherine Ann, born 6 April 1998.

Sarita is married to Chris Corona of Austin, Texas, and she has two stepchildren, Chase Jerome, born 3 March 1993, and Myles Cristopher, born 14 June 1995.

I went to high school in Kyle and played six-man football. I then attended Sul Ross College and South West Texas at San Marcos. I entered the air force in the summer of 1954 as a second lieutenant and went through flying school in Bartow, Florida, in AT-6s and Goodfellow Air Force Base at San Angelo, Texas, in one of the last classes of B-25s. I left the air force in 1957 and went down to join my folks on their ranch in Mexico just west of Muzquiz, Coahuila. I left there in 1960 and moved back to Austin, where I joined the Joe Crow Real Estate Company on West 6th Street where we opened a ranch real estate department in that firm. I obtained my real estate license in August 1960. I have been active in ranch real estate from that day to this, some 44 years of busting through the brush of some fine ranch property from Austin, Texas, to the Big Bend. I have looked at just about every ranch that ever came on the market from Austin to Silver City, New Mexico, over the years. However, as I have now "gotten longer in the tooth," I no longer venture so far from our lovely home near Driftwood, Texas.

I married Karen Koock in September 1959. We were divorced in 1974. In 1985 I married Betty Richardson Mielcarek of McAllen, Texas. She is a valley native, born in Alice, Texas, to Jay and Maria Salazar Richardson.

In 1993, in concert with several ranch real estate brokers, we formed the Texas Land Brokers Association and I was elected its first president. We started with five or six folks and now have over 200 active members.

Take Back Texas leaders Phil Savoy and Robert Kleeman on the left of Lt. Gov. Bob Bullock, and Marshall Kuykendall and T. J. Higginbotham on the right.

In 1994, when the local Austin radical environmental community started to cause tremendous trouble for private property owners in the Texas Hill Country, several of us formed Take Back Texas, and again, I was asked to be its president.

Marshall Kuykendall with Gov. George Bush in Waco

I have always been aware that we were an old Texas family with deep frontier and ranching roots. My parents, however, had no interest whatsoever in finding out about any of their ancestors as I did. One of the books in my library is authored by Colonel Cleland Early, one of my distant cousins, and it is dedicated to his father where he states: "Dedication to my father, Jacob Edward Early (1884-1982), who lived 98 years without knowing a grandparent, an uncle, aunt or cousin or from whence they came." And as my father would have said, "And didn't give a damn."

Marshall Kuykendall with Susan Combs and Governor Bush in Waco

Some twenty or thirty years ago, my interest in my family and its history took me to the Texas State Genealogical Library just east of the capitol building in the Lorenzo D. Zavala building. This building houses two of our fine research libraries in Austin, Texas, the State Genealogical Library and the State Library. The latter library contains all the records on any individuals who ever worked for and were paid by State of Texas.

I ventured into the Genealogical Library and asked the assistant if there was any information on the Kuykendalls. David, who has been there for many years, replied

Left to right, back row: Betty Kuykendall, Marshall Kuykendall, Gov. Rick Perry, Sarita Kuykendall, Marshall Kuykendall Jr, Front row: Jenny and Wylie Kuykendall.

Left to right, back row: Chris Corona; Sarita; Mary Alice holding Catherine; Kimberley Mielcarek; and Jerry Naiser. Seated: Wylie Kuykendall; Matthew Mielcarek; Betty; Marshall; Marshall Jr. with Jenny; Margaret. Front row on ground: Myles Corona; Haley Naiser; and Chase Corona.

that there was considerable information there and he just happened to have a pamphlet written by one of my cousins from Glen Flora, Texas. And, he asked, would I like to have it copied for 50 cents. It was two or three pages in length and was the story of Capt. Robert H. Kuykendall of Austin's Old 300 and his descendants. I reviewed it with with great interest and noticed that the last name on the last page was the name of my father. Well, needless to say, I was hooked forever. As my children will now tell all who will listen, "Do not bring up Texas history in front of Dad or the evening will be ruined forever and we will never get another word in edgewise." They are joking, of course.

Therefore, I am setting down all these stories and histories for several reasons. One, to satisfy my own curiosity about these amazing familes and two, to put my information into print where my family or others might be able to enjoy this information without having to crawl under my bed when I get to be 98 years old, looking for the old battered cardboard box full of all my stuff. And, I guess, three, would be that I am the last person to know who a bunch of these folks are or were and which picture is which and I'd better get into a publication before it is lost forever. Maybe my work will send you over to your grandmother's house to ask her what happened back in '06 so you won't have lost so much valuable history like I did early on in my life.

Marshall E. Kuykendall's 70th Birthday, 13 October 2002
Margaret, Marshall Jr., Kimberly Mielcarek, Marshall, Betty, Jerry Naiser, Mary Alice, Chris Corona, Sarita, Matthew Mielcarek. Photo taken at Matt's El Rancho in Austin.

Bill Hamlett, Karen Kuykendall, Mary Alice K. Naiser, and John Hamlett.

Darrell Royal and Marshall E. Kuykendall, 2000

MEK with Agricultural Commissioner Susan Combs, 2002

The Biographies

—ALLIED—

Will Moore, ca 1865

Chapter Twelve

William Erastus Moore

William E. (Will) Moore (1837-1902), pioneer Texas cattleman, was always known as Will Moore. He was born in Rahway, New Jersey, on 26 October 1837, the son of Robert Baxter Moore (b. Elisabeth, Union County, New Jersey, 11 April 1807; d. Indianola, Calhoun County, Texas, 16 September 1875) and Mary Crowell Layton[1] (b. Woodbridge, New Jersey, 10 January 1812; d. Ashby, Matagorda County, Texas, 12 April 1896). His father was of Scotch-Irish descent while his mother was French on her father's side and English on her mother's side. His great-grandfather on his mother's side was Christopher Marsh, who served in the American Revolution as a lieutenant in Captain Blanchard's troop of Lighthorse, Essex County, New Jersey. He was later commissioned a captain of the same troop.[2]

In this family seven children were born:

1. Joseph Layton—b. New York City, 11 April 1833.
2. William Erastus, b. Rahway, New Jersey, 25 October 1837.
3. Eudora Inez, b. Victoria County, Texas, 17 November 1847.
4. Spencer C., b. Indianola, Texas, 3 February 1850.
5. Adolph P., b. Indianola, Texas, 6 October 1852.
6. Robert Baxter Jr., b. Indianola, Texas, 23 July 1854.
7. Henry Edgar, b. Indianola, Texas, 21 December 1857.[3]

Will Moore started his education in Mobile, Alabama at five years of age, in the public schools of that city, and continued there until the family moved to the Republic of Texas. He was about thirteen years of age when the family moved to Indianola and he attended school in "Old Town," as the upper part of Indianola was called. The school was three miles away and across the bayou from his home and when the tide was high, Will would paddle across in a small skiff. His teachers of those years were Dr. Lewis, Professor Glass and Mrs. McFarlane.[4]

When Will was about sixteen years of age, he went hunting with some of his friends on Powderhorn Lake. They crossed in his skiff and as they were crossing, one of the boys tried to take his gun out from under one of the seats. The trigger caught on something and the weapon discharged, striking Will in the left side, just under his arm. He was badly powder-burned and filled with bird shot. It was a very close call, since the wound was so close to his heart. Dr. David Lewis dressed the wound and Will survived the ordeal.[5]

Mary Crowell Layton and Robert Baxter Moore, ca 1865

Will's father, R. B. Moore, moved from Victoria, and purchased a sizable tract of land from the Howerton brothers that was situated on the western part of the island. This purchase was made on 3 October 1848. The land was partially bound on the north by the lake, on the west and south by a bayou flowing from the lake and connecting with Powderhorn Lake on the east. His father built their home on a slight ridge fronting on the lake shore. There was a great deal of brush growing on this land which had to be cleared away to make room for a garden. The brush was used for fencing. When the family first moved to Indianola, there were only three or four houses. A Mr. Swartz, who had moved there from Galveston in 1844, built the first house. An old man by the name of Carrol built another house on the bayou, but he only lived there a short time before he died. Mr. Swartz and a man by the name of John Henry Brown buried him. Soon afterwards, Prince Carles de Solms arrived from Germany and also built a house there in anticipation of his emigrant friends arriving from Germany. The prince always tried to make as much display as possible and he would ride about town with long feathers in his hat.[6]

The land that Will's father bought was on the west side of Matagorda Bay, in Calhoun County, near a place called "Carles Haven." The senior Mr. Moore was a mechanic (builder) and contractor. He built and owned many rent houses in town until the great storm of 1875 when all was lost and Mr. Moore was killed. Since he was a trained mechanic and builder, he had a great part in building much of the original town of Indianola. That was his primary reason for moving from Victoria in the first place.[7]

Soldiers from the United States being sent inland to the frontier were landed in Indianola and emigrants from Europe arrived by the scores. Large quantities of merchandise for the interior towns and goods for the army posts were also landed there and shipped out by wagon to their respective destinations. Silver bullion brought up from Mexico in wagons and ox carts was shipped out of the new port built there destined for the U.S. Mint in New Orleans. Passengers came and went daily by stagecoach and in 1859, the "Western & Pacific Railway" built a line from Indianola to Victoria. It was later extended to Cuero, Texas.[8]

Mr. Dick Riener was the first photographer in town. His first pictures were daguerreotypes. He photographed the entire Moore family, but all the pictures were lost in the storm of 1875.[9]

Yellow fever and cholera was always a problem and in 1852 they both broke out and hundreds died from the dreadful epidemic. No words are adequate to describe the horrors of the time. There was no means for sanitation, few doctors, no trained nurses and little or no medicine. Will's brother Joe was stricken with the disease but somehow survived.[10]

Will's younger sister, Eudora Inez, known as "Dora" or "Aunt Doaty," wrote all the stories noted above. These are contained in her diaries and her "Recollections of Indianola" later printed in the *Wharton Spectator* and the *Bay City Tribune*. These and other of her writings were printed in the "Indianola Scrapbook" by the *Victoria Advocate* in 1936 as a Centennial project. Some of her stories were later used in a book titled, *Texas Tears and Texas Sunshine* that was published in 1985 by Jo Ella Powell Exley of Katy, Texas.[11]

Will Moore left school at the age of seventeen and was employed by the Hatch Bros. of Calhoun County as a cowboy. He started his career gathering and shipping cattle. In the fall of 1857, he was employed by James M. Foster, one of the pioneer cattlemen of that time. Before the Civil War and before the great trail drives started, most cattle gathered on the coastal plain at that time were trailed into Indianola to be shipped out to sea on ships. Indianola was the greatest port in Texas until the great storm of '75. Jim Foster was well known in cowman circles of south Texas and for years he had a monopoly on all cattle shipped by the Morgan Line out of Indianola. Will Moore was known as one of his able lieutenants. Will's wages for his first three months of employment was $15 per month. Many a young man got his start in the cattle business on the prairies around Indianola in those days, as did Will's friend Charles A. Siringo.

On the first day of January 1858, Will's wages were raised to $1 per day and he was furnished horses out of the company remuda to ride. He was then sent with a nephew of Mr. Foster's, Joe Collins, to assist in driving cattle from the western part of the state. On this trip, they were scheduled to gather 500 head of picked steers from the famous ranch of Thomas O'Connor of Victoria, and it was then that Will first experienced lavish hospitality from one of the early Cattle Kings of Texas. Upon arriving at the ranch, they found Mr. O'Connor just getting over an attack of fever, and they were compelled to wait several days until he recovered sufficiently to attend to their transaction. It may be thought that those days of waiting were boring, but Will stated that his entertainment there surpassed anything that it ever was his good fortune to participate in. He said that he had never forgotten the big "dun" calf Mr. O'Connor had killed, cooked and fed them at Foxes Ranch on Mellon Creek. He stated that it was the sweetest meat he ever ate.[12]

In the summer of 1859, Will was again with Collins up along the Brazos River, buying and shipping cattle from Harrisburg. He referred to one of the trips taken to that area as especially worthy of note. Among the herds purchased at that time, was one herd acquired from a man named Can Greer. Will tells the story:

> We were to have pick of the herd, which Collins considered the choicest of the area. Greer was dissatisfied and said we were leaving better steers than we were taking. Collins was an excellent judge of cattle and he replied that we had selected some "cows" that would outweigh any steers that were left in the herd. Mr. Greer was a man of "sporting proclivities" and at once offered to wager his best horse, a famous race horse named Bay Dick, which many stockmen of south Texas remember, against the horse Collins was riding, if his best steer didn't outweigh the cow that Collins had cut out. The bet was promptly accepted, and when the cow and steer were dressed out, the cow netted 619 lbs and the steer netted only 573 lbs.

The cow sold for $10 and the two boys went on their way laughing, and taking with them the famous race horse. After this, Will remained in the Harrisburg area for some time and shipped many herds from that place.[13]

In the fall of 1860, Foster & Co. was dissolved and the Collins Bros. started buying and shipping on their own and they employed Will to work for them. He remained with them until April of 1861, when all the gulf ports were blockaded by "Yankee Squadrons" and a stop was put to shipping any more cattle by sea.[14]

When the Civil War broke out, Will's sympathies were with the South's cause, notwithstanding the fact that he had been born in the north. He and several others went to Matamoros, Mexico, for a 4-horse wagon load of black powder for use at Fort Esperansa. On his return, when he had gotten as far as San Patricio (August 1864), he found a letter waiting for him there from James Collins informing him that several of the boys were getting ready to start for the war in Virginia and asked Will to join them. Will left immediately and made the ride to Indianola in two days and found the boys ready to leave.[15]

Benjamin Franklin Terry and Thomas S. Lubbock had been at the First Battle of Manassas on 21 July 1861. After the battle, they hurried home to call for volunteers with the desire to form their own regiments. It was to this call to fight that the boys were responding.[16]

Those first men joining from Indianola were James and Joseph Collins, Hays Yarrington, John Coates, Dan Hoffman, and Will E. Moore.[17]

Will joined Company "K" of the 8th Texas Cavalry, better known as "Terry's Texas Rangers." The Company was composed of some 2,000 men under Capt. S. P. Christian. The date Will joined was 17 September 1861.[18]

Colonel Augustus Buchel of Indianola also raised a Regiment of Cavalry. Will's brother Joseph Layton was a member of that outfit as was Abel H. (Shanghai) Pierce, his brother John E. Pierce and Wylie M. Kuykendall. These men were from the Demings Bridge area of Matagorda County.[19]

Confederate records of Will Moore in Company K, the 8th Texas Cavalry.

When Will's regiment was first formed, the boys had expected to be sent to Virginia, but were sent instead to Bowling Green, Kentucky, where the regiment was fully formed and made operational. In the very first battle the regiment was involved in, they lost their famous leader and commander, Gen. Benjamin F. Terry. This was at Woodsboro, Kentucky. When General Zollicoffer was killed at "Fishing Creek," Will was with the party sent under a flag of truce to recover the body.[20]

Will had four horses killed out from under him during the war. One of them held his head up very high, a fact which saved Will's life when a bullet struck the horse between the eyes, the bullet having been meant for Will.[21]

Will was dangerously wounded at Murfreesboro, Tennessee, in July 1862, when he was shot completely through the body. He was taken to a nearby plantation and left for dead, however, an old Negro man took charge of him and he survived. He was later moved to a home in the area. While convalescing, the lady of the plantation sent him some of her husband's clothes to wear. He was so impatient to rejoin his unit that he left before his wound had completely healed. It broke open again later, but he stayed with his company and refused a discharge on account of it. One of the records state that he was shot through the hip and that the ball was removed some years later before his death and that he was never disabled because of it.[22]

Will had participated in the battles of Wootsonville, Shiloh, and Murfreesboro (where he was wounded) and he rejoined his company in November 1862 in time to participate in the battle of Stone River.[23]

His old comrade, Hays Yarrington wrote:

> We went out and served together until my capture at Nashville just three weeks before the end of the war. He (Will) was dangerously wounded near Murfreesboro on July, 13, 1862. I got him to a place of safety. The tide of battle was against us and we moved from there to McMinnville via Woodbury. He was a brave and efficient soldier and very popular with the regiment.[24]

Will was promoted from private to sergeant in December 1863 and the records state he fought with the regiment through 29 February 1864, where on the last record roll that is on file, dated above, he was reported "present."

The records reflect that he had joined for the duration of the war and was sworn in by then lieutenant, later Captain J. W. Sparks. His paymaster for those early periods was Major Davis and Captain Botts. Later in 1863 and 1864, his paymaster in Company K was Captain Bartholomew. Remarks shown on his file in the Texas State Archives state:

Name & Rank:	Moore, W. E. Pvt.
Comm. Off:	Walker, John G., Capt.
Organ:	Co. K, Terry's Texas Rangers, 8th Cav.
Elist:	Sept. -61
Disch	Descrip:
Remarks:	R&F 130; Wounded at Murfreesboro, A splended soldier.[25]

After April 1865, Will transferred over to the Shannon Scouts, and was with that unit until the end of the war on scouting duty. Alexander Shannon, his commander, was later to become the postmaster at Galveston, Texas.[26]

In the early part of 1864, all available Texas troops had been ordered from Texas into Louisiana. At the battles of Mansfield and Pleasant Hill, many Texas boys lost their lives. Col. Augustus Buchel was mortally wounded while leading his regiment, the "Texas," in the charge at Pleasant Hill.[27]

Will's brother, Joseph, was badly wounded in the same battle and died shortly thereafter near Alexandria, Louisiana.[28]

In the early part of the war when it was evident that Indianola was to be captured by the federals, Colonel Van Dorn ordered all the wharfs and railroad bridges burned. The bridge over the bayou was spared because it led to the cemetery. While the federals were in town, some rebel youths gathered up on the prairie west of town. A regiment of the Yankees with cannon went out and fired several rounds at them. This may have given rise to the statement about a battle having been fought in the streets of Indianola.[29]

Will returned home in August 1865, in the company of friends that he had left with four years earlier. He came through New Orleans and had to pawn his gold pocketwatch in order to get the money to make passage to Galveston, and on to his home. He got home without a cent in his pocket. He found all his family well, but entirely destitute of money, horses or cattle, which had been killed by the Yankees or stolen by the "sneaks" as Will termed those who had stayed away from the war and preyed on those who had been left behind. He remained home only fifteen days when he started back at his old active work of gathering cattle and in a short time had rounded up 450 head of cattle in Jackson and Matagorda counties for Dillon & McChesney. He then drove them overland to New Orleans. He returned home in December of that same year and went back to work for his old employers, James Foster and Sam Allen. Mr. Foster owned a ranch at Chocolate, Texas, about five miles from Port La Vaca. Will furnished his own horse and received $2 per day. He drove cattle all over western Texas for the next few years and experienced many ups and downs which was typical for those times.[30]

In those early days, they carried their money in leather belts filled with $20 gold pieces. It was dangerous business as Indians and outlaws were prevalent in the country and were always on the lookout for some new prey.

Will stayed with a lone rancher who was killed by the Indians the night after he had left him. The family heard that Will had been killed also and were greatly relieved to see him ride up some time later, alive and well.[31]

Will's brother Joseph's family had a ranch on the prairie about three miles from Indianola and all the cattle that had been bought were penned and fed in these corrals until they could be shipped to New Orleans or Cuba. When the cattle were ready for shipping, they were driven into town along the bay shore, one man taking the lead and the others riding on the land side, until they reached their destination. Once, while driving the cattle along the shore, Will had a steer break out and swim into the bay. Will said the last time he saw him, he was halfway to Cuba.[32]

In the spring of 1867, Will quit Foster and went to work for Shanghai Pierce, and was in his employ for something like a year when Allen, Poole & Co., secured his services and upped his wages to $3 per day. They were large stock owners and shippers

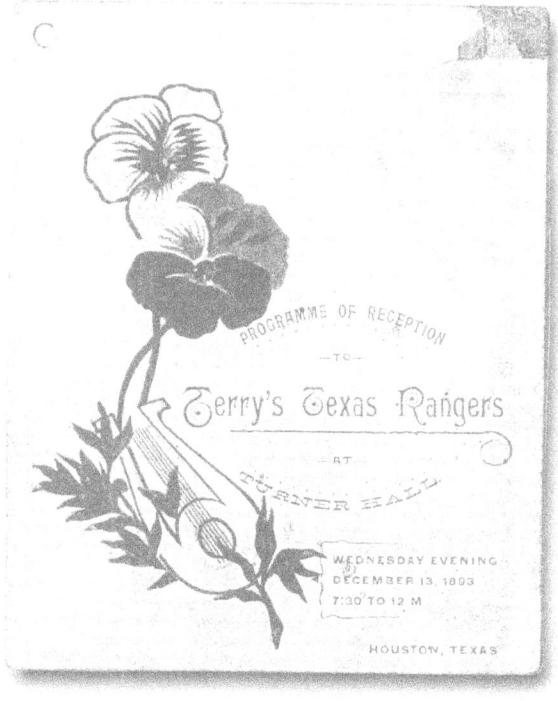

Terry's Texas Rangers Reunion, 1893, Houston, Texas.

of their day. In May 1870, he moved to Matagorda County and in the winter of 1870 was again in the employ of Joseph Collins and Wm. Bishop, driving cattle from Leon County to Indianola. In 1871, he was working again for Shanghai Pierce and in the winter of '72, he was buying cattle in the country west of San Antonio for W. B. Grimes.[33]

A few names of the men who shipped from and through the port of Indianola in those days were: Shanghai Pierce, Jack Elliot, John Adkins, Hays Yarrington, Jim and Joe Collins, Will E. Moore, and Wiley M. Kuykendall.[34]

In 1872, Will quit the cattle business, bought a boat, and started hauling goods and freight in around the Indianola, Matagorda, and Tres Palacios area. He continued this operation until sometime in '86. In '82, Will opened a store in partnership with his brother, H. E. Moore, at Demings Bridge and carried it on with success until 1891, when he moved to Ashby, Texas, just a few miles south of present-day Blessing, Texas. He owned a 1,500 acre ranch there for some time. It was there that he built and ran a store and was postmaster for many years.[35]

Will's first marriage occurred on 24 May 1866, when he married Augusta (Gussie) Butterfield. Gussie was a native of Kentucky. The marriage was short-lived, however, because she died two years later. On 15 December 1869, Will married Mary C. Swift of Concrete, Texas. She was the daughter of the prominent merchant and one of the founders of the town of Seguin, Arthur Swift and Margaret Mackey Baker. Both of her parents died of the fever before the war and she had been raised by her grandfather, Judge James McCulloch Baker of Gonzales County. Will probably met her at the college in Concrete, Texas. Four children were born to them, a son and three daughters:

Mary Swift and Will Moore, ca 1869

1. St. Leges, b. 29 September 1870, Matagorda County, d. the same day, buried at "The Oaks" near Ashby.

2. Margaret Martha (Maggie), b. 1 October 1871, at Indianola.

3. Mary, b. 18 May 1874, at "The Oaks."

4. Ella, b. 11 June 1877, at "The Oaks," d. 27 October 1883 of consumption, at Demings Bridge.

Will's beloved wife, Mary, died at their home in Matagorda County on 17 December 1878, at the age of 33. She is buried in the little cemetery at Ashby, Matagorda County, Texas, just a few miles south of present-day Blessing, Texas.

Will's daughter, Maggie, later married R. G. "Gill" Kuykendall, the son of Will's old friend and fellow cowman, Wiley M. Kuykendall.

After Mary's death, Will married a third time to his brother's widow, Kate A. Seaman

Moore, daughter of Charles Seaman, on 5 June 1881. Five children were born of this union:

1. Cecil Hamilton, b. 7 April 1882, at "The Oaks."
2. Vera, b. 9 December 1884.
3. William Ashby, b. 28 May 1887.
4. Winfred, b. 29 December 1890, d. 25 May 1892 at Ashby.[36]
5. Gladys, b. 3 April 1893.[36]

Will Moore and his wife, Mary, had settled on Wilson's Creek, a branch of the Tres Palacios not far from Ashby, just south of present day Blessing, Texas. (Ashby, Texas, where Will's store and post office once stood, no longer exists. Only Ashby Cemetery exists today, where many of the Moores are buried.) Eudora (Aunt Doaty), Will's sister, was living with Will and Mary at the time of the great hurricane and storm of 1875 and tells the following story:

Mary Swift Moore and baby, ca 1875

> The wind blew very hard the night of the 16th of September. A part of Will's house was blown from its blocks. During a lull in the storm, Mr. Jack Elliott, who lived a half a mile away, came to see how his daughter and family were doing. They lived on the opposite side on the creek from Will's house. When Mr. Elliott reached his daughter's house, the wind was blowing from the different direction, (the eye of the storm had passed directly over this part of the area and that was one of the reasons that so much damage was done to the whole region) and as he attempted to unsaddle his horse, the saddle was blown from its back.

In the course of a few days, rumors of the terrible conditions reached Will's brother, Dolph. He was living on the east side of the Colorado River near where Bay City now stands. Dolph came and got Will and the two of them went by boat to see what was left of Indianola, where their parents still lived. Aunt Doaty finally heard that Shanghai Pierce had been down to the coast surveying the damage, so she saddled a horse and rode over to the "Rancho Grande" seven miles away to find out the news. Shanghai gave her the sad news that their father, Robert Baxter Moore, had been killed in the storm but that the elder Mrs. Moore had survived.[37]

After Will and Dolph surveyed the terrible destruction, they located their mother and were able to bring her back to Will's house. Mrs. Moore told them that the wind had blown for two days until the water finally started coming into their home on the morning of the 16th, so they carried all their belongings upstairs. Before the night was over, the water was nearly up to the second story of the house. The senior Mr. Moore and a Miss Corrine Miller were in the back room on the north side of the house. In their fear that the house would collapse at any moment, they all tried to exit the structure thinking they could tie themselves to a chinaberry tree that was standing in the yard by means of a bed sheet. Will's mother Mary was the only one who made it. The house disintegrated just as the family made their dash for the tree and the family figured Robert Baxter was crushed as the building collapsed and was killed by the falling structure. Corrine was either standing on or near a large wardrobe when the house caved in and some way, no one knows how, she ended up inside the piece. The elder Mary Moore stated that the house gave way some time about 7 P.M. She had tied herself to the tree in the yard, and as the water receded, she would lower herself into it to keep warm. The branches of the tree had whipped her terribly and the family stated that many weeks passed before all the stripes on her frail body went away. At daybreak on the morning of the 17th, she noticed a light on in a house not far away and as soon as the water had gone down enough to allow her to get loose from the tree, she was able to make her way there. She entered the house and found some Negroes there in an upper room crouched by a furnace of coals. She warmed herself there and later made her way over to another house owned by Albert Mylius, who took her in.

About noon the same day, word was received that Corrine Miller had been found alive floating inside the wardrobe by some men who happened to be passing by. They heard sounds and groans coming from the cabinet and opened it up and found her inside. She was unable to walk and the passersby got her out and carried her over to the Mylius house also. It seems that particular house was one of the only homes still standing in the area.[38]

Will's brother, Spencer, was living on the other side of Powderhorn Lake. It was he, who after much searching, located their father's body where it had been washed upon the shore. All of the Moores' houses that were near the coast were blown away. Later, when Will went looking around his parents' house site, he found the family Bible. It was in a dilapidated condition, but he tore out the center section containing the family register and gave it to his sister Dora to copy. His parent's marriage certificate was also found in the Bible in good enough condition to keep. It was dated July 2, 1832.

One of Will's friends, Jim Crain, saved many lives during the storm. He was riding a big black powerful horse and he swam him out in the water to rescue people and carry them to high ground. The people clung to the saddle, stirrups, and even the tail of the horse. Jim Crain had been a comrade-in-arms with Will during the war and was also in Terry's Texas Rangers.[39]

As soon as it was safe enough to do so, Spencer Moore moved his mother and Corrine by boat over to Will's house which was inland enough to be on higher ground. Food, which was very scarce, was brought in from the interior to feed the neighbors. All the barrels of flour were opened and dug into hoping that the centers would be dry enough to make bread. Hogs were plentiful and the men killed all they needed and fed everyone. Every conceivable tale persisted. From everyone drowning, to an old Negro woman who saved herself from drowning by floating completely across the Bay on a feather mattress.[40]

As stated earlier, after the death of Mary Swift Moore, Will married his brother's widow. Kate had married Spencer on 24 May 1871 in Port Lavaca. Spencer died from yellow fever in Texarkana while on a business trip. (1879) They had been married eight years and had four children: Selkirk Seaman, Oce Ann, David Lewis M. (d. at birth), and Addie May.

Will Moore took all the children in as his own when he and Kate married. As stated earlier, Kate Seaman was originally from Biloxi, Mississippi.[41]

Will and his wife, Mary Swift, had joined the Methodist Church on 11 August 1875, at a camp meeting at Elliott's Ferry on the Colorado River, under the ministry of the Rev. S. J. Phair. Will became recording steward of the church. The church was built on land that he donated.

Upon the organization of the "White Man's Union" after the Civil War, Will was elected its first president and was re-elected every year thereafter until failing health compelled him to decline further service. He had also been county commissioner of Matagorda County for several years. Will was a Mason and he had also been postmaster at Ashby since its founding in August 1890. At the time of his death, he was director of the First National Bank of Port Lavaca.[42]

Kate Moore

Will E. Moore died very suddenly at his home at Ashby, Matagorda County, Texas, on 5 June 1902. The Rev. O. N. Morton conducted the funeral service at the Ashby Chapel. After the church service, Will was buried in the nearby Ashby Cemetery by the Masons, according to their beautiful custom. Will had been in declining health for two years but he had never been bedridden. He had suffered from Brights Disease for several years and this contributed to his heart failure and death. His last Will and Testament is as follows:

Will Moore, ca 1900

State of Texas   }
County of Matagorda}

I, W. E. Moore of Ashby, Texas, being of sound mind and memory do make, publish and declare this to be my last Will and Testament, To Wit:

First—All my debts shall be fully paid.

Second—I give, devise and bequeath to my son Hamilton Moore eleven shares of stock in the First Natl. Bank of Port Lavaca, Texas

Third—I give and bequeath to my

Will on porch of his home at Ashby, Texas, ca 1900

son William Ashby Moore ten shares of stock in the First Natl. Bank of Port Lavaca, Texas, they to hold said stock until Hamilton Moore is twenty-five years old.

Fourth—I give devise and bequeath to my daughter Maggie M. Kuykendall and Mary Inez Whaley all my rights and title into any lands now owned by me in the C. G. Cox League of land share and share alike.

Fifth—I give and bequeath all the residue and remainder of my Estate both real and personal to my beloved wife Kate A. Moore, she to make such disposition of the Estate for the benefit of our children as she deems best to have and to hold to her my said wife and to her heirs and assigns forever.

Sixth—I nominate and appoint my said wife Kate A. Moore to be the Executrix of this my last Will and Testament without bond.

In witness whereof I have hereunto set my hand and seal this day of June 12th 1901.

                              signed W. E. Moore (seal)

Signed sealed and delivered as and for his last Will and Testament by the above named testator in our presence who have at his request and in his presence and in the presence of each other signed our names as witnesses thereof.

                              Clay Moore, M.D.
                            Frank Shoaker[43]

On the 19th of August, 1912, Kate Seaman Moore, received the "Cross of Honor" during the Confederate reunion of "Old Times" at Camp #1428 at Bay City, Texas.[44]

Obituaries found in the Museum at Bay City, Texas:

Mr. W. E. Moore died last Thursday at his home at Ashby, Matagorda County, aged about 65 years. Mr. Moore was a prominent and highly respected businessman. He was one of the directors of the First National Bank of Port Lavaca, and had many friends in Calhoun County. He had recently bought, or bargained for, Mrs. C. Sterry's fine residence at this place, for $3,000, intending to move here with his family. Having sold his place at Ashby, it is likely the family will come to live in Port Lavaca. The deceased had suffered from Brights disease the past few years and this was probably the cause of his death.[45]

W. E. Moore passed away at his home at Ashby, Texas, Thursday morning, June 5th, at 6 o'clock. The deceased had been in bad health for several years and lately went to a health resort for his health, but did not improve any and so he returned early. Lately he had feeling a great deal better and was up early walking around the morning of his death. Death resulted from heart failure. Mr. Moore was 65 years of age and leaves a great many near relatives, both in Bay City and Matagorda County to mourn his death. He was a good man, was highly respected by all and will be greatly missed by all who knew him.[46]

Capt. Wm. E. Moore Dead

With profound sorrow, our people heard on June 5th that Capt. Wm. E. Moore had died very suddenly at his home in Ashby, a little after arising for the day. His son, Ex-sheriff Moore, and wife, his daughter, Mrs. Hugh Phillips, and his nephew, J. D. Moore, left immediately taking Rev. O. N. Morton and Wm. Walker, undertaker, with them. Capt. Moore's brother, D. P. Moore, was just ready to go with them, when his wife became alarmingly ill and he had to remain with her. However, she was so much improved next morning that Mr. Moore went over to the funeral. Capt. Moore was one of the country's oldest, most useful and best loved citizens, and his death will be universally regretted. Upon the organization of the White Man's Union, he was elected the first president and was re-elected till failing health compelled him to decline. He was a good man, foremost in all good works, and we shall not soon look upon his like again. He was one of our dearest friends, and we feel a keen sense of personal loss in his death and most deeply sympathize with the bereaved family. May God comfort them as none other can.[47]

MOORE: William E. Moore died June 5th, 1902. Rev. Morton of Bay City, performed the funeral service at Ashby Chapel, after which the Masons buried him according to their beautiful custom. He had been in bad health for over two years, but had never been confined to bed. His mind was clear and active up to the very last. He was born in Rahway, N.J., October 26th, 1837, but came with his parents to Texas immediately after annexation,* and lived for a number of years at Indianola. During the war he was a member of Terry's Texas Rangers, and was dangerously wounded at Murfreesboro, Tenn. It was a pleasure to him to attend the reunions of his regiment and meet again the remnant of his old comrades. He, with his wife, joined the M. E. Church August 11th, 1875 at a camp meeting near Elliott's Ferry, on the Colorado, under the ministry of Rev. St. Johns Phair and others. He lived at Ashby for over thirty years and during that time all the Methodist preachers found a welcome at his home. He was a man of unflinching courage and integrity of purpose, and was not afraid to die, for he had perfect trust in his Savior. He leaves a wife and six children, besides other near and dear relatives and friends, to feel the loneliness of life without him. (His sister Dora)

(* incorrect, the family had moved to Texas just before annexation.)[48]

Moore Family Members Buried in the Cemetery At Ashby, Matagorda County, Texas

Mary Crowell Layton Moore, b. 10 January, 1812, d. 12 April 1896.
Eudora Inez Moore, 1847-1933
William E. Moore, born Oct. 26, 1837, died June 5, 1902
Mary C. Swift Moore, Wife of W.E. Moore, born July 3, 1846, died Dec. 17, 1878
Winifred Moore, infant dau. of W.E. & Kate Moore, born Dec. 29, 1890, died May 25, 1892
Ella Moore, youngest dau. of W. E. & Mary Moore, born June 14, 1877, died Oct. 27, 1880
Kate Seaman Moore, Wife of W.E. Moore, born May 9, 1853, died April 27, 1941

Moore Family Members Buried in the Cemetery at Old Indianola, Calhoun County, Texas

Robert Baxter Moore, born April 11, 180, died Sept. 16, 1875 age 68
Joseph Layton Moore, born April 11, 1833, died June 14, 1864 age 31
Robert Baxter Moore Jr., born July 23, 1854, died June 29, 1867 age 12
Spencer C. Moore, born Feb. 3, 1850, died Jan. 18, 1879 age 29
D. L. Moore, born May 10, 1877, died May 17, 1877 age 7 days[49]

Birth and Death Records of the Moores as Recorded in the Moore and Kuykendall Family Bible

BIRTHS
W. E. Moore, b. 26 October 1837 in New Jersey.
Mary C. Swift, b. 3 July 1846, Concrete, Texas.
St. Legis Moore, b. 29 September 1870 in Matagorda County, Texas.
Maggie M. Moore, b. 1 October 1871 at Indianola, Texas.
Mary Moore, b. 18 May 1874 at The Oaks, Matagorda County, Texas.
Ella Moore, b. 11 June 1877 at The Oaks, Matagorda County, Texas.

DEATHS
Maggie V. Swift, d. 7 July 1871 at Concrete, Texas, in the 21st year of her life.
St. Legis Moore, son of Wm. and Mary, d. 29 September 1870 at The Oaks.
Martha Swift, wife of W. O. Collins, d 11 January 1874, of consumption, in the 26th year of her life.
Mary C. Swift, wife of W. E. Moore, d. 17 December 1878, of consumption in the 33rd year of her life at her home in Matagorda County, Texas.
Ella Moore, d. 27 October 1883 at Demings Bridge, Matagorda County, the youngest child of Mary and W. E. Moore.
Winifred Moore, d. 25 May 1892 at Ashby, Texas.

William E. Moore, d. 5 June 1902 at his home in Ashby, Texas, in his 65th year.
Eudore Inez Moore, d. 8 November, at 8 P.M. on the ranch near Buda, Texas. She would have been 86 on November 11th.⁵⁰

Genealogy

1) Marshall Early Kuykendall (13 October 1932, Austin, Texas) m. 20 September 1959, Austin, Texas, to Mary Karen Koock (19 November 1937, Austin, Texas). Issue: Marshall E. Jr., Mary Alice, and Sarita.
2) Wylie Moore Kuykendall (b. 3 March 1899, Ashby, Texas, d. 11 October 1976, Austin, Texas) m. 16 July 1926, San Marcos, Texas, to Alice Hamlett (27 October 1910, Temple, Texas). Issue: R.G. and Marshall E.
3) Margaret M. (Maggie) Moore (b. 1 October 1871, Indianola, Texas, d. 4 January 1950, Buda, Texas) m. 21 August 1890, Ashby, Texas, to Robert Gill Kuykendall (b. 15 May 1870, Matagorda County, Texas, d. 19 December 1905, Buda, Texas). Issue: Marion, Dorothy, Wylie, and Wm. Isaac.
4) William Erastus Moore (b. 26 October 1837, Rahway, New Jersey, d. 5 June 1902, Ashby, Texas) m. 15 December 1869, Concrete, Texas, to Mary C. Swift (b. 3 July 1846, Concrete, Texas, d. 17 December 1878, Ashby, Texas).
5) Robert Baxter Moore (b. 11 April 1807, Elisabethon, New Jersey, d. 16 September 1875, Indianola, Texas) m. 2 July 1832, New York, New York, to Mary Crowell Layton (b. 12 January 1812, Woodbridge, New Jersey, d. 12 April 1896, Ashby, Texas).
6) Safety Layton (b. New Jersey, d. New Orleans, Louisiana) m. Hetty Marsh (b. 10 October 1785, New Jersey, d. 5 May 1870, Newark, New Jersey).
7) Captain Christopher Marsh (b. 7 May 1742, Woodbridge, New Jersey, d. 26 October 1810, Woodbridge, New Jersey) m. Ann Brown (b. 5 May 1749, Woodbridge, New Jersey, d. 2 December 1813, Woodbridge, New Jersey).
8) Daniel Marsh (b. 25 February 1705, Rahway, New Jersey, d. 1 November 1756, Elisabethon, New Jersey) m. Mary Rolph.
9) Henry Rolph (b. 26 September 1678, Cambridge, Massachusetts, d. ca 1722, Elisabeth, New Jersey) m. Mary Connelly.
Judge Henry Rolph-1715, Judge of Court of Common Pleas and Quarter Sessions, Middlesex County, New Jersey.
Reference: *Monnette's First Settlers of Ye Plantations of Piscataway and Woodbridge, Olde East New Jersey*, Vol. IV, page 543.⁵¹

Biography

The entire biography on William Erastus Moore (my great-grandfather; my father's mother's father) was made possible by basically two individuals plus Kuykendall family files in my possession. My dear cousin, Martha L. Moore of Bay City, Texas, contacted me in 1986 and gave me her entire file on her uncle Will Moore that she had compiled over many, many years of personal research. She is a member of the DAR and the genealogy back to Henry Rolph (1678) was her sole work and hers alone.

The second person was Eudora Inez Moore, "Aunt Doaty" (Dora). Aunt Doaty lived and died on the Kuykendall ranch at Buda, Texas, from 1901 until her death in 1933. She wrote an extensive daily diary, copies of which are in the possession of close family members who allowed me to copy freely from them. Her "Recollections of Old Indianola," where she lived for many years, was the backbone of this biography on her brother, Will Moore.

Top left: Childhood photo of Martha Moore
Top right: Ellen Swift Partain, sister to Mary, the wife of Will Moore
Bottom left: Mrs. Pinchem
Bottom right: Uncle Ben Kuykendall

Joe Morris and Mattie Morris

Unknown Matagorda County Neighbors

More Unknown Matagorda County Neighbors

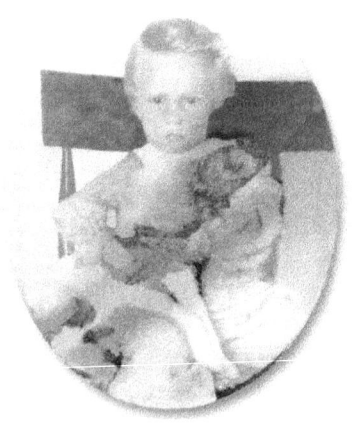

Chapter Thirteen

Arthur Swift

Arthur Swift was a prominent resident of Gonzales and in 1841 he was elected or appointed tax collector and constable in the town of Gonzales, as stated in *A History of Guadalupe County*, published in 1951 by Willie Mae Weinert.

No man of other early years of Seguin's history presents a more glamorous picture than does Arthur Swift. He was one of the original shareholders of the town. At the time of his death in 1855, his wealth was estimated at around a quarter of a million dollars in the inventory on file in Guadalupe County. Arthur Swift, Andrew Neill, and James Campbell were partners in the development of the upper half of the Humphrey Branch League. (This is Seguin west of Walnut Branch and extending to the west beyond the location of Texas Lutheran College.) The land was sold to James Campbell on 9 April 1840 by court order, four years after the death of Thomas R. Miller, who fell at the Alamo. The land was part of the estate of Thomas R. Miller. It appears that the money to actually close the deal was put up by Arthur Swift and Andrew Neill and that these three in their agreement stipulated, that if any of the three should die during the partnership, the remaining partners should inherit the share of the deceased member. So, upon the death of James Campbell (killed by Indians in 1841), Arthur Swift came in for his shares of James Campbell's part of the "Upper Half" of the Humphrey Branch League.

All of this section of Seguin lying west of Walnut Branch was first called Guadalupe City, but later became a part of the City of Seguin. When the county was organized in 1846, Swift used his influence to have the county commissioners move the designated route of the road from Seguin to San Antonio. Travelers at that time crossed the ferry about where the driveway extending through the Max Starcke Park reverses its course on the north bank of the Guadalupe River. At that spot Joseph

Johnson had a ferry that connected with the San Antonio road on the southside of the Guadalupe River. The road the county "kept up" was routed by "Swift's Ferry." The old Swift Ferry was operated just below the present bridge on the new highway to San Antonio, Hwy 90.

Swift's own concrete home was located about where the Starcke Furniture Store now stands. He and his first wife, Margaret Baker Swift, and their four daughters, Margaret, Mary, Eleanor, and Martha, lived in this homestead. (Mary married Will Moore and Eleanor married Partain)

After the death of Margaret, Swift married Philadelphia Borden daughter of Gail Borden, although the probate records of Guadalupe County seem to indicate this marriage was unknown in Seguin.

Thomas E. Partain

Arthur Swift was a Captain in the Texas Army during the Vasquez Campaign and a Minute Man in the Texas Ranger Force, a Son of Temperance, a stockholder in the Seguin High School Corporation, a shareholder in two groups of men who formed a company to "found" the village of Seguin in 1838. The estate records show that the store he owned was located where the Krezdorn Jewelry store now stands.

Arthur Swift was buried in a small cemetery just west of Texas Lutheran College, (in downtown Seguin) in the far northwest corner in the sunken area which in the old days was surrounded by a concrete fence. His grave, along with his first wife, Margaret, is unmarked.

1. Arthur Swift, b. ca. 1810 probably in Tennessee, married Margaret Mackey Baker, daughter of Judge James McCulloch Baker of Tennessee.

2. John Swift, b. 17 Oct. 1774, Louisa County, Virginia, married on 12 July 1805 to Mary Polly Anthony (1784-1870). He died on 6 September 1838 in Henry County, Tennessee.

3. Richard Swift, b. 16 Aug. 1732, Hanover County, Virginia, d. ca. 1784, Louisa County, Virginia, married Mary Terrell, who was born on 23 November 1740.

4. Rev. William Swift, b. ca. 1696, Kent, England, d. ca. 1734, Hanover County, Virginia, married Dianah Hodgkin on 12 June 1722 at St. Dunstan's Canterbury, England.

This information was furnished me by Hugh Swift of Abilene, Texas.

It is very probable since the Swifts, Bakers, and McCullochs all migrated into Texas from Tennessee, that the three families are more intertwined than indicated. Certainly, the Bakers and the McCullochs are related, why would the good Judge be named James McCulloch Baker if that was not the case? We have no information on who his parents were but a good guess would be that his mother was a McCulloch.

Chapter Fourteen

Captain Abner Kuykendall of Austin's Colony

Abner Kuykendall (ca. 1777-1834) Frontiersman; Colonist; Captain of Militia; was one of Stephen F. Austin's earliest members of the Old 300. He was the eldest son of Adam and Margaret Hardin Kuykendall and was probably born in Rutherford County, North Carolina. Adam Kuykendall had owned a piece of land there that he sold to Jos. Carpenter in October 1779, which was located on (K)Nob Creek.[1]

Adam, Abner's father, probably moved over the mountains into what is now eastern Tennessee either soon after the sale or just after the Battle of Ramsour's Mill which occurred on 20 June 1780.[2]

Three years later, in 1783, Adam appears as a taxpayer in Greene County (separated from Washington County) and shows to be a co-signer on a $10,000 bond with Col. Joseph Hardin (his father-in-law) in the August court in the same county. Adam's father, Peter Kuykendall, died between February and May of 1783 and in the "Will," Adam received five shillings. The "Will" is recorded in Washington County, Tennessee.[3]

Abner's father Adam Kuykendall, received "Land Warrant" #1604 in payment from North Carolina for his services during the Revolutionary War that was located in Davidson County, Tennessee (later to divide into two parts, with Davidson on the west and Summer County on the east). These lands were to be laid off in what was known as "Middle Tennessee." This is stated because Adam later shows up on the tax list for Summer County, Tennessee, in 1788 and 1789. In 1790 he appears on a jury list for that county, and was excused from jury duty along with his brother, Matthew, in 1791.[4]

Later, in 1792, Adam's signature appears on a "List of the Male Inhabitants" of Logan County, Kentucky, along with *Abner*, his son. It states he is located in the "Village of Red Banks," the present name of Henderson, Kentucky, on the red banks of the Ohio River. Abner would be fifteen years old at this time. (Note: it was first Logan County out of Russellville, Kentucky, then Christian County, and lastly, Henderson, County, Kentucky.[5]

On 23 December 1794, the court in what was then Logan County, Kentucky, appointed commissioners "to view" a road from Red Banks on the Ohio River to Russellville, keeping on the south side of the Green River. Morton Maulding, *William Gates*, Reason Bowie, and West Maulding were the commissioners. Those appointed by the commissioners to plan the road were: Benjamin Hardin, Morton Maulding, Ab Hardin, James Stewart, John McCombs, and Joseph Worthington. (These names are noted here because Abner Kuykendall, who would be sixteen by now, would soon marry Sally Gates the daughter of the above mentioned William Gates.)[5]

Adam Kuykendall and his family were on the tax rolls for Logan County, Kentuck, (at Red Banks), in 1793 and again in 1795. In 1797 this area of Logan County was changed to Christian County and he again shows up on record. In 1799 the county name and area was changed again, this time to Henderson County, and Adam was on that roll also. Adam's name appears on the tax rolls for the county again on 1 October 1800, 1801, 1802, 1803, 1804, and 1809, a five year skip.[7]

Records state "on Tuesday, the 2nd of July, 1799, the First Court of Criminal Common Law and Chancery Jurisdiction held its sitting in the village of Henderson, Kentucky. A grand jury was then empaneled, consisting of citizens of the area. *William Gates* served as a member of this first grand jury. Records further reflect that as late as the July term of 1810, the Court Records further reflect that as late as the July term of 1810, the Court appointed *Abner Kuykendall*, William Gates, and Humphrey Barnett to view a road from the town of Henderson to the main fork of Highland Creek. The road crossed "Canoe Creek" about 100 yards above the old ford on the Tract to "Diamond Island."

By this time Abner would be married to Sally Gates, the daughter of William Gates and Catherine Hardin Gates. Catherine Hardin was the daughter of John Hardin.[8]

Adam and Margaret Hardin Kuykendall probably had all of their children at this time: Abner born ca. 1777; Amos, born ca. 1781; Robert H. born in 1790, Joseph, born ca. 1791, Peter born ca. 1797; there are no more birth dates for when the younger children, Sally and Adam Jr., were born.[9]

After Adam Kuykendall shows up on the 1804 Tax List in Henderson County, Kentucky, there is a several year time lapse before he reappears there again. The reason for this lapse is because he shows up on a "Memorial," along with his sons *Abner*, Amos, and Robert north of the Ohio River in Indiana Territory, dated 16 March 1808. The Memorial is addressed to William Henry Harrison, governor of the Indiana Territory and is signed by many settlers of the area.[10]

There have been no deed records to date found for the family in the Indiana Territory. As noted earlier, Adam and the family appear south of the Ohio River in Henderson County on the tax list of 1809.[11]

Shortly after March 1808, it is obvious that the Kuykendalls and the related families of the Gates and the Hardins began their move into Missouri Territory (Arkansas). The records show that *Abner Kuykendall* was in Arkansas (Missouri Territory) at the *Cadron Settlement* at least as early as 15 February 1810, when Abner and his brother, Amos, were witness to a "Power of Attorney" from John Bain to Patrick Darby. The records reflect that Adam Sr. and William Gates lived nearby at the same time. Records show that Abner's land joined the "northwardly shore of the Arkansas River at the first rock bluff where Murphy has been for some years passed, the same Abner and Sally (Gates) his wife, having actually inhabited and cultivated upon the lands aforesaid for three or four successive years prior to the said 12th of April, 1814." Abner Kuykendall and his family left Cadron some time prior to 16 May 1820, because on that date they sold their pre-emption claim to Benjamin Murphy, identifying themselves as residents of Hempstead County, Arkansas. Their land claim at the Cadron Settlement was on South frl. ½ Sec. 7, and NW frl. ¼ Sec. 18, T-5-N, R-14 West.[12]

Many of the migrating families of the period crossed the Mississippi River at the Chickasaw Bluffs (Memphis, Tennessee). They walked or rode horses and mules all the way to the Cadron Settlement. Probably the most popular mode of travel was by water in flat-bottomed keel boats that they floated down the Ohio and the Mississippi River. When they came to the mouth of the Arkansas River they poled and pulled themselves upstream until they reached the Cadron Settlement which was located near the mouth of Cadron Creek where it empties into the Arkansas River.[13]

Adam and Margaret Hardin Kuykendall and their sons settled near a point on the Arkansas River known as "Red Hill" which is below the mouth of Cadron Creek. No deed for old Adam's pre-emption claim has ever been found.[14]

Other settlers in the area were Jacob Pyeatt, a Revolutionary soldier, and his family who settled at "Crystal Hill" on the Arkansas River ca. 1812. Soon after their arrival at that place, the increase in immigration created a need for a ferry, and Jacob established one which ran between his home and that of Samuel Gates on the south side of the river (Arkansas). This is noted because Samuel was the son of William Gates, was a brother-in-law to Abner Kuykendall (Abner would name one of his sons after Samuel), and was the son-in-law of Jacob Pyeatt.[15]

Abner Kuykendall, along with his brothers, Joseph and their respective families, left Arkansas Territory (Pecan Point-Red River area) for Texas in October 1821, probably in company with his father-in-law, William Gates. In Nacogdoches, the group met up with another brother, Robert H. Kuykendall, who researchers state had been scouting in Texas for some time. Those left behind in Arkansas near the Cadron were Adam and Margaret Hardin Kuykendall, Abner's parents, and Amos, Peter, Adam Jr., brothers and several sisters.[16]

The settlers and their families left Nacogdoches in late October and reached the junction of the Brazos River and the La Bahia road on 26 November 1821, where they remained camped for a month. There they found Andrew Robinson camped on the west side of the Brazos River. In the last few days of December, the entire group of Kuykendalls, along with the allied families of the Boatrights, the Gillelands, and others crossed the Brazos River on make-shift rafts and by swimming their livestock. They made camp inland a short distance near a pretty running stream, an area that they had scouted a few weeks previous. The following morning, 1 January 1822, they named the creek "New Years Creek." Abner and his family decided to stay and settle in that area. New Years Creek is in present day Washington County, Texas. Abner's land was located three or four miles south of the present village of Independence, Texas. It has been recorded by most researchers that these families were the very first of Austin's Old 300 to enter the proposed colony.[17]

Even though he was only a small child at the time, J. Hampton Kuykendall, one of Abner's younger sons, remembers Stephen F. Austin's visit to their camp in this location and states in his *Reminiscences* "that it was very cold and that there was a light snow on the ground at the time." In November 1822, Abner Kuykendall rented his farm to a Mr. Wheat and moved his family back to the Brazos River to a point five miles below the La Bahia Road. When he returned to the farm some time later, Josiah H. Bell, William Gates (his father-in-law), and Samuel Gates (his brother-in-law) were living there.[18]

In December 1822, an election for civil and militia officers was held at the home of Josiah H. Bell. Bell was elected alcade; Samuel Gates as captain and Abner's son, Gibson, was elected lieutenant.

Early in the summer of 1823, Abner and Gibson went to Natchitoches, Louisiana, for supplies for the family. They took two packhorses, which they loaded with salt, sugar, and coffee, items in very short supply in the colony.

In the latter part of the summer of '23, the Tonkawas a stole a horse from Abner. He pursued them in the company of two of his sons, Gibson and Barzillai, along with Thomas Boatright. They went through the village of San Felipe and were joined by Colonel Austin and additional men. They found the Indians under Chief Caritas camped about 6-8 miles below Fort Bend. The horses were returned and the offending Indians were given 50 lashes each.

In November 1823, Abner decided to move 30 miles farther down the Brazos River and settled on its west bank about 8 miles above the village of San Felipe. The farm was located just a short distance above the mouth of "Mill Creek." Here they raised a fine crop. This is in present day Austin County. Abner's wife, Sallie Gates Kuykendall, died sometime during this year. Abner never remarried, preferring as J. Hampton states, *"to raise all his children by himself with out having to subject them to a step-mother."*[19]

In spring 1824, Colonel Austin, along with Captain Abner and his sons, Gibson and Barzillai, led an expedition against the Carankaways down to La Bahia (Goliad) and back. They were joined by Jared E. Groce and thirty of his Negro slaves, all mounted and armed by Groce. The church officials at La Bahia negotiated a peace for the Indians and the militia returned to San Felipe and disbanded.

A few days after their return, Abner and his son Gibson were again on another expedition against the "Cokes" below San Felipe in the "Damons Mound" area. They encountered a herd of buffalo and killed one for food. At Bell's Landing (Columbia), they left their horses and proceeded down river in boats. No Indians were found and they returned once again to San Felipe. Gibson Kuykendall state that the total distance traveled by his father and himself in those last two months was in excess of 800 miles.[20]

In July 1824, Stephen F. Austin granted Abner Kuykendall one and one half leagues and two labors of land in what are now, Fort Bend, Washington, and Austin counties. In 1831, he received another league of land for services. They are listed as follows:

7-7-1824	1 League 4428 acres Ft. Bend County West Side Brazos River Below Richmond, Texas
7-7-1824	½ League 2214 acs. Washington Co.- On New Years Creek and Kuykendall Creek between Brenham and Independence.
7-8-1824	2 Labors 354 acs. Austin County West Side Brazos River just above the mouth of Mill Creek.
4-24-1831	1 League 4428 acres Lee County On Yegua Creek (For services against the hostile Indians)[21]

The census of March 1826, lists Abner Kuykendall as a stock raiser and farmer; a widower, aged over fifty. His household included two servants, four daughters, and eight sons.[22]

In the spring of 1826, Austin initiated a campaign against the "Wacos" and the "Tawacanies," whose depredations had become too frequent to be allowed. Abner and his son Gibson left their home on May 17 to rendezvous with the militia where the San Antonio road crossed the Brazos River. The force amounted to about 190 men. Aylett C. Buckner was elected captain, and Horatio Christman and William Hall were elected subordinate captains. It rained in torrents and the men had to continually unscrew the breech plugs from their rifles to extract and replace the incombustible powder. They crossed the Little Brazos River at flood stage. The expedition arrived within 3 to 4 miles of the "Tawacanie" village. Gibson, along with his uncle, Robert H. Kuykendall, and three others were ordered to swim the swollen stream and reconnoiter the village. It was found abandoned. The tired and hungry men ate some of the Indian corn at which time, Captain Buckner ordered them back home and at the original point of rendezvous on the Brazos, the expedition was disbanded.

Gibson's mention of Capt. Robert H. Kuykendall in his journal is important because it would be the last time he is shown to be on an active Indian campaign. Sometime shortly thereafter, while in an Indian fight, the blow from a rifle barrel would crush his skull and he would linger on ineffectively until his untimely death in late 1830.

Gibson Kuykendall wrote:

"In the fall of 1826, after the campaign against the Wacos and the Tawancanies, the "Fredonia" disturbances commenced. In Nov. or Dec., Austin sent my father (Abner), William Hall and Francis W. Johnson to Nacadoches to see the leaders of the rebellion and endeavor to dissuade them from rash measures, they were unable, however, to effect anything. After fathers return to San Felipe, the Mexican and Colonial forces moved against the Revolutionists. So large a proportion of the men of the Colony was sent on this service that Austin deemed it prudent to order my father with eight men to "range" the country between the Colorado and the Brazos along the San Antonio road to prevent any inroad of the "wacos" or other northern Indians. This service he performed until the termination of the Fredonia troubles. The men he had with him were B. (Barzillai) Kuykendall, W. (William) Kuykendall, (sons), Early Robbins, Thomas Stevens, John James, James Kiggans, John Walker, and J. Furnash.

At this time the San Antonio road, except where it crossed the Brazos, was 30-40 miles above the outmost settlements."[23]

Abner was a successful farmer and stock raiser and always participated actively in the life and business of Austin's colony. He was elected head (captain) of the colony's militia in 1829. Abner Kuykendall's official commission as captain of militia is dated "Leona Vicario, July 24th, 1829," and is signed by Governor Viesca. The commission entitles him "*Captain de la Compania de Infanteria de la Villa de San Felip de Austin.*"[24]

As stated, Abner was a captain of several expeditions against the Indians. In 1829 an expedition was organized in Austin's colony headed by captains Oliver Jones and Barlett Sims. Abner Kuykendall commanded 100 men on the expedition. At the mouth of the San Saba, where it enters the upper Colorado River, Captain Abner Kuykendall and his men were joined by a company of 38 men raised from De Witt's colony and commanded by Captain Henry S. Brown.[25]

In 1830 Austin sent a group which included Abner to (Fort) Tenoxtilan (near present day Caldwell, Texas) to discuss with the Mexican authorities how to prevent Indian depredations against the colony. In the same year, Abner served on a committee at San Felipe to supervise the building of a jail. He was sixth Regidor at San Felipe in February of 1832 and at the time of the Anahuac disturbances, Abner led a group of from 40 to 60 men to assist the Anahuac citizens.

On 18 May 1831, the Catholic priest Father Michael Muldoon met with many families and their neighbors at the home of Capt. Abner Kuykendall 21 miles above San Felipe. While there he baptized more than one hundred persons and married four couples, two of whom had been married some years previous by "Bond." J. Hampton Kuykendall, the younger brother of Gibson states in his papers that they were very fond of Father Muldoon and that they always considered themselves "Muldoon Catholics."[26]

The Abner Kuykendall who listed himself as a farmer from Tennessee when he applied for land at the mouth of Yegua Creek in May of 1831, has been listed as a possible son of Capt. Abner Kuykendall. This is erroneous. This man, or Abner (II) as he is referred to by researchers, was the son of Matthew and Nancy Johnson Kuykendall. He and his sons would later move to Bell County and their descendants would settle Bell, San Saba, and Llano counties.[27]

In June 1834, while attempting to arrest a man named Joseph Clayton in San Felipe, Abner was critically stabbed in the side of the neck. He lingered near death for about a month and was attended nearly every day by Dr. Robert Peebles. He probably died on 25 July 1834 (the last entry in Dr. Peebles' journal) because that was the day they also hung Joseph Clayton for the murder of Captain Abner Kuykendall: [28]

> "San Felipe; July 25, 1834—Witnessed this day the execution of Joseph Clayton who was condemned and executed for the murder of an old man named Abe Kuykendall."
> —Underwood

> "My father told me that the boys(sons of Abner), Gibson and Barzillai had Clayton in chains and the moment the old man died, they drug Clayton out and hung him."
> —T. R. Kuykendall

This was to be considered the first legal execution in the Colony.

Abner Kuykendall was married to Sarah (Sally) Gates. She was the daughter of William and Catherine Hardin Gates. Sally preceded Abner in death ca. 1823 just after they entered Austin's Colony. Her grave has never been found and was presumed to be located somewhere in Washington County, Texas. Abner never remarried. It has been stated that after Abner's death he was buried just south of old Independence, Texas but his grave has never been found. He was probably buried just north of San Felipe near the Brazos River on land that the family owned but gravestones were very scarce in those days and the location has never been located.

The known children of Abner and Sally Gates Kuykendall were:

Gibson (1802-1861), who served on many early Indian campaigns and were commanded the reserves at Harrisburg in 1836;

Barzillai (1806-1873), who also served under his father on many expeditions against the Indians and under his brother in 1836 and against the Mexican invaders of 1842;

William (1808-1862), (later children would call him William Abner) who served also in the Indian campaigns and who provided livestock and grain to the Texian Army in 1836;

Jonathon Hampton (1815-1880), the self taught, Texas History Scholar, who was in the "Run-away Scrape" and served under his brother Gibson at Harrisburg in 1836; with his brothers in the invasions of 1842; and with his nephews in the Civil War; would later write his recollections about the early days of Austin's Colony;

Samuel Gates (twin) (1821-1865), named after his uncle;

Wyatt Hanks (twin) (1821-1842), named after a long time friend, Wyatt Hanks. Hanks would later be wounded and die on the Mier Expedition of 1842, his remains would later be re-buried on "Monument Hill" at LaGrange, Texas;

Marinda (1812-?);

Elisabeth (1820-1835);

Adam (1814-1850) named after his grand-father; and

Sarah (?-d. before 1834).[29]

"San Felipe De Austin
7 August 1834"

"To the honorable judge of the first instance of the Jurisdiction of Austin, the petition of Gibson Kuykendall, Brazillai Kuykendall, William Kuykendall, Adam Kuykendall, and Miranda Kuykendall, wife of James Cooper, all major heirs of Abner Kuykendall, deceased most respectfully represent that their ancestor, Abner Kuykendall, late a resident of this jurisdiction departed this life on the 28th of June last, leaving for heirs in the descending line your petitioners together with: J. Hampton Kuykendall and Elisabeth Kuykendall, minor children of the said Abner Kuykendall over the age of puberty; all of whom are brothers and sisters of your petitioners by the whole blood. That the said Abner Kuykendall left considerable property consisting of two leagues and a half land with the exception of one Labor, and a stock of cattle and horses, hogs, etc., and one Negro boy, etc. Wherefore your petitioners pray that the nine children of said Abner Kuykendall above named may be admitted and declared by your Honor to be the universal heirs of the succession of their said father; and that the Curators and Tutors may be appointed to the said minor heirs by your Honor; and that your Honor will cause an estimative inventory of all property of the said Abner Kuykendall, deceased and cause the same to be delivered into the hand of his said heirs and successors and as in duty bound your petitioners will ever pay."

(signed) William B. Travis
Atty. for Petitioners

"San Felipe de Austin
this 7th day of August 1834"

"Having read and considered the foregoing petition and being satisfied of the truth of the facts therein set forth, it is by reason thereof and of the law, ordered, adjudged and decreed, that Gibson Kuykendall, Brazillai Kuykendall, William Kuykendall, Adam Kuykendall, Miranda Kuykendall, J. Hampton Kuykendall, Elisabeth Kuykendall, Wyatt H. Kuykendall, and Samuel G. Kuykendall be, and they are hereby admitted as, and declared to be the universal heirs of Abner Kuykendall, deceased, hereby vesting in them all the rights, powers, and privileges legally appertaining to them as the heirs of said succession; and that Gibson Kuykendall be and is hereby appointed Tutor to Wyatt H. and Samuel G. Kuykendall on his giving bond and taking the oath prescribed by law; and that a commission from this court be appointed to make an estimative inventory of all the property belonging to the succession of the said Abner Kuykendall, deceased, and to deliver the same into the possession of the aforesaid heirs and successors. This I have decreed. And I sign the same in conformity with the law in the town of San Felipe De Austin this 7th day of August, 1834."

(Signed) David G. Burnet

Abner Kuykendall's Will is recorded in Austin County, Book A-155; and Book B-167, at Bellville, Texas.

Barzillai, William, Abner (Adam), Miranda, wife of Jas. Cooper, and Gibson, for himself and curator for J. Hampton, and tutor for Wyatt H. (Hank) and Samuel G., universal heirs of the succession of Abner Kuykendall. Elisabeth, another minor, died soon after her father and before the estate was divided. Gibson K., asked administration for the estate. J.W. Benton was estate attorney.

The court appointed Wm. Pettus, Wylie Martin, and Wm. Cooper to divide all land held in common—2½ leagues to be divided into 8 parts—1 league in Washington County, 1 in Fort Bend County, and ½ league on New Years Creek.

There was much delay and the court was petitioned again. I. G. Swisher, Horacio Chrisman, Jas. Clark, John Allcorn and Jacob Stevens, citizens of Washington County were appointed to divide the Washington County lands; and Henry Jones, Michael Young, John H. Perkins, Gilliand (RH II) Kuykendall and Joseph Kuykendall to divide the Fort Bend County land.

The estate was appraised and inventoried at $6,978.50 by Jas. H. Baxter and Wm. Pettus, and was witnessed by Stephen Townsend, John Douglas, and Sam Douglas and signed by Gibson, Brazilla, William, Adam, Miranda Cooper by Jas. Cooper, her husband, and Gibson for the minors with Francis Adams and Dr. Robert Peebles as securities.

The first petition was in August of 1834 with Gibson asking administration on J. Hampton Kuykendall and Elisabeth Kuykendall, minor children of said Abner over the age of puberty and Wyatt H., and Samuel G., minor children under the age of puberty, all brothers and sisters of Gibson K., by whole blood. Signed by Barzilla, William, Adam, and Miranda Kuykendall.

Judge David G. Burnett granted that Gibson Kuykendall be administrator for J. Hampton, 17 years old, Jas. Cockran, as security. Oliver Jones was security for Elisabeth Kuykendall (died before division) and witnessed by C. B. Stewart, W. B. Allcorn, Geo. Ewing, and Isaac Best.

The land was divided into 8 equal parts and was surveyed by Nathaniel Peck, with J. Hampton Kuykendall and Robert (RH II–Gill) Kuykendall as chain carriers.

The estate was finally settled in September 1838, with Judge Robert M. McNutt, as Acting Judge.[30]

Chapter Fifteen

Captain Gibson Kuykendall of Austin's Colony

Gibson Kuykendall (1802-1861) Frontiersman—Colonist—Captain of Texian Militia—was the son of Captain Abner Kuykendall of North Carolina and Sarah (Sally) Gates Kuykendall. He was probably born near Henderson (Red Banks), Kentucky. His father had moved there ca. 1792, when the entire family moved into that area from Tennessee. His father's name shows up on a "List of Male Inhabitants" of Logan County, Kentucky. It states they were located at "Red Banks," the present name of Henderson, Kentucky.[1]

In 1810 the family moved into north central Arkansas (Territory of Missouri) and settled near the mouth of Cadron Creek on the east side of the Arkansas River. The village that was created there would be called the "Cadron Settlement." In 1820 the family moved into southwest Arkansas, Hempstead County, near Pecan Point on the Red River and it was from that area that they would immigrate into the Mexican Province of Texas in the fall of 1821.[2]

In his recollections Gibson states:

"My father, Abner Kuykendall, and his brother Joseph, with their families, left Arkansas Territory for Texas in October 1821. At Nacogdoches they were joined by their brother Robert, who had for some time been residing west of the Sabine. The three families crossed the Brazos River at the La Bahia road on the 26th day of November, 1821. We found Andrew Robinson and family camped on the west side of the river. Robinson had preceded us two or three days. His was the first immigrant family that crossed the Brazos River. Here we all camped for about a month. About the first of January 1822, my father and Thomas Boatright moved ten miles west of the Brazos River and settled near New Years Creek, about four miles south of the present town of Independence."³

In June, Gibson, his father, and his uncle Amos Gates went to the mouth of the Colorado River to meet a ship loaded with provisions. His father bought two barrels of flour for which he paid $25 a barrel. This flour would produce the first bread that the family had in over seven months.

In November 1822, Gibson's father rented his place on New Years Creek to a Mr. Wheat and moved the family back over to the Brazos River five miles below the crossing of the La Bahia road. When he returned, Josiah H. Bell, William Gates (*father of Amos and father-in-law of Captain Abner*), and Samuel Gates, the son of William, were living there.

In December an election for civil and militia officers was held at the house of Josiah H. Bell. Bell was unanimously elected alcalde, Samuel Gates, captain, and Gibson Kuykendall as *lieutenant*.

Early in the summer of 1823, Gibson and his father went over to Natchitoches, Louisiana, for supplies of salt, sugar, and coffee for the family. They carried these supplies on two pack horses.

In the latter part of the summer of 1823, some Tonkawas stole a horse from Gibson's father and several from Mr. Wheat. Gibson, his father, Thomas Boatright and Gibson's brother, Brazillai, pursued the thieves to a point just below Fort Bend on the Brazos. Finding the Indians encamped on the banks of Big Creek, the settlers returned to the village of San Felipe and reported to Stephen F. Austin. Austin raised a few men and the group, some thirty in number, returned to the Indian encampment where the chief named Carita returned all of the stolen horses and the Indian thieves involved were all given fifty lashes.

In November 1823, Gibson's father moved about thirty miles farther south down the Brazos River and settled on the west side of the river just above the mouth of Mill Creek. Here they cleared the land for farming and the following season raised their first good crop of corn. (*This is just upstream from San Felipe.*)

Gibson's mother, Sarah Gates, died sometime during 1823. Her grave has never been found. His father never remarried, preferring as J. Hampton stated, "*to raise all his children by himself with out having to subject them to a step-mother.*"

In the spring of 1824, the Indians again raided the area and Gibson's father lost all of their good horses, some thirteen in number. They pursued the Indians but were unable to retrieve any of their horses.

In July of the same year, Stephen F. Austin lead an expedition against the Carancawas, Gibson's father and his brother, Brazillai, were members of this expedition. After returning from this sojourn, Gibson and his father went on another trip looking for the Coke Indians in the "Damon's Mound" area. Gibson states that when they crossed the Bernard River they encountered a herd of buffalo and killed one for food.

In late spring 1826, Austin again raised a large company of men to make a campaign against the Carancawas and the Tawacanies. Gibson and his father joined the expedition about 17 May 1826. The entire force contained some 190 men and included Gibson's uncle, Robert H. Kuykendall. The expedition marched in heavy rain to the

Little Brazos river area. The Indian villages were found but no Indians were present and the expedition returned home toward the La Bahias crossing on the Brazos and disbanded.

In the fall of 1826, the disturbances known as the "Fredonia Rebellion" were started. Gibson states in his recollections: "In November or December, Austin sent my father, Judge Ellis and Francis W. Johnson to Nacogdoches to see the leaders of the Fredonians and endeavor to dissuade them from rash measures. They were, however, unable to do anything. After their return to San Felipe, the Mexican and Colonial forces marched against the revolutionists. So large a proportion of the men of the colony was sent on this service that Austin deemed it prudent to order my father with eight men to range the country between the Colorado and the Brazos along the San Antonio road to detect any inroads of the Wacoes or other northern tribes." This service was performed until after the terminations of the Fredonian troubles. These men he had with him were B. (Brazillai) Kuykendall, W. (William) Kuykendall, (Gibson's younger brothers) Early Robbins, Thomas Stevens, John Jones, James Kiggans, John Walker, and J. Furnaish. At that time the San Antonio road, except at the point where it crosses the Brazos, was from thirty to forty miles above the outmost settlements.[4]

In 1827 Gibson received a quarter-league of land as a single man. This was a Mexican Land Grant. Then in 1828, after his marriage to Elizabeth Leakey, he again petitions the Mexican authorities for additional land as follows:

Lord Commissioner Citizen Gaspar Flores

Town of San Felipe
March 29, 1828

Forward this petition to Citizen Esteban Austin for him to report hereinafter whether the applicant has the circumstances required by law, and whether (the land applied for) is private property.

Flores (Rubric)

I, Gibson Kuykendall, a native of the United States of the North, having lived in this Dept. for six years before you with the greatest respect appear and declare: that whereas in May of the past year I petitioned a quarter league as a single man, which is situated on Palmito (Mill) Creek above this town, which I cultivated and upon which I have established my house, family, and property, and whereas I have later acquired the new station of matrimony and have not yet received title of ownership for said tract, I beg that, pursuant to the provision of the Colonization Law of this state dated March 24th, 1825, and the powers that are vested in you as Commissioner to distribute lands in the 2nd colonization enterprise of Empressario Austin, you will please put me in possession of said tract and likewise grant me and give me possession of the augmentation to which I declare myself entitled as a married man by said law. By virtue of this, I want three quarters of a league to complete a league north and adjoining the league granted to Joel Lakey above this town of Austin, understanding fully that I (am) ready to comply with all that said colonization law requires, subjecting myself in all cases to the laws of this Federation in force and to the special laws of this state. Therefore, I beg you to please do as I have set forth, for therein I shall receive grace and justice.

Town of Austin, March 26, 1828
Gibson Kuykendall (signed)

Lord Commissioner:

Pursuant to your foregoing decree and the declaration of the applicant Gibson Kuykendall in his petition, I must say that he is one of the colonists introduced by me under my contracts with the Supreme Govt. of this State, and what he declares in his petition is true: he is a married man of good habits, well known industry and honesty, and there is no obstacle to his being granted the tracts he requests, for both are vacant; and I consider him by law entitled to be given possession of them. They comprise one league.

Town of Austin, May 12,1828
Estevan F. Austin (Rubric)

In accordance with the declaration of Empresario Austin in his foregoing report, I order that the tract requested by the interested party be surveyed by the Surveyor Horacio Chrisman and the corresponding title of ownership be issued him.

Town of Austin, May 13, 1828
Gaspar Flores (Rubric)[5]

The record states that the quarter league of land mentioned above is located on the east margin of the east branch of Palmito Creek known as Mill Creek (east side), and from the upper corner of Barzillai Kuykendall's tract on said creek to a point adjoining Early Robbin's tract on said creek. The other tract of three quarters league (an augmentation for marrying) was situated on what was called Caney Creek, back of Joel Lakey's league, and from there it adjoined tracts granted to John Elam and Samuel Miller. In addition to the Mexican Land Grants, Gibson received three more Bounty Grants and one grant issued under the Court of Claims under the Legislative Act of 1856. Also see Miller: "Received Bounty Warrant # 3740 for 640 acres from S War on 23 June 1838 for service from 1 Mar. to 1 Oct. 1836. 707.6 acres in Leon Co., were paid to him on 15 July 1862. Patent #222, Vol. 11, Abstract 474, Sup. D. GLO File Rob Bty 816. Note: 640 acres were originally paid to him but a re-survey showed the tract to contain 707.6 or an excess of 67.6 acres."—"Received Donation Certificate #360 for 640 acres from S War on 8 Aug. 1838 for being on the baggage detail at Harrisburg. 640 acres were paid to him in Hamilton County in Dec. 1889. Patent # 224, Vol. 77, Abstract #475, GLO File Military Donation #644."[6]

Gibson married Elizabeth Leakey in 1828. She was a sister of Lydia Leakey who married Amos Gates. She was possibly the daughter of Joel Leakey. They had one son, Brazilla, b. 18 December 1829. Brazilla married Louisa A. West in Washington County in 1853. Elizabeth Leakey died prior to 1837 because on 19 October 1837, Gibson married a cousin, Martha Kuykendall, in Austin County. Martha was probably the daughter of J. L. and Elisabeth Kuykendall and a sister to T. P. (Thornton Peyton) and John Kuykendall. Martha was also a sister to Catherine Kuykendall, who was the first wife of Gibson's younger brother, Barzillai.

Gibson and Martha's children were: Julian (b. ca. 1838), Joseph A. (b. ca. 1840), Wyatt Hanks (b. ca. 1843), John (b. ca. 1847), Elisabeth (b. ca. 1850), William Thornton (b. ca. 1852), Sarah (b. ca. 1854), Martha L. (b. ca. 1856), and Pernelia (female), unknown.[7]

After his father, Capt. Abner Kuykendall's death at San Felipe in July 1834, Gibson was appointed by the court as guardian for J. Hampton and Elisabeth and tutor for Wyatt Hanks and Samuel Gates, his younger brothers and sisters.[8]

The records of the General Land Office of Texas do not have a record of Gibson having received land for his services during the Siege of Bexar. However, recent roster lists discovered deep in the old Austin Papers do indicated that Gibson and most of his brothers were present around San Antonio during the months of October and November 1835. William, however, is the only brother to receive land for his services during that battle. The list is titled, "Muster Roll of Capt. R. Jones' Company, (signed) Daniel Perry, Orderly Sgt., Oct. 20, 1835." Those of the family who were present are: Thornton Kuykendall (son of Elisabeth), 4th Sgt., R. H. Kuykendall (son of Captain Robert, deceased), John Kuykendall (son of Elisabeth), Adam Kuykendall (son of Captain Abner, deceased, and brother to Gibson) and Gibson.[9]

In early 1836, when the alarm was first given by Gibson's younger brother, J. Hampton Kuykendall that the Mexicans were about to invade Texas, the citizens and neighbors of Austin and Washington counties formed militia companies and converged on the village of Gonzales. Gibson Kuykendall was elected lieutenant then captain of Company E, 1st Regiment, under Edward Burleson, general; Major McNutt, commander. He and all the others participated in the "Runaway Scrape." When General Houston split the army into two parts to proceed toward San Jacinto, Gibson was ordered to command the reserves at Harrisburg and was unable to participate at the battle. He petitioned his commander to allow him to go with the others but his request was denied by Houston. Researchers have hinted that there were bad feelings and jealousy between the Kuykendalls and Houston and that's why his request was denied. It was also felt by some that since Gibson had been a militia commander for nearly ten years that he should certainly be allowed to take part in the battle. It was not to be. Capt. Gibson Kuykendall, along with most of his younger brothers, Brazilla, William, J. Hampton, and Adam, and his cousins, Thornton P. and John Kuykendall, all of whom were serving in his company, were left to guard the wounded and the baggage at Harrisburg.[10]

"This is to Certify that Gibson Kuykendall entered Capt. McNutt's Company March 1st, 1836 as First Lieutenant and was elected Captain on the 8th of April in the Volunteer Army of Texas and is this day honorably discharged. Camp at Victory, May 30th, 1830."

A. Somervill, Lt. Col. Comg.
1st Regt. T.V.

"I certify that G. Kuykendall enrolled himself as a volunteer in the Army of Texas and was elected first Lieutenant and performed his duty as an officer up to the eighth of April and was elected Capt. and is entitled to pay up to this date.
Done in Camp at Victory, May 3th, 1836."

A. Somervill, Lt. Col. Comg.
1st. Regt. T.V.

"Received of Gibson Kuykendall two beeves for the use of Capt. Skurlock's Company for which the Treasury of Texas will pay ten Dollars each."
July 30th 1836

Theodore Bissell
asst. qt/ Master

"Received of Gibson Kuykendall five Hogs for the use of Capt. Skurlock's Company for which the Treasury of Texas will pay thirty Dollars."
July 31st 1836

> Theodore Bissell
> qt. Master

"Mill Creek Texas August 18 1836
Received of Gibson Kuykendall one beef at eight dollars for Capt. Home's troops."

> B.J. Revill
> assistant quartermaster

"Caney Creek Brazos River Oct. 1st. 1836.
I hereby Certify that Gibson Kuykendall entered the service as first Lieutenant in Capt. Cleveland's Company (now under my command) 1st Regt. 1st. Batl. Texas Army on the first day of July last and has served up to the present date making three months, he is thereby honorably discharged."

> B.F. Reavill, Capt.
> H.N. Cleveland
> Lieut. Col. 1st. Regiment, 1st Brg.

Republic of Texas]   "This day appeared Gibson Kuykendall and
Austin County   ]   after being duly sworn sayeth that the Republic of Texas is justly due him fifty eight dollars for beef and pork furnished the Army and he has the rights for that Amount and that he is in no way indebted to the government nor has he received anything from the government for said receipt and he the said Kuykendall further more authorizes Adam Kuykendall to present the same to the Auditor for the purpose of having them audited. Sworn to before me, Brazilla Kuykendall, Justice of the Peace for said county this May 22nd 1837."

> B. Kuykendall
> District No. 3[11]

A person desiring land after the revolution of 1836 was required to appear before a board of land commissioners in his county of residence where he could make application and answer questions specified by the constitution and the laws that had been enacted. The Boards of Land Commissioners began operation in early 1838 and some of the minutes of the first hearings are as follows:

Thursday, March 15th, 1838. Claim # 197.
Gibson Kuykendall presented his claim for one labor of land and took and subscribed the oath presented by Law (to wit). I do solemnly swear that I was a resident

citizen of Texas at the date of the Declaration of Independence, that I did not leave the country during the campaign of the spring of 1836 to avoid participation in the struggle, that I did not refuse to participate in the war, that I did not aid or assist the enemy, that I have not previously received a title to my quantum of land and that I conceive myself justly entitled under the Constitution and Laws to the quantity of land for which I apply."

(signed) Gibson Kuykendall

"B. Kuykendall and J. H. Kuykendall witnesses for the same deposed that the claimant arrived in this country in the year of 1821, that he is a man of family and has remained a Citizen of this Country till the present date. Whereupon the Board after having investigated said claim issued to the claimant a certificate for one labor of land."[12]

"I do hereby certify that the following list contains truly and faithfully a representation of all the tax due from each person in the County of Austin.

Given under my hand and seal of office this 20th July 1840.
Alexander Somervell, Clerk County Court,
Austin County and ex-officio Assessor.
Per J. Hampton   Kuykendall, D.C.C. A. C. &.

"Gibson Kuykendall has 900 acres of land, 25 town lots, 5 slaves, 20 cattle and 2 horses."[13]

The census of 1850 for Burleson County Texas shows Gibson as follows:[14]

#102. Gibson Kuykendall	48M Farmer $3000	Ky
Martha	32F	Mo
Brazillai	20M	Tex
Zulema	12M	"
Joseph A.	10M	"
Wyatt H.	7M	"
John	3M	"
Elizabeth	1F	"

In the 1860 census, Gibson was listed as a farmer in Burleson County Texas with his address as Evergreen, Texas. It is shown as follows:[15]

#493 Gibson Kuykendall	58M Farmer 4200-4989	Ky
Martha	46F	Ark
Wyatt H.	16M	Tex
John	13M	"
Elisabeth	10F	"
William	8M	"
Sarah	6F	"
Martha	4F	"

Gibson Kuykendall died on 1 December 1861. In his inventory of property is listed several thousands of acres of land in Burleson and Washington counties, a herd of cattle, sheep, hogs, work mules, oxen, and six Negro slaves. To date no grave has ever been found for any of the family members.

There is little or no evidence noted about the family after Gibson's death, however a Mrs. Martha Kuykendall married Mr. R. Lockhart in Bell County, Texas, on 29 November 1867. Then in the 1870 census of Bell County the following information exists:[16]

> "Bell County, Salado Beat # 4"
> R. Lockhart, 59 years old from Tenn.,
> Martha, his wife, 49 years old from Texas
> William, 17, possibly young Wm. Kuykendall
> Kuykendall (female) 20, possibly Elisabeth
> Angelina Kuykendall, 17
> Ruth Kuykendall, 14

The 1870 Census of Washington County Texas shows Joseph A. Kuykendall, Gibson and Martha's son, living at Evergreen, Texas, along with his wife, Sarah, and their three children. Also living with them are Joseph's two younger brothers, John age 21 and William age 18 and a Ms. Harriet Kuykendall, age 30, and her three little boys, Joseph, John and George.[17]

Chapter Sixteen

Barzillai Kuykendall of Austin's Colony

Barzillai (Brazilla) (B.) Kuykendall (ca. 1806-1873)—Frontiersman, colonist, Indian fighter, member of the colonial militia. He received a "labor" of land in Austin's first colony as one of the "Old 300." He was the son of Capt. Abner Kuykendall of North Carolina and Sarah (Sally) Gates Kuykendall. (Biblical names are predominate throughout the history of the family in colonial America. See II Samuel 19:31-33.) In all of the colonial records of the Mexican period and the Republic of Texas period, his name is divided equally between the two spellings, there are two occasions where he signed his name both ways. However he normally signed his name simply, "B. Kuykendall."

He was either born near Henderson, Kentucky, or in the Territory of Indiana because the family moved north of the "River Ohio" ca. 1806-1808. His father, Abner, appears on the census rolls for Logan-Christian-Henderson County, Kentucky, during those years and his name reappears on a "Memorial to the Governor of the Territory of Indiana" on 16 March 1808, just north across the Ohio River from Henderson.

In 1810, the family moved into northcentral Arkansas (Territory of Missouri) and settled near the mouth of the Cadron Creek on the east side of the Arkansas River. The village that was created there would be known as the "Cadron Settlement." In 1820 Abner and his family moved into southwest Arkansas near "Pecan Point" on the Red River. It was from that area that they would immigrate into the Mexican Province of Texas in the fall of 1821.

His brother Gibson states in his *Recollections*: "My father, Abner Kuykendall, and his brother, Joseph, with their families, left Arkansas Territory for Texas in October 1821. About the first of January 1822, my father and Thomas Boatright moved ten miles west of the Brazos River and settled near New Years Creek, about four miles south of the present town of Independence."

In the latter part of the summer of 1823, some Tonkawa Indians stole a horse from Barzillai's father and several from a Mr. Wheat. Barzillai, along with his father, his brother Gibson and Thomas Boatright, pursued the Indians to a point just below present day Richmond, Texas, on the Brazos. Finding the Indians camped on the banks of Big Creek, the men returned to San Felipe and reported the news to Austin. Stephen F. Austin raised a few more men and the group, some thirty in number, returned to the Indian encampment where after some negotiation, the Indian chief, Caritas, returned all of the stolen horses to the settlers and the Indian thieves involved were given fifty lashes.

In November 1823, Barzillai's father moved the family thirty miles farther south and settled on the west side of the Brazos River just above the mouth of Mill Creek. They then cleared the land and raised one of the first good crops since being in the colony.

Barzillai's mother, Sarah Gates, died during this same year of 1823. His father never remarried.

Barzillai received title to one "labor" of land in Austin County west of the Brazos River on 7 August 1824 as one of Stephen F. Austin's original "Old 300."

The disturbances known as the "Fredonia Rebellion" started in the fall of 1826. Austin sent Barzillai's father to Nacogdoches to try and settle the matter. After Abner's return, being unable to quell the problem, the Mexican and colonial forces marched from San Felipe to put down the rebellion. So many men were needed on that expedition, that Austin thought it necessary to order Capt. Abner Kuykendall and some of his men to patrol the San Antonio road between the Brazos and the Colorado rivers to prevent any inroads by the Waco Indians or any other northern tribes. Nine men in all were on that detail, which included Barzillai and his brother William.

On 27 April 1828, Brazilla received his second tract of land in Austin's second land dispersal. It was ¼ league and ¼ labor located on the east bank of Mill Creek and adjoining land owned by his brother Gibson. This was just north of the present village of New Bremen in Austin County.

On 22 August 1829, Stephen F. Austin wrote Capt. Abner Kuykendall a long letter of instructions that he take command of a group of the settlers and pursue a party of some fifteen Indians and one white man who had stolen some horses and that when he caught them that he was authorized in the name of the government to capture and "kill the said robbers, be them Indians or whites." Barzillai Kuykendall wrote:

"The above order was received the evening of the same day it was written, and in obedience thereto the ensuing morning, father, accompanied by brother William and myself, started for the Colorado, where we arrived the same evening and were joined by eight men, most of whom were old frontiersmen, to wit: Norman Woods, John F. Berry, Hazlitt, Elijah Ingram, John Williamson, Thomas Thompson, Seaborn Jones, and _____. We now counted eleven men, and father resolved to pursue the Indians without losing further time to increase our force. We forded the Colorado at the crossing of the La Bahia road and had proceeded eight or nine miles up the west side of the river, when about noon, we discovered people moving about an old cabin. As we knew the inhabitants of this neighborhood had, some time previously been driven from their homes by the Indians, this circumstance excited some surprise, and Hazlitt and another man were dispatched on foot towards the cabin to ascertain the character of its visitors. The rest of us sat in our saddles concealed by a point of woods."

"In order to approach near the house, Hazlitt and his companion had to pass through a corn-field. They had not proceeded far in the field when an Indian shot an arrow at Hazlitt and raising a war-whoop, fled towards the cabin. As he ran straight between two rows of corn, Hazlitt shot him in the back. The instant we heard the alarm we galloped forward and saw five Indians on foot, running up the river, evidently aiming to get to a thicket on its bank, two or three hundred yards above the cabin. Spurring our horses to their best speed, we intercepted them a short distance below the thicket. As we dismounted each man dropped the coil of his tethering rope from the pommel of his saddle and charged the Indians on foot. They were now compelled to fight us in the open prairie or leap down the precipitous bank of the river. They chose the latter alternative. Norman Woods shot one as he was in the act of leaping off the bluff. The remaining four threw away their arms and plunged into the Colorado. As they swam towards the opposite shore we plied them with two or three rounds of rifle balls, and sank two midway in the river. The remaining two reached the opposite shore with mortal wounds from which we could distinctly see the blood flowing. One of them uttered a few words in a very loud voice and almost instantly afterwards our ears were assailed with terrific yells from the thicket just above us, accompanied by a flight of arrows and discharge of fire-arms. Turning towards our unexpected assailants, we saw several of them running towards our horses. We also ran in the same direction, and all the Indians, except two, returned to the thicket. These two Indians succeeded in reaching our horses, of which each selected and mounted one and drove all the rest, save two, before them—yelling and firing off their guns to frighten the horses and urge them to greater speed. The two men whose horses were left, mounted them and pursued the Indians, the rest of us following as fast as possible on foot. After traveling nearly a mile and a half, we discovered our horses standing in a grove. Suspecting a ruse we approached them with caution, but found no enemy. Having now recovered all our horses but two (those of Thompson and Williamson) we returned to the scene of action, but every Indian had disappeared. The one shot by Woods was still alive, sitting under the bank. Deeming it an act of mercy to put an end to his sufferings, Woods shot him in the head. After collecting the arms of the defeated Indians, consisting of bows and arrows and one or two shotguns, we went into the field to look for the Indian shot by Hazlitt. We did not find him but picked up his belt which had been cut into by the rifle ball. This satisfied us that he had received a mortal wound. His body was afterwards found outside the field. The remains of the two who reached the opposite side of the river were also found afterwards—making six killed. Not one of our party was hurt, though Berry, after the engagement, fainted from the effect of the heat and over-exertion. There were at least forty or fifty of these Indians—Wacoes and Tawacanies. They were all provided with ropes and bridles and had doubtless come on a stealing expedition. The survivors left the Colorado without committing any depredations.—That evening we traveled about five miles on our return and slept at a spring about three miles above the present town of La Grange.

Immediately after father returned home and reported to Col. Austin, he received the following order.

'You will call a muster of your company and endeavor to raise volunteers to go against the Indians. If you cannot get volunteers enough to make one forth the number of men composing your company, you will raise them by draft. You will rendezvous at this place with at least one forth the men composing your company on the 12th September next, armed and equipped as the law directs, with provisions for a campaign of forty days. By the order of S. F. Austin.'

Oliver Jones, adjt.

"The different companies convened on the east side of the Colorado River about twelve miles below La Grange, between the 15th and 20th September, 1829. The entire force of nearly one hundred mounted men was placed by Austin under the command of my father."

On their way north toward the San Saba River the men spent the second night at Alum Creek at the point where it was crossed by the San Antonio road. From there the guide led them north until they crossed the San Gabriel River and then proceeded to the head of the Salt Branch of the Lampazos. Scouts were dispatched and upon their return two days later, reported having found a large encampment of Indians on the west bank of the Colorado River two or three miles below the mouth of the San Saba. The command was again ordered on the march and after a short distance, halted to await nightfall, so that an all night march could be made in order to attack the Indians at dawn the following day. The march had proceeded for several hours when the Mexican guide declared that he was unable to find his way. The men were obliged to wait until the morning to proceed. Suspecting the faithfulness of the guide, Capt. Abner Kuykendall decided not to use him any further and early the next morning sent six men, William Dever, Amos Gates, Seaborn Jones, Jefferson Pryor, another white man and a Chickasaw Indian named John on foot to explore the route to the Colorado River, supposedly some two or three miles from their camp, and search for a crossing.

Barzillai wrote: "They had proceeded about a mile and a half when they discovered twenty-five mounted Indians who charged towards them, yelling like demons. Our men ran back towards our camp and when the Indians pressed them too closely, turned and presented their guns and the Indians halted or slackened their pace. This was repeated several times. At length, John the Chickasaw, began to fail, and fall in the rear. The Indians could have shot or speared him but seemed intent upon making him prisoner. They ran up by his side and one of them caught him by the hand. At this critical juncture, John's friends again turned and pointed their guns at the pursuers, which enabled John to extricate himself and rejoin his party, who now had made a stand in a clump of bushes. Meantime the loud cries of the Indians had been heard at our camp and the whole command was hastening to the rescue. When William Dever perceived that succor was close at hand he shot one of the Indians and it was believed mortally wounded him. At this moment our whole force came up and the Indians fled at full speed. We pursued them as rapidly as the nature of the ground and a due degree of caution would permit. When we arrived at the Colorado River we forded it at the same place where the Indians had crossed.—John Shipman and I were ordered to dismount and proceed on foot in advance of the command. We walked briskly to the top of the hill, and looking down into the smooth, level prairie in a bend of the Colorado beheld it almost literally covered with mounted Indians, men women and children, flying from their encampment to the yellow cedar-brakes in the adjacent hills. We hastened back and reported and the command advanced at a gallop. We charged into the camp of Indians just as the last one mounted his horse to leave it. He was shot down by Holmes Petyon and Seaborn Jones. Nearly all the Indians had by this time gained the cover of the cedar-brakes. Detachments were sent a few miles in pursuit, but no Indians were found except a few squaws, who, when overtaken were riding slowly along apparently unconscious of danger or indifferent to it. When spoken to they made no reply. Indeed, neither by look nor gesture did they manifest recognition of our presence. Of course they were not molested.

"We encamped upon the ground evacuated by the Indians. Their conical, buffaloe skin lodges were still standing, and within them we found their entire store of winter provisions, namely, several hundreds of bushels of corn and beans, and a quantity of dried buffaloe meat. Many buffaloe robes were also found and on the fires were still boiling several kettles of corn and beans—all of which property was consigned to the flames or otherwise destroyed. The site of this encampment was very beautiful and had apparently often been temporarily occupied by the Indians; but there were no traces of agricultural operations. Early the ensuing morning, Capt. Henry Brown with a company of thirty men from Gonzales, rode into our camp. One of Capt. B's men who had traded with the Wacoes and Tawacanies at their villages on the Brazos, recognized the body of the Indian killed the day before, as that of a Tawacanie chief. It is also worthy of remark that the deceased was dressed in a hunting shirt and vest, one of which garments had belonged to Williamson and the other to Thompson and were tied to their saddles when the Indians took their horses in the fight in Wood's Prairie on the 25th of August.

"This day we commenced our homeward march—When the expedition reached the San Gabriel, it was disbanded and the men, in small squads, returned to their homes by different routes."

"In the month of November 1830, a Chickasaw Indian brought intelligence from the frontier that a party of eleven Wacoes were on their way to the neighborhood where I resided (22 miles northwest of San Felipe) for the purpose of stealing horses. The approach of the Indians was confirmed by one of my neighbors. He stated that they were on foot and well provided with ropes and bridles. The day this news was received a few of the neighbors armed and assembled for the purpose of attacking the Indians, who, we learned were camped near the residence of James Stephenson, on Caney Creek. As the Indians outnumbered our little party, William Cooper and I rode nearly all night to raise more men. At the dawn of the next day, with a force of eleven men, precisely that of the Indians, we stole upon their camp which was a little grove on the bank of a spring branch within less than a hundred yards of Stephenson's house. Favored by a gully and a dense fog, we approached within thirty feet of the Indians (part of whom had not yet risen), before they perceived us, at which moment we delivered our fire. One of the Indians fired and William Cooper fell, exclaiming that he was shot. The Indians ran and were pursued by our leader, Adam Lawrence, who reloaded his rifle and fired at them again, but further pursuit was prevented by the fall of young Cooper, who was shot through the heart and expired in a few minutes.

Late in the morning the trail of the Indians was followed as far as the bottom of Caney Creek, some five or six hundred yards. Seven red stripes marked their course across the prairie and two or three conically shaped pieces of spongy, rotten wood, with which these Indians are generally provided to plug their wounds, were picked up on their trail, saturated with blood. The carcass of one of the Indians was afterwards found in the Caney bottom. Seven of the eleven never reached home as will appear in the sequel. One shotgun, several bows and arrows, and ropes, and bridles fell into our hands. It was my painful duty to take the news of young Cooper's death to his parents who resided about five miles from the spot where he was killed. Of the eleven men engaged in this affair only the following are recollected, viz: Adam Lawrence, Thomas Stevens, Adam Kuykendall (Barzillai's younger brother), Charles Gates (Barzillai's uncle), George Robinson, William Cooper, B. (Barzillai) Kuykendall.

About a fortnight after the above events, Colonel Austin sent father, with six or seven men, of whom I was one, to Tenoxtitlan, then a recently established military post on the Brazos, garrisoned by one or two companies of Mexican Regulars under the command of Captain Ruis.

The object of our mission—had reference to the relations of the colonists and the Wacoes and Tawacanies. When we arrived at T. several northern Indians and two or three Wacoes were there.—One of the Wacoes informed the Mexicans that in the late affair on Caney they had sustained a loss of seven men, which corresponded well with my opinion."[1]

Barzillai Kuykendall married his cousin, Catherine Kuykendall, ca. 1828-30. She was the daughter of J. L. and Elisabeth Kuykendall and a sister of T. P. (Thornton Payton), John, and Martha Kuykendall (Gibson Kuykendall's second wife). Barzillai and Catherine had four children:

Joseph, b. ca 1834; Sarah, b. ca 1836; Lucinda, b. unknown; and Martha, b. ca 1839.[2]

Barzillai's father, Capt. Abner Kuykendall, was critically wounded by a man named Clayton that he was attempting to arrest on the streets of San Felipe in June 1834 and he died the following month. He was probably buried on his farm just north of San Felipe above the mouth of Mill Creek. His grave has never been found.

The records of the General Land Office do not record that Barzillai was in the Siege of Bexar. However, recent findings do indicate that Barzillai was indeed there with the rest of his family, ready to "do battle," if called upon. The records have him in a election roster of men under Burleson. He and his brother William were on the list: "The foregoing is the result of an election held on in Capt. F. W. Johnson's Company for Colonel 6 Nov. 1835."[3]

On 6 February 1836, "Brazilla" applied for an additional ¾ league of land for augmentation due to marriage. The land was located between the rivers, adjoining Price's League, and was noted to be in Austin's 5th Land Colony. The request was later denied.[4]

In late February 1836, when the alarm was first given by Barzillai's younger brother, J. Hampton, that the Mexicans were about to invade Texas, the citizens and neighbors of Austin and Washington counties formed militia companies and converged on the village of Gonzales. Barzillai's older brother, Gibson, was elected lieutenant, then captain of County E., 1st Regiment, under Edward Burleson, general; Major McNutt, commander. He and the others participated in the Run-Away Scrape. When General Houston split the army into two parts to proceed to the battle at San Jacinto, Capt. Gibson Kuykendall and all of his company was ordered to remain at Harrisburg and guard the wounded and the baggage, hence neither Barzillai nor any of the immediate family participated in the actual battle. His other brothers in the company were Gibson, William, J. Hampton, and Adam. His cousins, who were also his brother-in-laws, Thornton P. and John Kuykendall were in the same company.[5]

"I certify that B. Kuykendall Enrolled himself in the volunteer Army of Texas for Three Months as a Private commencing March 1, 1836 & has ever since performed his Duty & is now honorably Discharged.
Camp at Victoria May 30th, 1836"
"A. Summervill Lt.Col. Comg.   G. Kuykendall Capt."

"Mills Creek July 6th, 1836"
"Received of Brazilla Kuykendall one Beef appraised at fifteen dollars for the use of my company."

H. N. Cleveland-Capt.

REPUBLIC OF TEXAS
COUNTY OF AUSTIN

"This day appeared before me, Robert McNutt, Justice of the Peace, Barzillai Kuykendall, who upon being duly sworn states: That the discharge for the term of three months, dated Victoria, May 30, 1836, signed G. Kuykendall, Capt. and A. Sommervill, Lt. Col. Com'g., 1st Regt. T. V., is just-true and correct and also the receipt dated Mills Creek July 5th, 1836 for one beef at fifteen dollars signed by H. N. Cleveland, Capt.

And the aforesaid Barzillai Kuykendall further saith on oath that from, or on account of Govt., he has received but one pair of shoes to the price of which he cannot swear."

B. Kuykendall

"Sworn to and subscribed
before me this 1st day of
May 1837"
Robt. McNutt[6]

A person desiring land after the revolution of 1836 was required to appear before a Board of Land Commissioners in his county of residence where he could make application and answer questions specified by the constitution and the laws that had been enacted. The Boards of Land Commissioners began operation in early 1838 and some of the minutes of the first meeting are as follows:

"Thursday, 15 March 1838"
No. 196

Brazillai Kuykendall presented his claim for three quarters league and one labor of land, and took and subscribed the oath prescribed by law, to wit: I do solemnly swear that I was a resident Citizen of Texas at the date of the Declaration of Independence, that I did not leave the Country during the Campaign of the Spring of 1836 to avoid participation in the struggle, that I did not refuse to participate in the war, that I did not aid nor assist the enemy, that I have not previously received a title to my quantum of land and that I conceive myself justly entitled under the Constitution and laws to the quantity of land for which I now apply."

signed   "Brazillai Kuykendall"

J. H. Kuykendall and Gibson Kuykendall deposed that the claimant arrived in this Country in the year 1821, that he is a man of family and that he has been a resident Citizen of Texas at the date of the Declaration of Independence, and has remained a Citizen of this Country to the present date.

Whereupon the Board after having investigated said claim issued a certificate for three quarters league and one labor of land.[7]

In 1840, Barzillai shows up on the Tax rolls for Austin County as follows:

Austin County

I do hereby certify that the following list contains truly and faithfully a representation of all the tax due from each person in the County of Austin, in conformity with the general inventory as made from the inventory of the parties, and that a just and true estimation of the tax has been made in conformity with the provisions of "An Act to Raise Public Revenue by Direct Taxation" approved January 16, 1840 and supplement passed by the succeeding Congress—
Given under my hand and seal of office this 20th July 1840
Alexander Sommervill, Clerk County Court, Austin County
& ex-officio Assessor. Per. J. Hampton Kuykendall, D.C.C.A.c.&"
"Kuykendall, Barzillai" Poll 1—T1111   1tl (town lot) 7 cattle[8]

In the year 1842, the Mexicans invaded Texas twice, marching into San Antonio on both occasions. These two adventures are known as the "Vargas" and "Woll" campaigns. The Kuykendall family was active in both invasions and is documented as follows:

This is to certify that upon the invasion of the Western frontier of Texas by the Mexican forces under General Basquez in the spring on 1842, the undersigned knows that Barzillai Kuykendall went from the county of Austin armed and equipted for the purpose of assisting in repelling the invasion and that we saw the said Kuykendall in the Army as far west as the Guadalupe River.

John C. Lee

Williamson County Jan. 22, 1852   J. H. Kuykendall

State of Texas } Personally appeared before me, Levi
County of Williamson} Asher, a Justice of the Peace in and for the county of Williamson, John C. Lee and J. H. Kuykendall whose names are inscribed to the above certificate and upon oath declared that the facts therein stated are true.
January 22th, 1852 Levi Asher JP

  I, Barzilla Kuykendall, do hereby nominate constitute and appoint A. J. Bell my agent and attorney in fact for one and in my name to present to the Treasurer of the State of Texas my audited draft for services rendered in what is known as the Vasquez Expedition in 1842 and to receive and accept for the payment thereof hereby ratifying and confirming the acts of my said attny in the Business aforesaid and fully authorizing him, the said A. J. Bell, to do all that he might or could do in the premises aforesaid. Given under my hand and scroll for seal the 10th of Feby. 1854.
                B. Kuykendall

       #1876
     Barzillai Kuykendall
~~~~~~~~~~~~~~~~~~~~
Service on the Vargas
Campaign in 1842
~~~~~~~~~~~~~~~~~~~~
Certificate issued
to each of the above
for thirty one 50/100
dollars.
May 23rd 1853
"Jno. M. Swisher"
Auditor[9]

State of Texas } Before me Jno. P. Osterhart, a Notary Public
County of Austin} for said county duly commissioned and sworn personally appeared B. Kuykendall, Cambell Longley & John C. Lee, who upon oath say that when the western frontier of Texas was invaded by the Mexicans under Gen. WOLL in the fall of 1842 that B. Kuykendall went from the county of Austin and was seen as far west as the County of Fayette—armed and equipped to assist in repelling the invaders
      B. Kuykendall
        Campbell Longley
        John C. Lee

 Sworn to & subscribed before me
   To certify which I hereunto
   set my hand & affirm my
   official Seal this 10 Feby.
   1854, Jno.P.Osterhart,Notary Pub.

#3978—Reced. Feby. 13th, 1856, full payment for the within certificate from the State of Texas.
            A. J. Bell
            Kuykendall, Barzilla[10]

Sometime after the birth of their last daughter (Martha), Barzillai's first wife, Catherine Kuykendall, died. There has been no marriage certificate found for his second marriage to Elisabeth, but their first child, Solomon, was born ca. 1849. He was followed by William H., born ca. 1852, and Nancy, born ca. 1855.[11]

The 1850 of Washington County, Texas, shows the following information:[12]

	Washington Co.	
B. Kykendale	45M Farmer 3000	Indiana
Elisabeth	30 F	Tex
Joseph	16 M	"
Sarah	14 F	"
Maranda} (Twins)	11 F	"
Martha }	11 F	"
Solomon	1 M	"

The 1860 Census of Washington County is as follows:[13]

	Washington County, 1860	
B. Kuykendall	54 M	Ark
Elisabeth	38 F.	North Carolina
Solomon	12 M	Tex
W. H.	8 M	"
Nancy	5 F	"

The 1870 Census of Washington County is as follows:[14]

	Washington County 1870	
Kurkyndall, Brazil	65 M 3000-1100	Ind.
Elisabeth	49 F.	North Carolina
Solomon	21 M. Farmer	Tex
Wm. H.	19 M. Farm Assist.	"
Nancy	15 F.	"

The State of Texas }
County of Bastrop} Know all men by these presents that I, B. Kuykendall, of the County of Washington and state aforesaid fordivers good causes and considerations me hereunto moving being desirous on my part to settle and arrange the rights of my daughters by my first marriage with Mrs. Catherine Kuykendall to-wit: Mrs Martha L. Orvell, wife of Thomas A. Orvell and Mrs. Lucinda O. Thurmond wife of William Thurmond of Bastrop County they being entitled to their respective shares of their mother's interest in our headright league of land and being of full age and capable of attending to their own business in their respect I hereby transfer relinquish and forever quitclaim unto Mrs. Martha L. Orvell of said County and State the following tract piece or parcel of land being a part of our said headright in full satisfaction and settlement of her interest in said league of land as heir of her said mother Catherine same described and bounded as follows to-Wit: (land description), containing 800 acres of land by estimation—In witness where of I have hereunto set my hand and affixed my seal using a scroll for seal this 2nd day of March A D 1870.[15]

"B. Kuykendall" (seal)

General Land Office
Austin, Texas—Nov. 28, 1872

This is to certify that there is on file in this office a Bounty Warrant No. 4176 issued by Geo. W. Schockley, Secretary of War of the late Republic of Texas, on the 8th day of August 1838, to Barzillai Kuykendall, for services rendered by him in the Army of said Republic from the 1st day of March until the 30th day of May, 1836, having been honorably discharged.

In testimony thereof, I hereunto sign
my name and affix the impress
of the seal of said office this
day and year ___above written.
  J. Gross
   Commissioner

The State of Texas }
County of Blanco }

I hereby certify that I know Brazillia Kuykendall Late of Washington County and knew him to be in the Army that separated Texas from Mexico in AD 1835 and know him to be in the Battle at the taking of San Antonio the same year. I believe he was there in his Bro. Gibson Kuykendall's Company and I knew him in the Army in 1836 in his brother Gibson Kuykendall's Company in the 1st. Regiment commanded by Col. Ed. Burleson and knew him to be at the Battle of San Jacinto though not in the engagement but was in detail with the Entire Company Guarding the baggage.

And I further certify that I am not interested in the Said Brazillai Kuykendall getting a pension as a Veteran as this certificate entitles him to as an heir or relative and that I further certify that I am informed that Brazillai Kuykendall is dead and died at his home in Washington County Texas.
  John Ingrum

The State of Texas }
County of Blanco } "I certify that the foregoing and within certificate was duly sworn to by John Ingrum to me well known as a creditable Citizen of Blanco County." On this the 3rd day of November AD 1874.
  In testimony whereof I hereunto
  sign my name and affix the
  seal of office on the day and date above named.
  "John B. Finkle"
  JPP no.3BC & ex-oficio N. Public
  for Blanco County[16]

The State of Texas}
County of Lee } On this the 22nd day of October AD 1874 personally appeared before me, C. M. Leates, a Justice of the Peace, and ex-oficio, a Notary Public of said County, William H. Kuykendall, Nannie Kuykendall, Lucinda Thurmond, wife of Wilson Thurmond, and Martha Orvell, wife of Thomas A. Orvell,

of the County and state aforesaid, who being first duly sworn by me according to law, make the following declaration in order to obtain the pension provided for the descendants of survivors of the Revolution which separated Texas from Mexico. That your petitioners are the only legitimate children and legal descendants of Barzillai Kuykendall, who served as a Soldier in the military service of Texas between the first day of January AD 1832, and the fifteenth day of October AD 1836, in the revolution which separated Texas from Mexico, that said Barzillai Kuykendall died on the 31st day of March AD 1873; that he left a widow, Elisabeth Kuykendall surviving him, who died on the 10th day of April AD 1873; that your petitioners, William H. Kuykendall and Nannie Kuykendall, are the only legitimate descendants of said Barzillai Kuykendall, deceased, by his said wife, Elisabeth Kuykendall, deceased, and that said Lucinda Thurmond and Martha Orvell are the only legitimate descendants of said Barzillai Kuykendall, deceased, by a former marriage, that no prior application has been filed in their behalf, or by the father or mother; that petitioner Nannie Kuykendall is a minor under twenty-one years of age, and that Robert N. Atchinson of said County is the legally approved guardian of her estate; that said applicants hereby appoint James Shepard and Searcy of the law firm of Shepard & Searcy of the city of Austin and the state aforesaid, their attorneys to prosecute the above claim, that their residence is in Lee County, and their post office address is Giddings in said county and state; that said decedent, Barzillai Kuykendall, left no grand-children surviving him whose parents are dead.

Sworn to and subscribed]	Lucinda C. Thurmond
before me, C. M. Seale, a]	M. L. Orvell
justice of the peace of Lee]	Nannie Kuykendall
County and state aforesaid]	W. H. Kuykendall
and ex-oficio Notary Public there of]	Robert N. Atkinson
as witnessed my name and seal of office]	Guardian for Nannie K.
this 22nd day of October AD 1874.]	

#907
PENSION CLAIM
of   BARZILLAI KUYKENDALL
WASHINGTON COUNTY TEX

APPROVED DECEMBER 21st
1874
Amount of Pension $250.00[16]

The heirs of Barzillai Kuykendall filed for probate in Washington County, Texas, in AD 1880.[17]

As stated above, Barzillai Kuykendall, one of the last of "Austin's Old 300," died at his home in Washington County, Texas, on 31 March 1873, and his wife Elisabeth died one month later. To date no grave has ever been found for either one.

Chapter Seventeen

William Kuykendall of Austin's Colony, 1810–1862

William (Abner) Kuykendall (ca 1810-1862)—Colonist, Indian fighter, rancher, son of one of Stephen F. Austin's earliest members of the "Old 300." He was the son of Capt. Abner Kuykendall of North Carolina and Sarah (Sallie) Gates Kuykendall of Tennessee. He was probably born about the time that the family started their move from the Kentucky-Indiana area to the Territory of Missouri (Arkansas).

Shortly after March 1808, it is obvious that the Kuykendalls and the related families of the Gates and the Hardins began their move into Missouri Territory (Arkansas). Abner Kuykendall, William's father, and their respective families, left Arkansas Territory for Mexico (Texas) in October 1821, probably accompanied by Abner's father-in-law, William Gates, and all of his sons and daughters

The settlers and their families left Nacogdoches in late October and reached the Brazos River and the junction of the La Bahia road on 26 November 1821, where they remained camped for about a month. They made camp inland a few miles in an area that the boys had scouted previously, next to a pretty clear running stream on the evening of 31 December 1821. The following morning, they named the stream "New Years Creek" in honor of their campsite. This area is located in the present "league of land" that was later granted to Abner Kuykendall about five miles north of Brenham on the road to Independence in Washington County, Texas. Abner and his family, along with the Boatrights, decided to stay in this area.

In November 1822, Abner Kuykendall rented his farm to a Mr. Wheat on New Years Creek and moved the family back over to the Brazos River to a point five miles below the La Bahia road.

In November 1823, Abner again decided to move his family about 30 miles farther down the Brazos River. He settled on its west bank about eight miles above the village of San Felipe. The farm was located just a short distance above the mouth of Mill Creek. Here the family raised one of their first good crops since moving to Texas. The location is in southeast Austin County.

William's mother, Sallie Gates Kuykendall, died sometime during the year of 1823.

The disturbances known as the Fredonia Rebellion started in the fall of 1826. Austin sent William's father (Abner) to Nacogdoches to try and settle the matter. After Abner's return, being unable to quell the problem, the Mexican and colonial forces marched from San Felipe to put down the rebellion. So many men were needed on the expedition, that Austin thought it necessary to order Capt. Abner Kuykendall and some men to patrol the San Antonio road between the Brazos and Colorado rivers to prevent any inroads by the Waco Indians or any other northern tribes. Nine men in all were on that detail, which included young William Kuykendall and his older brother, Barzillai.

Between the periods of 1821 and 1826, William's older brothers, Gibson and Barzillai accompanied their father on many expeditions during the Indian Wars of the period but this is the first mention in their memoirs of the appearance of William. He was about 16 years old at this time and his father probably couldn't keep the young man out of the frays any longer.[1]

On 29 April 1828, William Kuykendall received his first land grant of ¼ league (1,107 acres) of land. It was located on the east side of the east fork of Mill Creek in present day Austin County.[2]

On 22 August 1829, Stephen F. Austin wrote Capt. Abner Kuykendall a long letter of instructions that he take command of a group of the settlers and pursue a party of some fifteen Indians and one white man who had stolen some horses and that when he caught them that he was authorized in the name of the government to capture and "kill the said robbers, be them Indians or whites." Barzillai Kuykendall wrote: "The above order was received the evening of the same day it was written, and in obedience thereto the ensuing morning, father, accompanied by brother William and myself, started for the Colorado, where we arrived the same evening and were joined by eight men." This experience is given in the biography on Barzillai.[3]

The *1830 Citizens of Texas* shows William having received ¾ league of land and one labor in Austin County.[4]

William Kuykendall married Eliza M. Carothers (Caruthers) on 6 November 1834 by Bond in Austin County. She was the daughter of Thomas Carothers. William and Elizabeth had nine children who survived infancy: Thomas Hampton, b. 1836; William b. 1839; Jane E., b. 1842; Catherine, b. 1844; Margaret b. 1845; Eliza-no date; Levantha-no date; Mary Ella-no date; Talbot Chambers-no date.[5]

William's father, Capt. Abner Kuykendall, was critically wounded by a man he was attempting to arrest named Clayton on the streets of San Felipe in June 1834 and he died the following month of July.[6]

The following men were issued Donation Certificates for 640 acres of land for having participated in the Storming and Capture of Bexar
(San Antonio), December 5th through the 10th, 1835: Kuykendall, William[7]

William appears on several Muster & Roster Rolls of men who participated in the Siege of Bexar.

      Election Results-FW Johnson for Col. 6 Nov. 1835.
 A list of Volunteers belonging to Capt. Bradley's Company Now present Nov. 21st 1835.
 A list of men who have this day volunteered to remain before Bexar—Nov. 24th 1835. Signed by Edw. Burleson & W.T. Austin.[8]

It has been stated that William was with his brother Capt. Gibson Kuykendall at Harrisburg, but he does not show up on the official muster roll.

 Received of William Kuykendall one large Sorrell horse for ____ on account of the Government of Texas. Which horse has been appraised at two hundred dollars,
June 20th, 1836   By order of Brig.
            Genl. Green.

I hereby certify that I was one
of the appraisers of the above
named horse and the above
is a correct certificate.
May 7th, 1838. H.N. Cleveland

      Texas June 21st—1836
 This government of Texas will pay Wm. Kuykendall five dollars for corn furnished Capt. Blunt's Company on the their march to join the army at head quarters
        W. L. McDonald
        Quartermaster

In Camp near Cureathersis? Texas July 29th, 1836
I certify that William Kuykendall has this day furnished my company with five dollars worth of corn on our march to join the Army which the Government will account for.
        Rich. Hooper, Capt.

(Admit this to Audit
May 6th, 1838.)   A.S. Thurston
      Q M Genl.

      Colorado November 20th 1836
This is to certify that Wm. Kuykendall Entered the Ranging service in my company on the 20th of July and for which time he is here by Honorably discharged from this service.
        John Polk
        Capt.
        Ewd. Burleson
        Col. Com'ding detach.
        of Rangers

"William Kuykendall"
filed 27th June 1837
Examined same day
admitted to audit for
$153.75
Military
16 June 1836
Ent. 27th June 1837
N. draft 3333. N.
Approved 28 June 1837
E. M. Pease, Controller

"A Joint Resolution for the benefit of WILLIAM KUYKENDALL"
"Resolved by the Senate and House of Representatives of the Republic of Texas in Congress assembled that the auditor of public accounts is hereby required to audit and allow the claim of WILLIAM KUYKENDALL for two hundred and five dollars for a horse and corn furnished the Army of Texas,

(signed) Joseph Rowe

Approved

Speaker of House
of Representatives,
Mirabeau B. Lamar
President of the Senate[9]

24th May 1838
SAM HOUSTON

As stated earlier, a person desiring land after the revolution of 1836 was required to appear before a board of Land Commissioners in his county of residence where he could make application and answer questions specified by the constitution and the laws that had been enacted. The Boards of Land Commissioners began operation in early 1838 and some of the minutes of the first hearings are as follows:

25 January 1838

No. 98. WILLIAM KUYKENDALL appeared and presented his claim for three quarters of a league and one labor of land and took & subscribed the following oath to wit: I do solemnly swear that I was a resident of Texas at the date of the Declaration of Independence, that I did not leave the country during the campaign of the Spring of 1836 to avoid participation in the Struggle, that I did not refuse to participate in the war, that (114) I did not aid or assist the enemy, that I have not previously received a title to my quantum of land and I conceive myself justly entitled under the Constitution and Laws to the quantity of land for which I now apply.

(signed) William Kuykendall

James Cochrane deposed that the applicant was a resident Citizen of Texas in 1829, was a Citizen at the Declaration of Independence, was married before that time and has resided in the Republic to the present date & J. Ham. Kuykendall deposed that if his memory does not err and if tradition is true, the said William Kuykendall emigrated to Texas some time in the year of our Lord eighteen hundred and twenty one and that he has resided in the Country to this date and was married before the Declaration of Independence.

Wherefore the Board issued to said William Kuykendall a Certificate for three quarters of a league and one labor of land, it being so much of his headright not heretofore received.

San Felipe de Austin January 26th 1838. The Board of Land Commissioners met pursuant to adjournment.[10]

I do hereby certify that the following list contains truly and faithfully a representation of all the tax due from each person in the County of Austin, in conformity with the general inventory as made from the inventory of the parties, and that a just and true estimation of the tax has been made in conformity with the provisions of an entitled "An Act to Raise a Public Revenue by Direct Taxation" approved January 16th 1840 and supplement passed by the succeeding Congress—

Given under my hand and seal of office this 20th July 1840. Alexander Somerville, Clerk County Court, Austin County & ex-officio Assessor. Per. J. Hampton Kuykendall, D.C.C.A.C. &

POLLS	LAND	OTHER PROPERTY	
Kuykendall, Wm. 1	S3510	1 sl(slave)	35 cattle[11]

This is to certify that upon the invasion of the Western Frontier of Texas by the Mexican forces under Vasquez in the spring of 1842, the undersigned know the William Kuykendall went from the County of Austin Mounted and Armed, to assist in repelling the invasion and that we saw the said William Kuykendall in the Army as far west as the Guadalupe River—

Williamson County}   John C. Lee
January 22nd 1852 }   J. H. Kuykendall

State of Texas   }   Personally appeared before me, Levi
County of Williamson}   Asher, a Justice of the Peace in and for the County of Williamson, John C. Lee and J. H. Kuykendall who acknowledged that they signed the above certificate and declared that the facts set forth therein are true—
Sworn to this 22nd of January 1852.   (signed) Levi Asher, JP

1876
William Kuykendall

~~~~~~~~~~~~~~~~~~~~

Services on the Vargas
Campaign in 1842

~~~~~~~~~~~~~~~~~~~~

Certificate issued to
each of the Above
for thirty-one dollars
May 23rd 1853
Jno. M. Swisher
Auditor
Samml. B. Shank
Compt.[12]

Some of the notable newcomers to the county between 1845 and 1850 were: William Kuykendall, a son of Capt. Abner Kuykendall. William came to this county in the late 1840s and settled near Mesquite Landing. J. Hampton Kuykendall lived in the county at various times. The Kuykendalls bought land owned by Willard Richardson, who then was the owner and editor of the *Galveston News*. The children of William intermarried with local families. Thomas married Cordelia Martin, daughter of Robert; William Jr. (later Judge William of McMullen County) married Kate Spaulding Byrne, daughter of Thomas K. Byrne, and niece of Captain James W. Byrne; T. C. (Talbot Chambers) married Alzena Dubois, daughter of Lucas Dubois of Saluria; Mary Kuykendall married Albert Teal of Lamar.

The year 1852 saw the last Indian fight in Refugio County and the expulsion of the Karankawas from the county and probably from Texas—the savages fled to Mexico. In 1851 or 1852 they reappeared at their old camping grounds at the mouth of the Guadalupe River and along the shores of Hynes Bay. Shortly they reverted to their old habits of killing and driving off cattle and livestock and committing petty thefts.

One morning William Kuykendall and his sons, Thomas, William and Talbot, happened unexpectedly upon the Indians in camp on the bluffs of Hynes Bay, the site being in the present Duncan pasture. The Kuykendalls got away without being detected, and reported the location of the Karankawas to the surrounding white settlers. It was decided immediately to form a posse and drive the Indians out of the county.

The posse met at Fagan's ranch and elected John Hynes as its leader. Included in the posse were John Hynes, Captain, William Hynes, William Fagan, Nicholas Fagan, John Fagan, Thomas O'Connor, William Kuykendall, Thomas Kuykendall, Talbot C. Kuykendall, John O'Brien, Michael Whelan, Dr. R. W. Wellington, Alfred S. Thurmond, Carlos de la Garcia, James W. Byrne, Martin L. Byrne, Moses Simpson, Walter Lambert, Charles G. Norton, John R. Baker, and Samuel Townsend.

The settlers rode towards the Indian camp and headed down the bluff, hoping to take the enemy by surprise. In this they were successful, but the Indians put up a stiff fight and wounded some of the citizens. (Captain de la Garcia was probably one of those wounded). It was not until several of the Indians had been killed and a number wounded that the Karakawas broke and left the battlefield in flight. John Hynes is known to have killed one of the braves. This was the end of the Karankawas in Refugio County.[13]

William Kuykendall died in Refugio County at Hynes Bay on 27 February 1862. His son, Judge William K. of McMullen County, stated in his *Civil War Diary*:

> Some time during the summer of 1862, a Regiment was organized by consolidating Yager's and Taylor's Battalion, which was designated as the 1st Regiment of Texas Cavalry and August Buchel was appointed Colonel; W. O. Yager, Lt. Col.; and Meyers, Major. But I am digressing, I must now return to the camp of instruction at Victoria. It was while at this camp (camp located on Spring Creek, three miles above Victoria on the east side of the Guadalupe River) that I received a message that father was dangerously ill at his home at Ingleside, in San Patricio County.
>
> Brother (T.C.) and I at once applied to the Captain for a permit to visit our sick

parent, the permit was refused by the commanding officer, Col. Garland. I saddled my horse and advised the Captain that I should go to father with or without a permit. Brother followed my example and within a few hours we were hastening with all possible speed to Ingleside, about seventy-five miles distant. Our worst fears were realized on reaching home to find our father hopelessly ill, his death ensuing on the 27th of February, a few days after our arrival.[14]

No grave has ever been found for William Kuykendall.

Chapter Eighteen

J. Hampton Kuykendall

Jonathon Hampton Kuykendall (1816-1880), a scholar of the Republic of Texas, was misidentified in the original *Handbook of Texas* and some archival papers as James H. Kuykendall. He always went by the name of Hampton or Hamp. A self-taught scholar, he was well versed in Spanish, Latin, history and geology.[1]

Hampton was the son of Capt. Abner Kuykendall and Sallie Gates. Sallie was the daughter of William Gates and Catherine Hardin. Hampton was named after his father's neighbor, friend and possible cousin, Jonathon Hampton. Jonathon Hampton had been traveling in the group with the family for many years. He had been in Kentucky with them and moved with them over into Indiana Territory in 1808 and then followed them on down into Missouri Territory (Arkansas) after 1810.[2]

J. Hampton was born on 15 November 1816, probably at or near the "Cadron Settlement" on the east side of the Arkansas River just below the mouth of Cadron Creek. His father had settled there in 1810.[3]

JHK accompanied his father and other family members to Texas in the fall of 1821, when the family joined Austin's Colony as one of the earliest members of the old original "300." "Young as the writer then was (referring to JHK), he distinctly remembers Austin and his companions, who visited his father's camp (New Years Creek) on the morning of January 1, 1822. A 'norther' then prevailed and a light snow covered the ground."[4]

In all of his memoirs and reminiscences, he makes little or no comment about himself after his arrival into Texas until his statement that he was residing in Chihuahua, Mexico, in early 1836, when he learned of the possible invasion of Texas by Santa Anna. However his later writings done on his own or at the request of others contain considerable information about his older brothers Gibson, Barzillai, William, his father, and his uncle, Capt. Robert H. Kuykendall. His *Reminiscences* housed at the Barker History Center are filled with stories by his brothers Gibson and Barzillai that go into great detail of the early days of the colony and especially the early Indian wars. This information was, however, greatly enhanced by the recent discovery of his previously unpublished California manuscript. In that document, written after his ventures in the Mexican War or 1846-7, he goes into great detail about the early days of the colony, himself, his father, talks of his mother's death, and the fact that he indeed gave the very first actual warning of the invasion of Texas by Santa Anna. This scholar and his writings form the backbone of all writings done on this particular family.[5]

Excerpts from a portion of the California manuscript state:

> My father, Abner Kuykendall, a North Carolinian by birth, but raised in Kentucky, emigrated to the Territory of Indiana about the year 1804 or 1805. Whence in a few years, he removed to the territory of Arkansas, where he resided several years where I was born.
>
> In the autumn of 1821, he emmigrated to Texas as a Colonist under the contract made by Moses Austin with the Vice-Regal Government of Mexico, the fulfillment of which contract had, by the death of the original Empresario, devolved on his son, Stephen F. Austin.
>
> My father and his brothers Robert and Joseph and families and two or three other families were the first families that settled west of the Brazos River. The vast expanse of country extending from San Antonio to Nacogdoches was then only inhabited by various tribes of hostile Indians. My father and my uncle Robert were for many years prominent leaders of the Colonists in their Indian Wars. Such of my brothers as were of age (Gibson, Barzillai and William) to bear arms were also active and efficient as was also my lamented cousin, the late noble hearted, and by nature, highly endowed, Robert H. Kuykendall. (Son of Capt. RHK.)
>
> The hardships, the privations, the dangers, and the romantic deeds of the early Colonists should here engage for a brief space my pen, did my proposed limits admit of it, but the less interesting subject of auto-biography alone, now engross these pages.
>
> So various, rapid and exciting have been the political events of this country; so multiplied, intense, and in the main, painful. My own thoughts and emotions; So many revolutions have been wrought by time and experience in my mind; So great a change is apparent in the social condition and even the physical face of the country—So many new men have crowded upon the stage and so many of the "old familiar faces" have become invisible forever, that the review of my boyhood's days is like casting back the Mental Ken "beyond a Million Seas."—Hence, ideas and emotions constitute the true horologe of the soul.
>
> Some sexagenarians retain much of the freshness of youth, and some young men are as gray at heart as if they had not been born before the flood.
>
> From childhood I have been sensitive, irritable and melancholy. During that period I was noted for a thousand times chided for a dreamy abstraction of mind. As boyhood verges upon youth the most gorgeous visions were developed. I had an intense desire to travel—to see forign countries—for the "distant and the dim" albeit they "lend enchantment to the view" of all, presented illusions to my imagination experienced, perhaps, by few. I became moody, restless and discontented. I loathed the labor

of the farm and soon became rebellious. My father was at times a stern man and not unfrequently corrected me with some severity. But is was to no avail. I was fond of reading and resolved to educate myself—In those early days books were scarce—but I eagerly devoured all I could procure. My partial friends soon began to regard me as a prodigy of erudition. My father was proud of my talents and thought me destined for a great man. Alas! Mistaken parent!

I must not omit that my good mother died when I was only eight years of age. My father never remarried again; for although several of his children were young (three being younger than myself) he preferred bringing us up by himself to the risque of introducing a bad step-mother into his family. He was exceedingly anxious to give his children at least a plain education, and notwithstanding this was very difficult in a new country, he partially succeeded.

At the age of sixteen (fall of 1833) my father absolved me from all allegiances to his authority. I had the option of entering the mercantile career as a clerk for W. C. White & Co., or of studing the law. I chose the law. I had made little progress when the declining health of Mr. Lesassier—the gentleman who had very kindly offered to direct my studies, compelled me to abandon for a time, the under taking. At this juncture, my passion to travel was revived by meeting with Mr. Thomas McQueen, an educated but rather eccentric gentleman, who had once been my tutor for a short time. He was on the point of visiting Monclova, the seat of Government of the State of Coahuila and Texas, for the purpose of transacting important business with the Govt. for Austin and Williams—Empresarios of a Colonial grant to which there was a rival claim. He was anxious that I should accompany him and as an inducement represented the facilities I would have to acquire the Spanish language—an acquisition at that period of great importance in Texas—especially to lawyers. I eagerly embraced the proposal, after consulting my father—who gave me some precuniary assistance.

We set out from San Felipe in high spirits, but our journey terminated most disastrously a days ride west of San Antonio. Traveling by night in rough hilly country, we were ambuscaded and attacked by a party of about twenty Comanches. The Indians were concealed in a dense thorny thick (chaparral) at the side of the road and the blaze from the muzzles of their guns flashed in our faces. Simultaneously we were assailed with a flight of arrows and deafened with hideous yells. McQueen fell from his horse at the first discharge of firearms. At the onset I was riding a few feet in advance of McQueen and my horse bounded several yards forward before I could rein him in. I instantly dismounted to assist my companion, Who, I could perceive, was on his feet in the road, almost within arms length of the Indians, cursing and yelling most furiously. I attempted to tie my horse to a bush but he drew the rope out of my hand and escaped. I flew to the side of McQueen, who was still exposed in the road with his gun presented at the Indians who were in the thicket within five paces of him; that he was not shot dead was almost a miracle. But the Indians who had firearms had discharged them, and those that had bows and arrows could not use them with effect on account of the brush. I proposed that we should remove to the thicket on the opposite side of the road. We did so, pursued by the Indians. We Crouched low in a fallen tree top to await our foes. Our horses were near us in the thicket and McQ. directed me to endeavor to recover one or both. I attempted to do so but was too closely pursued by the Indians. In the act of turning upon my pursuers with my gun presented, an arrow pierced me below the left eye, which so completely paralyzed me for an instant that my gun dropped from my hands. Before I had recovered from the shock they might have knocked me on the head and scalped me, but were too intent upon catching our horses to give me a finishing blow. With the exertion of all my strength, I drew out the shaft and rejoined McQueen. It was very dark in the thicket and the Indians though approaching us on their bellies were invisible for more than a minute. At length one rose to his feet in an open space and fired at us, instantly others rose and fired, several balls and arrows striking a small tree behind which we knelt. I attempted to shoot the first Indian that rose, but in holding for some minutes my gun to my wounded cheek, the blood wetted the lock of my gun and the percussion cap would not explode. My companion however fired and the Indian fell so near we could see him writhing. Again all was silent and no Indians visable. We crawled a little further into the treetop, and the Indians silently dragged away their slain Chief, (for such I afterward learned he was). In a short time the hills echoed with the howlings of the savages as they withdrew in a northen direction & gradually became inaudible from distance. By this time my companion was so weak from loss of blood that he thought he was dying. Indeed I thought so too. He had received three wounds, one in the neck, and one in the throat with arrows, both very slight, and one with a musket ball through the left side, the ball entering a short distance below and to the left of the navel and lodging near the backbone. He had also received a slight flesh wound in the thigh by the explosion of a belt pistol when he fell from his horse. With pocket handkerchiefs, I stanched the blood as well as possible. The night was cold and frosty (15th of Feb) and never did I hail the rising sun with half the pleasure as on the morning following. I assisted my companion to the road and we sat in the sunshine till we were somewhat revived. We found our saddle bags in the road, they had fallen from our saddles and had not been noticed by the Indians. I concealed them in a clump of prickly pears. McQueen thought with my assistance he could travel that day to the first water, about eight miles on the road to San Antonio. We set out, I carrying ours arms and giving McQ. some support on my shoulder. We reached water after sunset. My companion was unable to proceed any further. We passed another miserable cold night & early the succeeding morning I set out for San Antonio, leaving McQueen concealed in the reeds on the margin of the pool where he could crawl to water. I reached San Antonio at sunset, having traveled thirty odd miles. I told my tale as well as I could (for my throat was so inflamed that I could hardly articulate) and a party went out immediately & brought in McQueen. Poor fellow, he died in about a month, having suf-

---

In *Sketches of Early Texians* by JHK, he writes:

On the 15th of Feb. 1834, Thomas McQueen and the writer, who was then a youth, set out from San Antonio for Monclova, at that period the Capital of the State of Coahuila and Texas. Several miles west of San Antonio we met Deaf Smith returning homeward from the Medina River. He was alone as he loved to be, and informed us that he had been searching the banks of the Medina for cypress timber. Four or five hours after we met Smith and some time in the night, we were fired upon and both wounded by Indians, who captured our horses. In attempting to make our way back to San Antonio, my mortally wounded companion broke down, leaving concealed in the high grass near the margin of a pool of water called "El Charcon," I traveled on as fast as my weak and suffering condition would permit, to San Antonio, where I arrived at sunset on the 17th. By nightfall Deaf Smith had started at the head of a party of eight Mexicans to succor McQueen, who in due time was brought to San Antonio where he died of his wounds.
—JHK Papers "Sketches of Early Texians"
Box 2-R-74, Barker Texas History Center, Austin, Texas.

fered a thousand deaths. Like a prodigal son, I returned to my father's house, where I was welcomed."[6]

It is not stated where he got his education, but he was evidently quite studious, because in May 1834, while living with his father at or near San Felipe, he was employed by William B. Travis as a law clerk. Travis said, "made contact with J. Hampton Kuykendall with approbation of his father, to live with me three years and study law and help me in my office."

California manuscript: "William Barrett Travis of Alamo fame, was at this time in the practise of law at San Felipe. He offered me the use of his books and his instruction for my assissitance as a clear in his office. I accepted the terms. But Travis's practice being rather extensive, I soon found out I had made a bad bargain. I had little time to devote to reading. Hard labor at the desk and the irritation of my still uncicatrized wound rapidly undermined my health and to complete my depression, my father was basely assassinated in the streets of San Felipe."[7]

The employment by Travis was short lived, because JHK's father was badly wounded the following month of June 1834, by a man named Clayton and he subsequently died on 25 July 1834 at San Felipe.[8]

The *Journal of Ammon Underwood* states: "San Felipe: July 25th 1834,—Witnessed this day the execution of Joseph Clayton who was condemned and executed for the murder of an old man by the name of Abner Kuykendall."[9]

When I interviewed T. R. Kuykendall of Tilden, Texas, he told me, "My father told me that the boys, Gibson and Barzillai, had Clayton in chains and the moment their father died, they drug Clayton out of the jail and hung him."[10]

The California manuscript states: "Being dissatisfied with Mr. Travis, I went to (West) Columbia (Texas)[11] to study under the late William H. Sack, Esq.—But my health contined to decline. I was advised to travel. I made a hasty visit to my brothers & went off to Chihuahua, Mexico, in capacity of clerk for Mr. J. W. Magoffin.[12]

Later, young Kuykendall went to Chihuahua, Mexico, to work in a mercantile store and learn the Spanish language when he learned of Antonio Lopez de Santa Anna's preparation to invade Texas. At great personal risk, he escaped from Mexico to warn the colonists of the danger. Riding overland, he arrived at Goliad on 16 February 1836. His report to Col. James Walker Fannin was probably the first authentic news of the impending invasion. The California manuscript states: "At San Patricio we found a company of New Orleans Greys under the command of Captain Cooke.[13] The Irish residents of the town and colony were in the act of departing eastward in anticipation of the approaching invasion. With Captain Cooke we remained a day and continued our journey at a much abated pace to Goliad. The fortress of this place was garrisoned by about 300 men principally of volunteers from the U.S. under the command of Colonel Fannin.[14] We gave him the first reliable information of the approaching invasion, upon which information he founded a dispatch to the Provisional Gov't. of Texas." This dispatch is published in *Footes History of Texas*:

Headquarters, Army of Texas, Ft. Goliad, Feb. 16th, 1836. To HIS EXCELLENCY, J. W. ROBINSON, and GENERAL COUNCIL: "Since my communication of the 14th inst., enclosing several documents, received from various sources, from the interior, in relation to the movements of Santa Anna. Mr. Pantallion and young Mr.

Kuykendall have arrived here, only five days from Matamoras. Both of these gentlemen are known to me, and likewise to most of the people of middle Texas; and their statements, confirming in the smallest particular my former intelligence, may be confidently relied on."[15]

JHK went on to San Felipe to inform Governor James M. Robinson. On February 20, he enrolled in Captain Robert McNutt's Company "E" of Burleson's Regiment of Texas Volunteers encamped at Gonzales. This company was later commanded by his older brother Gibson.

JHK participated in the retreat (Runaway Scrape) by Houston's army from Gonzales until they were ordered to remain at Harrisburg. Houston ordered Capt. Gibson Kuykendall to remain behind at Harrisburg and guard the reserves, the baggage and the sick (everyone had the measles) while he, Houston, marched over for the fateful battle at San Jacinto. JHK's brother, Gibson, tried repeatedly to be allowed to take his company with Houston over to San Jacinto, but for reasons not known today, Houston would not allow it. Everyone concerned was quite bitter about Houston's actions because Gibson had been a well-known Captain of Texas Militia for many years.[16] JHK's own personal account of the 1836 campaign was first published in the Quarterly of the Texas State Historical Association in 1904.[16]

After JHK's initial three months enlistment was up (March-June) he re-enlisted on 1 July 1836 for another three months in a company first commanded by H. N. Cleveland and then later by Captain Reavill (Reville). The said company was attached to the Regiment of Texas Volunteers, Col. E. Morehouse, Commander. JHK is listed on the roster as a noncommissioned officer.[17]

Researchers have assumed that the H. Kuykendall listed on the Texas to Santa Fe Expedition of 1841 was JHK, but that is erroneous. He has been confused by a possible cousin, Henry Kuykendall, who was indeed on the expedition.

JHK was elected to the House of Representatives of the Sixth Congress of the Republic of Texas from Austin and Fayette counties in the early winter of 1842 and also in the special session from June 27 to July 19, 1842.[18]

In the spring of 1842, while between sessions, JHK was again in the service of his state, joining others in the Texas Militia on a campaign to repel the Mexican invaders under Gen. Rafael Vasquez. He joined the militia again after the summer session the following fall to ride against Gen. Adrian Woll, both Mexican commanders had attacked San Antonio.

To Wit

This is to certify that upon the invasion of the Western Frontier of Texas by the Mexican forces under Gen. Vasquez in the spring of 1842, the undersigned knows that J. Hampton Kuykendall went from the County of Austin, mounted and armed, to assist in repelling the invasion and that he saw the said Hampton in the Army as far west as the Guadalupe River.

Signed,
B. Kuykendall
(Barzillai Kuykendall)

State of Texas   )   I do hereby certify that upon
County of Austin)   the invasion of the Western
Frontier by the Mexicans under Woll in the fall of 1842, J. Hampton Kuykendall, mounted and armed, accompanied me from the County of Austin to San Antonio de Bexar to assist in repelling the invaders.

> signed,
> Samuel G. Kuykendall
> (Samuel Gates Kuykendall)[19]

In the 1842 campaigns against the Mexicans, JHK's younger brother, Wyatt Hanks, decided to remain on the ill-fated Mier Expedition over the objections of his brothers, JHK and Samuel G.—"Family members stayed up all night trying to persuade WHK not to stay on the Mier Expedition." WHK was badly wounded during the Mier battle and subsequently died there in December 1842. In later years, the remains that could be found of these men, along with Dawson's Company, were removed to Monument Hill just south of La Grange, Texas, and reburied. A beautiful monument stands there today in their honor.—JHK was later appointed executor to settle Wyatt Hank's estate in Washington County, just one county over from Austin County.[20, 21]

It is at this point that JHK wrote his poems about the battles of 1842. They are to be found in the California manuscript, which is in my possession:

STANZAS

"Written in the Valley of the San Antonio immediately after the invasion of the Mexican forces under Genl. Woll, the battle of Salado, and the Massacre of Capt. Dawson's Company, Sept. 1842."

1.
No classic land could ever boast
A fairer vale or lovier stream,
Than thou, sweet San Antonio dost;
Thy magic beauties well beseem,
Creations of some fairy dream;
So swift thy crystal waters glide,
So brightly in the sun they gleam,
So soft repose on either side,
Thy vibrant banks in floral pride.

2.
So vocal are thy groves with song,
So fragrant is the balmy air,
Such gentle zephrs steal along;
Such murmuring streamlets sooth the ear,
And yet, all peaceful as appear,
These Haleyon scenes, the God of War,
Delights to make his havoc here,

And banner'd legions from afar,
Have hither come these fields to mar.

3.
Here kindred armies met to fight,
And fell like sere leaves long ago,
"Twas then in succor of the right,
Impelled by valors generous glow,
(Which none but Freedom's sons may know)
That first the Anglo-Saxon blood,
In this fair vale did fairly flow;
And later times have seen renew'd,
The deathful strife and crimson flood.

4.
Here Texas led her chivalry,
To meet the hosts of Mexico,
Round Bexars walls the battle cry,
Has often pierced from foe to foe,
And death been dealt in many a blow,
And loud and deep the cannons roar,
Was thunder'd from the Alamo,
And hill and dale and rivers shore,
Baptised have been with human gore!

5.
Since here the Spaniard made his home,
Twice fourscore years have flown away,
And since the Bigot rear'd each dome,
Which in this vale stands lone and gray,
And worn by war and times decay,
"Twas then the prairie chicken wild,
Were doomed to feel tyrannic sway,
Their blood each temple-stone defiled,
Shed by the scourge of Christians mild!

6.
And ever as the wanderer winds,
His devious way oe'r hill and dale
A mouldring wooden cross he finds,
To mark where once a Christian fell,
And many a tale the aged tell,
Of bloody deeds of by gone time,
When, on their ears the Indian yell,
Came frequent as the church bell chimes.
And each day told of savage crime.

7.
The Prairie Wolf and Carion Crow,
Here long have held their carnival,
And human bones bleached white as snow,
Scattered amidst the rank grass tall,
Or shaded by the dense nopal,
Are frequent to the eye displayed,
And in the skull's decaying wall,

The rattle snake his coil has laid,
And threats man from his ambuscade!

8.

O heaven! shall man's unhallowed wrath,
Forever curse this lovely vale,
Shall blood besprinkle every path,
And death on every side assail!
E'en now I hear the orphan's wail!
E'en now upon Salados plain,
The earth is strewn with corpses pale,
And in yon grove the foeman slain,
With blood Salado's fountains stain!

9.

Ye whose romantic bosoms glow,
At narrative of martial strife,
Whose souls are smit with martial show.
And stirr'd by trumpet, drum and fife,
To long for warrior's glorious life;
Could ye behold these putrid slain,
And view this land with sorrow rife,
Happily like him who sings this strain,
Ye might not long for war again!

In October of 1846, JHK decided to seek employment as an interpreter with the American Army in Mexico under the command of Gen. Zachary Taylor. En route he stayed overnight at his brother William's house on Garcitas Creek near present day Victoria, Texas. It was at this juncture that JHK recorded the last known information about his first cousin, R. H. (Gill) Kuykendall, one of his fondest boyhood friends. The California Manuscript records this poem:

TO ROBERT H. KUYKENDALL

My friend in boyhoods balmy days,
We sported o'er these plains,
But memories of those happy hours,
Is all that now remains.

2.

How often did our simple hearts,
Then yearn for manhood's years,
Ah! little deem'd we that our wish,
Would bring us woes and tears!

3.

And now we stand on life's mid Arch,
Our friendship unestranged,
Our hearts are true to boyhood's pledge,
Though all things else have changed!

4.

We've chased the phantom happiness,
A long and weary round,

As erst we chased the butterfly,
But her we have not found!

5.
And every step we've ta'en in life,
Seems further from the goal,
And every sunny-winged hope,
Has flitted from the soul!

6.
Our span will soon be measured out,
Our brief career soon close,
And in our mother's earths embrace,
We'll find at last repose!

7.
And in the grave of dreams may come,
Be they of boyhood's days,
Ere time unseal'd the fount of grief,
Ere fancy dimmed the rays!

After leaving Garcitas Creek, JHK went on into Mexico, serving as a mule skinner, aide and interpreter, until the fall of 1847. At that time he left Mexico for Texas, going by boat first to New Orleans, then overland home by November of that year.[22]
The California manuscript states:[23]

In the autumn of 1846, shortly after the battle of Monterrey, I set out for the purpose of joining the American Army in that city. In Victoria on the Guadalupe, I met with Mr. James Grant, an old acquaintance, who was about departing for the same destination in company with a number of Mexican Traders from the Rio Grande.[24]

At the solicitation of Mr. Grant, I joined this company for the journey, though not without some reluctance as the Mexicans had quite a banditti appearance. We arrived safely, however, on the banks of the Rio Grande, but shortly afterward, Mr. G., who was a British subject, having been appointed an agent H. B. M.'s Consul at Matamoras to transact some business for the Consulate at Monterrey, trusted too much as was his wont, to the Mexican amity, and was murdered by the "guerrilleros, between Cerralvo and Marin."

When I stopped at Matamoras, I purposed to remain but a few days, and to continue my journey to Monterrey. But an accident befell me which occasioned a long detention. My lodgings were in a "garret" or third story of a private boarding house. The second night of my occupancy, after reading until about 9 Oclk., I laid aside my book to descend to the parlor on the ground floor—but being in an abstracted mood, I descended only the first flight of stairs to a balcony and stepped over the railing. I fell about twenty feet on a brick pavement, where I lay insencible several hours before I was found. When consciousness returned I was in the hands of a surgeon who was stitching a deep gash under my chin. My wrists were severly strained and both knees badly contused. I was confined to my room several weeks. My money was entirely exhausted. I owed a bit to the surgeon and was boarding at the rate of a dollar and a half a day. I had sought in vain for employment and was not aware that I had a friend in the city. I was in great distress.

Wandering one morning, mechanically through the city, I found myself before the door of the U.S. Quartermaster. A gentleman was standing in the door to whom I addressed some inquiry. Upon his turning to reply, we instantly recognized each other. It was Hiram J. Hughes of Texas, whom I had long known. Upon ascertaining my situation, he generously lent me a sum of money sufficient to disembarrasse me. He was in charge of several hundred mules belonging to the United States Army. The mules were herded in the vicinity of Matamores by Mexican Muleteers. As I was unable to obtain better business, I enrolled my name as a herdsman for the salary of $25 per month.

In this capacity I continued about four months, some times lodging of nights in the thatched huts (jacales) of the ranchos within a circuit of six or seven miles of Matamores, and sometimes sleeping in the open field. Robbery and murder were of daily occurrence in the neighborhood, and Americans, whether soldiers or citizens, could not venture out of the city in small parties, without immanent danger of losing their lives. But both Hughes and myself, though constantly exposed, escaped unmolested.

Notwithstanding my uncongenial avocation, the ever impending danger, and the scenes of blood and violence which occasionally sickened my heart, I spent many pleasant hours wandering with my gun along the "reedy" shores of the Rio Grande and the chaparral in quest of the Mexican hog And armadillos. I became, however, much disgusted with the occupation of Mulers, and learning that my qualifications would ensure me profitable employment in Camargo, I repaired thither in the month of May, and was immediately appointed Clerk and interpreter of the Spanish language in the U.S. Quarter Master's Dept at that place, with the salary of seventy five dollars per month, and rations.

My duties proved onerous and my health was much impaired by confinement, which constrained me, whenever my presence in the office was not indispensable, to make trips on steamers to Reynosa and other points on the Rio Grande. On the same account I also accompanied as interpreter, a detachment of Dragoons and Rangers, commanded by Major Graham, in pursuit of Canales, the (mullero) Garesilla Chieftain.[25]

The immediate occasion of which was this.—A detachment of Rangers under Captain Baylor had recently ventured out too far from the American post, in pursuit of a small party of the enemy, and imprudently paused to rest a day or two in the haunts of the Guerillos, where they were attacked by superior numbers, and defeated, with the loss of several men. Upon the reception of this news, Major Graham was ordered out with a choice detachment of upward of one hundred men for the purpose of chasing the guerillos into the interior & thereby to stop their depredations on the high road from Camargo to Monterrey, which had lately become very troublesome. Major Graham expected to find Canales still in the vicinity of Aldamos—indeed he was within two miles of that village when we arrived, but was well aware of our approach (but at that time we were not out of his proximity) and prepared to evade us. After refreshing men and horses at Aldamos, we continued our march for the place of Capt. Baylor's discomfiture. In half an hour we discovered a dense cloud of dust rising to the south of us about a mile and a half distant, This, we were informed by the rancheros, was the retreating force of Canales, but the River San Juan and an impenetrable chaparral intervened between the two forces, which deterred our commander from attempting to reach the Mexicans till we should find a road leading in their direction or the country should become sufficiently open to admit marching without a road. Thus we marched several miles up the San Juan, the Mexicans keeping pace with us at about the same distance, but suddenly, they left the valley and entered the hills, and such was the roughness of the country that our commander deemed in unnecessary to pursue. By the time we had arrived at Baylor's battleground, and scaring away clouds of ravens from the carcasses of the slain Rangers, we dug shallow graves with hatches and knives and having buried the remains, resumed our march. Most of the men of the village we visited fled at our approach, leaving their women and children and old men. The guerillo ranks were chiefly composed of the inhabitants of the towns in the valley of the San Juan. They were always on the alert, and no celerity of movement could surprise them.

Having fulfilled his orders, Major Graham determined to march direct to Monterrey. The weather was excessively warm and our horses much jaded when we arrived at the beautiful town of Cadereyta, distant twenty-five miles from Head Quarters, and we were glad of the necessity of resting a day or two in the delicious orange groves of that place. Major Graham and Lieut. Wood of the Dragoons and Lt. Pope of the Topographical Engineers, were all high-toned, intelligent gentlemen, and I was so highly pleased with them, the hospitality of the very respectable inhabitants of Cadereyta, and the luxurious shades of the groves, that I would fain have lingered for many days.

Upon leaving Cadereyta for the Head Quarters of the Army, we traveled nearly north parallel with the Sierra Madre "first range" of which loomed high into the heavens six or eight miles to our left, though seemingly, such is the purity of the atmosphere, within half that distance. The highest peak called "la silla" or the saddle, which overlooks Monterrey on the south, Lt. Pope informed me, had been found by triangulation to be six thousand six hundred feet above the city. Though more than eleven years had elapsed (1836) since I looked upon these same mountains, I found, by comparing them with their image in my mind, that my memory had preserved their likeness with "Daguerreotype" correctness. But mountains have ever been a passion with me; hence their images on my memory are durable as to be "a Joy forever." Indeed, no man whose soul is at all in harmony with nature can look upon mountains and the magnificent atmospherical phenomena of which they are the frequent theater, without experiencing an exhalation of intellect and a spontaneous impulse of devotion and enthusiasm such promted Howitt to exclaim:

"Now, bless God for the mountains"!

On my former visit to Mexico, in ascending to a great mountain in the state of Coahuila, I experienced that lively and joyous sense of existence so well described by Rosseau, I made an humble attempt to describe my own sensations in verse.

The Head Quarters of the American Army were situated about three miles from the city of Monterrey, in a beautiful grove—principally composed of liveoaks, through which dashed a bold mountain stream. The few days I remained here were very pleasantly spent riding about visiting many objects of interest in the vicinity of the city. Wilst at Head Quarters, I had a good opportunity of observing the servile homage paid to that plain and very ordinary gentleman, Gen. Zachary Taylor, and his spavined war-horse, "Ole Whitey."[26]

Every visitor to the camp, except my humble self, seemed to regard it as a great and immortal honor to shake hands with, or have a word addressed to him by "Old Zack," and I verily believe, had the Genl. condescended to bestow a kick on the seat of honor of his admirers, they would have regarded it as a sanctification of that region of the animal economy. We should certainly cheerfully render all reasonable honor and rewards to him, "whose word or voice has served mankind," but the pigmy is elevated to Alpine heights, and when the "poor radish," intoxicated by REPUBLICAN adulation,"

> Assumes the God,
> Affects to nod,
> And seems to shake the spheres. Who can
> resist a feeling of ineffable contempt and
> derision for both the idol and it's worshippers?

From Monterrey, I returned to Camargo with the "Express" which was escorted by twelve men,—through the most perilous part of the route & from (marked out) to Carralvo, we traveled by night. We, however, narrowly escaped the Guerillos. Signal lights on the hillsides, freshly slain mules, and burning vehicles, indicated their recent depredations and continued proximity.[27]

When I arrived at Camargo, I found Mr. A. B. Castle, who was one of the clerks in the Q. M. department, preparing to return to the United States. When the war with Mexico commenced, Mr. C. was a student of Medicine at Lexington, Kentucky, but catching the enthusiasm of the times, he volunteered as a private in the regiment of Kentucky Foot & served 12 months in Mexico. He was anxious to return to Lexington in time to attend the course of medical lectures in that city, to commence in Nov. ensuing. My heart being feeble, I resolved to return to Texas, accompanying M. Castle as far as New Orleans. Herein I acted foolishly. I was getting handsome pay and possessed the confidence of the head of the Q. M. department at Camargo, at that time presided over by Capt., since Major, O'Brien, a clear headed, efficient and very gentlemanly officer.

We took the steamer at Camargo, in October 1847. Upon arriving at "Brazos Lantiago.[28]

No steamer was up for New Orleans, and being impatient of delay, we took passage in a small schooner. We had head-winds during the whole voyage, and were twelve days at sea. When we made the Balize, our provisions and water was quite exhausted. With great joy we hailed the "Cressant City." My companion and myself took lodgings at the "Conti Street Hotel," which had for some time been closed in consequence of the recent epidemic (yellow fever), and was just re-opening. Having replenished our wardrobes, we strolled through the city, regaling ourselves with the many good things of which we had long been deprived and which we relished with extraordinary zest. We were both fond of reading and restored to the Bookstores, selecting and purchasing such works as suited our respective tastes. After the departure of Mr. Castle for Louisville, I continued in New Orleans for several days. In the "populous solitude," I felt very sensibly, the loss of my friend. I have not heard of or from him since we parted in N. Orleans. Should his years be prolonged, I predict for him eminence in the profession he has chosen. He was one of the most amiable and kind hearted of men, and where ever he may be, I invoke for him "perpetual benedictions."

"From N. Orleans, I took passage on the steamship "Yacht" for Galveston, where I found the Yellowfever still raging. It was also at Houston. Upon my arrival at the latter city, I took the stage for Richmond on the Brazos, where I had relations and many old friends.[29]

Remaining here a few days, I continued my journey in the adjoining county of Austin. My brother(s) had, some months before, received intelligence that I was dead, and were not undeceived until a few days before my arrival."[30]

JHK was very interested in geology and spent some time trying to get the State of Texas to set up a geology department and to make a geology survey of the State and appoint him as the leader of such a venture.

TO WIT: (1851) Letter to Bell:

"His Excellency
PH Bell, Governor
Austin

Austin County October 18th, 1851

Governor,
   Most of us have hobbies and often different on at different periods of our lives. For a few years past my favorite study has been Geology and Mineralogy. It is therefore possible that I overrate the importance of these sciences, yet I cannot but think your Excellency will concur with me in the opinion there exists within the limits of our State great mineral wealth which would be revealed by the researchers of science under the patronage of the State.
   You are doubtless aware that the Federal Government has caused Geological surveys to be made of most of her territories, and aside from the scientific interest which such researches possess, mines and minerals have been discovered and pointed out, which but from the light of science would long have remained unrevealed.
   There is still remaining to the State an unappropriated domain of great extent, the value of which would be much enhanced should it prove to abound (as doubtless does), in mineral wealth. But, I humbly conceive that if Texas did not possess an acre of vacant domain, a mineralogical survey of the State would still be highly useful.
   In settled portions of the State there are inexhaustible quantities of minerals scarcely less valuable than the priceless metals, the names, nature and value of which are not dreamed of by the unscientific, otherwise, intelligent proprietors.
   I need not to labor to impress you with the importance of ascertaining by the means I have dictated, the mineral resources of the State the subject of doubtless already received a share of your thoughts.
   Should you think proper to recommend to the Legislature a small appropriation for a Geological survey of the State or any portion of it, and should your recommendation be adopted, I trust you would not deem me unqualified for "a place." There are always so many who "crowd preferments" gate, to the great annoyance of those high in office that I shall not often trouble you with solicitation. Should you think me qualified for and deserving of any favor I flatter myself that importunity will be unnecessary.
   Trusting that you will not regard this communication as obtrusive,
   I remain, dear Sir,
   Your obt. sevt. and friend,
   JHK[31]

Also in 1851, JHK wrote a stinging rebuttal to a speech made by Sam Houston in the Congress of the United States, regarding the retreat of the Texas Army from Gonzales (1836). JHK contended that some of the important facts were different from what Houston stated in his speech.[32]

This was the same year that JHK moved to La Grange, Texas, and was editor (for three months during the summer) of the *Texas Monument*. It was during this period that he helped in establishing the Statue on Monument Hill just south of La Grange honoring the Dawson men and the Mier men that were killed in 1842.

In 1853, he and others made a trip out through North Central Texas and he describes the event in his journal in great detail as to timber, terrain, and minerals inspected.

> Went up the middle Yequa to String Prairie settlement (Burleson County) across East Yegua to a tributary of Brushy Creek. From here to the San Gabriel on to Donohoes Creek, crossed it and on to Dorres Creek. Course taken nearly due north to a point midway between the Colorado and the Brazos—May 12—Entered Valley of the Little River, crossed the Salado a short distance below the "Mill." through Bellton, the county seat of the new frontier county of Bell. Deer in the area are very scarce and buffalo have not been seen within a days ride for nearly two years.
>
> Travel to the valley of Cow House Creek, up a valley to a Sugar Loaf shaped hill. Descending the Sugar Loaf, we cross the military road from Austin to Fort Gates on the Leona River. Camped on the bank of Cow House Creek, traveled up the valley of Cow House then over into the area of the "Lampazos." Found the Lampazos deep but fordable. Descended from this area into the valley of the north branch of the Gabriel—May 17—This morning our company divided, a party of three making a "bee line" for home and four including the writer of this journal continuing on (into) the Hamilton Valley for the purpose of exploring that section and the gold mines beyond the Colorado. Within five or six miles of Hamilton's Valley, we met Capt. Ogden of the U.S. Army in charge of the Delaware tribe of Indians, numbering about 300 men, women, and children, and much cattle. For several years past, the Delawares have been pursuing a nomantic life between the Colorado River and the Rio Grande and are now by order of the U. S. Government on their way to the territory assigned them on the Red River—On to the ridge overlooking Hamilton Valley. Camped near Hamilton. Fort Groghan is nearby but will soon be moved further out. Left and crossed the Colorado, the ford was deep and the current swift and strong. Went on over the hills and down to the banks of the Llano River. About one-half hour before sunset, we encamped three miles south of Pack Saddle Mountain and about the same distance north of the "diggings."—May 19—Leaving camp we met several men returning from the diggings. They informed us the prosperity of the gold was not worth the working.
>
> Reached Sandy Creek, one mile down the creek brought us to the "Morman Diggings." Here we found a log cabin and the dwellers themselves were Mormans. All the gold they had found could not have been worth more than 50 cents.
>
> Having accomplished our object in visiting the mines, a little before noon we set out for home via Austin, which is about 80 miles distant. From the diggings to Morman Ferry on the Colorado River is 14 miles. Camped this night at Morman Ferry and Backbone Creek.—May 20—Went through Mormans Village, after six miles we entered the road from Austin to Fort Groghan.—May 21—Rode into town for breakfast. Here our little party dispersed and here ends my journal.[33]

JHK's attempt to get the state to set up a geology department and to get himself appointed its head never came to pass.

In the spring of 1862, at the age of 47, JHK again rallied to the aid of his state and joined the Confederate Army at Gen. H. E. McCulloch's camp. The camp was located on Spring Creek, three miles above Victoria, Texas, on the east side of the Guadalupe River.[34]

JHK had always been quite close to his brother William, who lived nearby, and JHK enlisted in the company with William's two sons, young William (later Judge William K. of Tilden, Texas) and T. C. Kuykendall. His grandnephew, Wiley Martin Kuykendall, was also in the same company with them. JHK's father and Wylie's grandfather were brothers. Two distant Kuykendall cousins from Bell County were in the same Regiment also.

Upon joining the company, JHK wrote the following: "In that hour, when we shall have engage the enemy in deadly conflict, when the cannons angry roar is heard and the bullets fall around us like hail, may the noble reputation of our State be uppermost in our minds."[35]

JHK had joined what was considered to be one of the elite cavalry units of the state at the time, but only William and his brother T.C. saw any action. They both would be sent later with their unit into Louisiana and would see action against the Union General Banks.

The unit that JHK joined was known as Capt. James C. Borden's Company, Col. Augustus Buchel's Regiment, Yager's Battalion, Texas Mounted Volunteers, also known as Company D., Yager's Battalion, Texas Mounted Volunteers.[36]

In his papers, JHK simply states that he was with his company near Brownsville, "guarding the Rio Grande River against blockade runners."[37]

In his writing career JHK wrote many articles for newspapers and periodicals, including the *Texas Almanac*. The articles dwelt principally with the Indians and early Texas history and are considered authoritative. His essays on "The Carankawa Indians" and "Aboriginal Antiquities of Texas" were reprinted in DeWitt Clinton Baker's *A Texas Scrapbook* in 1875, and show "an intelligent mind, with excellent powers of observation and description," according to science scholar S. W. Geiser.[38]

This basically ends the forty years of journals about Texas that JHK wrote and rewrote during his entire life, from stories and reminisces written about the early Texas settlement of Austin's first 300 colonists up and including the Civil War period.

It is obvious that JHK wrote and rewrote his memoirs several times. He probably had the complete history of Texas written at one time which would have covered the earliest days of the colony, but in one of his fits of deep depression, depressions that he had throughout his life, and because he could not get this early history published, he, like Richard Burton's wife, took all his papers out into his courtyard and burned them.

> "One fool lolls his tongue out at another
> and shakes his empty noodle at his brother.

> The journal to which these remarks are prefactory is one several similar records of my peregrinations in Texas and Mexico, none of them were ever published and are now either lost or destroyed."

(*Note*: The discovery of the unpublished California manuscript in 1989 by the author does away with this claim.)

I never but once seriously entertained the meditated intention of giving anything to the world in 'good black print.' Being in possession of many facts relating to the colonial history of Texas and many others being accessible to me, I purposed, some years since, to publish my materials for the benefit of the future historian. But meeting with no encouragement I "abandoned the design and burned my papers." The sufferings of the State have never been truly described, duly acknowledged or adequately rewarded and never will be. Few in number at first, they are now dwindled to a handful and the remnant are passing away like the swift Alpine torrent, to the land of the Spirits. A few years more and the last linger will have departed. Then indeed the historian and the legislator will essay to do them justice. But 'what is fame to a dead ephemera?' Or what ghost ever pined for posthumous bread?[39]

About the time that Aransas County was created from Refugio County in 1871, JHK moved to Rockport, Texas, where for a time he edited the *Transcript*. Later while employed by Aransas County to translate the Spanish records at Refugio into English and separate the documents of the two counties, J. Hampton Kuykendall died. It is assumed that this was around 1880. Because of the flooded conditions of the Mission River, JHK could not be buried in the Protestant cemetery and so he was buried in an unmarked grave outside the north fence of the Catholic cemetery in Refugio. In recent years, local historians raised a plaque in his honor, along with several other early residents, and that plaque can be seen today just outside the main gate to the Catholic cemetery on the west side of Refugio, Texas. To this day, no death date has ever been found, nor has a single obituary in any newspaper been located. It is a pity.[40]

By 1880, JHK's nephews, sons of his brother William who had died in 1862, and their families had moved from the Garcitas Creek area near Victoria, Texas, over to Tilden, Texas, in present day McMullen County. When William (later Judge) got word of JHK's death (ca 1880?), he hitched up his team to a wagon and made the trip over to Refugio, Texas, to pick up all his uncle's personal belongings. When Judge William returned, his wagon was full of books and handwritten ledgers that his uncle JHK had written over so many years. JHK had never married, living his whole life by himself as a bachelor.[41]

It should be interesting to note that after William returned with the ledgers, he then wrote the forth volume that is now on file at the Barker History Center in Austin. It contains mostly ranch bookkeeping information and cow prices of the period from 1880-1897, but hidden right in the middle of the ledger he stopped, and at the request of his daughter, wrote a stirring account of his activities during the Civil War. It is superb.

In this last volume, William makes no mention of the death of J. Hampton Kuykendall, but family members place it around 1880.[42] Read the Commissioner Court records that follow on the next page.

JHK's family were not governors, but two had been legislators, JHK himself (in Texas) and his uncle Amos was one of the early members of the Arkansas Territorial legislature. They probably didn't stay in one place long enough. They were frontiersman and Indian fighters. Captain Abner, his father, and Capt. Robert H. Kuykendall, his uncle, were Stephen F. Austin's first choices as militia captains of the colony. Both men were badly hurt while serving the colony in this capacity; Robert against the Carankawas, and Abner while arresting an outlaw and subsequently both died as a result of these encounters. Had either or both been alive in 1836, it is felt by most family members that one of them would have commanded the bulk of the army of the republic during the war in 1836, not Houston.

For 200 years up until this time, JHK's ancestors had always been on the edge of the frontier of America. At the first sign of danger, they were always ready to defend or fight and could nearly always be found on a militia roster when needed, whether up the Hudson against the French in the early 1770s, or at Kings Mountain, South Carolina, against the British under General Ferguson in the 1780s. Then later, in 1812, they are again with Jackson at New Orleans fighting against the British.[43]

When called on to do so, JHK and his brothers, Gibson, Barzillai, William, Samuel G., Adam, and Wyatt H., joined almost every militia company that was formed in the colony, the Republic and the state, from 1822 up until the time of their deaths. JHK's uncle Robert died ca 1830; his father in 1834; his brother Wyatt on the Mier in 1842; his first cousin R.H. by the Indians or outlaws in 1846, and two second cousins during the Civil War. All died in the defense of Texas.

One hundred years prior to JHK's death, another militia captain in Tennessee stood in front of his company in which three Kuykendall brothers were included and said: "Let the enemy come, whoever he may be, for even on the good days ... we sleep upon our rifles."[44]

Be it remembered that on the 7th day of June 1880 a special term of the County Court of Refugio County was begun and holden in and for Refugio County at the Court House thereof in the Town of Refugio on the 7th day of June 1880

    Present: L. M. Rogers, County Judge
    B. F. West   }
    F. C. Heard }   County Commissioners
    P. H. Fagan }
    J. Williams, Sheriff
    R. P. Clarkson, Clerk

Be it ordered adjudged and decreed by the Court that J. H. Kuykendall be and is hereby allowed the sum of Five Hundred dollars for transcribing Book A, B. & C, Records of Deeds and Titled Grants into a new Book and that the same shall be allowed and paid unto the said J. H. Kuykendall upon the completion, comparing and approval of the said transcript of said Records A, B, & C, and that said transcript shall be a true copy of the original Records in every particular, excepting that in transcribing said records he shall spell all words correctly if any said words in the original shall not be correctly spelled, but in no case to substitute one word different from the original. In case he should find any instrument of Record intended to be in Spanish if the same should contain any English he shall be required (to) put the whole in Spanish, leaving said English word in brackets and to show what Spanish word he has used in place of the English; the County Clerk is ordered to have said transcript made either through himself or a sworn deputy.

The minutes of the Court having been read and approved it is ordered that the Court adjourn to next regular term.

Attest:
R. P. Clarkson

Be it remembered that on the 8th day of November 1880 a regular term of the Hon. the County Commissioners Court was begun and holden in and for Refugio County,

>Present, L. M. Rogers, County Judge
>F. C. Heard   }
>B. F. West   }   County Commissioners
>Floyd Carpenter }
>J. Williams, Sheriff
>R. P. Clarkson, Clk. C. Cst. R. C.

The Court being duly opened the following account was presented and ordered paid to wit:

Be it ordered adjudged and decreed by the Court that whereas Johnathon Hampton Kuykendall[45] who had received ($40) Forty Dollars towards the payment of his transcribing the County Records A. B. and C, and since the payment of the same the said J. H. Kuykendall having departed this life the County Commissioners Court having examined the amount of work done by him the said Kuykendall, Book A. having been transcribed and Book B. to page 109 on to half of said page 109, find the sum now due him to be the sum of One hundred and Sixty Dollars and the same is now ordered paid to Thomas Kuykendall as the lawful heir of the said J. H. Kuykendall.

The Minutes of the Court having been read examined and approved the Court adjourned to the next regular term.

Attest:	L. M. Rogers County Judge
R. P. Clarkson	Thos. C. Heard, County Com.
Clk. R. C.	B. F. West, County Com.[46]

Chapter Nineteen

Joseph Kuykendall of Austin's Colony

Joseph Kuykendall (1794-1873)—Frontiersman, colonist—was one of Stephen F. Austin's earliest members of the Old 300. He was the son of Adam and Margaret Hardin Kuykendall. Joseph was probably born near Henderson, Kentucky. The family had just moved there from the "middle Tennessee" district.[1]

In 1792, Adam Kuykendall's signature appears on a "List of the Male Inhabitants" of Logan County, Kentucky, along with his eldest son, Abner. It is shown by later census records that Joseph would be born between 1792 and 1794 while the family was at Henderson, Kentucky.[2]

After Adam Kuykendall shows up on the 1804 tax list in Henderson County, Kentucky., there is a several year time lapse before he reappears again. The reason for this lapse is because he shows up on a "memorial," along with Joseph's older brothers, Abner and Robert, north of the "River Ohio" in Indiana Territory. The memorial is dated 16 March 1808 and is addressed to William Henry Harrison, governor of the Indiana Territory. There have been no deed records found for the family north of the Ohio River, however, Adam did reappear on another tax list in Henderson County, Kentucky, in 1809.[3]

Shortly after March 1808 the family began their move into Missouri Territory. (Arkansas). Abner Kuykendall and his family left the Cadron Settlement prior to 16 May 1820. Joseph and his brothers, Abner and Robert H., began their moves into the southwest corner of Arkansas, which would lead to their entry into the Mexican Territory of Texas in the following year of 1821. No deed record has been found for Joseph in Conway County, Arkansas.[4]

In early 1821, Joseph Kuykendall's name appears on a "memorial" along with his brother, Abner, to the president. This memorial was signed by many of the men who had been with old Adam in Indiana in 1808 and would soon become some of the first of the "Old 300" to enter Texas. The memorial has been quoted in other write-ups.

The memorial was signed by some 300 settlers among whom were: Joseph Kuykendall, Abner Kuykendall, Wm. Shannon, John Shannon, Owen Shannon, John Tumlinson, Jonathon Hampton, Wyatt Hanks, Wm. Gates, Samuel Gates, Charles Gates, Wm. Rabb, John Rabb, and A. Rabb, to name only a few who would later appear as members of the Old 300. The family later sued the U.S. government for the loss of their improvements but they were never compensated.[5]

The movement of the Indians onto the settlers' lands, coinciding with the opening of the lands in Texas by Stephen F. Austin in the middle of 1821, was the propelling force that moved all the families into the Mexican Territory of Texas.[6]

The settlers and their families left the disputed Arkansas Territory area around Pecan Point (the Red River) sometime before October 1821, because it was late in October of that year that they appeared in Nacogdoches and united with their brother, Robert H. Kuykendall, who the records state "had been living west of the Sabine" for some time.

> Robert and Joseph Kuykendall saw Moses Austin near Nacadoches, they had just been routed from Arkansas by the US (Government) granting the land to the Choctau and Chicasaw Indians;. They left Arkansaw September 1821—reached the Brazos & crossed it October, 1821, where Washington now stands; Robt. and Joe K.—left 1st day Janry 1822 for Colorado & stopped 12 miles below La Grange; remained there 2 or 3 years, sold his place to Ross and removed 5 miles below Richmond where he has lived ever since, this was Joe; Buckner and Peter Powell came to the Colorado soon after Joe Kuykendall— Bill Gibbons & Chas. Garret, came with their families with the Kuykendalls—-They parted near the Trinity, Gibbons and Garret took the upper road and settld at the Atuscasito crossing on the Brazos. Garret died 1849 at Joe Kuydndal on the Brazos.[7]

About Christmas 1821, Robert H. and Joseph Kuykendall and Daniel Gilleland planted the first settlement on the Colorado near the present site of Columbus. On 16 August 1823 James Cummins was elected alcalde of the District of Colorado by the citizens of the area. Those voting were: Joseph Kuykendall, Jacob Betts, Seth Ingram, Wm. B. Dewees, Thomas Gray, Charles Garrett, Daniel Gilleland, Micader Reeder, Jesse Burnum, James Ross, Thomas Williams, Robert Kuykendall, Thomas Jamison, and Rawson Alley.[8]

In the March 1823 first census of the Colorado district, Joseph Kuykendall states that he is 29 years of age and his wife, Rosanna, is 25, that he is a farmer with horses, hogs and farming tools. Researchers have not been able to locate a marriage license between Joseph and Rosanna nor a last name for her. It is thought that they got married after the family entered Arkansas Territory.[9]

Joseph also appears on the 1826 census of Texas as being between 25 and 40 years of age, wife (same), as a farmer and stockraiser. Joseph next appears on the 1830 citizens of Texas list as having received one labor of land from the Mexican government in August 1823 in Fort Bend County. He also received title to a sitio of land in Fort Bend County on 8 July 1824.[10]

In November 1830, the *ayuntamiento* of San Felipe de Austin appointed Joseph a commissioner to choose the best route for a road from San Felipe to Marion.[11]

Joseph Kuykendall was not active in the early Indian campaigns that his brothers Abner and Robert were so involved in (along with Abner's many sons). He did however furnish goods to the army and was in one company for a short while in the summer of 1836. There has been some speculation that Joseph was a cripple and therefore not able to be involved.

To Wit:
  Received of Mr. John H. Pickens of Kirkindolphs eight hund. lbs Beef valued @ $20.00 for the New York Volunteers.

              John Geraghty, Qty Master

May 13th, 1836

I hereby certify that Joseph Kuykendall entered my company on the fifteenth day of July and served faithfully up to the fifteenth of October making three months and is this day honorably discharged.
October 15th, 1836

              John P. Gill, 1st Sarg.
              for W.H. Secrest, Capt.
              of Columbia Cavalry.

Received of Joseph Kuykendall one Beef Steer some time about the first of May 1836, weighing Eight hundred pounds for the use of the Detachment under my command that was ordered on the retreat of the Mexican Army, this 29th November 1837.

The above beef I consider   Ewd. Burleson
worth three dollars per   Col. of 1st Regmt.
hundred pounds.   Volunteer Army.

              Ft. Bend Dec. 27th 1837
 Mr. MOODY,
        Sir, in sending me the others, my government says you only sent my pay for three months service and pay for one horse valued By Col Burleson therefore there remains in your office Pay for one horse valued at one hundred Dollars and beef valued at fifteen dollars which was reced to Mr. Pickens—Please send the above by Mr. Dobson and am ablige,
 Yours
       signed   Joseph Kuykendall

I certify that the horse which Joseph Kuykendall gave to Capt. Secrets as certified by him was for a mare which at the time belonged to Kuykendall. The horse was placed in service and used and I believe Kuykendall justly entitled to pay for the horse. I believe the valuation one hundred fifty dollars reasonable and just.
Houston 24th May 1838   Thomas J. Rusk
              late Brig. Genl.
              T.A.
    Let this be audited 25th May 1838.
              A. S. Thurston

AUDITORS OFFICE
Houston, 28 Nov. 1837

"This day came Joseph Kuykendall and says the annexed instrument is just, true and original, and is the only one that he has offered for liquidation: that he owes the government nothing on his account, or on account of any other person.
Sworn to before,
(Rubric) ~~~~Auditor[12]

During the Run-away Scrape, Joseph Kuykendall and John R. Fenn were captured briefly by the Mexican Army as they were attempting to cross the Brazos above Fort Bend. Joseph was able to convince the Mexican commander that he was not involved in the revolution and the officer gave Joseph a pass.

> El Col. Juan Bringas, Com'dt. jr., el E.S. P'se de la seccion de Vanguardia.-En viatudo de haberse procurando el ciduo Joseph Kuykendall, y no daber hecho armas el Ejercito, se lo extiendo el presente resguardo pa que pueda permancer tranquilo y sin ser molestado.—Fort Bend, April 12 de 1836—signed—Juan Ma Bringas

After their release, they made there way into the dense cane bottoms and joined the women and children and later made there way toward Harrisburg. The steamboat *Yellowstone* passed while they were in hiding and they could see the bullet holes in the side of the boat caused by the Mexicans shooting at the boat as it passed their position. It is in this write-up that the author states that Joseph Kuykendall is a cripple which is probably the reason he did not serve in but one of the militias.[13]

The following are some early notes on Texas that were published in 1838 and 1839 in the *Hesperian* magazine of Columbus, Ohio. They were titled "Notes on Texas":

> "Crossing the Brazos": We crossed the stream ourselves in a small dugout or canoe and swam our horses by our side. A distance of four miles again brought us upon the prairie. Here again was presented a picture in natural scenery which is seldom excelled. In the eye's wide limit we could see immense herds of cattle in colors as various as the hues of the kaleidoscope and as plump and as round as the stall-fed ox, scattered in all directions or collected in groups beneath clusters of verdant trees, which were intersperced over the green earth like so many small islands in the ocean. Nothing claimed to be monarch of all we surveyed but the noisy bull who moved over the plain with the importance of an emperor and who, when he saw us among his subjects, by pawing the earth, seemed to convey the idea that we had got into the wrong parish.
>
> As the sun was about to set, we came upon the habitation of a herdsman upon the borders of the Brazos timber, having traveled in our devious course near forty miles during the day. KUYKENDALL, the name of our host is a fair specimen of the early settlers of Texas in point of originality and peculiarity of character, as well as in pursuits and mode of life. He immigrated from the States to this country fifteen years ago, with nothing of this world's goods but a few cattle which, with great patience and labor, he drove from beyond the Sabine. He settled himself upon a league of land on the Brazos, as beautiful as the heart of man could wish and which, under the colonization law, cost him nothing but the trifling fees of the officers commissioned to put immigrants in possession of their rights. Without any attention to agriculture or with scarce an exertion of any kind but simply from the increase of his little stock, he now finds himself blessed with abundant means to bring within his reach all of this world's goods that men generally think necessary to their comfort and happiness. His cattle,

after having been scattered and driven off in great numbers by the troops of Santa Anna and heavy drafts upon them to supply the army of Texas, still number upwards of two thousand.

The abandoned appearance, even of a garden spot, which was in ruins, led me to think that our host had determined to prove an exception to the primal curse that man has to live by the sweat of his brow. If such was the case, everything went to show that he was not disappointed. If universal testimony is entitled to credit, stock of the horned kind will double every three years, making an allowance of twenty per cent for annual loss, so that, admitting our host to have two thousand head of cattle, which will readily sell for six dollars apiece, the aggregate value would be twelve thousand dollars, and the one third of this, to wit, four thousand dollars, would be the yearly addition to his wealth, simply from the increase of his stock. All this, too, to use his own language, without any more labor than is required to mark and brand the calves. The prairie, both winter and summer, furnishes the most abundant and nutritious pasture, and even salt is not necessary for the stock, as the dew is highly impregnated with the saline properties of the sea.

The situation of this man, removed from the ordinary perplexities and difficulties of life, with nothing to do but recline beneath the green trees and watch the daily increase of his wealth in the growth of his cattle, reminded me of the speech of Meliboeus to the sheppard Tityrus, jealous of the too easy tenor of his pastoral life. Before the Revolution, the Texian found a market for his cattle at New Orleans, where there were driven in large droves, and at the island of Cuba. Since that period, a law has been passed which prohibits any cattle being driven out of the country, as, in time of war, they are the main dependence for the subsistence of the army, as well as the people generally. This law of self-preservation is as difficult to enforce as are all the others which conflict with the interest or avarice of a people. Cattle are still driven across the Sabine, notwithstanding the great exertions of the authorities to prevent it.

As it was not yet dark, I persuaded our host to go with me to the cow yard, where were collected such as had calves. They were about sixty in number, and so far as rings, streaks, and speckles are concerned were evidently descended from the stock of the patriarch of Israel. The bellowing and bleating and constant agitation of the whole, and one or two Negroes in the midst busy in taking a little milk from all, formed a laughable and novel scene. The cows were generally of a fine, large size, equal, if not superior, in this respect to the stock in the United States but admitted to be inferior for all the purposes of the dairy. This has been disputed with great apparent justice by many who contend that if the cow of Texas does not yield the same quantity of milk that is generally given by those of the North it is only because the Texian has so many that he is not able to give them the attention, that is always necessary to bring them to the greatest perfection. This argument is certainly good, so far as the quantity of milk is concerned, but not the quality.

The evening was spent in listening to our host recounting the adventures of himself and his family with the army of Mexico, which passed by his door on their way toward the Brazos. Santa Anna was at least successful to some extendt in emulating Napoleon in the rapidity of his movement, for it seems he frequently came upon the inhabitants by surprise. Upon the arrival of the enemy at the house of Kuykendall, he was absent. His wife discovered them at a distance and commenced a retreat with her children but was pursued and fired at by the soldiers. She, however, with her little ones, escaped into the woods, where they lay concealed in canebrakes until the enemy passed, when she made her way to Harrisburg, the headquarters of many inhabitants. Kuykendall was not so fortunate. The enemy came upon him when he least expected it, and in his attempt retreat, two platoons were ordered to fire upon him, which did so with out effect, although the distance was not over twenty-five yards. This may be given as an instance, among many that might be adduced, to prove the total incapacity of the Mexicans in the use of firearms.

Although our host was not injured, he thought it prudent to surrender. The treatment he received was such as might be expected from those who thought it an act of heroism to fire upon his wife and children. After some suffering and many difficulties, which are too long for narration, he made his escape. Much insight into the character of a people as well as their invaders may be had from the incidents which often escape the notice of general history, which I choose to interlard, not only for such purpose but to give variety to the dry and perhaps, to many, uninteresting description of the country.

The county of Fort Bend was created by an act of the legislature on 29 December 1837. Thirteen of the original grantees of Mexican land grants appear on the list of the 128 signers. Joseph Kuykendall was among that number.[14]

Joseph and Rosanna lived on their league of land just south of Richmond, Texas. In January 1839 Joseph deeded a tract of land out of his league to Ignatius S. Johnson. Joseph would live on his land until his death in 1873.

FT BEND COUNTY

A general inventory of all taxable property returned by individuals situated in Ft. Bend County prior to the 1st of June 1840.

Kuykendall, J.   T2222   13 sl.   27 h.   1000 catt.   1 stud[15]

Joseph Kuykendall's wife, Rosanna died in 1848. She was buried on the league line between the Jane Long League and the Joseph Kuykendall League. The marble slab had two names inscribed on it:

Charles Garrett	Rosanah Kuykendall
Died 1847	Consort of
Age 51	Joseph Kuykendall
	Born Feb. 1, 1800
	Died May 29, 1848

The location of the marker was about one half mile NE of FM 762 on the above described boundary, just south of Richmond, Texas in Ft. Bend County The marker has not been seen for several years.

In the probate proceedings for the county during the June term in 1849 there is a simple statement of Rosana's death stated: "The Succession of Rosannah Kuykendall, Dec., Minutes of the Probate Court, recorded in Vol. B., page 496, Probate Records of Ft. Bend County Texas." There were no children from this marriage.

In January 1849, Joseph married Miss Eliza Jane Jones. The license issued on 16 January 1849 was returned and filed on 27 January. The rites were solemnized on 18 January by the Hon. C. C. Dyer, Chief Justice of Fort Bend County.[16]

The 1850 census records of Fort Bend County show Joseph as follows:

Joseph Kuykendall	59 M Farmer $15,000	Kentucky,
Eliza Jane	23 F	Ky
Robert H.	12 M	Tex
Wiley M.	10 M	Tex
William Stevenson	20 M Overseer	Ky

Note: Researchers have thought that the two boys listed above were sons of Joseph and are listed as such on old research work. That is erroneous. The two boys are sons of old Joseph's nephew, R. H. (Gill) Kuykendall, who was killed ca 1846 by outlaws or Indians while on a trip from the Victoria area to San Antonio. Gill was the eldest son of Joseph's older brother, Captain Robert. They would live with Joseph for several years.[17]

The census records in 1860 show Joseph as 66 years old, a farmer with a property value listed at $33,300–$88,700, and show him from Kentucky. Eliza is listed as 32 years of age, also from Kentucky, and the two boys are no longer living with their uncle.[18]

Joseph lived all his life on his land just south of Richmond, Texas. While other members of the Kuykendall family were very active in the affairs of the Civil War during 1861-1865, Joseph was not. It goes back to the fact that perhaps Joseph was a cripple and the fact that the old man just didn't involve himself in affairs outside his own plantation. In order to be able to vote, citizens had to obtain a pardon from the commanding general of the region after the war. One such request is as follows:

E. M. Pease
Recommending Jos Kuykendall for Special Pardon.
                                             Austin 2nd Sept. 1865
Dear Gen.
   In regard to the application of Mr. Jo Kuykendall of Ft. Bend County I would state that he is upwards of seventy years of age, was one of Austin's early colonists, he is not a man of much general intelligence or education, and never takes any particular part in Public Affairs, and exercises no particular influence in the community, although he has aquired a fine estate—-He has the reputation of being a worthy man and a quiet inoffensive Citizen, and I think he may be pardoned at once.

                                             Truly your friend,
                                             E. M. Pease[19]

On 31 March 1862, Joseph Kuykendall wrote his "Last Will and Testament" and deeded by "Deed of Gift" all the lands and holdings that he possessed to his wife Eliza J. Kuykendall while keeping for himself a "life estate." Eliza Jane filed all these instruments in October 1873, stating that Joseph was dead. They are as follows:

   Estate of Joseph Kuykendall

                          WILL AND ORDER
March 31, 1862
Filed, Oct. 31st, 1873.
   In the District Court of)
   Fort Bend County   )   In Vacation before William P. Huff
                                     Clerk of the District Court in and for Fort
Bend County in the matter of the Estate of said Joseph Kuykendall, deceased
   Be it remembered that on this the 24th day of November A.D. 1873, before William P. Huff the Clerk of the District Court in and for Fort Bend County, in Vacation came on for a hearing and consideration the petition of Eliza Jane Kuykendall of said County for the probate of a certain instrument of writing pro-

duced before me, purporting to be the last Will and Testament of the said Joseph Kuykendall of Ft. Bend Co., deceased.

Petitioner praying that she be appointed and confirmed as the Executrix of said last Will & Testament and on hearing and reading of the Testimony of Walter Andrus one of the subscribing witnesses to said last Will and Testament and which testimony was reduced to writing and sworn to and attached to said last Will and Testament which said Last Will & Testament is as follows, as also the testimony of said Walter Andrus, to-wit:

**** **** **** ****

The State of Texas)
Ft. Bend County) "In the name of God. Amen:-

I, Joseph Kuykendall of the County of Ft. Bend and the State of Texas, being of sound mind and disposing memory and considering the uncertainty of life and believing that every one should prepare for death, do make and declare the following to be my last Will & Testament. I hereby revoking and annulling all former Wills and Codicils.

Item 1st. I require, after my death that all my just debts shall be promptly paid off and discharged, by my executors hereinafter named or the survivors or survivor of them.

Item 2d. I bequeath and devise all the residue of my Estate, both real, personal, and mixed of every nature and description whatever, after the payment of all my debts, to my dear and beloved wife, Eliza Jane Kuykendall and her heirs forever.

Item 3rd. I hereby nominate, appoint and constitute my dear wife Eliza Jane Kuykendall, James B. Sullivan, and Allen Kuykendall Executors of this my last Will & Testament with full and ample power to them or the survivors or survivor of them to execute the same without any further action of the County Court being had in relation to the settlement of my Estate than the probate and registration of this my last Will & Testament and the return of an inventory of the Estate.

In testimony whereof, I, Joseph Kuykendall have signed, sealed, (using a scroll for my seal) and published this Will, this 31st day of March in the year of our Lord one Thousand Eight Hundred and Sixty two in the presence of the subscribing witnesses.

Witnesses: Joseph Kuykendall (Seal)
W. Andrus
W. S. Jones

Both the Deed of Gift and the Last Will and Testament were accepted by the court and Eliza Jane Jones was make executrix of the estate by the court on 24 November 1873.[20]

Researchers have stated the Joseph Kuykendall died on 25 October 1873, but to date that record has not been found. There is speculation that Joseph was buried in a crypt on the line between his estate and that of the Jane Long League. That crypt has been located about a half mile northeast of FM 762 on the boundary of the two leagues, just south of Richmond, Texas. The location is just off the pavement at a point on the highway called Crabs Switch. Interestingly, Eliza Jane married this Mr. Crabb some time after Joseph's death and that's when the name change occurred.

And so, with the death of Joseph Kuykendall, ends the chapter on the lives of the first of old members of Austin's Colony. Joseph, along with his older brothers, Captain Abner and Captain Robert H., were among the very first five families to enter Texas in what was to be the opening of the great migration into the state. They were in the very first group to cross the Brazos River to its west bank on those fateful early days of November 1821.

Rev. M. D. Early, ca 1900

Chapter Twenty

The Reverend Dr. Marshall Daniel Early, D.D., Baptist Minister, 1846-1918

Marshall D. Early was born near Rome, Floyd County, Georgia, on 30 September 1846. His father and mother were John Sharp Early (b. 20 July 1810, Whitley County, Kentucky; d. March 1878, buried Jefferson, Texas) and Mary Faulkner (b. Texas, m. 10 July 1837, d. 30 September 1846, buried in Summerville, Georgia). John Sharp Early's boyhood home was south of New Zion Church between Moonshine and Hollow on the Moonshine Hollow Road near cross roads #1083 in Whitley County, Kentucky.[1] His mother died at his birth and was buried in Summerville, Georgia.

The 1850 census of Chattooga County (Summerville), Georgia, shows John Sharp Early and wife, Hannah J. Early, aged 28, and five children. Marshall was not listed. John Sharp Early moved to Summerville after the death of his first wife.[2]

Marshall's father and family moved to Clark County, Arkansas, in 1858 when Marshall was 12 years old. Their home was probably located just a short distance out of Arkadelphia, Arkansas, on the Old Hollywood Road.[3]

When the Civil War started, Marshall persuaded his father to let him join the Confederate Army. He was quite large for his age (14) and in 1862 enlisted as a private in Company K of William A. Crawford's Brigade, Brigadier James Fleming Fagan's Cavalry Division, John D. McNabe, Captain. It was also known as the First Arkansas Cavalry (Trans-Miss. Dept.). His unit saw extensive action against the Union army commanded by General Steele and General Banks in the spring and summer of 1864. After Confederate General Price's Missouri Expedition (August 29 to December 2, 1864), Crawford's Arkansas Cavalry, along with most of the units that traveled with that column, retreated into northeast Texas. Extremely worn out by the exertions and losses of that campaign, the regiment took no further active part in the war. The regiment officially surrendered at Galveston, Texas, in early June 1865, but it had really ceased to exist by that date as most of the cavalry had already disbanded by mid-May 1865.[4]

It has been stated by family members that Marshall joined the ill-fated Shelby Expedition and went with that group into Mexico in the summer of 1865. That is not so. This group of men refused to be repatriated and decided not to take the oath of allegiance that was required at the time. They marched as a unit, from northeast Texas to the Mexican border at Eagle Pass, Texas, crossing the Rio Grande River at that point into the village of Piedras Negras, Coahuila (supposedly burying the Confederate flag in the river as they crossed in early July 1865). They were on their way to join Emperor Maximillian's forces in Mexico City and/or offer their services and their good Sharps rifles if he, Maximillian, would have them. They fought several skirmishes in crossing Texas, but their troubles didn't really begin until they entered Mexico. They had a pretty hot contest on the edge of Piedras Negras when the local militia confronted them. They shot themselves loose from this problem and literally had to skirmish all the way to Queretaro and Mexico City, a thousand or so miles away. Sadly, many of the brave men who had survived the whole Civil War were killed during this march. This group of soldiers stayed in Mexico for several years, until many returned to the United States. Marshall obviously did not accompany these men since the records reflect that he joined the church and got married in the fall of 1865 in Arkansas.[5]

It has been told by family members that Marshall's Negro man-servant and his horse his father had given him, stayed with him throughout the war.

Soon after returning home to Clark County from the war in the late summer 1865, Marshall joined the Mt. Bethel Baptist Church on 29 August 1865. Records state: "after preaching by Bro. Tate, the church opened the door for reception of members when W. J. Rowe, Marshall D. Early, Isabel Meadows and Sarah A. Lowery came forward and related an expression of Grace and were received into the fellowship of the church when baptised."[6]

Marshall married Mary Jane Rowe, daughter of Andrew Rowe (ca 1826-1864) and Martha Ann Conway Rowe (1829-1870), on 24 September 1865 at Arkadelphia, Clark County, Arkansas, with the Rev. James Wilson presiding. They were married in the presence of their parents.[7] Marshall was 19 and Mary was 16 at the time.

Andrew Rowe, Mary Jane's father, was wounded 30 April 1864 at the battle of Jenkin's Ferry in south central Arkansas and subsequently died a day or so later. He was buried on 5 May 1864 in an unmarked grave at the Old Mt. Bethel Cemetery. On 23 February 1865, Martha Ann married Joseph B. Langley. (There is an Old Conway Cemetery 2 miles west of Hollywood, Clark County, Arkansas.) The four Rowe brothers who came to Clark County and Garland County, Arkansas, from Lawrence or Jefferson counties, Alabama, were Wm. Jackson Rowe, John Wesley Rowe, Andrew Rowe, and Pierson Rowe. They probably came from Alabama in the company of some Conway families who moved about the same time. Martha Ann Conway was born in

Morgan County, Alabama, on 18 September 1829. She married Andrew on 18 February 1848. She died in Clark County, Arkansas, on 19 September 1870. Her parents were James H. and Angeline Jackson Conway, both born in South Carolina.) The father of these four men was John Rowe, b. 4 June 1789 in South Carolina. He died in Jefferson County, Alabama, in 1849. John Rowe's parents were Benjamin Rowe, b. 16 April 1758 in Halifax County, Virginia, and Ruth O'Neil, b. 10 June 1770. Benjamin died on 2 May 1848 in Lincoln County, Tennessee, and is buried in the Riutt-Wells Cemetery. Benjamin Rowe was a Revolutionary soldier. The mother of the four men was Elisabeth Rhodes, b. 7 Jan. 1793(?) and died in Jefferson County, Alabama, after the census of 1850. She was the daughter of Joseph Rhodes and Rachel Pearson. This information was given to me in 1987 courtesy Wanda J. Karnes, 1711 Magnolia Drive, Fort Smith, Arkansas 72903.

Marshall and Mary Jane had three daughters and one son: Ella, b. 10 September 1866, Maggie, b. 4 June 1873, Faye, b. 4 August 1876, and an infant son who died shortly after birth.[8]

Bethel-Union Baptist Church, a church just outside of Arkadelphia, asked in December 1870 that Marshall be ordained and sent to their church as pastor. Ordination was denied by Mt. Bethel, so he asked to be dismissed from their membership in January 1871. Bethel-Union welcomed him into their church and ordained him on 13 May 1871.[9]

Bethel-Union is now known as the DeGray Baptist Church, the name being changed on 12 December 1874, at the suggestion of Marshall. He served as pastor of that church from 1871 to 1878.[10]

Mt. Bethel Baptist Church Book Minutes: After divine service on Saturday before the fourth Lord's Day in May A. D., 1870, Mt. Bethel Church met in conference. Item #6 "opened the door for general business when the church granted license to Bro. M. D. Early to exercise his gift to preach or in any way he thinks proper."[11]

Bethel Union—December 17, 1870. The church met in conference Saturday before the third Lord's Day in December. The committee appointed to wait on Bro. Browning were present and made their report, Bro. Browning declined taking charge of the church. The committee was then discharged. An election then took place for pastor, and Bro. Marshall Early was chosen. Brothers Thos. Cook, L.B. Cash, and E. W. McBrayes were appointed to a committee to meet the church at Mt. Bethel in conference and request that Bro. Early be ordained for us to the full work of the ministry.[12]

Mt. Bethel Church met in conference. Item #5 opened the door for general business when a delegation of Bros. Thos. Cook, E.W. McBrayes and Lewis Cash from Bethel-Onion Church requested that the church ordain Bro. M. D. Early to preach the gospel (if the church thought him worthy) so that he can take care of their church. Resolved that Bro. Early preach in Trial Summer at the next regular conference meeting. On motion, conference adjourned until the next day.[13]

After divine service on Saturday before the Lord's Day in January 1871, Mt. Bethel Church met in conference. Item #6 opened the door for general business when letters of missions were granted to Bro. M. D. Early and his wife, Sister Mary Early, and Sister Isabelle Waldrope. No further business, conference adjourned.[14]

After divine service on Saturday before the Lord's Day on February AD 1871, Mt. Bethel Church met in conference. Item #5 called for references when the committee on the ____ was continued. The reference of ordaining Bro. M. D. Early was brought forward from previous conference. Resolved as the officers of the church refused to act their part in the ordination in behalf of the church and when the door for general business was opened, Bro. Early withdrew his letter from the church that the reference be dropped.[15]

After preaching by our worthy and esteemed Bro. Marshall Early, the church met in conference, L. B. Cash called to the chair pro-tem. Brother Early was then elected moderator April 8, 1871, after services conducted by our esteemed Bro. Marshall Early, the roll of male members was called, other business was attended to and Bro. Early came forward and connected himself and wife with us by letter, the right hand of fellowship was extended to Sister Early when she may visit us. The church unanimously voted that Bro. Early be ordained at our next meeting,—May 31, 1871— Bro. Early was ordained to the full work of the ministry and Bro. Bledsoe to the office of deacon.[16]

Marshall was doing missionary work from (Bethel-Union) DeGray Church to Okalona, Arkansas, when his daughter, Alice Forbes Early (known always as Faye to others and Mona to her children), was born on 4 August 1876. Marshall's beloved wife, Mary Jane Rowe Early, died in late April 1879 and was buried in the church yard at the DeGray church, about fifteen miles from Arkadelphia, Arkansas. Later that fall, their infant son also died and was buried in the same place. Mary's family lived nearby on farms around a small village named Hollywood.[17]

When the De Gray cemetery was moved to higher ground because of a lake that was built, these graves were lost. The current DeGray Church has no knowledge of their whereabouts.[18]

When Marshall left the church at DeGray to go elsewhere, the church wrote him the following letter:

(To The) Rev. M. D. Early

The subjoined resolutions were adopted at the DeGray church, Clark County, Ark., April 13th, 1878. Brother Early has resided and labored among us seven years, his labors not being confined to this community but in almost every section of the county. The Lord accompanied his labors with abundant grace; consequently, their fruits abound. He has moved to Hope, Homestead Co., and thence to Little Rock, Arkansas.

1. Resolved that the DeGray church and the congregation worshiping this day in this house do hereby declare that we most highly esteem our pastor, Rev. M. D. Early, as pastor friend, and brother, and that we sincerely regret his removal from our midst to a distant part of the state, for we shall miss him in the social, the pulpit, the church, and every good work.

2. Resolved that we do most cheerfully commend him to the good will and kind offices of all men.

3. Resolved that we hereby assure him the we most heartily appreciate and com-

mend his zeal and fidelity in performing the social and pastoral duty and in preaching the gospel.

4. Resolved that we hereby tender him our truest thanks for his labors of love, and do most earnestly entreat for him both now and ever the loving and tender mercy of our heavenly father and the holy fellowship and all-sufficing grace of our Lord Jesus Christ, the head of the church, the shepherd and bishop of our souls.

5. Resolved that we hereby instruct the clerk of the church to inscribe these resolutions in our minute book and to present a copy to our beloved and to furnish the Western Baptist with a copy for publication.

E. Clingan
F. Flecher   Committee
J. Bledsoe

Done in conference on Saturday before the second Lord's Day in April A.D. 1878.
                N. J. Davis, Mod
                Thos. Cook, Clerk

After the death of his wife, Mary Jane, Marshall sent his daughters to live with friends and family members. Faye (Mona) was sent to live with "Grandma Jackson" in Dadenelle, Arkansas, for three years.

In 1880, Marshall's name appeared in records as having attended the state convention from the Lonoke Baptist Church (est. 1869), "Caroline Association." He also held a pastorate at Dardenelle, Arkansas. He had married again during this time to Miss Elisabeth (Betty) Faulkner and she accompanied him to Lonoke (1881).[19]

It was in Lonoke that Marshall became good friends with J. P. Eagle, who lived on a large plantation nearby called "Richwoods." Mr. Eagles would later become governor of Arkansas. Soon thereafter, Mr. Eagles married Miss Mary Kavanaugh Oldham. Mary Eagle and Betty Early became fast friends and were leaders in home and state church work. Miss Ann Armstrong, the first president of the Baptist Missionary Union in the south was often a visitor in the Early home. Mrs. Eagle and her mother were elected delegates to the Southern Baptist Convention in Washington, D.C., from the state of Arkansas. A woman delegate was an unknown quantity at the time and much controversy was stirred over seating them. It was finally done and has been the custom ever since.[20]

In 1881, he was granted a leave of absence from Lonoke, Arkansas, for a rest. However, he labored in Eureka Springs and other places traveling 500 miles in four weeks and preaching 19 sermons. He was elected secretary of the foreign mission by the Arkansas Baptist State Commission for the convention year.[21]

From 1883-1885, Marshall attended the state convention from Lonoke, Arkansas. He was approved as missionary pastor at Morrilton, Arkansas (est. 1860—Dardenelle-Russellville Association). He served for two years.

In 1886-1888, he became pastor of the Second Baptist Church in Little Rock and was appointed corresponding secretary for the state convention for one year and was re-appointed. After Marshall's move to Little Rock, where the state missionary headquarters were located, his old friend and neighbor from Lonoke, Arkansas, J. P. Eagle was elected governor of Arkansas.

After two years in Merrillton, Papa was elected Superintendent of Missions for the state with headquarters in Little Rock where we went to live. Several events of interest happened there. The J. P. Eagle referred to at Lonoke ran and was elected governor of the state. At the time, it was said my father knew every man in Arkansas by name and he campaigned for his friend. At the inauguration, Governor Eagle led the grand march with my mother (on his arm) and Mrs. Eagle on the arm of my father.— In the summer vacation months, Papa often took me with him when he held meetings over the state. On these trips we traveled by train on a clergyman's pass. One trip was made through the apple country of northwest Arkansas, not so famous then as now. A narrow gauge railroad was laid through the orchards from Rogers to Bentonville where we were going. The trees swept the side of the small coach and Papa reached out and pulled an apple from a tree. Another trip was made to Fayetteville where Arkansas University is now located. We stayed with the family of Mr. Wells who was first president of the school. He had been (?) in Merrillton where we knew him. The Old Main Building was the only one then and it was surrounded by the tall corn cultivated by the students to help pay their tuition. It was more an industrial school then. Later we went down to Arkadelphia, Papa and (my) mother were (had been) married near there, where her people lived in a small village named Hollywood, in the hills about fifteen miles away. We went to visit two of my great uncles, one a brother of my mother's father(Andrew Rowe) and the other a brother of her mother (Martha Ann Conway). These were uncle Sil Conway and uncle Jack Rowe. Her name (Faye's mother) was Mary Jane Rowe and she is buried in the DeGray Church yard a few miles away.[22]

The Arkansas Baptist State Convention decided to purchase a house and property in Arkadelphia (Ark) and establish Arkadelphia Baptist High School in 1876. Marshall's name, among others, was on the original corner stone. He was a member of the first Board of Trustees of the school. The board was instructed to develop a four year college and its first meeting was held on 6 April 1886, at which time the board chose the location and the name of the school. Using the original building of the old blind school, Ouachita Baptist College was opened in 6 September 1886. The first building, Old Main, was added in 1888 and towered over the campus until it burned in 1949.[23]

Though Marshall is not listed as one of the trustees who planned this building, it is believed that this is the building which contained the cornerstone bearing his name. After the fire of 1949, the stone was lost in the rubble.

> Back in Arkadelphia, Papa laid the cornerstone of Ouachita Baptist College, his name is engraved on the stone. Many years later I made a special trip to that school to see the name on the cornerstone. I met the president who insisted on showing me about and later my visit was written up in the school paper. Several old timers I met remembered my family, calling them by name.[24]

The first annual catalog of Ouachita Baptist College listed the trustees as follows:
Announcement
The Ouachita College
Male and Female
Arkadelphia, Arkansas
1886-87

Board of Trustees:
John Hart, President, Morrilton, Arkansas
A. B. Miller, D.D., V. P. , Little Rock, Arkansas
A. J. Fawcett, Secretary, Pine Bluff, Arkansas
A. W. Files, Treasurer, Little Rock, Arkansas

J. P. Eagle, Lonoke; C. D. Wood, Monticello; B. R. Womack, D.D., Dardenelle; W. E. Atkins, Prescott; A. J. Kincaid, Searcy; W. F. Locke, Alma; J. B. Searcy, and V. B. Izard, Forest City; Jasper Dunagin, Rogers; W. A. S. Sayle, M.D., Morrilton; M. D. Early, Little Rock; W. P. Webb, Ozark; J. K. Brantley, Little Rock.[25]

In 1889, Marshall's name does not appear in the Arkadelphia Baptist State Convention minutes but there is a reference in the womens' committee minutes that they were called to another state.[26]

In 1889, after three years in Little Rock, Marshall was called to the church in Talladega, Alabama.[27]

> After three years in Little Rock, when I was twelve years old, Papa was called to the church in Talladega, Alabama, in the deep south where tradition held sway. Each family had their own pew with a name plate on it. The family all sat together. A much loved, former pastor had died there and his name, Dr. Rowan, had not been removed, though another (Pastor) had come between him and Papa.[28]

Later in 1889, Marshall was elected by the State Missions Board of Tennessee and moved to Memphis to establish a church in the suburbs of that city. It was called the Trinity Baptist Church, but was later moved to a new location and the name was changed to LaBelle Place Church.[29]

From 1889-1893, Marshall attended the Southern Baptist Convention from Memphis, Tennessee.[30]

In 1894, Marshall was elected as the State Superintendent of Missions in Texas at Waco, Texas, and his family went to Waco to live.

> That was the year 1894 and Papa had been called to Texas, to be Superintendent of Missions for the Baptists, and we went to Waco to live. My (step) mother died on June 19th, (1894) the first I knew of emancipation day. No one showed up and the wife of a prominent Judge who lived nearby came to help, a Mrs. West. She (stepmother) is buried in Oakwood among many of the older families, the Carrolls, Neffs, Morrows, and others.

In 1894-1895, Marshall attended the Southern Baptist Convention from Waco, Texas and in 1896 was appointed Corresponding Secretary of the Texas Convention. Later he resigned. A copy of the resignation letter states:

> Baptist General Convention of Texas
>
> Brethern of the Convention: I hereby respectfully and fraternally regret that my name not be considered in connection with the office of Corresponding Secretary for the new year.
>
> Very heartily do I appreciate the magnanimity with which the convention last year conferred this high honor upon me. And as faithfully as I have known how have I la-

bored to do deserve the confidence expressed by your almost unanimous endorsement in a recent vote of the years work, with which I was mainly charged as the most responsible servant of the board and the convention. And I do now, most heartily, tender to the board my thanks for the manly support it extended me throughout the year. The reasons prompting my course are these:

The responsibilities of the work under the conditions of the field the past year have been too crushing for me. I do not, therefore, feel that I could consider a proposition to stand under the responsibility another year.

To all who have prayed for me and helped me, sincerest thanks. Any one who, without intent, has embarrassed me in the discharge of my official duty, thereby increasing my burden, I pray to God to enable me to fully forgive and forget.

I will not trespass upon your time further than the expression of the ardent plea for my successor, whoever he may be to wit: that you pray for him and accord him your confidence and cooperation.

Very faithfully, your brother,
M. D. Early[32]

On 2 July 1895, Marshall married Bettie Lee Faulkner. A daughter, Mary, was born the following year on 2 July 1896.[33]

In September 1896, Marshall attended the Southern Baptist Convention in Washington, D.C., and while there, he and his group were guests of President Grover Cleveland at the White House.

> In September of 94, I entered Baylor University where two of the happiest years of my life were spent. There were no really outstanding events to write about. Papa took me to the Southern Baptist Convention in Washington DC, where I went to the White House to a reception in the Blue Room and met Grover Cleveland, the President at the time.[34]

In 1897-98, Marshall attended the Southern Baptist Convention from Meridian, Mississippi (Chickasahay Baptist Association). He served part of the year as pastor of the 15th Avenue Baptist Church in Meridian, Mississippi.[35]

In 1899, Marshall attended the Southern Baptist Convention from Morristown, Tennessee.[36]

While in Tennessee, he attended a convention of Confederate Veterans at the Wm. B. Tate Camp #72 U.C.U.'s on 4 April 1902 at Morristown, Tennessee, and was elected an alternate to attend the 12th Annual Convention the following year in Dallas, Texas.[37]

The Ouachita Archives at Arkadelphia, Arkansas, held no church records of Marshall's activities from 1900 to 1903.

In 1904, Marshall attended the Southern Baptist Convention from Newport, Tennessee; in 1905 from Burlington, Kentucky; and in 1906-7, from Blackwell, Oklahoma.

In 1908-1910, Marshall attended the convention from Lawton, Oklahoma, and the D.D. first appeared after his name. It has been surmised that Marshall received his D.D. degree from either the Southwest Seminary at Waco, Texas, or the seminary in Louisville, Kentucky. This is incorrect. Those schools did not grant that particular degree at that time. In those early years their only doctorate was Doctor of Theology.

While Marshall was pastor at Blackwell, Oklahoma (if indeed he was pastor), and possibly after he went to Lawton, Oklahoma, he received the Doctor of Divinity (D.D.) from the Oklahoma Baptist College at Blackwell. This school was founded by action of the Oklahoma State Convention in 1899 and continued until 1914.

Indications in the records of Marshall's involvement on the Education Commission (Board) in 1906, show that commission being charged with the task of attempting to unify Baptist education in what was the Oklahoma Territory. The fact that he was pastor at Blackwell, Oklahoma, and a trustee of the school there, leads one to believe he received the D.D. degree from there.

In 1906, one year before statehood, there were two conventions of Baptists in the Oklahoma Territory (western portion of the state) and Indian Territory (eastern portion of the state). In the latter, the land was divided into five tribal nations for the Indians. In 1906, those two areas of Baptist conventions merged to form the present Baptist General Convention of Oklahoma.

Four hundred persons attended and M. D. Early was chairman of the committee in reorganization, at any rate, he initially presided and called the meeting to order and presented the organizational report. He is listed in that year's Annual (1906) as a messenger from Blackwell. As the records indicate in 1907, he was a minister at Lawton, Oklahoma, and a messenger. In 1908, he was not listed as a messenger. In 1909, he was a member of the board of directors for the convention, a trustee of the Oklahoma Baptist College at Blackwell, an ordained minister at Lawton, and a messenger from Lawton to the convention.

The records of the Blackwell, Oklahoma, church were completely destroyed by fire, ca 1950, and nothing was saved.[38]

From 1911 to 1913, Marshall attended the convention from Monticello, Kentucky, and from 1914 until his death in 1918, he attended the convention from Stanford, Kentucky.[39]

> A number of pastors have come into the state since the last session held 18 years ago [June 1909], they were presented to the convention body as follows: M. D. Early, pastor at Monticello, etc.[40] Minutes of the Seventh Annual Session of the Wayne County (KY) Association of Baptists held with the church at Monticello, Kentucky, September 1 and 2, 1910. Sermon introductory to the business of the Association was delivered by Bro. M. D. Early. J. H. Shearee, moderator, etc., and proceeded to business by inviting brethren to seat with us as follows: M. D. Early from the Comanche County Association Oklahoma, etc.
>
> 1911 minutes of the Eighth Annual Session of the Wayne County Association of Baptist held with the church at Steubenville, Wayne County, Kentucky, August 31, and September 1st. A sermon introductory to the business of the Association was delivered by Bro. M. D. Early, etc.[41]

> 1912 minutes of the Nineth Annual Session of the Wayne County Association of Baptists held at the church at Liberty, Wayne County, Kentucky, September 5 and 6. Met September 5, a sermon introductory to the business of the Association was delivered by Bro. M. D. Early. He was appointed to the "Home Missions" committee to report the following year and did so in 1913 by letter to the Association as pastor from Monticello, Kentucky.[42]

For nearly forty years, Marshall Daniel Early had been a leader of Baptist groups from Arkansas, Alabama, Texas, Tennessee, Oklahoma, and Kentucky. For 33 years in succession, he attended the Southern Baptist Conventions with notables like Pendleton, Graves, Jeter, Broadus, Boyce Eaton, and other giants of the church.[43]

Marshall had been the pastor at Monticello, Kentucky, before going to Stanford.[44] At the time of his death, he was a member of the Kentucky Board of Missions. He had been a close friend of "Champ" Clark and others prominent to the national affairs and was indeed one of the big men of the Baptist denomination.

Marshall died at Stanford, Kentucky, on 13 March 1918 of uremic poisoning. Dr. E. J. Brown was in attendance. An immense throng including the Governor of Kentucky attended the funeral services.

Lincoln Lodge #60, F. and A. M., of which the deceased was a member, conducted the beautiful Masonic ritual at the grave site. The church service prior to burial was held at the First Baptist Church of Stanford conducted by Dr. Porter of Lexington, Kentucky, and Dr. Truett of Dallas, Texas. The burial followed at the Buffalo Springs cemetery and Marshall was buried in grave #1, Section 6, Lot #276½.[45]

The Kentucky Baptist newspaper, *Western Recorder*, Thursday, 21 March 1918:

Rev. M. D. Early, D. D.

The death of this noble man and minister, on March 12th, at his home in Stanford, Ky., brings sorrow to his multitude of friends. At the recent meeting of the State Board, of which he was an honored member, he seemed in the best of health, and with his usual cheerfulness and optimism. In the afternoon session of the meeting, he was called to the Chair by the Moderator, and presided with his accustomed grace and wisdom. We little thought that we would so soon be called upon to chronicle his going.

For many years, this Christian warrior had fought the good fight of faith and had justly earned the rest that remaineth for the people of God. He had served as Secretary of State Missions for Arkansas and Texas, and occupied a number of important pastorates. Wherever he labored, he was faithful, and the blessings of the Lord rested upon his labors.

Blessed with an unusually strong mind and a splendid voice, it was but natural that crowds should wait upon his ministry. His intense earnestness and evident sincerity challenged the love and admiration of his fellow men. We have know but few more vigorous preachers. His preaching was distinctly evangelistic, and therefore missionary. The mighty cause of missions had no truer friend than M. D. Early, and by his words and gifts, he still lives in the lands afar.

For more than forty years, he has been a familiar figure in the meetings of the Southern Baptist Convention, and he will be sadly missed in these gatherings. Few among us enjoyed so large an acquaintance or were blessed with so many friends.

It was a matter of keen regret that, owing to the funeral of one of our soldier boys, in our own church, that we were unable to attend the funeral services.

May the Gospel he so faithfully preached be the stay and consolation of the sorrowing wife and children.[46]

Chapter Twenty-One

Colonel Joseph Hardin
Father-in Law of Adam Kuykendall

Joseph Hardin (1734-1801) was the son of Benjamin Hardin II, who came from Virginia to Anson County, North Carolina, in 1752. Joseph was supposedly born near Richmond, Virginia, on 18 April 1734. Benjamin II, Joseph's father, was born ca 1705 possibly in Virginia and he was the son of Benjamin I and wife, Sarah. The older Hardin's "Wills" were probated in Virginia in 1734 and 1750 in the counties of Surry and Isle of Wight, respectively. When Benjamin II moved to Anson County, North Carolina, in 1752, his sons Benjamin III, Joseph, and John came with him, along with his daughters, Sarah, who was the first wife of Frederick Hambright[1], and Rebecca, who researchers think married John Kuykendall (1721-1763), son of old Matthew Kuykendall (1690-1752). The earliest record of the family in North Carolina is an order of 28 March 1753, issued by the governor to the surveyor general concerning land in Anson County, North Carolina, for Benjamin Hardin II. Joseph's father died in February 1764. Benjamin II married Catherine "Lamkin"(?) and John Hardin supposedly married Elisabeth Kuykendall, probably the daughter of old Matthew (1690).

When Mecklinburg County, North Carolina, was formed from Anson County in 1762, these families were in the new county. Joseph's brother, Benjamin III, was commissioned a captain of militia in that county on 25 January 1764.[2]

Tryon County, North Carolina, was formed from Mecklinburg County in 1768 and again, the families were present in that county. Joseph's name first appears in that county when he is named justice of the peace in April 1772. He was a member of the safety committee of Tryon County and a signer of the famous Tryon County Association Resolution on 14 August 1775.[3]

Joseph Hardin was a member of two of the provincial congresses which met over the protest of the English governor, Josiah Martin. The first popular assembly in opposition to royal authority met at Newbern on 25 August 1774. The group met again April 1775 and through their actions the governor terminated the royal rule in North Carolina and left the state. On 21 August 1775, the third congress met at Hillsborough. One hundred and eighty-four members took their seats and Joseph Hardin was a member from Tryon County. This congress proceeded to raise troops and organized two regiments of five hundred men each. Also raised in each of the six districts, were ten companies of fifty men each, called a battalion. These battalions were known as the Minute Men. The following men were appointed from the Salisbury District: Thomas Wade, colonel; Adlai Osborne, lt. colonel; and Joseph Hardin, major.

Joseph Hardin was a member of the congress that met in November 1776 not only to make laws but to form the first constitution of the state.[4,5]

While the colonists were considering their grievances against England, the Indians took advantage of the situation and began to give the settlers considerable trouble. Early in 1776, General Griffin Rutherford, with nineteen hundred men, led an expedition against the Cherokee and destroyed their farm and all their crops and provisions and compelled them to sue for for peace. Joseph Hardin was one the captains of light horse in that expedition.[6,7]

Tradition states that Joseph Hardin was in the battle of King's Mountain, South Carolina, but in the roster of men at the battle in Pat Alderman's *The Over Mountain Men*, only Abraham Hardin(?), Joseph Hardin Jr., and Joseph Sr.'s brother, John Hardin are shown. Joseph Hardin did fight at the battle of Ramsour's Mill, North Carolina. This was in Lincoln County, North Carolina, not far from his home. This was a battle between the Tories and the Whigs.[8]

Joseph Hardin bore three military titles. He was appointed major of the Minute Men in 1775, captain of light horse in the Cherokee Expedition of 1776, and in the same year was a captain in Locke's Battalion of General Allen Jones' Brigade in which organization he served at Ramsour's Mill; and finally he was made colonel but no record of the commission has been found to date. However, the North Carolina Historical Commission has issued a certificate of a manuscript record in one of the Revolutionary Army Account Books showing monies paid to "Colonel Hardin" in 1779. Furthermore, land grants totalling 8,100 acres to "Colonel Joseph Hardin" are on record in the land office at Nashville, Tennessee, having been copied from the North Carolina official records. He is addressed as "colonel" both in 1785 and 1788 in the record of letters by a resident of Greene County, Tennessee and the governor of North Carolina.[9]

All of the facts indicate that he was appointed to the rank of colonel either during or immediately following the Revolutionary War.

Some time during the latter part of the Revolutionary War, Joseph Hardin moved his family across the mountains to that section of North Carolina which in 1783 became Greene County (now Tennessee). Samuel Cole Williams in referring to this change of location on the part of Hardin says: "When his section (of North Carolina) was overrun by the British and the Tories, he fled over the mountains."[10]

It is believed that the Hardins and other related families (Adam Kuykendall and his family) moved across the mountains for reasons of safety. The removal took place just previous to, or immediately following the Battle of Ramsour's Mill.[11]

Dr. George Mellon says that when Hardin's section of the state of North Carolina was overpowered and overrun by the British, that his farm and all his property was confiscated and that he fled with his family and moveable possessions across the mountains into East Tennessee and settled on the Roaring Fork of Lick Creek in Washington County in the area known later as Greene County, Tennessee.[12]

This area was then still in Washington County, North Carolina, and in the North Carolina Assembly of 1782, Joseph Hardin represented the county in the formation of the new county of Greene, and became one of its first county court members: "Greene County was erected out of Washington County. The first court consisted of Joseph Hardin, John Newman, Geo. Doherty, James Houston, Amos Bird, and Asahel Rawlings. Daniel Kennedy was elected clerk, James Wilson, sheriff, and Wm. Cocke, attorney for the state."[13]

It was at this time that Joseph Hardin became involved in the formation of the "State of Franklin." The growth of these areas was so rapid and they were so far removed from the seat of government in North Carolina, that a convention was called in August 1784 at Jonesboro, Tennessee, in order to form a new state. Messrs. Cocke and Hardin were appointed as a committee to prepare a plan for organizing a new state. They reported the following day recommending that a convention be elected for the purpose of framing a constitution for the new state. The report was adopted and the convention was called to meet in Jonesboro in the month of September 1784.[14]

For some reason, the convention was postponed until November but adjourned without taking any action. Nevertheless, the new state adherents persisted and the election of deputies for the constitutional convention was held, five men from each county being chosen as follows: "For Washington County, John Sevier, Wm. Cocke, John Tipton, Thomas Stewart, and Rev. Samuel Houston. For Sullivan County, David Looney, Richard Gammon, Moses Looney William Cage, and John Long. For Greene County, James Reese, Daniel Kennedy, John Newman, James Roddye, and Joseph Hardin."[15]

This convention formed and agreed upon a constitution for the new state to be submitted to a future convention to meet on 14 November 1785 at Greeneville. A legislature was elected and met at Jonesboro for organization. John Sevier was elected governor, Landon Carter, speaker, and Thomas Chapmen, clerk of the House of Commons.[16]

Later Landon Carter was made secretary of state and William Cage, state treasurer, and Joseph Hardin was elected speaker of the House in his stead.[17]

The constitutional convention met at Greeneville, which was the capital and after some discussion and a win by a small majority, the state was named after Benjamin Franklin, or "The State of Franklin." After some difficulty adopting a constitution of their own making and at the suggestion of Wm. Cooke, the members adopted the constitution of North Carolina with some modification.[18]

North Carolina never recognized the new state and much confusion reigned on both sides. The militia was called out and only the cool heads of the settlers prevented considerable bloodshed. John Sevier was arrested but allowed to go free after some of his old comrades in arms from the Kings Mountain days put up the bond money. An act of pardon was extended to all who participated and even Sevier was admitted to the Senate of North Carolina when he was elected the next year from Greene County. Joseph Hardin was also accepted as a member of the assembly from Greene County in 1788. He had been an active and faithful new state adherent and was one of the last to take the oath of allegiance to North Carolina.[19]

At one time the governor of North Carolina wrote that he had no reply to his demand that Sevier and his party lay down their arms except from "Colonel Hardin."[20]

Dr. Ramsey gives a vindication of the State of Franklin which states: "The foundation of a new state was only a question of time. In all the letters, manifestos and proclamations of the Gov. of the parent state, the separation is spoken of as not a right unto its self, but desirable, and at the proper time, expedient." Another author declared the state to be not uncalled for, but only premature.[21]

North Carolina finally ceeded the western territory to the United States government and it was accepted by congress on 2 April 1790. On June 8 of that year, William Blount was commissioned governor of "The Territory of the United States South of the River Ohio."[22]

The number of the inhabitants had increased greatly and Governor Blount issued an ordinance declaring that the people were entitled to a Territorial Assembly. Elections were held in all counties on 22-23 December 1793. Thirteen men were elected: "David Wilson of Sumner Co; Leroy Taylor & John Tipton of Washington Co; George Rutledge of Sullivan Co; Joseph Hardin of Greene Co; William Cocke and Joseph McMinn of Hawkins Co; Alexander Kelly & John Beard of Knox Co; Samuel Wear & Geo. Doherty of Jefferson Co; James White of Davidson Co; and James Ford of Tenn. County.[23]

The governor called the new legislature to meet in Knoxville on the 4th Monday of February 1794. "Haywood" tells us that they "appointed David Wilson, Esq., their Speaker, and Hopkins Lacy, Esq., their Clerk."[24]

This was the "First Territorial Assembly" of which Hale and Merritt take no account. Neither does Garrett and Goodpasture, but they state that the August meeting was in fact the first session. Ramsey in his "Annals" agrees with Haywood, and Judge Williams in his "Lost State of Franklin" states that Joseph Hardin was a member of both the "First" and "Second" territorial assemblies and that he was speaker of the House of the second assembly.[25]

The work of the first session was unimportant in comparison to the second, which may account for the failure of some authors to consider the first. A long memorial was addressed to congress, setting forth the territory's grievances against the Indians and appealing for aid, constituted the chief work of the first. The second session which met in August 1794 had a distinguished service. Dr. Ramsey states: "The instincts, the sagacity and discernment of the constituents, had not been at fault in the selection of their public servants. Perhaps no other deliberative body, was ever more distinguished for identity and familiarity with the interests, the wishes and wants of those for whom they acted, and none could have surpassed them in honesty, promptness and zeal."[26]

Hardin, seconded by Mr. Doherty, was ordered that a message be sent to Wm. Blount, Esq., To Wit: "Sir: The House of Representatives are now met agreeably to your *preregation,* and are ready to proceed to business:. It was ordered that Messes. Hardin and Wear wait on his Excellency with the message. The "Body" adopted its rules then and they are listed in Ramsey, page 624. A committee was then appointed to report what bills of a public and general nature should be considered. The committee was composed of Mr. White, Mr. Cocke, Mr. Hardin, Mr. Wear, & Mr. Doherty.[27]

On the 28 August, the chairman, Mr. Hardin, reported: "An act to regulate the Militia of this Territory; and act to establish the Judicial Courts, and to regulate the proceedings there-of; an act making provision for the poor; and act to enable Executors and Administrators to make rights for lands due upon bonds of persons deceased; an act declaring what property is to be taxable, and the mode of collecting the tax there-on; an act to levy a tax for the support of Government for the year 1794; an act to provide for the relief of such of the militia as have been wounded by the Indians in the late invasions."[28]

These various subjects were referred to committees appointed to consider them and Ramsey says "that the members were selected for their special qualifications in view of past experience and training." Joseph Hardin served on two of them, namely, to make provision for the poor, and to declare what property was taxable.

The assembly passed many laws necessary to the organization of the new counties covering most of the subjects recommended by Joseph Hardin's committee. An act which deserves special notice was the act pensioning disabled soldiers and militia men and the widows of those who had died in service. This was twelve years before the U.S. Congress would pass a similar act. The assembly also recounted the Indian atrocities on the border and appealed to congress for help on the matter, It gives its attention to road building and education. Two colleges were established, Greeneville College, now called Tusculum College, of which Joseph Hardin was a trustee, and one called Blount College, which later became the University of Tennessee at Knoxville.[29]

The legislature worked very hard, assembling at 7:00 every morning and in only 37 days, the body enacted some of the most important laws that were passed by any state during the period. Before their adjournment, the two houses agreed that when the census was taken, as they had previously voted, the opinion of the people should be asked as to the probable admission of the territory into the Union as a state. The session was brought to an end on 30 September 1794.[30]

There was no further account of Joseph Hardin being active in the territorial assembly although they met the following June. On 1 June 1796, Tennessee was admitted into the Union and John Sevier was made governor. There is only one reference showing Joseph Hardin in a political appointment under the state of Tennessee. On 8 August 1796, he was named one of a committee of three electors from Greene County, in conference with three electors from each of the other counties in his district, to choose a presidential elector.[31]

In view of Joseph Hardin's constant activity in governmental affairs from the outbreak of the revolution until 1794, one cannot think that he voluntarily resigned from service. He was now only sixty years of age and was making provisions for his family. In 1795 he bought 2,000 acres of land in Knox County on Silver Creek which is known as Hardin's Valley and then moved his family from Greene County to that location. It has been stated that he later went down the Tennessee River in 1815 to the present Hardin County, Tennessee, and selected his 3,000 acres granted for military service.[32]

It has been determined by later research that it was probably Joseph Hardin Jr. and his family who went down the river to Hardin County in the group with the Brazeltons. The most plausible reason then for Col. Joseph Hardin's retirement from active public affairs must have been ill health. He lived only six more years if the 1801 death date is correct. The other reason that it probably was Joseph Jr. and not the colonel was the fact that he would have been 81 years old at the time and probably too old to made such an arduous journey. (Some researchers state that the colonel came from Kingston, Roane County, Tennessee, in 1815 with surveyors and chain carriers, and located his military claim to 2,000 acres on the lower Tennessee River, along with grants of 1,000 acres to each of his sons, and then he returned to his home in Knox County, Tennessee.)

In June 1816, his son James conducted a party of 26—four families—and settled these lands which lie in what is now known as Hardin County, Tennessee, which was named in honor of the colonel. These settlers traveled in two groups, one by boat down the Tennessee River, and the other over land to bring the livestock. In the boat party were the Goodens and the Brazeltons, including Solomon Brazelton and his family. Coming by land were James Hardin and his family, Joseph Hardin Jr. and his family, Mrs. Ellender Thacker and her family, and John Brazelton, which made in all, 22 persons. In 1817, James Hardin's four brothers, Gibson, Amos,[33] Robert, and Benjamin moved out of Roane County, Tennessee, into the new area of Hardin County, Tennessee, settling around Cerro Gordo, at the time known as White's Ferry.[34]

Col. Joseph Hardin married Jean Gibson (b. 1742, d. 25 March 1817) in 1762. She was the daughter of Walter and Margaret Jordan Gibson. Margaret Jordan was the daughter of Deborah Singletary Jordan.[35] After Walter Gibson died, Margaret married Colonel James McAfee in Tryon County, North Carolina. It was McAfee who remembered his son-in-law, Col. Joseph Hardin, and his stepdaughter, Jean, in his "Will" after he died. Jean is possibly buried in the Hickory Creek Baptist Cemetery next to the colonel but there is no marker. Joseph and Jean had fourteen children, nine sons and five daughters:[36]

1. Joseph Jr. (twin)(b. 22 January 1763, d. 1850, Antoine Twp, Clark County, Arkansas). Joseph was a twin to John. Both were in the Revolutionary War and both were captains. Records of their land grants are filed in the land office in Nashville, Tennessee. He married Fannie Douglas on 22 January 1799 in Knox County, Tennessee. Their children were: Joseph III, who married Mary Simpson; Abraham Kuykendall Hardin who married Elisabeth Wilson; Benjamin, who married Mary Sorrells; James, who married Nancy E. Cocke; and Mary, who married John Cocke.

2. John (twin) (b. 22 January 1763, d. 22 September 1788) married Rebecca Carter on 14 November 1787 in Greene County, Tennessee. He was killed by Indians at Lookout Mountain while serving under General Martin. He requested his unborn son be named after him. Col. Joseph Hardin was appointed guardian of his son, John Jr., who later married Claussa Newman.

3. Jane Ann(1764-1832) married Alexander Virtchworth Goodin in 1784. He was the son of Alexander and Jane (Virtchworth) Gooden. He was born 24 December 1762 in Culpepper, Virginia, and d. 1 April 1844 in Henry County, Missouri. Their children were: Robert; Joseph; Hannah, who married Mr. Kinman; Mary (Polly), who married John Brummett; Benjamin; Eleanor (Ellen), who married James L. Warren;

Amos Hardin; Jane Gibson, who married Ben Ogan; Celia, who married Jasper Sullens; an unnamed infant; and Mahala. Jane Ann's great-grandson, Dr. J. W. Blankinship of California, along with Major Hardin of Hardin's Valley, were responsible for placing the monument at the grave of Col. Joseph Hardin.

4. James, b.?, d. 4 July 1826 in Hardinsville, Hardin County, Tennessee, served in the Tennessee Legislature in 1815 representing Knox County. His wife was probably Elender (Nelly) Goodin, whom he married ca 1793. Nelly, her sons, and in-laws moved to Kentucky after James' death. Their children were: Joseph, Benjamin, James Jr., Jane Kizzie, Margaret, Mary Elisabeth, and Elender.

5. Benjamin (1st) was killed by the Indians at Licklogin in Green County ca 1788. This Ben had been ransomed from the Indians, but ran away and was never seen again.

6. Robert (1st) was killed by Indians at Flinn's Lick, Kentucky, ca 1788. Before leaving on the campaign, he requested his mother name her next born after him because he felt he was going to be killed. He *was* killed and his mother named her next child Robert II.

7. Elender married a Thacker (according to DAR). Possibly daughter unknown. Son James had a daughter named Ellender. Current research states this might be in conflict with Ellender Brazelton, daughter of John and Hannah Gooden Brazelton, who married John Thacker. Ellender and her sons, Shepard and William Thacker, were members of the land party that traveled with the Hardins, Brazeltons, and Goodens when they moved to Hardin County, Tennessee, in 1816. Her father was John Brazelton.

8. Mary E. (This probably should be Salley Hardin who married John Gallaher in 1797 in Knox County, Tennessee.)

9. Margaret, b. before 1760, d. after 1830 in Conway County, Arkansas, married Adam Kuykendall ca 1776 probably in Mecklinburg County, North Carolina.[37,38] Their children were: Abner, who married Sarah Gates; Amos, who married Elizabeth ____; Robert H., who married Sarah Ann Gilleland; Peter, who married Sarah ____; Adam Jr., who married Falbray Goza; and Sally, who married Mr. Blount. The Margaret shown in the 1850 census of Conway County, living with Peter Kuykendall, is not Peter's mother. She died in the 1830s. (Marshall E. Kuykendall of Austin, Texas, is descended through Margaret and her son Robert H. Kuykendall and Sarah Ann Gilleland.)

10. Benjamin (2nd, not to be confused with old Benjamin II) b. 28 December 1780, d. 24 August 1840, Liberty County, Texas (possibly Red River County, Texas), was in the Tennessee Legislature in 1823-25. He later moved to Texas and was prominent in politics. He married Martha Ann (Patsy) Barnett on 7 December 1801. She was the daughter of William Barnett. Their children were: (1) Joseph B., who married Arabella Adams; (2) William Barnett Hardin, who married Ann Holshaussen; (3) Robert E., who married Nancy Brinson Dixon; (4) Benjamin P., who married, first, Clara Robinson, and then Mary Ann ____?; (5) George W.; (6) Elisabeth Ann, who married Moses Wells; (7) Jane, who married Moses Tracy; (8) Easter Mary, who married, first, James Clements, and then Robert Hooker; (9) Martha Balch, who married Emanuel Clements; (10) Rev. James Gibson Hardin, who married Mary Elisabeth Dixon (this couple were the parents of John Wesley Hardin, the famous Texas gunfighter); (11) Gibson; (12) and a male child that died in infancy.

11. Amos, b. 25 February 1780, d. 1840 Hardin County, Tennessee, married Mary

Gallaher on 26 April 1796, daughter of James Gallaher Sr. and Mary ____ of Pennsylvania. Amos was the head of the family that remained in Know County, Tennessee. He was a large land owner, a minister in the Baptist church and a school teacher. Their children were: (1) Gibson; (2) George G., who married Cynthia Calloway; (3) Sarah, who married Jacob Butler; (4) John G., who married Sarah Gallaher?; (5) Jane Gibson, who married John Fleming; (6) James, who married Sarah Hope; (7) Amos Jr., who married Letitia Montgomery; (8) Mary E., (conflict with Sally, above), who married Major W. Wilkerson; (9) and the Rev. Robert W. Hardin, who married Amanda King. (Amos's grandson was Major Wm. Hardin, who assisted in the erection of the monument to the colonel.)

12. Rebecca, married Ninian Steele 8 June 1782 in Greene County (possibly Washington County, Tennessee). They moved to Hardin County, Tennessee. Possible children were: James H.; Robert; Sarah; Mary, who married William Wilkerson; and Benjagie??, who married ____ Briley.

13. Gibson, b. 1777, d. 11 May 1847 in Hardin County, Tennessee, married first Sarah Gallaher on 24 May 1800 in Knox County, Tennessee. She was born 2 December 1788, d. 24 July 1826. They moved to Hardin County, Tennessee, where he reared his family. They had six children. He then married Margaret Alvira Cobb on 2 January 1827 in Knox County, Tennessee. Children unknown.

14. Robert (2nd) D.D., b. 3 January 1789, d. 4 September 1867, married first on 3 January 1807 Margaret McAlpin (b. 26 September 1788, d. 11 October 1853), and they had one child, Alexander McAlpin Hardin, who married Elisabeth Robertson. Robert then married Mrs. Mary (Davidson) Hunter (b. 5 September 1827, d. 19 December 1903) on 24 December 1854. Their children were: Rev. Robert Emmett, who married Anna Price; Mary Ophelia, who married James Lindsey Cochran; Thomas Alexander (twin), who married first Eliza Tennyson, then married Susie Wade; Joseph Converse Hardin I (twin), d. in infancy; and Joseph Converse II, who married Emma Tate. Robert, the father, became a Presbyterian minister and was made Doctor of Divinity by Center College at Danville, Kentucky. He served as a commissioner to the general assembly of his church which met in Philadelphia in 1828, making the trip to and from that city by horseback. He died and was first buried at Union Church but later his remains were removed to Lewisburg to rest beside his second wife, Mary.[39]

Col. Joseph Hardin lived to see Tennessee become the second state to join the Union west of the mountains. Freedom and independence were the keynotes of his life. He died on the anniversary of the Declaration of Independence, 4 July 1801, and lies buried in the Hickory Creek Baptist Cemetery (now known as the Mt. Pleasant Baptist Church Cemetery) near Concord and north of Lenoir City in western Knox County, Tennessee, in the community known as Hardin's Valley. In recent years a monument has been erected by descendents which reads:[40]

JOSEPH HARDIN
FARMER   SOLDIER   STATESMAN

Born April 18, 1734, in Virginia of English Ancestry
Died July 4, 1801, in Hardin's Valley, Tennessee
A strict Presbyterian, stern and fearless in discharge of duty
Loved and trusted by his friends, feared by his enemies

Major 2nd N.C. Minute Men, Salisbury District, 1775
Captain Tryon Co., N.C. Light Horse, Cherokee Expedition, 1776
In battle of Ramsour's Mill and at King's Mountain, 1780
Colonel for Western Counties (Tenn.) 1788
Lost three sons in Tennessee Indian Wars
Member Committee of Safety, Tryon Co., N.C. 1775
Member Provincial Congress at Hillsborough, 1775 and at Halifax, 1775
Member General Assembly of N.C. 1778-79 and (from Tenn.) 1782-88
Organizer State of Franklin, Jonesboro, 1784-85
Member General Assembly, Territory South of the Ohio, Knoxville, 1794[41]

Because of his military services during the Revolutionary War and Indian wars, he received 3,000 acres in 1785 from North Carolina in the middle district, now Hardin County, Tennessee, which was later named for him.[42]

It should be noted that Joseph Hardin's sister Rebecca married John Kuykendall, son of old Matthew (1690-1754) and it is thought by most researchers that John Hardin's wife was Elisabeth Kuykendall, possibly a daughter of old Matthew and sister to John Kuykendall. Adam Kuykendall, son of Peter, whose "Will" was recorded in Washington County, Tennessee, in 1783, married Margaret Hardin, daughter of Colonel Joseph, and Adam's brother Matthew married Jane Hardin, daughter of John and Elisabeth Hardin. Matthew and his wife, Jane, were cousins.[43]

All three Hardins brothers were veterans of the Revolutionary War. There are several outstanding histories on Joseph Hardin noted in this paper. A copy of the affidavit from Davidson County, Tennessee, showing the land grants to Colonel Hardin shows he received a total of 8,100 acres of land from military grants between 1788 and 1801. It further states that John Hardin was granted 1,000 acres in military grants. It is also stated in the records that Benjamin III, brother to John and Joseph, either bought or was given Land Grant #1604 in Davidson County, Tennessee, from Adam Kuykendall. The grant reads:

State of N.C. No. 1604. Grants

Know Ye that we have granted unto Benjamin Hardin Sr. (III) assignee of Adam Kuykendall, a private in Continental Line of said State, 388 acres in our county of Davidson on both sides of the Sulphur Fork of Red River, beginning at a white oak and dogwood trees to heirs of Wm. Hood's corner. Runs with their line, east 10 chains to a Poplar, then south, 30 chains to a large white oak, then west 65 chains to a dogwood and white oak then north 18 chains and 50 links to a white oak to M. Gilkinson's line. With line east 4 chains to an elm said Gilkinson's corner with his line north 50 chains to a white oak and hickory, east 51 chains to a stake on said Hood's line with said line south to the beginning. To hold to said Benjamin Hardin, his heirs and Assigns forever.

(signed) J. Glasgow, sec.,
R. Weakley, D.S.,
James Gilkinson,
Alec Martin,
Samuel Hardin (C.C.)[44]

John Hardin, born prior to 1734, brother to Col. Joseph Hardin, as stated above was married to Elisabeth Kuykendall. Elisabeth was probably the daughter of old Matthew (1690). Their possible children were: (1) John Jr., who married Mary Karr. (2) Jane Hardin, who married Matthew Kuykendall. Matthew was the son of Peter and was a brother to Adam Kuykendall. (3) David Hardin married Sarah Gist. (4) Moses Hardin married Orpha Hassell. (5) Rebecca Hardin married John Parks. (6) Betty? married Robt. Agnew. (7) Margaret married Macajah Hancock. (8) Sarah? married Jacob Sanders.[45]

Benjamin Hardin III, was probably born ca 1736 in Virginia, a brother to both John and Joseph. He was supposedly married to Catherine "Lamkin"? Their children were: (1) Joab Hardin married three times. First to Sarah Drake; second to Miss Peel and third to Holly Bagley. (2) Sarah Hardin married Euel Lamkin? (3) Margaret Hardin married Henry Hicks? (4) Benjamin Hardin Jr., also known as Benjamin IV or "Benjamin, the Pensioner," was born 15 March 1764 in Mecklenburg County, North Carolina. He married Elisabeth Scott on 31 December 1782 in Mecklinburg County, North Carolina. He died 2 April 1848 in Christian Township, Independence County, Arkansas. Benjamin IV, the teenage soldier in the Revolution, attained the rank of colonel, whereas his father attained the rank of captain. (5) Samuel Hardin b. ca 1766, married Susannah Davis and moved to Howard County, Missouri. (6) George Hardin married Lydia? (7) Jacob Hardin. (8) Catherine Hardin, born ca 1766, married William Gates. Their daughter, Sarah, married Abner Kuykendall, son of Adam. They all went to Texas (except Adam) with Stephen F. Austin in 1821. Catherine died in 1826 and is buried in the Gates cemetery in Washington County, Texas, just south of Washington-on-the-Brazos. A monument has recently been erected in their honor.[46]

As stated earlier, Benjamin III would aquire a tract of land from Adam Kuykendall in Davidson County, Tennessee. The deed states that Benjamin III is the assignee of Adam Kuykendall, "a private in the Continental Line." There has been a lot of speculation as to who the private in the C.L. is, due to the way the deed is written. It is believed now that the statement pertains to Adam Kuykendall. Benjamin III later moved to Logan County, Kentucky, and died there on Clifty Creek, ca 1801.[47]

Both Benjamin III and his son, Benjamin IV, were in the Revolution. Both were in the battles of Kings Mountain, Ramsour's Mill (as was Joseph), and the Cowpens. Benjamin III was captain of his companies in which Ben IV served. Ben IV also spent a year in a mounted rifle company commanded by Capt. John Newman.[48]

Benjamin IV, and his wife moved from the Holston River area in east Tennessee to the area near Nashville, Davidson County, Tennessee, in 1793, then later moved to the part of Logan County, Kentucky, that in 1798 became Livingston County, Kentucky. From Livingston County, Ben. IV, along with his brother Joab and their wives, moved in 1815 to the White River area of what is now known as Independence County, Arkansas. Interestingly and also very confusing to the researcher, is the fact that Ben. IV's son Joseph moved ahead of him to Arkansas in late 1810 and lived in Lawrence County, Arkansas. At the time of his death in 1826, he would be a colonel in the Third Regiment of the Territorial Militia of Arkansas and also sheriff of Lawrence County. This designation of colonel has confused him many times with his uncle, Col. Joseph Hardin of Knox County, Tennessee. To also confuse matters further, Col. Joseph Hardin's (Knox County) son, Joseph Jr., also moved to Arkansas and lived not far from his "cousin" Joseph, sheriff of Lawrence County.[49]

It should also be noted that Adam Kuykendall and his entire family, along with the Gates, all who intermarried with the Hardins, matched the Hardins almost step by step in their long journeys, that started in North Carolina before the Revolution, wound Tennessee and Kentucky, down into Arkansas, almost year for year, with many of the children ending up in Texas.[50]

The other Joseph Hardin noted above, Joseph Hardin Jr./Sr., son of Col. Joseph Hardin of Knox County, Tennessee (later known as Joseph Sr.—hence the reference as Jr./Sr.), was born on 22 January 1763 in Tryon County, North Carolina, and was a twin to John, who was killed at the Battle of Lookout Mountain. Some sources state that he was born in South Carolina. That is quite plausible when one realizes that old Tryon County spilled over into what is now known as South Carolina. Joseph Jr./Sr. was probably married to Fanny Douglas in Knox County, Tennessee. He was a captain in the Revolutionary War and representative of North Carolina, Tennessee, and Arkansas in the various state legislatures. He was issued a land grant of 1,000 acres for services rendered, which was located in Hardin County, Tennessee, and known as the "middle district." He and his brother James, along with the Brazeltons, some of whom floated down the Tennessee River and others who went overland, moved to that area in 1816. From there, he moved into Kentucky, where a county was also named for the family, then into northern Arkansas, settling near Batesville and Walnut Ridge. This was known as "Union Township" of Lawrence County which was many miles northwest of Davidsonville. He later moved farther south into Hempstead to what is now Clark County, Arkansas, and settled near present day Hope, Arkansas. Joseph Sr./Jr. was speaker of the House in 1820 and a representative from Clark County to the Arkansas legislature in 1827-1829. Joseph Sr./Jr. died in Clark County, Antoine Township, Arkansas, ca 1850. Children of Joseph Sr./Jr. and Fanny were: (1) James Hardin, who married Nancy Ellen Coche on 8 September 1831. (2) Benjamin Hardin, who married Mary Sorrells on 7 September 1832. (3) Mary Hardin, who married John Cocke on 29 August 1841. (4) Joseph Hardin Jr., who married first Mary Simpson, and second Sally Cornelius. (5) Abraham Kuykendall Hardin, born ca 1813 in Tennessee, married Elisabeth (Betsy) Wilson on 25 September 1828, at Hope, Hempstead County, Arkansas. Betsy was born ca 1811 in Cape Gireadeau, Missouri, and died on 4 June in either 1862 or '63. She was the daughter of the famed statesman, John Wilson.[51]

Here is a statement from Dr. Craig's writings:

Thirty-two of the current seventy-five counties in Arkansas were formed in whole or in part, out of the area originally encompassed by "Old" Lawrence County This area is represented by the Northeastern, the North Central and much of Northwestern portions of present day state of Arkansas. The original Seat-of-Justice of "Old" Lawrence County was called "The Town of Lawrence." Early in 1817, the name of the town was changed to "Davidsonville."

Within "Old" Lawrence County, Missouri Territory/Arkansas Territory, lived three Joseph Hardins, all related. One Joseph Hardin settled in the area ca 1811, which was four years prior to the establishment of Lawrence County. In 1815, he was a member of the commission which selected the site for the original "Seat-of Justice" and helped lay out the town of Lawrence, later called Davidsonville. He served as the first deputy sheriff, and was later appointed sheriff. He was colonel of the Third Regiment of Militia of Arkansas, hence the title of Dr. Craig's compilation: "Colonel Joseph Hardin of Davidsonville." He died there in Davidsonville on 25 August 1826.

The other two Joseph Hardins of "Old" Lawrence County were related to Joseph Hardin of Davidsonville via collateral branches of the Hardin Family. The other two Joseph Hardins were Joseph Hardin Sr. (known above as Jr./Sr.), and his son Joseph Jr. They settled in Lawrence County ca 1816. By the early part of 1825, they had moved to Hempstead County, later Clark County, Arkansas.

It should be noted that a James M. Kuykendall became sheriff of the county after Joseph Hardin's death. He was the son of Joseph Kuykendall, who died in Pulaski County, Arkansas, in 1828. (He was a cousin of Adam Kuykendall's family.)

Copy of Affidavit, showing Land Grants
to
Colonel Joseph Hardin
of
Knox County Tenn.
State of Tennessee
Davidson County

Know all men by these presents that I, W.B. Leech, Attorney-at-law, address 916 Independent Life Bldg., Nashville, here-by certify and make oath that I have examined the records of North Carolina Military Grants Entries and Warrants, on file in the State Land Office at Nashville, Tennessee and I find recorded the following to Joseph Hardin Sr. in Book "North Carolina Grants" Nos. 1 to 2662, also Book "A," page 30, N.C. Military Grants, 1788-1803:

No.	Acres
318	600 acres
445	800 acres
670	1,000 acres
924	200 acres
1619	3,000 acres
2118	1,000 acres
2119	1,000 acres
2129	500 acres
Total	8,100 acres

Also Grant No. 317 for 400 acres, marked "withdrawn." I also find on said records that Joseph Hardin Jr. by warrant No. 2128 was granted 1,000 acres on May 10, 1784. I also find John Hardin in Book "A," page 3, was granted 1,000 acres on July 10, 1788.

State of Tennessee
Davidson County

(SEAL)   Personally appeared before me, J. H. Tidman, Notary Public, W. B. Leech, with whom I am personally acquainted and who made oath in the form of law that the statements made in the above instrument are true to the best of his knowledge, information, and belief.
Sworn and subscribed to before me, this the 24th day of June, 1931.
T. H. Tidman
My commission expires 9th day of July 1933.[52]

Bibliography

Dropped Stitches in Tennessee History, 1897, by John H. Allison
History of Hardin County Tennessee, 1885, by B. G. Brazelton.
History of Tennessee, 1900, by Garrett and Goodpasture.
Civil & Political History of Tennessee, 1823, by John Haywood.
History of Tennessee, 8 Vols., 1913, by Hale & Merritt.
Article on Colonel Hardin in the *Knoxville Sentinel*, 1915, by Dr. Geo. Mellon.
N.C. Grants, No. 1 to 2662, Land Office, Nashville, Tenn.
N.C. Military Grants, 1788-1803, Book "A," Nashville, Tennessee.
Annals of Tennessee, 1860, by J.G.M. Ramsey.
Colonial Records of N.C., Vol. X., by W.L. Saunders .
Historical Sketches of N.C., (2) Vols., 1851, by John H. Wheeler.
History of the Lost State of Franklin, 1924, by Samuel Cole Williams.
History of East Tennessee by Goodspeed.
The French Broad-Holston Country.

All of the information in this paper was furnished in its entirety by J. Oran Hardin, Rt.1., Box 2290, Crewe, Va. 23930; Anita Miller, 6502 Petain Ave., Dallas, Texas 75227; Ethel Monday, 3520 Hendrix Ln., Knoxville, Tennessee 37921, and Dr. Marion Craig of Arkansas. The effort by the present compiler is not to detract from any of their research, which was arduous, but simply to put the facts about the family in an order that is easily read.

Records and Notices

Chapter Twenty-Two

Kuykendall Texas Death Notices 1903–2000

AN INDEX TO PROBATE BIRTH RECORDS
TEXAS DELAYED
BUREAU OF VITAL STATISTICS

These death notices are from the Texas State Health Department that are stored at the Texas State Genealogical Library in Austin, Texas. They contain all the normal spellings of the name: Kuykendall, Kuyrkendall, Kirkendall, Kuydendale, Kuydendall, Kuykendahl, Kuykendal, Kuykendale, Kuykendoll, Kuykundoll, Kuykindall, Kuykindoll.

SURNAME	FIRST	COUNTY	DATE	FILE#
1903-1940				
Kirkendall	Charles David	Taylor	9-10-12	1224587
Kirkendall	Fannie Lou	Ill.	4-26-86	1019433
Kirkendall	Bunijan Inf. Of	Jasper	12-9-06	83703
Kirkendall	T. P. Inf. Of	————	5-7-10	18574
Kirkendall	Wily, Inf. Of	Van Zandt	10-2-10	38199
Kirkendall	C. H., Inf. Of	Hill	12-1-12	43500
Kirkendall	C. H., Inf. Of	Hill	12-1-12	43501
Kirkendall	Ed., Inf. Of	Callahan	8-19-12	26157

SURNAME	FIRST	COUNTY	DATE	FILE#
Kirkendahl	Augs, Inf. Of	Victoria	7-6-14	24511
Kirkendahl	Aug, Inf. Of	———	3-24-17	12644
Kirkendall	Loronzo, Inf. Of	Hardin	10-2-17	46531
Kirkendall	Chas. Everitt, Inf. Of	Galveston	9-20-18	46590
Kirkendall	Chas. M.	Taylor	5-31-18	26967
Kirkendall	Roy	Taylor	9-17-18	49426
Kirkendall	Wilson Welburn	Hardin	7-12-18	35262
Kirkindal	Y. C., Inf. Of	Franklin	2-7-18	7823
Kirkendoll	Lottie Juanita	Newton	3-20-20	16449
Kirkendoll	Raymond Jr.	Garza	8-24-20	42181
Kirkindale	F. C., Inf. Of	Franklin	9-16-20	48343
Kirkendall	Burtis Evandus	Hardin	4-6-04	263907
Kirkendall	Charles Bunion	Hardin	7-30-84	429058
Kirkendall	Commodore Stanley	Harris	4-2-16	669661
Kirkendall	Earl	Colorado	4-5-09	538832
Kirkendall	Evalee	Callahan	3-24-13	858288
Kirkendall	John Lawrence	Hill	6-2-11	563521
Kirkendall	Lindsey Lowell	Ohioll	10-7-76	900374
Kirkendall	Ruby	Taylor	7-8-14	694404
Kirkendall	Thurman Graham	Johnson	9-11-09	688407
Kirkendall	Vera Francis	Hardin	6-22-19	829186
Kirkendoll	Alton Lee	Scurry	1-14-00	188448
Kirkendoll	Doris Faye	Garza	3-13-24	316866
Kirkendoll	Gladys Jean	Garza	4-26-22	316863
Kirkendoll	Joan	Garza	7-31-28	316865
Kirkendoll	Ray Del	Garza	2-14-26	316864
Kirkendoll	Sarah Lois	Callahan	8-19-12	445603
Kirkendall	Carlos Gusten	Walker	4-14-?	010563
Kirkendall	Edith L.	Hill	12-14-?	23311
Kirkendoll	Michael Raye	Jefferson	3-63-?	191908
Kirkindall	Fannie R.	Hardin	4-7-?	150626
Kirkendoll	Mirle T.	Smith	5-10-?	095712
Kirkendall	Charles Everett, Inf.	Galveston	1-11-22	2777
Kirkendall	Gussie Earlene	Smith	3-19-22	18155
Kirkendall	Chas. Everett	Galveston	5-2-23	27118
Kirkendall	Doris	Taylor	1-4-23	6024
Kirkendall	Ida	Hardin	6-13-23	33274
Kirkendol	Agnes	Taylor	11-12-23	72189
Kirkendoll	J.F., Inf. Of	Knox	1-29-23	4429
Kirkendoll	James M., Inf. Of	Dallas	10-3-24	65316
Kirkindall	Charles Rex	Franklin	4-15-24	23699
Kirkendall	Ethel	Hardin	11-1-25	78343
Kirkendall	Flora	Galveston	3-9-25	18027
Kirkendoll	John T., Inf. Of	Hamilton	7-22-25	46421
Kirkindall	Arthur	Jasper	2-26-25	12080
Kirkindall	Juanita M.	Dickens	2-6-25	10142
Kerkundall	Carlyle J.	Hill	11-4-25	78940

SURNAME	FIRST	COUNTY	DATE	FILE#
Kirkendall	Therman Eugene	Johnson	2-12-26	11785
Kirkendall	Tommie Olean	Hardin	7-27-27	45722
Kirkendall	Bettye Jo	Dallas	12-3-28	100702
Kirkendall	Mittie	Jasper	5-16-28	36619
Kerkyndall	Margie, Inf. Of	Taylor	5-7-28	39074
Kirkendall	Maridith Eliane	Harris	5-10-29	40263
Kirkendoll	Reece Philip	Johnson	9-4-29	79701
Kirkendol	Roger	Taylor	8-23-21	51032
Kirkendall	Donald Lee	Tarrant	6-10-30	55761
Kirkendall	Kenneth Ray	Hardin	8-27-30	71545
Kirkendoll	Ben Long, Inf. Of	Smith	7-28-30	65298
Kirkendoll	Tom, Inf. Of	Howard	5-7-32	38882
Kirkendall	Margreda	Liberty	7-2-32	59021
Kirkindole	Charles E., Inf. Of	Franklin	1-1-32	3363
Kirkindall	Mary Louise	Hardin	2-12-33	12668
Kirkendoll	Ben Long, Inf. Of	Smith	7-3-34	56024
Kirkendoll	Maxine	Hardin	2-25-35	13528
Kerkendal	Willey G., Inf. Of	Montague	1-30-35	7014
Kirkendahl	Mary Frances	Hardin	7-8-36	5202
Kirkendoll	Minnie Ann	Franklin	4-9-36	2899
Kirkendoll	Sammy Louise	Jasper	10-31-36	8117
Kirkendall	Elouise	Hardin	11-6-37	93670
Kirkendall	Bobby Dean	Smith	3-16-38	8241
Kirkindoll	Thomas James	Gregg	12-10-38	108349
Kirkendall	La Vonne	Taylor	10-7-?	93571
Kirkendoll	Patsy	Hardin	9-25-?	78001
Kirkendoll	Ivy Thomas	Hardin	1-2-40	4349
Kirkendall	Preston ?yne	Uvalde	1-9-40	81510
Kirkendoff	Cleo	McLennan	3-8-40	?5824
Kirkendall	Marianne Yates	Midland	10-8-41	102169
Kirkendoll	Hiram Bernard	Bowie	1-19-41	962
Kirkindall	Linda Carroll	Jasper	4-20-41	35477
Kirkendall	John Franklin	Hardin	9-28-42	89397
Kirkendall	Roland Ray	El Paso	7-20-42	62936
Kirkendoll	Benny Ray	Potter	4-1-42	39775
Kirkendoll	Reba Lee	Victoria	7-25-42	70246
Kirkindoll	Almo, Inf. Of	Jefferson	5-26-42	47164
Kirkendall	Charles Byron Jr.	Galveston	4-12-43	42270
Kirkendall	Jimmy March	Jefferson	6-11-43	67376
Kirkendall	Shirley Faye	Cooke	7-16-43	74940
Kirkendall	Timothy James	Bexar	12-30-43	158047
Kirkindall	Harrell Dee	Hardin	7-16-43	77873
Kerkuedall	Charles Lenny	Coryell	4-7-43	40385
Kirkendall	Barbara Joe	Harris	11-9-44	138119
Kirkendall	Rodger Dale	Hardin	5-26-44	53265
Kirkendoll	Ira Raymond	Taylor	8-17-44	100387
Kirkendoll	Iris Kay	Wichita	4-20-44	48532

SURNAME	FIRST	COUNTY	DATE	FILE#
Kerkendall	Riley Marshall	Grayson	2-12-44	18393
Kirkendall	Dona Gail	Johnson	11-2-45	133779
Kirkendall	LaFay	Jackson	1-19-45	7974
Kirkendall	Ostrich	Jackson	10-30-45	120104
Kirkendall	Robert Biel	Lamb	3-28-45	33664
Kirkendoll	Horace Lee	Jefferson	3-20-45	33025
Kirkendoll	James Inf. Of	Galveston	8-23-45	63591
Kirkindall	Sandra LaVern	Hardin	12-27-45	143851
Kuydendale	J. L.	Llano	2-4-25	7339
Kuykendahl	Charles, Inf of	Lavaca	3-24-20	11269
Kuykendal	George Clark	Travis	5-30-40	25837
Kuykendal	Loreno	Taylor	1-25-24	3219
Kuykendal	Russell Lathen	Dallas	9-30-39	41397
Kuykendale	Rowens Bob	Dallas	10-23-32	41679
Kuykendoll	Eddie	De Witt	7-19-32	29484
Kuykendoll	Wade Willis	Cooke	11-27-18	48495
Kuykindall	Lovell Coffman	San Saba	4-16-21	11873
Kuykundoll	William Haskel	Lamar	7-11-28	31567
Kuykendall	A.D. Inf of	Coryell	3-27-18	11140
Kuykendall	A.L.	Harris	5-26-21	14143
Kuykendall	A.R.	McLennan	2-17-19	7836
Kuykendall	A.W.	Ochiltree	7-24-21	20506
Kuykendall	Abe	Harris	5-14-27	16542
Kuykendall	Abner	Bexar	7-24-10	12650
Kuykendall	Addie	Harris	11-17-37	55466
Kuykendall		DeWitt	6-28-25	21338
Kuykendal	Charley	Lavaca	7-1-18	29216
Kuykendal	Elbert	Lavaca	7-1-18	29217
Kuykendal	Emma	Matagorda	12-22-35	58200
Kuykendal	Ernest	Lavaca	6-10-18	25678
Kuykendal	George Agnes	Red River	3-31-39	15094
Kuykendall	Alfred	Wharton	12-10-05	60629
Kuykendall	Alice	Lamar	8-22-27	27937
Kuykendall	Alverta B.	Galveston	1-31-19	2287
Kuykendall	Alvie, Inf of	Lampasas	3-27-18	12940
Kuykendall	Alzena	Refugio	4-12-25	15552
Kuykendall	Andrew B.	Bexar	5-7-16	10857
Kuykendall	Anna	Lavaca	8-18-28	36262
Kuykendall	Anna B., Mrs	San Saba	6-6-40	30024
Kuykendall	Anna C.	Collin	1-3-29	1462
Kuykendall	August Buschell	Young	6-5-38	30605
Kuykendall	B. H.	Van Zandt	3-8-32	14329
Kuykendall	B. W.	Wharton	5-11-18	23052
Kuykendall	Barney	Howard	4-21-12	10619
Kuykendall	Ben M.	Dallas	9-17-39	41310
Kuykendall	Beulah	Nueces	3-2-34	14570
Kuykendall	Brazile	McMullen	1-1-16	2284

SURNAME	FIRST	COUNTY	DATE	FILE#
Kuykendall	Buelah Mae	Harris	2-11-33	8379
Kuykendall	Byrd	Wharton	3-18-37	18537
Kuykendall	C. D.	Stephens	8-19-39	39655
Kuykendall	Callie	McLennan	5-18-35	24958
Kuykendall	Calvin Willie	Dallam	7-11-33	31409
Kuykendall	Carline Yvonne	Travis	1-19-38	5079
Kuykendall	Carrie, Mrs	Bexar	8-15-23	23026
Kuykendall	Charle Wm.	Lavaca	2-23-19	7678
Kuykendall	Charles, Inf of	Taylor	6-8-18	26547
Kuykendall	Charles Emery	Gillespie	2-27-39	7523
Kuykendall	Charles P.	El Paso	2-20-32	8478
Kuykendall	Charles Wm.	La Salle	1-23-16	2111
Kuykendall	Clara	Freestone	5-1-40	23313
Kuykendall	Clara S., Miss.	Bexar	6-24-30	27215
Kuykendall	Claudina	Floyd	11-19-26	38130
Kuykendall	Cora, Miss.	Bexar	7-4-21	18474
Kuykendall	Cordelia	Bexar	2-3-27	4006
Kuykendall	Daniel	Bexar	11-20-20	33893
Kuykendall	David	DeWitt	11-17-13	23007
Kuykendall	David O.	Grayson	12-20-37	60297
Kuykendall	Derrie M.	Red River	8-8-20	27569
Kuykendall	Dollie	Limestone	7-27-23	21903
Kuykendall	Dorado	Lavaca	2-13-35	9077
Kuykendall	E.D., Inf. Of	Tarrant	12-3-29	61414
Kuykendall	Earl, Inf. Of	Montague	6-25-15	13568
Kuykendall	Edgar Wayne	Gregg	8-29-28	35239
Kuykendall	Edith	Bexar	7-13-16	15805
Kuykendall	Edna Mae	Wilson	8-2-30	42308
Kuykendall	Edwin S.	Tarrant	12-25-40	57590
Kuykendall	Effie Hilburn	Montague	4-30-36	22192
Kuykendall	Elizabeth	Lubbock	2-27-23	12941
Kuykendall	Ella	McLennan	6-26-35	29773
Kuykendall	Ella Mae	Dallas	9-15-40	41063
Kuykendall	Elleen, Inf. Of	McLennan	7-19-22	21329
Kuykendall	Emma	Bexar	5-2-30	22126
Kuykendall	Emma, Mrs.	Gray	6-18-28	25864
Kuykendall	Emma E.	Gregg	10-20-38	45754
Kuykendall	Emma Lee	Lavaca	6-5-34	28702
Kuykendall	Emma Missouri,Mrs	Harrison	9-16-39	42483
Kuykendall	Ernest Vernon	Bosque	8-10-25	28218
Kuykendall	Eugene Guy	Montague	9-7-26	32704
Kuykendall	Eula Mae	Grayson	12-11-18	56225
Kuykendall	Everette Vernon	Bosque	8-10-25	28221
Kuykendall	F.	Hunt	5-13-32	21899
Kuykendall	Fannie	Bexar	5-14-30	22016
Kuykendall	Fannie	Lavaca	8-15-36	41939
Kuykendall	Faye	Lavaca	6-19-40	26286

SURNAME	FIRST	COUNTY	DATE	FILE#
Kuykendall	Frances Lucille	Bexar	1-16-26	159
Kuykendall	Frances	Lavaca	5-16-24	17174
Kuykendall	Frank	Bexar	7-3-17	18078
Kuykendall	Frank	Presidio	2-6-34	9382
Kuykendall	Frank	Presidio	2-6-34	9387
Kuykendall	Frank	Wilson	8-4-20	28134
Kuykendall	Frank James	Lamar	2-16-39	8864
Kuykendall	George D.	Harris	3-3-19	10228
Kuykendall	George Gray	Navarro	8-17-03	44040
Kuykendall	G.M.	Williamson	2-9-36	12061
Kuykendall	Geo. W.	Grayson	8-5-32	34410
Kuykendall	George W.	Montgomery	10-14-26	35935
Kuykendall	George W.	Tom Green	2-23-25	8201
Kuykendall	Ginsey	Van Zandt	3-21-23	10472
Kuykendall	Harell	Jefferson	3-21-25	10940
Kuykendall	Hattie Hosea, Mrs.	Harris	7-2-30	34686
Kuykendall	Hendy	Harris	4-8-20	14005
Kuykendall	Ida Jane	Bexar	5-12-39	21700
Kuykendall	Ira	Bexar	4-12-21	9607
Kuykendall	Ira	Bexar	2-10-32	5300
Kuykendall	Iris	Bexar	1-31-27	463
Kuykendall	J. D. Mrs.	Hunt	5-14-29	26333
Kuykendall	J. D.	Tom Green	9-30-35	44274
Kuykendall	J. F., Inf. of	Montague	7-16-17	20019
Kuykendall	J. H.	De Witt	12-22-33	53288
Kuykendall	J. M.	Brown	6-25-35	27033
Kuykendall	J. M.	San Saba	12-19-35	58928
Kuykendall	J. N.	Dallas	3-8-16	6218
Kuykendall	J.Raymond, Inf. of	Lamb	2-1-32	7804
Kuykendall	J.Richard	Howard	6-8-29	31265
Kuykendall	J. W.	Bell	2-14-22	3379
Kuykendall	J.W., Inf. of	Bexar	5-18-16	10858
Kuykendall	J. W.	Lubbock	12-2-24	39715
Kuykendall	Jack	Bosque	7-31-37	34778
Kuykendall	Jack Wayne	Bexar	1-29-38	539
Kuykendall	Jacob	De Witt	2-12-19	6486
Kuykendall	James	Taylor	1-21-27	3429
Kuykendall	James Humphrey	Dallas	10-4-36	48769
Kuykendall	James M.	Panola	5-19-24	17542
Kuykendall	Jesse	Wharton	3-30-06	60648
Kuykendall	Jewel Eva	Dallas	4-22-26	13586
Kuykendall	Jim M.	Bell	5-20-21	12523
Kuykendall	Joan	Hunt	3-2-35	14148
Kuykendall	Joe, Inf. of	Harris	3-17-29	16194
Kuykendall	John	De Witt	4-20-25	13618
Kuykendall	John	Lavaca	2-11-27	6146
Kuykendall	John	Wheeler	11-26-22	32992

SURNAME	FIRST	COUNTY	DATE	FILE#
Kuykendall	John Alice	Lavaca	5-23-25	18903
Kuykendall	John Belton	Hill	2-21-10	12651
Kuykendall	John Ed	McLennan	9-10-34	42016
Kuykendall	John Holder	Potter	9-28-28	41002
Kuykendall	John J.	Taylor	1-26-18	4650
Kuykendall	John Wood	Tarrant	7-7-34	34247
Kuykendall	Joseph	Bexar	3-5-17	6390
Kuykendall	Joseph	Collin	11-1-04	12467
Kuykendall	Joseph Brazillian	Bexar	11-25-35	49667
Kuykendall	Joseph Edgar	Bexar	12-22-33	53534
Kuykendall	Josephine	Williamson	11-3-16	26662
Kuyykendall	Julie Ann	Gray	11-17-35	51369
Kuykendall	Kathren Zenia	Bosque	10-10-22	27803
Kuykendall	Kathryn	Lubbock	4-20-38	19519
Kuykendall	Kittie	Lavaca	8-28-09	40787
Kuykendall	L.P. Mrs	Eastland	2-20-30	7540
Kuykendall	Laura	Harris	7-6-35	33350
Kuykendall	Laura	La Salle	12-12-34	55661
Kuykendall	Laura	Lavaca	2-2-18	8365
Kuykendall	Laura	Tarrant	4-6-34	19863
Kuykendall	Laura	Williamson	4-30-35	21464
Kuykendall	Laura Ann	San Saba	9-17-19	27869
Kuykendall	Lee, Inf. of	De Witt	9-24-20	28863
Kuykendall	Leevell	Bexar	1-31-18	642
Kuykendall	Lela Bell	Deaf Smith	7-31-36	35288
Kuykendall	Lemer	Parker	3-27-10	12652
Kuykendall	Leon, Mrs.	Lavaca	7-11-27	24327
Kuykendall	Lester Lee	Nolan	7-8-40	34381
Kuykendall	Lettie	De Witt	9-24-15	19464
Kuykendall	Lillie	Bexar	10-23-18	35205
Kuykendall	Lillie	Bexar	12-4-11	25607
Kuykendall	Lillie	Hill	9-14-28	40066
Kuykendall	Liman	Bexar	5-16-17	12146
Kuykendall	Lindy M., Mrs.	Tarrant	3-12-24	10625
Kuyykendall	Lucinda R.	Navarro	6-13-40	29649
Kuykendall	Lucy, Mrs.	Harris	9-29-29	44830
Kuykendall	Lula D.	Tarrant	5-9-27	17889
Kuykendall	M. J.	Bell	5-15-13	9724
Kuykendall	Malissa	Nueces	2-29-36	10507
Kuykendall	Mamie	Williamson	7-12-33	35059
Kuykendall	Mamie Kerr	El Paso	2-2-37	8090
Kuykendall	Mandalma	Hamilton	8-3-25	29397
Kuykendall	Margaret	Bexar	6-8-28	24401
Kuykendall	Margaret	Harris	2-9-35	8030
Kuykendall	Margret Josefine	Navarro	10-31-18	44009
Kuykendall	Mari Lynn	Grayson	10-28-26	34984
Kuykendall	Martha	Lavaca	2-6-34	8783

SURNAME	FIRST	COUNTY	DATE	FILE#
Kuykendall	Martha H.	Galveston	5-31-36	25695
Kuykendall	Martin L.	Dallas	2-17-22	4117
Kuykendall	Mary	Bexar	5-2-21	12834
Kuykendall	Mary	Denton	12-18-32	51259
Kuykendall	Mary	De Witt	7-14-29	34719
Kuykendall	Mary	Lavaca	3-23-35	14628
Kuykendall	Mary	Travis	9-24-39	71667
Kuykendall	Mary Alice	Lavaca	8-20-37	42394
Kuykendall	Mary Ann	Harrison	10-14-36	50223
Kuykendall	Mary Elizabeth	Taylor	1-29-37	5203
Kuykendall	Matthew Hardin	San Saba	6-6-10	12654
Kuykendall	Matthew W.	San Saba	3-6-17	8615
Kuykendall	Maud	Stephens	9-5-37	47648
Kuykendall	Maud Ester	Lavaca	10-1-20	32625
Kuykendall	May, Mrs.	Limestone	1-30-30	4012
Kuykendall	Melton	Collin	1-5-29	1489
Kuykendall	Merrick Culumbas	Eastland	6-28-39	27660
Kuykendall	Milylos	Lubbock	12-3-27	41616
Kuykendall	Minerva	Lavaca	9-30-17	25646
Kuykendall	Minnie	Milam	12-30-20	39628
Kuykendall	Mittie B.	Rusk	5-17-38	24975
Kuykendall	Mont, Inf. of	Panola	4-3-15	8612
Kuykendall	Montreville Lafayette	Dallas	1-3-29	1748
Kuykendall	Myra	Bexar	5-18-16	10859
Kuykendall	N., Inf. of	Cooke	9-2-13	18534
Kuykendall	Nancy Ann	San Saba	3-20-24	10504
Kuykendall	Nancy D.	Irion	9-23-34	41518
Kuykendall	Nancy L.	Coryell	3-7-27	8115
Kuykendall	Nathan	Bexar	3-16-40	12449
Kuykendall	Nathaniel	Grayson	10-10-37	50227
Kuykendall	Nellie, Miss.	Harris	11-11-40	50657
Kuykendall	Nora	Colorado	11-24-30	52059
Kuykendall	O. N. Jr.	Fannin	11-21-33	50154
Kuykendall	Paul, Jr.	San Saba	7-13-34	34102
Kuykendall	Pearl	Bexar	6-4-40	26625
Kuykendall	Peter R.	El Paso	3-5-38	12472
Kuykendall	R. B., Mrs.	Potter	3-15-35	15287
Kuykendall	R. D., Inf. of	Hunt	8-30-30	40295
Kuykendall	R. D., Inf. of	Lavaca	3-26-29	16959
Kuykendall	R. N., Inf. of	Cooke	12-15-18	54763
Kuykendall	R. O.	Rusk	12-4-37	62639
Kuykendall	R. W., Mrs.	Bell	12-7-24	37212
Kuykendall	Rainbart	Bexar	3-3-21	6557
Kuykendall	Randal	Lubbock	3-6-29	17066
Kuykendall	Ransom Bradshaw	Montague	11-21-35	53020
Kuykendall	Robert (Bob)	Rusk	6-28-35	30189
Kuykendall	Robert Baylor	Johnson	11-24-32	47622

SURNAME	FIRST	COUNTY	DATE	FILE#
Kuykendall	Rosi	Harris	1-18-39	2678
Kuykendall	Rowena	Limestone	7-25-23	21902
Kuykendall	Ruth	Bexar	4-11-14	7210
Kuykendall	S., Inf. of	Limestone	1-29-30	4011
Kuykendall	S. B.	Cooke	1-28-37	1237
Kuykendall	S. E., Jr.	Tom Green	7-3-29	37725
Kuykendall	Samuel Gates	Bee	8-12-33	35275
Kuykendall	Sarah Margrate	Midland	11-4-36	56229
Kuykendall	Sharlett	Wharton	3-11-40	16957
Kuykendall	Sparks	Williamson	6-14-34	30334
Kuykendall	Sterling Price	Collin	3-8-19	9223
Kuykendall	Susan	Milam	7-4-39	34567
Kuykendall	Susan C.	Collin	12-3-37	59061
Kuykendall	Susan E.***	Matagorda	9-26-20	29946
Kuykendall	Sylvester	Nueces	7-20-34	33806
Kuykendall	T. N.	Taylor	4-17-18	18557
Kuykendall	T. T.	Foard	12-4-23	35300
Kuykendall	Thomas Calvin	Palo Pinto	5-14-33	24566
Kuykendall	Thomas J.	Harris	5-13-34	22952
Kuykendall	Tilman S.	Johnson	4-14-36	21556
Kuykendall	Tom	Lavaca	11-16-26	39132
Kuykendall	Tom Wiley	Brown	4-9-26	13125
Kuykendall	V. Maedelle, Mrs.	Dallas	5-8-40	22680
Kuykendall	Verialee	Harris	3-29-29	16155
Kuykendall	Vernon J.	Bexar	4-13-14	7141
Kuykendall	Violet	Tom Green	6-14-34	29835
Kuykendall	W. K.	Taylor	7-4-18	29948
Kuykendall	W. L.	Refugio	3-24-34	70683
Kuykendall	W. R., Inf. of	Travis	12-8-29	61625
Kuykendall	W. T.	Matagorda	9-27-19	27238
Kuykendall	W. W.	Hunt	9-9-33	42008
Kuykendall	Wanda Ruth	Gregg	1-5-39	2313
Kuykendall	Wiley M.***	De Witt	1-31-20	1115
Kuykendall	Willard, Inf. of	Dallam	6-21-32	24647
Kuykendall	William Edward	Montague	3-24-16	7630
Kuykendall	William Elvert	Lamb	4-17-38	70410
Kuykendall	Wm. Green Marshall	San Saba	7-4-13	16295
Kuykendall	William H.	Bexar	2-22-39	5933
Kuykendall	William Johnson	San Saba	4-26-13	9229
Kuykendall	William L.	Lynn	1-10-34	3679
Kuykendall	Wm. Thornton	Burnet	3-23-37	13433

1946

Kuydendall	Alford J.	Grayson	8-21-46	36458
Kuykendall	Alice	Dallas	3-8-46	11792
Kuykendall	Crowder Tenny Jr.	Kendall	6-30-46	27962

SURNAME	FIRST	COUNTY	DATE	FILE#
Kuykendall	George W.	Navarro	12-19-46	56246
Kuykendall	Katie Laura	Dallas	9-22-46	40360
Kuykendall	Loyd	Hill	10-30-46	46128
Kuykendall	Marie Coley	Jefferson	2-6-46	8729
Kuykendall	Rebecca Sappington	Panola	8-17-46	38154
Kuykendall	Richard Laymon	Bexar	3-11-46	10897
Kuykendall	T. H.	Tarrant	1-17-46	5090
Kuykendall	Thomas Lee	Ellis	12-21-46	54510
Kuykendall	William T.	Tom Green	9-1-46	43030

1947

SURNAME	FIRST	COUNTY	DATE	FILE#
Kuykendal	Minnie J.	Dallas	4-21-47	15936
Kuykindoll	A. C.	Harris	5-30-47	21339
Kuykendall	Alveria	McClennan	12-17-47	52318
Kuykendall	Annie L.	Harris	7-19-47	29939
Kuykendall	Eva	Dallas	8-28-47	33411
Kuykendall	J. C.	Eastland	4-12-47	16135
Kuykendall	James Wm.	Potter	5-30-47	83457
Kuykendall	John Landon	Baily	8-09-47	32324
Kuykendall	John Patrick	Harris	5-12-47	21170
Kuykendall	Lilly Louise	Kimble	3-16-47	12852
Kuykendall	Luther John	Cottle	6-08-47	24477
Kuykendall	Maggie	De Witt	8-05-47	33590
Kuykendall	Paul Edward	Johnson	1-05-47	3119
Kuykendall	Rachel	Williamson	8-09-47	36465
Kuykendall	Silas J.	Hunt	6-09-47	26066
Kuykendall	Simon, Inf. of	Navarro	7-13-47	31072
Kuykendall	Sol	Cooke	2-26-47	80699
Kuykendall	Thelma Gene	Kendall	6-09-47	26267
Kuykendall	Thomas R.	Bexar	11-28-47	44729
Kuykendall	William Amos	McMullen	10-24-47	88769

1948

SURNAME	FIRST	COUNTY	DATE	FILE#
Kuykendall	Alma	Bee	11-16-48	45920
Kuykendall	Byron A.	Gonzales	6-03-48	83993
Kuykendall	Elizabeth	Dallas	12-01-48	51224
Kuykendall	Fowler David	Deaf Smith	12-24-48	51637
Kuykendall	Joseph Edwin	Howard	6-05-48	26485
Kuykendall	Lewis Martin	Montgomery	1-04-48	3893
Kuykendall	Mary	Bexar	11-29-48	45986
Kuykendall	Mattie Lugene	Tarrant	7-09-48	32187
Kuykendall	Minor	Grayson	12-26-48	52130
Kuykendall	Norman A.	Archer	9-13-48	37494
Kuykendall	Ruphard P.	Bexar	2-07-48	5698

SURNAME	FIRST	COUNTY	DATE	FILE#

1949

SURNAME	FIRST	COUNTY	DATE	FILE#
Kuykendoll	Louis A.	Garza	1-8-49	1877
Kuykendall	Eberbelle	Bell	12-30-49	62663
Kuykendall	Harlan Edward	Denton	7-03-49	32981
Kuykendall	Janie Ruth	Potter	1-1-49	3924
Kuykendall	Jessie R.	Bexar	5-25-49	21399
Kuykendall	Juanita	Kerr	2-8-49	7769
Kuykendall	Lillie R.	Panola	12-3-49	60554
Kuykendall	Lorena	Lavaca	12-27-49	60025
Kuykendall	Lovie	Lavaca	5-1-49	24022
Kuykendall	Matthew	Bexar	8-11-49	36993
Kuykendall	Ola Boyd	Harris	10-20-49	48796
Kuykendall	Ronald	Gregg	1-24-49	9664
Kuykendall	Rony	Gregg	1-15-49	9659
Kuykendall	Susan	Harrison	3-16-49	20549
Kuykendall	Sylvester	Fort Bend	7-12-49	33192
Kuykendall	Walter	Wichita	2-24-49	9245
Kuykendall	Will	Lubbock	2-2-49	7931

1950

SURNAME	FIRST	COUNTY	DATE	FILE#
Kuykendall	Cora Mylissa	La Salle	4-5-50	26313
Kuykendall	Ethel	Van Zandt	6-28-50	45538
Kuykendall	Katherine M.	San Saba	2-21-50	15702
Kuykendall	Keith Rembert	Nueces	10-3-50	49489
Kuykendall	Maggie Moore	Hays	1-4-50	2563
Kuykendall	Margarett Ann	Kendall	6-14-50	29193
Kuykendall	Marie Louella	Gregg	12-7-50	58317
Kuykendall	Reeves W.	San Saba	12-6-50	60469

1951

SURNAME	FIRST	COUNTY	DATE	FILE#
Kuykendoll	Leona Francis	Taylor	1-21-51	15787
Kuykendall	Bill	Potter	7-10-51	37496
Kuykendall	Clara Ellen	Llano	9-7-51	48205
Kuykendall	Claude	Wichita	8-6-51	44712
Kuykendall	Edgar Owen	Gregg	12-26-51	66473
Kuykendall	Ellen	Wharton	2-4-51	10503
Kuykendall	Frank	Nueces	10-18-51	53770
Kuykendall	Helen G.	Galveston	7-26-51	41086
Kuykendall	Jessie Carol	Donley	7-24-51	40683
Kuykendall	John W. Jr.	Rusk	2-12-51	9679
Kuykendall	Kattie Lee	Tarrant	11-15-51	59550
Kuykendall	Lola Mae	Kendall	7-10-51	36523
Kuykendall	Louis D.	Llano	1-10-51	3441
Kuykendall	Mable Zora	Donley	7-24-51	40682

SURNAME	FIRST	COUNTY	DATE	FILE#
Kuykendall	Mary Elnora	Lamar	2-17-51	8849
Kuykendall	Myrtle T.	Hill	10-24-51	57975
Kuykendall	Olive Gaye	Denton	3-25-51	23662

1952

Kuykendall	Alfred Lee	Potter	12-19-52	62596
Kuykendall	Harriet	Lavaca	12-4-52	61851
Kuykendall	Hector Owen	Harrison	4-27-52	18542
Kuykendall	Iva Thornton	Llano	12-19-52	61948
Kuykendall	John	Lavaca	5-3-52	24316
Kuykendall	Julius	Karnes	8-27-52	45206
Kuykendall	Lonny Don	Gray	9-8-52	44084
Kuykendall	Mary Brobst	La Salle	4-28-52	24294
Kuykendall	Terri Jo	Dallas	6-5-52	27414
Kuykendall	Vernon Boiser	Jim Wells	5-31-52	45162
Kuykendall	William Ive	Lamar	1-1-52	3130

1953

Kuykendall	Claud Horton	Ellis	9-18-53	45593
Kuykendall	Earnest	Lavaca	6-6-53	31759
Kuykendall	Flora	De Witt	11-22-53	55504
Kuykendall	Isaac Tom	Gray	10-24-53	50912
Kuykendall	John	Gaines	12-8-53	61435
Kuykendall	Lena	Travis	7-31-53	43636
Kuykendall	Louis J.	Van Zandt	3-30-53	16633
Kuykendall	Maggie Ruth	Potter	5-3-53	26785
Kuykendall	T. E.	Tom Green	9-5-53	48465

1954

Kuykendall	Annie Vivian	Cherokee	6-11-54	26717
Kuykendall	Burton L.	Howard	9-28-54	45263
Kuykendall	Callie	Lavaca	8-1-54	40476
Kuykendall	Clent	Howard	5-5-54	23551
Kuykendall	Cora	Harris	5-27-54	22780
Kuykendall	Gilbert L.	Bexar	12-7-54	58289
Kuykendall	James Issac	La Salle	1-16-54	491
Kuykendall	Joe	Lavaca	12-13-54	62169
Kuykendall	Johanna C.	Goliad	1-25-54	2005
Kuykendall	Judy Faye	Howard	10-15-54	61648
Kuykendall	Margie Ann	Dallas	5-29-54	21562
Kuykendall	Mary E.	Burnet	6-5-54	26546
Kuykendall	Rosa Mae	Dallas	6-26-54	27268
Kuykendall	Roscoe	Harris	1-6-54	2649

SURNAME	FIRST	COUNTY	DATE	FILE#

1955

SURNAME	FIRST	COUNTY	DATE	FILE#
Kuykendall	John Abner	Bell	12-27-55	64942
Kuykendall	Allen D. Sr.	Schleicher	12-28-55	63597
Kuykendall	Calvin C.	Gray	2-22-55	7185
Kuykendall	Cora	Grayson	3-09-55	12532
Kuykendall	Frances B.	Gonzales	12-29-55	65242
Kuykendall	James Earl	Montague	8-11-55	40871
Kuykendall	James Wm.	Galveston	11-12-55	60651
Kuykendall	James Able II	Taylor	12-25-55	64136
Kuykendall	Jesse Brentz	Willacy	5-02-55	26292
Kuykendall	John Hubbard	Brown	1-20-55	762
Kuykendall	Leonard Ben	Johnson	12-02-55	62261
Kuykendall	Lucy	Liberty	12-20-55	62564
Kuykendall	Middleton J.	Cherokee	3-28-55	11284
Kuykendall	Myra B.	Lavaca	3-07-55	13980
Kuykendall	Peggy Zene	Navarro	1-18-55	3837
Kuykendall	Reese	Harrison	2-05-55	29274
Kuykendall	Willie	Lavaca	7-02-55	35184

1956

SURNAME	FIRST	COUNTY	DATE	FILE#
Kuykendall	Albert Teal	La Salle	9-30-56	60231
Kuykendall	Callie	Gonzales	8-04-56	42138
Kuykendall	Ed	Howard	12-01-56	65891
Kuykendall	Eddie D.	Gaines	4-11-56	19228
Kuykendall	Emmett L.	Howard	9-25-56	48839
Kuykendall	George Thomas	Gregg	5-30-56	30688
Kuykendall	James Henry	Lynn	3-23-56	15050
Kuykendall	James Doyle	Andrews	12-10-56	62087
Kuykendall	Jessie H.	Dallas	9-17-56	47031
Kuykendall	John A.	Hartley	8-12-56	43048
Kuykendall	Larry Wayne	Tom Green	6-17-56	33372
Kuykendall	Lillian D.	Bexar	5-01-56	23301
Kuykendall	Neoma	Dallas	9-06-56	46836
Kuykendall	Willis H.	Gonzales	11-03-56	58648

1957

SURNAME	FIRST	COUNTY	DATE	FILE#
Kuykendall	Alvie B.	Lampasas	6-17-57	32818
Kuykendall	Charles Allen	Dallas	12-20-57	66539
Kuykendall	Clara Bell	Cochran	9-2-57	53361
Kuykendall	Dave	Navarro	8-7-57	45545
Kuykendall	Debra Diane	Navarro	8-18-57	45541
Kuykendall	Ila Eula	San Saba	9-18-57	51445
Kuykendall	James C.	Lamb	11-27-57	62655
Kuykendall	Julia T.	Harris	1-22-57	2759

SURNAME	FIRST	COUNTY	DATE	FILE#
Kuykendall	Maggie McRae	Bexar	5-4-57	23525
Kuykendall	McCluskey	Potter	11-11-57	63449
Kuykendall	Samuel K. Jr.	Travis	7-21-57	46714
Kuykendall	Ted Dawson	Dallas	10-18-57	60213
Kuykendall	Thomas Robert	Atascosa	5-26-57	23339
Kuykendall	Vernon P.	Bexar	5-2-57	23540
Kuykendall	William G.	Grayson	2-1-57	8049
Kuykendoll	Ruby Lee	Colorado	7-25-57	36013

1958

Kuykendall	Arthur Louis	Bell	11-5-58	59839
Kuykendall	David, Inf. of	Navarro	10-25-58	70669
Kuykendall	Ella	Lavaca	9-14-58	52074
Kuykendall	Eugenia Ellen	Taylor	3-9-58	18529
Kuykendall	Eula Bell G.	Llano	6-2-58	34737
Kuykendall	Henry	Gonzales	4-22-58	21528
Kuykendall	Jeffery K.	Ector	2-27-58	14624
Kuykendall	Joe Glenn	McCulloch	7-3-58	40698
Kuykendall	Johnnie	Harris	9-11-58	50747
Kuykendall	Josiah Judson	Potter	10-2-58	58514
Kuykendall	Martha Ellen	Dallas	1-18-58	1797
Kuykendall	Stella	Travis	8-29-58	59324
Kuykendall	Sylvia	Harris	6-26-58	33718
Kuykendall	Tilmon M.	Falls	7-31-58	38611

1959

Kuykendall	Charlotte	Tom Green	12-26-59	71960
Kuykendall	Dudley Bryan	Dallas	05-23-59	25579
Kuykendall	Ethel L.	Bexar	01-27-59	595
Kuykendall	Jim	Tom Green	10-09-59	58708
Kuykendall	Maggie L.	Harris	11-05-59	61985
Kuykendall	Mary Ann	Uvalde	03-28-59	23808
Kuykendall	Mary E.	Montgomery	03-07-59	16498
Kuykendall	Mary Aulena	Johnson	10-31-59	63257
Kuykendall	Minnie S.	Gray	12-12-59	68394
Kuykendall	Pere Moran	Eastland	05-28 59	25872
Kuykendall	Robt. Lee	Bexar	05-25-59	24569

1960

Kuykendall	Albert Sidney	Atascosa	11-9-60	69342
Kuykendall	Bonnie	Harris	7-8-60	42112
Kuykendall	Emma Lee	Rusk	5-13-60	32144
Kuykendall	Eula Louise	Llano	11-17-60	77039
Kuykendall	Evelyn Mae	Kendall	5-3-60	37236

SURNAME	FIRST	COUNTY	DATE	FILE#
Kuykendall	Jesse Ellison	Tom Green	5-9-60	32765
Kuykendall	Robt. Frank	Harris	2-22-60	10264
Kuykendall	William W.	Johnson	7-12-60	43397
Kuykendall	Willie Mae	Bexar	9-23-60	51932

1961

Kuykendall	A. D.	Harris	12-29-61	76356
Kuykendall	Addie Jane	Dallas	3-18-61	14048
Kuykendall	Bethria C.	Lampasas	2-10-61	10246
Kuykendall	Charles C.	Tarrant	12-15-61	74048
Kuykendall	Dorthy L.	Victoria	5-5-61	36810
Kuykendall	Edward Sidney	Fort Bend	8-20-61	45492
Kuykendall	Jeffie	Johnson	9-2-61	53112
Kuykendall	Lafayette	Kendall	6-27-61	35032
Kuykendall	Lovell Lewis	Lubbock	1-26-61	4339
Kuykendall	Royce Lee	Grayson	10-9-61	64249
Kuykendall	Thelma B.	Potter	1-8-61	35854
Kuykendall	William T.	Dallas	1-24-61	7902

1962

Kuykendall	Andrew	Bexar	10-15-62	59969
Kuykendall	Carl Monroe	Tarrant	12-9-62	78958
Kuykendall	Claude	Kerr	8-1-62	50707
Kuykendall	Ernest Clyde	Harris	2-2-62	16735
Kuykendall	Eureina B.	Potter	12-20-62	78105
Kuykendall	George	Wharton	2-10-62	19966
Kuykendall	Green	Williamson	5-23-62	39605
Kuykendall	James Oliver	Lubbock	12-13-62	77250
Kuykendall	John Oscar	Harris	5-5-62	29854
Kuykendall	William Louis	Bexar	7-4-62	40194

1963

Kuykendall	Bert L.	Taylor	3-14-63	20752
Kuykendall	Delores Jan	Terry	4-20-63	27702
Kuykendall	Erick	Bexar	12-10-63	74168
Kuykendall	Rhoda	McLennan	3-29-63	26576
Kuykendall	Shellie M.	Lavaca	12-16-63	78323
Kuykendall	Walter E. Sr.	Dallas	12-4-63	75268
Kuykendall	William	Frio	4-28-63	30706

1964

Kuykendall	Abby Buster	Bell	9-12-64	54333
Kuykendall	Arthur	Lavaca	1-24-64	4586

SURNAME	FIRST	COUNTY	DATE	FILE#
Kuykendall	Beaulah	Colorado	12-30-64	75322
Kuykendall	Billy Joe	Tarrant	3-17-64	19724
Kuykendall	Elwell R.	Bexar	1-28-64	259
Kuykendall	Isaac Henry	Atascosa	12-26-64	81532
Kuykendall	John Raymond	Cochran	9-13-64	55266
Kuykendall	Herbert Z.	Johnson	3-29-64	24695
Kuykendall	James Kyle	Lavaca	4-5-64	24916
Kuykendall	John K.	Harris	1-2-64	3626
Kuykendall	Kenneth D.	Tom Green	10-16-64	67001
Kuykendall	Louis D. Jr.	Bexar	11-30-64	68082
Kuykendall	Margaret E.	Midland	12-11-64	79482
Kuykendall	Nora Myrtle	Bexar	11-5-64	68074
Kuykendall	Purches Pearl	Dallas	7-12-64	41850
Kuykendall	Texana	Travis	6-6-64	39870
Kuykendall	Tom	Gregg	2-11-64	9458
Kuykendall	William Q.	Tarrant	7-7-64	46299
Kuykendall	William Lee	Harris	1-11-64	3767

1965

Kuykendall	Camilla J.	Montgomery	12-8-65	84263
Kuykendall	Don Ivan	Walker	10-8-65	67716
Kuykendall	Gracie B.	Panola	2-28-65	18802
Kuykendall	Henry	Bexar	12-14-65	74738
Kuykendall	Hugh L.	Eastland	1-23-65	1774
Kuykendall	Joe Woody	Lamar	9-11-65	58662
Kuykendall	Laura Blanche	Wichita	9-4-65	60685
Kuykendall	Lee	McCulloch	4-21-65	32033
Kuykendall	Mary	Lamar	4-27-65	31827
Kuykendall	Minnie H.	Tarrant	6-23-65	39722
Kuykendoll	Willie	Tom Green	2-19-65	12189

1966

Kuykendall	Alma	Taylor	5-23-66	34869
Kuykendall	Clara Ellen	Potter	8-3-66	61551
Kuykendall	Eddie	Harris	2-9-66	10150
Kuykendall	Ella	Wise	7-17-66	49419
Kuykendall	Essie M.	Harris	12-16-66	81134
Kuykendall	Ethel J.	Tarrant	12-29-66	84541
Kuykendall	Fannie M.	Galveston	4-13-66	23517
Kuykendall	Hazel	Matagorda	8-16-66	54350
Kuykendall	Hicks	Lavaca	5-11-66	33271
Kuykendall	James Faires	Tarrant	3-22-66	27130
Kuykendall	James Monroe	Montague	5-21-66	33747
Kuykendall	John Angus	Harrison	9-13-66	59910
Kuykendall	Maggie Jane	Gray	5-24-66	30731

SURNAME	FIRST	COUNTY	DATE	FILE#
Kuykendall	Mathilde C.	Harris	5-16-66	53243
Kuykendall	Mattie E.	Kaufman	12-9-66	82544
Kuykendall	Nina Cecil	Gregg	5-29-66	30824
Kuykendall	Tenny Lee	Travis	10-30-66	69767
Kuykendall	Timothy Kent	Nueces	8-19-66	54586
Kuykendall	Warren Uyless	San Saba	5-17-66	34311
Kuykendall	Wiley Venton	Lampasas	8-16-66	54002
Kuykendall	William S.	Fannin	2-6-66	8572
Kuykendall	Zella	Harris	12-4-66	81138

1967

Kuykendall	Charlie F.	Harrison	11-24-67	080692
Kuykendall	Clay Willborn	San Saba	4-26-67	026728
Kuykendall	Daisy Mae	Lavaca	1-12-67	004324
Kuykendall	Daisy Miles	Gregg	6-2-67	038127
Kuykendall	Dorthy Ann	Cooke	3-28-67	022125
Kuykendall	Emanual W.	Travis	7-18-67	048488
Kuykendall	Jim Cannon	Rusk	7-12-67	047742
Kuykendall	John H.	Galveston	11-19-67	072053
Kuykendall	John Samuel	Harris	10-24-67	065849
Kuykendall	Martha C.	Tarrant	2-5-67	012263
Kuykendall	Mary Ann	Bexar	7-26-67	042632
Kuykendall	R. B. Jr.	Gregg	12-21-67	079568
Kuykendall	Rhoda Bell	Grayson	4-8-67	023600
Kuykendall	Robt. Darmon	Midland	2-10-67	011445
Kuykendall	Ruby Faye	Panola	8-18-67	060832
Kuykendall	Ruth Wharton	Travis	9-14-67	061953
Kuykendall	Sara E.	Gregg	10-21-67	065341

1968

Kuykendall	Allie Lee	Harris	4-21-68	027755
Kuykendall	Arthur James	Atascosa	4-4-68	024110
Kuykendall	Ben	Eastland	10-11-68	069754
Kuykendall	Delia	Taylor	9-12-68	066552
Kuykendall	Elmer Ernest	Bexar	1-11-68	000473
Kuykendall	Elmer Silas	Johnson	4-30-68	036442
Kuykendall	Elmo Franklin	Gregg	9-20-68	063425
Kuykendall	Erna M.	Bexar	3-25-68	016358
Kuykendall	Etta Gregory	Johnson	6-11-68	043581
Kuykendall	Finis Lefler	Travis	6-6-68	045627
Kuykendall	Henry Albert	Gonzales	12-14-68	085662
Kuykendall	Herbert	Falls	9-3-68	062981
Kuykendall	Hoyt Wesley	Howard	12-6-68	087533
Kuykendall	Johnny Wyne	Potter	8-8-68	058935
Kuykendall	Kuy Sparks Sr.	Fort Bend	5-14-68	034329

SURNAME	FIRST	COUNTY	DATE	FILE#
Kuykendall	Laurie Ann	Fort Bend	7-17-68	063108
Kuykendall	Lillie Goff	McCulloch	10-10-68	072941
Kuykendall	Lizzie Lee	Bell	1-16-68	000177
Kuykendall	Luther	Harris	9-9-68	071759
Kuykendall	Mary H.	Montague	1-28-68	013765
Kuykendall	Mary Olene	Atascosa	8-19-68	053483
Kuykendall	Mattie	Bexar	11-7-68	075580
Kuykendall	Opal May	Gray	6-10-68	041632
Kuykendall	Ruse Webb	Tarrant	7-7-68	052377
Kuykendall	Simon	Navarro	11-26-68	080302
Kuykendall	Simon Adolph	Callahan	8-21-68	054345
Kuykendall	Uylesses V.	Harris	2-25-68	019975
Kuykendall	Wylie R.	Rusk	3-5-68	022236
Kuyrkendall	Bulah Mable	Hunt	4-14-68	028608
Kuyrkendall	Clarda Abner	Fannin	10-31-68	077520

1969

Kuykendall	Alta Lena	Tarrant	9-2-69	067697
Kuykendall	Alvin Ray	Colorado	8-7-69	054664
Kuykendall	Amos M.	Grayson	4-7-69	025552
Kuykendall	Avilona	Gregg	2-28-69	017905
Kuykendall	Betty Annette	Dallas	8-6-69	055046
Kuykendall	Blake Abe	Jack	2-5-69	035005
Kuykendall	Eva Bell	Reagan	2-13-69	012963
Kuykendall	Fowler	Potter	11-19-69	082009
Kuykendall	Gerry Houston	Montague	6-18-69	051515
Kuykendall	Harry	Nueces	10-9-69	095106
Kuykendall	Helen	Bexar	1-10-69	000461
Kuykendall	Henry Clay	Gray	10-16-69	071808
Kuykendall	Ivan	Montgomery	4-17-69	028253
Kuykendall	James Mark Sr.	Travis	9-27-69	075888
Kuykendall	John Henry	Bexar	9-3-69	061573
Kuykendall	John Schuyler	Mills	1-17-69	005174
Kuykendall	Katie Martin	Hill	3-24-69	019330
Kuykendall	Lilah M. R.	Lamar	1-11-69	004719
Kuiykendall	Mary Ellen	Taylor	1-15-69	006174
Kuykendall	Myrtle	Haskell	4-16-69	026973
Kuykendall	Raymond R.	McLennan	5-20-69	035941
Kuykendall	Thomas	Dallas	3-31-69	024677
Kuykendall	Tom	Lavaca	8-7-69	058698
Kuykendall	Virginia Mae	Dallas	9-17-69	070920
Kuykendall	Vivian B.	Harris	1-5-69	003442
Kuykendall	William C.	Harrison	5-18-69	034680
Kuykendall	Willis Grice	Burnet	1-1-69	000992
Kuykendoll	Viva- Infant	Victoria	11-18-69	091885

SURNAME	FIRST	COUNTY	DATE	FILE#
1970				
Kuykendall	Alford R.	Montague	7-23-70	059237
Kuykendall	Alice H.	Cameron	4-3-70	024441
Kuykendall	Charles D.	Hill	10-24-70	089205
Kuykendall	Charles R.	Harris	10-1-70	072640
Kuykendall	Edgar	Gaines	12-21-70	087270
Kuykendall	Effie M.	Llano	2-3-70	021000
Kuykendall	George R.	Atascosa	12-6-70	084343
Kuykendall	Ida Laura	San Saba	1-17-70	006335
Kuykendall	James A.	Dallas	6-5-70	048224
Kuykendall	Jennie V.	Dallas	6-27-70	048230
Kuykendall	John P.	Ward	3-2-70	023205
Kuykendall	Lilliana L.	Harris	8-20-70	057334
Kuykendall	Lillie	Taylor	11-9-70	083391
Kuykendall	Mary A.	Nueces	6-23-70	044260
Kuykendall	Oscar	Bexar	3-21-70	016021
Kuykendall	Raymond J.	Harris	2-17-70	011267
Kuykendall	William T.	Camp	3-13-70	016708
1971				
Kuykendall	Abbie L.	Tarrant	12-25-71	091780
Kuykendall	Bertie	Montgomery	3-13-71	028534
Kuykendall	Blanche H.	Tarrant	6-18-71	044364
Kuykendall	Claude H. Sr.	Cullin	4-23-71	023705
Kuykendall	Dunrell	Harris	7-27-71	049084
Kuykendall	Eleo B.	Cooke	3-4-71	015660
Kuykendall	Ethel M.	Bexar	5-16-71	030963
Kuykendall	Euel J.	Nolan	8-29-71	059034
Kuykendall	Everette W.	Crane	4-1-71	023811
Kuykendall	Faye S.	Dallas	11-4-71	086291
Kuykendall	Frederick T.	Harris	9-16-71	064737
Kuykendall	Ira D.	Harris	6-19-71	041687
Kuykendall	Jacob D.	Tom Green	8-16-71	060234
Kuykendall	Lashawd R.	Bexar	3-25-71	014762
Kuykendall	Leo	Nueces	7-29-71	059152
Kuykendall	Leonard R.	Webb	2-23-71	022083
Kuykendall	Martha J.	Terry	1-5-71	006235
Kuykendall	Mary F.	Grayson	3-3-71	017507
Kuykendall	Scott	Harrison	3-15-71	018855
Kuykendall	William K.	Wise	1-9-71	006749
Kuykendall	William R.	Dallas	8-12-71	055187
Kuykendall	William R.	Burnet	12-14-71	085014

SURNAME	FIRST	COUNTY	DATE	FILE#
1972				
Kuykendale	Olive	Harris	8-5-72	059568
Kuykendall	Ada N.	Dallas	5-12-72	034227
Kuykendall	Benjamin F.	Upshur	12-5-72	096382
Kuykendall	Benjamin F.	Smith	5-25-72	039093
Kuykendall	Dorthy	Potter	8-4-72	062079
Kuykendall	Edgar W.	Galveston	4-21-72	027210
Kuykendall	Ella	Galveston	4-9-72	035501
Kuykendall	Evelyn	Harris	12-20-72	091717
Kuykendall	Florence	Potter	10-19-72	085473
Kuykendall	H. B.	Wichita	3-6-72	024048
Kuykendall	Henry C.	Bexar	8-18-72	056215
Kuykendall	Homer H.	San Saba	6-16-72	046763
Kuykendall	James W.	McLennan	6-20-72	046007
Kuykendall	Joseph P.	Tarrant	4-23-72	031287
Kuykendall	Kimberley A.	Travis	5-3-72	047757
Kuykendall	Lucy J.	Llano	1-29-72	029923
Kuykendall	Maye	Freestone	3-13-72	027146
Kuykendall	Rachel	Jim Wells	2-18-72	013083
Kuykendall	Raymond J. Jr.	Harris	2-10-72	011606
Kuykendall	Robert B.	Bexar	9-5-72	064320
Kuykendall	Roxie	Dallas	4-23-72	034610
Kuykendall	Shannon R.	Dallas	12-3-72	090032
Kuykendall	Zeldon	Atascosa	12-20-72	097015
1973				
Kuykendahl	Rothie	Travis	11-4-73	098882
Kuykendall	Alberta	Harris	11-7-73	084925
Kuykendall	Arvil	McLennan	1-22-73	005164
Kuykendall	Audrey	Cherokee	3-24-73	026649
Kuykendall	Bobby D.	Madison	6-30-73	096721
Kuykendall	Claude J.	Harrison	11-22-73	095258
Kuykendall	Diana L.	Taylor	4-25-73	032978
Kuykendall	Fannie B.	Fort Bend	5-18-73	036776
Kuykendall	Hulet C.	Bexar	2-23-73	017224
Kuykendall	Ira H.	Bexar	3-27-73	016855
Kuykendall	James F.	Panola	4-8-73	031918
Kuykendall	Jennie M.	Potter	12-25-73	097512
Kuykendall	John W.	Gregg	1-27-73	011035
Kuykendall	Katherine	Taylor	7-28-73	065300
Kuykendall	Margie L.	Van Zandt	3-4-73	024732
Kuykendall	Mark T.	Howard	2-12-73	012928
Kuykendall	Melton D.	Wichita	3-29-73	049681
Kuykendall	Mollie A.	Tarrant	10-11-73	088432
Kuykendall	Ollie M.	Gregg	11-18-73	084596

SURNAME	FIRST	COUNTY	DATE	FILE#
Kuykendall	Raymond R.	Travis	7-26-73	056931
Kuykendall	Sallie J.	Gregg	1-9-73	002670
Kuykendall	Samuel	Tarrant	9-8-73	072563

1974

Kirkendall,	John L.	Hardin	10-17-74	074953
Kuykendall,	Alma H.	Dallas	4-20-74	024252
Kuykendall,	Annie A.	Bexar	9-14-74	063215
Kuykendall,	Arthur L.	Gregg	9-26-74	065864
Kuykendall,	Bessie	Nolan	6-1-74	044962
Kuykendall,	Carl L.	Travis	5-17-74	038037
Kuykendall,	Carl R..	Taylor	9-28-74	070244
Kuykendall,	Charles J.	Gregg	6-11-74	041920
Kuykendall,	Colleen	Grayson	11-11-74	090088
Kuykendall,	David S.	Tarrant	8-28-74	070097
Kuykendall,	George	Harris	2-8-74	009848
Kuykendall,	George, Jr.	Harris	7-5-74	058988
Kuykendall,	Gertie	Harris	3-9-74	018622
Kuykendall,	Herman H.	Mongomery	12-23-74	100545
Kuykendall,	Jack	Potter	10-23-74	077544
Kuykendall,	John W.	Panola	1-30-74	012508
Kuykendall,	Maggie A.	Tom Green	4-17-74	029916
Kuykendall,	Mary E.	Eastland	10-22-74	073991
Kuykendall,	Matthew W.	Travis	8-21-74	070577
Kuykendall,	Mattie M.	Bexar	3-10-74	014679
Kuykendall,	Millie A.	Dallas	1-17074	001539
Kuykendall,	Olivia B.	Navarro	5-8-74	044946
Kuykendall,	Ordamy	Harris	7-19-74	058985
Kuykendall,	R. C.	Dallas	1-5-74	001531
Kuykendall,	R. D.	Nueces	11-24-74	094134
Kuykendall,	Roma D.	Tarrant	6-9-74	045910
Kuykendall,	Tom G.	San Saba	3-21-74	020995

1975

Kirkendoll,	James O.	Gregg	8-25-75	059043
Kirkendoll,	Ruby V.	Lubbock	10-29-75	084407
Kurkendall,	Stanley	Colorado	11-13-75	087998
Kuykendall,	Bertha A.	Harrison	6-12-75	060842
Kuykendall,	Dock	Tarrant	10-1-75	078375
Kuykendall,	Edward L.	Montague	6-12-75	045946
Kuykendall,	Edwin D. Sr.	Tarrant	6-17-75	047065
Kuykendall,	Erna F.	Grayson	6-2-75	042736
Kuykendall,	Ima L.	Tarrant	9-11-75	070542
Kuykendall,	James F.	Tarrant	6-9-75	047064
Kuykendall,	Jasper F.	Coleman	4-2-75	025006

SURNAME	FIRST	COUNTY	DATE	FILE#
Kuykendall,	Katie E.	Wise	7-1-75	055782
Kuykendall,	Loman A.	Ector	10-24-75	074336
Kuykendall,	Lottie E.	Bexar	12-21-75	086842
Kuykendall,	Mason	Nueces	6-29-75	046087
Kuykendall,	Minnie M.	Burnet	3-30-75	033127
Kuykendall,	Rita K.	Taylor	1-24-75	006110
Kuykendall,	Robert H.	Ellis	8-7-75	058338
Kuykendall,	Rush	Bexar	2-18-75	007215
Kuykendall,	Sarah	McLennan	6-18-75	045745
Kuykendall,	Sires M.	Fannin	12-20-75	089790
Kuykendall,	Waylan E.	Atascosa	1-30-75	015639
Kuykendall,	William M.	Bexar	6-30-75	040067
Kuykendall,	Winton	Montgomery	1-24-75	013341

1976

Kirkendoll,	Ben L.	Smith	9-25-76	071090
Kuykendall, Cora P.		Burnet	10-17-76	073540
Kuykendall,	Coy F.	Bexar	6-12-76	041945
Kuykendall,	Evia S.	Tarrant	4-7-76	032327
Kuykendall,	Ida B.	Van Zandt	6-11-76	048985
Kuykendall,	Ila M.	Taylor	8-28-76	064237
Kuykendall,	Irene H.	Lubbock	9-2-76	070015
Kuykendall,	J. A.	Atascosa	3-7-76	015259
Kuykendall,	James E.	Bexar	5-29-76	033875
Kuykendall,	James O.	Williamson	12-24-76	102118
Kuykendall,	James P.	Bosque	5-14-76	042351
Kuykendall,	John C.	Walker	7-17-76	056470
Kuykendall,	Mamie E.	Harris	5-19-76	037021
Kuykendall,	Mathonia	Bell	6-21-76	041636
Kuykendall,	Nona E.	McLennan	3-18-76	022361
Kuykendall,	Thenia J.	Dallas	6-30-76	051528
Kuykendall,	Wiley M.***	Travis	10-11-76	079979

1977

Kirkendall,	Christopher S.	Hardin	4-7-77	034936
Kirkendoll,	Flossy F.	Smith	9-28-77	070448
Kirkindall,	Donald L.	Smith	2-20-77	012911
Kuykendall,	Annie M.	Howard	3-7-77	020043
Kuykendall,	Charles J.	Dallas	3-20-77	016290
Kuykendall,	Crofard E.	Gray	12-6-77	092176
Kuykendall,	Edna E.	Wilson	11-16-77	088043
Kuykendall,	Frances H.	Lavaca	8-14-77	061680
Kuykendall,	Greenup M.	Williamson	11-22-77	098094
Kuykendall,	Johnny B.	Grayson	9-7-77	066922
Kuykendall,	Lester R.	Lamar	1-18-77	011704

SURNAME	FIRST	COUNTY	DATE	FILE#
Kuykendall,	Luther E.	Rusk	6-19-77	045650
Kuykendall,	Mamie L.	Montague	10-6-77	078366
Kuykendall,	Marion E.	Tarrant	5-13-77	038759
Kuykendall,	Marshall L.	Bexar	8-3-77	056568
Kuykendall,	Nannie D.	Tarrant	2-17-77	030566
Kuykendall,	Nettie L.	Grayson	9-7-77	066918
Kuykendall,	Oscar	Colorado	1-2-77	000956
Kuykendall,	Ruby H.	Jefferson	5-2-77	036802
Kuykendall,	William C.	Harris	6-9-77	043388
Kuykendall,	William L.	Tom Green	6-12-77	046547
Kuyrkendall,	Oscar N.	Hunt	3-12-77	020081

1978

SURNAME	FIRST	COUNTY	DATE	FILE#
Kirkendoll,	Katherine A.	Henderson	8-25-78	062870
Kirkindall,	Jessie M.	Montgomery	3-21-78	022359
Kuykendall,	A. C.	Lamb	1-25-78	004125
Kuykendall,	Amanda M.	Harris	10-2-78	100546
Kuykendall,	Annie L.	Bexar	3-27-78	025544
Kuykendall,	Blanche	Bexar	3-11-78	015924
Kuykendall,	Charles R.	Webb	6-7-78	048941
Kuykendall,	Christy A.	Tarrant	2-6-78	013937
Kuykendall,	David J.	Navarro	7-13-78	055613
Kuykendall,	Emmett A.	San Saba	12-31-78	102802
Kuykendall,	Eula M.	Potter	5-2-78	047565
Kuykendall,	Gary D.	Sutton	4-3-78	031693
Kuykendall,	Henry L.	Gray	11-4-78	093441
Kuykendall,	James E.	Hamilton	6-18-78	052996
Kuykendall,	James N.	Potter	9-28-78	080242
Kuykendall,	Jewell D.	Grayson	10-6-78	077296
Kuykendall,	Katherine L.	Gregg	3-12-78	019161
Kuykendall,	Laura M.	Liberty	12-24-78	102393
Kuykendall,	Lee E.	Montague	7-19-78	079807
Kuykendall,	Lloyd, Sr.	Galveston	8-12-78	061100
Kuykendall,	Lola M.	Lubbock	3-18-78	021924
Kuykendall,	Millie P.	Travis	5-13-78	040715
Kuykendall,	Myrtle A.	Potter	8-26-78	072285
Kuykendall,	Nell E.	Harris	11-28-78	094290
Kuykendall,	Robert	Howard	3-30-78	021253
Kuykendall,	Thomas E.	Webb	10-14-78	081948
Kuykendall,	William E.	Hopkins	10-22-78	078923

1979

SURNAME	FIRST	COUNTY	DATE	FILE#
Kirkendall,	Clifford	Andrews	8-12-79	057090
Kirkendall,	John Vaughn	Callahan	3-29-79	014896
Kirkendoll,	Kenneth	Jefferson	10-26-79	086917

SURNAME	FIRST	COUNTY	DATE	FILE#
Kuykendall,	Beulah Wms.	DeWitt	9-5-79	066630
Kuykendall,	Donald Webb	Wichita	7-2-79	089947
Kuykendall,	Ella Marie	Tom Green	7-17-79	056402
Kuykendall,	Ethel Lillie	Bexar	5-14-79	032563
Kuykendall,	Harley G.	Wichita	1-3-79	005353
Kuykendall,	Henry E.	McLennan	2-16-79	011253
Kuykendall,	John Wm.	Grayson	2-28-79	016380
Kuykendall,	Leora	Lubbock	9-22-79	070280
Kuykendall,	Louise	Harris	10-16-79	085915
Kuykendall,	Loyd E.	Dallas	10-3-79	074888
Kuykendall,	May Lura	San Saba	2-4-79	012160
Kuykendall,	Ollie Lucius	Harris	6-30-79	052767
Kuykendall,	Ollie Mae	Dallas	6-7-79	042129
Kuykendall,	Patricia Ann Bunton	Harris	5-11-79	035910
Kuykendall,	Rachel C.	Travis	1-25-79	005103
Kuykendall,	Randall Gray	Llano	2-24-79	029649
Kuykendall,	Roy D.	Zapata	7-11-79	081531
Kuykendall,	Susie Matilda	Cass	5-31-79	049689
Kuykendall,	Treery Wayne	Dallas	4-20-79	024391
Kuykendall,	Theodore	Archer	5-2-79	032143
Kuykendall,	William Monroe	Bosque	10-24-79	091579

1980

Kirkendall,	Cedric L.	Nueces	6-1-80	046887
Kirkendall,	Neoma Kathern	Hutchinson	12-6-80	097948
Kirkendall,	William A.	Potter	8-25-80	065541
Kuykendall,	Amelia White	Harris	4-28-80	036212
Kuykendall,	Annie Louise	Harrison	11-16-80	088600
Kuykendall,	Arnold James	Uvalde	3-13-80	031087
Kuykendall,	Charles Albert	Orange	4-11-80	029313
Kuykendall,	Clinton Lane	Ellis	2-16-80	016290
Kuykendall,	Eda Mae	Lubbock	12-16-80	098953
Kuykendall,	Elizabeth Coffey	Brazos	7-16-80	050794
Kuykendall,	Ellie Mae	Rusk	7-1-80	100205
Kuykendall,	Gene Pickett	McLennan	1-17-80	002869
Kuykendall,	Gladys Gray	Grayson	3-29-80	026253
Kuykendall,	Glenn Everett	Lubbock	9-10-80	08256/
Kuykendall,	Jesse Lee	McCulloch	5-21-80	046429
Kuykendall,	Jessie Newton	Montague	10-28-80	089596
Kuykendall,	Jewel Nettie	Llano	9-5-80	082443
Kuykendall,	Jimmie	Matagorda	4-17-80	028877
Kuykendall,	Joseph B.	Bexar	11-21-80	085807
Kuykendall,	Larry Don	Brazos	1-11-80	000720
Kuykendall,	Laura Mundine	Travis	3-26-80	031014
Kuykendall,	Marvin Arlin	Dallas	8-24-80	060607
Kuykendall,	O. L.	Potter	1-28-80	003345

SURNAME	FIRST	COUNTY	DATE	FILE#
Kuykendall,	Rodger Dale	Bexar	7-15-80	049970
Kuykendall,	Ruby Estelle	Dallas	8-22-80	060608
Kuykendall,	Sarah Elizabeth	Archer	5-28-80	040559
Kuykendall,	Sarah Jean	Tarrant	8-10-80	066090
Kuykendall,	T. L.	Dallas	9-28-80	069639
Kuykendall,	Tessie Irene	Gregg	5-2-80	034902
Kuykendall,	Walter, Sr.	Lavaca	8-25-80	064579
Kuykendall,	William Issac(Ike)	Blanco	9-12-80	068678*

1981

Kirkendoll,	Steven Dan	Galveston	3-27-81	027697
Kuykendall,	Billie Joe	Brown	1-2-81	001097
Kuykendall,	Elmer Emitt	Bell	11-1-81	087329
Kuykendall,	Fannie Ethel	Gonzales	1-29-81	009524
Kuykendall,	Hazel Erlene	Lubbock	9-10-81	084195
Kuykendall,	Howard Lee	Harris	2-21-81	019939
Kuykendall,	Ima Lee	Lubbock	11-1-81	102006
Kuykendall,	Inez	Tarrant	9-23-81	085925
Kuykendall,	James Henry	Gregg	5-23-81	045423
Kuykendall,	Johnathon Ray	Galveston	11-1-81	099176
Kuykendall,	Kirby K.	Harris	3-27-81	019352
Kuykendall,	Laura Eolia	Brazoria	11-24-81	105522
Kuykendall,	Lula M.	Nueces	6-3-81	048163
Kuykendall,	Mary June	Galveston	11-2-81	099188
Kuykendall,	Maxine	Bexar	2-13-81	006643
Kuykendall,	Motano	Bexar	10-2-81	077963
Kuykendall,	Norman Grady	Denton	6-13-81	044741
Kuykendall,	Orvell Thorp	Lubbock	1-28-81	012487
Kuykendall,	Robert	DeWitt	9-5-81	080282
Kuykendall,	Thomas G.	Henderson	11-18-81	108476
Kuykendall,	Zudora	Harris	9-4-81	082297

1982

Kirkendall,	Commodore Stanley	Hood	10-3-82	084442
Kirkendall,	Luella Marie	Jefferson	1-17-82	010597
Kuykendall,	Derrell Melton	Van Zandt	6-7-82	051024
Kuykendall,	E. L.	Lamar	11-20-82	105028
Kuykendall,	Etta D. Catherine	San Patricio	6-11-82	049621
Kuykendall,	George Richardson	Jack	12-8-82	104510
Kuykendall,	Gus Melvin	Potter	6-7-82	049384
Kuykendall,	Hazel Waller	Travis	6-8-82	050703
Kuykendall,	Isaac Lee	Ellis	12-14-82	101992
Kuykendall,	Mac Randall	Dimmitt	8-15-82	080857
Kuykendall,	Marion M.	Nueces	7-4-82	067167
Kuykendall,	Mona Kay	Dallas	6-2-82	044478

SURNAME	FIRST	COUNTY	DATE	FILE#
Kuykendall,	Phillip Rayburn	Ector	3-12-82	035506
Kuykendall,	Robert Lee	Potter	11-2-82	096951
Kuykendall,	Walter Clarence	Smith	9-2-82	087111
Kuykendall,	Willie, Jr.	Victoria	6-2-82	051048

1983

Kirkendall,	Herbert Leslie	Hutchinson	4-30-83	031898
Kirkendoll,	Donald Ray	Galveston	7-16-83	057186
Kirkendoll,	Pashion Eliz.	Harris	7-6-83	067735
Kirkendoll,	Roger Mack	Howard	6-17-83	049897
Kuykendall,	Ben Frank	Johnson	2-26-83	022651
Kuykendall,	Bettie	Montague	9-24-83	089158
Kuykendall,	Bobby Gene	Yoakum	12-14-83	115949
Kuykendall,	Cosette E.	Houston	8-19-83	068734
Kuykendall,	Dean Wilson	Bexar	11-28-83	091793
Kuykendall,	Earnest Walker	Lampasas	12-11-83	113431
Kuykendall,	Eldridge Lowe	Potter	8-30-83	070498
Kuykendall,	Hattie Pearl Foster	Tarrant	5-17-83	052509
Kuykendall,	Hector Owen	Smith	1-11-83	005679
Kuykendall,	John O.	Nueces	8-29-83	070171
Kuykendall,	John T.	Cass	10-1-83	082944
Kuykendall,	Kristi Diane	Tarrant	12-3-83	108391
Kuykendall,	Kyle David	Harris	8-24-83	077554
Kuykendall,	Lucindy Lee	Van Zandt	11-18-83	115864
Kuykendall,	May (NMN)	Dallas	6-23-83	056129
Kuykendall,	Minnie Mae	Bosque	1-9-83	016849
Kuykendall,	Minnie Viola	DeWitt	5-5-83	046615
Kuykendall,	Mollie	Caldwell	2-15-83	007915
Kuykendall,	R. C.	Bell	12-15-83	100082
Kuykendall,	Richard Caleb	McLennan	8-8-83	069690
Kuykendall,	Ruby	Harris	8-29-83	077028
Kuykendall,	Rubye Jewel	Taylor	11-26-83	099184
Kuykendall,	Wanda Lou	Tarrant	8-22-83	080245
Kuykendall,	William Scott	San Saba	1-25-83	005649
Kuykendall,	William Wilford	San Saba	5-19-83	042445

1984

Kirkendall	Ida Isabell	Harris	5-9-84	041819
Kirkendall	Wilson Wilburn	Liberty	7-13-84	061036
Kuykendall	Christopher Lee	Dallas	6-15-84	047694
Kuykendall	Erick, Jr.	Bexar	6-28-84	046551
Kuykendall	Helen Sepher	Brown	8-15-84	065809
Kuykendall	Herbert Gray	Rusk	7-20-84	062612
Kuykendall	Hobart Berlan	Nueces	9-17-84	081924
Kuykendall	Ida May	Tarrant	8-8-84	073574

SURNAME	FIRST	COUNTY	DATE	FILE#
Kuykendall	James Monroe, Jr.	Bell	6-18-84	046035
Kuykendall	Leslie Jacob	Dallas	12-27-84	113350
Kuykendall	Lloyd Paul	Cherokee	2-6-84	008251
Kuykendall	Melvin B.	El Paso	4-2-84	030921
Kuykendall	Monroe Dietrich	Bexar	3-10-84	016963
Kuykendall	Robert E.	Rusk	1-24-84	005558
Kuykendall	Ronnie	Uvalde	2-8-84	015736
Kuykendall	Ruby Cleora	Midland	8-7-84	072078
Kuykendall	Sarah Katherine	San Saba	3-22-84	025207
Kuykendall	Sherman NMN	Colorado	9-28-84	085816
Kuykendall	Singuita Starlet	Bexar	11-30-84	112717
Kuykendall	Tyman R.	Bexar	12-19-84	102951
Kuykendall	Virgil Claude	Midland	12-11-84	109506
Kuykendall	William Guy	Tarrant	9-8-84	083178
Kuykendall	William R.	Potter	4-11-84	034963
Kuykendoll	Beulah	Bowie	10-22-84	085296

1985

SURNAME	FIRST	COUNTY	DATE	FILE#
Kuykendall	Amos Ralph	Frio	12-6-85	107496
Kuykendall	Annie Lila	Travis	11-5-85	103392
Kuykendall	Edessa	Taylor	7-5-85	065266
Kuykendall	Elba Isles	Lamar	7-1-85	062963
Kuykendall	Elbert Price	Lubbock	2-9-85	024155
Kuykendall	Ella Mae	Dallas	10-19-85	086950
Kuykendall	Ellen Gertrude	Dallas	2-19-85	019974
Kuykendall	Emmett J.	Harris	10-6-85	099862
Kuykendall	Evelyn	Nueces	8-6-85	073969
Kuykendall	Harold Dean	Harris	5-13-85	052299
Kuykendall	Heather Michele	Grayson	2-28-85	010080
Kuykendall	James Arlyn Jr.	Dallas	1-1-85	002312
Kuykendall	La Wanda Kay	Harris	9-11-85	080027
Kuykendall	Lawrence Owen	Dallas	4-24-85	039914
Kuykendall	M. C.	Randall	11-11-85	102265
Kuykendall	Mary Elizabeth	Bexar	1-10-85	046910
Kuykendall	Rosie Lee	McLennan	3-26-85	034670
Kuykendall	Ruth	Potter	2-19-85	015033
Kuykendall	Tena G.	Lubbock	1-19-85	014026
Kuykendall	Tiffany Evette	Galveston	9-17-85	088579
Kuykendall	Ura Z.	Yoakum	5-14-85	046316
Kuykendall	Velma Lee	Moore	9-1-85	110992
Kuykendall	William Graham	Harris	9-1-85	080191
Kuykendall	Zada Lorene	(blank)	3-20-85	400856

1986

SURNAME	FIRST	COUNTY	DATE	FILE#
Kuykendall	Arie N.	Tarrant	11-25-86	113589

SURNAME	FIRST	COUNTY	DATE	FILE#
Kuykendall	Danny	Harris	1-27-86	018768
Kuykendall	David Alan	Collin	5-31-86	049119
Kuykendall	George Paul	Lubbock	3-4-86	033615
Kuykendall	Geo. Washington	Grayson	10-9-86	089397
Kuykendall	Glen Dale	Coleman	3-29-86	015009
Kuykendall	Gregory Lewis	Harris	2-4-86	019945
Kuykendall	James Bryant	Dallas	8-13-86	068672
Kuykendall	John Holmes	Dallas	11-9-86	096998
Kuykendall	Lucinda	Falls	2-7-86	009008
Kuykendall	Mary E.	Nueces	12-8-86	112223
Kuykendall	Mary Hermoine	Taylor	2-15-86	012293
Kuykendall	Mary Ruth	Midland	9-19-86	082802
Kuykendall	Minnie Rebecca	Uvalde	8-19-86	075376
Kuykendall	Duet William	Mclennan	3-30-86	082694
Kuykendall	Rickey Gwynn	Tarrant	1-9-86	004768
Kuykendall	Roland McCoy Sr.	Van Zandt	1-8-86	005487
Kuykendall	Ruth Edwards	Midland	7-1-86	073256
Kuykendall	Ulyss Chick	Dallas	3-13-86	015563
Kuykendall	Violette Raydell	Burnet	7-17-86	057816

1987

SURNAME	FIRST	COUNTY	DATE	FILE#
Kirkendall	Alfred Damon	Jefferson	6-23-87	053087
Kirkendall	Frank	Jasper	1-25-87	004134
Kuykendall	Benton Luther	Dallas	3-23-87	018532
Kuykendall	Clarence	Bexar	12-31-87	116664
Kuykendall	Connie Jack	(blank)	12-29-87	401417
Kuykendall	Curry Bennett	Harris	3-23-87	042896
Kuykendall	David Walter	Panola	3-19-87	035166
Kuykendall	Donal Earl	Gray	12-15-87	109754
Kuykendall	Dortha Lois Arnold	Bexar	12-8-87	106238
Kuykendall	Edith Berene	Bexar	9-6-87	076814
Kuykendall	Etta Lee	Taylor	2-4-87	014979
Kuykendall	Genevieve Rebecca	Potter	9-24-87	084023
Kuykendall	Georgia	Mills	6-25-87	063859
Kuykendall	Mattie McCarter	Ellis	1-5-87	060061
Kuykendall	James Byron	Greg	5-18-87	041161
Kuykendall	Lorraine Louise	Tarrant	4-22-87	055248
Kuykendall	Marie	Grayson	9-29-87	090077
Kuykendall	Melvin Baldwin, Jr.	Harris	4-28-87	042494
Kuykendall	Ola C.	Travis	2-28-87	015325
Kuykendall	Robert E.	Taylor	9-16-87	085491
Kuykendall	Sara Lucile	Dallas	10-18-87	088506
Kuykendall	Vera Allen	Fannin	8-9-87	089687
Kuykendall	Webster Van Buren	Dallas	5-17-87	039514
Kuykendall	William Quince	Hood	1-15-87	004037

SURNAME	FIRST	COUNTY	DATE	FILE#
1988				
Kirkendall	Content Lansing	Harris	11-10-88	102757
Kirkendall	Elmer Leroy	Kerr	2-20-88	015320
Kirkendoll	Jane Agnes	Taylor	1-1-88	017762
Kuykendall	Alla Ray	Eastland	4-19-88	033275
Kuykendall	Beverly Jean	Harris	1-22-88	003775
Kuykendall	Cynthia Jo	Travis	11-6-88	106430
Kuykendall	Doyle	Dallas	12-22-88	119832
Kuykendall	Eloise Foscue	Harris	10-26-88	093805
Kuykendall	Emily L.	Wichita	5-14-88	060016
Kuykendall	Fannie David	Harris	6-19-88	065166
Kuykendall	Faye Lonetta	Dallas	10-21-88	091261
Kuykendall	George Boles	Bexar	11-8-88	099332
Kuykendall	James Glenn	Upshur	12-3-88	118292
Kuykendall	Lois Lee	Wood	2-13-88	018926
Kuykendall	Mable	Bexar	10-30-88	089691
Kuykendall	Margie May	Comal	12-1-88	108873
Kuykendall	Marie	Nueces	3-4-88	027530
Kuykendall	Marie (NMN)?	Johnson	1-3-88	005113
Kuykendall	Mary Louise	Tom Green	1-20-88	007337
Kuykendall	Nina Catherine	Harris	3-14-88	045898
Kuykendall	Oma F.	Grayson	10-28-88	120631
Kuykendall	Richard	Harris	7-12-88	064362
Kuykendall	Robert	Harris	1-3-88	003763
Kuykendall	Samuel	Smith	9-22-88	097344
Kuykendall	Thelma Josephine	Tarrant	10-8-88	097880
Kuykendall	Tom Groves Jr.	Medina	2-11-88	015770
Kuykendall	Vera Theatt	Hutchinson	11-19-88	104121
Kuykendall	Vickie Lyn	Tom Green	12-5-88	122713
Kuykendall	Virginia Merle	Fannin	8-24-88	082934
Kuykendall	Walter Hilton	Eastland	6-30-88	062947
Kuykendall	Willie O.	Bexar	12-15-88	119237
Kuykendall	Wilson H.	Wichita	2-19-88	018672
Kuykendall	Winnie Bell	Harris	2-21-88	035306
Kuyrkendall	Jewel Irene	Fannin	12-10-88	110781
1989				
Kirkendall	Clara Elizabeth	Colorado	10-26-89	110739
Kirkendall	Lloyd Harold	Gregg	5-13-89	043513
Kirkendall	Matthew Thomas	Jasper	6-12-89	055284
Kirkendall	Pearl	Wharton	12-16-89	125271
Kuykendall	Asner Caldwell	Bell	6-14-89	059488
Kuykendall	Bessie Lorene	Dallas	2-23-89	020258
Kuykendall	Bruce Davis Jr.	Tarrant	3-28-89	038008
Kuykendall	Claudie B.	Bexar	1-7-89	008971

SURNAME	FIRST	COUNTY	DATE	FILE#
Kuykendall	Daniel Hugh	Atascosa	1-9-89	000073
Kuykendall	Fay Glen	Tom Green	8-16-89	078453
Kuykendall	Georgia Katherine	Randall	4-3-89	047439
Kuykendall	James Bromley	Galveston	6-2-89	052941
Kuykendall	Lemuel	Moore	7-23-89	066760
Kuykendall	Louise Frances	Tarrant	4-23-89	048397
Kuykendall	Mabel	Wharton	6-27-89	069481
Kuykendall	Mary Irene	Ft. Bend	11-24-89	112597
Kuykendall	Monte Clinton	Tarrant	5-6-89	047917
Kuykendall	Nora Anna	Rusk	12-28-89	117609
Kuykendall	Paul Edward	Lubbock	11-2-89	116491
Kuykendall	Rowena	Dallas	3-27-89	031151
Kuykendall	Sam Houston	Mills	10-14-89	096041
Kuykendall	Seawilla	Lavaca	2-26-89	014522
Kuykendall	Susan Diane	Navarro	12-15-89	117082
Kuykendall	Thurston Edmond	Armstrong	2-19-89	008017
Kuykendall	Vernon Olive	Nueces	12-27-89	126021
Kuykendall	William Emett	Andrews	3-29-89	028464

1990

SURNAME	FIRST	COUNTY	DATE	FILE#
Kuykendall	Ada O.	Victoria	11-17-90	110987
Kuykendall	Allen Hearn	Tarrant	4-29-90	050376
Kuykendall	Beatrice M.	Lavaca	11-2-90	108094
Kuykendall	Dan Michael	Wise	10-25-90	111408
Kuykendall	Doniqua Donshay	Dallas	5-5-90	043379
Kuykendall	Dudley Bryan Jr.	Tarrant	2-9-90	012418
Kuykendall	Earnest Layfette	Harrison	3-27-90	036012
Kuykendall	Edward Melton	Dallas	3-8-90	029607
Kuykendall	Flossie Jane	Dallas	11-1-90	103833
Kuykendall	Jack Louie	Moore	5-11-90	049026
Kuykendall	Jeneva	Nueces	3-21-90	038674
Kuykendall	John Brice	Ector	8-6-90	075246
Kuykendall	John Kenneth	Harris	7-19-90	077387
Kuykendall	Joyce	Williamson	3-27-90	041007
Kuykendall	Leroy Vivian	Harris	10-12-90	096882
Kuykendall	Lillian P.	Gregg	1-11-90	013621
Kuykendall	Louis Delong	Bexar	8-10-90	072798
Kuykendall	Lynnell Helen	Lubbock	2-7-90	037500
Kuykendall	Mary Mangum	Jim Wells	5-9-90	048006
Kuykendall	Perry Thornton J.	Wichita	12-22-90	125972
Kuykendall	Samuel Cornelio	Falls	5-18-90	044902
Kuykendall	Victor Marvin	Bexar	6-17-90	052302
Kuykendall	Walter Lewis	Montague	7-24-90	069710
Kuykendall	Willie Mae	Nacogdoches	4-8-90	038126

SURNAME	FIRST	COUNTY	DATE	FILE#
1991				
Kirkindall	Aundee Mona	Bexar	8-22-91	090362
Kuykendall	Amber Louise	Navarro	12-23-91	123225
Kuykendall	Billie Jean	Lamar	7-12-91	064357
Kuykendall	Bobby Elmo	Dallas	10-25-91	105453
Kuykendall	Cecil	Lamar	10-20-91	105372
Kuykendall	Cloma Leona	Llano	5-17-91	043013
Kuykendall	Clovis Alexander	Fannin	9-28-91	095609
Kuykendall	Earnest L.	Gregg	7-13-91	068721
Kuykendall	Eddie Ray	Denton	7-7-91	069019
Kuykendall	Ethel H.	Bexar	3-30-91	027839
Kuykendall	Grace May	Bexar	9-11-91	084588
Kuykendall	James Eric	El Paso	10-26-91	101528
Kuykendall	James Ewing	Tarrant	9-2-91	095756
Kuykendall	Jerry Don	Harris	6-27-91	066421
Kuykendall	Jess Echols	Tarrant	8-22-91	070473
Kuykendall	Leona Syble	Tarrant	8-22-91	079326
Kuykendall	Mildred Mavis	McCulloch	10-31-91	111998
Kuykendall	Rose Agnes	Brazos	1-20-91	027163
Kuykendall	Thelma Fern	Montague	10-12-91	112524
1992				
Kirkendall	Jannie Merle	Cass	7-5-92	061742
Kirkendall	John Lawrence	Galveston	2-6-92	005446
Kirkendall	Margaret Beatrice	Jefferson	1-10-92	007635
Kuykendall	Anita	Dallas	1-22-92	006081
Kuykendall	Billy Jack	Howard	10-16-92	096836
Kuykendall	Charley Carrol	Cooke	8-9-92	077988
Kuykendall	Collins B.	Bexar	3-12-92	021565
Kuykendall	Foster Marvin	Llano	10-27-92	107425
Kuykendall	Ila Mae	Llano	9-17-92	087859
Kuykendall	J. R.	Midland	7-8-92	065123
Kuykendall	James David	Dallas	7-14-92	068001
Kuykendall	Joe Stanley	Denton	8-22-92	077982
Kuykendall	John Henry	Collin	12-29-92	129585
Kuykendall	Kurtis Lynn	Montgomery	1-25-92	044008
Kuykendall	Lura Inez	Harris	8-7-92	072821
Kuykendall	Lyda Elizabeth	San Saba	2-14-92	015286
Kuykendall	Madie Belle	Tom Green	6-22-92	057342
Kuykendall	Maurine J.	Bexar	9-16-92	088170
Kuykendall	Melissa Elnora	Dallas	7-22-92	068815
Kuykendall	Michelle	Harris	6-15-92	062753
Kuykendall	Robert M.	De Witt	2-27-92	020355
Kuykendall	Ruby Jewel	Jim Wells	6-17-92	073712
Kuykendall	Thomas Calvin	Wharton	1-19-92	007995

SURNAME	FIRST	COUNTY	DATE	FILE#
Kuykendall	Willie T.	Liberty	10-18-92	109200

1993

SURNAME	FIRST	COUNTY	DATE	FILE#
Kirkendall	Doris Marquerite	Bexar	12-15-93	120125
Kirkendall	Earl Alexander	Colorado	3-13-93	041982
Kirkendall	John Wilburn	Hardin	12-27-93	132045
Kirkendall	Sonya Rayelaine	Jasper	11-14-93	113028
Kirkendoll	James Edward	Harris	4-10-93	030363
Kuykendall	Albert Frederick	Tarrant	6-20-93	058532
Kuykendall	Alice Hamlett	Travis	8-27-93	087105*
Kuykendall	Arnold Walter	Webb	6-29-93	074077
Kuykendall	Aubrey Leon	Dallas	3-21-93	027864
Kuykendall	Bertha Lee	Dallas	7-7-93	062704
Kuykendall	Celeste	Nueces	5-21-93	055753
Kuykendall	Clara Jane	Potter	8-25-93	081395
Kuykendall	Dwayne Winston	Dallas	1-21-93	006338
Kuykendall	Edith Cordella	Tarrant	12-1-93	123846
Kuykendall	Elnora Ann	Angelina	6-29-93	065974
Kuykendall	Eva	Taylor	7-15-93	067138
Kuykendall	Frank Russell Sr.	Bexar	3-1-93	016520
Kuykendall	Jahew C.	Harris	8-3-93	084821
Kuykendall	James Loyd	Tom Green	4-2-93	029823
Kuykendall	Julius	Harris	8-23-93	097010
Kuykendall	Lucy Archer	Coryell	10-12-93	130921
Kuykendall	Marion Johnson	Llano	7-11-93	067280
Kuykendall	Mary June	Galveston	7-4-93	062962
Kuykendall	Rodney A.	Gregg	11-7-93	114870
Kuykendall	Ruby K.	Hamilton	11-23-93	117289
Kuykendall	Velma E.	Tarrant	3-3-93	023406
Kuykendall	Walter E. Jr.	El Paso	1-8-93	007568
Kuykendall	Wanda L.	Ellis	12-5-93	134242
Kuykendall	William H.	Dallas	6-21-93	067784
Kuykendell	Bedford Lee	Haskell	2-2-93	011648

1994

SURNAME	FIRST	COUNTY	DATE	FILE#
Kirkendall	Meda Mae	Gregg	6-4-94	064336
Kirkendoll	John Henry Jr.	Jefferson	6-18-94	066042
Kuykendall	Ada Mae	Dallas	5-22-94	049412
Kuykendall	Anna	Sabine	11-10-94	118544
Kuykendall	Annabelle Bennett	Bexar	12-4-94	121030
Kuykendall	Annie Mae	Harris	1-5-94	004652
Kuykendall	Crowder Teenie	Bexar	11-30-94	117611
Kuykendall	Edmund Charles	Cherokee	3-10-94	028936
Kuykendall	Elvan E.	Mason	4-30-94	050842
Kuykendall	Emma	Guadalupe	8-5-94	081420

SURNAME	FIRST	COUNTY	DATE	FILE#
Kuykendall	James William	Lubbock	10-20-94	110865
Kuykendall	Joyce Ellen	Tarrant	9-23-94	099840
Kuykendall	Julia Ruth	Lamb	8-17-94	087983
Kuykendall	Kenney Lewis	Llano	6-13-94	059728
Kuykendall	Lula Mae	Wharton	2-26-94	032959
Kuykendall	Mabel Leota	Tarrant	4-24-94	040829
Kuykendall	Margaret Jean	Tarrant	10-4-94	103549
Kuykendall	Mary Vesta	Lubbock	2-26-94	022237
Kuykendall	Melton Columbus	Wichita	6-11-94	061377
Kuykendall	Otto O. Sr.	Dallas	7-3-94	071278
Kuykendall	Perley Lucretia	Potter	5-26-94	055532
Kuykendall	Ralph Belton	Dallas	8-26-94	093668
Kuykendall	Ruby Glenda	Montgomery	1-16-94	010792
Kuykendall	Samuel Orland, Jr.	Bexar	10-1-94	003350
Kuykendoll	Ollie Myrtle	Lampasas	1-10-94	003350

1995

Kirkendoll,	Edwin Neal	Dallas	11-20-95	118079
Kuykendall	Alva Sterling	Taylor	6-18-95	063870
Kuykendall	Archie Houston	Wichita	11-28-95	134087
Kuykendall	Barbara Leon	Denton	11-25-95	116009
Kuykendall	Billie Jo	Tarrant	11-4-95	109966
Kuykendall	Billy Don	Nolan	7-14-95	079814
Kuykendall	Billy Joe	Cooke	2-13-95	019393
Kuykendall	Clarice Nancy	El Paso	3-7-95	032725
Kuykendall	David Erwin Jr.	Collin	4-26-95	053733
Kuykendall	David M.	Bexar	8-13-95	080168
Kuykendall	Dora Shelton	Wharton	5-18-95	054825
Kuykendall	Evelyn Gertrude	Dallas	5-31-95	031888
Kuykendall	Hilton Foye	Harris	12-16-95	128006
Kuykendall	Ima Cleo	Lubbock	1-11-95	001832
Kuykendall	J. D.	Navarro	12-16-95	124055
Kuykendall	James C.	Bexar	12-27-95	139693
Kuykendall	James Mark Jr.	Travis	5-18-95	047124
Kuykendall	James V.	Harris	3-22-95	024871
Kuykendall	John Doyle	Montgomery	2-9-95	014754
Kuykendall	Karl	Bexar	11-30-95	122721
Kuykendall	Kathleen	Harris	5-15-95	053201
Kuykendall	Kenneth Allert	Ft. Bend	2-4-95	012097
Kuykendall	Lindsey Mack	Gregg	7-4-95	069399
Kuykendall	Mary Elizabeth	Atascosa	1-6-95	006829
Kuykendall	Mary L.	Nolan	8-19-95	085243
Kuykendall	Perry Thornton	Young	12-22-95	133167
Kuykendall	Reed Alan	Midland	4-1-95	034087
Kuykendall	Robert	Bexar	3-21-95	027178
Kuykendall	Theo Marie	Tarrant	9-19-95	091108

SURNAME	FIRST	COUNTY	DATE	FILE#
Kuykendall	Tony	Dallas	8-11-95	082792
Kuykendall	Virgie Lura	Johnson	4-14-95	042540
Kuykendall	Virgie Victoria	Moore	8-27-95	007972
Kuykendall	Viva	Harris	1-7-95	005262
Kuykendall	Woodrow Wilson	Hill	3-21-95	031399

1996

SURNAME	FIRST	COUNTY	DATE	FILE#
Kirkendale	Brian Anthony	Harris	1-8-96	016851
Kirkendall	Carlton Tony	Wharton	4-13-96	038831
Kirkendall	Riley Ruben	Harris	7-2-96	076396
Kirkendall	Timothy George	Dallas	6-10-96	056413
Kuykendall	Angela Kaye	Montgomery	2-1-96	026497
Kuykendall	Bill Arland	Dallas	4-8-96	036204
Kuykendall	Conway Ellison	Potter	3-30-96	035466
Kuykendall	Edward Thomas Jr.	Denton	11-16-96	115524
Kuykendall	Edwin Dillard Jr.	Hood	9-22-96	098756
Kuykendall	Eva Mae	MClennan	9-6-96	088921
Kuykendall	Fay	Harris	3-17-96	041283
Kuykendall	George	Harris	7-19-96	095626
Kuykendall	Gus Olen	Bexar	5-26-96	051006
Kuykendall	Ikie Thomas	Potter	8-12-96	083539
Kuykendall	James Barton	Bexar	10-17-96	110259
Kuykendall	Jerry Lonza	Johnson	5-14-96	064702
Kuykendall	Jodie Ross	Lamar	4-12-96	044592
Kuykendall	Johnnie Mary	Johnson	9-21-96	113340
Kuykendall	Lanelle	Bexar	7-10-96	079071
Kuykendall	Lillian Gladys	Gregg	11-10-96	117667
Kuykendall	Mary Lou	Gaines	5-19-96	050577
Kuykendall	Melba Joyce	Wichita	7-29-96	088853
Kuykendall	Mildred K.	McMullen	10-30-96	117512
Kuykendall	Mima Elizabeth	Dallas	1-2-96	010294
Kuykendall	Minnie Bell	Gregg	7-7-96	082783
Kuykendall	Norman Andrew	Wichita	8-1-96	088852
Kuykendall	Raymond Arlene	Johnson	12-21-96	138678
Kuykendall	Ruby Geneva	Montgomery	10-12-96	107721
Kuykendall	Thomas Robert Jr.	Live Oak	10-3-96	101143
Kuykendall	Willie Lee	Gonzales	6-8-96	073972

1997

SURNAME	FIRST	COUNTY	DATE	FILE#
Kirkendall	Donald Ray	Harris	11-12-97	120151
Kirkendall	Thurman Graham	Crosby	5-21-97	052114
Kuykendall	Betsy J.	Brazos	10-7-97	103485
Kuykendall	David Butler	Brazos	8-12-97	086516
Kuykendall	E. L. Jr.	Montgomery	9-6-97	099382
Kuykendall	Edith	Frio	6-15-97	080361

SURNAME	FIRST	COUNTY	DATE	FILE#
Kuykendall	Eunice	Harris	4-7-97	050611
Kuykendall	Harry Kenneth	Hidalgo	12-15-97	135605
Kuykendall	Hazel Viola	Dallas	8-18-97	093653
Kuykendall	Ivalene	Wichita	11-6-97	144548
Kuykendall	Ivory George	Mclennan	4-13-97	040284
Kuykendall	Jacky Earl	Grayson	4-19-97	040521
Kuykendall	James Ray	Harris	11-27-97	127441
Kuykendall	Joe Bailey	Hood	4-14-97	036446
Kuykendall	Rena May	Dallas	2-1-97	009079
Kuykendall	Rodger Webb	Kerr	10-1-97	100812
Kuykendall	Ruby Mae	Harris	4-20-97	041434
Kuykendall	Tommy Leon	Dallas	12-26-97	133696

1998

SURNAME	FIRST	COUNTY	DATE	FILE#
Kuykendall	Addie Ruth	Jack	3-26-98	028923
Kuykendall	Amanda Dawn	Panola	7-26-98	101716
Kuykendall	Claire Jane	Harris	11-19-98	127667
Kuykendall	Clara Madelyn	Atascosa	12-20-98	135266
Kuykendall	Claude	Harrison	2-2-98	013104
Kuykendall	Clifford Lee	Lubbock	1-17-98	027449
Kuykendall	Corinne Aldine	MClennan	2-20-98	019345
Kuykendall	Dewey Wayne	Dallas	3-17-98	037580
Kuykendall	Don	Midland	5-13-98	049888
Kuykendall	Elva Nona	Dallas	6-18-98	067125
Kuykendall	Fannie Mae	Nueces	9-7-98	103827
Kuykendall	Frances L.	Tom Green	10-24-98	112939
Kuykendall	Gladys Pearl	Bexar	3-24-98	034883
Kuykendall	Harold Dalton	Brazos	12-10-98	133745
Kuykendall	Harold Dean	Gregg	5-15-98	053975
Kuykendall	Helen Aline	Moore	3-30-98	031910
Kuykendall	James Clyde	Hood	11-19-98	120494
Kuykendall	Jerry Wayne	Dallas	8-7-98	104248
Kuykendall	John Malvin	Potter	6-3-98	058038
Kuykendall	Madison William	Brazoria	12-9-98	142517
Kuykendall	Marguerite	Ector	7-17-98	078444
Kuykendall	Phyllis	Mclennan	12-26-98	137598
Kuykendall	Prudence Kaye	Bexar	5-10-98	049247
Kuykendall	Ronnie Lynn	Harris	10-22-98	115647
Kuykendall	Sarah Ruth	Bowie	7-1-98	072718
Kuykendall	Suzanne	Hunt	7-23-98	090014
Kuykendall	Varina B.	Montgomery	7-7-98	090635
Kuykendall	Wanda Lee	Gray	6-13-98	06225

1999

SURNAME	FIRST	COUNTY	DATE	FILE#
Kirkendall	Kevin	Galveston	(blank)99	19990103

SURNAME	FIRST	COUNTY	DATE	FILE#
Kirkendall	Ethel	Hardin	(blank)99	19990424
Kirkendoll	Ben Wiley	Dallas	(blank)99	19990924
Kirkendolph	Arlena	(blank)	(blank)99	19990714
Kuykendall	Elsie Victoria	Hood	(blank)99	19990121
Kuykendall	Janet Lea	Galveston	(blank)99	19990212
Kuykendall	Perle Dale	Walker	(blank)99	19990222
Kuykendall	Rose M.	Bexar	(blank)99	19990226
Kuykendall	Roger Lynn	Lubbock	(blank)99	19990311
Kuykendall	Savannah	Bexar	(blank)99	19990321
Kuykendall	Forrest	Travis	(blank)99	19990407
Kuykendall	James Levi	Tarrant	(blank)99	19990504
Kuykendall	Cleone	Brown	(blank)99	19990510
Kuykendall	Marjorie Fay	Jefferson	(blank)99	19990521
Kuykendall	Charles	Tarrrant	(blank)99	19990603
Kuykendall	Mazie Fay	Harrison	(blank)99	19990609
Kuykendall	Myrtle G.	Travis	(blank)99	19990704
Kuykendall	Stella	Crane	(blank)99	19990712
Kuykendall	Margaret Amy	Smith	(blank)99	19990724
Kuykendall	Hilton F.	Harris	(blank)99	19990727
Kuykendall	June	Grayson	(blank)99	19990728
Kuykendall	Ida	Galveston	(blank)99	19990803
Kuykendall	Ina Bell	Tarrant	(blank)99	19990824
Kuykendall	Byron Amil	Brazoria	(blank)99	19990831
Kuykendall	Neva Jean	Van Zandt	(blank)99	19990915
Kuykendall	Anna Adele	Hunt	(blank)99	19990924
Kuykendall	Herbert Roger	Tarrant	(blank)99	19991006
Kuykendall	Audrey Jean	Schleicher	(blank)99	19991113
Kuykendall	Cora Elizabeth	Gregg	(blank)99	19991118
Kuykendall	Oleta Ruth	Mclennan	(blank)99	19991204
Kuykendall	Dorothy	Ector	(blank)99	19991230

2000

SURNAME	FIRST	COUNTY	DATE	FILE#
Kirkendall	Gladys Lavenia	Jasper	7-29-00	page 1389
Kirkendall	Margaret Daneda	Out of state(?)	7-13-00	page 1389
Kirkendoll	Audrey Emmaline	Jefferson	3-9-00	page 1389
Kuykendall	Anna Mae	Bexar	12-26-00	page 1419
Kuykendall	C. J.	Camp	3-13-00	page 1419
Kuykendall	Calvin Lucius	Victoria	2-28-00	page 1419
Kuykendall	Carlyle James	Tyler	6-18-00	page 1419
Kuykendall	Edwin Donovan	Dallas	2-22-00	page 1419
Kuykendall	Elvin Gus	Tarrant	11-30-00	page 1419
Kuykendall	Eunice Maxine	Dallas	3-6-00	page 1419
Kuykendall	James Lovell	Llano	7-7-00	page 1419
Kuykendall	James Melvin	Gregg	11-1-00	page 1419
Kuykendall	John Ryan	Dallas	6-21-00	page 1419
Kuykendall	Lee Allen	Wichita	1-3-00	page 1419

SURNAME	FIRST	COUNTY	DATE	FILE#
Kuykendall	Marlene Mae	Brazoria	7-17-00	page 1419
Kuykendall	Mary Helen	Wichita	1-3-00	page 1419
Kuykendall	Mary Janis	Tarrant	8-11-00	page 1419
Kuykendall	Minnie Clarine	Colorado	1-4-00	page 1419
Kuykendall	Peggy L.	Bexar	9-14-00	page 1419
Kuykendall	Troy Lee	Tarrant	8-3-00	page 1419
Kuykendall	Tyler Neil	Tarrant	6-22-00	page 1419
Kuykendall	Victor A.	Midland	9-1-00	page 1419
Kuykendall	William	Tom Green	6-28-00	page 1419
Kuykendall	Willaim Glen Sr.	Grayson	9-7-00	page 1419
Kuykendall	William Martin	Ellis	4-10-00	page 1419
Kuykendall	William T.	Gregg	9-17-00	page 1419

Chapter Twenty-Three

Kuykendalls (Texans) in the Civil War 1861-1865

This is a complete list of all the KUYKENDALLS from Texas who served in different military units during the Civil War. The first list contains 57 Confederate soldiers and one Union soldier. The second list contains 58 soldiers who served in the Texas State Troops (TST), Texas Militia (TM), Texas Volunteer Infantry (TVI), and the Frontier Troops (FT). The first list will be referred to as the "CSA" and the second list will be called the "Militia." The names are repeated on several occasions on both lists. The last 12 names of the TST list are not alphabetical, and are listed as they were found with some different spelling.

This CSA roster of men can be found in the National Archives in Washington, D.C., and are also available on microfilm in the Texas State Library and Archives (Genealogical Section), Zavala Bldg., Austin, Texas. The film is shown as: "The Index to Compiled Texas Confederate Service Records in the National Archives."

The film is listed under "Texas Military," K's, roll #227-20 for the Confederates and the roll for the Union soldier is listed under "Texas Military Volunteer Union Soldiers Who Served in Organizations from the State of Texas," National Archives microfilm copy #M-393-1.

The records enclosed simply show the name, rank, and organization in little or no detail with a very few having a bit more information for the CSA. The militia list, however, shows a great deal of information, and the two overlap. For complete records on any individual listed, write the Military Archives Division, National Archives and Records Center, Washington, D.C., 20408.

The genealogy was furnished by this author and Gifford White of Austin, Texas. The information on the military units are by White and this author.

Shown on the pages to follow are the names on the index cards as they are shown in the archives, with original punctuation.

Roster of Kuykendalls from Texas in the Civil War

(1) **KUYKENDALL, A.**
Co. F, 8 Texas Cavalry
(Terry's Regiment)
(1 Texas Rangers)
(8 Texas Rangers)

CONFEDERATE
Private
Ref. Notes: Look under Joseph. B. Kuykendall)
The 8th Tex. Cavalry Regt. was known as Terry's Texas Rangers. The 1st Col. of the Regt. was Benjamin Franklin Terry. The Rangers were mustered into CSA servive at Houston on 9 September 1861. The enlistment was for the duration of the war. Each man was required to furnish his own horse and arms. Later at Bowling Green, Kentucky, the Rangers were organized as the 8th Texas Cavalry Regiment. The regiment was formally paroled at Greensboro, North Carolina, on 28 April 1865. The 8th Texas saw more action than almost any other Texas unit during the war.

(2) **KUYKENDALL, A. S.**
Co. K., 4 Texas Cavalry
(4 Reg't. Texas Mtd. Vols.)
(1 Reg't Sibley's Brigade)

CONFEDERATE
Private
Reference Card originally filed under(pensil) KUYKENDALL, M.S.
Ref. Notes: Look under J. M. Kuykendall, John Kuykendall, or M. S. Kuykendall.

(3) **KUYKENDALL, ABRAHAM**
Co. A., Well's Batt'n. Texas Cavalry
Formed by consolidation of Scanland (Montague Co.) and Gillett's Squadrons and Capt. Miller's Co., Texas Cav.; consolidated with Good's Battl. of Texas Cavalry late in 1864 or early 1865 to form part of Well's Reg't. Texas Cavalry.

CONFEDERATE
Private
Enlisted: March 3, 1861, at Ft. McCulloch; enlisting officer; Capt. Scanland. 8 Years. Last paid, Sept. 30, 1862.
   (In pensil) *"See also Abe Kuykendall-Well's Regt. Texas Cavalry"*
Ref. Notes: See John Kuykendall; Possibly Abraham Kuykendall, son of Abraham (1793-North Carolina) and Lydia (unknown) Kuykendall) born ca 1824 in Tennessee. He is a brother to the John noted above. There is a note under "Abe Raykendall" that states he was "absent in arrest Choctaw Nation."

(4) KUYKENDALL, ALLEN
Co. D., Griffin's Batt'n Texas Infantry
(Griffin's Reg't Texas Inf.)
(21 Reg't or Batt'n Tex. Inf.)

Reg't broken up in Nov. 1864. Four of the companies being consolidated with six companies of the 11th Batt'n. Texas Inf. to form the 21st Reg't. Texas Inf. The other two companies were transferred to the 13th Regiment Texas Infantry.

CONFEDERATE
Private
Ref. Notes: See M. J. Kuykendall; Bk. 1, 0781, Pension Application. Comanche Co. Enlisted at Goliad.

(5) KUYKENDALL, B.
Co. F ?, 12 Texas Cavalry
(Parson's Reg't. Mtd. Vols.)
(4 Texas Dragoons)

CONFEDERATE
Private.
Ref. Notes: Possibly Barzillai Kuykendall, son of Gibson & Elisabeth Leakey Kuykendall. McMullen Co., Texas. Louisa A. West-see militia #2. There is a Benjamin Kuykendall listed from Nacagdoches Co., Texas, who married Margaret F. Curtis.

(6) KUYKENDALL, E. B.
Co. L, 11 Texas Infantry
(Robert's Regiment)

CONFEDERATE
Private–2 Lieutenant
Originally filed under (pensil) *Kuykendall, Elijah R.*
Ref. Notes: See James J. Kuykendall; P. K. Kuykendall; Peter Kuykendall; see militia #3.

(7) KUYKENDALL, ELIJAH R.
Co. L., 11 Texas Infantry
(Robert's Regiment)

CONFEDERATE
Private–2 Lieutenant
Ref. Notes: See E. G. Kuykendall; See militia units # 3; B. 1837; brother to J. J. Kuykendall, pg. 13, second section. See O. M. Robert's "Confederate Military History" Vol. XI, Clement Evans, Editor. Eld. Elijah Robinson Kuykendall, of Grand Saline, Texas, is one of the earliest settlers of the county. Jesse was the grandfather who lived in N.C. Peter was his father's name who preached in Tenn. His family moved to Van Zandt Co., Texas, in Feb. 1848. Oct. 18, 1858, he married Nancy Ann Bratcher. She died in 1881. In 1882, he married Mrs. M. J. Smith. In 1862, he volunteered into the Confederate service and served until the surrender, in Texas, Arkansas, and Louisiana.

(8) KUYKENDALL, E. R.
Co. C., 14 Texas Infantry
(Clark's Reg't. Texas Infantry)

CONFEDERATE
Private
(Ref. Notes: None)

(9) KUYKENDALL, E. R.
Co. E., 1 Regiment Cavalry
Texas State Troops
(6 Mos., 1863-4)

CONFEDERATE
(Ref. Notes: None)

(10) KUYKENDALL, G. M.
Co. K., 19 Texas Infantry

CONFEDERATE
Private
Ref. Notes: Son of Middleton Kuykendall, possibly Geo. M. Kuykendall of Panola Co., Texas. Married Miss M. M. Kinard (?) See W. A. Kuykendall.
See A History of Panola Co., Texas; Panola Co. Historical Asso., pages 231-232: George M. Kuykendall, son of Middleton Kuykendall, Sr., and Marian W. Branch Kuykendall.Middleton Sr., and two sons served in the Civil War, William Asher and George Middleton. Wm. Asher died during the war in Pine Bluff. Ark. in 1863. W A. K., was a private in the 18th Texas Inf.

(11) KUYKENDALL, GEORGE R.
Co. B., 8 (Taylor's) Batt'n. Texas Cav.
(Taylor's Batt'n. Mtd. Rifles)
Consol. about May 1863 with 3 (Yager's) Batt'n and Ware's Co., Texas Cav. to form 1 (Yager's) Texas Cav.

CONFEDERATE
3 Lieutenant–3 Lieutenant
See Also: 1 Yager's Texas Cav.
Ref. Notes: George Richardson Kuykendall, b. 3-8-1840, d, 1-25-1908. Lived Finis, Jack Co., Texas. Son of Abner Kuykendall (II) and Maria Duff Kuykendall. He married Eliza Caroline Willis on 22 June 1864. This particular Geo. R. Kuykendall was wounded at the battle of Plesant Hill and returned to Bell Co., Texas, after that battle. Note: There was also a Geo. R. Kuykendall, son of James Kuykendall and Dorcus Reynolds Kuykendall, who was killed in the war.

(12) KUYKENDALL, GEORGE R.
Co. K., 1 (Yager's) Texas Cav.
(1 Texas Mtd. Rifles)

Formed about May, 1863, by consolodation of 3 (Yager's) and 8 (Taylor's) Batt'n. and Ware's Co. Texas Cavalry.

CONFEDERATE
2 Lieutenant–2 lieutenant
See Also; (pensil) *8-Taylor-Battn., Texas Cav.*
Ref. Notes: Son of James & Dorcus Reynolds Kuykendall. There were two Geo. R's from Texas that were in the war. The other Geo. R. K., is the son of Abner and Maria Duff Kuykendall from Bell Co., Texas. This particular George R. Kuykendall, who was born on 3 April 1840, was killed during the war.

(13) **KUYKENDALL, J. B.**
Co. F., 24 Texas Cavalry
(Wilkes' Regiment)
(2 Texas Lancers)
(2 Reg't. Carter's Brig.)
Became Co., 1, Granbury's Consolidated Texas Brigade, about 9 April 9 1865.
Private

(14) **KUYKENDALL, J. H.**
Co., D., 1 (Yager's) Texas Cav.
(1 Texas Mtd. Rifles)
Formed about May 1863, by consolidation of 3 (Yager's) and 8 (Taylor's) Batt'n. and Ware's Co. Texas Cavalry.

CONFEDERATE
Private
See also: (pensil) *3-Yagers-Battn-Texas Cav*
J. H. Kuykendall was the son of Capt. Abner Kuykendall and Sally Gates Kuykendall. He was a member of the Old 300.

(15) **KUYKENDALL, J. H.**
The index card was filed twice with the same information.

(16) **KUYKENDALL, J. M.**
Co. A. (E)? 1 Batt'n. Texas Sharp Shooters
(Bennett's Batt'n.)

CONFEDERATE
Private
Ref. Notes: There is a J. M. Kuykendall from Hunt Co., Texas (30 April 1822-20 May 1874), who married Jenette Stofer 5 Nov. 1866. See Texas Militia # 55.

(17) **KUYKENDALL, J. M.**
Co. C., 4 Texas Cavalry
(4 Reg't Texas Mtd. Vols.)
(1 Reg't Sibley's Brigade)

CONFEDERATE
Private
Originally filed under (pensil) *Kuykendall, John*
Ref. Notes: See # 16. See also A. S. Kuykendall, CSA # 2.—There was a John M. Kuykendall from Goliad Co., Texas. See # 23 in this section.
The 4th Regt. Tex. Cav. was organized about Oct. 1861 with ten companies, A to K. It was also known as the 1st. Regt. Sibley's Brigade Tex. Mtd. Vols., and as the 4th Regt. Tex. Mtd. Vols.

(18) **KUYKENDALL, J. W.**
Co. G., McCord's Frontier Regiment
Texas Cavalry

CONFEDERATE
Private
Ref. Notes: See Militia #54. Born 1844?

(19) **KUYKENDALL, JAMES**
Co. C., 14 Texas Cavalry
(Johnson's Reg't Mtd. Vols.)
(1 Regiment Johnson's Brigade)

CONFEDERATE
Private
Ref. Notes: See: Wm. Kuykendall; See #19 of the Militia; A James H. Kuykendall, Co. K., 14th Tx. Cav., died in Georgia, May 1862, buried in the Natl. CSA Cemetery.?

(20) **KUYKENDALL, JAMES A.**
Co. A., Waul's Texas Legion
(Infantry, Cavalryt, and Artillery)
After the fall of Vicksburg, the Cavalry Batt'n was known as Willis's Batt'n of Texas Cav., serving later in _____ Company, Texas Cav. In 1864, part of the Artil'y Batt'n. and the remainder was transferred to the 2d Texas Field Batr'y. The Infantry Regiment as _____ was consolidated in 1864 to form the _____ Texas Infantry.
Private
Ref. Notes: See: Joseph A. Kuykendall, Llano Co., Texas; See Wyatt H. Kuykendall; See: Sarah Mickelborough; See: #12 Militia (JH)?

(21) **KUYKENDALL, JAMES J.**
Co. J., 11 Texas Infantry
(Robert's Regiment)

CONFEDERATE
Ref. Notes: See E. B. Kuykendall; See Eilijah Kuykendall; Possibly James J. Kuykendall of Van Zandt Co., Texas, married to Martha J. Hatton. B. 14 April 1818. See: Militia #13.

(22) KUYKENDALL, JOHN
Co., A., Well's Batt'n. Texas Cavalry
Formed by the consolidation of Scandland's and Gillett's Squadron and Capt. Miller's Co. Texas Cav., and subsequently formed part of Well's Reg't . Texas Cavalry.

CONFEDERATE
Private
This was John Lewis Kuykendall son of Abraham (1793) of Coffee Co., Tenn., and Lydia (unknown) Kuykendall. This John was born ca 1832 in Bond Co., Ill. He was married to Lydia Jane Fry in Gainesville, Cooke Co., Texas, ca 1859. This John joined Cooper's Company in the Indian Territory. He was subsequently court-martialed ca 1863 for desertion by the Confederacy and was shot about three miles north of Fort Arbuckle in the Chicksaw Nation I. T. His grave has been lost. His record states: "Absent without leave since June 27th 1863." Info. courtesey Sharon Taylor of Eunice, NM.
See also: (in pensil) –Raykendall, Well's Regt. of Texas Cav.
Ref. Notes: See: Abraham Kuykendall. Note: There were two John Kuykendalls of Cooke Co., Texas.

(23) KUYKENDALL, JOHN
Co. C., 4 Texas Cavalry
(4 Reg't. Texas Mtd. Vols.)
(1 Reg't Sibley's Brigade)

CONFEDERATE
Private
Ref. Notes: Probably same as #17, J. M. Kuykendall; There was a John M. Kuykendall of Goliad County, Texas; Comm. Off: Hampton, Geo. James, Capt.; Mus. in San Antonio, Tx., S. 9, 61 for the war; Mus. Off; Lt. A. Shaass, CSA; Age, 25; Mus. Roll dtd. S. 11-61 to Ap. 30-62; En. Victoria, Tex.; En. Roll Off; Geo. J. Hampton; V. H; $75; eq; $15; Remarks: 1 horse killed Feb. 21, 62; Name appears in column of names as Jno. Kuykendall. Captured at Bayou Teche, La., 14 Ap. 1863, paroled May 11, 1863. Appears as a prisoner of war who surrendered and was paroled at Victoria, Texas, prior to Aug. 8th, 1865. This John Kuykendall is probably the same man who was killed by vigilantes in Goliad County just after the war. This info. courtesy Doris Norman, Moscow, Idaho.

(24) KUYKENDALL, JOSEPH A.
Co. A., Waul's Texas Legion.
(Infantry, Cavalry, and Artillery)

After the fall of Vicksburg, the Cavalry Batt'n. was also known as Willis's Batt'n. of Texas Cav., serving later in _____ Company Texas Cav. In 1864, part of the Art'l. Batt'n. became the 1st Texas Field Battn. And the remainder was transferred to the 3rd. Texas Field Battr'y. The Infantry Batt'n. were consolidated in 1864 to form Timmon's Reg't. Texas Infantry.
Private.

Originally filed under: (pensil) *Kuykendall, James A.*
Ref. Notes: See James A. Kuykendall: See Wyatt H. Kuykendall; Probably the son of Gibson Kuykendall, b. ca 1840 and married to Sallie A. Mickleborough Kuykendall.

(25) **KUYKENDALL, JOSEPH A.**
Ibid.

(26) **KUYKENDALL, JOSEPH B.**
Co. G., 8 Texas Cavalry
(Terry's Regiment)
(1 Texas Rangers)
(8 Texas Rangers)

CONFEDERATE
Private
Originally filed under (in pensil) *Kuykendall, Joseph C.*
Ref. Notes: See A. K. Kuykendall; possible son of old Barzillai Kuykendall, b. 1834; Llano Co., Texas.

(27) **KUYKENDALL, JOSEPH C.**
Ibid.

(28) **KUYKENDALL, M.**
Co. C., 1 Battalion Cavalry
Texas State Troops
(6. Mos, 1863-4)

CONFEDERATE
Ref. Notes: This is Matthew Johnson Kuykendall of Bell County, Texas. Enlisted as a private in Halley's Texas Company but was immediately transferred in the Texas State Troops as 1st Lieutenant under his brother-in-law, Capt. S. Green Davidson in Co. C. of the Texas Cavalry. He made a big expedition into West Texas after Indians in Feb. of 1861. After passing Fort Chadbourne in San Angelo, Capt. Davidson was killed in the ensuing fight on the 22nd of Feb. 1861 and Matt assumed command of the company. In May of 1861, M. J. Kuykendall enlisted in Co. K., 1st Texas Cavalry under Col. Augustus Buchel. This company saw extensive action in the Loiusiana campaigns. MJK's brother, Robert Baylor Kuykendall, also of Bell Co., was in the same company. James Swan Bigham was the Capt. in command of Co. K. Matthew Kuykendall resigned his commission toward the end of the war and joined another company as a Private.
See #29 to follow.
See The History of Bell County: Bell County in the Civil War by Geo. W. Tyler; pub. by Naylor Press of San Antonio, Texas, in 1936. MJK was the son of Abner and Maria Duff Kuykendall. He was born in Fayette Co., Texas, on Sept. 6th, 1838, and died in Texas on May 15th, 1913. He was married twice, first to Mary Louisa Cabler, and second to Thurza Smithwick. He had six children by Cabler and one child by Smithwick. MJK was originally buried in the Moffat Cemetery in Bell County, Texas. Also see: E. R. Kuykendall.

(29) KUYKENDALL, M. J.
Co., G., Griffin's Batt'n. Texas Infantry
(Griffin's Reg't. Texas Inf.)
(21 Reg't or Batt'n. Tex. Inf.)
Batt'n was broken up in Nov. 1864 with four of the companies being consolidated with six companies of the 11th Batt'n. Texas Inf. to form the 21st. Reg't. Texas Inf. The other two companies were transferred to the 12th Reg't. Texas Infantry.

CONFEDERATE
Private
Ibid. See #28.

(30) KUYKENDALL, M. J.
Co. F., 1 McCulloch's Texas Cavalry
(1 Texas Mtd. Riflemen)
Subsequently formed part of 8 (Taylor's) Batt'n. Texas Cav.

CONFEDERATE
1 Lieutenant.
Originally filled under (in pensil) *Kuykendall, Matthew J.*
Ref. Notes: See #'s 28 & 29 this section.

(31) KUYKENDAL
Co. F., 1 McCulloch's Texas Cavalry
(1 Texas Mtd. Riflemen)

CONFEDERATE
Originally filed under (in pensil) *Kingkindall, R. George*
Ref. Notes: Same as #28, 29, and 30.

(32) KUYKENDALL, M. S.
Co. K., 4 Texas Cavalry
(4 Reg't. Texas Mtd. Vols.)
(1 Reg't Sibley's Brigade)

CONFEDERATE
Private
Ref. Notes: See: John or J. M. Kuykendall

(33) KUYKENDALL, P.
Co. (?), 19 Texas Cavalry
(Locke's Regiment)

CONFEDERATE
Private/Sergeant
Ref. Notes: Unknown.

(34) KUYKENDALL, P. K.
Co. I., 11 Texas Infantry
(Robert's Regiment)
CONFEDERATE
Private
Originally filed under (in pensil) *Kuykendall, Peter E.*
Ref. Notes: See *P. E. Kuykendall;* See #27 in the Militia section.

(35) KUYKENDALL, PETER E.
Co. I., 11 Texas Infantry
(Robert's Regiment)
CONFEDERATE
Ref. Notes: See: *P. K. Kuykendall;* possibly *P. E. Kuykendall* from Van Zandt Co., Texas. Married Mary Ann Hunt. See: #27 in the Militia section

(36) KUYKENDALL, ROBERT
Co. D., 6 Texas Infantry
(3 Texas Infantry)
Became Co. A. Grabury's Consolidated Texas Brigade about April 9th, 1865.
CONFEDERATE
Private
Ref. Notes: This is Robert H. Kuykendall III, son of R.H. Gill Kuykendall and Electra Shannon Kuykendall. He was born ca 1838 and died in 1863. The 6th Texas Infantry was organized at Camp McCulloch, Victoria Co., Texas, in mid-1861. Company D was formed by men from Matagorda Co., Texas. The 6th Texas Infantry served on both sides of the Mississippi River but served on the west side until its capture at the fall of Fort. Hindman (Arkansas Post) January 11, 1863. A large number of these men were imprisoned by the Federals at Camp Butler, near Springfiled, Ill. It is there that RHK III died as a prisoner of war on 20 April 1863 and is buried in grave #378 in the National Cememtery there.

(37) KUYKENDALL, ROBERT
Co. D., 6 Texas Infantry
(3 Texas Infantry)
Became Co., A., Granbury's Consolidated Texas Brigade about April 9, 1865.
CONFEDERATE
Private
Originally filed under (in pensil) *Kuykendall, Robert.*
Ref. Notes: Same as #36.

(38) KUYKENDALL, ROBERT
Co., B., 8 (Taylor's) Batt'n. Texas Cav.
(Taylor's Batt'n. Mtd. Rifles)
Consol'd about May 1863 with 3 (Yager's) Batt'n. and Ware's Co. Texas Cav. to form 1 (Yager's) Texas Cav.

CONFEDERATE
Private
See also: (in type) 1-Yagers' Texas Cav.
Ref. Notes: There was a Robert Kuykendall, b. ca 1840 in South Carolina, who was from Gonzales Co., Texas. He was a doctor in Gonzales after the war. He married Eliza Coe in 1868. He had a brother, James C. Kuykendall, b. ca 1832 in South Carolina, who also lived in Gonzales Co., Texas. See "The History of Gonzales Co., 1850-1900," by Marjorie Burnett Hyatt (1980), published by The Clan MacBean Press, Cut & Shoot, Texas 77301.

(39) KUYKENDALL, ROBERT
Co., K., 1 (Yager's) Texas Cav.
(1 Texas Mtd. Rifles)
Formed about May 1863 by consolidation of 3 (Yager's) and 8 (Taylor's) Batt'n. and Ware's Co. Texas Cavalry.

CONFEDERATE
Private
See Also: (in pensil) 8-Taylors-Batt'n, Texas Cav.
Ref. Notes: This is Robert Baylor Kuykendall, b. Dec. 25, 1845, d. June 4, 1875. He married Callie Milam. They lived in Cleburne, Texas. RBK was the son of Abner and Maria Duff Kuykendall. This Robert was in the same company with his brother, George Richardson Kuykendall. Robert B. and Callie Milam Kuykendall had six children. Interestingly, there was a "Boaz" Kuykendall and a Will Kuykendall in this same company. These are unknown men.

(40) KUYKENDALL, S. M.
Wilson's Co., Bean's Battalion
Texas Reserve Corps.

CONFEDERATE
Unknown

(41) KUYKENDALL, SAMUEL
Co. G., Baylor's Reg't Texas Cavalry
(2 Reg't. Arizona Brigade)

CONFEDERATE
Private
Ref. Notes: A Sam Kuykendall and a Simeon Kuykendall were in Co. G. under Capt. R. B. Halley. There was also a William Kuykendall added to the roster at a later date. This is possibly Samuel Kuykendall of Bell Co., Texas, who married Anna Warick on Feb. 6, 1857. See The History of Bell County, pg. 220. These people mustered in the Confederate Army on Jan. 1, 1863, at Camp Salado, Bell Co., Texas.

(42) KUYKENDALL, SIMON
Co. G., Baylor's Reg't. Texas Cavalry
(2 Reg't Arizona Brigade)

CONFEDERATE
Private
Ref. Notes: Unknown. Possible son of Abraham Kuykendall. There was a Simon Kuykendall born on Feb. 2, 1822, who died in Erath, Dublin Co., Texas, on May 10, 1902.

(43) **KUYKENDALL, SIMON**
Co. F., Sauleys (?) Scouting Battalion
Texas Cavalry
Composed of men detailed from Baylor's, Chisolm's, Crump's (?), and Madison's Reg't Texas Cavalry.

CONFEDERATE
Private
Ref. Notes: See #42, for Simon Kuykendall, son of Abraham Kuykendall.

(44) **KUYKENDALL, T. C.**
Co., D., 3 (Yager's) Batt'n. Texas Cav.
(3 Batt'n. Mtd. Rifles)
(Yager's Batt'n. Mtd. Vols.)
Consol'd. about May 1863, with 6 (Taylor's) Batt'n. and Ware's Co., Texas Cav. to form 1 (Yager's) Texas Cav.

CONFEDERATE
Private–Corporal
See also: (in pensil) 1 Yager's Tex. Cav.
Ref. Notes: Talbot Chambers Kuykendall was the son of old William and Eliza M. Caruthers Kuykendall. His grandfather was Capt. Abner Kuykendall of Austin's Old 300. His brothers William and Thomas Hampton Kuykendall served in the same company, as did his cousin, Wiley Martin Kuykendall. Little is known about T. C. Kuykendall. His birth date is unknown and he could be the Talbot Kuykendall who died of lockjaw about 1912-13 and is buried in an abandoned grave in a field near Austwell, Texas. His family had lived in the area during and just after the Civil War. Old notes state he might have been married to Aljena Dubois or Alizena Givens? William Lucas Kuykendall could have been their son.

(45) **KUYKENDALL, T. C.**
Co., D., 1 (Yager's) Texas Cav.
(1 Texas Mtd. Rifles)
Formed about May 1863 by consolidation of 3 (Yager's) and 8 (Taylor's) Batt'n. and Ware's Co. Texas Cavalry.

CONFEDERATE
Corporal–Corporal
See also: (in pensil) *3-Yagers-Texas Cav.*
Ibid, same as above.

(46) KUYKENDALL, W. A.
Co., H., 19 Texas Infantry

CONFEDERATE
Private
Originally filed under: (in pensil) Kuyrkendall, W. A.
Ref. Notes: Possible son of Middleton and Marian W. Branch Kuykendall. If so, his name is William Asher Kuykendall, who joined the Confederate service in Wallace's Co. as a private and died during the war in 1863 at Pine Bluff, Arkansas. He was from Panola Co., Texas. See "A History of Panola County, Texas," by the Panola County Historical Asso., pages 231 and 232. The history states that father Middleton Kuykendall and his two sons, George Middleton and William Asher Kuykendall, all served in the war. NOTE: There was a W. A. Kuykendall in Fannin Co., Texas (Honey Grove) 1818-1902?

(47) KUYKENDALL, W. A.
Ibid, same as above.

(48) KUYKENDALL, W. C.
Co., C., 14 Texas Cavalry
(Johnson's Reg't Mtd. Vols.)
(1 Reg't Johnson's Brigade)

CONFEDERATE
Originally filed under: (in pensil) Kuykendall, William
Ref. Notes: There was a Wm. C. Kuykendall in Red River Co., Texas. There was also a Wm. C. Kuykendall in Rusk Co., Texas. Names attached to old notes show Elizar J. McAnear and Susannah E. McCollum? Also see William Kuykendall, son of James Kuykendall.

(49) KUYKENDALL, WILLIAM
Co. C., 14 Texas Cavalry
(Johnson's Reg't. Mtd. Vols.)
(1 Reg't. Johnson's Brigade

CONFEDERATE
Private
Ibid, same as above.

(50) KUYKENDALL, WILEY
Co., D., 1 (Yager's) Texas Cav.
Formed in May 1863 by consolidation of 3 (Yager's) and 8 (Taylor's) Batt'n. and Ware's Co. Texas Cavalry.

CONFEDERATE
Private
See also: (in pensil) 3-Yager's-Battn.-Texas Cav.
Ref. Notes: Wiley Martin Kuykendall was the son of R. H. Gill Kuykendall and Electra

Shannon Kuykendall. His grandfather was Capt. Robert H. Kuykendall of Austin's Old 300. He was born in Fort Bend County, Texas, on Oct. 22, 1839, and died in De Witt County, Texas, on January 31, 1920. He married Susan E. Pierce, sister of Abel Head (Shanghai) Pierce on 22 April 1869 in Matagorda Co., Texas. See bio.

(51) KUYKENDALL, WILEY
Co., D., 3 (Yagers) Batt'n. Texas Cav.
(3 Batt'n. Mtd. Rifles)
(Yager's Batt'n. Mtd. Vols.)
Consol'd. about May 1863 with 8 (Taylor's) Batt'n. and Ware's Co. Texas Cav. to form 1 (Yager's) Texas Cav.

CONFEDERATE
Private–Sergeant
See also: (in pensil) *Yager's Tex. Cav.*
Ibid, same as above.

(52) KUYKENDALL, WILLIAM
Co., C., 7 Texas Cavalry
(7 Reg't. Texas Mtd. Rifles)
(3 Reg't. Sibley's Brig.)

CONFEDERATE
Private
Ref. Note: see A. S. Kuykendall and John Kuykendall

(53) KUYKENDALL, WILLIAM
Co., D., 1 (Yager's) Texas Cav.
(1 Texas Mtd. Rifles)
Formed about May 1863 by consolidation of 3 (Yager's) and 8 (Taylor's) Batt'n. and Ware's Co. Texas Cavalry.

CONFEDERATE
Private
See also: (in pensil) 3-Yager's-Battn.,-Texas Cav.
Ref. Notes: Judge William Kuykendall was the son of old William and Eliza M. Caruthers Kuykendall. He was the grandson of Capt. Abner Kuykendall of Austin's Old 300. He was born in Austin County, Rep. of Texas, on the 13 May 1839. He died in McMullen County, Texas, on 31 Dec. 1922. He married Kate S. Byrne on 31 Dec. 1868 in Lamar, Refugio County, Texas. He served in the same company with his brother, T. C. Kuykendall, and his cousin, Wiley Martin Kuykendall. His unit saw extensive service in the Loiusiana campaign and he wrote about it in a letter to his daughter which is located in the J. H. Kuykendall Papers, the Barker Texzas History Center, UT Austin, Austin, Texas.

(54) KUYKENDALL, WILLIAM
Co., D., 3 (Yager's) Batt'n. Texas Cav.
(3 Batt'n. Mtd. Rifles)
(Yager's Batt'n. Mtd. Vols.)

CONFEDERATE
Private
See also: (in pensil) 1 Yagers Tex. Cav.
Ibid, same as above.

(55) KUYKENDALL, WILLIAM C.
Co. H., 6 Texas Cavalry
(Stone's Reg't.)
(2 Texas Cav.)

CONFEDERATE
Private
Ref. Notes: William Cliff Kuykendall, son of Abner and Maria Duff Kuykendall, was born on 26 Dec. 1835, probably in Austin Co., Texas, and was killed at the battle of Corinth, Miss., on 4 Oct. 1862. The 1860 census of Bell Co., Texas, shows W. C. Kuykendall, 25, farmer, from Texas; his wife, Nancy M. Hamilton Kuykendall, 20, and young J. A. (John Abner) Kuykendall, 8 mos. old. They had a daughter in 1861 named Willie. John Abner Kuykendall later married Lily Cavanaugh and Willie later married Robert Estis. No further details on them.

Co. H., mustered in at Belton, Bell Co., Texas, was under the command of Col. B. Warren Stone (who was subsequently killed), then later Col. L. S. Ross. The company saw extensive action in Miss., Tenn., Alabama, and Georgia. This company first started out as a cavalry company but was later dismounted in the spring of 1862 and all of the horses were sent back to Bell County. (History of Bell County in the Civil War.)

(56) KUYKENDALL, WYATT H.
Co., A., Waul's Texas Legion
(Infantry, Cavalry and Artillery)
After the fall of Vicksburg, the Cavalry Batt'n. was also known as Willis's Batt'n. of Texas Cav., serving later in Steel's Command Texas Cav. In 1864, part of the Art'l. Batt'n. became the 1st Texas Field Batt'y. and the remainder was transferred to the 2nd Texas Field Batt'y. The Infantry Batt'ns were consolidated in 1864 to form Timmon's Reg't. Texas Infantry.

CONFEDERATE
Private
Ref. Notes: Wyatt Hanks Kuykendall was the son of Capt. Gibson and Martha Kuykendall. (Gibson's 2nd marriage to his cousin Martha K.) WHK was born ca 1843-44 as per the census for Austin County, Texas, in 1860. There is no known death date. WHK's grandfather was Capt. Abner Kuykendall of Austin's Old 300. WHK was named for Gibson's brother by the same name who was wounded and died on the Mier Expedition in 1842. He served in the same company with his brother, Joseph A. Kuykendall (See #24) Little else is know about this man.

(57) KUYKENDALL
Co., A., Steele's Command Texas Cav.
Organized in 1864, principally of members of McCabe? Cavalry Battalion, Wauls' Texas Legion.

CONFEDERATE
Private
No further details.

(58) KUYKENDALL, SAMUEL
Co., E., 1 Texas Cavalry
Pvt.
See also:
(in pencil) Union Army

KUYKENDALL, SAMUEL
Co., E., (in pensil) *1 Texas Cav.*

*(in pencil) Kuykendall, Samuel
Union Army from Texas*

Muster Roll of the Kuykendalls
In the Texas State Troops
Before the Civil War

(1)
Name & Rank:	**Kuykendall, B.**, 1st Corpl.
Comm. Off.	Boswell, R. P. Capt.
Organ:	MC, Evergreen Guards, Wash. Co., 23rd Brig. TST
Enlist:	May, 1861
Descrip:	
Remarks:	R&F 77: Co. able to furnish horses but lack arms. HQ Evergreen Comm. July 25-61. Elec. Certf. With roll.

Ref. Notes: Barzillai (Zilla) Kuykendall, the only child by Capt. Gibson Kuykendall and his 1st. marriage to Elizabeth Leaky, was b. on 18 Dec. 18 1829, probably in Washington Co., Texas and d. on 2 January 2 1916 at Tilden, McMullen County, Texas. Barzillai married Louisa A. West (Tenn.) and they had two sons, James West Kuykendall and Isaac West Kuykendall. It is from this particular line that most of the McMullen Co. K's descend.

Also: "The Muster Roll of the 23rd Brigade: Capt. R. P. Boswell's Company of Evergreen Mounted Guards, Washington County, July 1861," from the "History of Lee County, Texas, pages 381–382, Texas State Gene. Library, Lorenzo de Zavala Bldg., Austin, Texas.

(2)
Name & Rank:	**Kuykendall, B.**, Pvt.
Comm. Off:	Mullen, John W., and Peace, Wiley J., Capt.
Organ:	Williamson Bowies, 4th Regt. TC, Col. Wm. H. Parsons Commdg. TST.
Enlist:	Au. 18-61 at Georgetown; mus. In 0.22-61 at Camp Hebert, Austin Co., for 12 mos.
Disch:	Serv. To c.28-61: 7 days at $12—$2.80: mus. out 0.28-61 at Camp Hebert
Descrip:	Age 25
Remarks:	R&F 85; En. Off. Capt. Peace; Mus. Off. Col. Parsons, Appraisers A. M. Maddux & Wm. J. Stokes; due for Cloth. $.97, usc of horse $2.80, mileage $12; Total pay $18.57; trav. 120 mi. to place of rendez. Co. reorganized S. 14-61 and new officers elected; Co. comm.. S. 30-61: 1 MR dtd, Au. 27 to 0.28-61, 1 valuation roll dtd. Au. 27-61 and 1 PR dtd. Au. 27 to 0.28-61. Name not on valuation roll; according to MR, served only 6 days.

Ref. Notes: unknown.

(3)
Name & Rank:	**Kuykendall, E. R.** Pvt.
Comm. Off:	Harrison, Jas. M., Capt.
Organ:	Co. E, Roberts' Regt. TVI, CSA
Enlist:	F. 22-62 at Canton for 12 months.
Disch:	
Descrip:	Age 25
Remarks:	R&F 90; En. Off. J. M. Harrison: Mus. Off. Col. O. M. Roberts; trav. 9 mi. to place of rendevous; Co. called into service by BG P. O. Hebert; sta. at Camp Lubbock Ap. 30-62; 1 MR.

Ref. Notes: See: Confederate #7: Elijah R. Kuykendall of Canton, Van Zandt Co., Texas. He was a brother to J. J. Kuykendall, #13. His father was Peter Kuykendall and his grandfather was Jesse Kuykendall of North Carolina and Tenn.

(4)
Name & Rank:	**Kuykendall, G. R.** Pvt.
Comm. Off:	Barton, James M., Capt.
Organ:	Cav. Co. Col. M. F. Locke's Regt., CSA
Enlist:	
Disch:	
Remarks:	R&F 109; Co. mus. into serv. of state on S 16-61 serv. O 31-61: M. F. Locke Mus. Off.;

Ref. Notes: Possibly George Richardson Kuykendall, born 3 April 1840, son of James and Dorcus Renolds Kuykendall. If so, he enlisted at Quitman, Texas, in Company G. of the 10th Texas Cav. on 25 Sept. 1861 and remained with that unit until killed in action on 24 June 1862 at Lauderdale Springs, Miss.(Info. from Kay Clark, San Angelo, Texas)

(5)
Name & Rank:	**Kuykendall, George W.**, 2nd Sgt.
Comm. Off;	Neuhaus, Charles, 1st Lt.
Organ:	Co. B, Young Co., Pr. No. 2, 1st Front. Dist., Maj. Wm. Quale Commdg., TST
Enlist:	F. 2-64 in Young Co.
Disch:	Served 17 days at $2.50—$42.50
Descrip:	Age 23
Remarks:	R&F 43; En. Off. Lt. Neuhays; Mus. Off. Maj. Quale; 1 shotgun; Co. org. under Act D. 15-63; 2 MR dtd. F2-64 & Je. 27-64 & 1 PR dtd. F.2-64 to Je. 1-64.

Ref. Notes: Unknown

(6)
Name & Rank: **Kuykendall, H. A.**, Pvt.
Comm. Off: Tompkins, Jno. B., Capt.
Organ: Co. for Beat No. 1, Parker Cty., 20th Brig. TM
Enlist: Sept. 31-'61
Disch:
Descrip:
Remarks: R&F 55; Arms: 1 Rifle; Co. Comm. N.21-'61; 1 mus. Roll;
Ref. Notes: *Unknown*

(7)
Name & Rank: **Kuykendall, J. K.**, Pvt.
Comm. Off: Robison, Wm. F., Capt.
Organ: Co. for Comanche Co., 2nd Frnt. Dist; Maj G. B. Erath, Comd. TST
Enlist: Feb. 6, 64, at Comanche. Served 20 days.
Age 18, b (1846)
Disch:
Descrip:
Remarks:
Ref. Notes: *Unknown.*
From 1857 to 1873, Indians made numerous raids into Commanche country and thus delayed its growth and development. Two Frontier Regiment companies, composed of men of the county, were organized to combat the Indians during the Civil War. (Comanche Co. History)

(8)
Name & Rank: **Kuykendall, J. A.**, Pvt.
Comm. Off: Boswell, R. P. Capt.
Organ: MC Evergreen guards, Wash. Co. 23rd Brig. TST
Enlist: May 1861
Disch:
Descrip:
Remarks: R&F 77; Co. able to furnish horses but lack arms. HQ Evergreen Comm. July 25-61; Elec. Certf. With roll.
Ref. Notes: *Joseph A. Kuykendall, (b. 4 Dec. 1839-Austin co., d. 21 Oct. 1913, Llano Co.), son of Gibson and Martha Kuykendall. Half brother to Brazillia. See #1 in this militia section. See #24 and 25 in the Confederate section.*
J. A. Kuykendall married Sarah (Sallie) A. Mickleborough (Michelboro). They lived in Wash. County until 1877, then moved to Blanco County for two years then to Llano County in 1879. They had several children. Two of their children were William H. Kuykendall, b. 6 June 1860, Lee Co., Tx; d. 22 Feb. 1939 in Bexar County Tx. He is buried in the San

Jose Cem. there, and a son, I. T. Kuykendall, b. in Lee County Tx. On 21 April 1873. Both JAK and his wife Sallie are buried in the Llano City Cemetery. No further info.

(9)
Name & Rank:	**Kuykendall, J. A.**, Pvt.
Comm. Off:	Searcy, Oliver C., Capt.
Organ:	Co. of Hallettsville, Lavaca Cty., TM
Enlist:	Je. 6-61
Disch:	
Descrip:	
Remarks:	R&F 74; Hdqrs. At Hallettsville; 1 muster roll
Ref. Notes:	*Unknown*

(10)
Name & Rank:	**Kuykendall, J. C.**, Pvt.
Comm. Off:	Houston, W. Y., Capt.
Organ:	Co. G., Terry's Texas Rangers, 8th Cav. CSA
Enlist:	Sept. '61
Disch:	Nat.: Kentucky
Descrip:	
Remarks:	R&F 87; Information on this card from roll compiled by John M. Claiborne for the reunion in Galveston, Feb. 20 '82.
Ref. Notes:	*Unknown*

(11)
Name & Rank:	**Kuykendall, J. H.**, 3rd Corp.
Comm. Off:	Robison, William F., Capt.
Organ:	Co. for Comanche Co., 2nd Front. Dist., Maj. G. B. Erath commdg., TST
Enlist:	F. 6-64 at Comanche; mus. In same day at same place.
Disch:	Served 20 days at $2.25—$45.
Descrip:	Age 45
Remarks:	R&F 49, 67; En. & Mus. Off. Frank M. Collier, 1 rifle; last pd. Je. 1-64; Co. org. under Act D. 15-63; 1 MR for F. '64 & 1 PR dtd. F.6 to Je. 1-64. Listed as Pvt. On MR.
Ref. Notes:	*Unknown*

(12)
Name & Rank:	**Kuykendall, J. H.**, Pvt.
Comm. Off:	Rowland, J. C. Capt.
Organ:	Co. A., Cav., Waul's Legion, CSA
Enlist:	1862 in Washington County
Disch:	
Descrip:	
Remarks:	R&F 104; Co. org. with Jesse G. Thomas as Capt.; officers

	resigned at Vicksburg & Rowland & others elected; certified copy of roll dtd. D. 31-62 signed by D. C. Thomas May 6, 1903.
Ref. Notes:	*Unknown*

(13)
Name & Rank:	**Kuykendall, J. J.,** Pvt.
Comm. Off:	Harrison, Jas. M. Capt.
Organ:	Co. E., Robert's Regt. TVI, CSA
Enlist:	F. 22-62 at Canton for 12 months
Disch:	
Descrip:	Age 34
Remarks:	R&F 90; En. Off. J. M. Harrison; Mus. Off. Col. O. M. Roberts; trav. 9 miles to place of rendezvous; Co. called into service by BG P. O. Hebert; sta. At Camp Lubbock Ap. 30-62: 1 MR.
Ref. Notes:	*James Jefferson Kuykendall was the brother of Elizah R. Kuykendall of Van Zandt County Texas. His father was the Rev. Peter Kuykendall and his mother was Prudence Terry Kuykendall; his grandparents were Jesse Young and Jean Hall Kuykendall of North Carolina & Tenn. See #7 of the Confederate section. JJK m. Martha Hatton and they had three children.*

(14)
Name & Rank:	**Kuykendall, J. T.,** Pvt.
Comm. Off:	Bounds, Joseph M., Capt.
Organ:	Co. of Collin Co. Inf. Vol., Col. Wm. C. Young's Regt., 15th Brig. TM; Tr. CSA.
Enlist:	June 12, 1861 at McKinney for 12 mo. Unless sooner discharged.
Disch:	
Descrip:	Age 20
Remarks:	R&F 96; J. M. Bounds En. Off.; Joseph Bledsoe & E. R. Ashford Apprs.; Comm. Sept. 4, 1861; Val. Gun $30; Pistol 10; Knife $2.; Blanket $6. 0.2-61 Co. was mustered into 11th Tex. Cav. CSA. Served as Inf. until July, 1861, when mounted & served as Cavalry. One muster roll & one payroll. Amt. of pay $43.30; Allowance for clothing $15.65, for use of horse $26.80; Stoppages $6; Balance paid $79.75.
Ref. Notes:	*Unknown*

(14-A)
Name & Rank:	**Kuykendall, J. T.,** Pvt.
Comm:	Bounds, Joseph M., Capt.

Organ:	Co. TVI, Collin Co.; Young's Regt.
Enlist:	Je. 12-61 at McKinney
Disch:	
Descrip:	Age 20
Remarks:	R&F 109; J. M. Bounds En. Off.; John Shields Muss. Off.; Roll read D. 24-62. awol Aug. 27th.
Ref. Notes:	*Ibid, above.*

(15)

Name & Rank:	**Kuykendall, J. W.**, Pvt.
Comm. Off:	Calhoun, R. N. Capt.
Organ:	Co. in Beat No. 4, Williamson Co., 27th Brig. TM
Enlist:	N. 2-64
Disch:	
Descrip:	
Remarks:	R&F 44; Co. comm.. D. 7-61; John T. Flint, Aid; 1 MR.
Ref. Notes:	*Unknown*

(16)

Name & Rank:	**Kuykendall, J. W.**, Pvt.
Comm. Off:	Cureton, J. J. Capt.
Organ:	Co. of Rangers, Stephens Co., Fr. Regt. TST, Col. J. M. Morris, comdg.
Enlist:	Jan. 2-63 at Belknap.
Disch:	Jan 2-63 by reentry into service.
Descrip:	
Remarks:	R&F 132; N. White, En. & Mus. Off.; Co. enr from counties: Young, Jack, Palo Pinto, & Parker. Clothing due from enlistm. Clothing drawn $31.20. Co. org. under Act of Dec. 21-61. 3 Mus. Rolls; 1 gives date of enrollm & election of Capt. Cureton as Feb. 1-62; one date June 30-62 to Jan 31-63; one dated Mar 11-63. Wm. R. Peveler, Capt. Comdg. Co. after Nov. 62. Pay due from enlistment. This name appears only on roll dated June 30-62 to Jan 31-63.
Ref. Notes:	*Unknown*

(17)

Name & Rank:	**Kuykendall, J. W.**, Pvt.
Comm. Off:	Peveler, W. R., Capt.
Organ:	Co. I., Front. Regt., Col. Jas. M. Norris, commdg., TST
Enlist:	Mus. in July 5-62 at Cap Belknap
Disch:	Jan. 31-63 at Camp Balknap by reenlistment Jan. 2-63.
Descrip:	
Remarks:	R&F 123; Mus. Off. Lt. N. White; Co. org. under Act D. 21-61; Co. mus. out of serv. At Camp Belknap Jan. 31-63 by M. B. Loyd; I mus. roll dtd. Jan. 31-63.

Ref. Notes: *Ibid, same as above.*

(18)
Name & Rank: **Kuykendall, James**, Pvt.
Comm. Off: Brummitt, Harrison, Capt.
Organ: Farmersville Cav. Co., No. 1, Collin Co., 15th Brig., Frontier Troops.
Enlist: May 25, 1861
Disch:
Descrip:
Remarks: R&F 78; Co. org. exclusively for frontier protection at a point N. of line running W. from Waco & E. to Jefferson Co. Pledged to be in readiness at Gov. call or in emergency.
Ref. Notes: *Unknown*

(19)
Name & Rank: **Kuykendall, James**, Pvt.
Comm. Off: Garrison, Fleming H., Capt.
Organ: Co. in 1st Regt. TMV, Comd. By Col. M. T. Johnson, CSA
Enlist: Jan. 1-62 for 12 mos. Unless sooner discharged.
Disch:
Descrip: Age 21
Remarks: R&F 116; Mus. Off. Thos. J. Johnson; Apprs.; Jas. A. Hardin & T. S. Holt; Va. H. $140, HE. $15, Gun $25, Knife $5; Co. sta. At Camp Likens F. 15-62; 1 mus. roll dtd. Ja. 1-62.
Ref. Notes: *Unknown*

(20)
Name & Rank: **Kuykendall, James W.**, Pvt.
Conmm.Off: Greenwood, Bevily C., Capt.
Organ: Homeguard Co. for Charco Prec. No. 2, Gloliad City., 29th Brig., TM
Enlist: August, 1861
Disch:
Descrip:
Remarks: R&F 38; En. Off. Jno. W. Richardson; Elec. Certf. with roll; Co. comm. O. 24-61; 1 muster roll;
Ref. Notes: *Unknown*

(21)
Name & Rank: **Kuykendall, Limm**, Pvt.
Comm. Off: Damron, Milton W., Capt.
Organ: Co. in Beat No. 2, Bell Co., 27th Brig., E.S.C. Robertson BG, TM
Enlist: Jc-61
Disch:

Descrip:
Remarks: R&F 139; Co. com. Au. 31-61; belonged to Beat No. 2, but preferred to attach himself to another Beat for convenience of drill; 1 mus. roll dtd. Je-61.
Ref. Notes: *Unknown*

(22)
Name & Rank: **Kuykendall, M**. Pvt., 2nd Class
Comm. Off: Renfroe, J. P., Capt.
Organ: Cav. Co., TST; tr. To CSA
Enlist: Mar. 18-64 at Buena Vista, Shalby Co., for 6 months.
Disch:
Descrip: Age 49; Ht. 5.6; Eyes blue; Complexion & Hair light; Farmer
Remarks: R&F 91; En. Mus. Off. Capt. Renfroe; Appraisers Jesse Pope & J. P. McCarty; sta. At Buena Vista Mar. 18-64; Co. reorganized pursuant to Act. Of Legis. To provide for public defense of State & GO Nos. 13, 14, & 16 of Gen. J. B. Magruder; I1 mus. roll dtd. Mar. 18-64. Reenrolled; claims exemption as having a Horse grist mill grinding for the public.
Ref. Notes: *Probably Middleton Kuykendall of Beckville, Panola Co., Texas. MK's father was William and his grandparents were Matthew & Nancy Johnson Kuykendall of De Soto Co. Miss. See: Sons Geo. M. and Wm. Asher Kuykendall in the Confederate section. Middleton and his wife, Marian W. Branch Kuykendall are both buried in the Youndblood Cem., Beckville, Panola Co., Texas.*

(23)
Name & Rank: **Kuykendall, M. H.**, Pvt.
Comm. Off: Brown, John H., Capt
Organ: Fr. Regt. 2nd Fr. Dist. TST; Maj. G. B. Erath Comdg. San Saba So.
Enlist: O 1863 in San Saba Co., En. F. R. F 10-64
Disch: Service 14 days
Descript: Age 31; given as 30 on roll of 0-63
Remarks: R&F 122; W. R. Wood En. Off., G. B. Erath Mus. Off., Co., org. for local defense under 25% call for 6 mo. 0-63 & part of 31st Brig., Hdq. New Braunfels-later part Fr. Regt. Under Act D-15-63; Had Rifle
Ref. Notes: *Unknown*

(24)
Name & Rank: **Kuykendall, M. H.**, Pvt.
Comm.Off: Pitts, William A., Capt.
Organ: Volunteers from San Saba Cty, McCulloch's Regt., 31st Brig., CSA.

Enlist:	1862
Disch:	
Descrip:	
Remarks:	11 Vols. Roll certified April 8, 1862 by M. H. Wadsworth, C. J. of San Saba Cty. 1 Roll.
Ref. Notes:	*Unknown*

(25)

Name & Rank:	**Kuykendall, M. J.**, Pvt
Comm.Off:	Halley, R. B., Capt.
Organ:	Co. of Mtd. Ran. in Regt. Com. by Col. H. E. McCulloch Comdg. NW Front. of Tex., TST.
Enlist:	Feb. 15, 1861 in Bell Co. for 5 mo.
Disch:	Mus. out May 10-61; 2 mo. 26 da. at $25.; $71.66.
Descrip:	Age 22
Remarks:	R&F 65 & 66; En. Off. R. B. Halley; Val. H. $100; H. E. $40; Gun $20; Pistol $27; Pack H. $90. 140 miles to Rend. 205 miles from place of disch. Home $14.61. Total pay & allowance $86.27. Stoppages due Howard & Leig; $8.15. Balance paid $78.12. Due 10 days rations $8.15. Pack H. in serv. from 15th Feb. until May 10th. Co. 1 called into temp. serv. of the Convention by Col. Henry E. McCulloch. One M. R. dated Feb. 15, 1861; One payroll dated May 10, 1861.
Ref. Notes:	*This is Matthew Johnson Kuykendall, son of Abner and Maria Duff Kuykendall of Bell Co. Texas. See: Confederate Section: # 28, 29, & 30.*

(26)

Name & Rank:	**Kuykendall, N. H.**, 4th Sergt., (Pvt)
Comm. Off:	Gilbert, Singleton, 1st Lieu.
Organ:	2nd Fron. Dist., Eastland Cty., Maj. G. B. Erath, Comdg., TST
Enlist:	F. 9-64 in Eastland County
Disch:	Served 20 days at $2.50-Total $50.00
Descrip:	Age 36
Remarks:	R&F 45; En. Off. S. Gilbert; Mus. Off. Maj. G. B. Erath; 1 Rifle & 2 holsters; Co., org. under Act D. 15-63; 1 mus. roll dtd. F. 9-64 & 1 mus. & payroll dtd. Je. 1-64;
Ref. Notes:	*Unknown*

(27)

Name & Rank:	**Kuykendall, P. E.**, Pvt.
Comm. Off:	Harrison, Jas. M., Capt.
Organ:	Co. E., Robert's Regt., TVI, CSA
Enlist:	F. 22-62 at Canton for 12 months
Disch:	
Descrip:	Age 18

Remarks:	R&F 90; En. Off. J. M. Harrison; Mus. Off. Col. O. M. Roberts; trav. 9 miles to place of rendevous; called into service by BG P. O. Hebert; Co. sta. At Camp Lubbock Ap. 30-62; 1 MR.
Ref. Notes:	*Probably Peter E. Kuykendall of Van Zandt Co., Texas. Married Mary Ann Hunt. See Confederate section #35.*

(28)
Name & Rank:	**Kuykendall, R.**, Pvt.
Comm. Off:	Strobele, L. M., Capt.
Organ:	Co. F., Terry's Texas Rangers, 8th Cav., CSA
Enlist:	Sept. 61 in Lavaca Cty.
Disch:	Res.; Lavaca Cty., Texas
Descrip:	
Remarks:	R&F 117; Died at Nashville, Dec. –61; Information on this card from roll compiled by John M. Claiborne for the Reunion in Galveston, Feb. 20-82.
Ref. Notes:	*Unknown. These men in Co. F. were from mostly from Fayette Co., and a few were from Lavaca Co., Texas.*

(29)
Name & Rank:	**Kuykendall, R. B.**, Pvt.
Comm. Off:	Capt. E. R. Collard
Organ:	Co. Beat No. 3; Bell Co.; 27th Brig.; BG E. S. C. Robertson; TM
Enlist:	Je-61
Disch:	
Descrip:	
Remarks:	R&F 112; Com. Au. 21-61; 1 MR
Ref. Notes:	*This is probably Robert Baylor Kuykendall, son of Abner & Maria Duff Kuykendall of Bell Co., Texas. However, the company information is different than file #39 in the Confederate section.*

(30)
Name & Rank:	**Kuykendall, S.**, Pvt.
Comm. Off:	Campbell, J. R., Capt.
Organ:	Co., F., 23rd Brig., Jno. R. Sayles, Brig. Genl. TST
Enlist:	Jan 5-63 at Brenham for 3 months.
Disch:	
Discrip:	
Remarks:	R&F 75; Jno. R. Sayles, Brig. Genl., Insp. & Mus. Off.; stationed at Brenham. Date of roll Jan. 13-63.
Ref. Notes:	*Unknown*

(31)
Name & Rank: **Kuykendall, S.**, Pvt.
Comm. Off: Fouty, Clinto, Capt.
Organ: Mt. Pisgah State Guards, Inf. Co., Beat No. 4, Navarro Cty, 19th Brig., TM.
Enlist: August 1861.
Disch:
Descrip:
Remarks: R&F 38; Elec. Cert. with roll; Co. commissioned Sept. 18-61; Navarro, Ellis, Freestone, & Limestone counties compose the 19th Brigade. 1 MR dtd. August 24, 1861.
Ref. Notes: *Unknown*

(32)
Name & Rank: **Kuykendall, S.**, Pvt.
Comm. Off: Martin, J. B. B., Capt.
Organ: Co. for 2nd Front. Dist., Erath Co., Maj. Geo. B. Erath commdg., TST
Enlist: F. 1-64 in Stephenville
Disch: Served 2 days at $2—$4.
Descrip: Age 42
Remarks: R&F 82; En. & Mus. Off. W. E. Motheral; 1 shotgun; Co. org. under Act of D. 15-63; 1 MR dtd. F, '64 & 1 PR dtd. F.1 to Je. 1-64.
Ref. Notes: *Unknown*

(33)
Name & Rank: **Kuykendall, Sam**, pvt.
Comm. Off: Halley, R. B., Capt.
Organ: Co. of Mtd. Ran. in Regt. Com. by Col. H. E. McCulloch Comdg. NW Front. of Tex., TST.
Enlist: Feb. 15, 1861 in Bell Co. for 5 mo.
Disch: Mus. out May 10-62; 2 mo. 26 da. at $25.; $71.66.
Descrip: Age 25.
Remarks: R&F 65 & 66; En. Off. R. B. Halley; Val. H. $75; H. E. $25; Gun $20; Pistol $27. 140 miles to Rend. 205 miles from place of disch. Home $14.61. Stoppages due Howard & Leigh $5.70. Balance paid $80.57. Due 10 days rations $5.70. Draft in favor of R. B. Halley $75.00. Co. called into temp. serv. of the Convention by Col. Henry E. McCulloch. One M. R. dated Feb. 15, 1861; one payroll dated May 10, 1861.
Ref. Notes: *Unknown*

(34)
Name & Rank: **Kuykendall, Sam**, Pvt.
Comm. Off: Wilkinson, James, Capt.
Organ: Co., Bell Cty., 27th Brig., Genl. E. S. C. Robertson, comdg., TM.
Enlist: Jy. –61.
Desch:
Descript:
Remarks: R&F 69; Co. comm.. Aug. 21-61; 1 MR dtd. Aug. 18-61.
Ref. Notes: *Unknown*

(35)
Name & Rank: **Kuykendall, Samuel**, Pvt.
Comm. Off: Damron, Milton W., Capt.
Organ: Co. in Beat No. 2, Bell Co., 27th Brig., E. S. C. Robertson BG, TM.
Enlist: Je-61
Disch:
Discrip:
Remarks: R&F 139; Co. com. Au. 31-61; belonged to Beat No. 2, but preferred to attach himself to another Beat for convenience of drill; 1 mus. roll dtd. Je-61.
Ref. Notes: *Unknown*

(36)
Name & Rank: **Kuykendall, Simon**, Pvt.
Comm. Off: Wilkinson, James, Capt.
Organ: Co., Bell Cty; 27th Brig., Genl. E. S. C. Robertson, comdg., TM.
Enlist: Jy.-61.
Disch:
Descrip:
Remarks: R&F 69; Co. comm.. Aug. 21-61; 1 MR dtd. Aug. 18-61.
Ref. Notes: *Unknown*

(37)
Name & Rank: **Kuykendall, Thomas H.**, 2ng. Sergt.
Comm. Off: Doughty, Daniel C., Capt.
Organ: Co. B., 3rd Regt. 29th Brig., TST
Enlist: July 20 (in pensil) *1863* in Refugio Co. for 6 months.
Disch:
Descrip: Age 27
Remarks: R&F 70; Brig. Gen. Dunlap, En. Off.; L. M. Rogers, Mus. Off., Jno. Rabb & Robt. Dougherty, Appraisers. 50 miles to rendezvous. H: $350; HH: $50; Arms:$400. Co. stationed at Camp Magruder on Sept. 21-63. 1 Mus. Roll. Drafted.

Has either joined other organization or been discharged by reason of disability.
Ref. Notes: *There was a T. C. Kuykendall in Refugio Co., at this time, son of old William Kuykendall, but THK is unknown.*

(38)
Name & Rank: **Kuykendall, W. C.**, Pvt.
Comm. Off: Smith, John F., Capt.
Organ: Co. for Beat No. 2, Bell Cty., 27th Brig., Genl. E. S. C. Robertson Comdg., TM.
Enlist: July, 1861
Desch:
Descrip:
Remarks: R&F 116; 1 mus. roll for July, 1861;
Ref. Notes: *Probably William Cliff Kuykendall. See #55 Confederate section.*

(39)
Name & Rank: **Kuykendall, W. C.**, Pvt.
Comm. Off: Whittington, W. B. Capt.
Organ: Co. H., 6th Regt., TC Col. B. Warren Stone, cmdg., CSA
Enlist: Feb. 6-62 at Cantonment Washington for 12 mos.
Disch:
Descrip:
Remarks: R&F 75; Mus. Off. R.M.White; Enr. Off. D.R. Gurley; Dis. Ins., Arms, & Acc. Goo; Mil. Ap. Respectable; clothing-almost without; Last pd. Feb.28-62; 1 Muster & Pay Roll dtd. Aug. 31-62 to Oct. 31-62; Killed at Corinth Oct. 4-62.
Ref. Notes: *William Cliff Kuykendall, son of Abner & Maria Duff Kuykendall. See #55 Confederate section.*

(40)
Name & Rank: **Kuykendall, W. C.**, Pvt.
Comm. Off: Neuhaus, Charles, 1st Lt.
Organ: Co. B., Young Co., Pr. No. 2 , 1st Front. Dist., Maj. Wm. Quayle commdg., TST
Enlist: F. 2-64 in Young Co.
Disch: Served 18 days at $2-$36.
Desdrip: Age 35
Remarks: R&F 43; En. Off. Lt. Neuhaus; Mus. Off. Maj. J. Quayle; 1 rifle; Co. org. under Act D. 15-63; 2 MR dtd. F. 2-64 & Je. 27-64 & PR dtd. F. 2 to Je. 1-64.
Ref. Notes: *Unknown*

(41)
Name & Rank: **Kuykendall, W. H.**, Pvt.
Comm. Off: Rowland, J. C., Capt.
Organ: Co., A., Cav., Waul's Legion, CSA
Enlist: 1862 in Washingtron County
Disch:
Descrip:
Remarks: R&F 104; Co. org. with Jesse G. Thomas as Capt.; Officers resigned at Vicksburg & Rowland & others elected; certified copy of roll dtd. D. 31-62, signed by D. C. Thomas, May 6, 1903.
Ref. Notes: *Wyatt Hanks Kuykendall, the son of Gibson Kuykendall. See #56 of the Confederate section.*

(42)
Name & Rank: **Kuykendall, W. J.**, 1st. Sergt.,
Comm.Off: Brown, John H., Capt.
Organ: Fr. Regt. 2nd Fr. Dist., TST; Maj. G. B. Erath Comdg. San Saba Co.
Enlist: O. 1863 in San Saba Co.; En. F. R. F. 10-64
Disch: Service 14 days
Descrip: Age 33
Remarks: R&F 122; W.R.Wood, En. Off. G.B.Erath Mus. Off., Co. org. for local defense under 25% call for 6 mo. 0-63 & part of 31st Brig. Hdq. New Braunfels- later part Fr. Regt. Org. under Act D 15-63; Had rifle & pistol
Ref. Notes: *Unknown*

(43)
Name & Rank" **Kuykendall, W. J.**, 1st Sergt.
Comm. Off: Brown, John H., Capt.
Organ: San Saba. Troops, 31st Brig., TST
Enlist: O 1863 in San Saba Co.
Disch:
Descrip: Age 35
Remarks: R&F 122; G. Lohmitz Col. Comdg., 31st Brig., TST. Co. org. for local defense under 25% call for 6 mo. 0-63 & part of 31st Brig., Hdq. New Braunfels; Had rifle & pistol
Ref. Notes: *Ibid, above.*

(44)
Name & Rank: **Kuykendall, William**, Pvt.
Comm. Off: Damron, Milton W., Cpat.
Organ: Co. in Beat No. 2, Bell Co., 27th Brig., ESC Robertson BG, TM
Enlist: Je-61

359

Disch:	
Descrip:	
Remarks:	R&F 139; Co. com. Au.31-61; belonged to Beat No. 2, but preferred to attach himself to another Beat for convenience of drill; 1 mus. roll dtd. Je-61.
Ref. Notes:	*This person served in the same group with Sam, & Simeon Kuykendall of Bell Co., Texas. Unknown.*

(45)
Name & Rank:	**Kuykendall, William**, Pvt.
Comm. Off:	Garrison, Fleming H., Capt.
Organ:	Co. in 1st Regt. TMV, Comd. By Col. M. T. Johnson, CSA
Enlist:	Jan. 1-62 for 12 mos. Unless sooner discharged.
Disch:	
Descrip:	Age 26
Remarks:	R&F 116; Mus. Off. Thos. J. Johnson; Apprs.: Jas. A. Hardin & T. S. Holt; Val. H. $200, HE. $20, Gun $25, knife $10; Co. sta. At Camp Likens F. 15-62; 1 mus. roll dtd. Ja. 1-62;
Ref. Notes:	*Unknown*

(46)
Name & Rank:	**Kuykendall, Wm.**, Pvt.
Comm. Off:	Wilkinson, James, Capt.
Organ:	Co., Bell Cty., 27th Brig. Brig., Genl. ESC Robertson, comdg,. TM.
Enlist:	Jy.-61
Disch:	
Descrip:	
Remarks:	R&F 69; Co. comm.. Aug. 21-61; 1 MR dtd. Aug. 18-61.
Ref. Notes:	*Unknown*

(47)
Name & Rank:	**Kuyrkendale, A. M.**, Pvt.
Comm. Off:	Lyon, William C., Capt.
Organ:	Co. B., Panola Cty; 4th Brig. TST
Enlist:	Mus. in Ja. 17-63 for 3 months.
Disch:	
Descrip:	Age 38; Home Miss.; Height 5'10; Complexion Light; Eyes Blue; Hair Light; Occupation farmer;
Remarks:	R&F 66; Drury Field Mus. Off.; 1 SG; Disc. Limited; moderate instruc.; good mil. App.; few arms; limited acctrs.; No tents; clothing furn. By troops very good; 1 muster roll dtd. Ja. 17-63;
Ref. Notes:	*Unknown*

(48)
Name & Rank: **Kuyrkendale, G. W.**, Pvt.
Comm. Off: Lyon, William C., Capt.
Organ: Co. B, Panola Cty; 4th Brig. TST
Enlist: Mus. in Ja. 17-63 for 3 months
Disch:
Descrip: Age 18; Home Texas; Height 5'4"; Complexion Light; Eyes dark; Hair light; Occupation farmer
Remarks: R&F 66; Drury Field Mus. Off.; 1 rifle; Disc. Limited; moderate instru; good mil. App.; few arms; limited acctrs.; No tents; clothing furn. By troops very good; 1 mus. roll dtd. Ja. 17-63;
Ref. Notes: *Unknown*

(49)
Name & Rank: **Kuykendal, A.**, Pvt.
Comm. Off: Mackey, John, Capt.
Organ: Columbus Greys, 1st Class, Active Co., Colorado Couinty, TM
Enlist: July, 1861
Disch:
Descrip:
Remarks: R&F 73; Co. Comm. Au. 21-61; elec. Certif. with roll; Hdqrs. At Columbus; 1 mus. roll.
Ref. Notes: *Unknown*

(50)
Name & Rank: **Kuykendall, Allen**, Pvt.
Comm. Off: King, Jas. P., 1st. Lt.
Organ: Co. for Karnes Co., 3d Fron. Dist., TST
Enlist: F 18-64
Disch:
Descrip: Age 37
Remarks: R&F 46; Jas. P. King, En. Of. 1 Navy Pistol. Roll consists of all male citizens 15-50, in prt. of Karnes Co. W of Sdan Antonio R. Members of 29 Batt. 3d Rgt. TST on furlough were permitted to participate in org. as it is believed that when disbanded Mr 15-they will be allowed to enter the front. Org. Co. org. under D 15-63 act, 1 MR: F 18-64. (Over) Private Co. B., 29th Batt., 3rd Rgt., TST
Ref. Notes: *This is Allen Kuykendall, son of Moses and Ann Wand Kuykendall; brother to Granville Kuykendall; grandson of Matthew and Jane Hardin Kuykendall of Butler Co. Kentucky, Daniel C. Doughty's Spy Company, Co. B. 29th Brigade. Officers: Doughty, Capt.; Heard, 1st Lt.; Radford, 2nd. Lt; Allen Kuykendall, 2nd. Jr. Lt. Allen Kuykendall Pension application: Archives Tx. State Lib.,*

Austin, Texas
Application for Confederacy pension under the Act of
May 12, 1899.
Allen Kuykendall, Comanche County
75 years old
Residing in Comanche Co. 2 ½ years (in pencil) Post ofc Gap.
Came to Texas in 1859
Signed 26 July 1899
Affidavit by J. H. Thormton, identification
Another affidavit says that he enlisted from Goliad Co.
Allen Kuykendall was born in 1824 and died in 1910 and is buried in the Bluffton Cem. in Llano Co. Texas.

(51)
Name & Rank:	**Kuykendall, Allen**, Pvt.
Comm. Off:	Jones, C. C., Capt.
Organ:	Home Guards (Reserve Co.), Pr. No. 1., Bee Co., 29th Brig., BG H. P. Bee Commdg., TM
Enlist:	July, 1861
Disch:	
Descrip:	
Remarks:	R&F 98; En. Off. Geo. G. Kibbe; 1 rifle, 100 rounds of ammunition, 1 horse & 1 saddle; election certificate with roll; 1 MR.
Ref. Notes:	*Ibid; probably same as above.*

(52)
Name & Rank:	**Kuykendall, Allen**, 2nd Junr. Lieut.
Comm. Off:	Doughty, Daniel C., Capt.
Organ:	Co. B., 3rd Regt., 29th Brig., TST
Enlist:	July 20 (pensil) 1863 in Bee Co. for 6 months.
Disch:	
Descrip:	Age 39
Remarks:	R&F 70; Brig. Gen. Dunlap, En. Off.; L.M. Rogers, Mus. Off.; Jno. Rabb, & Robt. Doughty, Appraisers. No. of miles to rendezvous: 28; H. $300; HE: $100; arms: $300. Co. stationed at Camp Magruder on Sept. 21-63. 1 Mus. Roll. Drafted. Has either joined other organization or been discharged by reason of disability.
Ref. Notes:	*Ibid; same as above. These files on Allen Kuykendall are presented as found in the archives and were out of alphabetical order.*

(53)
Name & Rank:	**Kuykendall**, (blank), Pvt.
Comm. Off:	Upton, William F., Capt.
Organ:	Co. C., Cav. 22nd Brig., Genl. Wm. G. Webb, cmdg.,

	TST tr. to CSA.
Enlist:	Aug. 6-63 in Matagorda County for 6 mos.
Disch:	
Descrip:	
Remarks:	R&F 77; Enrolled under GO No. 28; Mus. Off. Wm. G. Webb; std. At Camp near Columbus, Texas Aug. 7-63; 1 MR dtd. Aug. 7-63; 1 Monthly Return for Sept. –63—1st Monthly of Co.
Ref. Notes:	*Unknown*

(54)
Name & Rank:	**Kuykendal, J. W.**, Pvt.
Comm. Off:	White, Newton, Capt.
Organ:	Co. Mtd. Volunteers, Front. Regt., Col. J. E. McCord, cmdg., TST.
Enlist:	Jan. 2-63 at Camp Belknap for 3 yrs. or War; Mus. in Jan. 2-63 at Camp Belknap.
Disch:	
Descrip:	Age 19 yrs.
Remarks:	R&F 67; 74; 82; 90; Enr. Off. & Mus. Off. H. C. Holman; Apprs.: R.C. Whittin, & H.E. Williams; Val. Of H$200, HE$40; Co. org. under Act of Dec. 21-61; Oath of Allegiance dtd. Jan. 2-63, with roll; $ MR dtd. Jan.2-63, Jan. 2 to Feb. 28-63, Feb. 28 to Apr. 30-63 & Apr. 30 to June 30-63; 1 Valuation Roll.
Ref. Notes:	*Unknown; See #18 in the Confederate section.*

(55)
Name & Rank:	**Kurkendall, Jesse M.**, 1st. Lieut.
Comm. Off:	Wilson, Jackson, Capt.
Organ:	Co. for Pr. No. 5, Hunt Cty, 14th Brigade, TM.
Enlist:	July 6-61.
Disch:	
Descrip:	Age—30 years.
Remarks:	R&F 79; Co. commissioned Oct. 10-61. 1 MR dtd. July 2-061. Name deleted on roll.
Ref. Notes:	*There is a J. M. Kuykendall from Hunt Co. See # 16 in the Confederate section.*

(56)
Name & Rank:	**Kurkendall, Thomas**, Pvt.
Comm. Off:	Pearson, E.A., Capt.
Organ:	Co. D., 6th Regt. TVI, Col. R.R. Garland commdg., CSA
Enlist:	Matagorda Co.; mus. in O. 4-61 at Victoria for the war.
Disch:	
Descrip:	Age 23
Remarks:	R&F 86; Mus. Off. Lt. Dinkins; 1 mus. roll.
Ref. Notes:	*Could be Thomas Kuykendall, the son of Capt. R. H. Kuykendall*

of Austin's Colony, b. 1829, but his age is wrong. Thomas(1829) lived in Matagorda Co., Texas at the time.

(57)
Name & Rank:	**Kirkenall, M. A.**, Pvt.
Comm. Off:	Cathey, William H., Capt.
Organ:	Co. 2nd Fr. Dist., TST, Johnson Cty., Maj. Geo. B. Erath Comdg.,
Enlist:	F. 1-64 at Stockton
Disch:	
Descrip:	Age 40
Remarks:	R&F 109; En. & Mus. Off. Wm.H. Cathey; Co. org. under act D. 15-63; 1 mus. roll dtd. F. 1-64, 1 payroll dtd. F.21 to Je. 1-64; On payroll 1st Lieut. Dillahunty is Comdg. Company and is Mus. Off.; Arms: shotgun & pistol;
Ref. Notes:	*Unknown*

(58)
Name & Rank:	**Kerkendall, J. R.**, Pvt.
Comm. Off:	Miller, W. F. Capt.
Organ:	Active Co., Prec. No. 5, Goliad Cty., 29th Brig., H. P. Bee Brig. Genl., TM
Enlist:	1861
Disch:	
Descrip:	
Remarks:	R&F 43; En. Off. Daniel Blackburn; Co. comm.. O. 24-61; 1 mus. roll; Co. had two musicians: 1 drummer and 1 fifer.
Ref. Notes:	*Unknown. Allen Kuykendall also served in the 29th Brig., in a different company.*

Notes

Chapter Two: The Indian War Paths and the Great Wagon Road
1. Research done by Eugene Kuykendall, Sloatsburg, New York.
2. References: *The Wilderness Road* by Robert L. Kincaid, *The Path of Empire in the Conquest of the Great West*, originally published in 1947 by Bobbs-Merrill Co., in the American Trail Series; "The Great Wagon Road" by Parke Rouse, Jr., from *Philadelphia to the South, How Scotch/Irish and Germanics Settled the Uplands*, published by the Dietz Press, Richmond, Va.; *Carolina Cradle, Settlement of the Northwest Carolina Frontier, 1747-1762*, by Robert W. Ramsey, published by the University of North Carolina Press, 1964; *History of the Early Settlement and Indian Wars of West Virginia: An Account of the Various Expeditions in the West, Previous to 1795*, by Wills De Hass, 1851, reprinted by McClain Printing Co., Parsons, W. Va., 1960-1998; *Frontier Forts Along the Potomac And Its Tributaries*, by William H. Ansel, Jr., published in 1984 and reprinted in 1995 by Fort Pearsall Press, Romney, W. Va; and *The Overmountainmen, Battle of Kings Mountain, Cumberland Decade, State of Franklin, Southwest Territory*, by Pat Alderman, 1970, reprinted with index in 1986 by the Overmountain Press, Johnson City, Tennessee.

These are the very best. They will make you want to leave home in the morning and go exploring.

Chapter Three: Maps
1. Kincaid, Robert L. *The Wilderness Road*, pgs. 47, 67, 72.
2. Alderman, Pat. *The Overmountainmen*, pg. 51, Donelson's river trip, 22 December 1779, Overmountain Press, Johnson City, Tennessee.

Chapter Four: The People
1. Price, Betty K. (BKP), researcher, Mt. Gilead, North Carolina.
2. Ibid.
3. Winn, Velma.
4. Hampshire County Deed Book 3, p. 161 and Deed Book 7, p. 159, Hampshire County, West Virginia.

Chapter Five: Adam Kuykendall

1. BKP and Gifford White, researcher, Austin, Texas: Division of Archives and History, Archives and Records Section; 109 E. Jones Rd., Raleigh, North Carolina 27611; also see Anson County, North Carolina Records, Wadesboro, North Carolina 28170; Lincoln County, North Carolina Records, Lincolnton, North Carolina 28092; Gaston County, North Carolina Records, Gastonia, North Carolina 28052; Rutherford County Records, Rutherfordton, North Carolina 28139; Chester County, South Carolina Records, Chester, South Carolina 29706; York County, South Carolina Records, York, South Carolina 29795; Lancaster County, South Carolina Records, Lancaster, South Carolina 29720; and Cherokee County, South Carolina Records, Gaffney, South Carolina 29340.

2. Philbeck, Miles, Chapel Hill, North Carolina.

3. BKP, Division of Archives.

4. *Kuykendalls of America* by Velma Winn, Vol. II, p. 182. (*Deed Abstracts of Tryon, Lincoln and Rutherford Counties, 1769-1786* by Brent Holcomb, 1977.) Division of Archives, etc. See file card 1225, Grant 1112, Bk. 13.39, issued 9-24-1754, Anson County, North Carolina, Wadesboro, North Carolina 28170. See file card 2078, Bk. 15-461, issued 11-15-1762. See file card 1504, Bk. 13, issued 15 November 1762.

5. Gifford White, Austin, Texas; Marshall E. Kuykendall personal files, Austin, Texas.

6. BKP, Division of Archives.

7. Ibid.

8. BKP. The State Records of North Carolina, Vol. XXII, p. 281. List of Capt. Samuel Cobrin's (Coburn) Company, Raleigh, North Carolina Genealogy, Fall 1967, p. 190, Members living in Lincoln and Gaston counties, North Carolina.

9. See the Great Wagon Road, etc. See *The Wilderness Road* by Robt. L. Kincaid, 1966. See *Western North Carolina—A History*, chapter X, p. 229-247, by John Preston Arthur, 1914, Ashville, North Carolina.

10. Dr. Gamblo's description furnished by BKP.

11. Lot #1, 420 acres, 10 June 1749, Lord Fairfax to Peter Kuykendall. *Kuykendall Families of America*, Vol. II, p. 25, by Velma Winn. Winn, Vol. III, p.s 124-133. See *A Forest of Many Trees*, p. 439, by Winn; See *Frontier Forts Along the Potomac*, pp. 118, 119, 120, and 121, by William H. Ansel, Jr. See *Writings of George Washington*, Vol. I, p. 275, by W. C. Ford, New York, 1889-1893.

12. Winn, *Kuykendall Families of America*, Vol. III, p. 225.

13. BKP. Will was filed in "WILL" Book I, 1779-1808, Washington County, Tennessee, Johnson City, Tennessee. Also see Tennessee State Library and Archives, 403 7th Ave., Nashville, Tennessee 37219, and Washington County, Tennessee. *Wills—1777-1872*, p. 2, by Goldene Fillers Burgner. Also see *Washington County, Tennessee, Marriages and Wills*, Vol. I, edited by Ethel Wheeler Smith. Transcribed from the Original Bonds and Licenses at the Courthouse, Jonesboro, Tennessee, by Ethel Depew Huffine and Ruth Stuart, 1961.

14. BKP, ibid.; Marshall E. Kuykendall files, Austin, Texas; hereafter referred to as the "MEK files"; Anson County Deed Records, Wadesboro, North Carolina; also Division of Archives; Buncomb County, North Carolina, records, Asheville, North Carolina 28807; Henderson County, North Carolina records, Hendersonville, North Carolina 28739.

15. Ibid.

16. Alderman, Pat. 1986, *The Overmountain Men*, pp. 122, 123, 127, Johnson City, Tennessee; MEK files; Pension Application of Matthew Kuykendall, dated 12 November 1832, recorded in Butler County, Kentucky.

17. Recorded in Book "AD," p. 83, Deed Records of Rutherford County, North Carolina, Rutherfordton, North Carolina 28139. Also see Archives.

18. Lincoln County records, North Carolina, Washington County, Tennessee, records, and Greene County, Tennessee, deed records, Greeneville, Tennessee 37743. See *Annals of Tennessee* by Ramsey, pp. 228-231, 242-243, 246-247. See *Over Mountain Men* by Alderman, pp. 117-128.

19. See Washington County Will, Washington County, Tennessee. Will Bk I, 1779-1808, Jonesboro, Tennessee 37659. Also *Kuykendalls of America*, Vol. II, p. 239, by Winn.

20. See Adam Kirkendall, Vol. I, p. 23, Folio 2, North Carolina Revolutionary Army Accounts, Division of Archives and History, Archives and Records Section, 109 E. Jones St., Raleigh, North Carolina 27611: Ramsey, p. 487, ibid. Also see *Tennessee Soldiers in the American Revolution*, by P. J. Allen. N.C. Revolutionary Army Accounts, p. 24, Raleigh, North Carolina, ibid. Sumner County Court of Pleas and Quarterly Sessions, 1787-1791, Tennessee State Library, Nashville, Tennessee 37219. Also see Montgomery County, Tennessee, deed records, Clarksville, Tennessee 37040. See Sumner County, Tennessee, records, 108 Courthouse, Gallatin, Tennessee.

21. Tax Rolls for Washington, Greene, Davidson, and Sumner counties, Tennessee. *The Annals of Tennessee*, "Capt. Robertson's route to French Lick," p. 195; also pp. 503-507, by J.G.M. Ramsey. Letters from the Tennessee Historical Society by Ann Toplovich, June 2002.

22. MEK files; Federal Census Map of 1790.

23. Patterson, Tommie Cochran. 1932. *Col. Joseph Hardin*; Biography on Col. Joseph Hardin, furnished by J. Oran Hardin of the Hardin Association, Crewe, Virginia. Also see Tennessee Archives at Nashville.

24. Patterson, Tommie Cochran. 1932. *Col. Joseph Hardin;* See biography on Col. Hardin in a later chapter of this book.

25. Patterson, Tommie Cochran. 1932. *Col. Joseph Hardin;* Surry County, Virginia, records, Surry, Virginia 23883; Isle of Wight County, Virginia, records, Isle of Wight, Virginia 23397. See biography on Col. Hardin in a later chapter of this book.

26. Patterson, Tommie Cochran. 1932. *Col. Joseph Hardin;* Ethel Monday of Knoxville, Tennessee, ibid.

27. Griffin, C. W. 1982. *History of Tryon and Rutherford Counties, North Carolina, 1730-1936*. See Department of Archives, North Carolina, ibid.

28. Patterson, Tommie Cochran. 1932. *Col. Joseph Hardin;* Deed Records of Anson County, North Carolina, Wadesboro, North Carolina 28170. Deed Records of Mecklinburg County, North Carolina, Charlotte, North Carolina. Deed Records of Rutherford County, North Carolina, Rutherfordton, North Carolina 28139. Dept. of Archives, ibid. Also see Joseph Hardin, Vol. I, p. 14, Folio 2; Vol. I, p. 59, Folio 4; Vol. I. p. 79, Folio 4, North Carolina Revo. Army Accounts, Archives & Records Section, ibid. Also see *Tennessee Soldiers in the Revolutionary War*, pp. 23, 24, by P. J. Allen, 1975, Gene. Publishing Co., Baltimore, Md. Also for Joseph, see Griffin, pp. 22-23, ibid. For Benjamin III, see Griffin, p. 70, ibid.

29. Patterson, Tommie Cochran. 1932. *Col. Joseph Hardin;* Dr. Marion Stark Craig of Little Rock, Ark.; J. Oran Hardin, Crewe, Virginia.

30. Greene County, Tennessee Deed Records, Greeneville, Tennessee 37743, Tenn. State Archives, Nashville, ibid. Butler County, Kentucky Records, Morganton, Kentucky 42261; Patterson, Tommie Cochran. 1932. *Col. Joseph Hardin.*

31. Allen, P. J. *Tennessee Soldiers in the Revolutionary War*. North Carolina Revolutionary Army Accounts, pp. 23-24, North Carolina Army Accounts, Raleigh, North Carolina, Vol. 1, p. 23, Folio 2. Register of the Kentucky State Historical Society, p. 156: List of the Male Inhabitants at Red Banks, 19 Nov. 1792. History of Henderson County, Kentucky, by Starling, pp. 27, 97, 102, 104, 107. See Tennessee State Archives, ibid. See Montgomery County, Tennessee, Deed Records, Clarksville, Tennessee 37040.

32. See Logan County Kentucky records, 23 Dec. 1794, Russellville, Kentucky 42276. *History of Henderson County, Kentucky* by Starling. Henderson County, Kentucky, Deed Records, Henderson, Kentucky 42420. Christian County, Kentucky, Deed Records, Hopkinsville, Kentucky 42240.

33. Winn, Velma. *Kuykendalls of America*. Vol. II, p. 297, Vol. III, p. 41. (Starling, p. 104.) See counties, ibid.

34. Starling, Judge E. L. *History of Henderson County, Kentucky*, pp. 103-107; Patterson, Tommie Cochran. 1932. *Col. Joseph Hardin*.

35. MEK files; Patterson, Tommie Cochran. 1932. *Col. Joseph Hardin*; "Annals of Tennessee" by Ramsey.

36. MEK files; *Over Mountain Men*, pp. 122, 123, 127 by Pat Alderman, 1986.

37. MEK files.

38. MEK files.

39. MEK files; Davidson County, Tennessee, Records; Donalson's Diary, pp. 197-198; the diary of the boat trip about Col. James Brown, pp. 508-515, both in *Annals of Tennessee* by Ramsey.

40. The Territorial Papers of the United States, Indiana, Vol. 1, Clarence E. Carter, editor, P.C.L. Library, University of Texas at Austin. (Also see American States Papers, Letters to William Henry Harrison, Public Lands section, published at Washington, D.C. by Gales and Seaton, Texas State Archives Bldg., 3rd Floor, Austin, Texas.) Also see Winn's *Kuykendall's of America*, Vol. II, p. 70.

41. *The Territorial Papers*, Vol. 2, p. 297.

42. Ross, Margaret Smith. "Squatter's Rights," part III, the Cadron Settlement, *Pulaski County Historical Review*, Vol. IV, #4, pp. 54-58, Dec. 1956. Little Rock 72243; Pulaski County Deed Book A, p. 223, Little Rock, Ark.; Arkansas County Probate Records, 1807-1810, p. 142, Arkansas History Commission, U. of A., Fayetteville, Ark. 72701.

43. Allsopp, F. W. *Early Days in Arkansas*, pp. 64-115, Barker History Center, U.T. Austin, File #F-411-TXC-2.

44. Arkansas Historical Quarterly, Vol. X, p. 126, University of Arkansas, Fayetteville, Arkansas 72701.

45. Pulaski County Historical Review: Vol. II, #3, 1955, Little Rock, Arkansas 72203; Arkansas Historical Quarterly, Vol. X-VI-23.

46. Winn, *Kuykendalls of America*, Vol. II, p. 321.

47. Census records of Conway County, Arkansas; Texas State Genealogical Library, Texas State Archives Bldg, Austin, Texas; MEK files; "Pioneers and Makers of Arkansas," "Old Men (and Women) Not Afraid to Move" by Shinn, pp. 159-160. (Shinn states that he visited the Widow Margaret Kuykendall in Conway County in the 1830s and noted her age at between 70 and 80 years.); Pulaski County Historical Review.

48. Census. Pulaski County Historical Review, Little Rock, Arkansas History Commission, One Capital Mall, Little Rock, Arkansas 72201.

49. Arkansas Census of 1830.

50. Pulaski Historical Review; Arkansas Historical Quarterly, Vol. X, p. 126, Fayetteville, Arkansas.

51. Arkansas Historical Quarterly, Vol. I, p. 58.

52. All of the above on Arkansas: Pulaski County Historical Review, Dec. 1856, Vol. IV, #4, "Squatters Rights, Part III, *The Cadron Settlement Prior to 1814*," by Margaret Smith Ross, Little Rock; Myra Vaughan's Notes: Pulaski County Deed Book A, p. 219; Pulaski County Deed Book B, p. 60; Little Rock; "Gazette," August 1, 1826; April 2, 1828; September 11, 1833; August 11, 1835; Tract Book 40, p. 118; Deed Vol. B., p. 536, County of Arkansas, Arkansas

Historical Commission.

53. Pulaski Historical Review, Dec. 1956.

54. Ibid., Sept. 1956.

55. MEK files; "WILL" in Davidson County, Tennessee, Records, Clarksville, Tennessee.

56. Pulaski County Historical Review, Squatters Rights, Part II, Crystal Hill; Maumelle; Palarm; Settlers Prior to 1814; Vol. IV, #3, Sept. 1956, by M. S. Ross, Little Rock. (Robert H. Kuykendall; descendants of; Barker Texas Historical Center, Austin, Tex., 1984; Arkansas County Deed Bk. B, p. 38-133, Arkansas Historical Commission, Little Rock; *The Life and Papers of Frederick Bates*, Vol. II, p. 240, Barker Historical Center; *The Hand Book of Texas*, Vol. II, p. 916, Tx. State His. Asso., Austin, Texas; Pulaski County Deed Book B., pp. 161, 200, 253, Little Rock.

57. MEK files.

58. Census Records of Conway County, Arkansas.

Chapter Six: Captain Robert H. Kuykendall of Austin's Colony

1. An Accurate List of the Male Inhabitants of Charlestown (Red Banks, Ohio) 19 Nov. 1792. "Letter & Petitions from Red Banks," 1792. Register of the Kentucky, State Historical Society, Vol. 25, Jan. 1927, pp. 155, 156, 157. Frankfort, Ky.: Researchers have never determined the middle name of Robert. It could be either Hardin or Hampton. If his grandfather Peter's wife was a Hampton, possibly Andrew Hampton's sister, then it could be Hampton. Interestingly, a Jonathon Hampton always traveled with the family, and Robert's brother would name one of sons, Jonathon Hampton. His father, Adam, however, was married to a Hardin. No proof of either has been found.

2. Tax Lists of Logan County, Christian County, and Henderson County, Ky., 1780-1800.

3. Starling, *History of Henderson County, Kentucky*, pp. 103-107.

4. Tax Rolls for Washington, Greene, Davidson, and Sumner County, Tennessee. *The Annals of Tennessee*, "Capt. Robertson's route to French Lick," p. 195, by J.G.M. Ramsey. First Texas Census. *Manuscript Letters & Documents of Early Texians, 1821-1845*, by E. W. Winkler

5. Petition to Harrison. Signed by 27 settlers including Adam, his sons, Abner, Amos, and Robert and Jonathon Hampton. *American States Papers: Messages and Letters of William Henry Harrison*, Vol. I, 1800-1811, p. 221, dated 2 July 1807. Published by The Indiana Historical Commission, Indianapolis, Indiana (1922).

6. Smith, Margaret Ross. *Pulaski County Historical Review*, "Squatter's Rights," Part III, The Cadron Settlement, Vol. IV, #4, pp. 54, 58, Dec. 1956, Little Rock, Arkansas.

7. Allsopp, F. W. *Early Days in Arkansas*, pp. 64-115, The Barker Texas History Center, Austin, Texas, Box F-411-TXC-2; Biographical and Historical Memoirs of Western Arkansas; "The History of Conway County," pp. 20-21. The Southern Pub. County, 1891.

8. #1. Arkansas County Deed Book B. p. 61; #2. Arkansas County Deed Book B., pp. 534-535; #3. Arkansas County Deed Book B., p. 536; Dept. of Archives, One Capitol Mall, Little Rock, Arkansas 72201.

9. MEK files.

10. Gatewood, R. L. *History of Faulkner County, Arkansas, 1778-1964*, p. 9; Pulaski County Historical Review, Dec. 1956, by Margaret Ross Smith, Little Rock, Arkansas.

11. Pulaski County Historical Review, Vol. IV, # 4, p. 1. Dec. 1956; The Arkansas Territorial Papers, Vol. XIV, pp. 756-757.

12. Shinn. *Pioneers and Makers of Arkansas*. "Old Men (and women) not afraid to move" pp. 159-160. Shinn states that he visited the Widow Margaret Kuykendall in the 1830s and noted her age at between 70 and 80 years. Pulaski County Historical Review; Conway County, Arkansas, census rolls for 1829-1850.

13. Patterson, Tommie Cochran. 1932. *Col. Joseph Hardin*; "Bio of Col. Joseph Hardin, Father-in-Law of Adam Kuykendall," by Marshall E. Kuykendall, 1989. Barker Texas History Center, Austin, Texas.

14. Ray, Worth S. *Austin Colony Pioneers*, pp. 1-2; Conway County, Arkansas, Census Rolls, 1829-1850. Pulaski County Historical Review, Vol. II, #3, 1955.

15. WILL Book A, p. 24, Pulaski County Arkansas, Little Rock, Arkansas; Shinn, *Pioneers and Makers of Arkansas;* MEK files; Pulaski, Vol. IV, #4, 1956.

16. Pulaski, Conway County Census Records.

17. "The Descendants of Robt. H. Kuykendall," McCrosky, Wharton, Texas 1962; *Six Months from Tennessee*, pp. 104-107, by Steeley, Pub., The Wright Press, P.O. Box 94, Paris, Texas 75460 (1982)

18. Pulaski, Vol. 4, #4, pp. 56, 63.

19. Steeley. *Six Months From Tennessee*.

20. MEK files; WILL of Wm. Gilleland; *Six Months From Tennessee*: Pulaski, Vol. IV, #3, pp. 43, 49, Sept. 1956.

21. Steeley. *Six Months from Tennessee*, pp. 48, 49, 103.

22. Steeley. *Six Months from Tennessee*, pp. 102-103. Electra Shannon, daughter of John Shannon of Montgomery County, Texas, later married R.H.(Gil) Kuykendall, son of Capt. RHK.

23. MEK files.

24. From the personal papers of Betty Kuykendall McCrosky, Glen Flora, Texas.

25. *The Hand Book of Texas*, p. 21; *Six Months from Tennessee*.

26. Pulaski, Vol. IV, #4; *The Hand Book*, Vol. I, pp. 976-977; "The Papers of M. B. Lamar" from the original papers in the Texas State Archives, Vol. IV, Part II, #2484, pp. 13, 14; "The First Emigrants Into Texas"; Information derived from Joe Kuykendall.

27. *The Hand Book of Texas*, Vol. I., p. 694 and Vol. II, p. 282; *History of the Island and City of Galveston*, p. 53, by Charles W. Hayes, Cincinnati, 1879, copyright 1974, Jenkins-Garrett Press, International Standard Book #0-89063-000-3; Jenkins Pub. Co., Austin, Texas.

28. *The Hand Book of Texas*, Vol. I, p. 976

29. J. Hampton Kuykendall Papers, "The Recollections of Gibson Kuykendall," The Barker Texas History Center, Austin, Texas.

30. Ray, Worth S. *Austin Colony Pioneers*, pp. 1, 2.

31. J.H.K. Papers, "The Recollections of Gibson Kuykendall."

32. J.H.K. Papers, "The Recollections of Duke."

33. J.H.K. Papers, "The Recollections of Gibson Kuykendall."

34. Winkler, ibid.

35. *Hand Book of Texas*, Vol. I, p. 958; personal papers of Betty Kuykendall McCrosky, Glen Flora, Texas.

36. Winkler, ibid.

37. J.H.K. Papers, "The Recollections of Duke."

38. J.H.K. Papers, "The Recollections of Ingram."

39. Austin Papers, Vol. II; *Bounty and Donation Land Grants*, by T. L. Miller. The General Land Office of Texas, Spanish Archives Division, Austin, Texas.

40. Personal papers of Betty Kuykendall McCrosky, Glen Flora, Texas.

41. MEK files.

42. Austin Papers, Vol. II, p. 296.

43. Austin Papers, Vol. IV, "R. Kuykendall to S.F. Austin," Barker Texas History Center, Box 2A-161, Austin, Texas.

44. Austin Papers, Vol. II, p. 311.

45. J.H.K. Papers, "The Recollections of Gibson Kuykendall"; personal papers of Betty Kuykendall McCrosky, Glen Flora, Texas.

46. *Texas Gazette*, 27 March 1830; personal papers of Betty Kuykendall McCrosky, Glen Flora, Texas; MEK files; Donna McCrosky Johnson, Bay City, Texas.

47. Personal papers of Betty Kuykendall McCrosky, Glen Flora, Texas; Starr Papers, "Diary of Wm. B. Travis," Barker Texas History Center, Austin, Texas.

48. Book A, p. 37. Matagorda County Deed Records.

49. Ibid., p. 268.

50. Personal papers of Betty Kuykendall McCrosky, Glen Flora, Texas; MEK files; Winkler, *Census of 1823*; additional information on Thomas Kuykendall and family furnished by Donna McCrosky Johnson of Bay City, Texas.

51. Colorado County Record Book "D," pp. 101-114, dated 24 Aug. 1842, Columbus, Texas; MEK files.

52. Deed Book "B," pp. 333-334, Matagorda County Deed Records, Bay City, Texas; personal papers of Betty Kuykendall McCrosky, Glen Flora, Texas.

Chapter Seven: R. H. (Gill) Kuykendall

1. *Pulaski County Historical Review*, "Squatter's Rights," Part III, The Cadron Settlement; Vol. IV, pp. 54-58. December 1956, by Margaret Smith Ross, Little Rock, Arkansas.

2. Wright, George W. "Visit through Texas, 1817," (Unpublished memoirs of G. W. Wright); *Six Months from Tennessee*," by Steely, p. 120, Henington Pub. Co., Wolfe City, Texas, 1983.

3. Steely. *Six Months from Tennessee*, p. 164.

4. *The Original Hand Book of Texas*, Vol. I, p. 21; *Six Months from Tennessee*.

5. Pulaski, Vol. IV, #4, ibid; *The Original Hand Book of Texas*, Vol. 1, pp. 976-977; The Papers of M. B. Lamar, from the original papers in the Texas State Archives, Vol. IV, Part II, #2484, pp. 13-14; *The First Emigrants Into Texas;* Information derived from Joe Kuykendall.

6. J.H.K. Papers, "The Recollections of Gibson Kuykendall."

7. Ernest W. Winkler Papers: 1875-1960. Barker Texas History Center, Austin, Texas.

8. J.H.K. Papers, "The Recollections of Ingram."

9. Personal papers of Betty Kuykendall McCrosky, Glen Flora, Texas; MEK files.

10. Wiley (Wyly) Martin; *The Hand Book of Texas*, 1986 ed., Vol. 4, p. 532; Washington H. Secrest, *The Hand Book of Texas*, 1986 ed., Vol. 5, p. 962.

11. Land Grant Application by RHK; "Land Grant Records," General Land Office of Texas, Spanish Archives Div., Austin, Texas; MEK files.

12. Certificate of Discharge of service for RHK from Wyly Martin, Texas State Archives, Lorenzo de Zavala Bldg., Austin, Texas.

13. Audited Military Claims 304-142-#648, Texas State Archives, Lorenzo de Zavala Bldg., Austin, Texas.

14. Bounty Land Grant to Robert H. Kuykendall (Jr.), Texas State Archives, Austin, Texas.

15. Transfer of Bounty Land Grant, General Land Office of Texas, Spanish Archives Section, Austin, Texas.

16. Fort Bend County Bounty, File #16, Land Warrant, Transfer of Bounty Grant, Pat. 72, Vol. 1, Abst. 274, GLO file; General Land Office of Texas, Austin, Texas, Spanish Archives Div.; MEK files.

17. Land Grant to RHK, General Land Office of Texas, Spanish Archives Section, Austin, Texas; MEK files.

18. Gamel, ed., *The Laws of Texas 1822-1897*, Vol. 2, pp. 529-530, 650-651; Election Returns, RG 307; Sec. of State Papers, Texas State Archives, Austin, Texas. Courtesy Bill Stein,

Ed. Nesbitt Memorial Library Journal, Vol. 6, No. 2, May 1996, Columbus, Texas.

19. Colorado County Record Book "D," pp. 101-114, dated 24 August 1842, Columbus, Texas; MEK files.

20. MEK files.

21. Vol. B, p. 20, Ft. Bend County Deed Records, Richmond, Texas; MEK files.

22. Colorado County Probate Records, Columbus, Texas; MEK files.

23. J. Hampton Kuykendall Papers, "Journal of Trip to Mexico," October 1846 to November of 1847, Vol. II, Book VII, Barker Texas History Center, UT Austin, Austin, Texas; J. Hampton Kuykendall, "The JHK California Manuscript," in MEK files.

24. Ft. Bend Co., Probate Book B, p. 342, Richmond, Texas; personal papers of Betty Kuykendall McCrosky, Glen Flora, Texas; MEK files.

25. "Biography of Wiley M. Kuykendall, 1839-1920," by Marshall E. Kuykendall, Barker Texas History Center, UT Austin, Austin, Texas; *Shanghai Pierce, a Fair Likeness*, by Chris Emmett, Norman, Okla. 1953, pp. 45, 47, 55, 82, 87, 139; *A Texas Cowboy*, by Charles A. Siringo, Umbdenstcck & Co., 1885, pp. 77, 79, 84, 90; *The History of the Cattlemen of Texas*, Johnson Printing & Advertising Co., 1914, p. 131; *The History of Matagorda County*, D. Armstrong County Pub., Houston, Texas, 1986, Vol. I, pp. 178-179. *Confederate POW's Buried in Northern Cemeteries*, p. 50, compiled from the Federal Records by Frances Ingmire and Caroline Ericson, 1986; MEK files.

26. *The California Manuscript*, MEK files.

Chapter Eight: Wiley Martin Kuykendall

1. A well known Texas colonist, who had joined the U.S. Army in 1805. He had been involved with Aaron Burr in the early 1800s. He was in the war of 1812 with Wm. Henry Harrison. He also served under Andrew Jackson at the battle of Horseshoe Bend and was promoted to captain for his gallantry. He killed a man in a duel sometime thereafter and was forced to resign his commission in the army. As a result, he came to Texas in 1823 to join Austin's Colony. Martin County on the lower Great Plains of Texas was named in his honor. *Handbook of Texas*, Vol. 4, p. 532.

2. R. H. Kuykendall married Electra Shannon on November 7, 1837, Simon Jones, J.P., presiding. Marriage License, Book A, p. 30, Austin County Records, Bellville, Texas, MEK files.

3. *Texas County Sheriffs*, p. 523, courtesy Sheriff's Asso. of Texas, 1601 S. IH35, Austin, Texas 78741.

4. Emmitt, Chris. 1953. *Shanghai Pierce, A Fair Likeness*, Norman, Oklahoma: p. 45; Matagorda County, Texas, census records of 1850 show Wiley and his older brother, Robert, living with his uncle Thomas Kuykendall.

5. *Galveston Daily News*, "Leisurely Living Follows Days of Much Labor," by S. M. LeSeave, October 23, 1913.

6. Cox, James. *Historical and Biographical Records of Texas Cattlemen, 1895*, p. 131.

7. Hawley Cemetery Association, Blessing Historical Foundation, Blessing, Matagorda County, Texas. Ruth and A. B. Pierce, Jr., 1977, pp. 18, 24, 25; MEK files.

8. National Archives & Records Service (NNIR) Washington, D.C., War Dept. Records Group #109. MEK files. Also, Confederate Archives, Hill Jr. College, Hillsboro, Texas.

9. National Archives, ibid.; MEK files.

10. National Archives, ibid., MEK files.

11. Simpson, Colonel Harold B., USAF (ret.). *Texas in the War: An Encyclopedia of Texas in the Confederacy*, pp. 125, 129. Confederate Archives, Hill Jr. College, Hillsboro, Texas; MEK files.

12. Confederate Records Center, Hill Jr. College, Hillsboro, Texas; MEK files.
13. Ibid.
14. 1946 War Dept. letter to Ella Kuykendall Dunn of San Antonio, Texas. Courtesy H. H. Phillips, Jr., San Antonio, Texas. Private collection.
15. James Hampton Kuykendall papers, 1822-1897, Barker Texas History Center, UT Austin, Manuscript Boxes 2-R-74, Vol. 3, "JHK's Journal written while in the Confederate Army. Vol. 4 of the JHK Papers contain the diary of Judge William Kuykendall of Tilden, Texas."
16. *Galveston Daily News*, "Leisurely Living," Oct. 23, 1913. MEK files.
17. Letter from Laura E. (Kuykendall) Veasey of Dickson, Texas, to Gil Kuykendall of Austin in the late 1960s. Laura was Wiley Kuykendall's granddaughter. She was the illegitimate child of Isaac (Ike) Kuykendall, son of Wiley and Susan.
18. Emmitt, *Shanghai Pierce, A Fair Likeness*, p. 45.
19. "I do hereby certify that the above named Wiley M. Kuykendall and Susan E. Pierce were duly joined in matrimony by me, this 22nd day of April AD 1869." (signed) W. H. Burkhart, Judge, Matagorda County, Texas. (Marriage Records, Vol. A. p. 161, Matagorda County Records, Bay City, Texas.)
20. Emmitt, *Shanghai Pierce, A Fair Likeness*, p. 47.
21. Ibid.
22. Kuykendall family Bible. Copy in MEK files.
23. Emmitt, *Shanghai Pierce, A Fair Likeness*, p. 82.
24. Siringo, Charles A. *A Texas Cowboy, or 15 years on the Hurricane Deck of a Spanish Pony*, p. 77.
25. Excerpt of a letter mailed from Indian Territory (Oklahoma) to Shanghai Pierce, mentioning Wylie, n.d.; *The Cowboys*, p. 31. Time-Life Books, 1980. Chicago, Ill.
26. *Galveston Daily News*, "Leisurely Living," Oct. 23, 1913. MEK files.
27. GWD–M. W. Rogers et ux and Annie L. Rogers to Wiley M. Kuykendall; 3,724.5 acres out of the Burr, Morey, Dusenberry, Brichin, Wilson, San Antonio Valley Ditch & Holderman Surveys, Hays County, Texas, dated September 12, 1903. Information compliments Zeb Fitzgerald, Hays County Abstract & Title Co., San Marcos, Texas. MEK files.
28. Kuykendall family Bible, copy in MEK files.
29. MEK files.

Chapter Nine: Robert Gill Kuykendall
1. Fenn, *Ft. Bend County History*.
2. A personal letter from the real estate broker in Ft. Worth (MEK personal files); General Warranty Deed; John L. Robinson Jr., & E. B. Robinson to R. G. Kuykendall; 11,073 acres out of the Moore, Gray, Beckham & Tatum Surveys, Hays County, Texas, dated June 14, 1902. Courtesy of Zeb Fitzgerald of the Hays County Abstract Co., San Marcos, Texas.

Chapter Twelve: William Erastus Moore
The Moore family moved from New Jersey to Mobile, Alabama, and lived there from 1 Jan. 1840 until 1845. In 1845, the family moved to the Republic of Texas and Will's father bought 85 acres in Victoria County, Texas, on 18 Nov. 1845 from Hiram Warren. The land was located three miles below the present town of Victoria, Texas, on the east side of the Guadalupe River. He paid the sum of $500. The transaction was recorded in the Victoria County Clerk's office, Republic of Texas, on 24 Nov. 1845, in Book #2, folio 847. R. B. Moore later sold this land and moved to Indianola, Texas.
1. Cox. *Historical and Biographical Record of Cattlemen in Texas*, pp. 621-622.

2. Martha Moore of Bay City, Texas.
3. Cox. *Historical and Biographical Record of Cattlemen in Texas*, pp. 621-622.
4. Cox. *Historical and Biographical Record of Cattlemen in Texas*, pp. 621-622.
5. Eudora I. Moore, copies in MEK files.
6. Ibid.
7. Ibid.
8. Ibid.
9. Ibid.
10. Ibid.
11. MEK files
12. Cox. *Historical and Biographical Record of Cattlemen in Texas*, pp. 621-622.
13. Ibid.
14. Ibid.
15. Ibid.
16. MEK files
17. MEK files
18. Martha Moore of Bay City, Texas. Roster of Terry's Tx Rangers, by John M. Claiborne
19. Martha Moore of Bay City, Texas.
20. Confederate Veterans Magazine, Sept. 1902, p. 418, Nashville, Tenn
21. Eudora I. Moore, copies in MEK files.
22. Ibid.
23. Goodspeed. 1894. Memorial & Genealogical Record of SW Texas, pp. 626, 627.
24. Confed. Mag., ibid
25. Natl. Archives & Records Center, Washington, DC, Confederate Section.
26. Goodspeed. 1894. Memorial & Genealogical Record of SW Texas, pp. 626, 627.
27. Texas Hand book, Vol. I, p. 799. Tx State His. Asso, Austin, Texas
28. Goodspeed. 1894. Memorial & Genealogical Record of SW Texas, pp. 626, 627.
29. Eudora I. Moore, copies in MEK files.
30. Cox. *Historical and Biographical Record of Cattlemen in Texas*, pp. 621-622.
31. Eudora I. Moore, copies in MEK files.
32. Ibid.
33. Cox. *Historical and Biographical Record of Cattlemen in Texas*, pp. 621-622.
34. MEK files
35. Goodspeed. 1894. Memorial & Genealogical Record of SW Texas, pp. 626, 627.
36. Goodspeed. 1894. Memorial & Genealogical Record of SW Texas, pp. 626, 627; Cox, *Historical and Biographical Record of Cattlemen in Texas*, pp. 621-622; Kuykendall-Moore bible
37. Eudora I. Moore, copies in MEK files.
38. Ibid.
39. Ibid.
40. Ibid.
41. Martha Moore of Bay City, Texas.
42. Obituaries filed by Martha Moore in Matagorda County Museum, Bay City, Texas.
43. Ibid.
44. Martha Moore of Bay City, Texas.
45. Martha Moore of Bay City, Texas.
46. Martha Moore of Bay City, Texas.
47. Martha Moore of Bay City, Texas.
48. Eudora I. Moore, copies in MEK files.
49. Kuykendall-Moore bible

50. Ibid.

51. Martha Moore of Bay City, Texas.

Chapter 14: Captain Abner Kuykendall of Austin's Colony

1. Land recorded in Book AD, p. 83, Deed Records of Rutherford Co., North Carolina, Rutherforton, North Carolina 28139; North Carolina Archives, Raleigh, North Carolina; Marshall E. Kuykendall, "Biography on Adam Kuykendall, Son-in-Law of Col. Joseph Hardin of Tennessee," 1989, The Texas State Genealogical Library at Austin; *The California Manuscript*, MEK files, where JHK states that "my father was a North Carolinian by birth."

2. J.G.M. Ramsey, *Annals of Tennessee*, pp. 503-507. MEK files

3. Washington County Wills, Washington County, Tennessee, Will Book I, 1779-1808, Jonesboro, Tennessee 37659; Winn, *Kuykendalls of America*, Vol. II, p. 239; Tax Rolls for Washington and Green counties, Tennessee.

4. Adam Kirkendall, Vol. 1, Folio 2, North Carolina Revolutionary Army Accounts, Division of Archives and History, Archives and Records Section, 109 E. Jones St., Raleigh, North Carolina 27611; Tax Rolls of Sumner County, Tennessee.

5. Register of the Kentucky State Historical Society, p. 156; List of the Male Inhabitants at Red Banks, 19 Nov. 1792; Starling, *History of Henderson County, Kentucky*, pp. 27, 97, 102, 104, 107.

6. Logan County Deed Records, Russellville, Kentucky 42276; Starling, *History of Henderson County, Kentucky*, pp. 27, 97, 102, 104, 107; Henderson County Records, Henderson, Kentucky; Christian County Deed Records, Hopkinsville, Kentucky 42240.

7. Winn, *Kuykendalls of America*, Vol. II, p. 297 and Vol. III, p. 41. Starling, *History of Henderson County, Kentucky*, p. 104.

8. Starling, *History of Henderson County, Kentucky*, pp. 103-107; MEK files of the Hardins and the Gates.

9. MEK files.

10. The Territorial Papers of the United States, *Indiana*, Vol. I., Clarence E. Carter, ed. PCL Library, University of Texas at Austin; American States Papers, "Letters to Wm. Henry Harrison," Public Lands Section, published at Washington, D.C. by Gales and Seaton, Texas State Archives, Zavala Bldg, 3rd Floor, Austin, Texas; Winn, *Kuykendalls of America*, Vol. II, p. 70.

11. Ibid.

12. Pulaski County Historical Review; "Squatters Rights," part III, the Cadron Settlement, Vol. IV, #4, pp. 54-58, Dec. 1956, by Margaret Smith Ross, Little Rock, Arkansas 72243; Pulaski County Deed Book A, p. 223, Little Rock, Ark.; Arkansas County Probate Records, 1807-1810, p. 142, Arkansas History Commission, U. of A., Fayetteville, Arkansas 72701. Present State of Arkansas was created as a county from Missouri Territory on 31 December 1813; *High Lights of Arkansas*, by Dallas T. Herndon, 1922.

13. Allsopp, F. W. *Early Days in Arkansas*, pp. 64-115, Barker History Center, U.T. Austin, File #F-411-TXC-2.

14. Gatewood, R. L. *History of Faulkner County, Arkansas, 1778-1964*, p. 13; Plate Five, Ownership of the Cadron Community, 1808-1820, Vol. X, p. 126, Arkansas Historical Quarterly, U of A., Fayetteville, Arkansas 72701.

15. Pulaski Historical Review, "Squatters Rights," part II, "Crystal Hill"; Maumelle; Palarm; Settlers Prior to 1814, Vol. IV #3, Sept. 1956, by M. S. Ross, Little Rock, Arkansas.

16. MEK files; Betty McCrosky's papers, 1952, Wharton, Texas, in possession of the writer.

17. "Recollections of Capt. Gibson Kuykendall," in J. H. Kuykendall's "Reminiscences of

Early Texans," *Texas Historical Asso. Qtly*, Vol. 7, July 1903, p. 29. Also referred to as the "Papers of Jonathon Hampton Kuykendall (JHK) and William Kuykendall; in Four Vols., Vol. #1, 1822-1829, Four Books, Book I, pp. 42 to 61. Barker History Center, U.T. Austin; *Austin Colony Pioneers*, pp. 1-2, by Worth S. Ray, Pemberton Press, 1970; MEK files.

18. Ibid., pp. 31-32; JHK's recollection of Austin's visit to his father's camp, from comments of Thrall's *School History of Texas*, p. 53; JHK papers, "Recollections of Gibson Kuykendall," p. 46; JHK papers, "Recollections of Barzillai," pp. 13-38.

19. JHK papers, "Recollections of Gibson," pp. 46-47; JHK 1849 Calif. unpublished papers, p. 84; MEK files.

20. JHK papers: "Recollections of Gibson," pp. 52, 53, 54.

21. Donation and Bounty Land Grants, by Miller; Index to Field Notes & Plats, Spanish Archives General Land Office of Texas, Stephen F. Austin Bldg., Austin, Texas.

22. First Census of Austin's Colony, 1826, Spanish Archives Vol. 54, p. 13, General Land Office of Texas, SFA Bldg., Austin, Texas.

23. JHK papers, "Recollections of Gibson," pp. 56, 57, 58, 59, 60; reference to Capt. R.H. Kuykendall from MEK files.

24. Austin papers; JHK papers, "Recollections of Barzillai," pp. 13-38. Barker History Center.

25. John Henry Brown, *History of Texas*, Vol. I, pp. 157-158; "Recollections of "Barzillai and Gibson" in JHK papers.

26. Austin Papers; JHK papers, "Recollections of Barzillai"; JHK papers, "Sketches of Early Texians, Father Michael Muldoon," p. 44. File Box #2-R-74. Barker Texas History Center, Austin, Texas.

27. "A History of the Kuykendall Family in Texas." A Masters Thesis (The Descendants of Abner Kuykendall), by Ann Delaney, East Texas State Teachers College, August 1942. Texas State Genealogical Library, Austin.

28. Dr. Robert Peeble's Medical Journal states that he, Peebles, attended Abner Kuykendall on 25 July 1834. Barker History Center, Box 2-J, #135, UT-Austin, Texas; "Journal of Ammon Underwood," Texas State Archives; His. Qtly., Vol. 32, p. 127, Austin, Texas; oral history: T.R. Kuykendall of Tilden, Texas, to MEK.

29. *The California Manuscript*, MEK files; genealogical information from the files of Gifford White, Austin, Texas; McCrosky papers, Wharton, Texas, 1952; Texas State Library, Austin, Texas.

30. "Succession of Abner Kuykendall," Probate Records of Austin County Texas, Bellville; Affidavit of Andrew Dilworth of San Antonio, Texas; MEK files.

Chapter 15: Captain Gibson Kuykendall of Austin's Colony

1. Register of the Kentucky State Historical Society, p. 156: "List of the Male Inhabitants at Red Banks, 19 Nov. 1792; *History of Henderson County, Kentucky*, by Judge E. L. Starling, pp. 27, 97, 102, 104, 107.

2. Pulaski County Historical Review: "Squatters Rights," part III, the "Cadron Settlement," Vol. IV, #4, pp. 54-58, Dec. 1956, by Margaret Smith Ross, Little Rock, Arkansas 72243; Pulaski County Deed Book A., p. 223, Little Rock, Ark.; Arkansas Probate Records, 1807-1810, p. 142, Arkansas History Commission, U. of A., Fayetteville, Arkansas 72701.

3. "Recollections of Capt. Gibson Kuykendall" in J. H. Kuykendall's "Reminiscences of Early Texans," Texas State His. Asso. Qtly., Vol. 7, July 1903, p. 29. Also referred to as the "Papers of Jonathon Hampton Kuykendall (JHK) and William Kuykendall; In four Vols., Vol. #1, 1822-1829, Four Books, Book I, pp. 42-61. Barker History Center, U.T. Austin, Texas.

4. "Recollections of Gibson. Sarah Gates Kuykendall, "JHK 1849 Calif. unpublished

Papers," p. 84, MEK files.

5. Index to Field Notes and Plats, Spanish Archives Section, The General Land Office of Texas, Stephen F. Austin Bldg., Austin, Texas.

6. Original survey maps of Austin and Washington counties, Texas. The quarter league of land was located very near the present village of New Bremen in Austin County on Mill Creek. The three quarters league is located in S.E. Washington County a short distance above Caney Creek and just west of the Brazos River. Land Grant Index, pp. 1907-1908, Spanish Archives of the General Land Office of Texas, SFA Bldg., Austin, Texas; *Bounty and Donation Land Grants of Texas 1835-1888*, p. 402, by T. L. Miller.

7. MEK files; Inez Napier, Houston, Texas, and Gifford White, Austin, Texas.

8. Probate records of Capt. Abner Kuykendall recorded at Bellville, Austin County, Texas, 1837-38.

9. Austin papers IV, Box 2 A160: "Muster Roll of Capt. Jones' Co., Oct. 20, 1835," Barker Texas History Center, Austin, Texas.

10. J. Hampton Kuykendall papers, Recollections of the Runaway Scrape by JHK; "Capt. Robert H. Kuykendall of Austin's Colony" by Betty McCrosky, 1956, The Texas State Genealogical Library, Austin, Texas.

11. "Muster Rolls of the Texas Revolution," pp. 41-42, and "Audited Military Claims," file # 304-142, The Texas State Archives, Zavala Bldg., Austin, Texas.

12. Minutes of the Board of Land Commissioners of Austin, County, Texas, 1972, p. 85, by Gifford White, Austin, Texas.

13. "The 1840 Census of Texas" p. 4, 1966, by Gifford White, Austin, Texas.

14. 1850 Census of Texas from the records of Gifford White.

15. 1860 Census of Texas from the files of Gifford White.

16. Bell County Marriage Book, Belton, Texas, Bell County Census of 1870, Texas State Genealogical Library, Austin, Texas.

17. "1870 Census of Washington County," by Gifford White.

Chapter 16: Barzillai Kuykendall of Austin's Colony

1. JHK Papers, "Recollections of Barzillai," MEK files.

2. Genealogy furnished by Gifford White of Austin, Texas, and Gertrude Boyd of Corpus Christi, Texas.

3. Austin papers IV, Barker Texas History Center, box 2A-161; Elections Results-FW Johnson for Col.

4. Stephen F. Austin's Register of Families, Book II, pp. 95-96, General Land Office of Texas.

5. J. Hampton Kuykendall Papers, Recollections of the Runaway Scrape. The Muster Roll of the Texas Revolution, San Jacinto List, p. 42; "Companies left at the Upper Encampment under Major McNutt to guard the sick and the baggage." General Land Office of Texas, SFA Bldg., Austin, Texas.

6. Audited Military Claims, File # 304-142; The Texas State Archives, Austin, Texas.

7. Minutes of the Board of Land Commissioners of Austin County, Texas, p. 84, by Gifford White of Austin, Texas.

8. The 1840 census of Texas, pp. 1, 4, by Gifford White of Austin, Texas.

9. "Audited Debt Claims," File # 304-226; the Texas State Archives, Zavala Bldg., Austin, Texas.

10. Ibid.

11. Genealogical information furnished by Gifford White, Austin, Texas, Gertrude Boyd, Corpus Christi, Texas, and MEK.

12. The 1850 Census of Washington County, Texas, by Gifford White of Austin, Texas.
13. Ibid., 1860.
14. Ibid., 1870.
15. Deed Records of Bastrop County, Vol. P. pp. 210-211, Bastrop, Texas.
16. Republic of Texas Pension Claims, File # 304-66, Texas State Archives, Zavala Bldg, Austin, Texas.
17. Probate Records of Washington County Clerk's Office, Brenham, Texas 77833.

Chapter 17: William Kuykendall of Austin's Colony

1. JHK Papers, "Recollections of Gibson and Barzillai," MEK files.
2. Mexican Land Claims Book, dated 1832, Bellville, Austin Co., Texas.
3. JHK Papers, "Recollections of Barzillai," MEK files.
4. An Alphabetical List of Returns from Different Boards of Land Commissioners, Book A, p. 157, Records of the General Land Office of Texas; by Gifford White, Austin, Texas.
5. Genealogical information from MEK files, Gifford White of Austin, Texas, and the SRT membership files of Andrew Dilworth of San Antonio, Texas.
6. Probate Records of Abner Kuykendall, dated 1837-38, recorded at Bellville, Austin County, Texas. "Biography of Capt. Abner Kuykendall of Austin's Colony," 1989, by Marshall E. Kuykendall of Austin, Texas, Texas State Library, Austin, Texas.
7. The Muster Rolls of the Texas Revolution, from the collection of L. W. Kemp, on file at the Alamo DRT Library; p. 254, by the Daughters of the Republic of Texas.
8. Austin Papers, IV, Barker Texas History Center, Box 2A-161; Austin, Texas.
9. "Audited Military Claims" for Wm. Kuykendall, file # 304-102, Texas State Archives, Zavala Bldg., Austin, Texas.
10. Minutes of the Board of Land Commissioners of Austin County Texas, p. 43, by Gifford White, Austin, Texas.
11. (S) means land in acres owned under survey based on a grant but without final title confirmed by the GLO, the 1840 Census of the Republic of Texas, p. 4, by Gifford White, Austin, Texas.
12. "Audited Debt Claims," File # 304-226; the Texas State Archives, Zavala Bldg., Austin, Texas.
13. Huson, Hobart. 1953. *Refugio, A Comprehensive History of Refugio County from Aboriginal Times to 1953*; Vol. I, pp. 531, 539, 540, 552, 553, Refugio, Texas.
14. "The Papers of J. Hampton Kuykendall and William Kuykendall" Vol. IV, Book 16, pp. 21, 22, File Box 2-R-74, The Barker History Center, UT-Austin, Texas.

Chapter 18: J. Hampton Kuykendall

1. Warder, Oran. *Sketches of Early Texans*. Barker Texas History Center, Austin, Texas.
2. Marshall E. Kuykendall Papers, Barker Texas History Center, Austin, Texas.
3. J. Hampton Kuykendall Papers, Vol. II, Book VII, p. 15; Barker Texas History Center, Austin, Texas.
4. "Thralls School History of Texas," comments from, p. 53; Barker Texas History Center, Austin, Texas.
5. JHK Papers, Barker Texas History Center, Austin, Texas.
6. *The California Manuscript*, MEK files.
7. Turner, Martha Ann. *William Barrett Travis, His Sword and His Pen*, Chapter V, p. 55.
8. Dr. Peebles Medical Journal, where he states that he, Peebles, attended Capt. Abner Kuykendall on 25 July 25 1834. Barker Texas History Center, Austin, Texas, Box 2-J, #135.

9. "Journal of Ammon Underwood," Vol. 32, p. 127, Texas State His. Qtly. Texas State Archives, Austin, Texas.

10. Oral history, T. R. Kuykendall of Tilden, Texas, to MEK.

11. West Columbia, Texas; *Hand Book*, Vol II, p. 882.

12. JHK Papers: "As he (Travis) passed through Columbia, I was in the act of departing thence for the interior of Mexico and we traveled the same road together for thirty miles. That night, the 16th of April, 1835, we lodged at Mrs. Powell's, and on the morning of the 17th, we shook hands and bade each other, what proved to be, a final adieu." *Sketches of Early Texians, W. B. Travis*, pp. 4-5, Barker Texas History Center, Austin, Texas.

13. *Hand Book of Texas*, Vol. II, p. 406.

14. Ibid., Vol. I, p. 582

15. Foote, Henry Stuart. *Texas and the Texans*, Vol. II, Chapter VII, p. 210. *Hand Book of Texas*, Vol. I, pp. 616-617; "Calender of Papers of M. B. Lamar," p. 46, edited by Michael R. Green, Texas State Archives, Austin, Texas.

16. JHK Papers, Barker Texas History Center, Austin, Texas. "Kuykendall's Recollection of the (San Jacinto) Campaign." Vol. IV, pp. 291-306, the Qtly of the Texas State His. Asso., Eugene C. Barker, ed.

17. "Republic of Texas Payment for Services: Republic Pension." File # 306-66, Texas State Archives, Zavala Bldg, Austin, Texas.

18. JHK: Republic of Texas Payment for Service, Civil Services, File 304-18, Texas State Archives, Zavala Bldg., Austin, Texas.

19. JHK: Republic of Texas Payments for Services: Debt Claims. File # 304-226, Texas State Archives, Zavala Bldg, Austin, Texas.

20. Oral history, T. R. Kuykendall of Tilden, Texas, to MEK.

21. JHK Papers: "Journal of Trip to Mexico, October 1846 to November 1847"; Vol. II, Book VII: Barker Texas History Center, Austin, Texas.

22. Ibid.

23. *The California Manuscript*, MEK files, Chapter IV, pp. 99-110.

24. "Contrabandistas: Commanded by Jose Castilla"; JHK Papers, Vol. II, Bk. VII, p. 4. November 1, 1846. Barker Texas History Center, Austin, Texas.

25. JHK Papers: Aug. 1847, "Antonio Canales"; *Hand Book of Texas*, Vol. III, p. 141.

26. *The California Manuscript*, MEK files. *Hand Book of Texas*, Vol. 6, p. 222.

27. Dr. A. B. Castle, of Lexington, Kentucky, to whom this (Calif.) manuscript was originally written. MEK files.

28. JHK Papers: "Arrived Brazos Lantiago 6 Oct. 1847." Barker Texas History Center, Austin, Texas. "Brazos Santiago Pass"; *Hand Book of Texas*, Vol. I, p. 718.

29. Uncle Joe Kuykendall's plantation was on the south side of Richmond, Texas. Joseph was the younger brother of Abner and Robert. MEK files.

30. JHK's older brothers, Capt. Gibson and Barzillai Kuykendall. MEK files.

31. JHK Papers: "Letters of J. Hampton Kuykendall, Vol. II, Book VIII, pp. 1-30, 1851-52. Barker Texas History Center, Austin, Texas.

32. JHK Papers: Vol. II, Book XI, pp. 1-32. Barker Texas History Center, Austin, Texas.

33. Ibid., Vol I, Book II, pp. 1-32.

34. JHK and William Kuykendall Papers: Vol. IV, p. 31. Barker Texas History Center, Austin, Texas.

35. JHK Papers: Vol. III, Book VXII. Barker Texas History Center, Austin, Texas.

36. National Archives & Records Service (NNIR), Washington, D.C. 20408, War Dept. Records, Group 109.

37. JHK and William Kuykendall Papers: 1862-1866, Vol. III, Book XII, Journal of JHK

in the Confederate Army on the Rio Grande. May 27-Dec. 28, 1862. Barker Texas History Center, Austin, Texas. (Note: William Kuykendall's comment: "Enlisted 3 January 1862, father's home was Ingleside in San Patricio County.")

38. Geiser, S. W.; *Men of Science in Texas, 1820-1880*, IV; Field & Laboratory, July 27, 1959, p. 118. (111-60)

39. JHK Papers: Vol. II, Book VIII, "Letters of JHK," "Proposed History of Texas." Barker Texas History Center, Austin, Texas.

40. Huson, Hobart. 1953. *Refugio, A Comprehensive History;* Rooke Foundation, Vol. II, 1953-55, Woodboro, Texas.

41. Oral history: T. R. Kuykendall of Tilden, Texas, to MEK relating his father's statement about the death of JHK and the trip made by his Uncle Billy (Wm. Kuykendall) to get JHK's personal journal and belongings and bring them back to the ranch at Tilden.

42. JHK and Wm. Kuykendall Papers, Vol. IV, Barker Texas History Center, Austin, Texas.

43. *N. Y. Historian*, Vol. I, p. 442. Johanne Kuykendall volunteered in 1717 in expedition against Canada.

44. Alderman, Pat. *Overmountain Men*, Col. Seviers addressing his men, p. 198

45. The first time his name appears completely spelled out.

46. Commissioners Court Minutes, Refugio County, Texas, Vol. 2, p. 124, 124, and Vol. 2, p. 132, 133, 139.

Chapter 19: Joseph Kuykendall of Austin's Colony

1. Sumner County Court of Pleas and Quarterly Sessions, 1787-1791; Tenn. State Library, Nashville, Tenn. 37219; Sumner County Deed Records, 108 Courthouse, Gallatin, Tenn.; Matthew's Revo. Pension Application, recorded in Butler County Kentucky. MEK files.

2. Register of the Kentucky State Historical Society, p. 156: "List of the Male Inhabitants at Red Banks, 19 Nov. 1792; Starling, *History of Henderson County*, pp. 27, 97, 102, 104, 107.

3. The Territorial Papers of the United States; *Indiana*, Vol. I., Clarence E. Carter, ed., PCL Library, University of Texas at Austin; American States Papers; "Letters to Wm. Henry Harrison," Public Lands section, published at Washington, D.C. by Gales and Seaton, Texas State Archives, Zavala Bldg., 3rd Floor, Austin, Texas; Winn, *Kuykendalls of America*, Vol. II, p. 70; Henderson County Kentucky Tax List, Henderson, Kentucky.

4. Pulaski County His. Review; "Squatter's Rights," part III, the Cadron Settlement, Vol. IV, #4, pp. 54-58, Dec. 1956, by Margaret Smith Ross, Little Rock, Arkansas 72243; Pulaski County Deed Book A, p. 223, Little Rock, Ark.; Arkansas County Probate Records, 1807-1810, p. 142, Arkansas History Commission, U. of A., Fayetteville, Arkansas 72701.

5. The Territorial Papers of the United States, Arkansas, Vol. 19, pp. 384, 385, 386, 387, 388, by C. E. Carter, ed. PCL Library, U. of T. at Austin; the Papers of Betty McCrosky of Wharton, Texas, 1952, Texas State Libray; MEK files.

6. Papers of Betty McCrosky of Wharton, Texas, 1952, Texas State Library.

7. The papers of M. B. Lamar, from the original papers in the Texas State Archives; Vol. IV, Part II, # 2484, p. 13-14. "The First Emigrants Into Texas." Information derived from Joe Kuykendall.

8. Barker, Eugene C. *Texas History*, p. 69. "The Austin Papers," edited by Barker.

9. Winkler, E. W. *Manuscript Letters and Documents of Early Texians, 1821-1845*.

10. "The 1830 Citizens of Texas," Report No. 1, the General Land Office of Texas, p. 157, by Gifford White of Austin, Texas; Lester Bugbee, "The Old 300," Qtly of the Tx State His. Asso., Vol. I (1897-1898).

11. J. H.Kuykendall, "Reminiscences of Early Texans," Vol. VII (1903-1904).

12. "Audited Military Claims," Joseph Kuykendall, file #304-142. The Texas State Archives, Zavala Bldg., Austin, Texas.

13. Jenkins, John H. *The Papers of the Texas Revolution, 1835-1836*, Vol. 5, p. 442; *The History of Ft. Bend Co.*, p. 93-102, by Sowell.

14. Muir, Andrew Forest, ed. *Texas in 1837: An Anonymous, Contemporary Narrative*, pp. 65-69. The University of Texas Press at Austin; *The History of Ft. Bend Co.*, p. 87, by Wharton.

15. Ft. Bend County Deed Records, Deed Book A, p. 138. "The 1840 Census of Texas, p. 45, by Gifford White of Austin, Texas.

16. Marriage License Record, Book A., p. 30, of the Ft. Bend Co. Marriage Records, Richmond, Texas.

17. Census records of Ft. Bend Co., Texas, for 1850, by Gifford White of Austin; information on Gill Kuykendall from MEK files.

18. Census Records of Ft. Bend Co. for 1860, by White.

19. "Pardons during Reconstruction," File #109, Application for Special Pardon for Joseph Kuykendall, Adj. Generals Office; Texas State Archives, Zavala Bldg., Austin, Texas.

20. The Estate of Joseph Kuykendall, recorded in Probate Records of Fort Bend County, Texas, in Vol. D, pp. 597, et seq., Richmond, Texas.

Chapter 20: Rev. Marshall Daniel Early, Baptist Minister

1. Compliments, Col. Cleland E. Early of Pasadena, Texas. 1988.

2. Col. J. M. F. Jr. Williamsburg, Va. MEK files.

3. Mortgage Book N, p. 241, Clark County Deed Records. Arkansas Baptist Historical Commission, Ouachita Baptist University, Arkadelphia, Arkansas, Archives 71923, Pamela R. Dennis, Archivist, 1987.

4. Confederate Research Center, Hill College, PO Box 619, Hillsboro, Texas 76645. Col. Harold B. Simpson, Curator. 1985.

5. It has been stated by family members that Marshall joined the Confederate Ordinance Dept. under Gen. Magruder(?) and later under McCabe.

6. Minutes of the Mt. Bethel Church Book, Clark County, Arkansas. Ouachita Archives.

7. Marriage license filed, October 16, 1865, Clark County Arkansas. Marriage Book D, p. 338.

8. Letter from Mary Early Archer to Col. JMF Jr. Williamsburg, Va.

9. Ouachita Baptist University, Arkadelphia, Arkansas, Archives 71923, Pamela R. Dennis, Archivist, 1987.

10. Ibid.

11. Ibid.

12. Mt. Bethel Church Book, December 1870 AD.; Ouachita Baptist University, Arkadelphia, Arkansas, Archives 71923, Pamela R. Dennis, Archivist, 1987.

13. Mt. Bethel Church Book, January 1871 AD; Ouachita Baptist University, Arkadelphia, Arkansas, Archives 71923, Pamela R. Dennis, Archivist, 1987.

14. Mt. Bethel Church Book, February 1871 AD; Ouachita Baptist University, Arkadelphia, Arkansas, Archives 71923, Pamela R. Dennis, Archivist, 1987.

15. Bethel-Union Church, March 11, 1871; Ouachita Baptist University, Arkadelphia, Arkansas, Archives 71923, Pamela R. Dennis, Archivist, 1987.

16. Mt. Bethel and Bethel-Union Church Book Minutes; Ouachita Baptist University, Arkadelphia, Arkansas, Archives 71923, Pamela R. Dennis, Archivist, 1987.

17. Letter from Faye to her children dated 1967. Mary Jane Rowe Early was the daughter of Andrew Rowe and Martha Ann Conway. Obituaries found in the Clark County Library at Arkadelphia from the *Southern Standard Newspaper*: "May 3rd, 1879—Mrs. Marshall D. Early,

the wife of Rev. Marshall D. Early, pastor of the Third Baptist Church in Little Rock, died at her residence in that city on last Wednesday of Pneumonia. Her (remains) were brought down to this place Thursday morning to be carried out in the country for internment. Rev. W. A. Forbes ____ the remains and the bereaved family to conduct the burial services."—Sept. 27th, 1879—"Son of M. D. Early." Rev. M. D. Early has had occasion to again visit our city on a sad mission. He arrived Thursday morning with the remains of his little son, aged about one year, who died in St. Louis last Tuesday. It was but few months since Mr. Early brought the remains of his wife to this place for burial. We sympathize deeply with the bereaved in his affliction. The funeral took place at the De Gray Church a few miles from town, Rev. W. A. Forbes, officiating." MEK files.

18. 1990 trip by MEK to Arkansas.

19. Betty Faulkner (1844-1894) was from Ireland, County Cavern. Her family brought her over to New Orleans as a child and that was where she was educated. She was an accomplished pianist and the children all grew up to strains of an "organ in the parlour."—Letter from Faye to her children. MEK files.

20. Letter from Faye (Mona) to her children, 1967. MEK files.

21. Ouachita Baptist University, Arkadelphia, Arkansas, Archives 71923, Pamela R. Dennis, Archivist, 1987.

22. Letter to my Children. Faye E. H. 1967. Ouachita Baptist University, Arkadelphia, Arkansas, Archives 71923, Pamela R. Dennis, Archivist, 1987. Mississippi Baptist Preachers, L. S. Foster, St. Louis, Mo., p. 39. Mississippi Baptist Historical Commission. Sylvanus G. Conway-b.1835-d.____, was born in Alabama and reared in Clark County, Arkansas. He married first, Sarah J. Thomas, and second, Anna Thomas. In 1862, he enlisted in the infantry in Co. H., under Capt. Greene and served until the end of the war. Goodspeed, *History of Southern Arkansas*. MEK files.

23. Ouachita Baptist University, Arkadelphia, Arkansas, Archives 71923, Pamela R. Dennis, Archivist, 1987.

24. Ouachita Baptist University, Arkadelphia, Arkansas, Archives 71923, Pamela R. Dennis, Archivist, 1987; Letter to My Children, Faye E. Hamlett, 1967. MEK files.

25. Ouachita Baptist University, Arkadelphia, Arkansas, Archives 71923, Pamela R. Dennis, Archivist, 1987.

26. Ibid.

27. Reid, Avery Hamilton. 1967. *Baptists in Alabama, Their Organization and Witness*, p. 141. Reference: Mrs. M. D. Early's work with the "Women's Mission Society," Mississippi Historical Commission.

28. Letters to my Children, Faye E. Hamlett, 1967. MEK files.

29. Ibid.

30. Ouachita Baptist University, Arkadelphia, Arkansas, Archives 71923, Pamela R. Dennis, Archivist, 1987.

31. Letters to my Children, Faye E. Hamlett, 1967; Elisabeth (Betty) Faulkner Early, 1844-1894. MEK files.

32. Ouachita Baptist University, Arkadelphia, Arkansas, Archives 71923, Pamela R. Dennis, Archivist, 1987.

33. Bettie Lee died on 18 August 1945 in Orlando, Florida, and was buried in Houston, Texas. Letter from Mary Early Archer to Col. JMF JR.

34. Letters to my Children, Faye E. Hamlett, 1967.

35. *The Baptist Record*, December 23, 1897, p. 1, column 5, Mississippi Baptist Historical Commission, P. O. Box 51, Clinton, Miss. 39056, Alice G. Cox, Librarian, 1987.

36. Ouachita Baptist University, Arkadelphia, Arkansas, Archives 71923, Pamela R. Dennis, Archivist, 1987.

37. Copy of reunion certificate, MEK files.

38. Complete Oklahoma information and history indicated above compliments of Dr. J. M. Gaskin, Director of History, Historical Commission and Society, Baptist General Convention of Oklahoma, 1141 North Robinson, Oklahoma City, Okla. 73103; Ouachita Baptist University, Arkadelphia, Arkansas, Archives 71923, Pamela R. Dennis, Archivist, 1987.

39. Ouachita Baptist University, Arkadelphia, Arkansas, Archives 71923, Pamela R. Dennis, Archivist, 1987.

40. *A Period of Baptist Achievements, 1910-1918*, Chapter XXXII.

41. Ouachita Baptist University, Arkadelphia, Arkansas, Archives 71923, Pamela R. Dennis, Archivist, 1987.

42. Ibid.

43. Ibid.

44. Monticello is 40 miles west of Williamsburg, Whitley Co., Kentucky, from whence MDE's father, John Sharp Early, came. Information from Col. John M. Ferguson, Williamsburg, Va.

45. Death certificate, obituary notices, MEK files. Grave location compliments of the Stanford-Lincoln County Chamber of Commerce, Margaret T. Gabriel, Secretary, 6 August 1985.

46. Compliments: Stanford University, University Library, Special Collection Department, Birmingham, Alabama 35229, Shirley L. Hutchens, Archivist. 1985.

Chapter 21: Col. Joseph Hardin, Father-in-Law of Adam Kuykendall

1. Hunter, C. L. *Sketches of North Carolina*, p. 325.

2. Craig, Marion Stark, M.D. *History of the Benjamin Hardins*, Little Rock, Arkansas.

3. Sanders, W. L., *The Colonial Records of North Carolina*, p. 162.

4. Wheeler, John H. *Historical Sketches of North Carolina*, I, p. 64. Joseph would continue to represent Tryon Co. again in 1778 and 1779.

5. Williams, Samuel Cole. *The Lost State of Franklin*.

6. Ibid., p. 297. Congress also ordered Joseph Hardin to consider raising some Companies of Rangers to protect the frontier against the Indians.

7. Saunders, Vol. X, p. 924.

8. Wheeler, *Historical Sketches,* pp. 231-232.

9. Saunders, XXII, pp. 648 & 716.

10. Williams, *The Lost State of Franklin*, p. 297.

11. Patterson, Tommie Cochran. 1932. *Col. Joseph Hardin*, p. 9.

12. Dr. Geo. Mellon, article in the "Knoxville Sentinel," Dec. 14, 1915; Patterson, Tommie Cochran. 1932. *Col. Joseph Hardin*, p. 9.

13. Garrett and Goodpasture, *History of Tennessee*, p. 135.

14. Ramsey, J.M.G. *Annals of Tennessee*, pp. 288-289; Haygood, John. *History of Tennessee*, p. 76; Garrett and Goodpasture, *History of Tennessee*, p. 90; Hale and Merritt. *History of Tennessee*, Vol. I, p. 132.

15. Ramsey, J.M.G. *Annals of Tennessee*, p. 292.

16. Ibid.

17. Allison, John H., Judge. *Dropped Stitches in Tennessee History*, p. 28.

18. Garrett and Goodpasture, *History of Tennessee*, p. 92.

19. Williams, *The Lost State of Franklin*, p. 297.

20. Saunders, Vol. X., p. 296.

21. Ramsey, J.M.G. *Annals of Tennessee*; Saunders, Vol. X, p. 296.
22. Garrett and Goodpasture, *History of Tennessee*, p. 105.
23. Hale & Merritt, Vol. I, p. 195.
24. Haygood, John. *History of Tennessee*, p. 313.
25. Williams, *The Lost State of Franklin*, p. 298.
26. Ramsey, J.M.G. *Annals of Tennessee*, p. 626.
27. Ibid., p. 44.
28. Ibid., p. 625, 626.
29. Ibid., p. 627, 629.
30. Ramsey, J.M.G. *Annals of Tennessee*, p. 635.
31. Allison, John H., Judge. *Dropped Stitches in Tennessee History*, p. 97.
32. Williams, *The Lost State of Franklin*, p. 298.
33. Apparently Amos visited Hardin County but returned to East Tennessee. His grave is near his father's in the Mt. Pleasant Baptist Cemetery.
34. Brazelton, E. G. *History of Hardin County, Tennessee*.
35. Deborah Singletary was possibly the daughter of Carolina and Ithamar Singletary; Abstracts & Wills of Bladen County, North Carolina, 1734-1900, pp. 4, 81, 90.
36. Patterson, Tommie Cochran. 1932. *Col. Joseph Hardin;* Anita Miller of Dallas, Texas, 1989.
37. Shinn, *Pioneers and Makers of Arkansas*, pp. 159-160.
38. Census of 1830, Conway County, Arkansas.
39. Ibid
40. Patterson, Tommie Cochran. 1932. *Col. Joseph Hardin.*
41. Ibid.
42. Ibid.
43. MEK files.
44. Velma Winn Papers, MEK files; Gifford White, Austin, Texas.
45. Patterson, Tommie Cochran. 1932. *Col. Joseph Hardin*; Oran Hardin of Crewe, Va.; Anita Miller of Dallas.
46. Washington County Texas Historical Society, Brenham, Texas. List of the cemeteries in Washington County, Texas.
47. Gifford White, Austin, Texas; Ethel Monday, Knoxville, Tennessee.
48. Dr. Marion Craig of Little Rock, Arkansas, "Col. Joseph Hardin of Davidsonville."
49. Ibid.
50. MEK files.
51. Total information on Joseph Jr./Sr. furnished by Ethel Monday, Knoxville, Tennessee.
52. Affidavits of Land Grants to Colonel Joseph Hardin in Tennessee.

Index

—A—
———, Cassie, 151
Abel, Henry S., 56
Allcorn, Elizah, 47
Allcorn, Elliot, 47
Allcorn, James, 47
Allcorn, John, 210
Allcorn, Mary Ann, 47
Allcorn, Nancy (Mrs. Elizah), 47
Allcorn, Thomas, 47
Allcorn, W. B., 211
Allcorn, William, 47
Allen, David Lavern, 160, 161
Allen, LaVerne, 151
Allen, Poole & Co., 189
Allen, Sam, 189
Alley, Rawson, 259
Andrus, Walter, 265
Ann (nine-year-old mulatto), 41
Archer, B. T., 62
Arkansas Post, 42
Armbruster family, 152, 153
Armstrong, Ann, 271
Armstrong, Charles M., 146
Armstrong, John, 146
Armstrong, Martin, 16, 17
Arnett, Winnie, *see* Winnie Arnett Phillips (Mrs. H. H., Sr.)
Arnold, Edgar, 160
Asche, F. B., 146
Asher, Levi, 228, 236
Atchinson, Robert N., 231
Atkins, W. E., 273
Austin, Moses, 45, 46, 60, 240, 259
Austin, Slim, 134
Austin, Stephen F., 10, 37, 39, 42, 45, 51, 54, 71, 206, 213, 215, 221, 223, 225, 232, 233, 239, 240, 255, 258
Austin, W. T., 234

Austin's Colony, 265
Austin County, 64, 71, 206, 207, 210, 215, 216, 217, 218, 221, 227, 228, 233, 236, 244, 245, 252

—B—
Baehr, C. A., Major, 142
Bain, John, 33, 36, 59, 205
Baker, DeWitt Clinton, 254
Baker, John R., 237
Baker, James McCulloch, Judge, 94, 98, 190, 202
Banks, General, 267
Barber, Will, 136
Barber, Will G., 134
Barker, ———, 54
Barnard, Joseph H., 63
Barnet, Pumley, 55
Barnett, Doug, iv
Barnett, Humphrey, 30, 39, 204
Barnhart, F. H., Captain, 142
Barton, Bob, 134
Barton, Jim, 134
Bassett, Bill, 160
Bastrop, Baron de, 47, 51
Battle, Mills M., 66
Battle, Willis M., 66
Baxter, Jas. H., 210
Bay City Tribune, 185
Baylor, Captain, 249, 250
Baylor University, 274
Beard, John, 280
Beaty (Betty) family, 17
Bell, A. J., 228
Bell, Josiah H., 206, 213
Bell, P. H., Governor, 252
Benharm, C. G., Lieutenant, 146
Berry, Bill, 147
Berry, Harold, 146, 147
Berry, John F., 221, 222
Berry, Roy, 146

Berry, William, 146
Best, Isaac, 211
Betts, Jacob, 259
Bickerstaff's Old Field, 24
Biography of Col. Joseph Hardin, 28
Bird, Amos, 279
Birdwell, Sherman, 131
Bishop, Wm., 190
Bissell, Theodore, 216, 217
Black, Coach, 159
Bledsoe, ———, 270
Blocker, Joe, 112, 116
Blocker, William B. (Bill), 122
Blount, Reuben J., 34
Blount, Sally Kuykendall (daughter of Adam-1758), 283
Blount, Wiley, 34, 37
Blount, William, 280
Blunt, Captain, 234
Boatright, Betsy, 47
Boatright family, 205, 232
Boatright, Richard, 47
Boatright, Thomas, 47, 212, 213, 221
Boone, Daniel, 7
Boothe, S. P., Dr., 88
Borden, Capt. James C., 254
Bowie, Reason, 29, 204
Bradford, Maj. William, 59
Bradley, Captain, 234
Brantley, J. K., 273
Brazelton, John, 282
Brazelton, Solomon, 282
Bringas, Col. Juan, 261
Broadus, ———, 276
Brown, E. J., Dr., 276
Brown, Henry S., Captain, 208, 224
Browning, ———, 269
Buchel, Col. Augustus, 72, 186, 188, 237, 254
Buckeye Ranch, 87, 111
Buckner, ———, 46, 259
Buckner, Aylett C., 207
Bullock, Bob, Lt. Gov., 176
Bunton, L. D., 139
Bunton, Mary (Mrs. Pete), 139
Bunton, Pete, 134, 135, 139
Burleson, Edward, Colonel, 216, 225, 226, 230, 234, 244, 260
Burnett, David G., Judge, 210, 211
Burnum, Jesse, 259
Burris, John, 34
Burris, Thomas, 34
Burton, Courtney, 146, 147, 175
Burton, Sarita, 175
Bush, George, 177
Butler, Mike, 144, 146
Byrne, James W., Captain, 237

Byrne, Kate Spaulding, *see* Kuykendall, Kate Spaulding Byrne
Byrne, Martin L., 237
Byrne, Thomas K., 237

—C—
Cabaniss, Charlie, 134
Cabniss, M., 133
Cadron Creek, 33
Cadron Settlement, 33, 35, 40, 41, 59, 205, 212, 220, 239, 258
Cage, William, 279
Calhoun, John C., 59
Camp H. E. McCulloch, 73
Campbell, James, 201
Campbell, William, Colonel, 24
Canales, ———, 249
Carankawa Indians (also Carancawa, Carankaway), 206, 213, 255
Cardwell, O. M., 142
Cardwell, W. W., 142
Carothers (Caruthers), Eliza M., *see* Kuykendall, Eliza M. Carothers
Carothers, Thomas, 233
Carpenter, Floyd, 257
Carpenter, Joseph, 23
Carpenter, Saml., 23
Carter, Landon, 279
Carwell, O. W., 134
Cash, L. B., 269, 270
Cash, Lewis, 269
Casneau, William, 57
Cassidy, Patty, 127
Castle, A. B., 251
Cayuga Indians, 5
Chapmen, Thomas, 279
Chickasaw Bluffs, 33, 40, 205
Chickasaw Indians, 223, 224
Chief Carita (also Caritas), 206, 213
Chief Dragging Canoe, 28
Chief Tallantusky, 41
Childers, Cecil, 142, 146
Childs, James L., 160
Christman, Horacio (Chrisman, Horase, Horatio), 207, 210, 215
Clark, William, Governor, 41
Clark, Jas., 210
Clarkson, R. P., 256, 257
Clayton, ———, 233, 243
Clayton, Joseph, 208
Clement, Rachael, 124
Cleveland, Grover, 274
Cleveland, H. N., Captain, 217, 226, 234, 244
Cleveland, Mrs., 112
Coates, John, 186
Coburn, Jonathon, 21
Cochrane, James (Cockran, Jas.), 211, 235

Cocke, William, 279, 280, 281
Coddy, James, 21
Colder, John D., 66
Collins, James (Jim), 186, 190
Collins, Joseph (Joe), 185, 186, 190
Combs, Susan, 177, 180
Confederacy of Six Nations, 5
Conway, Angeline Jackson, 269
Conway, James H., 269
Conway, Martha Ann, 272
Conway, Sil, 272
Cook, Thos, 269, 271
Cook, Vernon, 150
Cooke, Captain, 243
Cooper, James, 209, 210
Cooper, William, 210, 224, 225
Cope, Nora, 118
Corona, Chase Jerome, 176, 178
Corona, Chris, 176, 178, 179
Corona, Myles Cristopher, 176, 178
Corona, Sarita Kuykendall (daughter of Marshall E., Sr.), 171, 176, 178, 179
Coulter, H. K., Captain, 146
Covert, Clarence, 162
Covert, Polly Blanton, 159, 162
Cox League map, 84
Crabs Switch, 265
Craig, W. H., Captain, 146
Craig, Marion, 287, 288, 289
Crain, Jim, 192
Crawford, William A., 267
Crawford's Arkansas Cavalry, 268
Crawford's Brigade, 267
Creeks, see Kirkendall's, Dutchman's, Fishing
Crews, Mrs. Earl, 138
Croft, Sutton, 133, 134, 142
Cruseman, Mr. and Mrs., 135
Cruze, Curry, 135
Cruze, Joe, 111, 112, 124, 134, 135, 155
Cruze, Will, 112
Cummins, James, 47

—D—
Dalton, Jack, 160
Damon's Mound, 213
Darby, Patrick, 59, 205
Darby, Patrict, 33
Davis, Jefferson, 139
Davis, N. J., 271
Dawson, Captain, 245
Decker, Charles, 148
Deckhard Rifle, 24
Deckrow, Elijah, 72
Deckrow, Emma, 72
Deckrow, Matilda, 72
Delaware Indians, 253
Delheryea, James, 21

Dever, William, 223
Dewees, Wm. B., 259
Dobbs, Arthur, 17
Dobson, George M., 63
Doherty, Geo., 279, 280, 281
Donaldson, Sidney, 133
Donalson, John, Colonel, 31
Dorman, Owen, 160
Douglas, John, 210
Douglas, Sam, 210
Douwes, Stijintje, 9
Dubois, Alzena, see Kuykendall, Alzena Dubois
Dubois, Lucas, 237
Duchassin, Joseph, 34
Duke, Thomas M., 50
Dunagin, Jasper, 273
Dunn, Electra (Ella) Miranda Kuykendall, 76, 88, 89, 113, 121
Dunn, T. B., 108, 109
Dunn, Winnie Arnett, see Phillips, Winnie (Mrs. H. H., Jr.)
Dutchman's Creek, 15, 21
Dutton, George, 134
Dyer, C. C., 263

—E—
Eagle, J. P., Governor, 271, 272, 273
Eagle, Mary Kavanaugh Oldham, 271
Earl of Granville, 17
Early, Alice Forbes (Faye) (Mona), see Hamlett, Alice Forbes Early
Early, Cleland, Colonel, 177
Early, Elisabeth (Betty) Lee Faulkner, 271, 274
Early, Ella, 269
Early, John Sharp, 267
Early, Maggie, 269
Early, Mary, 274
Early, Mary Faulkner, 267
Early, Mary Jane Rowe, 268, 269, 270, 271, 272
Early, Marshall Daniel, Rev., 170, 255, 266-276
Earp, Icabod E., 68
Earp, Matilda, see Kuykendall, Matilda Earp
Easton, Reuben, 34
Eaton, Boyce, 276
Edmonson, Clarence, General, 165
El Fortin Ranch, 163
Elam, John, 215
Ellebrocte, Hilman, 134
Elliot, Jack, 190
Elliott, Jack, 191
Elliott's Ferry, 193, 195
Ellis, Judge, 214
Enfield Realty Company, 133
English, Bailey, 45
English, William, 59
Ewing, Geo., 211

—F—
Fagan, James Fleming, 267
Fagan, John, 237
Fagan, Nicholas, 237
Fagan, P. H., 256
Fagan Ranch, 237
Fagan, William, 237
Fain, Earnest, 146
Fairfax, Thomas Lord, 10, 21, 22
Fannin, James Walker, Colonel, 243
Farish, S. P., 146
Faulk, John Henry, 166
Faulk, Lynn, 166
Faulkner, Elisabeth (Betty) (Bettie) Lee, see Early, Elisabeth (Betty) Faulkner
Faulkner, Mary, see Early, Mary Faulkner
Fawcett, A. J., 273
Featherston, C. H., 146
Fenn, John R., 57, 261
Ferguson, Corinne (Mrs. John), 128, 150
Ferguson, General, 24, 256
Ferguson, Jack, 129
Ferguson, "Ma," Governor, 137
Ferguson, Major, 24
Files, A. W., 273
Finkle, John B., 230
First Arkansas Cavalry, 267
Fishing Creek, 15
Fitzgerald, John, 65
Flanakin, William, 35
Fleming, Alton, 134
Fleming, L. S., 133
Fleming, O. D., 133
Fleming, Patrick, 66, 67
Flores, Gaspar, 214, 215
Floyd, Aubrey, 142, 146
Floyd, Jay, 146
Ford, James, 280
Fort Bend County, 206, 210, 259, 263, 264
Fort Groghan, 253
Fort Kuykendall, 22
Fort Tenoxtilan, 208
Foster, James M., 185, 189
Foster, Mr., 125
Franklin, State of, 279, 280
Frazier, William, 34
Fredonia Rebellion, 214, 221
Frontier Troops (FT), 346-364
Furnaish, J., 207, 214

—G—
Gainer, Henry A., 56
Gainer, Jimmie (Mrs. Carl Haggard), 56
Gainer, Wilburn Harry, 56
Gainer, William Thomas (Bill), 56
Gainor, Sarah Ann, see Kuykendall, Sarah Ann Gainor (Mrs. Thomas)

Galveston News, 237
Gamblo, Harry Y., Dr., 18
Gammon, Richard, 279
Garcia, Carlos de la, 237
Garland, Colonel, 73, 238
Garrett, Charles (Garret, Chas.), 46, 259, 263
Gates, Amos, 213, 215, 223
Gates, Catherine Hardin, 30, 40, 204, 209, 239
Gates, Charles, 225, 259
Gates family, 205
Gates, Lydia Leakey, 215
Gates, Sally, see Kuykendall, Sally Gates
Gates, Samuel, 36, 45, 205, 206, 213, 259
Gates, William, 29, 30, 33, 34, 36, 39, 40, 45, 46, 204, 205, 206, 209, 213, 232, 239, 259
Geiser, S. W., 254
Geraghty, John, 260
Gibbons, Bill, 46, 259
Giberson Dairy, 152
Gibson, Jean, see Hardin, Jean Gibson
Gibson, Margaret Jordan, 282
Gibson, Walter, 282
Gill, John P., 61, 260
Gilleland, Daniel, 47, 259
Gilleland, James, 10
Gilleland, Nancy Johnson (Mrs. William), 36, 45, 57
Gilleland, Robert, 36
Gilleland, Sarah Ann, see Kuykendall, Sarah Ann Gilleland (Mrs. RHK)
Gilleland, William, 10, 36, 45, 57
Gilleland family, 205
Glass, Anthony, 46
Glen Flora, Wharton County, Texas, 53, 54
Goetzmann, William H., Dr., xiii, 22
Gold, Jack, 160
Goza, Aaron, 34
Graham, Major, 249, 250
Graham, Murray, 133, 134
Graham, Niles, 133, 134
Grant, James, 248
Grant, Samuel, 56
Graves, ———, 276
Gray, Thomas, 259
Great Wagon Road, 18
Green, Betsy, 36
Green, General, 234
Green Pastures, 166
Green, T., 34
Greenhaw, Doc (John Greenhawe), 138, 140, 153
Greenhaw, Herman, 136, 138
Greenhawe, John, see Doc Greenhaw
Greer, Thomas, 34
Griggs, Asa (Mrs. T. K. McCrosky), 57
Grimes, W. B. G., 72, 75, 190
Groce, Jared E., 206
Gross, J., 230

Gross, Maggie, 112
Gross, Mrs. Will, 112
Guttery, Truman, 160

—H—
Hacker, Frederick, 37
Hacker, Margaret, 34
Haddon, John, 55
Hagedorn, Alton, 160
Haggard, Archie, 56
Haggard, Carl, 56
Haggard, Ward, 56
Haggard, Wilburn, 56
Hall, Helen (m. Michaelis), 134
Hall, Mrs., 112
Hall, William, 207
Hambright, Frederick, Colonel, 28, 30, 277
Hambright, Sarah Hardin, 277
Hamlett, Alice Forbes (Faye) (Mona) Early, 127, 128, 131, 150, 153, 170 , 269, 270, 271
Hamlett, Alice, see Kuykendall, Alice Hamlett
Hamlett, John, 180
Hamlett, Marshall, 136, 150
Hamlett, William A. (Bill), 128, 131, 150, 170, 180
Hampton, Adam, 15
Hampton, Andrew, Colonel, 15
Hampton, Jonathon, 31, 45, 239, 259
Hampton, Mary see Kuykendall, Mary (Mrs. Petrus)
Hampton, Noah, 21
Hanks, Wyatt, 45, 245, 259
Hardin, Ab, 204
Hardin, Abraham, 278
Hardin, Amos, 28, 282, 283
Hardin, Benjamin, 28, 204, 282
Hardin, Benjamin (1st), 283
Hardin, Benjamin (2nd), 283
Hardin, Benjamin I, 28, 29, 277
Hardin, Benjamin II, 28, 29, 277
Hardin, Benjamin III, 26, 28, 39, 40, 42, 277
Hardin, Benjamin, Sr. (III), 285, 286
Hardin, Benjamin IV, 286
Hardin, Catherine, 28
Hardin, Catherine Lamkin(?), 277
Hardin, Catherine, see Gates, Catherine Hardin
Hardin, Elender, 28, 283
Hardin, Elisabeth Kuykendall (Mrs. John), 29, 277
Hardin family, 205, 232; Hickory Creek, 28; Knob Creek, 28
Hardin, Gibson, 28, 282, 284
Hardin, J. Oran, 289
Hardin, James, 28, 282, 283
Hardin, James Gibson, 29
Hardin, Jane (Mrs. Matthew Kuykendall, daughter of John and Elisabeth), 29
Hardin, Jane Ann (daughter of Col. Joseph and Jean), 28, 282

Hardin, Jean Gibson (Mrs. Col. Joseph), 26, 28, 282
Hardin, John (brother to Joseph), 28, 29, 40, 42, 204, 277, 278, 282, 285
Hardin, John Wesley, 29, 76, 77, 283
Hardin, Jonathan, 35
Hardin, Joseph (son of Benjamin IV), 29
Hardin, Joseph, Colonel (father-in-law of Adam Kuykendall), 10, 23, 25, 26, 28, 29, 30, 40, 42, 203, 265, 277-310
Hardin, Joseph, Jr., 28, 29, 30, 278, 281, 282
Hardin, Joseph, Jr./Sr., 287
Hardin, L., 133
Hardin, Margaret, 28
Hardin, Margaret, see Kuykendall, Margaret Hardin
Hardin, Mary E., 28, 283
Hardin, Mary Elisabeth Dixon, 283
Hardin, Rebecca, 28, 284
Hardin, Rebecca, see Kuykendall, Rebecca Hardin
Hardin, Rev. James Gibson, 283
Hardin, Robert (1st), 283
Hardin, Robert (2nd), 284
Hardin, Robert, 28, 29, 282
Hardin Robert II, 28
Hardin, Sarah (Mrs. Benjamin I.), 277
Hardin, Sarah, 28
Hardin, Sarah, see Hambright, Sarah Hardin
Harrison, William Henry, 31, 204, 258
Hart, John, 273
Harwell, Turner, 134
Hastey, T. W., Lt. Col., 146
Hawley Cemetery, 57, 65, 102
Hazlitt, ———, 221, 222
Heard, F. C., 256, 257
Heep, Dorothy, 134
Heep, Helen, 134
Heep, Herman, 119, 120, 122, 123, 126, 153
Heep, Mrs., 136
Heep, Mrs. Herman, 119, 134
Heep, Zoe, 134
Heimer, Hubby, 134
Heimer, Mr., 134
Heimer, Mrs., 138
Henderson, Col. Richard, 29
Hesperian, 261
Hestor, Mr., 122
Hickman, Kenneth, 146
Higginbotham, T. J., 176
History of Guadalupe County, A, 201
Hoffman, Dan, 186
Holcomb, Brent H., 17
Honey, Marge, 119, 120
Hooper, Capt. Rich., 234
Horton, Lt. J. B., 142
Hoskins, Dorothy Kuykendall (Mrs. Lawrence),

iii, 102, 104, 113, 115, 116, 118, 120, 121, 123, 126, 134, 136, 137, 143, 172
Hoskins, Elizabeth, 137
Hoskins, Florence, 137
Hoskins, Lawrence, 121, 123, 146
Hoskins, Lawrence Worth (son of Dorothy), 123, 131, 134, 137, 158
Hoskins, Marion K. (daughter of Dorothy), 131, 137, 172
Houston, James, 279
Houston, Samuel Rev., 279
Houston, Sam, 216, 226, 235, 244, 252
Hudson, Henry, 2
Huff, William P., 264
Hughes, Hiram J., 249
Hughes, Robt. F., 34
Humberson, Wynn, 146
Humphrey family, 17
Hurd, John, 168
Hurnden, Bill, 72
Hynes Bay, 237
Hynes, John, 237
Hynes, William, 237

—I—
Ike (slave), 66
Ingles, Wm., 41
Ingram, ———, 50
Ingram, Elijah, 221
Ingram, John, 37
Ingram, Seth, 259
Ingrum, John, 230
Innes, James, 18
Iroquois Confederacy, 5
Iturbide, Emperor, 47, 60
Izard, V. B., 273

—J—
Jackson, Andrew, General, 59
Jackson, Grandma, 271
Jacobsen, Luur, 1, 2, 9
James, John, 207
Jamison, Thomas, 259
Jay, H. D., Major, 142
Jenkin's Ferry, 268
Jeter, ———, 276
John (Chickasaw Indian), 223
John (slave), 66
Johnson, F. W., Captain, 225
Johnson, Donna McCrosky (Mrs. Hubert), 55
Johnson, Francis W., 207, 214
Johnson, Ignatius S., 263
Johnson, John, 36
Johnson, Joseph, 201-202
Johnson, Lyndon B., 148, 150
Jones, Allen, General, 278
Jones, Eliza Jane, *see* Kuykendall, Eliza Jane Jones

Jones, Henry, 210
Jones, John, 214
Jones, Oliver, 208, 211, 223
Jones, R., Captain, 216
Jones, Randall, 64
Jones, Seaborn, 221, 223, 224
Jones, W. S., 265
Jordan, Deborah Singletary, 282
Jordan, Margaret, *see* Gibson, Margaret Jordan
Joy, Jesse, 41

—K—
Karankawa Indians, 60, 237
Karnes, Wanda J., 269
Kelly, Alexander, 280
Kennedy, Daniel, 279
Kensie, Peter, 57
Kensie, Sarah Ann (Mrs. John Moore), 57
Kepler, Christopher, 34
Kerkendol, Robert H., 67; *also see* Kuykendall, Robert H., Jr.
Kiggans, James, 207, 214
Killam, Radcliff, 168
Kincaid, A. J., 273
Kinchelow, William, Colonel, 49
Kirkendall's Creek, 15
Kleeman, Robert, 176
Knisple, Barney, 129
Knutsen family, 146
Knutsen, O., Jr., 146
Koock, Karen, *see* Kuykendall, Karen Koock
Koock, Mary Faulk, 175
Kuykendal, Henry, 10
Kuykendall, Abner, Captain of Austin's Colony, 29, 30, 31, 33, 34, 36, 37, 39, 40, 42, 45, 46, 47, 55, 59, 60, 68, 203-211, 212, 215, 220, 221, 223, 225, 232, 233, 237, 239, 240, 243, 255, 258, 259, 260, 265, 283
Kuykendall, Abner II, 208
Kuykendall, Abraham, 10, 16, 17, 18, 22, 30
Kuykendall, Adam, Sr. (son of Petrus or Peter), 10, 14, 15-37, 39, 40, 42, 203, 204, 205, 209, 210, 211, 216, 217, 225, 226, 256, 258, 277, 278, 283, 285, 286
Kuykendall, Adam (son of Capt. Abner), 216
Kuykendall, Adam Jr. (son of Adam Sr.), 31, 36, 37, 42, 204, 205, 283
Kuykendall, Affray (Affay) (daughter of Peter-1783), 26
Kuykendall, Albert Benjamin (twin son of Capt. Robert H.), 56
Kuykendall, Alice Hamlett, 11, 93, 127, 128, 131, 132, 134, 136, 137, 138, 146, 150, 151, 152, 154, 164, 165, 167, 169, 171, 175
Kuykendall, Allen, 265
Kuykendall, Alzena Dubois, 237

Kuykendall, Amos, 30, 31, 33, 34, 36, 37, 42, 59, 204, 205, 283
Kuykendall, Angelina, 219
Kuykendall, Annie (Mrs. Henry S. Abel), 56
Kuykendall, Barzillai, of Austin's Colony (also Brazilla, Brazillai), 206, 207, 209, 210, 211, 213, 214, 215, 216, 217, 218, 220-231, 233, 240, 243, 244, 256
Kuykendall, Ben, 198
Kuykendall, Benjamin, 22, 30, 42
Kuykendall, Benjamin W., 56
Kuykendall, Betsy (Mrs. Amos), 33
Kuykendall, Betty, *see* Betty Kuykendall McCrosky
Kuykendall, Betty Richardson Mielcarek (Mrs. Marshall E.), 176, 178, 179
Kuykendall, Catherine (daughter of William of Austin's Colony), 233
Kuykendall, Catherine (Barzillai's first wife), 215, 225, 229
Kuykendall, Cordelia Martin, 237
Kuykendall, Cornelia (daughter of R. G. and Maggie), 102
Kuykendall, Cornelius, 15
Kuykendall, Dempsey, 42
Kuykendall, Dorothy, *see* Hoskins, Dorothy Kuykendall
Kuykendall, Dr. George Benson, vii
Kuykendall, Electra Miranda, *see* Electra (Ella) Miranda Kuykendall Dunn
Kuykendall, Electra Shannon (Mrs. R. H. Gill), 10, 64, 65, 71
Kuykendall, Elisabeth (Mrs. Amos), 42
Kuykendall, Elisabeth (Barzillai's second wife), 229, 231
Kuykendall, Elisabeth, 26, 209, 210, 215, 219, 225
Kuykendall, Elisabeth (daughter of Peter-1783), 26
Kuykendall, Elisabeth (daughter of Capt. Abner), 209, 210
Kuykendall, Elisabeth (Mrs. J. L.), 215, 225
Kuykendall, Elisabeth Elliot, 56
Kuykendall, Elisabeth I (daughter of Matheus), 16
Kuykendall, Elisabeth II (Elizabeth) (daughter of Matheus), 16, 28, 285, 286
Kuykendall, Eliza (daughter of William of Austin's Colony), 233
Kuykendall, Eliza Jane Jones, 263, 264, 265
Kuykendall, Eliza M. Carothers, 233
Kuykendall, Elizabeth (Mrs. Amos), 37, 283
Kuykendall, Elizabeth (daughter of Gibson and Martha), 218
Kuykendall, Elizabeth Leakey, 214, 215
Kuykendall, Emma, 57
Kuykendall, Ester, 102
Kuykendall, Eugene L., vii, 1
Kuykendall, Eugeone Burchell (Burshell), 76, 89

Kuykendall, Falbey (Falray, Falbray) Goza (Mrs. Adam Jr.), 36, 37, 42, 283
Kuykendall, George, 74, 219
Kuykendall, Georgia, 135, 136, 137, 139
Kuykendall, Gibson, Captain of Austin's Colony, 206, 207, 209, 210, 211, 212-219, 220, 226, 227, 230, 233, 234, 240, 243, 244, 256
Kuykendall, Gil (Gill) (son of Wylie and Alice), vii, 137, 138, 143, 154, 159, 163
Kuykendall, Harriet, 219
Kuykendall, Henry, 22, 244
Kuykendall, Isaac (Ike), 102, 112, 113, 114, 115, 116, 117, 120, 122, 123, 124, 125, 126, 131, 135, 137, 139, 153, 155, 158
Kuykendall, Isaac Bradford, 76, 89
Kuykendall, Isaac Green, 76, 86, 89
Kuykendall, Ishmal, 102
Kuykendall, J. L., 215, 225
Kuykendall, Jacob, 9, 16, 17, 22
Kuykendall, James (Jacobus), 16, 17, 18, 22, 33, 42
Kuykendall, James M. (son of Joseph Pulaski), 42, 288
Kuykendall, Jane, 26, 49, 56, 60, 65, 68
Kuykendall, Jane E., 233
Kuykendall, Jane Hardin, 285, 286
Kuykendall, Jannetje Westvael, 9
Kuykendall, Jennie Alice (Jenny) (daughter of Marshall E., Jr.), 178
Kuykendall, Jesse Young, 26
Kuykendall, John (son of Elisabeth), 216
Kuykendall, John (son of old John), 29
Kuykendall, John (1720-1767, son of Old Matthew), 10, 16, 17, 18, 22, 28, 29, 30, 42, 277, 285
Kuykendall, John (son of J. L. and Elisabeth), 215, 216, 218, 219, 225, 226
Kuykendall, Jonathon Hampton (J.H.K., J. Hampton K.), 45, 66, 67, 69, 74, 206, 209, 210, 211, 213, 215, 216, 218, 226, 227, 228, 235, 236, 237, 239-257
Kuykendall, Joseph (son of Barzillai), 225, 229
Kuykendall, Joseph (son of Ms. Harriet Kuykendall), 219
Kuykendall, Joseph (Pulaski) (son of John), 28, 30, 36, 42
Kuykendall, Joseph, of Austin's Colony, 30, 36, 37, 42, 45, 46, 47, 55, 60, 66, 68, 204, 205, 210, 212, 221, 240, 246, 258-265
Kuykendall, Joseph A. (son of Gibson), 215, 218, 219
Kuykendall, Joseph (Jose) Felix Trespalacios (Joseph F.) (son of Capt. Robert H.), 49, 56, 60
Kuykendall, Judge William, 254, 255
Kuykendall, Julian, 215
Kuykendall, (Mary) Karen Koock, 166, 167, 171, 175, 176, 180
Kuykendall, Kate (Mrs. Samuel Grant), 56

Kuykendall, Kate Spaulding Byrne, 237
Kuykendall, Kirk, 171
Kuykendall, Lamond (daughter of Bill), 11, 122, 124, 126, 134
Kuykendall, Laura Elisabeth (daughter of Isaac G.), 85, 88, 89, 112, 171
Kuykendall, Laura Jean, see Laura Jean Kuykendall Maxey
Kuykendall, Levantha (daughter of William of Austin's Colony), 233
Kuykendall, Lucinda (daughter of Barzillai), 225
Kuykendall, Maranda (daughter of Barzillai), 229
Kuykendall, Margaret (daughter of William of Austin's Colony), 233
Kuykendall, Margaret Hardin (Mrs. Adam), 10, 23, 30, 33, 36, 37, 39, 40, 42, 203, 204, 205, 233, 258, 283, 285
Kuykendall, Margaret Martha (Maggie), 11, 87, 93, 95-96, 97, 98, 102, 104, 105, 106, 107, 109, 111, 112, 115, 116, 117, 118, 121, 123, 126, 131, 132, 134, 135, 137, 139, 143, 155, 172, 173, 190, 194
Kuykendall, Margaret Williams (Mrs. Marshall E., Jr.), 175, 178, 179
Kuykendall, Marinda, 209
Kuykendall, Marion, see Marion Kuykendall Taylor
Kuykendall, Marshall Early, 11, 138, 143, 151, 161, 163, 164, 165, 171, 174-181, 283
Kuykendall, Marshall, Jr., 171, 175, 178, 179
Kuykendall, Martha (daughter of Barzillai), 225, 229
Kuykendall, Martha (Mrs. Gibson), 225
Kuykendall, Martha L. (daughter of Gibson), 215
Kuykendall, Martha Lockhart (second wife of Gibson), 215, 218, 219
Kuykendall, Mary (daughter of William), see Mary Kuykendall Teal
Kuykendall, Mary (wife of Petrus), 10, 15
Kuykendall, Mary (wife of Matheus), 9, 16
Kuykendall, Mary Alice, see Naiser, Mary Alice Kuykendall
Kuykendall, Mary Ella (daughter of William of Austin's Colony), 233
Kuykendall, Matheus (Matthew, Old Matthew) (1690), 9, 15, 16, 17, 18, 21, 22, 28, 277, 285
Kuykendall, Matilda Earp (second wife of R. H. Gill), 10, 65, 68
Kuykendall, Matthew (son of Peter), 23, 24, 26, 29, 30, 203, 286
Kuykendall, Matthew (De Soto County, Mississippi), 208
Kuykendall, Mattie Amanda (Mrs. John Harrison McCrosky), 56, 57
Kuykendall, Maxey (son of Robert Gill (1928)), 171
Kuykendall, Mildred Williams (Barber) (Mrs. Wylie), 11, 121, 122, 123, 124, 125, 126, 127, 132, 134, 136
Kuykendall, Miranda (daughter of Capt. Abner), 210, 211
Kuykendall, Molly (Mary) (daughter of Capt. Robert H.), 49, 56, 60
Kuykendall, Mrs. Gill (wife of R. H. Gill), 57
Kuykendall, Nancy (Nannie) (daughter of Barsillai), 229, 230, 231
Kuykendall, Nancy Johnson, 208
Kuykendall, Nathaniel, 22
Kuykendall, Pernelia (daughter of Gibson), 215
Kuykendall, Peter (Cooper County, Missouri),
Kuykendall, Peter, Jr. (son of Peter-1783), 26
Kuykendall, Peter (son of Adam), 31, 33, 36, 37, 42, 204, 205, 283
Kuykendall, Petrus (Peter-1719), 10, 15, 16, 17, 18, 21, 22, 23, 25, 26, 30, 203, 286
Kuykendall, R. H. (Gill) (Robert H., Robert H. Jr., RHK Jr.) (son of Capt. Robert H.), 10, 55, 57, 58-69, 71, 190, 211, 216, 240, 247, 256, 264
Kuykendall Ranch, 158
Kuykendall, Rebecca (daughter of Peter-1719), 26
Kuykendall, Rebecca Hardin, 277, 285
Kuykendall, Robert Baylor (cousin, of Bell County, Texas), 74
Kuykendall, Robert Gilden (Gil) (son of Bill), 11, 75, 89, 92-109, 131, 132, 171
Kuykendall, Robert (Gill) (son of Wiley), 49, 50, 76, 87, 111
Kuykendall, Robert H., Captain of Austin's Colony (1790), 9, 10, 30, 31, 34, 36, 37, 38-57, 59, 60, 68, 71, 179, 204, 205, 207, 212, 213, 240, 255, 258, 259, 260, 264, 265, 283

Kuykendall, Gilliand (R.H. II), 210

Kuykendall, Robert H. III (son of R. H. Gill), 65, 68, 263
Kuykendall Rodeo, 130
Kuykendall, Rosanna (Rosanah) (first wife of Joseph of Austin's Colony), 263
Kuykendall, Ruth (daughter of Gibson), 219
Kuykendall, Ruth (daughter of Peter), 26
Kuykendall, Sarah (Sallie, Sally) Gates (Mrs. Abner), 31, 33, 37, 40, 204, 206, 209, 212, 213, 215, 219, 220, 221, 232, 233, 239, 283
Kuykendall, Sally, see Blount, Sally Kuykendall (daughter of Adam-1758)
Kuykendall, Samuel Gates (twin son of Capt. Abner), 45, 209, 210, 215, 245, 256
Kuykendall, Sarah (daughter of Barzillai), 225, 229
Kuykendall, Sarah (Mrs. Peter), 42, 283
Kuykendall, Sarah Ann Gainor (Mrs. Thomas), 56
Kuykendall, Sarah Ann Gilleland (Mrs. Robert H.), 10, 36, 37, 45, 47, 49, 55, 57, 59, 64, 93, 283
Kuykendall, Sarah Hacker (Mrs. Peter), 37

Kuykendall, Sarita (daughter of Marshall E., Sr.), see Corona, Sarita Kuykendall
Kuykendall, Simon, 16
Kuykendall, Solomon, 229
Kuykendall, Susan Elizabeth Pierce (Mrs. Wiley M.), 11, 65, 75, 77, 81, 82, 85, 86, 87, 88, 89, 93, 102, 112, 121, 138
Kuykendall, T. P. (Thornton Payton) (son of J. L. and Elisabeth), 215, 216, 225, 226
Kuykendall, T. R., of Tilden, Texas, 208, 243
Kuykendall, Talbot Chambers (son of William), 74, 233, 237, 254
Kuykendall, Thomas (twin son of Capt. Robert H.), 56, 71, 75
Kuykendall, Thomas Hampton (son of William), 233, 237, 257
Kuykendall, Wilburne (Willie) (Mrs. Wilburn Harry Gainer), 56
Kuykendall, Wiley Martin (son of R. H. Gill), 10, 57, 65, 68, 70-91, 98, 112, 118, 121, 138, 173, 190, 254, 263
Kuykendall, William, Judge, of Tilden, Texas, 237, 255
Kuykendall, William Abner of Austin's Colony (son of Capt. Abner), 45, 67, 74, 207, 209, 210, 211, 214, 216, 219, 220, 221, 225, 226, 232-238, 240, 247, 254, 255, 256
Kuykendall, William H. (son of Barzillai), 229, 230, 231
Kuykendall, William Isaac (son of Robert Gill and Maggie), 102
Kuykendall, William T. (Thomas, son of Albert Benjamin-1829), 56
Kuykendall, William Thornton (son of Gibson), 215
Kuykendall, Wyatt Hanks (twin son of Capt. Abner), 45, 209, 210, 215, 218, 256
Kuykendall, Wylie (daughter of Gil and Jean), 171
Kuykendall, Wylie Moore "Bill," 11, 76, 81, 102, 104, 102, 107, 110-173, 186
Kuykendall, Wylie Williams (son of Marshall E., Jr.), 175, 178
Kuykendall, Zulema (daughter of Gibson), 218

—L—
Lacy, Hopkins, 280
LaFitte, Jean, 47
Lakey, Joel, 214, 215
Lamar, Mirabeau B., 60, 235
Lambert, Walter, 237
Lark (slave), 66, 68, 71
Lauderdale, Dr., 134
Law, Mrs., 124
Lawrence, Adam, 224, 225
Leakey, Brazilla, 215
Leakey, Elizabeth, see Elizabeth Leakey Kuykendall

Leakey, Joel, 215
Leakey, Louisa A. West, 215
Leakey, Lydia, see Lydia Leakey Gates
Leates, C. M., 230
Lee, John C., 227, 228, 236
Lemons, James, 34, 35
Lemons, John, 41
Lindeman, Mrs. Staten, 134
Locke, W. F., 273
Lockhart, Martha Kuykendall, see Martha Lockhart Kuykendall
Lockhart, R., 219
Long, Jane (League), 265
Long, John, 279
Longley Cambell, 228
Looney, David, 279
Looney, Moses, 279
Loudermilk, J. J., 73
Lovely, Maj. William L., 41
Loving, Geo. B., 100
Lowery, Sarah A., 268
Lowther, Harry, 150, 155
Lubbock, Thomas S., 186
Luurszen, Jacob, 1, 9

—M—
Magoffin, J. W., 243
Malone, Ross, 146
Mansfield, battle of, 73
Marsh, Christopher, 183
Martha (slave), 66
Martin, Cordelia, see Cordelia Martin Kuykendall
Martin, Josiah, 278
Martin, Robert, 237
Martin, Wiley (Wylie, Wyly), 61, 63, 64, 71, 210
Martinez, Antonio Maria, Governor, 46
Mather, J. T. (Tom), 146, 147
Maulding, Morton, 29, 204
Maulding, West, 29, 204
Maxey, Lattimer, 163
Maxey, Laura Jean (Mrs. Robert Gill Kuykendall), 163, 171
Maximillian, Emperor, 268
Mays, Clyde, 162
Mays, Harley, 162
McAfee, James, Colonel, 28, 282
McBrayes, E. W., 269
McCombs, John, 29, 204
McCrosky, Betty Kuykendall, vii, 57, 67
McCrosky, James Harrison, Jr., 57
McCrosky, John Harrison, 56
McCrosky, John Voss, 57
McCrosky, Peggy, 57
McCrosky, Peter, 57
McCrosky, Thomas Griggs, 57
McCrosky, Thomas Kuykendall, 57
McCulloch, Ben, 94

McCulloch, Henry E., General, 94, 253
McDonald, W. L., 234
McDowel family, 17
McDowell, Capt. Joseph, 22
McDowell, Col. Charles, 22, 24
McElmurry, Absalom, 34
McElmurry, John, 34, 35, 36, 41, 42
McFarland, Alexander, Colonel, 34, 35, 36, 41
McFarland, Lydia (Mrs. Alexander), 41
McKeller, Alden, 167, 168
McLendon, Betty Randolph (Mrs. J. H. McCrosky, Jr.), 57
McMinn, Joseph, 280
McNabe, Capt. John D., 267
McNeese, Ivy, 47
McNeese, John, 47
McNeese, Parrott, 47
McNutt, Robert M. (Captain, Major, Judge), 211, 216, 226, 244
McQueen, Thomas, 241, 242
Meadows, Isabel, 268
Mellon, George, Dr., 279
Meyers, Major, 237
Michaelis, Max, 163, 169
Mielcarek, Betty Richardson, *see* Kuykendall, Betty Richardson Mielcarek
Mielcarek, Kimberley (daughter of Betty Kuykendall), 178, 179
Mielcarek, Matthew (son of Betty Kuykendall), 178, 179
Mier Expedition, 245
Milican family, 17
Miller, A. B., 273
Miller, Anita, 289
Miller, Corrine, 191, 192
Miller, Samuel, 215
Miller, Thomas R., 201
Miller, Zack, 98
Milliken, Dudley, 146
Mina District, 47
Mitchell family, 161
Mohawk Indians, 5
Monday, Ethel, 289
Montague, Bill (William), 153
Montague Grocery, 152
Montague, Molly, 153, 159
Moody, Mr., 260
Moody, Weldon (coach), 160
Moore, Addie May, 192
Moore, Adolph P., 183
Moore, Augusta (Gussie) Butterfield, 125, 190
Moore, Cecil Hamilton, 191
Moore, David Lewis, 192, 196
Moore, Dolph, 124, 134, 191
Moore, Clay, Dr., 194
Moore, Ed, 124
Moore, Ella, 190, 196

Moore, Eudora Inez (Dora), 95-96, 102, 112, 115, 116, 119, 120, 123, 124, 126, 127, 130, 132, 135, 138, 139, 183, 185, 191, 196, 198
Moore, Gladys, 191
Moore, Hamilton, 193
Moore, Henry Edgar, 183, 190
Moore, Joe, 125, 185
Moore, John, 57, 72, 73
Moore, Joseph Layton, 183, 188, 189, 196
Moore, Kate A. Seaman, 190-191, 193, 194, 196
Moore, Margaret Martha (Maggie), *see* Kuykendall, Margaret Martha (Maggie)
Moore, Martha L., 197, 198
Moore, Mary (daughter of Will Moore and Mary C. Swift), 190
Moore, Mary C. Swift (Mrs. Will), 93, 94, 190, 191, 192, 193, 196, 202
Moore, Mary Crowell Layton (Mrs. Robert B.), 125, 183, 184, 196
Moore, Oce Ann, 192
Moore, Robert Baxter, 93, 125, 173, 183, 184, 191, 192, 196
Moore, Robert Baxter, Jr., 183, 196
Moore, Selkirk Seamon, 192
Moore, Spencer C., 125, 183, 183, 192, 196
Moore, St. Leges, 190
Moore, Vera, 191
Moore, William Ashby, 191, 194
Moore, William (Will) Eurastus, 93, 171, 182-200
Moore, Winfred, 191, 196
Morehouse, E., Colonel, 244
Morris, Joe, 199
Morris, Mattie, 199
Morrison, Robert B. (Bob), Dr., 163
Morrison, Moses, Lt., 50
Morrison, Verna Mae (Mrs. Robert B.), 163
Morton, O. N., Rev., 195
Muldoon, Michael, Fr., 208
Murphy, Benjamin, 34, 41, 205
Murray, John, 37
Mylius, Albert, 192

—N—

Naiser, Catherine Ann (daughter of Mary Alice Kuykendall Naiser), 176, 178
Naiser, Haley Nichole (daughter of Mary Alice Kuykendall Naiser), 176, 178
Naiser, Jerry (husband of Mary Alice Kuykendall Naiser), 175, 178, 179
Naiser, Mary Alice Kuykendall (daughter of Marshall E., Sr.), 171, 175, 178, 179, 180
Nance, Elizabeth, 124
Nance, Grace (Mrs. Laverne Allen), 115
Neff, Gov. Pat, 125
Neighbors, Allen, Dr., 127
Neill, Andrew, 201
New Orleans Greys, 243

Newell, James C., 34
Newman, ———, 50
Newman, John, 279
Ninety Six District, 17
Nolan, Mr., 112, 116
Nolen, Phillip, 46
Norton, Charles G., 237

—O—
O'Brien, John, 237
O'Brien, Major, 251
O'Connor, Thomas, 185, 186, 237
O'Quin, Leon, 146
Ogden, Captain, 253
"Old" Lawrence County, 287
Olive, Bill, 134
Oneida Indians, 5
Onondaga Indiana, 5
Orvell, Martha L. (daughter of Barzillai), 229, 230, 231
Orvell, Thomas A., 229, 230
Osage Indians, 41
Osborne, Adlai, 278
Osterhart, Jno. P., 228
Ouachita Baptist College, 272
Over Mountain Men, The, 278

—P—
Padilla, Gen. Juan Antonio, 54
Pantallion, Mr., 243
Partain, Eleanor (Ellen) Swift (Mrs. Thomas), 198, 202
Partain family, 124
Partain, Robert, 72
Parton, Nancy, 79
Patience (slave), 66
Patterson, Tommie Cochran, 28
Patton, Richard C., 45, 55
Pease, E. M., Governor, 235, 264
Pecan Point, 45
Peck, Nathaniel, 211
Peebles, Dr. Robert, 55, 208, 210
Pendleton, ———, 276
Peoples, Jack, 161
Peppar, Jim, 146
Perkins, John H., 210
Perry, Daniel, 216
Perry, Gov. Rick, 178
Pettus, Wm., 210
Petyon, Holmes, 224
Phair, Rev. S. J., 193
Phillips, H. H. "Hokey," Jr., 135
Phillips, Sylvanus, 36
Phillips, Winnie Arnett Dunn (Mrs. H. H., Sr.), 86, 122, 135
Pickens, John H., 260

Pierce, Abel Head (Shanghai), 11, 65, 75, 76, 77, 79, 102, 135, 186, 189, 190
Pierce family, 82, 120
Pierce homestead, 83
Pierce, Jonathon (John) E. (brother to Shanghai), 75, 76, 79, 186
Pierce, Miranda (sister to Susan P. Kuykendall), 81
Pierce, Susan, *see* Kuykendall, Susan Pierce
Pinchem, Mrs., 198
Pleasant Farm Plantation, 54
Pleasant Hill, battle of, 73
Polk, John, Capt., 234
Pool, Hogue, 151
Pope, J. C., 133
Pope, Lieutenant, 250
Porter, Dr., 276
Powell, Peter, 46, 259
Prendergast, Geo., 142
Price, Aaron, 34
Price, Betty Kuykendall, vii
Price, General, 268
Pryor, Richard (Cactus), 168
Pryor, Jefferson, 223
Puett, Frances, 124
Puett, Nelson, 123, 124
Pyeatt, Jacob, 36, 205

—Q, R—
Quiniones, Jesus Jamie, Gen., 146
Rabb, A., 259
Rabb, John, 259
Rabb, Wm., 259
Ragsdale, Bobby, 168
Ramsey, Dr., 280, 281
Ramsour's Mill, 23, 278, 279
Ratliff, York, 146
Rawlings, Asahel, 279
Rawls family, 161
Rawls, Grandpa, 161
Rawls, Jack, 161
Rawls, Junie, 161
Rawls Ranch, 161
Reavill (Reville, Reavill, Revill), B. F. (B. J.), Captain, 217, 244
Records and Notices, 291-364
Red Banks, 29
Reeder, Micader, 259
Reese, James, 279
Refugio County, Texas, 237
Reiner, Dick, 185
"Reminisces of Indianola," 123
Rhodes, Elisabeth, 269
Rhodes, Joseph, 269
Rhodes, Rachel Pearson, 269
Richardson, Jay (father of Betty R. Kuykendall), 176

Richardson, Maria Salazar (mother of Betty R. Kuykendall), 176
Richardson, Willard, 237
Robbin (Robbins), Early, 207, 214, 215
Robbins, Horrace, 146
Roberts, Wallace, 134
Robertson's route of 1779, 26
Robinson, Andrew, 47, 205, 212
Robinson, George (Bo), 175
Robinson, George, 225
Robinson, James M., Governor, 244
Robinson, J. W., 243
Robinson, Mama Al (Mrs. Al), 175
Robinson, Ralph, 133, 134, 138, 142
Roddye, James, 279
Rogers, L. M., Judge, 256, 257
Ross, Raleigh, Dr., 167, 169
Ross, James, 259
Rowan, Dr., 273
Rowe, Andrew, 268, 272
Rowe, Benjamin, 269
Rowe, Jack, 272
Rowe, John, 269
Rowe, John Wesley, 268
Rowe, Joseph, 235
Rowe, Martha Ann Conway, 268
Rowe, Mary Jane, *see* Early, Mary Jane Rowe
Rowe, Pierson, 268
Rowe, Ruth O'Neil, 269
Rowe, W. J., 268
Rowe, Wm. Jackson, 268
Royal, Carrell, 180
Rugeley, Mrs., 124
Ruis, Captain, 225
Rusk, Thomas J., 260
Russell, William, 42
Rutherford, Griffin, General, 278
Rutherford, Pat, 153, 162
Rutledge, George, 280

—S—
Sack, William H., 243
Saffell, Mrs. Herman P. (Arlene), vii
San Marcos Baptist Academy, 153
Santa Anna, Antonio Lopez de, General, 54, 239, 243, 262
Sargent, C. E., Captain, 142
Savoy, Phil, 176
Sayle, W.A.S., Dr., 273
Scarbrough, Lem, 123
Schlemmer family, 162
Schlemmer, Mr., 134
Schmeltekopf, Edward, 160, 161
Schnautz, Eugene, 160
Schockley, Geo. W., 230
Scivally, Herschell R., 146
Scott, D. M., Major, 146

Seale, C. M., 231
Seaman, Charles, 191
Searcy, ———, 231
Searcy, J. B., 273
Searight, Mr., 112
Secrest (Secrets), Washington H., Captain, 61, 260
Seneca Indians, 5
Sevier, John, Colonel, 24, 279, 281
Shank, Samml. B., 236
Shannon, Alexander, 188
Shannon, Charlotte (Mrs. John), 65
Shannon, Electra, *see* Kuykendall, Electra Shannon
Shannon, John, 45, 259
Shannon, Owen, 45, 259
Shannon Scouts, 188
Shannon, Wm., 259
Shearee, J. H., 275
Shelby, Isaac, Colonel, 24
Shelby Expedition, 268
Shepard, James, 231
Shipman, 224
Shoaker, Frank, 194
Siege of Bexar, 215
Sierra Hermosa Ranch, 163
Simon, Edward, 160
Simpson, Moses, 237
Sims, Barlett, 208
Siringo, Charles A., 76, 185
6th Texas Infantry, 68
Skidmore, Billy, 146
Skurlock, Captain, 216, 217
slaves, *see* John, Winny, Ike, Patience, Lark, Martha
Sledge, Jack, 118
Smith, Deaf, 242
Smith, Dean, 133
Smith, John, 72
Smith, John B., 72
Smooth Sailing, 142, 157
Solms, Prince Carles de, 184
Somervell (Somervill, Somerville, Summervill), Alexander, 216, 218, 226, 227, 236
Southwell, Wilson, 146
Spanish Alarm, 17
Spanish Camp, 54
Sparks, J. W., Captain, 188
Spaw, R. E., 101
Standlee, John, 35
Starke, L., 142
Steele, General, 267
Steiner, T. C., 133
Stephens, B. H., 142
Stephenson, James, 224
Sterry, Mrs. C., 195
Stevens, Jacob, 210
Stevens, Thomas, 207, 214, 225
Stevenson, J., 23

Stevenson, William, 263
Stewart, C. B., 211
Stewart, James, 29, 204
Stewart, Mr., 136
Stewart, Thomas, 279
Stewart, Virgil A., 64
Stocklin, Benjamin Franklin, 64
Storey, H.C., 115
Storey, Helen, 151
Storey, Jack, 115
Storey, Julia, 115
Storey, Nell, 115
Stubbs, Marcelle, 137
Stubbs, Mrs. Roy, 138
Stubbs, Roy, 123, 133, 134, 138, 142
Sullivan, Dan, 77
Sullivan, James B., 265
Swift, Arthur, 94, 98, 189, 190, 201-202
Swift, Hugh, 202
Swift, John (father of Arthur), 202
Swift, Margaret (daughter of Arthur), 202
Swift, Margaret Mackey Baker (Mrs.Arthur), 94, 98, 190, 202
Swift, Martha (daughter of Arthur), 202
Swift, Mary C., *see* Moore, Mary C. Swift
Swift, William, Rev. (great-grandfather of Arthur), 202
Swift, Richard (grandfather to Arthur), 202
Swift's Ferry, 202
Swisher, I. G., 210
Swisher, Jno. M., 228, 236

—T—
Tack, Grietje Aertze, 9
Tawacani (Tawacanie) Indians, 213, 222, 224, 225
Taylor, General, 73
Taylor, Gen Zachary, General, 67, 247, 250
Taylor, Leroy, 280
Taylor, Lester, Dr., 118, 120, 132, 135, 137
Taylor, Marion Kuykendall, 102, 104, 116, 118, 121, 132, 135, 136, 139, 154, 155, 165, 172
Teal, Albert, 237
Teal, Mary Kuykendall (daughter of old William of Austin's Colony), 237
Tenoxtitlan (fort?), 225
Terry, Benjamin Franklin, General, 186, 187
Terry's Texas Rangers, 186, 189, 192, 195
Texas Almanac, 254
Texas Gazette, 55
Texas Militia (TM), 346-364
Texas Monument, 253
Texas Scrapbook, A, 254
Texas State Troops (TST), 346-364
Texas Tears and Texas Sunshine, 185
Texas Volunteer Infantry (TVI), 346-364
Thacker, Mrs. Ellender, 282

Thomas, Isaac, 21
Thompson, Thomas, 221, 222, 224
Thurmond, Alfred S., 237
Thurmond, Lucinda O. Kuykendall, (daughter of Barzillai), 229, 230, 231
Thurmond, William, 229
Thurmond, Wilson (husband of Lucinda O.), 230
Thurston, A. S., 234, 260
Tipton, John, 279, 280
Toalson, E., 116, 134
Tone, Sarah Kuykendall, 57, 71
Tone, Thomas J., 55, 57
Tonkawa Indians, 221
Townsend, Samuel, 237
Townsend, Stephen, 210
Trammell, Nicholas, 34
Travis, William B., 55, 61, 210, 243
Trespalacios, J. F., Governor, 49, 60
Truett, Dr., 276
Tryon, William, 17
Tumlinson, John, 49, 50, 60, 259
Tuttle, Martin S., 33, 34
Tyler, Doyle, 160
Tyler, Ron, iv

—U, V—
Underwood, ———, 208
Van Dorn, Colonel, 188
Vargas campaign, 227
Varner, Martin, 45, 46
Vasquez Expedition, 228
Vasquez, Rafael, General, 227, 236, 244
Vaugine, Frances (Francis), 36, 40
Victoria Advocate, 185
Viesca, Governor, 208
Village of Cadron, 36
Voght, Mr., 138

—W—
W. C. White & Co., 241
Waco Indians, 214, 222, 224, 225
Wade, Thomas, 278
Walden, Elisha, 7
Waldrope, Isabelle, 270
Walker, Dr. Thomas, 7
Walker, John, 207, 214
Walker, John G., 188
Wallace, Charles (Charlie), 117
Waller, Mr., 122
Ward, George, iv
Ware, Captain, 73
Washington, George, 22
Washington County, Texas, 206, 207, 209, 210, 215, 216, 219, 226, 229, 230, 231, 232, 245, 286
Waters, Johnathon D., 66
Watson, J. A., Major, 146

Wayland, Mr., 134
Wayne, John, 164, 167
Wear, Samuel, 280, 281
Webb, W. P., 273
Webster, John, 34
Weeks, Luther E., 142, 146
Weinert, Willie Mae, 201
Wellington, R. W., Dr., 237
West, B. F., 256, 257
West, Louisa A., *see* Leakey, Louisa A. West
Westenfield Polo Field, 133
Western Recorder, 276
Westfall, Janetjen, 16
Westvael, Jannetje, *see* Kuykendall, Jannetje Westvael
Whaley, Mary Inez, 194
Wharton, A. B., Jr., 142
Wharton Spectator, 185
Wheat, Mr., 206, 213, 221, 232
Whelan, Michael, 237
Whisnant, Herbert, 124
White, Gifford, vii, 9, 330
White, James, 280, 281
White Man's Union, 193
Wier, Alton (Doc), 142, 146
Wightman, E. M., 54, 55
Wilhelm, Judge, 137
Williams, Mr. (Mildred Kuykendall's father), 123
Williams, Dr., 46
Williams, Dr. Rayworth, 146
Williams, Jim (father of Margaret Kuykendall), 175
Williams, John, 36
Williams, Joseph, 72
Williams, Judge, 280
Williams, Robert M., Judge, 55
Williams, Lois (mother of Margaret Kuykendall), 175
Williams, Mildred, *see* Mildred Williams Kuykendall
Williams, Mrs., 126
Williams, Nancy (Mrs. Thomas), 36, 47
Williams, Samuel Cole, 278
Williams, J., Sheriff, 256, 257
Williams, Thomas, 36, 45, 47, 59, 259
Williamson, John, 221, 222, 224
Wilson, David, 280
Wilson, James, 279
Wilson, James, Rev., 268
Wilson, Sammy, 119
Winn, Velma Kuykendall, vii
Winny (slave), 66
Woll campaign, 227
Woll, Adrian, General, 244, 245
Womack, B. R., 273
Wood, C. D., 273
Wood, Lieutenant, 250
Woodlawn Polo Club, 133
Woods, Andrew, 17
Woods family, 17
Woods, Norman, 221, 222
Worthington, Joseph, 29, 204
Wright, Claiborne, 45
Wyatt, Henry, 45

—Y, Z—

Yager, W. O., 237
Yarbrough, David, 36
Yarrington, Hays, 186, 188, 190
Yeamans, Horace, 72, 73
Yellowstone, 261
Young, A. V., Dr., 146
Young, Michael, 210
Young, Saml., 23
Zollicoffer, General, 187

KUYKENDALLS FROM TEXAS IN THE CIVIL WAR

Kuykendall, A., 331
Kuykendall, A. S., 331
Kuykendall, Abraham, 331
Kuykendall, Allen, 332
Kuykendall, B., 332
Kuykendall, E. B., 332
Kuykendall, Elijah R., 332
Kuykendall, E. R., 333
Kuykendall, G. M., 333
Kuykendall, George R., 333-334
Kuykendall, J. B., 334
Kuykendall, J. H., 334
Kuykendall, J. M., 334
Kuykendall, J. W., 334-335
Kuykendall, James, 335
Kuykendall, James A., 335
Kuykendall, James J., 335
Kuykendall, John, 336
Kuykendall, Joseph A., 336-337
Kuykendall, Joseph B., 337
Kuykendall, Joseph C., 337
Kuykendall, M., 337
Kuykendall, M. J., 338
Kuykendal, 338
Kuykendall, M. S., 338
Kuykendall, P., 338
Kuykendall, P. K., 339
Kuykendall, Peter E., 339
Kuykendall, Robert, 339-340
Kuykendall, S. M., 340
Kuykendall, Samuel, 340
Kuykendall, Simon, 340-341
Kuykendall, T. C., 341
Kuykendall, W. A., 342
Kuykendall, W. C., 342
Kuykendall, William, 342
Kuykendall, Wiley, 342-343
Kuykendall, William, 343-344
Kuykendall, William C., 344
Kuykendall, Wyatt H., 344
Kuykendall, 345
Kuykendall, Samuel, 345

KUYKENDALLS IN THE TEXAS STATE TROOPS BEFORE THE CIVIL WAR

Kuykendall, B., 346
Kuykendall, E. R., 347
Kuykendall, G. R., 347
Kuykendall, George W., 347
Kuykendall, H. A., 348
Kuykendall, J. K., 348
Kuykendall, J. A., 348-349
Kuykendall, J. C., 349
Kuykendall, J. H., 349-350
Kuykendall, J. J., 350
Kuykendall, J. T., 350-351
Kuykendall, J. W., 351-352
Kuykendall, James, 352
Kuykendall, James W., 352
Kuykendall, Limm, 352-353
Kuykendall, M., 353
Kuykendall, M. H., 353-354
Kuykendall, M. J., 354
Kuykendall, N. H., 354
Kuykendall, P. E., 354-355
Kuykendall, R., 355
Kuykendall, R. B., 355
Kuykendall, S., 355-356
Kuykendall, Sam, 356-357
Kuykendall, Samuel, 357
Kuykendall, Simon, 357
Kuykendall, Thomas H., 357-358
Kuykendall, W. C., 358
Kuykendall, W. H., 359
Kuykendall, W. J., 359
Kuykendall, William, 359-360
Kuykendall, Wm., 360
Kuyrkendale, A. M., 360
Kuyrkendale, G. W., 361
Kuykendal, A., 361
Kuykendall, Allen, 361-362
Kuykendall, 362
Kuykendal, J. W., 363
Kurkendall, Jesse M., 363
Kurkendall, Thomas, 363-364
Kirkenall, M. A., 364
Kerkendall, J. R., 364

www.ingramcontent.com/pod-product-compliance
Lightning Source LLC
Chambersburg PA
CBHW080723230426
43665CB00020B/2591